Yalta 1945
Europe and America at the Crossroads

This revisionist study of Allied diplomacy from 1941 to 1946 challenges Americocentric views of the period and highlights Europe's neglected role. Fraser J. Harbutt, drawing on international sources, shows that in planning for the future, Churchill, Roosevelt, Stalin, and others self-consciously operated into 1945, not on "East/West" lines but within a "Europe/America" political framework characterized by the plausible prospect of Anglo-Russian collaboration and persisting American detachment.

Harbutt then explains the destabilizing transformation around the time of the pivotal Yalta conference of February 1945, when a sudden series of provocative initiatives, manipulations, and miscues interacted with events to produce the breakdown of European solidarity and the Anglo-Soviet nexus, an evolving Anglo-American alignment, and new tensions that led finally to the Cold War.

This fresh perspective, stressing structural, geopolitical, and traditional impulses and constraints, raises important new questions about the enduringly controversial transition from World War II to a Cold War that no statesman wanted.

Fraser J. Harbutt is Professor of History at Emory University. After graduation from Otago University and a decade of law practice in London and Auckland, he received a Ph.D. from the University of California at Berkeley and later taught diplomatic, political, and legal history variously at the University of California Los Angeles, Smith College, and the University of Pennsylvania. He is the author of *The Iron Curtain: Churchill, America, and the Origins of the Cold War* (1986), which co-won the Society for Historians of American Foreign Relations Bernath Prize, and of *The Cold War Era* (2002). He has also published chapters in several edited volumes and many articles in such journals as *Diplomatic History, Political Science Quarterly,* and *International History Review.*

Advance Praise for *Yalta 1945*

"Professor Fraser Harbutt's latest book is a model of scholarship. It is elegantly written, a pleasure to read. It is thoroughly researched and employs archival materials hitherto overlooked or insufficiently mined. It abounds with shrewd insights and convincing portraits of British, Soviet, and American leaders as they wended their way through the final frenzy of World War II and sought to shape a new global order. With very great care, Harbutt demonstrates how the Yalta conferees were constrained by geopolitical realities, the burdens and 'lessons' of the past, and the multitudinous tugs of domestic politics in the UK, United States, and USSR. Harbutt in *Yalta 1945* makes a major contribution to that historiography centered on the Second World War and the early Cold War. His work amounts to a re-conceptualizaion, placing British statecraft and its European concerns at center stage in the Yalta contest of wills, rather than as a secondary drama to that featuring Stalin versus FDR. Particularly noteworthy is Harbutt's nuanced treatment of the Anglo-Soviet wartime relationship in 1944–45. This is an indispensable study for anyone trying to make sense of the mid-twentieth century's diplomatic dilemmas and violent turmoil. Harbutt's is international history as its best – lucid, judicious, and refreshingly original. A rare achievement, most impressive."

– David Mayers, Boston University

"*Yalta 1945* is a worthy addition to the trend of internationalizing Cold War studies. More than a study of Roosevelt, Churchill, and Stalin's last summit, Harbutt's treatment puts that pivotal moment in world history in its original wartime context. Reminding us that history is lived forward, he shows how the preconditions of Yalta, notably the Eurocentric power politics practiced by Churchill and Stalin, interacted with the universalism of Roosevelt's hopes for a postwar world order. The result was disorder and disagreements that eventually led to the breakdown of the wartime alliance and the onset of the Cold War. Harbutt's interpretation is revisionist in the best sense. He revises our Americocentric, East-versus-West perspective on Yalta and enriches our understanding of its place in the origins of the Cold War."

– Robert Messer, University of Illinois at Chicago

Yalta 1945

Europe and America at the Crossroads

FRASER J. HARBUTT

Emory University

CAMBRIDGE
UNIVERSITY PRESS

CAMBRIDGE UNIVERSITY PRESS
Cambridge, New York, Melbourne, Madrid, Cape Town, Singapore,
São Paulo, Delhi, Dubai, Tokyo

Cambridge University Press
32 Avenue of the Americas, New York, NY 10013–2473, USA

www.cambridge.org
Information on this title: www.cambridge.org/9780521856775

First published 2010

Printed in the United States of America

A catalog record for this publication is available from the British Library.

Library of Congress Cataloging in Publication data
Harbutt, Fraser J.
   Yalta 1945 : Europe and America at the crossroads / Fraser J. Harbutt.
      p.   cm.
   Includes bibliographical references and index.
   ISBN 978-0-521-85677-5 (hbk.)
      1. World War, 1939–1945 – Diplomatic history.   2. Yalta Conference (1945).
   3. Europe – Foreign relations – United States.   4. United States – Foreign
   relations – Europe.   I. Title.
   D749.H37 2009
   940.53′141–dc22   2008055955

ISBN 978-0-521-85677-5 Hardback

For Josie and Chris

Contents

Preface	*page* ix
Acknowledgments	xxv
Abbreviations	xxix
1	The Confusions of Yalta	1
2	Two Arenas: Europe and America	22
3	The Persistence of Europe, 1942–1943	79
4	The Making of the Moscow Order	139
5	Consolidation	183
6	Roosevelt's America: A World Apart	225
7	The Yalta Disorder	280
8	Aftermath	331
9	Reflections	398
Select Bibliography	409
Index	427

Preface

This book has its general origins in a preoccupation with the transition from World War II to the Cold War and in a growing conviction that, despite a voluminous and intellectually spirited historiography, it is not properly understood. More specifically, I have been interested in the part played in that transition, insofar as it affected the future of Europe, by the famous Yalta conference of February 1945. There, on the eve of victory over Hitler's Germany, Franklin D. Roosevelt, Winston Churchill, and Joseph Stalin met to shape a future that almost immediately turned to crisis and later to Cold War.

The meeting at Yalta continues to fascinate. The leading personalities seem as compelling as ever, each the subject of a vast biographical literature. The decisions supposedly made there – the reshaping of Poland, the postwar arrangements for Germany, the Far Eastern concessions to the Soviet Union, and the repatriation of unwilling Soviet soldiers, among others – are still seen as active or at least suggestive elements in the move from wartime alliance to Cold War confrontation. But Yalta has also had a long career as a potent symbol, conjuring up images of intrigue, betrayal, and failure. For many it is still a live issue, generating a passionate response among the Poles, French, Germans, Chinese, Koreans, and others who, in one way or another, began from an early stage to identify themselves as victims of the power politics allegedly practiced there by the victorious Allies.

I shall attempt to explain Yalta by presenting a fresh, internationally oriented perspective on Allied diplomacy during and immediately after World War II. This account challenges orthodox views by rejecting the familiar "East/West" conception that sees, so far as the political dimension is concerned, an intimately collaborative Anglo-American wartime leadership (Roosevelt and Churchill) coexisting uneasily and distantly with the indispensable but difficult Soviet ally. It asserts instead a "Europe/America" context. This has the effect of bringing to life two distinct wartime arenas: an Allied European sphere in which Britain and the Soviet Union, working together more closely than is generally understood, took a leading role; and a detached America intent on keeping European politics at arm's length. Up to the beginning of 1945, it was almost universally assumed that the postwar world would reflect that dichotomy, with a battered but still autonomous Anglo-Soviet–led Europe looking across the Atlantic to a benevolent, financially supportive but still politically distant United States. In fact, of course, things turned out very differently. At some point – in and around the time of the Yalta conference – the political situation was quite suddenly transformed. The Europe/America framework began to break down, and the East/West configuration came more plausibly into view. This reconstruction is an attempt to explain why and how this came about.

Many people – statesmen, thinkers, millions of deeply interested observers, as well as many historians – look back to Yalta to explain the origins of the Cold War. In this book I will try to look forward to Yalta from the perspective of wartime diplomacy. The approach is analytic and selective. I do not present a full narrative treatment of wartime diplomacy, even of the European affairs that are my main concern. Nor do I attempt to do justice to all the divergent views in this controversial field. I do, however, want to put in question what I believe it is fair to call the conventional view of Allied diplomacy and to suggest an alternative conception that may illuminate these profound issues and perhaps inspire, if not agreement, a sense of renewed curiosity.

We badly need to get this right, for there are profound, still contentious issues here: the conduct of Allied wartime diplomacy; the matter of Roosevelt's reputation; the question whether there was an Anglo-Soviet "road not taken" that, among other things, might have prolonged Britain's status as a Great Power; the possibility that the Cold War itself might have been avoided or at least have taken a different form; the still unresolved issue of Stalin's intentions; and beyond all this, the question of European-American relations, which is arguably again today a leading preoccupation of politicians, pundits, and editorialists on both sides of the Atlantic.

Yalta lies at the heart of the conventional East/West view. In broad terms, this view holds that, within the general ambit of tripartite diplomacy, political relationships during World War II essentially mirrored the strategic associations. Thus the United States and Great Britain, intimate partners for war, viewed themselves as linked in a "Western," or "transatlantic," outlook. From this foundation, united by a shared politico-cultural outlook and the bonds of democracy as well as market capitalism, they worked to accommodate or frustrate (opinions differ about this) their distinctively different "Eastern" or "other" partner, the Soviet Union. The emphasis is invariably upon the unique Roosevelt-Churchill relationship as a decision-making and directive agency, and upon the great summit conferences as crucial occasions where the two Western statesmen engaged meaningfully with Stalin. At Yalta, it is widely believed, the three leaders divided (or refused to divide – again, opinions differ) Europe, and created what has in recent years come to be a kind of all-explanatory mantra, the "Yalta Order." The political alliance associated with this order broke up only when Stalin (or Truman, as many revisionists think) violated the Yalta "agreements," leading soon afterward to the Cold War.

This East/West line of thought, with the United States in a leading role, has the appeal of logic and simplicity – always desirable in times of tension and complexity – and it captured a widespread public and media understanding during the Cold War era at a time when people looked back to wartime diplomacy for explanations of their predicament. It was reinforced not only by the events of the Cold War itself but by a historiographical tradition crowned by Churchill's own authoritative wartime memoirs, which were themselves permeated with Anglo-American and East/West conceptions. And remarkably, insofar as it assumed a powerful American component in wartime politics, the conventional view was strengthened rather than undermined by the eruption of a revisionist historiographical onslaught in the Vietnam-era United States. For the leading studies produced by that passionate movement – much of it sharp-edged, imaginative scholarship – were for the most part obsessively preoccupied with the role of the United States, and largely focused on issues of moral accountability and on politico-economic impulses rather than on objective reconstructive analysis.

Still, even during the Cold War years there were doubts and questions. Historians have often shown an awareness of the myth making associated with crucial events like Yalta, and of the manipulations of governments and vested interests. They have also complained at times of Cold War pressures, of being drawn into national-patriotic causes, of becoming, as the phrase has it, "chaplains on the pirate ship."[1] There was also increasing

---

[1] Coined, unsurprisingly, by A. J. P. Taylor in *Europe: Decline and Grandeur* (Harmondsworth, Middlesex, 1950), p. 20.

awareness, as the Cold War dragged on and European and other foreign researchers entered the lists, of a pervasive Americocentrism. It was perhaps a sense of this professional imbalance and of the need for a more international approach that led the doyen of American diplomatic historians, George F. Kennan, to greet the Cold War's end in 1989 with a call for "a sober reexamination" of its causes.[2] Rather surprisingly, this has not happened. Instead, as the first Soviet records began to make an impression upon the field, there appeared a book by Professor John Lewis Gaddis, a distinguished figure in the field, with the debate-closing title *We Now Know*. In earlier days this would surely have provoked an immediate revisionist response, perhaps entitled *Not So Fast*. There was a flurry of critical resistance, but one frequently hears it said that revisionism in this sphere, once so robust and iconoclastic, is a thing of the past.[3]

I hope this is not so. For we need, not least in order to get a just appraisal of the American role in the politics of Europe between Pearl Harbor and Yalta, a fresh, skeptical look at the conventional view. It is, I believe, an edifice with shaky foundations. The central East/West conception, for instance, seems largely founded not on the actual record of Anglo-American collaboration in European political affairs but on the failure to make a crucial distinction between the undeniably close Anglo-American partnership for the planning and waging of war, on the one hand, and the fundamentally different set of policies these two countries pursued in their European diplomacy, on the other. In fact, these were two very separate arenas, each with its own character – one overwhelmingly strategic (though certainly with political implications), the other mostly political and geopolitical – though the two did of course overlap and intersect at times. In truth, the United States and Britain had very different attitudes about and policies toward Europe and its future, and in their policies they followed very different trajectories.

Nor was the Roosevelt-Churchill combination, undeniably a remarkable partnership for the prosecution of the war, a functioning political authority in European affairs. The two statesmen, and their two countries, had very divergent views of the European future. They often clashed. Each often went its own way. It also seems likely, when we look closely at the record, that, for all their success in imposing their authority upon their

[2] *New York Times*, October 28, 1992.
[3] John Lewis Gaddis, *We Now Know: Rethinking Cold War History* (Oxford, 1997). For critical response, see Melvyn P. Leffler, "The Cold War: What Do We 'Now Know'?" *American Historical Reviews*, 104 (April 1999), pp. 501–524; and Carolyn Eisenberg, "We Now Know: Revisiting Cold War History," *Journal of American History* (March 1998), pp. 1462–1464.

national establishments, they were somewhat less powerful than popular legend and celebratory scholarship suggests, and had to listen to a variety of voices and impulses, some of which are still obscure.

Some of the famous tripartite conferences, one of World War II's most striking political art forms, similarly tend (at least insofar as the European political dimension is concerned) to receive disproportionate attention. The first of these, the Moscow and Teheran conferences that, at the end of 1943, brought American leaders physically into the European political milieu for the first time (only eighteen months from the end of a six-year-long war), were mainly concerned with strategy, personal relationships, and public morale. Like the Anglo-American strategic partnership and the Roosevelt-Churchill association – foundations of the Allied war effort in the West – they were crucially important for the furtherance of the war effort, less so in matters affecting the fate of Europe. Significantly, at both the 1943 conferences and at Yalta, the two primary concrete issues that the United States pressed were always the same: the establishment of the United Nations and Soviet entry into the Pacific war. Neither of these directly affected Europe. And while Yalta was infinitely more important than the earlier meetings (though not in the way generally believed), one is bound to question what is today its most widely credited outcome: the division of Europe and the ensuing "Yalta Order." There was in fact no division of Europe at Yalta. And one can only observe with amazement the ease with which the notion of a Yalta "order" caught on (and persists today) in the press and in world opinion as a description of the significant residue of a conference that was so obviously riddled with semantic confusion and deep political misunderstanding that it produced within a month the most serious crisis in the history of the "Grand Alliance" (another conveniently functional but misleading characterization, this one an appropriation from Britain's imaginative prime minister). The effect of these qualifications is surely to cast doubt upon the conventional wisdom.

A reason for the considerable interest in the Moscow and Teheran conferences, one suspects, is simply that the United States government, which carefully avoided the more European-focused gatherings, was a major participant in each. Yet most of the significant political activity affecting Europe between June 1941 and February 1945 took place in much less well-known contexts, and there is some force in the complaint of one British diplomatic historian that "although there are excellent historians of individual European countries and European culture in the United States they lack interest in European international politics."[4] Today the American

---

[4] D. Cameron Watt, "Britain and the Historiography of the Yalta Conference and the Cold War," *Diplomatic History*, 13, 1 (Winter 1989), p. 71, n. 11.

tendency to self-preoccupation is widely acknowledged by historians. At the same time, it is to a large degree understandable. Since the early nineteenth century visionaries from Simon Bolivar to Alexis de Toqueville had been predicting the political engagement of the United States with Europe. Contemporaries (and historians) might surely be forgiven for thinking, so tenacious and powerful was the American commitment to victory from 1941 to 1945, that the moment had at last arrived (as indeed it had, but not until February 1945). For many writers, especially after the Wilsonian false start, the argument from destiny has therefore been compelling. Further, the United States was arguably the only global power fully engaged in World War II, fighting two wars at full throttle, supporting its two allies in impressive material fashion, and posing credibly and uniquely as the foremost champion of a democratic, progressive future. When one adds to this the fact that the great majority of early Cold War historians were American and that United States governmental archives were the first to open their holdings for inspection, it is hardly surprising that Cold War historiography has tended to focus primarily on, and attribute profound effects to, American thought and action.

Another factor that tended to turn this healthy national partiality into a more obsessive introspection that left little room for the actions of other states was the almost universal post-1945 American public interest in, and indeed demand for, explanation and accountability concerning the Cold War's origins. Most great historical issues seem to revolve around a basic question. In this case historians were responding to a confused, anxious American audience that wanted to know: How is it that World War II led, not to the hoped for peace, but to the Cold War? The intense focus on that question did two things. First, it produced the explanatory paradigm I have called the conventional view, holding in essence that the key to the 1941–45 period and its aftermath, at least so far as Allied diplomacy was concerned, lay in the governing conception of a more or less like-minded United States and Britain positioning themselves in relation to a distinctly different Soviet Union. Second, it appears to have led many historians to produce, in full compatibility with and reinforcement of that paradigm, a hierarchy of relationships among the Big Three: a United States–Soviet political one characterized by deeply portentous initiatives, gestures, and personal relationships; a uniquely intimate and substantive Anglo-American strategic partnership; and finally, a distant third in American historiography and thinly developed even in European historiography, an Anglo-Soviet association that expressed itself occasionally (and only too predictably, in American eyes) in spasms of atavistic political behavior and was treated as of little consequence by American historians, who chose to follow instead the intriguing path of the inexorably rising United States, and were perhaps looking ahead prematurely to the era of superpower hegemony.

Out of ingredients like these came, within the framework of the conventional view, an impressive but overwhelmingly Americocentric historiography that, once launched successfully upon an expectant public and a warmly receptive political and military establishment, steadily took on some of the attributes of a powerful biological organism, adept at both energizing itself by harnessing reinforcing lines of inquiry and defending itself by carefully bypassing threatening impulses that might have suggested alternative scenarios.

Three illustrations that bear on the comparative neglect of the European dimension of wartime diplomacy show how this worked out in practice. The first has to do with the widespread tendency to link Churchill to Roosevelt. This has the effect of immediately making FDR a party to all Churchill's multifarious activities, and thus a much more significant figure in European affairs, for instance, than in fact he was. A reader in the World War II historiography produced in the United States may well get the impression that the three Allied powers were the United States, the Soviet Union, and Winston Churchill. This approach probably owes something to Harry Hopkins, who, during his pathfinding mission to London in 1941, cabled a delighted Roosevelt, who did not want to deal with a spectrum of British leaders, that "Churchill is the Government," and to Averell Harriman, who similarly affirmed that "[t]here is no other man in sight to give the British the leadership that Churchill does." This line was fully appropriated by many American historians, content to judge Anglo-American relations by the extraordinary Roosevelt-Churchill correspondence and perhaps overimpressed by Churchill's persistent courtship of the president. Other British leaders doing other things, notably in Europe, could thus be, and were, largely ignored. The effect was inevitably to exaggerate the American political role. For once wedded to Churchill in this way, FDR automatically comes to be seen as a major actor (often *the* major actor) in all important issues. In fact, however, his pre-Yalta involvement in European political affairs was, largely but not entirely by his own choice, fitful and only marginally consequential.[5]

[5] Robert Sherwood, *Roosevelt and Hopkins* (New York, 1950), p. 243. Harriman to Roosevelt, March 7, 1941, PSF, Box 50, Roosevelt MSS.

The second illustration appears to exhibit a self-protective turning away from the threat of potentially subversive thought. The occasion was the release in the early 1970s of the British diplomatic records for World War II. By this time the American archives had already been long available. The British records posed some threat to the conventional wisdom, and especially to Americocentric perspectives. For insofar as they posited a leading British role, they opened up a hitherto neglected, autonomous European dimension of Allied diplomacy. They revealed, for instance, a range of independent collaborations with the Soviet Union, led by the Foreign Office, looking to an agreed framework for postwar European security. Churchill himself had been actively involved in this. But few of the leading American Cold War historians of the day, distracted at the time by the intense orthodox-revisionist arguments of the Vietnam era, showed much interest in these admittedly voluminous records. Indeed, several fine scholars whom we think of as leading "Cold War historians" have made little or no use of the British material, preferring to probe ever more deeply into new sources at home, sources that throw ever more light on American policy, rather than contemplating the system-disturbing international dimension now on offer in London. This, I believe, is why we are still burdened with such concoctions as the "Yalta Order" (which carries the implication of a large role for Roosevelt in bringing about this fictitious result) and yet have been unable to come up with an alternative explanation of that intriguing meeting that can command public understanding. Ironically, Yalta was, in many respects, essentially an American revolt against a European "order" agreed upon months before within the long-developing Anglo-Soviet nexus.

The third example involves not a turning away from a potential source of subversion but a vigorous reaching out for reinforcement and perhaps for reassurance. For the sudden prospect in the early 1990s of access to Soviet diplomatic records stimulated in the United States all the appropriating and integrating energy that had been so significantly lacking in the British case twenty years earlier. There is surely no more eloquent manifestation of the commitment to a bilateral, East/West, and specifically United States/Soviet view of Allied wartime and Cold War diplomacy than the enthusiastic response of the American political and academic establishment to the chance to gain revelations from the great Soviet foil. Now, through the energetic midwifery of American foundations and universities, extensive support was given to American and Soviet scholars. The results, at least for the World War II years, have in fact been meager. No striking evidence of a crucially enhanced American role in Europe's affairs before 1945 has yet emerged. Indeed, it seems that, at least up to the Yalta conference, the Soviets looked to their British connections, not to the Americans, as they planned for the postwar.

I have undoubtedly in these observations unfairly flattened out some fine, variegated scholarship to make my point – which is, put very simply, that we should bring the Europeans much more fully into our thinking about World War II Allied diplomacy. For there are demonstrably enough flaws, gaps, and obvious distortions and imbalances in the conventional East/West view of Allied diplomacy in the early 1940s to raise an important question: Is there another scenario, with an evidentially stronger base, to take its place? Now that we are out of the Cold War cage and free from the intellectual pressures generated by that struggle, we can perhaps reach for, or at least consider the possibility of, a more satisfying account of its origins and its relationship to World War II. Let us therefore shelve the "traditional" categories and assumptions for a moment and with them the momentous inquiry: Why and how did the World War produce the Cold War? Let us pose instead a humbler question: What, as precisely as we can measure in light of evidence old and new, were the constituent relations of the three Allied powers during World War II?

As soon as we invoke this simpler perspective, fresh explanatory vistas begin to present themselves. We start to see Yalta as it appeared to contemporaries rather than as it seems to us in Cold War retrospect. We become more conscious of their past, of their predicaments, rather than of our own presuppositions. We see the politics of World War II not as a dress rehearsal for the Cold War but as rooted, more than we had thought, in prewar 1930s patterns. We become more conscious of the weight of Europe and its non-Nazi leaders in the wartime affairs of their own arena. We see more clearly the corresponding passivity of American diplomacy in its approach to Europe. And we become more aware of the continuing separation, up to the time of Yalta, of the European and American political worlds.

Above all, we become aware of a change in the significance, at least so far as European matters are concerned, of the three basic relationships I mentioned earlier. The Anglo-American nexus is, of course, still uniquely and intimately strong, but so far as its political character is concerned we feel more aware of its engagement, not with the future of Europe – which Roosevelt and Churchill tended to avoid – but with the European politics necessarily involved in the prosecution of the war and, much more seriously, with the shape of future worldwide economic competition. The postwar political architecture of Europe, except in the casual talk of Anglo-American leaders suddenly thrown together in the course of complex strategic operations, or during the occasional eruption of emotions engendered by the ambitions of irritating figures like de Gaulle, plays little part in Anglo-American relations before the autumn of 1944.

The other strong relationship now is the neglected Anglo-Soviet association – founded not only in the exigencies of a war fought on their continent but also in a natural concern with the politics of Europe during and after the catastrophe. Suddenly, events like Foreign Secretary Anthony Eden's meeting with Stalin in December 1941, the Anglo-Soviet Treaty of May 1942, and the connections culminating in the Churchill-Stalin agreements of October 1944 come to the fore as tangible reflections of a profound pattern of deeply felt concern for their own future among Europeans.

What then of the third relationship, that between the United States and the Soviet Union, in which so much of our forensic energy has been invested? This now seems from the overall record to have been less important and thin by comparison, characterized, at least in its European manifestations, by a combination of American detachment and Soviet reluctance to forge a closer association. Only at the very end of the war, when apparent British and Soviet excesses in the reordering of Europe forced President Roosevelt to engage more fully than he wished with the old continent's politics at Yalta, did this change significantly.

There is, therefore, I believe, a persuasive alternative scenario to that offered by the conventional view of Allied wartime diplomacy. It posits a more internationalist and specifically European reality. It stresses the importance of the Anglo-Soviet nexus, institutionalized by treaty, sanctioned by history, compelled by geopolitical logic, and, most importantly, demonstrable by reference to the historical record. There we find a growing partnership in European affairs evident in a range of negotiations and relationships as well as in various kinds of diplomatic and political cooperation and culminating in the Churchill-Stalin arrangements of October 1944. There too we see a political division of Europe (one that in its territorial aspects lasted through the Cold War) which, in its subsequent consolidation and working out, we might reasonably call the Moscow Order.

The case for this alternative scenario depends, of course, on a credible reordering of the significant events in light of the evidential record as it now exists. In this account some familiar events, including some that seem to show the United States as a dynamic actor in European affairs, recede in importance. These include FDR's persistent efforts to arrange meetings with Stalin, and even some of his personal interventions such as the declaration of "unconditional surrender" in 1943. At the same time other, less familiar events, particularly those signifying some kind of European political vitality – such as the Anglo-Soviet treaty of 1942, the intensive intra-European negotiations over the future of Poland, and the widespread dissemination of European geopolitical visions – become more prominent. A similar adjustment of priorities will be noticed in personal relationships. We will see less here of such Rooseveltian acolytes as Henry Wallace, Sumner Welles, and William Bullitt – names that appear in most American accounts of the period. We will see more of such people as Eduard Benes, Paul-Henri Spaak, and Ivan Maisky – names rarely found in American studies but more prominent in the work of European historians.

What then is the evidence for this heightened sense of European diplomacy? Significant facts and suggestive relationships have emerged from the Soviet archives, and (though my knowledge of Russian is very limited, and I have had to rely on better-equipped historians and professional researchers, whose help I gratefully acknowledge) I have been able to make some use of these. They tend, I believe, to support the argument I make here, especially the notion of a Soviet desire to avoid close ties with the United States and to make a partner of the British in wartime and postwar Europe. But, as everyone knows, the high expectations of 1989 have not been fulfilled. The new materials are selective and very limited (especially for the wartime period with which I am most concerned), and their release has often been guided by political and other criteria. I can therefore make no pretence to a definitive account, probably a mythical quest in any kind of diplomatic history.

There are basically three problems with the Soviet records. A major one has been the haphazard and difficult access since the warm but brief initial welcome in the early 1990s. Another is the lamentable paucity of the available wartime record so far, which works to hide from us that sense of plausible context and bureaucratic infrastructure that historians need for confident evaluation. (This is particularly true for the wartime period we are concerned with here.) Nearly all the admirable volumes based on Soviet records produced by the Woodrow Wilson Cold War project deal with the Cold War itself, not with the war period. There were apparently several "shredding" operations of the wartime papers during the Cold War, and Stalin himself, the man who was at the center but did much of his business on the telephone, seems to have covered his tracks well. Obviously there is much we shall never know. Stalin hated historians, whom he called "archive rats." At the October 1944 conference in Moscow, when Churchill offered an awkward apology for his earlier hostility to the Bolshevik regime, Stalin gracefully produced, as he was wont to do, a soothing Russian proverb:

"He who recalls the past should lose his eyesight."[6] To be fair, historians, who like to think they have the last word, have been taking their revenge ever since. But in many ways Stalin has won, for as we search for archival enlightenment we find that he has left us, to paraphrase his notorious proverb about the pleasures of calculated revenge, a dish served cold and with very little in the way of nutritious fare. And this is a pity, because the decision making on important issues was, it is generally agreed, in his hands. Indeed, so powerful was he that he felt able to reverse basic policy virtually overnight and make the Nazi-Soviet pact of August 1939 without even consulting the Politburo, or apparently any other political figure except his compliant commissar for foreign affairs, Vyacheslav Molotov.

On the other hand, in addition to the valuable glimpses into the work of the wartime diplomatic establishment now available, we have the benefit of some important revelations, notably the records of the postwar planning commissions established during 1943 under Maisky, the former ambassador to Britain, and Maxim Litvinov, the former ambassador to the United States. Further, there has been a proliferation of useful memoir literature in recent years. We also have the British Broadcasting Corporation's *Daily Digest of Soviet Broadcasts* for the entire war, an excellent, little-exploited source, at least for public policy. Using these and other sources we can show much of the reality of the Anglo-Soviet nexus, and from the smattering of more intimate sources we can convey something, at least, of the calculations that inspired the Kremlin's commitment to it, as we endure the long wait for a fuller enlightenment.

The most useful sources available today for a delineation of the European dimension, however, are the British wartime archives. These have not been fully exploited. One wonders if they will be in the future. The danger now is that the internationally oriented insights in the British archives will for a time be swamped by the lure of exciting new Soviet records, which, while in fact they appear to be steadily reinforcing the perspectives I am urging here, seem nevertheless to be leading many researchers back to congenial thoughts of a superpower bipolarity that is perfectly appropriate for the course of the Cold War itself but badly misleading for the World War II years, or even for the period between May 1945 and March–April 1946, when new political associations were still crystallizing and the range of postwar possibilities was still quite open and conjectural.

---

[6] Record of talks at the Kremlin, October 18, 1944, in PREM 3.434/7.

The British records are a useful corrective to any tendency toward narrowly nationalistic or excessively bipolar thinking. They tell us a great deal about large World War II issues, about Yalta's real significance, and about the unexpected emergence of the Cold War. There are a number of obvious reasons for this. One is the basic fact that Britain was much closer to both the United States and the Soviet Union than those two countries were to each other. Another is that Britain had worldwide interests and was both European and transatlantic in outlook and historic orientation. Inevitably, therefore, the British were close students and perceptive observers of each partner, the more so because Britain was in many respects the most vulnerable of the three powers and was in fact subjected to intense pressures from each of its better-endowed allies as the war progressed. Then too, London was the wartime capital of non-Nazi Europe, the home of many exile governments for whom it exercised a generally sympathetic custodial or at least fiduciary role. All this was reinforced by a comparatively efficient governmental machine, a tradition of worldliness and political sophistication, and a vast array of international connections. Britain's archives, therefore, were always likely to be a primary source for any historian interested in the international as opposed to the narrowly national diplomatic history of World War II.

What the British records seem to show, above all, is that while the war itself was always the governing concern of the Churchill government, this focus was accompanied by the development and elaboration of a European vision of postwar security based not on the creation of a successor to the League of Nations or on the vindication of the principles of the Atlantic Charter, but on a steadily growing Anglo-Soviet understanding about future security from which, partly by its own choice, partly by Anglo-Soviet preference, the United States was excluded. The resulting "Moscow Order" represented the short-lived triumph of traditional and geopolitical logic over the visionary ideas and economic multilateralism offered by what then seemed to be a politically very detached United States. In the end, Churchill and Foreign Secretary Anthony Eden forged with Stalin and Molotov what amounted to a European path. At the beginning of 1945, as the three leaders prepared for the Yalta conference, this was still generally expected in Paris, Berlin, and Madrid, as well as in London and Moscow, and even in Washington, to be the basis of postwar European political organization. Yet a few short weeks after Yalta all this lay in ruins.

Thus, from the viewpoint developed here, the Yalta conference turns out to be just as important as it appears to be in the conventional account, but for different reasons. It did not produce a division of Europe,

or a Yalta Order, or any other kind of coherent or integrating conception. In fact, we might with some justice speak of a "Yalta Disorder."
For President Roosevelt, who had up to this point openly or covertly
endeavored to subvert nearly all impulses toward European postwar
unity, came to Yalta determined to break down, or at least to weaken, the
now well-established Anglo-Soviet concert, which, by its sudden display
of vitality and activism, was threatening in late 1944 to destroy public
support in the United States for his policy of a postwar internationalism focused on a United Nations organization. In this he was, as we will
see, largely successful. The president's eccentric personal diplomacy, and
the various temptations it seemed to offer, worked to separate Churchill
and Stalin. But in publicly proclaiming the Yalta agreements a brilliant
success for American diplomacy, FDR presented the British leader with
an unintended opportunity, which Churchill quickly seized, to try and
create at last an Anglo-American front against the Soviets (now suddenly upstaged in the post-Yalta myth making) in defense of the supposed Polish settlement, a general regime of freedom and democracy in
Eastern Europe, and much else. And in this Churchill was partly successful. Ironically, therefore, the consequence of Roosevelt's Yalta success was
not the tripartite tranquility or the beneficent Yalta Order he had hoped
for, but the entanglement of the United States at last in the complex and
constraining politics of Europe.

Could the Anglo-Soviet concert have worked? Would it have avoided
the Cold War? Defenders of the conventional view of the Cold War's
origins may be inclined to dismiss such questions as inconsequential
and simply to ask whether it is worth studying this European "road not
taken." The short answer is that this road was taken. The geopolitical
arrangements made by Churchill and Stalin, in effect a political division
of Europe, founded on military realities, became a territorial framework
for continental Europe that lasted for nearly half a century. In this the
United States played no part. What did change were the presiding relationships. And here the United States played a crucial role. For the real significance of Yalta is that, in its erratic conference course and in its convoluted
aftermath, it brought about the political commitment to that now divided
Europe of the hitherto separate United States. Thus the Moscow and Yalta
conferences worked, together with the underlying military realities, to create the Cold War Order – the one creating the geopolitical architecture,
the other establishing (after a short crystallizing interval) the new political
relationships – within which Europe struggled to recover from the midcen-
tury catastrophe.

The argument here will be developed through three phases. We begin with a brief review of Yalta's image during the Cold War era, with a view to demonstrating in a rudimentary way the subjective character of much that we think we know about this event that is so deeply embedded in the conventional view of the Cold War's origins. The book then works into a more positive mode with three chapters that take the story, in a necessarily selective way, from the shocks of 1939 to the eve of the Yalta meeting in February 1945, tracing the origins and evolution of the Anglo-Soviet concert of power that was generally seen at the time as the likely framework for postwar European politics. These chapters will emphasize both the continuing efficacy of European diplomacy and the equally traditional detachment, despite a growing practical involvement in European affairs as the war progressed, of the United States. The third phase involves some further stage setting for Yalta, with a chapter exploring some of the distinctive features of Roosevelt's America and the ways in which the war influenced not only FDR's policies but also a range of official and private interests. By 1944 these elements were moving into position to shape and underpin that sudden and remarkable projection of American power and organization that was soon seen by everyone to be ushering in a new era. We then come, in two concluding chapters, first to the conference itself and then to its complex aftermath, which was in one sense transformative in breaking down the Anglo-Soviet nexus through two distinct crises in 1945 and 1946, yet in another way confirmatory in that it did not challenge (indeed, it tacitly endorsed) the structural, geopolitical division of the continent created earlier by the European leaders.

I should be clear about one thing. It is not my purpose to try to stamp out the East/West conception of Allied diplomacy and substitute for it an all-encompassing Europe/America framework. There is far too much tripartite activity and complex mixing for that, too many material American intrusions in Europe and interweaving relationships among the Big Three to justify a dogmatic generalization of that kind. It is really a matter of proportion. By bringing Europe more fully into the story of Allied diplomacy, and correspondingly reducing the supposed American role, I want not simply to challenge a prevailing Americocentrism but, more substantively, to render a truer portrait of the activities of the victorious combination, so that we can see these two great continental theaters as they really were, at least until February 1945: politically autonomous arenas that – despite the distortions caused by the obscuring Hitlerian overlay, the culturally imperializing character of the Anglo-American strategic partnership, and Churchill's spellbinding transatlantic oratory and persisting anticommunist animus – viewed each other as separate and distinct political worlds and expected that to continue.

Yalta is best seen as the end of the Grand Alliance. It was not, I think, the beginning of the Cold War, though its immediate aftermath did produce a crisis that in turn created conditions for future confrontation and made that outcome much more likely. The final denouement came in a second crisis in early 1946. Between these two clashes there were both spasmodic attempts to restore good relations within the tripartite association and, on the other hand, intervening causative events (such as the appearance of the atomic weapon) that created new tensions and would certainly need to be factored in to a fuller account of the Cold War's origins and consolidation than I am offering here. Nonetheless, the Crimean meeting remains central to any understanding of these later events as well, and also to an appreciation of the structural approach to the Cold War's origins. For Yalta set in train a process that produced, for the third time in just over thirty years, a situation in which the United States found itself gradually and uncertainly moving through the familiar British corridor toward a fateful confrontation with Britain's continental adversary. Even in the United States, where we instinctively resist deterministic explanation, this is surely a humbling reminder of the constraints on human action that seem to rear up repeatedly to frustrate the most creative statesmen of almost any era in modern history, even as they inspire the scholarly enterprise that tries to understand them.

Acknowledgments

It is a pleasure to acknowledge certain debts I have incurred while writing this book. In general, I have a strong sense of the obligation I owe to friends and fellow practitioners in the field of modern diplomatic/international history, and especially to the fellowship and collegiality of the scholars grouped in the Society for Historians of American Foreign Relations. These have been enriching associations.

Any field of study devoted to the recent diplomatic history of a Great Power that is still as active in the world as the contemporary United States is bound to be a feisty arena: effusive, articulate, and pulsing with emotion. But, as historians know only too well, the attractive lure of immediacy and relevance comes at a price. Current political and philosophical allegiances, continually refreshed and sharpened by the ongoing story, tend to shape inquiry into the past. It is sometimes hard to be objective. Dichotomous thinking flourishes. And fresh perspectives have to make their way against entrenched views that also function, far beyond their crystallization in the academic community, as a strongly defended treasure chest for politicians and polemicists who take a somewhat opportunistic view of the past.

Increasingly, however, we appear to be coming to terms with these hegemonial domestic constraints and breaking free of the Americocentrism that has long been their most obvious manifestation. One sign of this is the steady trend in recent years toward a more internationally oriented understanding of American diplomatic history, especially for the crucially transformative years of World War II and the early Cold War. This comes from a line of thought that draws its inspiration from distinguished scholars – W. H. McNeill and George F. Kennan in the United States,

Donald Cameron Watt in Britain, for example – whose work during the Cold War era urged the importance, when exploring the American role in world affairs, of wider views. I hope this book, with its central Europe/America focus, will help to reanimate that tradition.

My interest in the Europe/America juxtaposition goes back to my graduate training in the 1970s at the University of California at Berkeley. I began my studies with two stimulating courses, one in classic European diplomatic history with Raymond Sontag, the other in the history of modern American foreign relations with Martin Sherwin. Other teachers on that remarkable faculty – Lawrence Levine, Kenneth Waltz, and Michael Rogin, among others – are also gratefully remembered. I want to mention with appreciation Diane Shaver Clemens, who arrived to teach at Berkeley after I had completed my course work but who kindly chaired my dissertation committee. Her own book, *Yalta*, published in 1970 before any official British or Soviet records had become available, is a model analysis of a diplomatic negotiation. It has long been admired. Our mutual interest in this extraordinary meeting is entirely coincidental, but I have found her book very useful in the preparation of this study. The Yalta conference can of course be profitably viewed from a variety of angles, and I have benefited from participation in panel discussions about it with Robert Dallek, Robert Service, and Constantine Pleshakov and in informal discussions too numerous to mention, though several stimulating conversations with Holger Afflerbach are lodged firmly in my mind. I would also like to thank Robert Messer and Klaus Larres, who read the manuscript and offered helpful suggestions. All errors and shortcomings are of course mine alone.

I want to thank Svetlana Savranskaya of the National Security Archive for her help with Soviet and Eastern European research materials. She has been a splendid guide to many of us, including my own graduate students. I am grateful, too, for the insight I received at various points from participants in the events described herein, such as the Foreign Office's Sir Frank Roberts in London and Stanislaw Szwalbe, former vice-marshal of the Polish Sejm. I am deeply thankful to the many librarians in the United States and Europe (especially at the British National Archives at Kew) who have eased my way. There is an extraordinary volume of material to examine in this field, far beyond the ability of any lone scholar to fully comprehend, let alone master. One particularly values, therefore, collections like Warren Kimball's fine volumes on the Churchill and Roosevelt correspondence and the Woodrow Wilson Center's Cold War International History Project. We need more help of that kind.

The University Research Committee of Emory University gave much-appreciated support, as did Emory College in granting me timely leaves from teaching duties. I am grateful also to Lewis Bateman for his longtime encouragement and support of the project and to Emily Spangler, Mark Fox, and others at Cambridge University Press for their valued contribution, and to copy editor Russell Hahn for his scrupulous care and patience.

My greatest debt is to my family, above all to my wife, Marysia, whose fluency in Russian has been of enormous practical help, and whose warmth and vibrant personality have sustained me throughout. The engaged historian is, from a human viewpoint, a notoriously difficult proposition, a fact amply illustrated by the penitential eloquence one often finds in these familial tributes. The physical frame may still be present, but the mind becomes a wandering thing. It takes a very special person to understand this and eventually lead the time traveler back to a safe shore. And here, as friends and relations are always pointing out to me (needlessly, I might say), I have been exceptionally fortunate. I am also indebted, for their good-humored indulgence and interest, to my children, Josie and Chris, the bright lights in my personal firmament. The book is lovingly and thankfully dedicated to them.

Abbreviations

BBC Digest	British Broadcasting Corporation, world broadcasts
CAB	Cabinet papers (UK)
Correspondence	Warren Kimball, ed., *Churchill and Roosevelt*: *The Complete Correspondence*
COS	Chiefs of Staff (UK)
EAC	European Advisory Commission
FO	Foreign Office (UK)
FRUS	*Foreign Relations of the United States*
FRUS, Yalta	*Foreign Relations of the United States*, conferences at Malta and Yalta
HW	Intelligence files (UK)
INF	Ministry of Information papers (UK)
JCOS	Joint Chiefs of Staff (U.S.)
OSS	Office of Strategic Services (U.S.)
PHP	Post-Hostilities Planners (UK)
PMM	Prime ministers' meetings (UK)
PREM	Prime ministers' papers (UK)
SC	Security Council, United Nations
SCCA	Stalin's correspondence with Churchill and Attlee
SCRT	Stalin's correspondence with Roosevelt and Truman

SD   State Department (U.S.)
SOE   Special Operations Executive (UK)
T   Treasury papers (UK)
ULTRA   British intelligence intercepts (UK)
WM   Cabinet minutes (UK)
WP   Cabinet papers (UK)

The Confusions of Yalta

Yalta's tantalizing combination of political drama and deep public emotion, as well as the urge to understand an event that so obviously lies near the center of the break-up of what Churchill liked to call "the Grand Alliance," has engaged many historians. There is also a natural professional interest in transitions, in the way great conflicts end and lead into a new, often unanticipated phase. But Yalta, even when viewed simply as a technical problem in diplomatic history, presents more difficulties than most such cases. The conference lasted only ten days; it took place before the end of the war whose ravages it supposedly aspired to mend; and it was conducted in complete secrecy. The other great terminal conferences of modern history seem transparently clear by contrast. The 1815 Congress of Vienna is generally seen as a success because the plenipotentiaries knew each other and took their time. They wined, dined, and seduced their way through about a year of spasmodic activity. "The conference dances but it does not move," complained one observer.[1] Still, they created, at least temporarily (some would say for a century), a stable, post-Napoleonic order. The Paris Peace Conference of 1919 self-consciously followed this model; it also took several months, and though it is generally regarded as a failure today we at least have a clear record and a substantial measure of academic agreement as to the aims of the Great Powers and what was said and done.[2]

---

[1] Attributed to Prince Charles-Joseph Ligne. Tim Blanning, *Times Literary Supplement*, June 13, 2003.
[2] See Margaret Macmillan, *Paris 1919* (New York, 2002); and Charles K. Webster, *The Congress of Vienna, 1814–1815* (London, 1920).

Yalta was not a conventional, punctuating negotiation in this sense. Indeed, there was no such comprehensive peace conference after World War II. Instead, we see a string of often hastily arranged meetings between 1941 and 1946, several of which may be held to have contributed in some measure to the final outcome. Naturally, the three great summit conferences have drawn much attention: Teheran in 1943, a strategy-oriented meeting that saw the introduction of basic but not yet crystallized political themes; Yalta in February 1945, for better or worse a kind of creative, architectural moment; and Potsdam in mid-1945, a necessary confrontation with practical postwar problems. But, as will be seen, this narrow fixation on the three summits offers only a spurious clarity – a brilliant surface, certainly, but one that elevates the "Big Three" concept excessively and obscures and diminishes less glamorous negotiations and a number of other causative impulses.

The high public emotion that Yalta has always inspired is another problematic for the historian. The wide variety of entrenched perspectives is daunting. These include a bitter Polish interpretation, natural enough considering the territorial and political violations visited upon that tragic country; a deeply resentful French view, soon to become a generalized European sense of subjection to a United States–Soviet hegemony; a British suggestion of a hard-won victory prejudiced by tragically clumsy diplomacy on the part of the two emergent superpowers; a Soviet belief that President Harry S. Truman, abetted by Churchill and American capitalists, betrayed Roosevelt's well-intentioned Yalta commitments; a conservative charge in the United States that FDR had been either traitorous or incompetently naïve; and the Truman administration's conviction that Stalin had violated his Yalta pledges, especially his declared acceptance of Polish independence and Eastern European democracy.[3]

The natural corrective to a witches' brew of this kind would have been a full documentary account. None was made available until the official American record of Yalta was released in 1955. By that time politicians, editorialists, and memoirists had established the dominating, sharply edged images. Yalta had already become not only a primary cause of dissension between the United States and the Soviet Union, but also a symbol for the

---

[3] See, variously, R. Umiastowski, *Poland, Russia and Great Britain, 1941–1945, A Study of Evidence* (London, 1946); Arthur Conte, *Yalta ou le Partage du Monde* (Paris, 1966); Chester Wilmot, *Struggle for Europe* (London, 1952); Diane Clemens, *Yalta* (New York, 1970); Felix Wittmer, *The Yalta Betrayal: Data on the Decline and Fall of Franklin Delano Roosevelt* (Caldwell, Idaho, 1953); and Arthur M. Schlesinger, Jr., "Origins of the Cold War," *Foreign Affairs* (October 1967), pp. 22–52.

Europeans of their eclipse at the hands of the two supposedly hegemonic superpowers; a token for small countries of Great Power domination; and a harsh measuring point for many Americans of Roosevelt's reputation. By the time an authentic record had become available all these feelings were already deeply entrenched, as indeed they are to this day. Historians had already lost the battle for definition. Much of their effort thereafter was concerned with only half-successful attempts to discredit proliferating myths rather than with patient reconstruction.[4]

The Cold War inevitably brought its own distorting pressures. There was a widely felt need everywhere, but especially in the United States, whose citizens felt that they had been suddenly pitchforked into a role that cut right across their historical tradition of detachment from Europe, for quick explanations of the disappointing outcome of World War II and for justifications of the new, assertive postwar policies. Yalta – initially portrayed by the Big Three as a great success and then, within weeks, exhibited to the world as a failure – was quickly and perhaps inevitably seized upon as the crucially causative diplomatic event and was then caught up in a worldwide media whirlwind of partisanship and recrimination that only slowly spilled over into academic circles. Professional historians during the Cold War wrote books about Yalta that endeavored to be even-handed but that, as we will see, tended to mirror the political atmosphere of the day. It was difficult to be objective. There was an emphasis on answers and justification. Complexities were brushed aside as Yalta was made to serve, as it still does today, as a shorthand explanation of the origins of the Cold War, much as "Munich" has been used since 1939 as a catch-all reference point for the lead-up to World War II. And there is nothing more functional than today's conventional view, a distillation of Yalta's many diverse characteristics, that the three powers created there the postwar division of Europe as well as "Yalta orders" for that continent and Asia.

We are talking here, to be sure, of images, not reality. The creation of the symbolic Yalta (or Yaltas) is potentially a large, fascinating subject in cultural-intellectual as well as political terms. But my main purpose in this book is simply to offer an explanation of Yalta itself and not, except in

---

[4] The United States documentary record is in FRUS, *The Conferences at Malta and Yalta, 1945* (Washington, D.C., 1955). The British records are in PREM 3/51/4. The Soviet government's published account is *The Teheran, Yalta and Potsdam Conferences: Documents* (Moscow, 1960). Three varying perspectives on Yalta are found in John Snell (ed.), *The Meaning of Yalta: Big Three Diplomacy and the New Balance of Power* (Baton Rouge, La., 1956); Clemens, *Yalta*; and Russell Buhite, *Decisions at Yalta: An Appraisal of Summit Diplomacy* (Wilmington, Del., 1986).

these ground-clearing comments, to probe deeply into the epidemic imagery that has obscured its real significance. Still, having mentioned some
general reasons for the distortions, it seems appropriate to single out one
tangible cause that does establish some sense of connection between the
event and the image, and also helps explain the extraordinary fervor of the
widespread public emotion we have just noted.

This is the role of President Franklin D. Roosevelt. Yalta was in many
ways his conference. Stalin chose the remote site, to FDR's and Churchill's
dismay, but Roosevelt did most to stage-manage Yalta's form and character. He began by refusing to join the Europeans in the traditional task
of setting a preliminary agenda. Determined to control the conference's
presentation, he took with him carefully chosen domestic political figures
who could convey the right impression to the American people. He took
the lead in refusing any independent press coverage and selected a trusted
photographer whose group portraits of the three could be relied upon
to send out from the Crimea a striking image of Allied power and unity.
Viewed bleakly across six decades, these pictures are in fact disturbingly
suggestive far beyond the president's intentions: Roosevelt manifestly
haggard and ill; Stalin mostly aloof and in most photographs cold as a
statue; Churchill grimly brooding. But at the time the grainy newspaper
reproductions served the cause.[5]

More to the point, Roosevelt, by artful use of the language he had
persuaded the European allies to accept in the Declaration on Liberated
Europe, gave the world the impression, in the glowing vision he and his
associates created publicly after the conference, that he had been able to
bring about a surprising and deeply gratifying degree of harmony and
constructive promise among the Big Three victors, who would now go on,
under the hospitable auspices of a liberally refashioned world organization,
to build a progressive Wilsonian order of justice and goodwill.[6] This over-
sold vision, which Churchill later likened to "a franudulent prospectus,"
had profound consequences. Roosevelt, suddenly rendered defenseless
by death, was succeeded by Harry S. Truman, who took the view that the
Declaration was a treaty that Stalin, already acting unilaterally and oppres-
sively in Poland and elsewhere, was deceitfully violating. But an increasing

---

[5] For conference preparations and recommendations, see FRUS, *Yalta*, pp. 3–428. For
photographers and censorship, see Roosevelt to Churchill, January 22, 1945, in Warren
Kimball, ed., *Churchill and Roosevelt: The Complete Correspondence*, 3 vols. (Princeton,
1984), vol. III, p. 515 (hereafter cited as **Correspondence**, volume and page).

[6] The Declaration on Liberated Europe is in FRUS, *Yalta*, pp. 971–973.

number of Americans also blamed the supposedly naïve FDR, who now became for many of them (and for even more Europeans) a logical if not inevitable scapegoat for Yalta's failure to rein in the Soviets and for much else that was now going wrong in Europe. Alarming revelations of Roosevelt's secret dealings at Yalta – his willingness to give additional United Nations memberships to the Soviet Union, territorial concessions made to Stalin at China's expense, the forced repatriation of Soviet citizens – which emerged shortly after the conference and mostly after the president's death, stoked the fire. As Cold War tensions grew, he became the focus of McCarthy-era allegations that he had "sold out" Eastern Europe and China at Yalta. He was accused of treason by American right-wingers. Even some moderate American opinion was inclined to wonder whether Roosevelt's dubious public portrayal of Yalta had not led more or less directly to the breakdown of United States–Soviet cooperation.[7]

To put matters in this way, however, is not to endorse any particular view. The natural question, of course, is why President Roosevelt felt it necessary to act in this fashion, effectively creating two Yaltas. As we will see later, he had his reasons, perhaps very good reasons. Let us suspend judgment. My present purpose is simply to draw attention, in the briefest possible way, to some of the causes of the initial confusion that set Yalta off on a Cold War career of polemics, crises, and raw emotions, ending finally in the strangely distilled "Yalta Order" of today's common editorial usage. For the moment it is enough to note that in 1955 President Eisenhower published the documentary record of the conference. This had the effect of clearing Roosevelt of "betrayal" charges but left him branded as a "naïve" statesman who had not properly understood Stalin or Soviet/communist aims – a charge made by Churchill, with some delicacy but with crystal clarity, a year on so before in the final volume, *Triumph and Tragedy*, of his immensely influential war memoirs.[8]

We will return in a moment to the various ways in which Yalta was received in the United States. But first let us see how the combination of

---

[7] For the "prospectus" comment and letter, see Churchill to Roosevelt, March 8, 1945, *Correspondence III*, pp. 547–551; Harry S. Truman, *Memoirs*, Vol. 1, *Year of Decisions* (New York, 1955), pp. 15, 24–25, 71–72, 77, 82. See also Athan Theoharis, *The Yalta Myths: An Issue in United States Politics, 1945–1955* (Columbia, Mo., 1970), pp. 19–22, 29–33 and passim. For Stalin's reaction to post-Yalta events, see Fraser J. Harbutt, *The Iron Curtain: Churchill, America and the Origins of the Cold War* (New York, 1986), pp. 95–99.

[8] See Theoharis, *The Yalta Myths*, pp. 195, 200–202, 206–208 and passim. See also Winston S. Churchill, *The Second World War*, Vol. 6, *Triumph and Tragedy* (Boston, 1953), pp. 346–402.

Roosevelt's supposedly gullible Yalta diplomacy, American postwar hegemony, and Europe's misery and decline – all increasingly subsumed in the
"Yalta" indictment – encouraged a pervasive sense of victimization in the
old continent. This began immediately after Yalta with the understandably
bitter protests of the Polish exile government in London and their supporters
in the large Polish diaspora over the fate meted out by their supposed allies:
political subjection to the Soviet Union, and severe territorial amputation
in the east with as yet only vague compensation in the west, which, when
regularized, would leave postwar Poland even more beholden to Moscow
as the indispensable protector against German irredentism.[9] The French
were also aggrieved from the outset. They, especially General Charles de
Gaulle, resented their exclusion from the conference, manifestly signifying
their lost status. Yalta was henceforth seen in Paris as the symbol first of a
keenly disliked Anglo-American and then of a United States–Soviet hegemony. British writers, drawing on revived memories of President Woodrow
Wilson's alleged ineptitude in Paris in 1919, soon joined the parade of resentment, beginning in the early 1950s to suggest that Roosevelt had similarly prejudiced a hard-won victory by his irresponsible Yalta diplomacy.[10]

The circle of grievance soon widened. As they recovered some self-
confidence in international affairs, German spokesmen and writers in
the Federal Republic also began to look to Yalta as a prime source of
their postwar tribulations. By the mid-1950s, as the post-Stalin Soviets
began to talk seductively of "disengagement," we find German scholars
blaming "the punitive attitude" of the British and Americans at the conference for the division of their country. By this time the Italians were also
expressing the continental angst. The geopolitical theorist Luisi Bonnanti
complained that Italy's postwar political system, which was often in dis-
array, had been imposed by the victors at Yalta. Other views occasionally broke through. In 1958 an Italian academic journal even published a
pro-Roosevelt article by an American historian, though the editor found
it necessary to warn his readers in a prefatory note that the author had
not seen fit to mention FDR's errors at Yalta, for which, he pointed out,
Europe had suffered so much during the previous twelve years.[11]

---

[9] Umiastowski, *Poland, Russia and Great Britain*, pp. 436–441.
[10] Charles de Gaulle, *Memoirs of Hope: Renewal and Endeavor*, trans. Terence Kilmarton
(New York, 1971), pp. 199, 226. See also Roger Gromand, "De Gaulle et Yalta," *Revue
des Deux Mondes*, no. 9 (1982), pp. 629–634; and Wilmot, *Struggle for Europe*, p. 714
and passim.
[11] H. Herrschaft, "Zur Dokumentation von Jalta," *Militar Politsches Forum*, 4, 5 (1955),
pp. 21–31; Luisi Bonate, "L'Italia nel Nuova Sistema Internazionale, 1943–1948,"

"Eurocentrism" of this kind may perhaps be seen as a mirror image of what we think of as "Americocentrism." Both reflect a high degree of self-preoccupation. The most acute point of sensitivity for European commentators was the apparent subjection of their continent to the hegemonic Anglo-American and/or Soviet powers. They tended to see Yalta and all it stood for as an unwelcome and politically annihilating visitation from outside, an attitude summed up by the headline "Europe Out of the Game" that the French historian Jean Laloy gave to his discussion of the consequences of 1940.[12] The abdicatory failure or reluctance of continental European historians through the Cold War era to look for alternative explanatory scenarios that might have recognized some purposeful European political role in the wartime Allied coalition (Anglo-Soviet if not French) naturally reinforced tendencies in the United States to assume that there had been an all-encompassing American control of the significant events.

In general, it was the grievance-ridden French who most strenuously and creatively asserted the malign significance of Yalta, often attaching more blame to the American "false friends" than to Stalin's Soviet Union, which was treated by many Parisian intellectuals as at best a benign model and at worst a political force of nature whose excesses in the unfolding of history's design could be excused. One should not exaggerate French anti-American sentiment. It is demonstrable that Yalta served for millions of French and other Europeans through the Cold War as a kind of rallying point for Americophobic sentiment. But balancing this there was also a strong pro-American symbolism associated, for instance, with memories of Lafayette, World War I, and the Marshall Plan. For every Jacques Servan-Schreiber raising the alarm in his *The American Challenge* one can find a Jean Francois Revel celebrating American vitality, as he did in his book *Without Marx or Jesus*. Similarly with Yalta: Arthur Conte's critique of Yalta in *Le Partage de Monde* must be juxtaposed with the work of a number of other French historians, from Andre Fontaine to Pierre de Senarclens, who have challenged the notion that it led to an American-mandated division of Europe at the Crimean meeting.[13]

Comunita, 27 (1973), pp. 13–75; Walter Johnson, "L'Opinione Pubblica e la Politica Estera Americana," *Rassegna Italiana di Politica di Cultura*, 35 (1958), pp. 211–224.

[12] Jean Laloy, *Yalta: Yesterday, Today, Tomorrow* (New York, 1988), p. 8.

[13] Jacques Servan-Schreiber, *The American Challenge* (New York, 1969); Jean Francois Revel, *Without Marx or Jesus* (New York, 1984); Conte, *Le Partage du Monde*; Andre Fontaine, *Histoire de la Guerre Froide*, Vol. 1 (Paris, 1965); Pierre De Senarclens, *Yalta*

It was the French too who were initially instrumental in putting Yalta to constructive uses in Europe. During the Cold War era the continental lament was steadily transformed into a foundation of Europe-wide solidarity. At every stage in the postwar move toward unity – in the progressive social democratic Franco-British impulses of the late 1940s; during de Gaulle's federally oriented "Third Force" period in the 1950s and 1960s; and later with the idea of a new Europe built around Franco-German reconciliation and leadership – Yalta featured in at least some French public commentary not simply as a moment of unwanted division imposed from outside, but as a catastrophe to be transcended, a fresh point of departure. French President Francois Mitterand and German Chancellor Helmut Kohl were particularly focused on this. As Mitterand put it in 1989, "Yalta is the symbol of the division of Europe into zones of power or influence between the Soviet Union and the United States. I dream of a reconnected, independent Europe. I dream about it and I work for it." [14]

Effusions of this sort, looking beyond the grievances of the immediate postwar years to a larger European identity and the repudiation of "Yalta's dark legacy," repeatedly appeared in editorial comment at the anniversaries of the conference and steadily acquired an all-European character. In the 1980s, Eastern Europeans also began to see themselves as part of a continent-wide struggle against what many had long seen as Yalta's hegemonic superpower imposition, despite a natural sense of the difficult odds during the Cold War. The Hungarian intellectual George Konrad, writing in 1984, drew from the failure of the 1956 uprising against Soviet rule the pessimistic conclusion that "it is impossible to alter the Yalta system from inside by means of dynamic, uncontrolled mass movements." [15] But this jeremiad was confounded at the end of the decade as the success of the Polish Solidarity movement, the decisive emergence of Mikhail Gorbachev, and the collaboration of the United States came together in the late 1980s. One of the striking features of those heady days was the constant reference to a "Yalta Order," supposedly now being brought to a welcome close. The Cold War, whose origins had seemed so messy and complex to many, now appeared to have a clear start and finish, with the Yalta conference and the destruction of the Berlin Wall emerging to general approval as the respective political

---

(Paris, 1965); *Time*, April 13, 1987. See also Conte, "Le XXe Siecle," *Nouvelle Revue des Deux Mondes*, 5 (1979), pp. 289–294.

[14] *New York Times*, November 30, 1989.

[15] "The Post-Yalta Debate: George Konrad Interviewed by Richard Falk and Mary Kaldor," *World Policy*, 2 (1984/1985), pp. 451–466.

book ends. From the sharp-edged clarity of 1989, the whole world could now look back to Yalta as the foundational sin of the postwar era.[16]

How do British attitudes fit in here? It is a question that brings to attention a curious feature of the whole post-Yalta process, namely, the immunity from serious criticism of Britain and its wartime leader. Certain flinty European conservatives never let Churchill off the hook. In his war memoirs de Gaulle was still grumbling about the "endorsement given by the Anglo-Saxons at Yalta" to the Soviets. Alexander Solzenhitzen also wrote scathingly of "the cowardly pens of Roosevelt and Churchill."[17] But this is unusual. Most British commentators took their line from two influential books. The first to appear was reporter Chester Wilmot's *Struggle for Europe* (1952), which was fiercely critical of Roosevelt's supposed naivete at Yalta. Wilmot revived many of the old resentments about American diplomacy after the previous war and, in the words of one reviewer, "gave voice to the nagging anti-Americanism that lurked beneath the English sense of dependency and focused it on Roosevelt." Fast on the heels of Wilmot's book came Churchill's *Triumph and Tragedy* (1953), which faulted the former president with compelling and unique authority and gave these negative emotions a respectable gloss. Politically this thinking was perfectly compatible with the administrations of Truman and Eisenhower, with whom Britain was now collaborating closely, and who had also now turned away self-consciously from Roosevelt's supposed legacy.[18]

Triumph and Tragedy was the last of Churchill's six volumes on the Second World War. It included an artfully Brutus-like critique of Roosevelt's conduct at Yalta. The historian David Reynolds, in a recent book aptly titled *In Command of History*, suggests that "Churchill's main object ... was to prove that he had been a far-sighted prophet of the Soviet threat" and "to shift responsibility for Western mistakes on to the Americans." American liberal reviewers, with some solicitude for FDR's reputation, had seen this coming and had laid down a series of warnings as Churchill's previous volumes had appeared. Thus, as early as 1948, the pundit Anne O'Hare McCormick had expressed admiration for *The Gathering Storm* but predicted that when Churchill's account reached 1945 "the historian

---

[16] *New York Times*, April 13, 1988 (Fuentes), and February 17, 1990 ("Yalta II"): *The Sunday Times* (London), July 9, 1989.

[17] De Gaulle, *Memoirs of Hope, Renewal and Endeavor* (New York, 1971), p. 226.

[18] Wilmot, *Struggle for Europe*, p. 714 and passim; D. C. Watt, "Britain and the Historiography of the Yalta Conference and the Cold War," *Diplomatic History*, 13, 1 (Winter 1989), p. 79; Churchill, *Triumph and Tragedy*, pp. 346–402.

will have a hard time justifying the statesman." By that time, however, with Roosevelt and his closest associate, Harry Hopkins, long dead and the Cold War in an intense phase, Churchill had an undistracted global audience at his feet. While discreetly conveying an overall impression of his own percipience and a contrasting American credulity, he explicitly criticized FDR for his carelessly volunteered statement that no American troops would remain in Europe after two years and for making the Far Eastern deal with Stalin (which he called the "least defensible" agreement at Yalta) and went on to question Roosevelt and (more delicately) other American leaders for the post-Yalta failure to face up to the fact and implications of Stalin's violations.[19]

For the next two decades this line of thought, lumping Soviet expansionism and Rooseveltian naivete together as primary causes of the Cold War, appears to have been the accepted wisdom in British thinking about Yalta. As late as 1985 a respected columnist in *The Times*, David Watt, condemned "Roosevelt's fatuous belief in his own abilities to 'handle' Stalin in 1944 and 1945." Not that there was very much scholarly work in Britain on such topics during most of the postwar era. A traditional suspicion of "contemporary" history, combined, perhaps, with the perception of declining British power in a fast-changing world, seems to have inhibited the development of a school of Cold War historians. This was the reverse of the situation in the United States, where, following World War II, a heightened sense of national power, destiny, and purpose led many toward Cold War studies. But this juxtaposition, which has over time produced an unfortunate imbalance in the field, was not due simply to emotional distaste in Britain or to glory mongering in the United States. Much of the difficulty was that the British documents for the World War II era were released only in the 1970s, nearly two decades after the American Yalta documents had appeared. From that moment on, British (and later some American) historians began to break down, to some degree, the politically established Churchillian view of an intimate Anglo-American wartime relationship that came to grief with the fateful divergence at and immediately after Yalta, and to develop a more typically European perspective. But, in general, the Wilmot-Churchill perspective persists in much British thinking. One finds innumerable echoes of it in books such as R. W. Thompson's *Churchill and Morton*, where the author refers to "the sinister Roosevelt,"

---

[19] David Reynolds, *In Command of History: Churchill Fighting and Writing the Second World War* (London, 2004), pp. 138, 425, 434, 470.

and in right-wing periodicals like *The Spectator*, where articles cri̇
FDR quite frequently appear.[20]

The way in which Yalta moved in Europe during the Cold War yea.
from being simply a diplomatic stage on the way to the Cold War to being
lodged as a highly visible symbol of eclipse, then metamorphosing into
an inspiration for European unity and enhancement – all this deserves
closer attention. Even from this abbreviated review we can see some of
the ways in which it burst free from its moorings in the history of mid-
twentieth-century diplomacy to become a potent agent in modern politics, ministering variously to Polish anguish, French self-esteem, and
many other Europeans with wounds to salve. Much of this remains elusive. But perhaps we can push the analysis a little further by trying to
identify, not just the primary emotions of resentment and betrayal so
vividly on display in over fifty years of epidemic myth making, but also
something of the mental process that lodged Yalta's association with
the supposed shortcomings of American diplomacy in general, and of
President Roosevelt in particular, firmly in the European mind. And here,
I think, we can identify three facilitating steps.

The first simply refers to the natural conclusions many contemporaries
drew from the actual course of events. This began with the official and
public reactions to Roosevelt's ringing post-Yalta proclamation of a benign
postwar settlement with democracy, freedom, and elections for all (which
effectively bound Roosevelt and Yalta together, for better or worse), almost immediately followed by the tangible falsification of this vision. The
consequence was an accumulating disillusionment and, in Western Europe
generally, a high degree of cynicism that intensified as observers, struggling
with all their postwar privations and finding themselves reduced to a reluctantly spectatorial role in their American-led orbit, found answers of
a sort in the slowly emerging revelations about Yalta's secret deals. These
quickly took on a sinister cast. As the wartime collaboration unraveled and
socioeconomic as well as political conditions deteriorated, all the things
that were not working – the Polish political settlement, Eastern Europe's
difficulties, the stalled economic recovery, and much more – seemed trace-
able, at least in part, to Yalta. Stalin was, to be sure, widely viewed as the
principal villain, but Roosevelt was also held accountable for his supposed

---

[20] David Watt, *The Times*, February 8, 1985; John Colville, "How the West Lost the Peace
in 1945," *Commentary*, September 1985, pp. 41–47; R. W. Thompson, *Churchill and
Morton* (London, 1976), p. 150. For the comment that Roosevelt was "trying to figure out
how to turn most of Europe over to Uncle Joe," see *The Spectator*, February 13, 1993.

indifference to the fate of Europe and for his apparent naivete, as well as for his instrumental part in bringing about a suddenly dominant if not hegemonic United States.

The second, less obvious but significant step in the developing European indictment of Yalta (and of FDR as its leading culprit) was the casting adrift of the president, and thus of the reputation of American diplomacy, by those Europeans who one might have expected to defend him. Generally, Churchill has been seen as he portrayed himself, as an aghast but impotent observer of Roosevelt's irresponsible and naïve Yalta performance. A recent Polish-made film, for instance, insists that Churchill did his best for Poland at the meeting, while Roosevelt was indifferent. In all this imagery, Churchill's reputation doubtless benefited from a well-timed political volte-face. For within days of the Yalta conference Churchill was presenting himself as the champion of a noncommunist Europe by publicly defining the test of Yalta, much to Roosevelt's embarrassment, as Stalin's pledge of Polish independence. Feted by virtually all the insecure postwar Western European elites, he then initiated a campaign for European unity that culminated in his influential Zurich speech in 1946. The result has been that even as Cold War Britain lined up with the Truman administration (whose leading members were themselves disinclined to defend FDR) and sedulously cultivated its "special relationship" with Washington, British historians and other spokesmen have tended to identify their country through the years of decline as one of the European victims of Roosevelt's diplomacy at Yalta.[21]

A third step seems, in retrospect, to have folded the anti-Roosevelt conception conclusively into the mainstream Cold War narrative in Europe. Confounded by events, fastened posthumously with the blame for Yalta's sad outcomes by his influential British partner, FDR – or, to be more exact, his reputation – was then subjected to what was in the new Cold War context the unkindest cut of all – the warm embrace of the Soviet Union. For tentatively in the difficult weeks immediately following the conference, and then fulsomely and energetically as the Truman administration edged steadily toward confrontation, Roosevelt was, in inverse proportion to the criticism he was beginning to incur in the United States, taken up and celebrated in the Soviet and worldwide communist press as

[21] *A Forgotten Odyssey: The Deported*, film written and directed by Jagna Wright, Lest We Forget Productions (London, 2002); *Hansard*, February 27, 1945, pp. 1283–1284; Randolph Churchill, ed., *Sinews of Peace* (London, 1948), pp. 116–119.

Stalin's supportive wartime colleague and understanding collaborator in postwar planning. Was this genuine? To this day Roosevelt Street is a favorite promenade for strollers in Yalta. There are no such memorials to Stalin or Churchill. It was axiomatic during the Cold War to say that the Kremlin's instincts were entirely political and free of human sentiment. Still, it is remarkable that there are no hostile references to Roosevelt by Stalin on record. Even during the post-Yalta confusion and crisis Stalin told an inquiring Marshal Zhukov that the conference had gone well, that he trusted FDR not to violate the Yalta accords, and that "Roosevelt had been friendly." And there are sympathetic and respectful references elsewhere. We will revisit this relationship later. The point here is simply to record the downward trajectory of Roosevelt's reputation as a putative architect of postwar Europe.[22]

The sheer volume and variety of these bitter European perspectives on Yalta strongly suggests the need for further historical explorations of its course, contexts, and character. But what is most striking in virtually all of them is the powerful tendency one finds in many places toward what at this distance seems to be a self-interested politicization of the event. It suited governments, editorialists, and media pundits in "the West" to use "Yalta" as a kind of shorthand Cold War explanatory reference point – a usefully simple touchstone for the disappointments and confusions of the postwar. Conversely, Yalta quickly came to be seen in the Soviet sphere as a vindication of Stalin's well-intentioned, collaborative policies, endorsed by Roosevelt but treacherously subverted by Churchill and by FDR's successor. In the West it was soon judged a diplomatic disaster, exhibiting Stalin's bad faith. But Stalin's supposed guilt did not help Roosevelt. In the polarizing postwar atmosphere the fusion of Yalta, Roosevelt, and the fate of Europe, despite the divergent interpretations, was for many a convenient explanation and a salutary lesson in the virtues of "firmness" with antagonists.

Yalta, chameleonic in every sense except its fixation on Roosevelt's performance, was made to suit everyone. It suited the Soviets to assert Roosevelt's supposed concurrence as a justification of their consolidation in Eastern Europe and elsewhere around their periphery. It also suited the British, always anxious since Munich to disassociate themselves from the taint of appeasement, to blame the dead president for

---

[22] *New York Times*, April 14, 1985; Simon Sebag Montefiore, *Stalin: The Court of the Red Tsar* (London, 2003), pp. 475–476; Anthony Beevor, *The Fall of Berlin, 1945* (New York, 2002), p. 145

his concessionary approach to the Soviets. It especially suited Winston Churchill, who was eager after Yalta to rally the West against Soviet expansion, to gloss over the actual division of Europe he had effectively arranged with Stalin in October 1944 (of which more later), and to let the supposed Roosevelt-mandated division at Yalta come distractingly to the fore. It suited the diminished Western European states, coming after 1945 under powerful American influence, as an explanation of their unwelcome eclipse and later as a spur to regenerative unity. And, to look ahead for a moment, it suited President Harry S. Truman and American Cold War liberals as an explanation of the dangerously destructive Rooseveltian legacy of false optimism they saw themselves as laboring heroically to overcome.

For there have, of course, been several American Yaltas, too. The political context was different, but here too Yalta was detached from its roots and launched on a theatrical career of intrigue, illusion, and fragmentation, much of it inspired by a variety of narrowly national preoccupations. And we see in the United States, as in Europe, a process of assimilation into competing Cold War rationales, a fixation on Roosevelt, and finally a set of multivarious conclusions very much like those we have seen developing in Europe. Thus the first criticisms came, as one might expect, from the large Polish-American community and from a range of conservative, anti–New Deal elements in politics and the media, especially the Hearst, Paterson, and McCormick newspapers, whose persistent anticommunism and dour view of Soviet policy during and after the war may not unreasonably be characterized as a permanent Red Scare. And steadily thereafter, as in Europe, the transformation from initial euphoria to disillusionment as details of hitherto undisclosed Crimean deals leaked out and relations with the Soviet Union deteriorated, led to a wider, more generalized critique whose course and character was firmly shaped by the same three-stage process we have observed in the European arena. First, there was a course of events pushing Yalta and FDR's supposed blunders to the center of attention, where they were effectively exploited by a spearhead of politically aroused critics bent on using the apparently flawed record to promote specific causes. Second, we have the failure of many of FDR's erstwhile supporters to defend him, and third, his warm embrace by the American left. This process, it must be said at once, was far less straightforward than its European analog because Roosevelt never lacked American champions and was stoutly defended during much of the Cold War era by liberal historians who portrayed his Yalta conduct as that of a realist doing his best in response to conditions (especially in Eastern

Europe) that no American leader could have controlled. Nevertheless, the three impulses are readily identifiable, and their effect, as in Europe, was to fuse Yalta and Roosevelt's reputation into a referential center of Cold War explanation.[23]

In the United States the causative political events that shaped interpretations of Yalta came not just from the disheartening aftermath of the conference itself but also from the intersection of the deteriorating international climate with an intensified anticommunism in domestic right-wing circles. After their unexpected and bitter defeat in the 1948 presidential election – and even more forcefully after Senator Joseph McCarthy launched his witch hunt in 1950 against communists and radicals – the Republican Party began to use Yalta systematically as a bludgeon against the Truman administration and Democratic foreign policy. They exploited the revelations of Roosevelt's secret diplomacy, the adverse course of subsequent events in Europe and in Asia (where the Korean War presented further opportunities for recrimination after 1950), and the presence as an adviser at Yalta of State Department official Alger Hiss, who, in a sensational case, was convicted of perjury in 1949 after denying communist affiliations during the 1930s. The effect of all this was to entrench Yalta as a permanent mark against the Soviet Union, against a supposedly delusional or even traitorous Roosevelt and all his works in foreign policy, and against a liberal diplomacy that was vulnerable now to charges of incompetence and un-American behavior generally. Henceforth, Yalta bashing and anti-Roosevelt polemics from the right wing became in association a common feature of American politics. During the earlier period the conservative critique, following in the steps of the attacks made upon Roosevelt by Charles Beard and Charles Tansill for allegedly manipulating the United States into the war, found their most vitriolic expression in Felix Wittmer's 1953 book, *The Yalta Betrayal: Data on the Decline and Fall of Franklin Delano Roosevelt*. In the 1980s, the "naïve and blundering" condemnations came again from passionately critical books like Frederick Marks's *Wind Over Sand: The Diplomacy of Franklin Roosevelt* and Robert Nisbet's *Roosevelt and Stalin: The Failed Courtship* and from the polemics of

---

[23] The Hearst, Paterson, and McCormick newspapers were a very influential anti-Soviet and mostly anti-Roosevelt voice. Their daily readership together with that of the similarly anti-Soviet Gannett and Scripps-Howard chains has been estimated at some seventy million. Anne T. Golden, "Attitudes to the Soviet Union as Reflected in the American Press, 1944–1948" (Ph.D dissertation, University of Toronto, 1970), pp. 112–122.

neoconservative writers like Adam Ulam and Jeanne Kirkpatrick during the 1985 anniversary.[24]

The second facilitating stage we noticed in the European process – the passivity of those who might in other circumstances have defended FDR – is also evident here. Dominated by Cold War pressures, many of FDR's former associates and/or liberal supporters tended to side with the critique rather than with the now discredited celebration of Yalta. Former ambassador to the Soviet Union William Bullitt and the wartime military representative in Moscow, General John Deane, wrote critical accounts. Many erstwhile Roosevelt associates, laboring now in the more tightly integrated Truman administration, saw themselves as having to confront an expansionist Soviet Union that was very different from the accommodation-oriented ally conjured up in FDR's benign post-Yalta portrayal. Churchill played a direct role here too. During his visit to the United States in early 1946 he said very little in praise of the former president and – in a remarkably ostentatious omission – did not even mention him in his famous "Iron Curtain" speech of March 6, 1946, calling for an Anglo-American "fraternal association" against further Soviet expansion. Truman, who occasionally presented dutiful but tepid defenses of Roosevelt's Yalta effort, felt let down by his predecessor's failure to brief him effectively and remarked bitterly, "Heroes know when to die!" The memoirs of his administration, often enough by an eloquent refusal to discuss Yalta except in reference to its now seemingly obvious shortcomings, tend to imply a distinction between the two administrations, discreetly positing a well-intentioned but naïve Roosevelt leaving a most complex set of difficulties that his untutored successor triumphantly surmounted.[25]

It would be going much too far to interpret this as a liberal revolt against Rooseveltian diplomacy generally. FDR's historic significance is obviously much larger than the Yalta conference, and he has always had champions even on that inflammable issue among historians and liberal Americans. But concern about his Yalta performance was increasingly widespread and

---

[24] See Theoharis, *Yalta Myths*, pp. 39–129 and passim. See also Wittmer, *Yalta Betrayal*; Frederick Marks III, *The Diplomacy of Franklin Roosevelt* (Athens, Ga., and London, 1988); Robert Nisbet, *Roosevelt and Stalin: The Failed Courtship* (Washington, D.C., 1985).

[25] Truman, actually referring to Lincoln but believed to be meaning FDR, cited in William E. Leuchtenberg, *In the Shadow of FDR: From Harry Truman to Ronald Reagan* (Ithaca, N. Y., 1983), p. 40; Harbutt, *Iron Curtain*, p. 189. For memoirs, see William Bullitt, *The Great Globe Itself: A Preface to World Affairs* (New York, 1946); John R. Deane, *The Strange Alliance: The Story of Our Efforts at Wartime Cooperation with Russia* (New York, 1947); and generally Truman, *Year of Decisions*; and Dean G. Acheson, *Present at the Creation: My Years at the State Department* (New York, 1989).

left his reputation only thinly defended for several years into the postwar era. No less a liberal-progressive than Bruce Bliven, editor in 1945 of the *New Republic*, records in his autobiography, "I was staggered, like everybody else, at the concessions Roosevelt made to Stalin at Yalta, when these finally became known."[26] And the historian Athan Theoharis concludes, after persuasively tracing the impact of Yalta on American domestic politics and opinion, that "by 1950 many people had made the emotional appraisal that Yalta had created the problems of the postwar period."[27]

Against this growing tide of revulsion, to which former secretary of state Edward R. Stettinius's tepid 1949 memoir, *Roosevelt and the Russians,* offered little resistance, other Roosevelt intimates like speechwriter Sam Rosenman and State Department liaison Charles Bohlen worked behind the scenes to put Yalta in a better light. Bohlen, who had attended the conference as the president's principal interpreter, was especially active. His papers are full of letters to old New Dealers like Rosenman, memoirists like Stettinius, biographers like the playwright Robert Sherwood, who was writing about Hopkins, journalists like Walter Lippmann, and historians like the conservative William Henry Chamberlain and the liberal Arthur M. Schlesinger, Jr., all invariably taking the line that Roosevelt's policies had been directed to the creation of an "open world" and were being misunderstood and irresponsibly exploited. But these views made little headway in the enveloping Cold War atmosphere. Eventually a strong liberal defense of FDR's Yalta conduct did emerge. One could perhaps date this from Schlesinger's influential 1967 article on the "Origins of the Cold War," which blamed the postwar breakdown mainly on Stalin's supposed paranoia. Books by Robert Divine and James M. Burns stressing Roosevelt's "realism" followed in the late 1960s. Later studies by Robert Dallek and John Lewis Gaddis emphasized the difficulties he had encountered and his generally pragmatic and clear-eyed approach, further advancing a cause that has never lacked substantial academic support.[28]

The third element, the fateful embrace by the American left, effectively sealed for many the association of Roosevelt with Yalta's evident failures, much as it was doing in Europe. For Soviet hosannas to the dead president in

---

[26] Bruce Bliven, *Five Million Words Later* (New York, 1970), p. 261.

[27] Theoharis, *Yalta Myths*, p. 218.

[28] Edward R. Stettinius, Jr., *Roosevelt and the Russians* (New York, 1949); Bohlen to Rosenman, July 11, 1949, Box 1A, Folder R, and Bohlen to Harriman, February 15, 1950, Box 2, Folder H, both in Bohlen MSS, Library of Congress, Washington, D.C.; Schlesinger, "Origins of the Cold War" pp. 22–52. For Rooseveltian historiography, see Chapter 6 of this volume.

the international arena were echoed at home by an American left wing that was still influential and self-confident after the Democratic Party's 1944 election victory and was at least to some degree mobilized during 1945–46 to resist what it saw as the willful destruction of FDR's noble vision of co-operation with the Soviets. In the end this campaign – working through publications like the crusading New York daily newspaper *PM* (which played up, in the tense days of early 1946, what it saw as Roosevelt's statesmanlike efforts to accommodate legitimate Soviet needs against Churchill's supposed warmongering in the famous "Iron Curtain" speech), and in formal politics through union agitation and former vice president Henry Wallace's forlorn presidential campaign in 1948 under the aegis of the Progressive Citizens of America – went down to crushing defeat. But similar left-wing impulses appeared during the 1960s and 1970s, in response primarily to the actions of President Lyndon Johnson's administration in Vietnam, but also voicing a deeper perception that traced American failings in the post-1945 arena to Truman-era liberals who in the 1940s had, several revisionists argued, undermined Roosevelt's statesmanlike Yalta vision, shown a lack of sensitivity to legitimate Soviet needs, and sacrificed America's own domestic interests to meretricious Cold War priorities.[29]

Two notable Yalta books written from that critical perspective caught attention during the era of Cold War détente. In 1970, Diane S. Clemens's admirably analytic *Yalta*, exceptional in its broader international focus, portrayed the conference as a constructive negotiation later undone by Truman's determination to break "those agreements at Yalta which reflected Soviet intentions." Meanwhile, in the same year, Athan Theoharis confronted the conservative thesis in his *The Yalta Myths: An Issue in American Politics: 1945–1955*, which was designed to expose the perceived combination of insincerity and opportunism at work in right-wing attempts to exploit Yalta for domestic purposes.

Given this shared three-part process (and significant similarities in sentiment), it is not surprising that as the Cold War continued the hitherto parallel but distinct European and American versions of Yalta tended in some ways to converge, in the end bringing the self-proclaimed European

---

[29] See *PM*, March 6, 12, 1946; John M. Blum (ed.), *The Price of Vision: The Diary of Henry A. Wallace, 1942–1946* (Boston, 1973); Norman Markowitz, *The Rise and Fall of the People's Century: Henry A. Wallace and American Liberalism, 1941–1948* (New York, 1972); and Kevin Boyle, *The UAW and the Heyday of American Liberalism, 1945–1968* (New York, 1995). For criticisms of the Truman administration, see Lloyd Gardner, *Architects of Illusion: Men and Ideas in American Foreign Policy, 1941–1949* (Chicago, 1970), passim; Clemens, *Yalta*, pp. 267–291; and Theoharis, *Yalta Myths*, pp. 218–223.

victims of Yalta into a strange alignment with Roosevelt's domestic critics. The Europeans maintained a sense of grievance in these years, but at a much lower temperature. They were increasingly intent now upon freeing themselves from the hegemonic Yalta system. The 1985 anniversary, as we saw, inspired Mitterand and others, notably former German chancellor Helmut Schmidt, to proclaim a new European unity in the face of Yalta's rupture. Meanwhile, President Ronald Reagan, once a New Deal Democrat but now America's most conservative modern leader, had declared in a significant speech in Poland that he too had never accepted Yalta's division of Europe, implicitly acknowledging, as the Cold War began to show signs of winding down, at least a degree of American responsibility, albeit one conveniently fixed on the Democratic Party. Since then it has become an axiom in the public political arenas of both Europe and the United States that Roosevelt and Stalin (with Churchill still enjoying a curious immunity) divided Europe; that they established "Yalta orders" in Europe and Asia; and that Yalta is properly seen as the primary focal point and legitimate political symbol for politicians, editorialists, and pundits everywhere of the transition from World War to Cold War.[30]

But in fact there has never been any real or lasting consensus about the meaning of Yalta. In Europe and in the United States, it has always been enmeshed in politics and congenial national or ideological mythologies. Even in academic circles the specialized books on the conference have faithfully reflected the predominating impulses of the era in which they appeared. The historians who compiled the 1956 collection of articles *The Meaning of Yalta* – whose editor wrote, "Hesitantly, complainingly, suspiciously, but on the whole well, we assumed the responsibilities which our position enforced upon us" – captured much of the essence of postwar liberalism; Diane Clemens's 1970 defense of Roosevelt emerged from the leftist revisionist tide of that period; and Russell Buhite's balanced but conservatively tinged *Decisions at Yalta* (1986) stressed in Reaganesque fashion Stalin's "menacing, aggressive posture toward the rest of the world" and "Roosevelt's failure to grasp its full significance." These have not always been sharp divisions, and a range of views has appeared within these categories, which are far from ironclad. There have also been some strange alliances over the years. Early in the Cold War, for example, hard-edged conservatives and more hesitant but critical liberals tended to gang up on the Rooseveltian left. During the revisionist era, many left-wing

---

[30] See Buhite, *Decisions at Yalta*, pp. 129–137. For Yalta's impact in Asia, see Akira Iriye, *The Cold War in Asia: A Historical Introduction* (Englewood Cliffs, N. J., 1974), passim.

scholars and pundits joined conservatives in attacking both Roosevelt and (especially) Truman. In the more recent conservatively flavored period since 1980, military historians (who invariably identify armed force rather than diplomacy as the decisive agent in international affairs) have joined liberals in suggesting, against political conservatives, that Roosevelt's actions had not been decisive or destructive. [31]

In recent years American confrontations over Yalta's significance seem to have taken two predominant forms: public conservative eruptions at the ten-year anniversaries, reiterating the "sell-out" thesis, and refutations of that charge from liberal academic historians. The argument in 1985 was particularly passionate. Launched by the Harvard historian Adam Ulam (whose headline in the *New Republic* proclaimed "Forty Years after Yalta: Stalin Outwitted FDR and the West Still Pays"), it was quickly contested in spirited fashion by the liberal writer Theodore Draper. A general debate, which *Newsweek* called "A New War on Yalta: Neocons vs. the Liberals," quickly flared up.[32] Much the same thing happened in 2005 when President George W. Bush declared while on a visit to Latvia that the Yalta agreement, which he compared in characteristically free-wheeling historiographical style to the pre-war Munich agreement and the Nazi-Soviet Pact of 1939, had left the European continent "divided and unstable" and had "led to one of the greatest wrongs of history." This provoked yet another round in the ongoing struggle between conservative columnists and liberal historians.[33]

Many professional historians have watched the public career of Yalta – as symbol, icon, myth – with varying degrees of disapproval, bemusement, and fatalism. Of the "sell-out to Stalin" notion, for instance, the historian Robert Dallek concluded more than two decades ago that "the myth of Yalta will not go away." Nevertheless, academic passions have for more than half a century been almost as high as those in the public sphere, and it is not hard to see beneath the surface of ostensibly objective scholarship the same varied emotions and polemical instincts – European resentment, Americocentrism, present-minded Cold War preoccupations – we have noticed in the wider arena of Yalta debate. On the whole, reviews of the academic literature quickly vindicate the prediction by a historian in

---

[31] Snell (ed.), *Meaning of Yalta*, p. ix; Buhite, *Decisions at Yalta*, p. 136.
[32] Adam Ulam, "Forty Years after Yalta; Stalin Outwitted FDR and the West Still Pays," *New Republic*, February 11, 1985; Theodore Draper, "A Look at the Yalta Conference," January 16, 1986, and "Yalta and the Fate of Poland," May 29, 1986, both in *New York Review of Books; Newsweek*, April 28, 1986.
[33] *New York Times*, May 16, 2005.

1956, just after the release of the documentary record, that "[e]ven if Yalta should vanish as a political issue it will remain a problem of interpretation in history."[34]

This brief review has not probed very deeply into the extraordinary career of Yalta since 1945. But it is hoped that enough has been said to suggest the urgent need for a fresh look. As it happens, this book will advance a structurally oriented interpretation that is, so far as I can tell, rather different from those presented so far. In order to explain it properly and with a view to closing or at least narrowing the gap left by, on the one hand, a tendency on the part of the Europeans to neglect the wider significance of their World War II diplomacy, and, on the other, an American disinclination to take with full seriousness any diplomacy but their own, we must go back to the beginning, to the grim days of September 1939.

[34] Dallek, *Roosevelt and American Foreign Policy,* p. 541.

Two Arenas

Europe and America

In the first week of September 1939 great crowds appeared each day outside the British and French embassies in Warsaw. Poland was already under attack by Hitler's *Wehrmacht*, and bombs were falling on the capital. Yet the crowds were lively and optimistic. Allied diplomats were cheered loudly. Invigorating patriotic music was heard. It was widely expected that British and French planes were about to bomb Berlin and that Germany was about to be invaded from the west.

The diplomats, sick at heart, saluted the crowds from their balconies during intervals between the backyard destruction of codes and other compromising documents. One British official caught the BBC's short-wave broadcast. There was no martial music in London. The news seemed to be mostly about vacations and football scores.[1] As the days passed the truth sank in, and the Warsaw crowds dwindled and finally dispersed altogether. There was aerial action over the Third Reich, but the Royal Air Force dropped innocuous propaganda pamphlets, not bombs. There would even be a "second front." But it would come not in the form of an Anglo-French invasion of Germany but from a sudden Soviet attack two weeks later on Poland's virtually undefended eastern frontier.

This savage twist in the long history of Polish misfortune seemed to many observers at the time, not least to Americans viewing events from afar, the predictable outcome of the predatory impulses, dangerous intrigues, and desperate illusions that marked Europe in the 1930s, stigmatized memorably and indeed unanswerably as "the low decade." Among

---

[1] *Road to War*, final episode, November 29, 1988, Arts and Entertainment Channel.

the Poles it inaugurated a sense of betrayal at the hands of their Western allies that would persist during the following half-century of forced subjugation, at the hands first of Germany and later of the Soviet Union. Meanwhile, the fate of Poland became a crucial element in the European arena of Allied wartime diplomacy. The fundamental issue, which became clear almost as soon as Hitler's forces invaded the Soviet Union in June 1941, was Stalin's sustained campaign to get his new allies (especially Britain) to bestow some measure of acceptance and legitimation upon the Soviet wish to dominate, in some as yet undefined but potentially coercive way, most of postwar Eastern Europe. The British, anxious not to lose this crucial ally, and obedient in their diplomacy to a compound of geopolitical logic, historical precedent, and felt necessity, steadily showed themselves willing to pay the price. Poland, its interests stubbornly defended by its London representatives in exile, stood disconcertingly in the way. To gain some understanding of these political currents, and to set the stage for a discussion of the Anglo-Soviet treaty negotiations that first cleared a path to the outcome Stalin desired, we turn initially to a brief historically oriented review of British attitudes toward Poland and Eastern Europe.

THE BRITISH AND EASTERN EUROPE

Britain and France in September 1939 took the view that by committing themselves to war with Hitler's Germany they had fulfilled their obligation to Poland – "a matter of honour," as Britain's wartime prime minister later put it. But that is not the whole story. The French, already bound to come to Poland's aid by alliance and military convention, had given specific promises in May 1939 of immediate action by both the French air force and the army, to be followed by a major offensive by the bulk of her forces by the fifteenth day of the war. It soon seemed clear to the Poles that this had been a cynical maneuver to induce a sacrificial effort while the French prepared at leisure behind the Maginot Line.[2]

The British were also blamed. True, their military promises had been vaguer, but they had joined the French in undertaking to launch bombing attacks on Germany immediately after war broke out. From the outset, the attitude in London was that this would be a long war and that Britain

---

[2] Richard Overy with Andrew Wheatcroft, *The Road to War* (London, 1999), rev. ed., pp. 1–23. See also S. Newman, *The British Guarantee to Poland* (Oxford, 1976), p. 32; and A. Prazmowska, *Britain, Poland and the Eastern Front, 1939* (Cambridge, 1987), pp. 94–95.

and France should "conserve our resources and not fritter them away."
The British ambassador in Warsaw was told to impress upon the Poles the
fundamental need to defeat Germany ("the immutable aim of the allies")
and the importance of not undertaking precipitate action "merely for the
sake of maintaining a gesture."[3]

This last phrase conveys succinctly the combination of cold logic and
emotional insensitivity that was characteristic of Britain's attitude toward
the small Eastern European states during the interwar period. More specifically, it reflected a feeling that the Poles, having seized and shaped their
own independence after World War I, lacked a certain legitimacy. The
Poles were viewed as brave but unrealistic. Misled in part by their own
pretensions, they had ignored the hierarchies of modern European politics, especially the tendency of the so-called Great Powers to cultivate their
own relationships and interests while viewing the smaller states (apart
from those with whom they had special political or strategic relationships)
as pawns in the larger game. They had not drawn the right historical conclusions from the lack of support (except from France) that had attended
their rebirth after World War I. They had exaggerated their own strength.
They had dabbled in intrigues and expansionist schemes at the expense of
potential allies like Czechoslovakia. And they had not used the time that
Soviet and German weakness had given them until the late 1930s to secure
themselves better before the inevitable recovery of their two overbearing
neighbors.[4]

Above all, one must add, they had miscalculated their two allies:
France and Britain. From France they had reason to expect more, for
here there were historic political and cultural ties dating from Napoleon's
time. The French, moreover, had promoted and supported the great
post-1919 enlargement of Poland at Soviet and German expense, and
had reinforced this with a military convention in 1921 and an alliance
in 1925. Poland was the cornerstone of a French security system against
any German revival in Eastern Europe, one that also came to include
Czechoslovakia and Rumania. Until the mid-1930s, this arrangement had

---

[3] F.O. to Kennard, September 8, 1939, C13252/1359/18, F.O. 371.23092; Prazmowska,
Britain, Poland and the Eastern Front, pp. 182–183.
[4] Overy and Wheatcroft, *The Road to War*, p. 10, write, "The Western Powers saw Poland
as a greedy, revisionist power, illiberal, anti-Semitic, pro-German." See also W. Brian
Newsome, " 'Dead Lands' or 'New Europe'? Reconstructing Eastern Europe: 'Westerners'
and the Aftermath of the World War," *East European Quarterly*, 36, 1, (March 2002),
pp. 39–62, for an illuminating discussion of Anglo-French attitudes toward Poland and
Eastern Europe generally between the world wars.

some of the attributes of a functioning collective security system. But the Locarno treaty of 1925 had long since exposed the limits of the French commitment. Germany now formally guaranteed to France and Britain the postwar boundaries in the west. In return, the Western allies agreed to leave open the possibility of peaceful revision of Germany's postwar boundaries in the east. From this time on, it should have been apparent to France's eastern allies that the Paris politicians were inclined to see them as assets to French diplomacy, not the prospective beneficiaries of an actual obligation. From the Locarno pact until the surrender of Czechoslovakia at Munich in 1938, French policy was increasingly defensive, dependent upon the Maginot Line for security, and subsequently upon British leadership in negotiation.[5]

What then of Britain? Here the Poles could rely neither on historical ties nor on any serious sense of common purpose. The British had shared to some lukewarm degree the general liberal sympathy for partitioned Poland during the nineteenth century. Castlereagh had discreetly urged its cause at the Congress of Vienna. Alfred Lord Tennyson wrote a stirring poetic tribute to Polish courage decades later. More significant, however, were recent grievances that went back beyond the 1930s to Poland's revival after World War I. The British, it is worth remembering, of the three Great Powers that had shaped the Versailles peace conference of 1919 had been the least enthusiastic about the so-called "successor" states. They had clung to the hope of a Habsburg revival as long as that seemed possible, and had accepted the new fragmented Eastern Europe with reluctance and foreboding. Shortly after the war, they alienated themselves from the new Poland by prescribing – when asked by the Warsaw government in a moment of military desperation to arbitrate their frontier with the advancing Bolsheviks – a border based on ethnographic considerations, later famous as the "Curzon Line." Almost immediately Polish fortunes improved, and they subsequently took control of a much larger part of Soviet territory, an act still seen two decades later in London diplomatic circles as opportunistic.[6]

---

[5] R. Young, *In Command of France: French Foreign Policy and Military Planning, 1933–1940* (Cambridge, Mass., 1978), p. 242 and passim. French historical sympathy for Poland is discussed in S. Bonsal, *Suitors and Suppliants: The Little Nations at Versailles* (New York, 1946); and J-B Duroselle, *Clemenceau* (Paris, 1988).

[6] Margaret Macmillan, *Paris 1919* (New York, 2002), p. 221 and Chapter 17; Liverpool to Castlereagh, December 22, 1814, cited in C. K. Webster, *British Diplomacy, 1813–1815* (London, 1921), pp. 263–264; Norman Davies, *Heart of Europe: A Short History of Poland* (New York, 1984), p. 163.

But this skepticism about the restored Poland was only one aspect of a generalized negativity on the part of the British toward Eastern Europe. The region did have its British champions, among them the historian R.W. Seton-Watson, who devoted much of his distinguished career to a progressive interpretation of its past. Indeed, he went so far as to collaborate in the founding in 1916 of a periodical called *The New Europe*, dedicated to the postwar establishment of national, independent states following the anticipated collapse of the various sagging imperial structures. But events confounded these hopes. New states were indeed created, but they struggled with only marginal success for stability and independence during the interwar period.[7]

Above all, they received little political, economic, or moral support from the so-called West led by Britain and France, whose peoples, according to a persuasive recent account by the historian W. Brian Newsome, continued as they had before 1914 to look upon Eastern Europe and its Polish, Czech, Serbo-Croat, Slovene, and other nationalities as irredeemably inferior and culturally backward. Reinforcing these negative stereotypes, which doubtless served to flatter Western self-esteem at Eastern expense, were such luminaries as the poet-essayist Paul Valery in France and the historian Arnold Toynbee and the writer H. G. Wells in Britain. Many of the images current in interwar discourse and literature were highly derogatory, even when applied to comparatively strong polities like those of Poland and Czechoslovakia. The Balkan states, despite the occasional upbeat image cultivated by writers like Rebecca West, fared worse, attracting widespread references to "Asiatic savagery," primitive culture, and degenerate populations ruled by repressive regimes.[8]

Practical ties might have led to some reconsideration. But there was, so far as the British were concerned, only a small shared commerce with this region, not much warmth for the Slavs as a race, and after 1919 a strong sense of the London government's inability to influence events in this arena, along with a chronic concern that the French might involve them

[7] R. W. Seton-Watson, "Nationalism versus Internationalism," *The New Europe*, 14 (December 1916), pp. 317–320.
[8] Newsome, " 'Dead Lands' or 'New Europe'," pp. 39–40, 43–44, 52–55. The "Dead Lands" conception originated with the British diplomat J. W. Headlam, who wrote in 1917, "Across the continent of Europe from the Baltic to the Adriatic there runs a ... band of death ... nations and peoples broken up, wrecked and destroyed for more than a thousand miles." Headlam, *The Dead Lands of Europe* (New York, 1917), p. 5; Rebecca West, *Black Lamb and Grey Falcon* (London, 1941). See also W. H. McNeill, *Arnold J. Toynbee: A Life* (Oxford, 1989); H. G. Wells, *The Salvaging of Civilisation* (London, 1921); and Paul Valery, *Variete* (Paris, 1924), pp. 11–33.

there anyway. Finally, there was a growing sympathy through the interwar years for German complaints of unjust dispossession in the east following the edicts of the Paris Peace Conference. The tangible manifestations of these attitudes mark a familiar downward trajectory. They include Britain's refusal to do anything substantial to secure the new states of the post-Versailles order, its acceptance of the 1925 Locarno accords offering Germany the tacit prospect of reclaimed territory in Eastern Europe and the hegemony that would inevitably go with it, and finally, of course, the notorious Munich conference of 1938 sacrificing the Czechs to Hitler's ambition.[9]

There were, within this attitudinal drift, various particular, sometimes counterpoised "policies." But in general it seems fair to say that the fundamental aim of the British establishment in continental Europe between the wars was stability at almost any cost. There was considerable nostalgia for Habsburg Austria. Despite all its chronic deficiencies, it had been valued for its long custodial role in Central and Eastern Europe. For while stability was the aim, the method of achieving it was invariably some kind of Great Power control. It was much the same in the Mediterranean. For generations the British had propped up the fading Turks, partly to fence in expansionist Russia, but also to keep order in the fractious Balkans. Only Greece among the Sultan's rebellious dominions had a hold on the classically educated British elite.[10]

In recounting these impulses, with their associated conviction that the Great Powers had the right (usually seen congenially as the "responsibility") to order matters politically without too much concern for the sensitivities of the smaller states, we are establishing some context for a later consideration of the difficult relations between the British and the Poles during World War II. Attitudes like these also help us understand why, as they saw the revival of German power under Hitler in the 1930s, many British leaders, especially among the most ardently anticommunist elements of the Conservative Party, were inclined to view Germany's expansionary policies to the east with equanimity, if not with relief. Thus the British did nothing when pre-Hitler Germany began a "war of nerves" against Poland in 1932. The Tory Cabinets of the 1930s were, as is well known, slow to

---

[9] See Martin Gilbert, *The Roots of Appeasement* (New York, 1970), Chapters 15 and 16; and Overy and Wheatcroft, *The Road to War*, passim.

[10] For various perspectives on British foreign policies towards Europe and the Mediterranean, see D. Dilks (ed.), *Retreat from Power: Studies in Britain's Foreign Policy of the Twentieth Century* (2 vols., London, 1981); and T. G. Otte (ed.), *The Makers of British Foreign Policy: From Pitt to Thatcher* (London, 2002).

see the implications of Hitler's rise to power. They accepted the German reoccupation of the Rhineland in 1936 with hardly a tremor. Prime Minister Stanley Baldwin looked on with benevolence, saying that "if Hitler moves east I will lose no sleep."[11] His successor, Neville Chamberlain (widely called in continental Europe "J'aime Berlin"), showed his own brand of complacency and indifference when he told Tory colleagues in 1938 that he did not believe "the assumption that when Germany had secured the hegemony of Central Europe she would then pick a quarrel with ourselves." These were not rarified, elitist views. The decomposition that year of Czechoslovakia – the "far-away country" whose preservation Chamberlain had declined to protect – was effected at the Munich conference to generally enthusiastic public approval in Britain, though a growing section of opinion had profound misgivings. Only in March 1939, when Hitler swallowed the rest of that country, was there a sudden revulsion that led the Chamberlain government into bestowing upon Poland and Rumania the famous "blank check" guarantee – a quixotic reverse that was almost as striking as the fatal Nazi-Soviet pact to which almost inevitably, it seems in retrospect – it led.[12]

What stands out here for the historian is not only the familiar rhythm of pre-war appeasement, but also the inadequacy of much of the conventional wisdom about British diplomacy. How many times have we heard it said, echoing the famous dictum of Sir Eyre Crowe early in the 20th century, that the cardinal feature of British foreign policy historically has been to prevent the domination of the continent of Europe by a single great power? This is only marginally less mythic than the "Yalta Order." It at least needs substantial refinement, along with some careful geopolitical qualification. It seems to be a notion derived from imperial nostalgia and comfortable armchair rumination rather than a grasp of actual events. It would be interesting to embark on a close examination of the considerable head of steam built up variously by Philip II, Louis XIV, and Napoleon (not to mention ambitious despots further to the east) before their eventual English/British adversaries stirred themselves in a serious way. The lead-up to 1914 might seem an exception, for here there was a naval build-up, some diplomatic fence mending, and Sir Edward Grey's secret and unauthorized intrigues with the French. But even there Britain didn't do very much about Wilhelmine Germany until it was suddenly propelled into World War I by the Kaiser's shocking violation of Belgian neutrality. And as we have just seen, the

[11] Martin Gilbert, *Winston S. Churchill*, Vol. 5, 1922–1939 (London, 1976), p. 777.
[12] Overy and Wheatcroft, *Road to War*, pp. 101–120.

well-worn (and worn out?) Crowe adage hardly covers the appeasement years and the run-up to disaster in September 1939.[13]

The moral seems to be that it is notoriously difficult to generalize about the history of British foreign policy. The subject abounds in agreeable fictions. The idea that the empire was acquired in a fit of "absent-mindedness" is surely another. The historian Zara Steiner recently noted, with regard to the course of British diplomacy, "a far more irregular process of change than is so often assumed."[14] There has of course been a good deal of recurrent behavior over the centuries, and even a governing principle of sorts in the observable and well-documented tendency of the island nation to rouse itself when the would-be continental hegemon began to make threatening moves along or toward the continent's Atlantic seaboard. Historically, it was Western Europe and later the Mediterranean that Britain was inclined to protect, not Europe as a whole and certainly not Eastern Europe. It is significant that Britain, until well after World War II, saw herself as a global power, and some historians have pointed out the strains that extra-European interests long imposed on her capacity to prevail against serious continental challenges.[15] But so far as the fate of Europe is concerned, the example of the 1930s seems to suggest that, despite concern in some quarters, British governments were willing to see much of Central and Eastern Europe fall under the hegemony of Germany, with only the hopeful proviso that this be achieved in a moderate way and with suitable attention to face-saving devices and respect for British interests elsewhere. Similarly – and this is the point to which we will find ourselves moving in this account – a Soviet hegemony over postwar Eastern Europe was acceptable providing that, as with Germany earlier, British interests in Western Europe and the Mediterranean were not endangered. As will be seen, the Cold War began only when the Soviets stepped beyond Eastern Europe and threatened more cherished British interests in the Mediterranean and the Near East. It was a pragmatic and geopolitical approach, consistent with the Palmerstonian injunction that interests must determine diplomacy, sanctioned by long experience and, except for occasional spasms of public upset such as those inspired by the Bulgarian atrocities of the late nineteenth century and Hitler's threats and betrayals in early 1939, largely unaffected by distracting moralisms.

[13] Keith Wilson, "Sir Eyre Crowe on the Origin of the Crowe Memorandum of 1 June 1907," *Bulletin of the Institute of Historical Research*, 55 (1983), pp. 238–241.

[14] Zara Steiner, *Times Literary Supplement*, September 13, 2002.

[15] See, for example, Edward Ingram, *Britain's Persian Connection, 1798–1828* (Oxford, 1993), passim; and Corelli Barnet, *The Collapse of British Power* (London, 1972).

It is interesting to see how quickly this traditional British policy, with all its implied willingness to see some kind of division of Europe if no other principle of order was attainable, reappeared once the Soviet Union was propelled by Hitler into World War II and presented itself to Britain first as an ally and then as a political partner. There was historical sanction as well as geopolitical logic in this. For Britain and Russia had long seen each other as Europe's peripheral powers. The largest volume in the New Cambridge Modern History of Europe, 1493–1945, is aptly entitled *The Rise of Great Britain and Russia, 1688–1725*. It registers some scholarly awareness of this perception and ushers in a long era during which, despite their nineteenth-century imperial rivalry, stretching in its politico-strategic theater from the Balkans to the Caspian but erupting seriously only once, in the Crimean War of the 1850s, Britain and Russia showed a repeated tendency to come together in the face of a threat from the eruptive states that lay between them.[16]

This is a point of deep significance. Russian land power and British sea power had, as Soviet publications liked to point out during the war with Hitler, been the key to defeating Napoleonic France. The two allies had then played a dominating part in the peace settlements in their respective regions, putting their philosophical differences aside at the Congress of Vienna in the cause of continental order and political reconstruction. The two came together again in 1914–17 against Wilhelmine Germany, with much the same objective, only to have their ring-hoding alliance against the new continental threat go off the rails unexpectedly during the Bolshevik revolution. And in the confused, politically and ideologically charged prelude to war in 1939, they reached out tentatively to each other a third time with preliminary intimations and finally an effort, fatally feeble on the British side, to reconstitute the old association against Nazi Germany. This was essentially the logical and pragmatic convergence of the two great peripheral European powers – one presenting a territorial barrier, the other a sea wall – against the recurrently menacing center. The Soviets saw things in much the same light. Even in 1940, when the Nazi-Soviet Pact was in full operation and British fortunes seemed at their lowest ebb, we find Stalin scoffing at Hitler's hegemonic ambitions as "a physical impossibility ... since Germany lacks the necessary sea power." In like fashion, the Soviet ambassador to Britain, Ivan Maisky, urged upon Eden "the similarity of our historical development and the complementary nature of our national

---

[16] J. S. Bromley (ed.), *The New Cambridge Modern History: Vol. VI: The Rise of Great Britain and Russia* (Cambridge, England, 1970).

interests. We were both on the fringes of Europe. Neither of us wished to dominate Europe but neither of us would tolerate any other power doing so." Nor was the impulse to collaboration exclusively strategic or geopolitical. These were, after all, two long-rooted Great Powers that, despite very different systems and cultures, shared a hierarchical sense vis-à-vis smaller states and a compelling interest, though it often took a crisis to stimulate it, in the fate of Europe as a whole.[17]

It is not surprising, then, that as we come to the great turning point of June 22, 1941 – the sudden German onslaught on the Soviet Union – we find Prime Minister Winston Churchill, an arch anti-Bolshevik whose real passion, however, was not ideological polemics but Great Power politics, and who with sure historical instinct had worked hard in 1938–39 to promote an Anglo-Soviet nexus, immediately offering Joseph Stalin a partnership for war against Germany. He was so sure of support at home that he did not even bother to consult his Cabinet. True, the relationship was slow to develop. During the 1939–41 period Anglo-Soviet relations had been tense. On several occasions the British and French governments had contemplated military action against a Russia that was obviously cooperating fully with Hitler and was inclined to regard all warnings from London as dangerous intrigues. Even after June 22, 1941, Stalin was often churlish and mistrustful. The grievances of the immediate past – Munich still resented by the Soviets, the Nazi-Soviet collaboration a bitter memory for the British – persisted, and indeed remained as a partially subdued but easily identifiable undercurrent of tension throughout the war.[18]

There were other impediments to the development of a fuller understanding. The British initially doubted the Soviet capacity to hold out. Stalin from the start irritated London by calling stridently and unavailingly for an

---

[17] F. S. Northedge and Audrey Wells, *Britain and Soviet Communism: The Impact of a Revolution* (London, 1982), pp. 3–5 and Chapter 1. Stalin cited from German sources by Adam Tooze, *The Wages of Destruction: The Making and Breaking of the Nazi Economy* (London, 2006), p. 396. The notion of Britain and Russia as "peripheral" powers recurrently acting together against Central Europe is a counterpoint of sorts to the sense of destiny often associated with Alexis de Toqueville's famous prophecy, fulfilled in 1945, that the United States and Russia would eventually confront each other across a prostrate Europe. For Maisky, see Eden to Clark Kerr, January 5, 1943, F.O. 954/26. *Historical Journal*, (Moscow), December 1943.

[18] Winston S. Churchill, *The Second World War*, Vol. 3, *The Grand Alliance* (Boston, 1950), pp. 369–373. See, generally, Martin Kitchen, *British Policy Towards the Soviet Union during the Second World War* (London, 1986), pp. 56–99; and Steven Merritt Miner, *Between Churchill and Stalin: The Soviet Union, Great Britain, and the Origins of the Grand Alliance* (Chapel Hill, N. C., 1988), pp. 98–137.

immediate "second front" in France, and for supplies he suspected the British and Americans were withholding. The British ambassador in Moscow, Sir Stafford Cripps, was obliged to transmit protests from the Kremlin that the British "were prepared to fight to the last drop of Russian blood."[19] It was not until the first German drive faltered at the gates of Moscow in December 1941 that the British began to take the prospect of Soviet victory seriously. And it was partly in tribute to that possibility that Foreign Secretary Anthony Eden, responding to Stalin's intimation to Churchill on November 8 that he would welcome a visit from a British leader to open negotiations on "war aims and on plans for the postwar organization of peace," set off in December to establish a political dialog with Stalin and his foreign commissar, Vyacheslav Molotov. As he was traveling by train through northern England on the way to embarkation for the hazardous sea voyage, members of his party noticed some curious public agitation at a local station. Inquiries brought the sensational news of the Japanese attack on Pearl Harbor. Eden immediately telephoned Churchill. Should he proceed? The prime minister urged him on. He was himself already planning his first trip to Washington to discuss strategy with President Roosevelt.[20]

It is at this point, as we observe the two leading figures in the British government departing on alliance-building missions to east and west, that we first become sharply aware also of diverging streams in Allied relations that would soon mark the appearance of two distinct arenas – one strategic and Anglo-American, the other politico-diplomatic and Anglo-Soviet. The first, overwhelmingly more familiar, took Churchill to Washington, D.C., and led to the crystallization of his remarkable partnership with Roosevelt and to a tightly welded Anglo-American strategic and war-fighting combination that would last throughout the war. The second, much less well-known one, taking Eden to Moscow, led to an Anglo-Soviet alliance that was certainly occasioned by the war and had practical strategic implications, but was essentially political and directed particularly to the future shaping of Europe. These combinations did at times overlap and intersect. Thus Eden was handicapped in his encounter with Stalin by promises given to American leaders that he would make no territorial deals with the Soviets that might compromise the ideals of the Atlantic Charter. And in Washington, Roosevelt and Churchill kept Stalin broadly informed and

---

[19] Cripps to Eden, October 26, 1941, PREM 3.395/17.
[20] Stalin to Churchill, November 8, 1941, SCCA, pp. 33–34; Elisabeth Barker, *Churchill and Eden at War* (New York, 1978), pp. 234–235; Ivan Maisky, *Memoirs of an Ambassador*, trans. Andrew Rothstein (New York, 1967), pp. 221–231.

occasionally brought the Soviet ambassador, Maxim Litvinov, into their deliberations. But for the most part the two arenas remained separate and distinct, each with its own logic and preoccupations.[21]

At the time, so far as British and American public opinion was concerned, the stream of news issuing from the Washington meeting overshadowed the Anglo-Soviet developments. This is understandable. Undeniably, Pearl Harbor had converted the European war into a fully global confrontation. Then too we see in that meeting two uniquely charismatic world leaders consulting together, surrounded by the world's press, for nearly three weeks. The secret meetings in Moscow could not compete with that. Roosevelt and Churchill set in motion the full Anglo-American partnership for the conduct of the war, leading to an unprecedented fusion of resources and objectives. It is perhaps not very surprising that from this crucial point the Western memory of World War II, as it has been shaped by innumerable memoirists and historians, has taken an Anglo-American form, tracing the evolution through the fully explicated and well-remembered arguments between Washington and London over strategy (often with political implications, but usually more or less constructively resolved in the end) and then on to the vivid campaigns and the portentous "Anglo-American" encounters with the Soviet "other," notably at the great tripartite summit meetings with Stalin, who was presiding over an almost completely separate campaign in the east.

Still, this is an unbalanced picture, one that, for all its congeniality and historiographical monumentality, obscures a good deal of relevant history and blurs the vital distinction between a familiar Anglo-American war-fighting combination and the more obscure Anglo-Soviet association that, though much less intimate, was deeply political in the Clausewitzian sense and characterized by persistent, serious attempts by these two leading non-Nazi European powers not only to position themselves for the postwar era and to effect in advance of victory some crucial bilateral arrangements over the Europe they intended to conquer, but also, more generally, to create a mutually acceptable postwar structure for the continent. We will therefore simply take note of the profound event of the American entry into the war and the impressive arrangements created by Roosevelt and Churchill and try to commune more fully with the foreign secretary, now on his way through the icy North Sea and the forbiddingly dense forests of northern Russia in search of concord with Stalin.

---

[21] Dallek, *Roosevelt and American Foreign Policy,* pp. 317–324; Kitchen, *British Policy,* pp. 108–113.

EDEN AND STALIN

Eden, who had visited Stalin in 1935 and was eager now to forge a closer personal tie, did not anticipate any particular difficulty. There was ample recognition in London that he might be asked by the Soviets to approve their wartime annexations during the Nazi-Soviet partnership of the three Baltic states and of eastern Poland, as well as other recent gains at the expense of Finland, Rumania, and Norway. This was also feared by the United States secretary of state, Cordell Hull, a suspicious Wilsonian moralist where European politics was concerned, who had sent word urging that no such provocative or secret political decisions be taken. The War Cabinet, understandably concerned that any obvious breaches of the high principles of the Atlantic Charter – recently proclaimed by Churchill and Roosevelt at their August 1941 meeting off the Newfoundland coast – would upset American sensibilities, had also instructed Eden to avoid being drawn into such discussions. The foreign secretary brought some suitably anodyne drafts and apparently thought that once he had explained his transatlantic concerns to the supposedly desperate Soviet leaders – the German siege of Moscow had just been lifted and a Soviet counterattack successfully launched, but the overall situation still seemed to the British to be dangerously precarious – they would be glad simply to see him, and he would be able to confine the talks to wholesome generalities and emerge with a pleasing declaration committing the parties not to make a separate peace.[22]

Eden, a clever man in some ways but not a particularly shrewd one, was quickly disabused of this notion in his three Kremlin meetings with Stalin and Molotov. The Soviet leaders were surprisingly self-confident. As Stalin explained at their first meeting on December 16:

We are at the turning point now. The German army is tired out. Its commanders had hoped to end the war before winter and did not make the necessary preparations for the winter campaign. The German army today is poorly dressed, poorly led and losing morale. Meanwhile the USSR has prepared large reinforcements and put them into action in recent weeks. This has brought about a fundamental change on the front. ... We are advancing and will continue to advance on all fronts.[23]

[22] Hull to Winant, December 5, 1941, FRUS, 1941, I (Washington, D.C., 1958), p. 194. Eden's plans for Moscow were put before the War Cabinet in "Forthcoming Discussions with the Soviet Government," November 26, 1941, WP (41) 288. For the conditional approval, see WM (41) 124. See also Lloyd Gardner, *Spheres of Influence: The Great Powers Partition Europe, from Munich to Yalta* (Chicago, 1993), pp. 111–112.
[23] O. A. Rzheshevsky (ed.), *War and Diplomacy: The Making of the Grand Alliance* (*Documents from Stalin's Archives*) (Amsterdam, 1996), Document No. 4, pp. 11–22.

This upbeat assessment, apparently sincere, immediately thrust Eden into a disconcertingly different negotiating context. Historians comparing the virtually simultaneous discussions in Washington and Moscow often stress the intimacy and warmth of the former and the gloom and tension of the latter. But there is something paradoxical here. For while Roosevelt and Churchill were laying plans for what they expected to be a long, drawn-out war, Stalin was acting as though the Soviets were on the verge of full victory. It was time, he intimated to the astonished foreign secretary, to settle basic postwar arrangements for Europe.

To this end, Stalin presented Eden with drafts for a formal military alliance and an agreement for postwar reconstruction that spoke of non-aggrandizement and noninterference very much in the spirit of the Atlantic Charter. But to this unimpeachably wholesome document, destined for public consumption, was attached, in the manner of the Nazi-Soviet agreement of August 1939, a secret protocol that laid out a remarkably full conception of postwar Europe envisaging immediate British recognition of the postwar frontiers Stalin had gained during his collaboration with Hitler. The Baltic states and eastern Poland, which Stalin stressed had been Russian territory before 1918, would now revert to the Soviet Union. Further accessions would include gains at the expense of Rumania and Finland as well as the port of Memel. As for the rest of Europe, Germany was to be broken up, with the Rhineland, Bavaria, and Austria detached from the Reich and east Prussia given by way of territorial compensation to Poland. Stalin then urged Britain to take a similar lead in Western Europe, acquiring with Soviet approval military bases in Denmark, Norway, the Low Countries, and France to guard against any renewal of German expansionism. It was, as the historian Lloyd Gardner has written, "a bold proposal for what amounted to an Anglo-Russian diarchy to rule postwar Europe." An impressive geopolitical scenario for postwar Europe, with Britain clearly the chosen partner in a kind of hegemonic, continental condominium, it firmly excluded the United States, whose apparent desire to frustrate or constrain deals of this kind was openly and repeatedly resented by Stalin in his representations to Eden.[24]

Eden should not have been surprised. In a wide-ranging discussion with the British minister of supply, Lord Beaverbrook, a few weeks after

[24] The minutes of the three Eden-Stalin talks between December 16 and December 20, 1941, are in "Mr. Eden's Visit to Moscow," January 5, 1942, WP (42) 8, and in N109/G, F.O. 371.32874. See also Sir Llewellyn Woodward, *British Foreign Policy in the Second World War, Vol. II* (London, 1971), pp. 220–236, for selections.

the German invasion, Stalin had candidly proposed an Anglo-Soviet postwar alliance, a conception that Beaverbrook, an influential newspaper owner, later championed in Britain. Cripps had also warned in October that Stalin would want some assurance of recognition of the Soviet western frontier of 1941. A few days later Stalin cabled Churchill complaining that "there is no definite understanding between our two countries covering war aims and plans for the post-war organization of peace." There were a number of other, similar portents. Eden himself had raised the possibility of an alliance with the War Cabinet in October and had been authorized to discuss a possible treaty with Soviet ambassador Ivan Maisky. This issue was temporarily shelved as the Soviets pushed for diplomatic support in another direction, urging a reluctant British government to declare war on Hungary, Rumania, and Finland, each of which was providing troops for Hitler's onslaught. Britain had finally and with some reluctance done so on December 5. But it should have been clear that the Kremlin still wanted a comprehensive political agreement and that this was bound to come up for serious discussion during the foreign secretary's visit.[25]

Why then was Eden taken by surprise when he at last confronted Stalin in the Kremlin? Much of the answer seems to lie in the residual feelings of suspicion, dislike, and condescension toward the Soviet government – fading perhaps to some grudging respect as the Red Army seemed to be holding its position protecting Moscow in December – that the Foreign Office files reveal for the second half of 1941. Here, notwithstanding the drama of Churchill's famous immediate declaration of support, the actual policy was one of "reserve" – of waiting to see if the Soviet Union could survive before forming a serious political attachment or committing much in the way of material support, or making morally compromising political arrangements that would upset the Americans. The general expectation in early December was still for a German victory in the east. An endorsement of Soviet territorial demands – which had no intrinsic merit in British eyes and in fact challenged their sense of legitimacy – would in these circumstances not only upset the Americans but would also alarm Britain's Polish and Turkish allies. The historian Martin Folly, noting that "it came as a shock when Stalin did raise the issue as his main desideratum with Eden in Moscow," aptly remarks that the British inability to respond positively was not due solely to

[25] For Beaverbrook, see "Moscow Conference," October 8, 1941, WP (41) 238; Cripps to Eden, October 25, 1941, N6169, F.O. 371.29492; Stalin to Churchill, November 8, 1941, SCCA, p. 33. For Eden and the Cabinet, see WM (41) 102.

American constraints. "It was also a reflection of the vestigial unwillingness to consider seriously Soviet points of view".[26]

Eden's rejoinder the following evening, in which he attempted no denial of the political or geopolitical logic of Stalin's scenario, was consequently full of equivocations. On the one hand, he was quick to point out that he would have to consult the War Cabinet, the United States, and the Dominions before accepting any of the proposed territorial changes. This led Stalin, always very aggressive in the second meeting of any diplomatic sequence, to a series of bullying charges. He showed some understanding of the British government's obligation to the Poles but insisted that it must at least recognize the Soviet absorption of the Baltic states and some territory from Finland and Rumania, both of whom were now fighting on Germany's side. Soviet opinion would otherwise be horrified, he sanctimoniously exclaimed. Eden, taken aback, answered lamely that the Baltic states "have no diplomatic status with us." This was untrue. He disclaimed any prior knowledge of the Soviet claims, which was also incorrect and disingenuous. Much recriminating commentary about Anglo-Soviet relations in 1939–40 then followed, with Stalin's angry comments about the policies of the Chamberlain government drawing no defense or reproachful reference to the Nazi-Soviet pact from Eden. When the visitor raised the problem of certain American objections to the proposed course on the 1941 frontiers, Stalin tried to shame the foreign secretary with expressions of disgust at the British lack of independence. He threatened to refuse even a declaration if his wishes were not met.[27]

"In all," one unsympathetic historian writes, "Eden had given a feeble performance." Yet he did stand firm in refusing to make any compromising agreement in Moscow, though it is true that, anxious not to offend, he made his case almost entirely in terms of the need to consult the United States and the Dominions first, rather than in substantive argument or on grounds of equity or justice. He was sustained by the War Cabinet, which sent him a firm message on December 19 insisting that any agreement must conform to the Atlantic Charter and satisfy American opinion.[28]

At their third and final meeting the dictator again sneered at the foreign secretary for his evident lack of authority and for, in effect, kowtowing

---

[26] Martin Folly, *Churchill, Whitehall and the Soviet Union, 1940–1945* (New York, 2000), pp. 10, 17, 37.

[27] Eden-Stalin meeting, December 17, 1942, WP (42) 8.

[28] Miner, *Between Churchill and Stalin*, p. 192; Foreign Office to Eden, December 19, 1942, N7483, F.O. 371.32874.

to the Americans. He characterized the Atlantic Charter as a weapon consciously directed "against the Soviet Union." "Why," he asked, "does the restoration of our frontiers come into conflict with the Atlantic Charter?" Eden replied defensively, "I never said that it did." Then, accusing Eden of wanting to break up the Soviet Union, Stalin went on to insist that the question of the Baltic states was a simple matter between Britain and the Soviet Union. There was no need to involve third parties. He made one concession regarding Poland. "The Polish frontier," he said, "remains an open question and I do not insist upon settling that now. What I am most interested in is the position in Finland, the Baltic states and Rumania." But he emphasized that the Baltic states and the Soviet Union's western frontiers were "the main question for us in the war."[29]

In the end, Stalin had to accept the fact that Eden could not yet sign the desired agreement. But he had won the foreign secretary over, and Eden departed promising, "If you wish for it and attach great importance to this point then I will try and get a favorable answer for you upon it." Eden would remain faithful to this pledge. And indeed these 1941 exchanges, as well as later encounters, leave the impression that Stalin did achieve some kind of personal ascendancy over Eden, who became henceforth the leading protagonist of Soviet interests in London. Molotov, in his later recollections, characterized the foreign secretary as "spineless, too delicate, quite helpless." It was perhaps Eden's misfortune to suffer from what many would call an enviable problem. He was an exceptionally handsome, fastidious man in an era when politicians – a warty, motley crew in those pre-television years – did not have to care much about their personal appearance. An impeccably groomed scion of the British establishment with an affable personality, Eden had throughout his career to contend with thinly veiled suspicions of effeminacy. "Worth his weight in gold as a floorwalker in any West End store" was one typical taunt in the 1930s. This image dogged him throughout his career, its final barb being the cartoonist Vicky's notorious portrait of him during the catastrophic Suez Crisis of 1956 as a sheep in wolf's clothing. Much of this was unfair or false. In fact, Eden was physically brave, with a well-merited Military Cross for courage in World War I. He was also an active heterosexual who on several occasions hovered precariously on the verge of career-ending exposure in the brutal divorce courts of the pre-war era. More to the point, he was an intelligent, highly educated, experienced diplomat with a record of

[29] Eden-Stalin meeting, December 18, 1941, WP (42)8. Woodward, *British Foreign Policy in the Second World War*, Vol. 2, pp. 231–232.

resistance to the appeasement of Mussolini and Hitler. Part of his difficulty was that, like all British political leaders of this wartime era, he was deeply aware of Britain's vulnerability in material matters, and of the need to compensate for this in confrontations with the Russians or the Americans with displays of self-confidence and "front." But Eden did have a flaw. He was impressionable and highly strung. The records of his thinking and of his conduct at the various wartime conferences do leave the impression that – like Churchill in this respect, but without the prime minister's aggressive temperament and saving depth of psychological strength and political discernment – Eden was susceptible to the impression of power that Stalin was able to convey.[30]

Eden could hardly acknowledge any tendencies of this kind. But it was very much in character that he rationalized his Moscow experience and his subsequent support for Soviet aims by spreading the word in London that Stalin's belligerence stemmed not from power politics or from any semblance of personal aggressiveness but from a psychological state of chronic insecurity. The central issue, therefore – the "acid test," as Eden called it – was the need to gain Stalin's trust. Thus was a basis laid in the quicksands of psychology, as well as more substantively in realistic calculations of what the Soviet alliance meant to Britain, for a policy of accommodation frequently dressed up in the appeasement-conscious atmosphere of wartime London as a magnanimous strategy to reassure an insecure ally who badly wanted – in an axiom frequently voiced in the Foreign Office during the war – to "join the club" of reigning Great Powers.[31]

Stalin, who had actually shown extraordinary self-confidence rather than any kind of insecurity in the Moscow talks, continued to push the British for the bipolar treaty he wanted. The tone of the Soviets' relentless diplomatic campaign and of Anglo-Soviet relations generally was strongly influenced by the rapidly changing fortunes of war. Having survived Hitler's first onslaught and then driven the Germans back at the end of 1941, the Soviets were now remarkably optimistic. They and their

---

[30] Albert Resis (ed.), *Molotov Remembers: Inside Kremlin Politics: Conversations with Felix Chuev* (Chicago, 1993), p. 50. Eden's career and character may be studied in S. Aster, *Anthony Eden* (London, 1976); David Carlton, *Anthony Eden* (London, 1982); Randolph Churchill, *The Rise and Fall of Sir Anthony Eden* (London, 1959) – a hostile account; and Robert Rhodes James, *Anthony Eden* (London, 1987). A more recent, sympathetic review stresses Eden's European proclivities in contrast to Churchill's American focus: David Dutton, "Anthony Eden," in Otte (ed.), *Makers of British Foreign Policy*, pp. 219–237, 220.

[31] Eden paper, "Policy towards Russia," February 10, 1942, WP (42) 288.

supporters in the West talked of beating Hitler in 1942. The president
of the Czechoslovakian exile government in London, Eduard Benes, to
whom Eden paid considerable deference as a supposed oracle on European
politics, insisted that the Soviets would win the war virtually on their own
in 1942. The British, by contrast, reeling now from defeats in the Far East
at the hands of the Japanese, felt themselves to be going downhill. The
permanent under-secretary at the Foreign Office, Sir Alexander Cadogan,
lamented in early February, "We are nothing but failure and inefficiency
everywhere."[32]

The Russians exploited this situation with the combination of
encouragement and intimidation that soon came to be recognized as
representative of their political style. There was, on the one hand, a good
deal of harsh criticism in the Soviet media of the alarmingly poor British
military performance in early 1942. But, well aware of the need to support as well as pressure Eden in his campaign at home for the desired
treaty, the Soviet press made much of the Stalin-Eden meeting. *Pravda*
hailed it as "a turning point in relations between the Soviet Union and
Great Britain," reflecting the two powers' awareness that victory would
not be enough, that history's lesson was that war could come yet again,
and that there was therefore a need to prepare for "the postwar organization of peace and security." *Izvestia* characterized the "agreement" as
a "turning point in the relations of the two largest states in the world."
It showed "an identity of views" between the two countries that was "of
the greatest importance for the destinies of the peoples of Europe." The
United States was mentioned as "helping," but the whole emphasis was
on the European context. A few days later clearly inspired reports were
being circulated by Czech diplomats in Moscow saying how impressed
Stalin had been with Eden personally, how sure he was that the meeting
would have "good results," and reporting his conviction that Anglo-
Soviet relations would become "harmonious in mutual support and
loyalty."[33]

Eden bent himself energetically to the cause. On its face, this was a difficult task. He had now to ask the War Cabinet, which had applauded his
seemingly firm line in Moscow, to abandon the policy, set in May 1940,

---

[32] Sargent memorandum, January 22, 1942, F.O. 954/4. Alexander Cadogan diary,
February 12, 1942, in David Dilks (ed.), *The Diaries of Sir Alexander Cadogan, 1938–
1945* (New York, 1971), p. 433.

[33] *Pravda*, December 30, 1941; *Izvestia*, December 30, 1941. For the Czech informant
(Fierlinger), see Bruce Lockhart note, January 14, 1942, N344, F.O. 371.32874.

of not recognizing territorial changes made during the war. And he had to battle Churchill, who cabled from Washington on January 8 reminding his colleague that the Soviet accessions "were acquired by acts of aggression in shameful collusion with Hitler." British recognition would be "contrary to all the principles for which we are fighting and would dishonour our cause." Churchill continued, "There must be no mistake about the opinion of any British government of which I am the head, namely, that it adheres to those principles of freedom and democracy set forth in the Atlantic Charter and that those principles must become especially active whenever any question of transferring territory is raised." But Eden quickly found powerful support. His task was eased by the series of grave reverses Britain suffered at the beginning of 1942, which was now dispelling the short-lived public euphoria generated in London by the Soviet survival and the American engagement. Defeats at the hands of the Axis in North Africa, the devastating sinking of two capital ships off the Malayan coast, and the subsequent loss of Singapore all encouraged a conciliatory mood vis-à-vis the Soviet ally. Eden now found willing helpers in the War Cabinet, in the Foreign Office, and in the government generally, as well as in the press and among the public. *The Times* on December 29, echoing the Soviet press, declared that "in Europe, Great Britain and Soviet Russia must become the main bulwarks of a peace which can be preserved, and can be made real, only through their joint endeavour."[34]

Particularly strong in advocacy were Lord Beaverbrook, the influential cabinet minister and newspaper tycoon, who portrayed the ill-fated Baltic states as "the Ireland of Russia" and therefore vital to Soviet security; Lord Halifax, the former foreign secretary and now British ambassador in Washington, who weighed in urging that "[t]he future peace is going to depend very much upon Joe and ourselves being prepared to think and act together"; Sir Stafford Cripps, a major figure on the British left, who relinquished his ambassadorial post in Moscow in January to come home as a very effective champion of closer Anglo-Soviet ties, a cause that propelled him to a prominence that momentarily raised the possibility of a Cripps premiership; and some of the younger Chamberlainites who were still powerful in the Conservative party, among them R. A. Butler, who called for a realistic acceptance of Stalin's

---

[34] Churchill to Eden, January 8, 1942, N109, F.O. 371.32874; P. M. H. Bell, *John Bull and the Bear: British Public Opinion, Foreign Policy and the Soviet Union, 1941–1945* (London, 1990), pp. 67–88; *The Times*, December 29, 1942.

1941 frontiers and reminded Eden of the "truism," widely voiced as the debate intensified, that Britain took a closer interest in Europe than did the United States.[35]

But there was also significant opposition. Churchill continued to have serious reservations about any territorial deal with Stalin, partly out of visceral distaste, mainly for fear of American displeasure. And there was resistance on moral grounds to any recognition of Soviet claims over the Baltic states and Finland from the two most influential Labour leaders in Churchill's coalition War Cabinet, Deputy-Premier Clement Attlee and Minister of Labour Ernest Bevin. Opposition came also from a significant group of right-wing Tories in the House of Commons and, unsurprisingly, from the London-based Polish government in exile and their right-wing parliamentary supporters led by Victor Cazalet, who branded the looming deal as "a kind of inverted Munich."[36]

The challenge for Eden was also diplomatic. The various Dominion governments had qualms, especially over the sacrifice of the Baltic states. The Australian Cabinet was willing to proceed only on the grounds of "realism" and only if in return the Soviets would come into the war against Japan, a very unlikely prospect. The South Africans were lukewarm in support, with Premier Jan Smuts urging further talks and saying, "We can but do our best before acquiescing." The New Zealand and Canadian governments expressed understanding but soon sent word that they would not endorse the looming treaty.[37] Britain's continental allies were also anxious, especially the Polish government in London, which found little comfort in Stalin's decision not to press for the Curzon Line at this stage, and sought renewed affirmations of support from Eden. The Turks were, as always, fearful of Russian/Soviet designs on the Straits. Above all, the Foreign Office had to worry about the United States, where the Roosevelt administration was already showing deep concern over the unwelcome turn in the Moscow talks. How were they to be squared? Might President Roosevelt

---

[35] For Beaverbrook, see Kitchen, *British Policy*, p. 115. Halifax to Eden, January 12, 1942, F.O. 954/15. For Cripps, see Gardner, *Spheres of Influence*, pp. 121–122; Butler to Eden, March 13, 1942, F.O. 954/24. For the various factions, see Kitchen, *British Policy*, pp. 100–123.

[36] Churchill to Eden, January 8, 1942, N108, F.O. 371.32874. For Attlee and Bevin, see WM (42) 37th. CA; Kenneth Harris, *Attlee* (London, 1957), p. 197; Folly, *Whitehall*, pp. 91–92; Cazalet to Eden, April 17, 1942, F.O. 954/24; and Robert Rhodes James, *Victor Cazalet* (London, 1976), pp. 275–277; Kitchen, *British Policy*, pp. 115–116.

[37] Curtin to Churchill, rec'd. December 23, 1942, N171/G, F.O. 371.32874. Smuts to Eden, April 10, 1942, N1939; and Dominions Office to Cadogan, April 22, 1942, N1993, both in F.O. 371.32879.

redirect the emphasis to the Pacific, now the central preoccupation of an aroused American opinion?[38]

In London the issues were thrashed out in the War Cabinet. The foreign secretary tried to scotch any ideological concerns by insisting that Stalin was "a political descendant of Peter the Great rather than Lenin." He urged the importance for Britain of "really close and intimate collaboration and consultation with the USSR," elaborating the arguments on January 28 in a major paper entitled "Policy towards Russia" and in a series of subsequent written submissions. Eden interpreted Stalin's principal motive as a desire to pose "an acid test" designed "to see what value we attach to ... cooperation and what sacrifices of principle we are prepared to make in order to achieve it." To make the deal more palatable to his appeasement-conscious colleagues, and in condescending deference to Stalin's "oriental mind," Eden declared that it should not be an entirely one-way transaction. In return for the recognitions Stalin wanted, Britain should receive a "quid pro quo" including Soviet support for a Greek/Yugoslav Balkan federation (seen as protecting a British-oriented Mediterranean), a solid assurance of postwar cooperation, and, as already offered, support for the establishment of British bases in Western Europe.[39]

This "bargain" mentality, with its strong implication of a divided postwar continent, was very much of the European essence. Stalin had encouraged the traditionally detached British to think in terms of the mutuality of the proposed geopolitical settlement. Eden and the Foreign Office now accepted this approach, partly in service of Britain's own interests but also out of a belief that Stalin, presumably devoid of any elevated moral sense, would respect only a genuine bargain. Britain's future domination of Western Europe was one thing and to the British, historically skittish about continental entanglements, not an issue they wished as yet to take up with the mostly eager Western European exile governments. But the war was now creating new situations, and the Foreign Office was sympathetic to the prospective confederations in Central and southern Europe being shaped by several of the exile governments in London,

---

[38] Polish anxieties are discussed in Anita Prazmowska, *Britain and Poland, 1939–1943: The Betrayed Ally* (Cambridge, UK, 1995), pp. 114–138. The Eden-Stalin talks threw the Turks into "a fever of apprehension," according to Dixon memorandum, March 30, 1942, R 2108, F.O. 371.32879.

[39] Eden paper, "Policy towards Russia," January 29, 1942, WP (42) 48. Eden's later submissions to the War Cabinet in "Policy towards Russia," February 24, 1942, WP (42) 96; "Proposed Anglo-Soviet Treaty," April 5, 1942, WP (42) 144; and "USSR," May 18, 1942, WP (42) 198, repeat these points and enlarge the case in various ways.

two of which were, by the time Eden went to Moscow, already at an advanced drawing-board stage of development. One associated the Poles and Czechs, the other the Greeks and Yugoslavs. Both were ostensibly inspired and publicly justified as guards against future German aggression. But both inevitably bore the unacknowledged but recognized character of a revived anti-Soviet *cordon sanitaire*. In the case of most of their continental proponents (though not the Czechs) and also, discreetly, of the British Foreign Office, this was the primary appeal.[40] As one senior official put it, the confederations were "delicate growths" that required "all the encouragement we can discreetly give them. They will wither away all too easily if we withdraw such encouragement for fear of Soviet susceptibilities."[41] Here then, in the form of Soviet acceptance, was the price of British recognition of the 1941 frontiers, one that Eden, with German armies still deep within the Soviet Union, felt he could press with some prospect of success.

One can clearly see in these developments some of the elements and rationalizations that would lead the British and the Soviets to a fuller and more precise division of Europe later in the war. In the spring of 1942, however, the Germans and the war itself were still the controlling factors, and it was by no means certain that the Soviet Union would be able to survive the anticipated second Nazi onslaught. By February, Churchill, though still concerned not to offend the Americans, was wavering. After some spirited debate with his colleagues, and overriding the concerns of those who had no wish to turn the matter over to the Americans, he got the War Cabinet to agree to submit the whole issue to President Roosevelt together with a balanced statement setting out the pros and cons. But, in deference to Eden's objections, he delayed action on this. The Soviets were strongly opposed to any effort to bring the United States into the treaty negotiation. Ambassador Ivan Maisky told Eden on February 26 that this would mean delay and said he had made it clear to the United States ambassador to Britain, John Winant, "that the Soviet Government were not asking the United States Government to sign anything with them, they were only asking them to acquiesce in our signature." Meanwhile, the continuing pressure from the repeated military defeats and the growing public agitation "to help Russia," together

---

[40] For supportive Foreign Office attitudes toward the confederations projects, see Eden paper, "Forthcoming Discussions with the Soviet Government," WP (41) 288; and Prazmowska, *Britain and Poland, 1939–1943*, pp. 68, 142.

[41] Roberts minute, October 1, 1942, N4912, F.O. 371.32918.

with the persistence of Eden, Beaverbrook, and Cripps, all began to push the prime minister toward the endorsement of an Anglo-Soviet agreement more or less along the lines Stalin wanted.[42]

Significantly, however, the rationale was by this time becoming more complex. Increasingly, as the campaigning season approached, it began to seem less a matter of appeasing a self-confident Kremlin leadership looking forward to an imminent victory that would bring its power deeply into Central Europe that Eden had encountered in December (though this line of thought persisted in some quarters) than of doing what was necessary to keep the suddenly more uncertain Soviet Union of February and March engaged in the war. For through February the Soviet mood seemed to be wavering between hectoring self-confidence and rising concern as German preparations for a renewed spring offensive became ever more evident. On February 12 Maisky pushed more actively for a quick settlement and showed great concern about the "timetable" for the negotiation. Great significance was also attached to Stalin's Red Army Day speech on February 28, in which he carefully distinguished the German people from the Nazi regime. This was widely seen by anxious observers in London as, in the words of an indiscreet *Daily Herald* columnist, "a prelude to peace with Germany."[43]

It was, therefore, not only from the accumulation of British military setbacks and political concerns – and less now from a desire to get on good terms with a confidently expansionist Soviet government than from a growing fear that the Soviets might once again back away from the effort to find common ground with the pusillanimous British, make a deal with Hitler, as they had done in 1939, and thus slip out of the war – that Churchill came to see the treaty as a necessary deal. Stressing the now looming likelihood of an immense German spring offensive in the east, he cabled Roosevelt on March 7 that "the increasing gravity of the war has led me to feel that the principles of the Atlantic Charter ought not to be construed so as to deny Russia the frontiers she occupied when Germany attacked her. ... I hope therefore that you will be able to give us a free hand to sign the treaty which Stalin desires as soon as possible."[44]

[42] Eden to Baggallay, February 26, 1942, N1115, F.O. 371.32876; Kitchen, *British Policy*, p. 116.

[43] For Maisky, see Eden to Baggallay, February 12, 1942, N846, F.O. 371.32875. For Foreign Office reactions to Stalin's speech, see Dew memorandum, March 3, 1942, with telegrams and attachments in N1155, F.O. 371.32876. *Daily Herald*, March 1, 1942. The columnist was W. N. Ewer.

[44] Churchill to Roosevelt, March 7, 1942, *Correspondence*, I, p. 394.

THE TRANSATLANTIC GULF

We might usefully pause here to register, in Churchill's decision to refer the Anglo-Soviet treaty issue to Roosevelt, another defining moment in these early stages of the Big Three relationship. It went some way toward converting a hitherto self-consciously bilateral Anglo-Soviet negotiation into a problem of triangular diplomacy, presenting the full moral mess of European politics, fastidiously avoided wherever possible by the United States since 1919, to a reluctant American government that was still suffused, only a few weeks after Pearl Harbor, with the full flood of aroused idealism and patriotism. This seems a good moment, then, to digress briefly and ask ourselves, as contemporaries were now doing on both sides of the Atlantic, how much the Europeans and Americans of this tumultuous era really knew about each other.

The answer appears to be: not a great deal. Focusing first on European views of the United States, we see immediately that very few leaders of the wartime generation had any first-hand knowledge. Stalin, Hitler, and Mussolini never crossed the Atlantic. Churchill made several pre-1939 trips, but this was exceptional among the British elite. Official Anglo-American political links and visits were still quite rare before World War II. For members of the British establishment the imperial trails led to Africa, Asia, and the South Pacific, just as their habitual vacation paths took those who could afford it toward the beaches and casinos of the Mediterranean. On the other hand, the title of the British writer W. T. Stead's best-selling 1901 book, *The Americanisation of the World,* suggests an already solidly rooted familiarity with, and a mixture of hope and anxiety about, accelerating trends that would become much clearer when the United States came fully into the international arena after 1941.[45]

A snapshot view of certain categories of experience and thought will perhaps suffice to convey something of the reality. The historian Sigmund Skard, for instance, has shown us a wider informed opinion among Europeans than one might have expected. Surprisingly, perhaps, from the late 1800s on the pacesetter was not Britain but Imperial Germany. Its

---

[45] W. T. Stead, *The Americanisation of the World* (London, 1901). For American influences in Europe before 1939, see Frank Costigliola, *Awkward Dominion: American Political, Economic and Cultural Relations with Europe, 1919–1933* (Ithaca and London, 1984), pp. 140–267; Emily Rosenberg, "Cultural Interactions," in Stanley Kutler (ed.), *Encyclopedia of the United States in the 20th Century* (New York, 1996), pp. 698–708; and D. W. Brogan, "America and Britain, 1939–1946," *Yale Review*, 35, 2 (December, 1945).

leaders respected American vitality and material progress. Both Bismarck
and Kaiser Wilhelm II were keenly aware of actual and potential American
power, and starting in 1905 several German universities, and a few French
and Spanish ones too, offered courses in the study of American civilization. Skard found that even as late as 1900 the United Kingdom "held a
place in the rear as far as American Studies were concerned." The American
involvement in World War I understandably stimulated a deeper academic
commitment in Britain and led to endowed chairs in American history at
Oxford and Cambridge and also at London and St. Andrews Universities.
During the interwar years, though, Germany continued to lead the way,
with twenty-three Weimar-era universities announcing an average of one
specialized American course per semester up to 1933.[46]

At the secondary-education level, however, European traditional
school curricula in the years before World War II left little or no room for
American studies. Not until 1941 do we find the British Board of Education
making amends with summer instruction for teachers in American history. Determined efforts were then made to remedy the general ignorance
about the American story. The historian David Reynolds has traced this
volte-face, finding that "an ambitious programme to promote the study
of America was quickly set in train for elementary and secondary schools,
followed, though more slowly and less successfully, by action at the university level." On the continent, meanwhile, even at the university level there
had been a headlong retreat in the 1930s as interwar totalitarian regimes
came to power in Central and Eastern Europe. Paradoxically, American
studies atrophied there even as American popular culture became ever
more ubiquitous.[47]

So far as specific political images of the United States are concerned,
three negative reference points from the interwar period, each reflecting a
deeply felt European resentment, are illuminating. First, many articulate
Europeans appear to have taken a critical view of American diplomacy
after World War I, especially of Woodrow Wilson's allegedly erratic and
destructive course at Versailles, followed by what was widely seen as the
sullen American withdrawal from political responsibility. Second, there
was a widespread sense that reckless and selfish United States economic

[46] Sigmund Skard, *The American Myth and the European Mind* (Philadelphia, 1961),
pp. 38–58.
[47] David Reynolds, "Whitehall, Washington and the Promotion of American Studies in
Britain during World War Two," *American Studies*, 16, 2 (1982), pp. 165 and 166–188;
Skard, *American Myth*, pp. 73–74; *Reader's Digest*, December 1941, p. 10.

policies in the 1920s had undermined and frustrated Europe's recovery and even brought on the depression of the 1930s. A third grievance, especially among elites in the politically intense 1930s, was the supposedly subversive social impact of American mass culture. "Coming into contact with the peoples," one German Protestant cleric wrote, "one is constantly made aware that it is not socialism but Americanism that will be the end of everything as we have known it."[48]

To reinforce these more or less familiar markers of political attitudes, we might dip briefly into what little we know of the unguarded discourse of the leading figures. Mussolini, responding in the late 1930s to a suggestion by his mistress, Margherita Sarfatti, that he would be wise to cultivate better relations with the United States, declared with conclusive simplicity, "America doesn't count."[49] This was a widely shared European view. Hitler, much given to uninterrupted, highly generalized monologues, sometimes voiced admiration for American vitality and industrial techniques and even praised the New Deal until Roosevelt became critical of Nazi excesses. But, more typically, he saw the United States as hopelessly mongrelized, dominated by Jews, and, as Hollywood movies seemed to him to show, thoroughly decadent. He seems to have seen himself as Europe's standard bearer in a kind of transatlantic *kulturkampf.*[50] Stalin's views are more obscure. But the Soviet media routinely gave vent to conventional Marxist abuse of Wall Street capitalists, Southern racists, capitalist bosses, and Chicago gangsters, while literary people often took their line from Maxim Gorky's celebrated evisceration of New York in his book *The City of the Yellow Devil.*[51]

British pre-war leaders, keenly aware of American economic power and competition but mindful too of the republic's military potential and the familiar range of cultural affinities, were much more circumspect in their public references to the United States. Behind the scenes, notwithstanding a growing sense of the need to attach the Roosevelt administration to British interests, there was much ambivalence and even outright resentment. Neville Chamberlain's well-known 1938 declaration that at critical moments the Americans typically gave no help but words

---

[48] Cited in A. J. Nicholls, "End of a Republic," *Times Literary Supplement*, January 3, 1992.

[49] Adrian Lyttelton, "Mussolini's Femme Fatale," *New York Review of Books*, July 15, 1993.

[50] See the various references in Adolf Hitler, *Mein Kampf*, trans. Ralph Mannheim (Boston, 1999), Marriner edn., pp. 139, 566–567, 615, 644.

[51] Maxim Gorky, *The City of the Yellow Devil* (New York, 1921).

was a representative sentiment. As late as 1944 we find Anthony Eden's complaining that "[t]he Americans don't help themselves but are always ready to criticize the efforts of others." There was behind these attitudes a lively fear of American domination. Even in January 1940 Chamberlain was writing, "Heaven knows I don't want the Americans fighting for us. We should have to pay too dearly for that if they had a right to be in on the peace terms."[52]

Winston Churchill himself, though often appreciative of American vitality in private as well as in public expression, had confronted Wilson personally at Paris in 1919 and found fault with him subsequently in his literary account of the aftermath of the war. He was critical of American diplomacy and economic policy throughout the interwar period, telling the German ambassador in 1930 of his regret "that no one had adopted his suggestion made after the war, that the debtor and creditor nations, including Germany, should unite to form a common front against America."[53] This fear of dispossession by the better-endowed United States was deeply felt in Britain. Left-wing circles were hardly more positive. Ernest Bevin, Labour stalwart and wartime Cabinet minister, thought American life, which he saw at first hand, "bleak and soulless." Detroit, he noted after a 1926 visit, was "a hard, cruel city … no culture … No one talks to you except in dollars and mass production."[54]

Finally, at the more general level of ideas and images – hard for the historian to pin down but increasingly significant as international tensions grew and improved communications made for a world that seemed smaller than before – we can see that, excepting only the magnetic draw of transatlantic mass culture and some practical emulation of business and technological systems, characteristic American "models" – political, social, constitutional – seem to have held little appeal for Europeans during the interwar years. There had been much interest in American federalism at the turn of the twentieth century, and some of this persisted into the 1914–45 era as various European groupings were contemplated.[55] But, generally

[52] Chamberlain cited in Reynolds, "Whitehall, Washington and the Promotion of American Studies," p. 168. Eden note, January 17, 1944, C262, F.O. 371.38920.

[53] Winston Churchill, "Will America Fail Us?," *Illustrated Sunday Herald*, November 30, 1919; and Churchill, *The World Crisis*, Vol. 4, *1918–1928: The Aftermath* (New York, 1929), pp. 98–115, 118–119. See also Harbutt, *Iron Curtain*, pp. 9–15.

[54] Alan Bullock, *Ernest Bevin: Foreign Secretary, 1945–1951* (London, 1983), p. 144; Harbutt, *Iron Curtain*, pp. 132–133.

[55] Reynolds, "Whitehall, Washington and the Promotion of American Studies," p. 165. The pan-European impulses of the interwar years associated with Coudenhove-Kalergi and others drew somewhat on American experience, as did the wartime "confederation"

speaking, neither the distinctive American constitutional formulas nor the various rhetorical principles of Jeffersonian or New Deal democracy resonated deeply in Europe. During the nineteenth century the United States had indeed been a "beacon of freedom" for the European working classes. But industrial, urban, modern America was a more ambiguous, even threatening proposition. Furthermore, in the turbulent years before World War II European regimes intent on foiling "the elements of disturbance" and/or shaping the political course of what was increasingly called "mass society," were creating their own resonant models of acceptable behavior. Thus the Italian fascists proclaimed their "New Order"; the Nazis pushed their exclusivist Aryan warrior aspirations; the Soviets celebrated the "New Man." Even the British had their own, somewhat less theatrical, but cherished homegrown ideal, the cult of the unassuming English gentleman. This was much in vogue during the 1930s and later reached a kind of apotheosis in the mystique of the Battle of Britain pilots. The popular Yorkshire novelist J. B. Priestley eulogized this seemingly diffident but quietly heroic type as a congenial national contrast to the kind of vulgar personality supposedly produced by any close association with American mass culture.[56]

Needless to say, American views of interwar Europe were similarly unflattering. Doubtless Americans knew more about Europe than vice versa. There was a widespread if thin awareness of some elements of the British past, less so of continental history. But the proverbially forward-looking drive of American society and culture – its future-oriented ethos and its introspective political focus – meant that even after the sudden, unwelcome, and quickly liquidated engagement with the old continent in World War I there was really very little sense of transatlantic intimacy or even of a common destiny. Indeed, memories of the "European War," as it was often called, were mostly bitter in America too, but for reasons directly antithetical to those that fed anti-Americanism in Europe. Americans tended to believe that, having drawn them into the struggle,

projects. Despite the general policy of United States diplomatic avoidance, a plan for a large Eastern/Central Europe "confederation" was advanced without significant outcome by Sumner Welles and Adolf Berle: see Sargent minute, October 3, 1942, N4912, F.O. 371.32918.

[56] George D. Lillibridge, *Beacon of Freedom: The Impact of American Democracy upon Great Britain, 1830–1870* (Philadelphia, 1955); Chris Waters, "J. B. Priestley: Englishness and the Politics of Nostalgia," in S. Pederson and P. Mandler (eds.), *After the Victorians: Private Consciousness and Public Duty in Modern Britain* (London, 1994), p. 212 and passim.

the Europeans had been ungrateful for the decisive contribution of the United States to their ultimate deliverance. Had they not foolishly and selfishly rejected Woodrow Wilson's well-intentioned peace making? The lesson for the crisis-ridden 1930s, therefore, was generally held to be the incorrigibility of the Europeans, an assumption that, as the historian John Harper has recently reminded us, lay at the heart of Franklin D. Roosevelt's worldview.[57]

Cultural images reinforced these attitudes. The old, half-affectionate American measures of cultural comparison with Europe – Emerson's proud assertion of his compatriots' self-reliance, Mark Twain's humorous observations, Henry James's transatlantic subtleties – now seemed passé. The novels of Ernest Hemingway, John dos Passos, and F. Scott Fitzgerald lent some glamor to Europe in the immediate postwar years, but the predominant influence during the 1930s was the critical outlook now increasingly cultivated by modern American newspapers, many of which established impressive news-gathering facilities in Europe during the interwar years. They typically put a harsher, more dramatic cast on the almost continuous round of political confrontations that characterized the pre-war years in Europe and helped institutionalize unattractive stereotypes that the calmer overviews of writers like John Gunther could only partially dispel.[58]

American diplomacy in the interwar years was largely left to an unpopular, elitist State Department that was distrusted precisely because it seemed to commune too closely, in attitudes and outlook, with the politically tricky, perhaps more sophisticated Europeans. The universities contributed little to a deeper enlightenment. The close study of world affairs in the United States, to the limited extent that this existed, was mainly left to international lawyers and to ardent keepers of the Wilsonian flame. Increasingly, as World War II approached, émigrés from Nazi oppression like the political scientist Hans Morgenthau appeared. Their shocked reactions to the low level of informed opinion they found were often expressed in shrill, Cassandra-like warnings that raised anxiety in some elite circles but brought little in the way of political mobilization.[59]

---

[57] For a recent treatment of the critical views of Europeans held by Roosevelt and his contemporaries, see John L. Harper, *American Visions of Europe: Franklin D. Roosevelt, George F. Kennan, and Dean G. Acheson* (New York, 1994), pp. 7–131.

[58] John Gunther's *Inside Europe* (New York, 1938) was widely read.

[59] For a study of European émigrés in the United States, see Ellen G. Rafshoon, "Power over Principle: Hans J. Morgenthau and the Fate of Émigré Realism in America" (Ph.D. dissertation, Emory University, 2001).

It is perhaps an indication of the disdain and concern with which Americans regarded Europe in the interwar and early wartime years that the one quality they saw there that did register in a positive way was not, as one might assume, a display of functioning democracy such as that found in Britain, France, and a dwindling number of other countries. Nor was it the occasional show, here and there, of progressive reform. Rather, it was the fitful appearance of the impulse of regeneration, the redeeming element that the moral/religious sensibility instinctively looks for only in those who have sunk to the lowest depths. Where it seemed to appear, it was often applauded by many in the United States, whether it came from democrats or dictators, fascists or communists, capitalists or socialists. Thus Mussolini was greatly admired in the 1920s for his apparently successful efforts to bring order and revived pride to a hitherto (as many saw it) chaotic, decadent Italy. Stalin was sometimes lauded by liberals for avoiding the depression and creating a new, supposedly progressive society out of backward, ravaged Russia. Hitler was praised by many for creating order, reviving his economy, and restoring German self-esteem. And even Britain, under Churchill's leadership, was briefly able to redeem itself in American eyes during the glorious days of 1940, producing a brief positive feeling that Churchill tried with only limited success to maintain later in the war. The usually maligned Soviets achieved a similar epiphany with hitherto skeptical Americans following their great victory at Stalingrad.

All of which brings us back to our discussion of Allied diplomacy in early 1942. For unfortunately, so far as any prospect for productive tripartite political collaboration was concerned, Churchill's invitation to Roosevelt to pass some judgment upon the sensitive Anglo-Soviet treaty negotiations fell between two of these regenerative European moments. For now the British, reeling from humiliating defeats at the hands of both the Japanese in Asia and the Germans in North Africa, had largely exhausted the moral capital of 1940; and the Soviets, during this pre-Stalingrad period, had not yet had time to overcome traditional suspicions and build theirs up. The reception in Washington, consequently, was unlikely to be enthusiastic.

THE EMERGING ANGLO-SOVIET TREATY

So it proved, as we quickly see when we return to the story of the Anglo-Soviet treaty, now converted by Churchill's singular decision from the purely European negotiation Stalin and Eden had intended to a subject of "Big Three" triangular diplomacy. Eden had resisted the submission to Washington. The Soviets were also opposed to it. The State Department similarly wanted nothing to do with the matter. Eden's compromising Soviet diplomacy in Moscow, as soon as its purport became known in Washington, had already aroused passionate criticism and acute anxiety.

Cordell Hull was particularly incensed at Eden's Moscow conduct, which he had tried to head off. Always suspicious of European intrigue, he had asked Eden, even before his departure for Moscow, to avoid any commitments on the Soviet frontier question. Early in February, Halifax had been given the unenviable task of presenting him with Eden's explanation and the case for a territorially oriented deal with Moscow. This involved, Halifax stressed, the notion that the Soviet Union was an indispensable partner in the war. Indeed, he warned, it might win on its own and then go on to communize most of Europe unless there was a constraining treaty. Alternatively, if Stalin was rejected now, Churchill's government might fall and be replaced by a "frankly communist, pro-Moscow government." Hull was unmoved by these scarecrow scenarios.[60]

Now, in March, Halifax was obliged by Churchill's initiative to try again, this time in a series of acrimonious confrontations with undersecretary of state Sumner Welles, who was, if anything, even more inflexible. The proposed deal, Welles objected, "evidenced the worst phase of the spirit of Munich," hardly a tactful reminder to one of the leading figures in that now notorious settlement. Welles, seizing with relish the opportunity both to pronounce a personal anathema upon Chamberlain's closest associate and, more generally, to deliver what might reasonably be called the distilled judgment of the American people on the European diplomacy of the inter-war period, piled on the odium relentlessly, declaring that the Anglo-Soviet deal seemed designed to restore "the shoddy, inherently vicious kind of patchwork world order which the European powers had attempted to construct during the years between 1919 and 1939." The State Department, he advised, took a straightforward moral view. There should be no frontier agreements until after the war. American opinion would be shocked. The commitment to defeat Germany first, he threatened, might be abandoned in favor of the Pacific war. Halifax, a phlegmatic Yorkshireman, maintained his poise and finally won Welles's promise to consult the president. Two days later, the undersecretary was able to tell Halifax, with an air of

---

[60] *Memoirs of Cordell Hull* (New York, 1948), Vol. 2, pp. 167–70. Eden to Baggallay, February 26, 1942, N1115 F.O. 371.32876. Victor Rothwell, *Britain and the Cold War, 1941–1947* (London, 1982), p. 94.

ill-disguised satisfaction, that Roosevelt had studied all the documents and
had said that his impression of the whole matter could be summed up in one
word: "provincial."[61]

In fact, Roosevelt's position was not so simple. Yes, he consistently
refused to approve the Anglo-Soviet treaty. He had already burst out at a
press conference in late February: "Don't you think we might win the war
before we start determining all the details of geography, and boundaries,
and things like that?" But he now declined the State Department's urgings
to resist the deal openly. On the one hand, he criticized the European diplomacy to Welles and told him he was firmly opposed to the Anglo-Soviet
treaty on both moral and practical grounds. But in communication with
Churchill, and in discussions with Halifax and Beaverbrook (sent over by
Churchill to explain the British position), he was much more worldly, at
one point suggesting to Halifax that ultimately the crucial question of the
Baltic states, for instance, was "simply a question of presentation."[62]

Roosevelt, in conversation with Welles, referred to the probability of a
Soviet fait accompli if they recovered the Baltic states at the war's end, and
the inability of the United States or Britain to do anything about it, and said
he was going to say this to the Soviet ambassador, Maxim Litvinov. Welles
thought he had dissuaded the president from this compromising step but
was told to insist, as a condition of any possible quiet American acceptance
of a takeover, that Stalin agree to allow any citizen of the Baltic states who
so wished to emigrate with his or her property.

To this point FDR might be seen as acting in a spirit of realistic moderate statesmanship to counter the obdurate moralism of his advisers. But
on March 12, as he would often do during the war, he smudged the otherwise sharp distinction between American and European diplomacy scrupulously maintained by the State Department in a private talk he initiated
with Soviet Ambassador Maxim Litvinov. He offered the Russian reassurances of his concern for the Soviet Union's postwar security against
any renewed German threat. He stressed the importance of the Atlantic
Charter and the bad effect that premature territorial arrangements of
the kind contemplated by the treaty would have on American opinion.

---

[61] Memorandum of conversation, February 18, 1942, FRUS, 1942, III (Washington, D.C.,
1961), pp. 512–521; memorandum of conversation, February 20, 1942, ibid., pp. 521–
524. Welles, characterized by an official as "another Wilson only 20 years out of date,"
was unpopular in Foreign Office circles – Oliver Harvey diary, March 14, 1942, in John
Harvey (ed.), *The War Diaries of Oliver Harvey, 1941–1945* (London, 1978), p. 109.
[62] *New York Times*, February 5, 1942; Halifax to Eden, February 20, 1942, N931, F.O.
371.32876; Harbutt, *Iron Curtain*, p. 38.

He could not agree to any secret treaty, but said he did not foresee "any difficulties" over the border issues once the war was won. According to the Litvinov record, "He himself [FDR] had always thought it had been a mistake to separate provinces from Russia after the war and he thought Wilson had also been opposed to this. And therefore he assures Stalin in a personal way that he absolutely agrees with us."[63]

But Molotov, who had not wanted any American involvement, appears not to have been particularly impressed with this vague hint of long-term support. Rather, he saw an opportunity to take advantage of FDR's initiative and also of some clumsily ingratiating diplomacy by Churchill, who, having ostensibly passed the issue to the president, had immediately undermined the latter's judicial standing by telling Stalin ingratiatingly on March 12 that "I have sent a message to President Roosevelt urging him to approve our signing agreement with you about the frontiers of Russia at the end of the war." Molotov was now in a position to pressure the British toward the treaty. He quickly saw to it that Eden was apprised of Litvinov's report, which was being taken in Moscow as signifying American acceptance of Russia's security needs. Unaware of Churchill's subverting commitment to Stalin, Roosevelt appears to have believed that with his benevolent intervention he had personally seized control of the negotiation and that he could bring the Europeans to abandon the agreement altogether. In fact, his gate-crashing intervention through Litvinov, as the Foreign Office saw it, enraged Eden and his advisers. But this was of little concern to the president. Clearly expecting a favorable response from Moscow, he wrote ebulliently to Churchill on March 18: "I know you will not mind my being brutally frank when I tell you that I think I can personally handle Stalin better than your Foreign Office or my State Department. Stalin hates the guts of all your top people. He thinks he likes me better and I hope he will continue to do so."[64]

This was not simply a display of presidential vanity. FDR was also no doubt seriously concerned to avoid the threat to American public tranquility and to alliance solidarity posed by the treaty. But any hope that his private reassurances to Litvinov would head off Stalin's drive for a formal

---

[63] There is no fully reliable account of the Roosevelt-Litvinov meeting, but see the discussion and discordant reports of Halifax and Maisky cited in Hugh Phillips, "Mission to America: Maksim M. Litvinov in the United States, 1941–1943," *Diplomatic History*, 12 (Summer 1988), pp. 261–275.

[64] Churchill to Stalin, March 3, 1942 (received March 12), SCCA, p. 40. Kitchen, *British Policy*, p. 120. Roosevelt to Churchill, March 18, 1942, *Correspondence*, I, p. 421.

treaty with the British was soon exposed as illusory. The Soviet leader sat on the president's seemingly portentous message for two weeks and then simply acknowledged its receipt.[65] This casual response to an apparently helpful initiative from the American president, especially at a time when Lend-Lease material from the United States was beginning to grow, may seem remarkable. But the Soviets, still confident about their military prospects for 1942, had not yet taken the full measure of American power and potential and were not in an appeasing mood. Just as the typically aggressive Soviet media had criticized the early British failures in the Far East, so too the Soviet media had been hard on the Americans. On December 30 the leading commentator, David Zazlavsky, had scathingly condemned in *Pravda* the American decision to preserve Manila from Japanese destruction by declaring it an "open city." Under the headline "Petain Methods in the Philippines," Zazlavsky likened the American posture to that of a ladybird lying on its back and impotently waving its legs about and charged the commanders there with a cowardice that he contrasted with the resistance being put up by cities like Leningrad and London. Protests from United States representatives in Moscow (Churchill also remonstrated with Stalin) were met with reference to "the many unpleasant articles about the Soviet Union in America."[66]

Roosevelt, always temperamentally robust, was not at all deterred by this setback to his private diplomacy. Still eager to break down the dangerous treaty negotiation, he now moved from private assurances of postwar support on the Soviet frontier to more tempting hints of an early second front. At the beginning of April he had sent Army Chief of Staff George C. Marshall and his closest aide, Harry Hopkins, to London with plans drawn up by General Dwight D. Eisenhower's military planners for a build-up of approximately 48 divisions and 5,800 planes in Britain in anticipation of a large-scale invasion in April 1943, and for smaller emergency landings in the autumn of 1942 if either Germany or the Soviet Union seemed to be on the verge of collapse. Hearing from Hopkins that the talks with the British were going well, Roosevelt cabled Stalin on April 11 urging him to let Molotov – now thought to be preparing to go to London to complete and sign the hoped-for treaty – come to Washington beforehand to discuss "a very important military proposal" for the relief of his "critical western front." FDR baited the hook with a declaration that he wanted Stalin's advice "before we determine with finality the strategic course of

[65] Dallek, *Roosevelt and American Foreign Policy*, pp. 338–339.
[66] *Pravda*, December 30, 1942.

our common military action." Once again he got a damp response. Stalin waited until April 22 and then replied, agreeing to send Molotov but making it clear that he would arrive only after his visit to London, where he would presumably sign his treaty.[67]

As the campaigning season approached the Soviet leaders, for all their rising concern about some kind of second front, were still obsessively focused on the treaty they had long labored to extract from the reluctant British. They would of course have liked an early second front, but now that Japan was running rampant in the Pacific they did not expect it. Nor was the United States the obvious key to any such operation. It was clear that virtually no groundwork had been laid – no American troop build-up in Britain or stockpiled supplies – for a cross-Channel invasion. And, in any event, if there was to be an effective second front that year in Europe it would be the British who would have to assume the preponderant burden.

There is much evidence today that, despite the vigorous public campaign for a second front in the Soviet and worldwide communist and "fellow-traveling" press, the Soviet leaders did not really expect any significant Allied landings in France during 1942. They had made little of the issue with Eden in December, and the foreign secretary put it about on his return that no such enterprise was anticipated in Moscow. This was also Cripps's view, which he had been disseminating in political circles since his return in January to London, telling a meeting of members of Parliament on February 18 that "Stalin had never really taken the Second Front issue seriously and that since the outbreak of war in the Far East he had put it out of his mind completely."[68] By the spring there were indeed signs of rising Soviet anxiety and a notable intensification of the public campaign. But the treaty was still the main priority. As late as May 5 we find Maisky telling Eden that he did not see "any expectation that a second front could be formed before the autumn." It was for this reason, he continued, that "his government had hoped that we would be willing to agree to their draft of the treaty."

It is true that Molotov again raised the question of a second front upon his arrival in Britain in late May and was, as we will see, even more aggressive in his subsequent discussions of the matter in Washington. By

---

[67] Roosevelt to Stalin, April 11, 1942, FRUS, 1942, III, pp. 542–543; Standley to secretary of state, April 24, 1942, ibid., pp. 545–548; Dallek, *Roosevelt and American Foreign Policy*, p. 339.

[68] Law memorandum, February 19, 1942, N897/G, F.O. 371.32876.

this time the increasingly alarmed Soviets undoubtedly did want some kind of effective Allied effort in France in 1942. But in his published recollections Molotov conceded that he had known that Britain and the United States could not launch a significant second front in 1942. As he explained: "We knew they couldn't dare mount a second front but we made them agree to it. ... We didn't believe in a second front, of course, but we had to try for it." He intimated that the Soviet diplomatic efforts that year had been mainly designed to boost the morale of the Soviet people and to lay the foundation for later political pressure upon the Western powers. This is confirmed, as will appear, by the uses the Soviet authorities made of the Anglo-Soviet treaty when it was revealed to the world in June. What Stalin and Molotov seem to have wanted was a public promise from their allies, backed by the impression of strong solidarity given by the intended Anglo-Soviet treaty, that a second front was coming. Meanwhile, the treaty would, in addition to its desired territorial terms, reassure the Soviet people, legitimize the regime's leadership at home, and gain political leverage with the Western Allies for the future. But there was no expectation of strategically meaningful landings on the continent in 1942.[69]

It would appear that it was the Americans alone – and perhaps, in the end, only the military leadership and a few high officials – who consistently viewed any landings on the French coast in 1942 as a viable project. Marshall and Hopkins had returned to Washington in mid-April thinking they had received a positive British commitment. It soon became clear that this was not the case and that the president's emissaries had either been manipulated in some way or that they and their British hosts had misunderstood each other. Roosevelt continued to proclaim his support, notably in his talks with Molotov. But in June he swung over to the British view and settled with Churchill for what is sometimes called a "peripheral" strategy focused initially on the Mediterranean. Marshall and Hopkins, and also Henry Stimson, the influential secretary of war, had by this time in their frustration formed the view, which sharpened and radiated throughout much of the American political establishment later in the war, that the seemingly self-serving British were thinking above all of their own imperial

[69] Resis (ed.), *Molotov's Conversations*, pp. 46–47. Eden to Clark Kerr, May 5, 1942, N2385, F.O. 371.32880. In a recent study Geoffrey Roberts argues that Stalin would have welcomed a second front because "at best, it would happen and contribute to rolling back the Wehrmacht on the Eastern Front by drawing forces to the west; at worst, the threat would deter Hitler from redeploying too many troops from Western Europe." Geoffrey Roberts, *Stalin's Wars: From World War to Cold War, 1939–1953* (New Haven and London, 2006), p. 135.

and geopolitical interests rather than early victory and the common cause. The effect was to chill thoughts of political collaboration with the British in Europe and to strengthen the preexisting (and traditional) determination in Washington to concentrate on military victory first and leave postwar politics until it had been achieved.[70]

The two European powers, meanwhile, with the Soviets setting the pace, were operating from a very different (but also traditional) set of precepts. There was no shelving of politics. Through April and into May the Soviets continued to take the American diplomatic intrusion, despite its clear hint of a second front, with much less enthusiasm than Roosevelt had expected. Meanwhile, they redoubled the diplomatic pressure on the British government, sending draft treaties that, in typically provocative fashion, urged British acceptance in advance of highly self-interested secret treaties that they apparently wished to force later upon the Polish and other governments. They enlarged the original demands in certain ways, and now upset Eden by excluding the British quid pro quo of a Balkan federation. "It was despairing," a frazzled Eden complained to Maisky in May, "to try to negotiate with the Soviet Government when they invariably raised their price at every meeting."[71] Nevertheless, despite all provocations and disappointments, he labored on.

THE MAKING OF THE TREATY

The treaty negotiations, as they briefly assumed the triangular character imposed by Churchill on a host of unwilling participants, presented the British with a very difficult problem of political navigation. As Eden aptly remarked, "Soviet policy is amoral; United States policy is exaggeratedly moral, at least where non-American interests are concerned." In practice, a senior Foreign Office diplomat noted, "Our major diplomatic problem is to keep on good terms both with the United States of America and with Russia and to avoid choosing between them whenever possible."[72] But now, as spring approached and Soviet pressure intensified, it seemed they would have to choose. If Stalin were rejected, might he not turn again to Germany and leave the war? If his unwholesome demands were accepted, on the other hand, the Roosevelt administration (as well as the Dominions, the

---

[70] Dallek, *Roosevelt and American Foreign Policy*, pp. 339–347.

[71] Eden to Clark Kerr, May 5, 1942, N2385, F.O. 371.32880.

[72] Eden's remark is in "Policy towards Russia," January 28, 1942, WP (42) 48. Makins memorandum, May 10, 1942, N2221, F.O. 371.32880.

Turks, the Poles, and others) would be upset, and the principal American war effort might be diverted to the Pacific.

Eden and the Foreign Office stuck firmly to the Soviet option, continuing to make the case in a series of submissions to the War Cabinet and through Halifax to leading American figures. The argument was invariably grounded in a felt necessity. Without Soviet support Britain could not win the war and might well lose it. The Soviets, Eden told his colleagues, were bearing the brunt of the war and were about to face "perhaps a heavier military onslaught than the world had yet seen." Political collaboration was also needed because after the war the Soviet Union would be overwhelmingly dominant in a Europe where there would be "no counterweight." A bold front was put on this essentially accommodative diplomacy. Britain would be insist in return on the acceptance of her interests in Western Europe and seek some gestures of support for the various "confederation" projects in the east and south.[73]

Considerations of this kind – hard-headed, pragmatic, Palmerstonian in the emphasis on interests rather than ideals – summon up memories of independent action in palmier days. But the British felt acutely vulnerable in early 1942, and less robust impulses, psychological in character, coursed through the anxious deliberations. No one wanted to be accused of "appeasement," but the diplomats were only too aware that charges of this kind were bound to be voiced when the sacrifice of the Baltic states became public knowledge. Yet in fact the British had already set foot on the slippery slope in their Soviet diplomacy by reluctantly, in advance of Eden's mission to Moscow, declaring war on Finland, Rumania, and Bulgaria and now, in response to Maisky's request, by removing the Baltic states' representatives from the Diplomatic List, though they were allowed to retain their privileges. And even the ostensibly robust "quid pro quos" seem rather less impressive as compensatory measures of self-respecting assertion when one recalls that during the Moscow talks Stalin had actually invited Britain to act forcefully in Western Europe, and had also made it clear to Eden that he was not opposed to "federative" solutions in Europe. The Foreign Office was simply taking what was apparently on offer.

There was in all these calculations some resolve not to knuckle under to the Soviets completely. "We need to stand up to the Russians," noted one senior official. But there was a persistent desire to satisfy Stalin's "acid test,"

---

[73] The most cogent exposition is in Eden's "Policy towards Russia," January 28, 1942, WP (42) 48.

which Eden repeatedly described as being designed "to find out how far His Majesty's Government are prepared to make unpalatable concessions in order to obtain the postwar cooperation of the Soviet Union ... and what sacrifices of principle we are prepared to make in order to achieve it." The Baltic states were to be abandoned, that was clear. But the Poles, with whom Britain had a 1939 treaty binding them not to engage without consent in any negotiations with third parties affecting Polish territory, were also anxious about the situation. Eden sought to reassure them with a letter to the Polish prime minister, General Sikorski, affirming Britain's fidelity – soon to be jettisoned – to that commitment, and saying, "In any negotiation with the Soviet Government His Majesty's Government intend fully to safeguard the position of their Polish allies."[74] That, for the moment, calmed the Poles, who now had a swelling library of similar written reassurances they would later present reproachfully to the Foreign Office. There was also concern that the Turks, similarly watchful, might be tempted by the Anglo-Soviet flirtation to abandon their similar British treaty connection in favor of restored ties with their World War I German ally. If so, a senior official wrote, consideration should be given to offering a bribe to the Turks. In such a bribe compensation at the expense of Syria as well as Bulgaria would necessarily figure."[75] The contrast here – the eager inclination to accommodate the desires of the forceful Great Power; the quick resort to a manipulative diplomacy directed toward lesser powers supposedly standing in the way – is a foretaste of the way in which the developing Anglo-Soviet project would operate in and around Europe later in the war.

The British then, in these desperate times, were ready enough to sacrifice principle to keep the Soviets in the war. But the transatlantic predicament remained: how to square the distant, moralistic Americans. Paper promises and bribes would not be enough there. Had Roosevelt been implacably hostile it is unclear whether the British would have gone ahead. But FDR, perhaps chastened by Stalin's rebuff and anxious, like the British, to keep the Soviets in the war, was now helpful, making it clear he would not oppose, though he could not endorse, the projected treaty. But that still left American public opinion, supposedly wedded to the Atlantic Charter and plausibly expected to be highly critical of these ostensibly cynical displays of European realpolitik. Eden did his best to put it all in a good light. The Foreign Office bombarded Halifax with material proclaiming

---

[74] Warner minute, February 17, 1942, N927, F.O. 371.32876. For the Anglo-Polish treaty reference, see Rothwell, *Britain and the Cold War,* p. 163.
[75] Dixon memorandum, March 30, 1942, R2108, F.O. 371.32879.

that no secret protocols were involved and giving reassurances that Britain would try, as the president had insisted, to get the Soviets to allow free emigration from the Baltic states. The main emphasis, however, was educative: a grim realism and a continuing stress on the need to encourage the Soviets to resist the renewed German onslaught, and also on the bitter reproaches later generations were likely to voice if a rejected Stalin left the war or suffered defeat through some kind of Anglo-American moral obstinacy. The more provocative arguments urged at home – British interests and postwar geopolitics – were naturally played down in these transatlantic presentations. And most of the more bizarre rationalizations that bubbled up to explain to skeptical Americans the expected disappearance of the Baltic states – the notion that their inhabitants would in fact benefit from the Soviet's professed commitment to "a better life for all"; the assertion that Soviet minority policies had in the past been "conspicuously successful"; the claim that the integration of the Baltic states would be a wholesome tribute to American "federalism" – were wisely weeded out before transmission.[76]

The War Cabinet finally decided on March 25 to commit to Eden's treaty accepting the Soviets' 1941 frontiers, with the exception of the Polish lands. The foreign secretary now moved quickly to try and bring both his problems – the negotiations with the Soviets and the anticipated difficulty in putting any settlement across with American opinion – to a satisfactory conclusion. On April 13 he sent an eight-point draft to the Soviet government. It conceded the basic Soviet demands but, along with some conventional general terms, also referred ostentatiously to the Atlantic Charter, the right of emigration for inhabitants of the seized areas, and support for a Balkan confederation – all anathema in one way or another to Moscow.[77] Predictably, the Soviets raised objections and then quickly submitted two new proposals that the Foreign Office in its turn could not accept. One sought a British commitment in advance to any territorial agreement reached between the Soviet and Polish governments. The other looked to a "secret protocol" (a politically impossible method for the British) endorsing contemplated future treaties Moscow contemplated imposing on Finland and Rumania allowing Soviet military bases on their territory, envisaging also similar British defense agreements with

---

[76] For representative Foreign Office instructions on representations to American opinion, see cables from Eden to Halifax on April 19, 30 and May 13, 1942, in N2557, N2806, and N3075, respectively, all in F.O. 371.32880.

[77] Eden to Clark Kerr, April 13, 1942, F.O. 954/25A.

its Western European allies, and implying, we can see in retrospect, the Anglo-Soviet division of power in Europe that would take a fuller form in 1944. Eden, deeply depressed at this setback, expressed his fear that the whole negotiation seemed to be failing. At this point, Stalin himself intervened. Obviously concerned that the prize was slipping away, he complained to Churchill on April 22 that the British drafts "substantially depart on certain points from the texts of the treaties discussed during Mr. Eden's stay in Moscow." Nevertheless, he would send V. M. Molotov to London "for personal talks with a view to settling the issues holding up the signing of the treaties." That was not all. The strategic issue now came into play. Molotov's journey, Stalin continued, "is all the more essential as the question of a second front in Europe raised by Mr. Roosevelt, the United States President, in his latest message to me, inviting M. Molotov to Washington to discuss the matter, calls for a preliminary exchange of views between representatives of our two governments."[78]

Ironically, just as negotiations with the Soviets seemed to be bogging down in stalemate, Eden settled at last on a basic justificatory principle to lay before the Americans. He reminded Halifax on March 26 that "[t]his country, as a European Power for whom collaboration with a victorious U.S.S.R. after the war will be essential, cannot afford to neglect any opportunity of establishing intimate relations of confidence with Stalin." On April 19, he sent the ambassador a ringing assertion of British independence:

The time has come for us (and by implication the Americans) to accept our responsibilities as a European power and to show that we intend to play our part in the future settlement of Europe. This naturally involves collaboration and agreement with the Soviet Union to prevent the recurrence of German domination and aggression. This collaboration is equally essential for the United Kingdom, Soviet Union and all other European countries and we realise the necessity of preparing for it immediately.[79]

One wonders how this stoutly realistic declaration would have resonated with American opinion had the full treaty envisioned by Stalin gone ahead with all its anticipated territorial elements. As it was, even before Molotov arrived in London on May 21 to complete the political arrangements, the war itself began to supervene in a decisive way. Alert observers in London, mostly on the defensive in the drawn-out early stages of these negotiations,

---

[78] Eden to Clark Kerr, May 1, 1942, N2336, F.O. 371.32880; Stalin to Churchill, April 22, 1942, SCCA, pp. 44–45.
[79] Eden to Halifax, March 26, 1942, in WP (42) 144; Eden to Halifax, April 19, 1942, N2056, F.O. 371.32879.

now began to sense in Stalin's second-front reference some faltering of the Soviet spirit and started to adopt a strategy based, not on submission to an aggressively self-confident Moscow, but on the assumption that the threat of an "imminent German attack" might produce a more congenial outcome. The Joint Committee of Intelligence chief, Cavendish-Bentinck, noted on May 6 that "our principal motive was to keep the Russians in the war and to avert the danger of a separate Russo-German peace." The best course, therefore, was "to string out negotiations" until the German attack, for "if the Russians are suffering serious reverses they will be more amenable to reason." The Foreign Office's permanent under-secretary, Sir Alexander Cadogan, agreed. He defined this new approach as "keeping the Russians in play on our side" – the principal British objective – while haggling with them over their increasingly extreme demands. As he elaborated, "the object of the treaty was always to hold the Russians during a difficult period (now) when the German attack is pending but not yet launched and when the Russians might be frightened into a negotiation."[80]

But the Soviets seemed to be playing the game with iron nerves and gave no clear reason to think that these delaying tactics would work. In the first weeks of May they were as demanding as ever, and as Molotov's visit approached, a nervous Churchill urged Eden to try and convert dubious Cabinet members, noting, "I do not want to face a bunch of resignations." Eden took care to line up sympathetic American supporters such as the columnists Arthur Krock and Walter Lippmann, both of whom promised to help when the anticipated storm broke, as well as reluctantly offered but welcome State Department assistance, all designed to ease the transatlantic impact of the expected treaty.[81] Eden's fears that the Soviets, working on the sense of guilt they were doubtless still hoping to create in British minds, would be aggressive in the final negotiations seemed confirmed when Molotov touched down in Scotland on May 21 after a hazardous flight, and upon arrival in London immediately raised the terms by not only demanding acceptance of the two treaty drafts recently submitted but also insisting that the Soviet claim to Poland's eastern territories, which Stalin had shelved during Eden's visit to Moscow, be included after all in the treaty. Churchill and Eden immediately rejected this proposal, acceptance of which – politically impossible for the British at this stage,

---

[80] Cavendish-Bentinck to Sargent, May 6, 1942, N2524/G; and Cadogan memorandum, May 7, 1942, N2524/G, both in F.O. 371.32881.
[81] Churchill to Eden, May 13, 1942, F.O. 954/24. Halifax to Eden, May 10, 1942, N2467, F.O. 371.32880.

with the London Polish government watching events closely and public opinion as yet totally unprepared for such radical measures – would have caused general consternation. Yet now that Molotov was in London, it was clear that there must be some kind of agreement. To cover the situation, the adroit Cadogan made what turned out to be a decisive intervention. Increasingly aware of German preparations for the renewed offensive in the east, he was now inclined to suspect a Soviet bluff. He therefore drew up as an alternative to Molotov's aggressive demands, a simple treaty of military alliance and political association designed to last twenty years. All the vexing territorial clauses were unceremoniously dropped.[82]

In the end, Cadogan's insight proved correct. Eden had remained committed to his April draft and was willing to brave the anticipated American complaints, for, as his private secretary wrote at the time, "in assessing American criticisms we must bear in mind the unlikelihood of America cooperating in policing Europe after the war. Russia and ourselves are part of Europe and we must contrive to work together or be prepared to fight each other." After several difficult meetings and much haggling, during which Eden resolutely refused to address the Polish issue, Molotov (whose whole trip to Britain and the United States was carried out in strictest secrecy and not revealed until his safe return to Moscow) agreed to consider the now comparatively innocuous Cadogan draft. After some show of reluctance he sent it off to Stalin on May 23 with a recommendation that it be rejected. Meanwhile, he met with U.S. Ambassador John Winant at the latter's request. Winant stressed both the likelihood of American public upset over a treaty with territorial clauses and the compensating potential of Roosevelt's enthusiasm for an early second front. This must have been attractive to the foreign commissar. The Soviet leaders had not pressed the second-front issue during the first heady months of 1942. Now, though without high expectations, Molotov called for it at every opportunity. In talks with the ambassador, therefore, presumably unsure as yet how Stalin would react to the ostensibly disappointing bare-bones British draft, and eager in any event to promote a receptive, pro–second front mood with the Americans, Molotov was unusually pleasant.[83]

---

[82] Kitchen, *British Policy*, p. 122; Gardner, *Spheres of Influence*, pp. 137–139.

[83] Harvey diary, May 24, 1942, Harvey, *War Diaries*, p. 128; Winant to Hull, May 24, 1942, FRUS, 1942, III, pp. 558–563. Steven Miner, in *Between Churchill and Stalin*, p.288, notes the significance of the Soviet military reverses between May 20 and 30, 1942. There is still some question about the significance of Winant's intervention on Hull's instructions, with Gardner taking a positive view in Gardner, *Spheres of Influence*, pp. 137–139, and Kitchen, in *British Policy*, p. 122, asserting without

But it seems unlikely that Winant's intervention was in any way decisive in turning Molotov away from the territorial treaty that, though not perfect from a Soviet viewpoint, must now have seemed within his grasp. It is unclear whether Cadogan's minimalized draft treaty had already been sent to Moscow before the ambassador and Molotov, who met again on May 24, got down to fundamentals. What is clear is that a great battle began on May 20 and quickly turned against the Red Army, which had by May 30 lost more that 200,000 troops. The first stages of this debacle occurred near Kharkov between May 21 and 24. Stalin, presumably thinking that he had now lost the battle of timing with the shrewd procrastinators in London, was now ready, and perhaps even eager, to settle quickly for the simplified agreement. His instructions to Molotov on May 24 were characteristically trenchant:

We have received the draft treaty Eden handed you. We do not consider it an empty declaration but regard it as an important document. It lacks the question of the security of frontiers, but this is not bad, perhaps, for it gives us a free hand. The question of frontiers, or to be more precise, of guarantees for the security of our frontiers at one or another section of our country, will be decided by force.[84]

This effectively concluded the issue. All the embarrassing and provocative terms were dropped. The brief Cadogan treaty simply proclaimed the alliance and bound the two parties not to make any separate peace with the Nazis or any other German government that did not clearly abandon all aggressive impulses. It went on to pledge postwar collaboration against any later German revanchism or aggression. They would also assist each other in the reconstruction of Europe after the war. Much of the attraction the deal was expected to have for Europeans generally was that it was to be a twenty-year treaty of mutual assistance, thus offering the prospect of a long period of security for the postwar recovery. The treaty was quickly agreed upon and formally signed with Molotov

---

elaboration that the Eden-Molotov discussions "were not helped by the presence of the United States ambassador." Recent scholarship seems to make clear that the prompt to Stalin's change in policy was "the deteriorating military situation at home" (Roberts, *Stalin's Wars*, p. 115). For the argument, based on Soviet records, that Molotov's main purpose in Washington was now to create a sense of obligation on the part of the president, see Eduard Mark, "Revolution by Degrees: Stalin's National Front Strategy for Europe, 1941–1947," Working Paper No. 31, Cold War International History Project, Woodrow Wilson Center, Washington, D.C., p. 11.

[84] Stalin to Molotov, May 24, 1942, in Rzheshevsky, *War and Diplomacy: The Making of the Grand Alliance* (Amsterdam, 1996), pp. 122–123.

on May 26. As the British began to celebrate, Molotov departed for the United States, ushering in the last act of this initial drama in tripartite diplomacy.[85]

Molotov was now free to focus on the second-front issue. He had not received from the British, and seems not to have expected, any assurance of an early invasion of France. However unreal the prospect, he wanted to take advantage of the more positive attitude the Americans had been promoting, especially after his diplomatic "concessions" in London. Roosevelt welcomed him warmly to the White House on May 29 but was at first characteristically elusive and vague, though full of compliments and assurances of sympathy for Soviet security needs and regaling the visitor with his vision of the "Four Policemen" (the United States, the Soviet Union, Britain, and China) taking on postwar global responsibility. Molotov showed little interest in these visions and brushed aside the president's offer to have the State Department help the Soviet Union mend fences with Iran and Turkey. Hull similarly found his visitor unresponsive when asked about postwar issues. Clearly, the Soviet leaders did not – at this stage, at least – want any American political role in postwar Europe. Nor did the Russian show any reaction when Roosevelt inaugurated another tendency that would become habitual: inviting a deeper intimacy by criticizing British colonialism and remarking that Churchill wanted to bring back the now defunct League of Nations, one of whose last acts had been to expel the Soviet Union. Molotov quickly came to the point. Would there be a second front in 1942? FDR said he was thinking of landing ten divisions that year. Thirty-five was the necessary minimum, came the quick rejoinder. The following morning, at a full meeting with the president and the Joint Chiefs of Staff, Molotov made a more dramatic case, raising the possibility that "the Red Army might not be able to hold out." He then asked, "Could we undertake such offensive action as would draw off 40 German divisions?" Roosevelt turned to the army chief of staff, General George C. Marshall, and asked "whether developments were clear enough so that we could say to Mr. Stalin that we are preparing a second front?" Marshall answered affirmatively. At their third and last meeting, on June 1, the president authorized Molotov to tell Stalin that "we expect the formation of a second front this year." The military chiefs, now well aware of British reservations, must have doubted that any such substantial operation was feasible, at least on the European continent. In any event, as Molotov must have realized, any landings would be on a small scale. But Roosevelt, fully

[85] Ibid., Documents 36, 37, and 38, pp. 120–123.

aware of the renewed German threat now looming up, was determined to reassure the Soviets, even agreeing to a public communique, to be issued later when Molotov's secret mission was disclosed, saying that "full understanding was reached with regard to the urgent tasks of creating a second front in Europe in 1942."[86]

Molotov, seemingly satisfied with this generalized formula and no doubt pleased also to have in his briefcase a new United States–Soviet agreement on military supplies and other aid to bolster that relationship, then returned to London. He was promptly informed by Churchill, in unmistakably precise terms, that while the British government was sympathetic and would do the best it could to help, he could give no definite undertaking to launch a second front in France in 1942. Molotov clearly had not expected anything more from the British. He then departed, free of illusion, for the long homeward trip. In fact, Roosevelt was also well aware of the practical problems that made a substantial early second front in Europe virtually impossible. Within a few days of Molotov's departure he was pressing upon his advisers the advantages of Churchill's old idea of an Anglo-American invasion of North Africa, an initiative that would immediately and conclusively foreclose the option of any 1942 invasion of Europe. But the Soviets could hardly have shouted fraud. True, in the treaty negotiation the British had taken advantage of the sudden loss of nerve on the part of the Soviets as the German threat loomed up again. But so far as the second front was concerned, Churchill, whose government would necessarily be the primary agent in any short-term invasion of the continent, had been scrupulously honest.[87]

On the face of things, Molotov may seem to have suffered a double diplomatic defeat. He had received neither the desired geopolitical agreement nor a firm commitment to a second front. Soviet territorial aspirations remained ungratified, at least for the moment. The Soviets would have to fight alone again in 1942.

But this is rather deceptive. There were consoling benefits. For Stalin and Molotov had now established closer relations with their allies and had agreements to wave encouragingly in front of their own people during the coming crisis. For the longer term, they had put their allies on notice of their desires

---

[86] Memoranda of conversations on May 29, 30, and June 1, 1942, FRUS, 1942, III, pp. 566–568, 571–572, 575–583. Halifax to Eden, May 6, 1942, F.O. 954/24. These discussions are summarized in Gardner, *Spheres of Influence*, pp. 139–143, but see his notes 69 to 72 on p. 280 for evidentiary problems.

[87] Woodward, *British Foreign Policy*, Vol. 2, pp. 258–260.

and intentions in Eastern Europe and had received significantly supportive private undertakings. At the same time, they apparently felt they had created a sense of obligation that could be exploited in future. The historian Lloyd Gardner has also suggested that Molotov had gained an advantage in that Roosevelt had given "serious indications" that he "did not accept the peripheral strategy that the Russians suspected was really designed to allow Germany and the Soviet Union to exhaust themselves."[88]

In the end, the modified Soviet purpose was probably simply to get the best possible deal from the British in the form of the treaty and from the Americans in the form of promises of some kind of effective action in the west, all with high-sounding declarations and agreements that would help legitimize the Stalinist leadership and raise the morale of the Soviet people. Litvinov told Halifax later that he and Molotov had wanted to make the Washington communiqué "as terrifying as possible to the Germans" and thought that some exaggeration of the results would be legitimate. Historians have made us aware of the terrible fragility of the Soviet war effort in 1941, when massive losses and desertions had occurred.[89] The victorious comeback in December had briefly revived spirits but had led to overconfidence. By the spring of 1942 the issue of Soviet solidarity in the face of a looming threat must again have seemed the crucial problem. From this perspective, Molotov's failure to secure British acceptance of the old imperial boundaries was less important than the impressive-sounding treaty with London, the supply agreement with the United States, Roosevelt's public commitment to a second front, and the legitimizing and bonding impulses coming from his dramatic trip and the meetings with Churchill and Roosevelt. That these were seen as solid gains is suggested by the extraordinary media campaign with which the Soviets celebrated the secret Molotov trip when it was at last revealed to an astonished world on June 11.

THE ANGLO-SOVIET FOUNDATION

The Soviet media – print, radio, pamphlets – erupted. Celebratory exchanges between Stalin and Churchill and between President Kalinin and

---

[88] Gardner, *Spheres of Influence*, p. 139. Gardner points out here that the Soviets had achieved something significant in that the representatives of the Baltic states had now been removed from the Diplomatic List in London, and that the new treaty referred to the defeat of "Germany," not simply "Hitlerite Germany" – a reassurance to both sides.

[89] Halifax to Eden, June 4, 1942, F.O. 954/24. For the estimate that Soviet losses by the end of 1941 amounted to nearly 200 battle divisions and 4.3 million casualties, see Roberts, *Stalin's Wars*, p. 117.

King George V were published in the newspapers along with photographs of the signing ceremony in London.

There was also a seemingly genuine, immediate sense of public euphoria. An American Columbia Broadcasting Service correspondent in Moscow reported: "I was offered drinks by total strangers. This evening on broad squares were the largest crowds I have ever seen here, listening to street corner loudspeakers blaring out the good news." Throughout the Soviet Union workers' councils, factory delegations, and other groups met to record their approval. Cordial letters were exchanged between British and Soviet trade unions and between pairing cities. Plans were announced in Moscow for a literary festival in Gorky Park celebrating the achievements of H. G. Wells, George Bernard Shaw, Theodore Dreiser, and other acceptable authors. Lectures on the treaty were envisioned with "great enthusiasm."

It was not all emotion and symbolism. Much was made of the massive Royal Air Force raids on Cologne and Essen that Churchill had carefully staged to coincide with the treaty signing, and of the political implications of the agreements for the chronically isolated Soviet state. *Pravda* welcomed the news with the headline "The Strengthening of the Military Cooperation of Freedom-loving Peoples" and with glowing editorials calling the London treaty on successive days "an important milestone in the history of Anglo-Soviet relations" and "an important political landmark." The agreement with the United States was "a valuable supplement to the first agreement and linked to it by unity of purpose." A few days later, the Soviet press was able to announce that "world public opinion had also received news of the three power agreements with enthusiasm."

The treaty, *Pravda* declared, excluded any negotiation, armistice, or peace with Germany except by mutual consent. It also "opens up prospects for postwar collaboration between the USSR and Great Britain, collaboration which is to oppose any repetition of aggression, as well as to assist in the reestablishment of peace for the organization of security and economic prosperity in Europe." The wider implications were featured by Molotov in his report to the Supreme Soviet on June 18. He stressed that the treaty had "[g]reat political significance not only in Anglo-Soviet relations but for the further development of international relations in the rest of Europe." It would also promote "a reliable basis" for the further development of friendly relations "between these two countries and the USA."[90]

[90] For the Tass official statement on June 11, 1942, and articles and news, see *Pravda*, June 11, 12, 13, 1942. See also Columbia Broadcasting Service talk, June 12, 1942, Reel 73, *British Broadcasting Daily Digest of World Broadcasts*, BBC Archives, Reading, England;

It is noticeable here that the motivational propaganda emphasis was not on the promise of a continental second front, which few must have thought feasible, but on the political implications of the Anglo-Soviet treaty. It is not surprising, then, that the British official reaction was also upbeat. Churchill and Eden led the celebration. "Winston relieved and delighted," noted Cadogan. Old divisions and arguments about the morality of dealings with the communist state were swept away, at least for the moment. Eden received most of the official and press plaudits. He modestly gave credit to Winant, Sikorski, and others. He was well aware that he would have to face Stalin again on the issue of the Soviet frontiers. Meanwhile, however, he could view the scene with satisfaction. Molotov not only had abandoned the provocative territorial clauses but had also agreed during his visit to look favorably on the Central European confederations. Soon after his return to Moscow, he accepted Eden's proposal for a "gentleman's agreement" binding Britain and the Soviet Union not to pursue bilateral treaties with the lesser continental states pending the anticipated peace conference. Significantly too, in terms of British diplomacy, Eden and the Foreign Office now had an institutional basis for a sophisticated Europe-oriented policy to compensate for the comparatively minor role in Anglo-American relations left them by Churchill. Eden saw the episode in a Europe/America context. As he recalled in his 1965 memoir: "I had to judge how far in meeting the problem of Anglo-Russian relations I could, at the Foreign Office, insist on my point of view, how far be unreservedly for Mr. Churchill in his sentiment for his transatlantic allies."[91]

The treaty was also warmly received by the British public and press. *The Times,* as one might expect from its assiduous championship of Anglo-Soviet ties, was effusively complimentary. *The Sunday Chronicle* was impressed by the historical precedent, commenting, "There has always been a closer understanding between us and the Russians than between any other two great countries in Europe." In *The Observer* the emphasis was on "a great event in history" from which "the picture of a stable world begins unmistakably to emerge." *The Scotsman* was specific, thinking that "by this treaty Britain and Russia accept the main, but not the sole, responsibility for the future settlement in Eastern Europe." Beaverbrook's *Sunday Express* called it "The

and Wilson memorandum, June 17, 1942, N3132, F.O. 371.33018. For Soviet radio and Molotov reactions, see unsigned memoranda, June 17, 1942, N3247, and June 18, 1942, N3241, both in F.O. 371.33018.

[91] Anthony Eden, *The Reckoning* (London, 1965), pp. 267–268; Gardner, *Spheres of Influence,* p. 138; Kitchen, *British Policy,* pp. 122–133.

Great Treaty," and the conservative *Sunday Times* gave Eden "the highest praise." The socialist left was predictably less enthusiastic, with the *The New Statesman and Nation* looking to "a new balance of power in Europe" while finding it "inevitable" that "the states that lie on Russia's eastern frontier will strategically and politically come within the Soviet security sphere."[92]

This hard truth, glossed over in much of the British reaction, was the point that Axis propagandists were quick to exploit. Here the basic response was that the treaty signified a dramatic advance of the Bolshevik menace, which the British were now shamefully encouraging to Europe's detriment. From Berlin came sharp condemnations of "the Bolshevik-plutocratic alliance" and the "betrayal of Europe to Bolshevism." The Italian radio saw it as "one step further in the communist infiltration of Britain." Similar sentiments came from Hungary and Japan and from Spain, where the Franco press saw the gloomy prospect of a ruined Europe under Anglo-Soviet control. William Joyce, the notorious "Lord Haw-Haw" who broadcast regularly to Britain from Germany, scoffed at the Soviet promise not to pursue "territorial aggrandizement." "What is the word of a Bolshevik worth?" he asked. "Fidelity might conceivably be found in a brothel, but never in a Soviet promise." In general, the Nazi and pro-German media seem to have been somewhat rattled by these surprise developments, though they fought back with derisory comments about the proposed second front, which would surely be thrown back into the sea, and looked on the bright side with suggestions that Molotov's diplomacy was "the best proof that the situation in the Soviet Union is most critical."[93]

Non-Nazi Europe, on the other hand, was enthusiastic. This was true of all the exile governments in London. The Poles, deeply relieved that Soviet aspirations against their territory had been at least temporarily blocked, were fulsomely grateful to Eden. General de Gaulle, on behalf of the Free French, expressed "great satisfaction." The Norwegian foreign minister welcomed his country's enhanced security. His Czech counterpart, echoing President Benes, who characteristically viewed the whole development as a personal vindication of his vision for Europe, noted

---

[92] *Sunday Chronicle, The Observer*, the *Sunday Express, Sunday Times,* all on June 14, 1942; *The Scotsman*, June 12, 1942; *The New Statesman and Nation*, June 20, 1942. Several British publications (e.g., *The New Statesman*) stressed that the era of small states was now over, reflecting widespread British disillusionment with the Versailles system.

[93] For Axis responses, see Political Information Department memorandum, "Reactions to the Anglo-Soviet Treaty," July 11, 1942, N3859, F.O. 371.33019 (German and Italian); and for others, see unsigned memorandum, N3303, F.O. 371.33018.

that it had been "for twenty years the hope of Czech foreign policy to see the western powers and the great Soviet power in Eastern Europe collaborating in maintaining political and economic peace on the continent." The vulnerable neutral states on the continent, naturally more guarded, were nevertheless positive. The Swedish press, for instance, noted that for the first time in its history Britain was breaking down Russian isolation and identifying itself with the future of Europe. It also suggested, perhaps with a placatory glance at neighboring Germany, that the Anglo-Soviet accord lessened the danger of Soviet expansion. At the other end of Europe, the Turks, always anxious about Russian designs, were relieved and encouraged. And indeed, wherever one looks outside the enemy countries, one finds warm approbation. Hosannas poured in from the Dominions, relieved that there were after all no morally embarrassing territorial deals; from Chungking, where the besieged Chinese expressed full approval; and even from far-off Latin America.[94]

What of the American reaction? Here too Foreign Office observers found cause for celebration. They had made a treaty with their principal European ally on their own terms, and they had been able to do so without alienating their principal strategic partner. The Roosevelt administration was also off the hook, spared from having to explain an unmistakable departure from the Atlantic Charter to its own people. Roosevelt and the State Department issued approving statements. The now largely internationalist press was positive, with many publications accepting, the Foreign Office found, that "the treaty constituted part of the foundation of the postwar world." Even isolationist, anti–New Deal newspapers like the *Chicago Tribune* and the New York *Daily News* found little to criticize. Only the Roman Catholic and foreign language press were profoundly skeptical, insisting that the victorious Soviet Union would take what it wanted in Eastern Europe regardless of any treaty obligation.[95]

The euphoria in official London was tempered, however, by the tendency of some American politicians and columnists to claim transatlantic credit for the pared-down treaty. Roosevelt himself cabled congratulations to Winant for getting the treaty worked out "in thoroughly acceptable form." Vice President Henry Wallace noted FDR's assessment of his own role in

[94] For exile governments' and Dominions' reactions, see *News Chronicle*, June 12, 1942, and for Turks', see N3207/G, for Norwegians, see N2512/G, for Swedes, see N3108 and N3152/G, all in F.O. 371.33018. For world opinion generally, see notes in F.O. 371.33017 and F.O. 371.33018 and Wilson memorandum, July 19, 1942, N3859, F.O. 371.33019.

[95] For a review of American reactions to the treaty, see Political Information Department memorandum, July 11, 1942, N3859, F.O. 371.33019.

the early negotiations so far as the Baltic states were concerned. "He said
that he had stepped in and prevented the British and Russians from arriving at an accord that would give the Russians this area." Arthur Krock, in
The New York Times, wrote that Roosevelt "saved the day by insisting
that the treaty should recognize the principles of the Atlantic Charter,"
and Walter Lippmann suggested that "[w]e have contributed decisively
to this momentous undertaking." More serious, in British eyes, than this
seemingly unmerited self-congratulation was the less-than-momentous
resonance of this "European achievement" in the United States generally.
Foreign Office observers noticed that discussion of the treaty soon ceased,
becoming, in the words of one official, "a seven day wonder" that was
quickly swamped by war events, not least by Churchill's arrival on June
19, and then by the deeply embarrassing fall of Tobruk on June 21. The
war, to be sure, was steadily integrating the United States and Europe.
Politically, however, they remained two distinct arenas.[96]

Reviewing the overall foreign reaction a few weeks after the treaty
signing, the Foreign Office's Political Intelligence Department expressed
its satisfaction. Outside the areas of Axis control there was evidence of
widespread relief that Britain had saved Europe from Bolshevism, a line
taken even by the Italians before a reproving Berlin condemnation came
through. Neutrals were relieved that Britain was "going to play a full part"
in the postwar era. The Turks and Swedes, always liable to swing to the
Axis side, were clearly pleased that Eastern Europe had not been "sold" to
the Soviets. There was both relief that there would not, at least for the time
being, be a separate German-Soviet peace, and in general a new sense of
hope for the future.[97]

The Molotov mission, and the Anglo-Soviet treaty it produced, looks
even more impressive in historical retrospect. Conceived originally as the
capstone to a far-reaching design looking to at least the rudiments of a
division of postwar Europe that the Kremlin wished to take shape under
some form of Anglo-Soviet control, the treaty as it emerged was obviously
something much less, though it ended as an impressive register of British
and American support in a war that the Soviets had come to see in the
spring of 1942 was far from won. This was a pleasing outcome for the

---

[96] Ibid. See also Henry Wallace diary, December 31, 1942, in John Blum (ed.), *The Price of
Vision: The Diaries of Henry A. Wallace, 1942–1946* (Boston, 1973), p.160; *New York
Times,* June 14, 1942 (Krock); *New York Herald Tribune,* June 13, 1942 (Lippmann).

[97] Political Information Department memorandum, July 11, 1942, in N3859, F.O.
371.33019.

Roosevelt administration, which, notwithstanding the president's private diplomacy, was still officially and publicly determined to avoid any potentially compromising political collaboration with the Euopeans, and was therefore inclined to see the bare-bones Anglo-Soviet treaty as a triumphant vindication of its views and a sign that it need not worry, at least in the near future, about the European problem.

But, as we have seen, the rest of the world, including the Soviet government, was deeply interested in and more impressed by the political aspects of the whole affair. This was palpably true of all the European states involved. It was already widely expected that the Soviets, if they survived the renewed German onslaught, would dominate much if not all of Eastern Europe. They had now made it clear that they wished to do this in some sort of partnership with a Britain that they were encouraging to act somewhat similarly in Western Europe. And it is clear to us today, with the full record of their deliberations before us, that the British, despite pressures from far-off America, and reservations of their own as to the details, were likely to try and find ways to accommodate them.

Not that the new partnership was free of residual uncertainties. The Soviets remained suspicious throughout the war of Britain's obviously very close ties to the United States. And the British, for their part, were somewhat disconcerted to find Molotov actively courting the Free French and the Czechs during his time in London. A Foreign Office observer noted that "a very close understanding has developed between the Soviet Government, President Benes and General de Gaulle which may ... be found to have developed into a formal bloc." This was interpreted as "reinsurance" in case cooperation with the British and the Americans broke down.[98]

Beneath the power politics there were of course a variety of undercurrents and mixed emotions. Some uneasy Foreign Office consciences were on view in early 1942. Cadogan, for one, didn't like the deal with the Russians. In late February he noted, "Americans are sticky about it – quite rightly." Shortly afterward he called it "wrong" to be giving Stalin "all he wants." In April he lamented, "We're selling the Poles down the river and everyone will suspect we are going to do the same to them." By early May he was warning, "I believe still it would be better not to crawl to the Russians over the dead bodies of all our principles." It seems strangely fitting that it was his minimalized treaty that saved the day – at least for a time. But others were eager

---

[98] Scaife memorandum, October 12, 1942, N5414, F.O. 371.32918.

to deepen rather than divert the new ties with the Soviets. G. M. Wilson, a leading Foreign Office specialist in Soviet affairs, urged his colleagues to think in terms of a broader agreement addressing social, economic, and industrial issues. He envisioned talks with the Soviets on supra-national organization addressing such issues as transport, communications, banking, and raw materials. "Attractive, but I fear difficult to carry out" was one representative comment. Ideas like this, along with many other suggested ways to strengthen ties with Stalin's regime, were a constant feature of Foreign Office discourse throughout the war. In the anxious days of early 1942, however, the political/geopolitical issues were overwhelmingly dominant.[99]

In all this there was nothing a connoisseur of 1930s European diplomacy would have found unfamiliar. Historians have been understandably fascinated by the American role, which, however, has probably been exaggerated. The United States had been unable to turn its European allies from their preferred course. This would have been more obvious at the time, and to historians later, if the full treaty had been more completed. As it was, it was only the suddenly very imminent and dangerous renewal of the German threat, not susceptibility to American disapproval, that produced the Soviet diplomatic retreat and the modified treaty. The war still had a long way to go. But Europe had been given, for the first time, a clear view of the likely political framework of its post-Hitler future. And it had, the Axis powers apart, shown its strong approval.

There is much in this unique episode to fascinate the historian. We see here a range of revealing attitudes, emotions, and actions in a prolonged moment of flux and confusion as the three newly associated powers began to define and shape their relationships. Stalin's disturbing geopolitical initiative set the pace and led to a general scramble for influence and control in the Western democracies. It brought Churchill and Roosevelt under pressure from their respective diplomatic establishments. The two leaders began to court Stalin at each other's expense. We catch also early glimpses of tendencies that later turned into habitual behavior: Roosevelt's penchant for personal intervention far beyond American policy lines; Churchill's volatility as he tried to balance strategic collaboration with the United States and political cooperation with the Soviets; Stalin's steady purposefulness and reliance upon a bargaining mode of diplomacy. It is understandable that the story

---

[99] Cadogan diary, February 24, April 19, May 3, 1942, in Dilks (ed.), *Cadogan Diaries*, pp. 437, 446, 449. Wilson memorandum, April 30, 1942, and Warner note, May 1, 1942, both in N2221, F.O. 371.32880.

of Allied diplomacy is usually told in highly personalized terms and mainly with reference to the parts played by these three preeminent figures.

The deeper significance of this period emerges, however, only if we look at it in a more structurally oriented way. Here we can usefully juxtapose the Japanese onslaught, which set off events that brought Britain and the United States tightly together in their strategic partnership, with the very different Soviet political/territorial initiative that almost simultaneously began to drive them apart in their political preoccupations and practices. For the Western allies responded to Stalin in markedly different ways: the Americans offering military help largely because they could not accept the toxic politics; the British accepting the unsavory politics because they could not offer significant military help. The patterns thus inaugurated persisted into early 1945. The Americans would henceforth be strategically assertive but largely passive so far as Europe's political future was concerned. The British would often appear to both their allies to be dragging their heels in military matters but would be compensatingly forthcoming political partners for Stalin in Europe.

One should not exaggerate these contrasts. American leaders were not indifferent to events in Europe. They were watchful and suspicious. But the nonentanglement tradition, reinforced by the chilling display of European realpolitik on show in early 1942, led the Roosevelt administration to what was in the main a policy of avoidance and deferral toward the old continent, tempered by occasional interventions to sustain the Atlantic Charter vision and to frustrate option-closing Anglo-Soviet initiatives. It was, at least until the transformative exchanges at Yalta in February 1945, a diplomacy of glancing encounters, derived in large part from the lessons American leaders drew from their reluctant involvement in a negotiation characterized at its inception by Roosevelt as "provincial" and dismissed at its conclusion as "a seven-day wonder."

For the British, the renewed Anglo-Soviet association had more profound implications. At the beginning of December 1941 we see that Britain, though besieged and strained, was still a Great Power and the vital center of a vast, supportive global empire. By May 1942 things looked very different. The Japanese attacks had exposed the fragility of the British position in Asia and the Pacific. Any recovery there would be dependent on the United States. This theater, to which Churchill thereafter paid comparatively little attention, became for Britain a secondary concern, if not exactly the so-called forgotten war. Meanwhile, even as Britain's influence was receding elsewhere, Stalin's initiative was drawing the British deeply into European political affairs. This development, and the associated divisions over the projected second front, upset important elements in the United States and also strained relations with the far-flung Dominions, which were already turning ever more anxiously to the United States for security.

We should not let our knowledge of Britain's postwar rejection of a leadership role in Europe obscure the importance of these events. In essence they signified that even as their global influence was contracting (in large measure irretrievably), the British were, through Stalin's founding initiative and the medium of the ensuing Anglo-Soviet treaty, engaging more substantially than they had ever done in modern times with continental affairs. The principal spur in 1942 was felt necessity. Despite genuflections to the Atlantic Charter, the British government, haunted by memories of the German-Soviet agreement at Rapallo in 1922 and the Nazi-Soviet Pact of 1939, could not take a continuing Soviet war partnership for granted. But gradually, as the 1942 crisis passed and postwar planning became the central issue, it let itself be harnessed – not immediately but by stages, and never entirely submissively but generally in acquiescent recognition of the rise of Soviet power – to Stalin's geopolitical purposes, notably to a division of Europe, to a mode of diplomacy that emphasized bargaining, to a hierarchical approach over lesser states, and always with acute sensitivity to the logic of power.

Out of all these events – whether one judges them simply as stage setting or as deeply significant in themselves – came a tripartite alliance that, so far as the liberation and political reconstruction of Europe were concerned, would henceforth operate in two distinct arenas: an East/West field of strategic action in which the Soviets, on the one hand, and the Western allies, on the other, would wage war separately; and a Europe/America political theater based on a clear distinction between a detached America and an Anglo-Soviet partnership that was founded on the as yet unchallenged principle of continuing European autonomy.[100]

---

[100] Foreign observers were alive to many of these developments. Maisky noted in April 1942 that "the Empire was in a pretty parlous state." Boothby to Eden, April 16, 1942, F.O. 954/24. Gardner, *Spheres of Influence*, p. 147, cites *Time* noting on June 22, 1942, a "recent high Tory feeling that, in a world where the U.S. was daily growing stronger, a pact with Russia was a sound move for the preservation of European weight in the world of the future."

3

The Persistence of Europe, 1942–1943

To this point we have explored the early stages of Allied diplomacy in a more or less chronological fashion. One might well continue on this line, for the pattern we have seen up to the Anglo-Soviet treaty of May 1942 – of separate and divergent American and European political arenas – persisted almost to the end of the war. But from May 1942 to the first tripartite summit at Teheran in December 1943 there is a lull in the politics of the Grand Alliance. War and strategy dominate. Significant political events occur – notably the Anglo-American surge in the western Mediterranean, with its profound consequences in France and Italy; the Casablanca "unconditional surrender" proclamation; the carefully glossed-over German revelations in April 1943 of the murder at Katyn by Soviet operatives of thousands of Polish officers in 1940, an event that forced Britain into an even closer engagement with the Soviet leadership; and the drift of Eduard Benes toward a far-reaching deal with the Soviets. But by the summer of 1942 the difficulties associated with the first institutionalization of an Anglo-Soviet concert for Europe had been surmounted, and the challenges of 1944 that would test and then crystallize that combination still lay inscrutably ahead. This middle period is therefore a good moment, while still maintaining some semblance of a narrative thread, to turn to a more thematic approach and focus briefly on some of the relationships and attitudes that give some depth and meaning to the European characterization we are exploring.

During this period the British and the Soviets, having already regularized their relationship, steadily developed it with the support of leaders and elites in both countries and with the tacit recognition and approval of the increasingly active non-Nazi elements in Europe, who had, as we have just seen, greeted the Anglo-Soviet treaty as a promising, indeed indispensable, framework for their postwar security. From all this the United States was, except for an occasional burst of eye-catching "expeditionary diplomacy," studiously remote: focused on strategy and military victory; distracted by the Pacific struggle; confining its political involvement in Europe to the practical issues unavoidably raised by the war; and only slowly preparing to devote itself to the construction of a transcending postwar international organization, all the while leaving the uncongenial middle ground of Europe's politics to its two allies.

CHURCHILL AND EUROPE

This notion of a distinctly European non-Nazi politics during World War II, with its own logic, preoccupations, and issues entirely separate from those that concerned American leaders, deserves more attention than it has received from historians. It is symptomatic of the neglect of the European dimension that, while there have been numerous published studies of the relationship between Churchill and Roosevelt and even that between Roosevelt and Stalin (and indeed studies of the Churchill-de Gaulle and Roosevelt-Hitler relationships), no full treatment of the Churchill-Stalin relationship has yet appeared.[1] Yet they met on several momentous occasions for political discussion, twice without Roosevelt. They exchanged more than 500 messages during the war, mostly on topics involving Europe. Each stood, moreover, at the head of a political establishment that looked to the other, rather than to the United States, as the prospective postwar political partner in Europe. And the two states, or systems of power, that they led were the respective magnetic poles toward which other Europeans naturally gravitated.

A comparative Churchill-Stalin biography would be a fascinating enterprise. The contrasts are extraordinary. The two men – one the great self-styled romantic defender of a cherished status quo, the other a ruthless social engineer who once defined his postwar aim as a desire to make the Russian people "more human and less like beasts"[2] – stand at opposite ends of the twentieth century's politico-ideological spectrum. Their

---

[1] But see David Carlton, *Churchill and the Soviet Union* (Manchester, 2001), which has a chapter focused on Churchill and Stalin; and Steven Merritt Miner, *Between Churchill and Stalin*, which examines the 1939–42 period. There are, of course, innumerable references to the relationship in books and articles.

[2] Quoted in Roberts to Bevin, October 19, 1945, N14171, F.O. 371.47870.

backgrounds, personalities, sensibilities, and diplomatic styles were totally different. Unfortunately, the obvious dramatic possibilities are tempered by the fact that Churchill is so fully before us, owing to a voluminous literature and enormous media exposure, while Stalin remains, despite some new evidence, a deeply elusive figure, especially in his foreign policy, which, in the absence of much in the way of an inner history, has received very little scholarly attention. Such a study would surely seek to convey some impression of Churchill the committed European, as well as the more familiar figure of Churchill the celebrant of Anglo-American fraternity. He was of course both, reflecting the distinction just made.

Churchill had prepared himself for collaboration by portraying Stalin, in his 1937 book *Great Contemporaries*, as a practical man and brilliant party manager, contrasting him with the supposedly more radical Trotsky, whom he stigmatized as "skin of malice washed up in the Gulf of Mamora."[3] But his personal relationship with Stalin had been full of tension and suspicion during the period of the Nazi-Soviet pact and was not much better in the early months of co-belligerency. It came more constructively to life during Churchill's sudden visit to Moscow in August 1942, which was intended by the prime minister to establish a personal bond. During the long flight, Churchill recalled, "I pondered on my mission to this sullen Bolshevik state I had once tried so hard to strangle at its birth, and which, until Hitler appeared, I had regarded as the mortal foe of civilized freedom. What was it my duty to say to them now?" It was of course to convey the hard truth that there would be no second front in Europe in 1942, a task Churchill described as "like carrying a large lump of ice to the North Pole." Once in the Kremlin, Churchill was quickly subjected to the now habitual Stalin treatment. First came a reasonably cordial first meeting, during which Churchill gave one of his impressive strategic overviews, emphasizing the Royal Air Force's bombing successes and the virtues of the planned Anglo-American landings in North Africa as a preliminary to landings in France, which he envisioned as "the great operation of 1943." This was followed by disillusioning harsh accusations at the second meeting as Stalin virtually accused the British of cowardice. The angered prime minister responded that he would pardon the charge "only on account of the bravery of the Soviet troops." Churchill then launched into a passionate justification of the British war effort which the poor Soviet interpreter, inexperienced in

[3] Winston S. Churchill, *Great Contemporaries* (London, 1937), pp. 197–208.

the splendors of Ciceronian oratory, found it impossible to follow but which inspired the momentarily warmer Soviet leader to compliment his visitor on his "spirit."[4]

The week-long stay included several emotional encounters like this, as well as a crudely boisterous dinner reception that Churchill left early in evident disgust despite the urging of Stalin and Molotov to stay. By this time the British ambassador, Archibald Clark Kerr, was upset with both "prima donnas." It seemed they would part in acrimony. Clark Kerr was able to set up a final meeting. This went off a little more congenially, and finally the situation was saved as Stalin invited Churchill to his private apartment for a long night of drinking and reminiscing about past antagonisms and familiar historical personalities, from Trotsky to Lloyd George, with digressions on the first Duke of Marlborough and Napoleon, and most pleasingly a favorable review by Stalin of the ill-fated Gallipoli campaign of 1915, which had led to Churchill's resignation as First Lord of the Admiralty. His War Cabinet colleagues, waiting hungrily for hard news, must have been gratified to receive Churchill's triumphant cable reporting this unexpected benediction.[5]

So Churchill came away thinking he had established a bond, later receiving word from Molotov that Stalin felt the same way. Indeed, Stalin sent a message through Clark Kerr that "he was a rough man and begged that his roughness not be misunderstood."[6] It seems unlikely that Stalin was often "misunderstood" on this score, but in fact the true Soviet view of Churchill's visit was still hard to read. The prime minister was shown on film in the Soviet Union, which was good; but it soon transpired that his famous two-finger gesture was being officially interpreted not as a victory sign but as a reaffirmed promise of an imminent second front, which was not so good. The aftermath was further soured by the most widely read Soviet journalist, Ilya Ehrenburg, who in one sentence of his report managed to combine references to the dishonor of Marshal Petain, the existence of Major Quisling, and the British capitulation at Tobruk. Eden protested but received no explanation.[7]

---

[4] Winston S. Churchill, *The Second World War: Vol. IV, The Hinge of Fate* (Boston, 1950), pp. 472–502; Woodward, *British Foreign Policy*, Vol. 2, pp. 265–272; Harriman and Abel, *Special Envoy*, pp. 149–164; Gilbert, *Churchill*, VII, pp.173–208.

[5] Churchill, *Hinge of Fate*, pp. 472–502; Churchill to Attlee, August 15, 1942, F.O. 954/16.

[6] Clark Kerr to Eden, August 16, 1942, F.O. 954/24.

[7] Clark Kerr to Eden, August 20, 1942, ibid.; Clark Kerr to Foreign Office, August 23, 1942, ibid.

The clash of diplomatic styles is very evident here. Churchill was rarely at his best in these summit encounters. He was, when all is said and done, the brave, resourceful, and on the whole self-confident man of well-upholstered historical image. But in the presence of what he felt to be great power, for all the formidable "front" he invariably put on, he was as conscious as Anthony Eden of Britain's limited resources and consequently somewhat insecure. He was always anxious at the outset of these summit meetings, with Roosevelt as well as with Stalin, to begin by establishing a level of personal comfort. He usually accomplished this in the early days of the war by dazzling his hosts with one of the masterly strategic overviews for which he was famous. Later, as this became less effective, he developed the habit of quickly divesting himself, to the consternation of his associates, of his few negotiating cards. One Foreign Office observer noted at a later conference, "The PM, alas, gave away many points, as he always does."[8] Overall one often has the impression, observing Churchill at these meetings, of an extrovert but initially nervous dinner guest, thrusting his wine and flowers upon his startled hosts at the door and then, all tension thus dispelled or at least alleviated, moving quickly to the main event trailing ever-growing clouds of flattery, eloquence, and gravitas. Churchill's theatricality eventually irritated Roosevelt and was for the most part wasted in the Kremlin. Stalin, always intent on the bottom line, appears to have enjoyed the show but seems to have remained substantially unmoved.

This speculative excursus is intended only to suggest that the summit meetings are not necessarily the best and certainly not the only place to study Anglo-Soviet diplomacy. We can more fully understand the scope as well as the character of the Churchill-Stalin combination by comparing it to the much more distant Roosevelt-Stalin relationship. Then we see that it soon became a fully functioning working relationship with a range of openly addressed practical concerns. This comes out especially clearly when we compare the two Western leaders' correspondence with Stalin between, say, May 1942 and late 1943. For all practical purposes the two Europeans appear, from their cable exchanges at least, to be running the war against Germany with spasmodic, supportive interventions from the president. This is of course a distortion, for the crucial supply operation (and a large part of the British effort) already depended substantially on American resources. But the problem of getting materials to the Soviet

---

[8] Cadogan to Halifax, Jan. 10, 1944, Box. A4.410.4, Halifax MSS; Dixon diary, Oct. 10, 1944, Dixon MSS (Piers Dixon), London, England.

Union, notably through the north Russian ports, was mainly in the hands of the Royal Navy and British merchant shipping. Churchill therefore took the lead in explaining to the demanding Stalin the frequent delays and shortfalls caused by Germany's power to intercept the convoys with surface, air, and submarine forces based in northern Norway. These exchanges were, especially on Stalin's part, acrimonious and resentful. Churchill bent all his powers of eloquence and debate to explain and defend decisions that were indeed his to make. It was much the same with the second-front issue. Here too there was an irony. It was Roosevelt, not Churchill, who had promised a second front in Europe in 1942. But here too it was substantially Churchill's decision to make because the effort would have to be overwhelmingly British. It was therefore Churchill upon whom Stalin's wrath largely fell, and who took it upon himself, for two uncomfortable years, to try to explain the delays and strategic modifications that put off the invasion of France.[9]

The early relationship, then, was full of tension. Still, it was an engaged, functioning association, and Churchill and Stalin, even as they left Eden and Molotov to bring some institutional reality to the relationship, soon formed a kind of partnership that steadily enlarged to cover many political aspects of the European war. The war itself was the overwhelming issue in the critical years, 1941–43, and Churchill tried to make up for the second-front delay by stressing the devastation the Royal Air Force was creating in Germany. This, he urged, was causing great damage to German production and morale and was drawing the *Luftwaffe* away from the eastern front. But political issues, few of which found their way into the Roosevelt-Stalin correspondence, did come up and were invariably handled in a traditionally European way in which, despite much plain speaking and some bitterness, there was considerable mutual understanding and no visionary cant.[10]

The United States was not totally absent. But here Churchill pushed in vigorously, playing up his American associations when it was to his advantage. Indeed, he went to great lengths in his cables to Stalin to present himself by heavy implication both as the director of Anglo-American strategy and as the crucial interlocutor with Washington and therefore a key to the American war effort in Europe. Sometimes he played the role

---

[9] SCCA, pp. 11–80. For supply issues generally, see Kitchen, *British Policies,* pp. 65–75, 95–98, 129–130 and passim; *and* George Herring, *Aid to Russia, 1941–1946: Strategy, Diplomacy and the Origins of the Cold War* (New York, 1973). For second-front agitations, see Woodward, *British Foreign Policy,* II, pp. 257–264, 267–275.

[10] Roosevelt and Churchill to Stalin, Jan. 27, 1943, SCCA, pp. 86–88; Churchill to Stalin, March 2, 4, and 6, 1943, ibid., pp. 98–99, give examples of the Royal Air Force emphasis.

of tutor, offering his impressions of American economic, strategic, and political attitudes. Thus in early 1942 he took it upon himself to warn Stalin to curb provocatively critical Soviet press comment about the United States' inability to present immediate resistance to the Japanese in the Philippines, advice Stalin appears to have followed. A year later, when the State Department, in a rare initiative, offered to try and mediate an end to the Soviet-Finnish war, we find Stalin asking Churchill for his opinion. Churchill replied expressing doubt that the Finns would respond. Stalin decided not to take the offer up.[11]

More substantively, the two men acted together very much in the traditional "Great Power" mode when dealing with lesser states where they had established geopolitical interests. By the time the United States entered the war the Anglo-Soviet collaboration had already deposed the pro-Axis government in Iran and sent occupying troops to strengthen their long-standing dual domination of that strategically important country, which then became a crucial alternative to the North Atlantic for Lend-Lease shipments to the Soviet Union.[12] Later, in a little-known 1943 operation, Britain and the Soviet Union cooperated in Afghanistan, intervening to eliminate German influence in Kabul, despite protests from the stubbornly Wilsonian American ambassador, who did not think the war against Hitler justified this apparent violation of an independent state's sovereignty.[13] The more significant Turkish predicament also drew the two allies into a long drawn-out political discussion. Here was a British ally with long-standing, well-founded concerns about Russian expansionism. Britain had propped up the "sick man of Europe" through the nineteenth century, and this strategically vital country was still a primary British ally and client. The two allies had jointly reassured Turkey shortly after Hitler invaded the Soviet Union that they respected its sovereignty and accepted the Montreux Convention giving Turkey effective control of the Straits between the Black Sea and the Mediterranean. Stalin understandably showed keen interest in and support for Churchill's efforts to press Turkey into the war. They discussed the problems associated with Turkey's anxiety about Soviet intentions and its desire for an Anglo-Soviet guarantee before considering entering the war against

---

[11] Churchill to Stalin, Jan. 5, 1942, ibid., p. 38; Stalin to Churchill, Mar. 15, 1943, ibid., pp. 104–105.

[12] For Iran, see Churchill to Stalin, received Aug. 30, 1941, and Stalin to Churchill, Sept. 3, 1941, in ibid., pp. 18–22; Woodward, *British Foreign Policy in the Second World War,* Vol. 4 (London, 1975), pp. 412–441.

[13] Eden to Cripps, Oct. 10, 1941, and Nov. 14, 1941; Eden to Halifax, June 11, 1943, all in F.O. 954/1.

Germany. This was of course a potentially hazardous and politically sensitive matter for both powers. Yet they handled it in a very practical way.[14]

The acute interest of the British and the Soviets in these three countries derived not only from the German threat or even from their long-rooted historical confrontation in the region, but also from concerns for their postwar influence there. We are so used to thinking of the Cold War's origins in Eastern Europe that it is easy to forget the significance of this long band of countries along the border between Europe and Asia, later collectively known, with the addition of Greece, as the "Northern Tier." It was a more durable and more valued vested interest for Britain during World War II than the fate of Eastern Europe. The obsessive focus on events in Eastern and Central Europe by early historians of the Cold War's origins, and the comparative neglect of the Northern Tier until it makes a late-blooming appearance in 1944–47, is in many respects a distorted perspective, derived largely from the ubiquity of the Polish issue and the dominating East/West conception. In the end, the Northern Tier was the political arena where the durability of the Grand Alliance would be most significantly tested and, in the event, found wanting. Both arenas are of course crucially important, and one virtue of the Europe/America approach is that it forces us to think about their relationship and their respective claims to primacy as the forcing ground of the Cold War. But it is salutary to remember that Soviet domination of Eastern Europe, however vital it came to be later in mobilizing American public opinion for Cold War policies, had in substance been accepted by the governments of Britain and the United States by 1945. It was in the Northern Tier during the following year that preexisting tensions between the British and Soviets boiled over, with consequences that brought the United States into play and led directly to the Cold War.[15]

Having said that, it must be acknowledged that the political issue that really agitated the Anglo-Soviet relationship during the war itself was the future of Poland. The Polish tragedy hangs over World War II, touching many aspects of an Allied diplomacy that proclaimed a supportive outcome but, once confronted with the complexities of the problem, could not sustain a high moral tone. The German government's announcement

[14] Churchill to Stalin, Nov. 24, 1942, SCCA, pp. 78–79; Stalin to Churchill, Feb. 6, 1943, ibid., pp. 92–93; Woodward, *British Foreign Policy*, vol. 4, pp. 81–140; and Gilbert, *Churchill*, VII, pp. 562–564, 578–580, 595–598 and passim.

[15] See Bruce Kuniholm, *The Origins of the Cold War in the Near East: Great Power Conflict and Diplomacy in Iran, Turkey and Greece* (Princeton, N.J., 1980); and Harbutt, *Iron Curtain*, pp. 209–241.

in April 1943 that it had uncovered the bodies of 10,000 Polish officers allegedly killed earlier by the Soviets in the Katyn woods near Smolensk produced an immediate crisis. The Polish government called for an investigation by the International Red Cross, conveying the impression that it endorsed the German interpretation. Stalin promptly severed relations with the London Poles, who from that moment became the target of a worldwide communist press campaign of vilification. The ensuing difficulties within the Anglo-Soviet alliance were handled almost entirely by Churchill, with Roosevelt offering vague reassurances of his continuing support to Stalin and telling him that "Churchill will find a way" to curb the criticisms of the anguished Polish authorities in London. The prime minister, though fully aware that the Soviets were responsible ("There is no use prowling morbidly round the three-year old graves of Smolensk," he told Eden) earned Stalin's gratitude by censoring and generally damping down criticism of the indispensable ally.[16]

Churchill and Stalin also collaborated in pressing European interests on those rare occasions when the United States did seem to take a potentially intrusive interest of its own. Thus when the prospect of Italian surrender in 1943 brought an unwelcome Soviet demand for a tripartite armistice commission, Churchill opportunistically went behind the president's back and tried to enlist Stalin's support for a French seat. Yes indeed, Stalin replied, very much in the spirit of the concept of a divided, Anglo-Soviet Europe he had unveiled in 1941. And if you like, he added, you can put it forward as an Anglo-Soviet proposal. The resultant demarche did indeed oblige Roosevelt to agree to the desired commission, though he finessed the matter adroitly by ensuring that it would have no significant powers.[17]

We are used to the well-authenticated notion that Churchill was eager to bring American power and influence more fully into Europe, first against Germany, later as a security against Soviet expansion. But

[16] Stalin to Churchill, April 21, 1943; and Churchill to Stalin, April 24, 1943, both in SCCA, pp. 120–122. Churchill to Eden, April 28, 1943, PREM 3.354/8. Roosevelt to Stalin, April 26, 1943, SCRT, p. 61. For Churchill-Roosevelt exchanges on this issue, see *Correspondence*, II, pp. 388–402. See also Gilbert, *Churchill*, VII, pp. 384–385, 389–392, 664–665; Churchill, *Hinge of Fate*, pp. 759–761; and Dallek, *Roosevelt and American Foreign Policy*, pp. 400–401. See also Sarah Meiklejohn Terry, *Poland's Place in Europe: General Sikorski and the Origins of the Oder-Neisse Line, 1939–1943* (Princeton, N.J., 1980), pp. 337–340.

[17] Churchill to Stalin, Aug. 30, 1943; Stalin to Churchill, Aug. 31, 1943, in SCCA, p. 152; cf. Dallek, *Roosevelt and American Foreign Policy*, p. 415. See also, for Anglo-American tensions, Matthew Jones, *Britain, the United States and the Mediterranean War, 1942–1944* (New York, 1996), pp. 65–137.

here again the truth is more complex. On several occasions Churchill and Stalin exhibited a common interest in resisting potential American political intrusions. Stalin had made his concerns clear to Eden in December 1941, and, as we will shortly see, the Soviets maintained this line throughout the war, persistently attacking "Wall Street imperialism" in their media and showing extraordinary suspicion of American efforts to create airfields on Soviet soil, to send officials or journalists on investigatory missions, or to find other ways to infiltrate the tight Soviet cage. The British, anxious above all other concerns to enhance the wartime partnership with the United States, were of course infinitely more hospitable. But they too were self-protective. As early as August 1942 we find Churchill resisting the notion of stationing American troops in Iran on the grounds that it would lead to "friction" in a British sphere, though in the end he gave way there. Following the successful landings in western North Africa in November 1942, to cite another British inhibition, he resisted Roosevelt's wish to give General Dwight D. Eisenhower, the Allied theater commander, full political as well as military authority in the region. The British urged the separation of political and military responsibility, but again felt obliged to submit. Churchill was determined, however, not to let this happen in Sicily, the next theater of action, where, he petitioned FDR, Britain should be "senior partner." But Roosevelt, supported by his State and War Departments, rebuffed him yet again, insisting that because of the special American connections with Italy (he was doubtless thinking of domestic American politics) the government in Sicily should be given "as much of an American character as possible," with joint control and no senior partner. Once again Churchill felt he had to back down.[18]

But Churchill's apparent submission was deceptive. The British effort to assert political predominance in the Mediterranean simply moved to a lower level, and with the enlargement of the Italian campaign two developments conspired to give them an edge in that country. One was the sophisticated maneuvering and persistence of British officials and especially of Harold Macmillan, Churchill's principal political operative in the Mediterranean. The complex political problems that appeared after the invasion of the Italian mainland in 1943 enhanced the power of the more experienced British officials. FDR was also frustrated by the abdicatory reluctance of Eisenhower and finally of the War Department to assume what

---

[18] Jones, *Mediterranean War*, pp. 65–137; Churchill to Roosevelt, April 13, 1943, and Roosevelt to Churchill, April 14, 1943, in *Correspondence*, II, pp. 187–189.

quickly came to be viewed as burdensome political responsibilities. It was now Roosevelt's turn to back down. It was consequently the British who were mainly instrumental in creating the Badoglio government, to which Stalin gave impressive support. All this brought about, as the American Assistant Secretary for War John J. McCloy acknowledged in May 1944, "such a strongly British flavor as to destroy the President's directive for a joint rather than a senior partner arrangement." The British were also the beneficiaries of the London-backed (though hardly Anglophile) General de Gaulle's successful struggle against the United States–promoted Henri Giraud for control of the French National Council, now domiciled in Algiers. They were successful too in maintaining a controlling edge in the eastern Mediterranean, including Yugoslavia, where they worked vigorously and successfully to restrict the activities of William Donovan's OSS groups.[19]

In general, notwithstanding Roosevelt's intermittent assertiveness (in the Mediterranean war theater, or over de Gaulle's activities, for instance), the United States showed only a fitful, spasmodic desire to engage in European affairs. Consider, for example, the interesting contrast between the comparatively substantive Churchill-Stalin exchanges that we have been sampling and the much thinner Roosevelt-Stalin correspondence. The president in his messages to Moscow was invariably complimentary, reassuring, and characteristically optimistic. He periodically addressed the practical issues of war production, supply, and transportation. But he carefully avoided any potentially compromising European or other controversial issues, as indeed Stalin did in his mostly perfunctory replies. From his cables Roosevelt must have seemed to the Soviets, at least during 1942–43, preoccupied with two unpromising political purposes. One, hardly likely to inspire enthusiasm in Moscow while the western Allies were putting off a second front, was to get the Soviet Union involved in the war with Japan. FDR repeatedly warned Stalin about prospective Japanese attacks that never came and probably never seemed likely to come, given Japan's existing southward commitments and the insights of Soviet espionage. From this ostensibly self-interested supposition he urged Stalin to allow American survey parties into the Soviet Union to build airfields for the use

---

[19] McCloy to Hopkins, May 25, 1943, cited in Jones, *Mediterranean War*, p. 92. For de Gaulle and OSS, see ibid., pp. 65–96, 229–230. Dallek, *Roosevelt and American Foreign Policy*, pp. 377–379, 406–407, 458. See also John Charmley, "Harold Macmillan and the Making of the French Committee of National Liberation," *International History Review*, 4, 4 (November 1982); and Harold Macmillan, *War Diaries: Politics and War in the Mediterranean, January 1943–May 1945* (London, 1984), passim.

of American bombers. He also pressed unwanted American air squadrons upon an increasingly irritated Stalin, who clearly did not expect a Japanese attack and can hardly have wanted to provoke one in order to benefit the United States.[20]

Roosevelt's other objective, equally remote from European political issues, was to arrange a bilateral meeting with Stalin. A succession of emissaries, including former Republican presidential candidate Wendell Willkie, General Patrick J. Hurley, and former ambassador to Russia Joseph E. Davies, were sent to urge this. Indeed, much of Roosevelt's Soviet diplomacy comes down to his relentless efforts to get Stalin to meet with him, setting up meetings to arrange summit meetings. Stalin was mostly unresponsive, and not once during the war, despite repeated Rooseveltian invitations and hints, did he show interest in the prospect of a summit meeting without Churchill.[21]

It was not until March 1943, roughly three and a half years into World War II, that Foreign Secretary Anthony Eden made his first wartime visit to the United States. This set off alarms in Moscow, which may well by this time have begun to feel a proprietary interest in Eden. Maisky, perhaps encouraged by what the Soviets probably regarded as an authoritative editorial in *The Times* approving the concept of an Anglo-Soviet condominium for Europe, quickly enjoined him "not to enter into any definite commitments with the United States for any detailed settlement." The emollient Eden, no doubt recalling the similar injunction he had received from Hull as he prepared to go to Moscow in 1941, was again happy to give the desired reassurances. He found President Roosevelt eager to enlist his support for a world organization that did not envision the regional component the British preferred. Eden was depressed. True to form, the Americans were thinking in the large-scale visionary terms that the British had learned to view with suspicion. Only the prospect of reducing British politico-economic power seemed to be inspiring focused thought. Eden was particularly chilled when Hull presented him with his ideas for what was developing in the State Department into a National Declaration of Independence holding out the prospect of independence and self-rule to all peoples. It looked like a clear and familiar American threat to the British

[20] Roosevelt to Stalin, Dec. 16, 1941; Roosevelt to Stalin, June 17, 1942; and Stalin to Roosevelt, January 13, 1943, SCRT at pp. 17–18, 25–26, 50. For Maisky's concern about a possible Japanese attack, see Eden to Clark Kerr, July 14, 1942, F.O. 954/24.

[21] See, for instance, Roosevelt to Stalin, received April 12, 1942, SCRT, pp. 22–23; Roosevelt to Stalin, May 5, 1943, ibid., pp. 63–64; Roosevelt to Stalin, Oct. 5, 1942, ibid., pp. 34–35.

Empire. He refused to endorse it, sending word to Halifax that "we none of us liked Hull's draft."[22]

To Eden and his colleagues it seemed at this point that the United States – morally censorious, politically and economically threatening, not very sensitive to London's security concerns – was bent once again on presenting them with the old Wilsonian hemlock. This came at a moment when Anglo-Soviet relations were warming up, Stalin having in the post-Stalingrad euphoria finally called off the public campaign criticizing the British failure to produce a second front. It is not surprising, then, that Eden's experiences in Washington led to some significant soul searching in London about the future. His Cabinet colleagues endorsed his rejection of Hull's initiatives. Further, the whole episode stung Churchill into a vigorous defense of European interests. Until now he had actively discouraged Foreign Office or any other speculation about the postwar prospect as a dangerous time-wasting distraction. Now he emerged, presenting Eden with one of the most important of his wartime appraisals. Based partly on an evaluation, entitled "Morning Thoughts," that he had prepared for Turkish leaders some months before, it reveals Churchill as an essentially European statesman, fearful of postwar domination by either the Soviet Union or the United States.[23]

Despite his growing collaboration with Stalin, Churchill's view of the Soviet threat had persisted. In October 1942 he had told Eden, "It would be a measureless disaster if Russian barbarism overlaid the culture and independence of the ancient states of Europe."[24] Now he noted that "the overwhelming preponderance of Russia remains the dominant fact of the future." What could be done? His discussion of the United States in this connection is interesting. "We must not expect that the United States will keep large armies in Europe long after the war. Indeed, I doubt whether there will be any American troufts in Europe four years after the ceasefire." But he did not regard this as tragic because he was confident about Europe's future and suspicious, as he would continue to be through 1944, of the American plans for a world organization. Thus "United States assistance should be of a soothing and stabilizing nature. It could never extend to any form of

---

[22] *The Times*, March 10, 1943; Rowan to Churchill, Mar. 14, 1943, PREM 403/10; Eden to Churchill, March 29, 1943, F.O. 954/22; Victor Rothwell, *Britain and the Cold War* (London, 1982), p. 104; Eden to Halifax, May 26, 1943, F.O. 954/22. See also, for background on American universalist thinking about colonial issues and expanding independence, Wm. Roger Louis, *Imperialism at Bay: The U.S. and the Decolonization of the British Empire, 1941–1945* (Oxford, 1977), pp. 225–235.

[23] Eden paper, "The Foreign Secretary's Visit to Washington," March 30, 1943, WP (43) 130.

[24] Churchill to Eden, Oct. 21, 1942, PREM 4: 100/7.

rulership, whether exerted directly or through a world organization." The American threat, as Churchill conceived it, was clearly economic and political, the Russian one military and political. But there is here a strong sense of danger from both these rapidly developing power systems.

Where then lay the desired security? Churchill's answer is simply put. Europe must look to itself. Britain is "certainly not going to maintain large armies on the Continent for any lengthy period. Neither our finances nor our systems of recruitment would be equal to such a strain." Churchill puts his faith, rather, in the autonomous responses of the states of Western and Mediterranean Europe. Thus "it is a prime British interest that a strong France should be rebuilt and France can only be rebuilt round the French army." As for the rest, "the nations of Europe" will never consent to complete disarmament, while Russia preserves the greatest armaments in the world. "Even neutrals like Turkey, Siam and Sweden would want strong defenses. Above all Europe must be a self-governing entity, capable of managing her own affairs...." This could be achieved, not through a world organization (though he stressed, "Let us please FDR" by not opposing it), but through a regionally oriented Council of Europe.

In all this we surely see the persistence of 1930s attitudes about security and order. More significantly, we see that, far from being an unqualified champion of Anglo-American association, Churchill was already keenly aware of Britain's looming predicament – the fact that her two giant allies were likely to present her with quite different yet dangerously fundamental and possibly interacting threats. The Soviets, potentially dominant in and around Europe, would threaten Britain's fundamental geopolitical security. The Americans would restrain British political freedom of action and menace the empire and its economic recovery. In 1944, both these threats would materialize at the same time.

The underlying theme in Churchill's paper is the primacy of Europe in British interests, and the need to preserve a traditional kind of Europe – a continent-wide system characterized by proud, independent states willing to defend themselves; a Europe of the 1930s as it should have been if Churchill's pre-war warnings had then been followed. Thus Churchill had a postwar vision, too. But where Stalin seemed to be looking forward to Soviet aggrandizement, and Roosevelt apparently envisioned the expansion of freedom and American trade at British expense, Churchill looked forward to victory, certainly, but then back through a glow of nostalgia to the reconstitution of a very traditional Europe. He was prepared, as the next two years would show, to follow the Foreign Office and most of the British political and press establishment by making terms with Stalin in Europe,

even to the point of a de facto division of the continent. He was also willing
to please Roosevelt on the world organization while nonetheless calling for
a Council of Europe that would, he clearly hoped, maintain the independence of the old continent and keep American political influence at arm's
length. The flaw in the design was his inability to settle decisively on the
identity of the strong Western ally needed to help Britain balance anticipated
Soviet postwar power. At this point he was thinking of a more or less consolidated, traditional Europe. Later, as that illusion faded, he would focus on
an America that remained, under Roosevelt, frustratingly elusive; fitfully on
a France he could not bring himself to embrace while de Gaulle remained;
later still on the possibility of a morally unacceptable association with what
was left of German power in the spring of 1945; and finally on the United
States after all. Nonetheless, to the question raised in the spring of 1943 –
"Was there in prospect a viable European option for Britain in the postwar
era?'" – Churchill was clearly prepared to give an affirmative answer, even
as he worked in distinct and separate arenas with Roosevelt on strategy and
the war effort, and with Stalin on European political issues.[25]

THE BRITISH ESTABLISHMENT

One of the most durable barriers to a proper understanding of the British
wartime commitment to the politics of Europe has been the uncritical
acceptance by many historians of Harry Hopkins's initial assessment upon
his 1941 visit to Britain: "Churchill is the Government in every sense of the
word. ... I cannot emphasize too strongly that he is the one and only person over here with whom you need to have a full meeting of minds."[26] This
judgment, transmitted without qualification to President Roosevelt (who
was delighted to find that he need deal with the prime minister alone) was
confirmed by similar messages from another presidential emissary Averell
Harriman, and then further reinforced by Churchill's adroit cultivation
throughout the war of these two influential Americans, whom he persistently flattered and carefully integrated into his own small inner social and
business circle. Intimate associates like Beaverbrook and Brendan Bracken
functioned as weekend hosts, escorts, and guides to Whitehall. Churchill's
creation of this supportive inner circle and his loyalty and frequent submission to Roosevelt and his associates (despite many reservations and

---

[25] Churchill to Private Office, April, 1943; and note by Prime Minister, "The Structure
of Postwar Settlement," dated "April," all in PREM 4.30/3. Eden paper, "The Foreign
Secretary's Visit to Washington," March 30, 1943, WP (43) 130.
[26] Sherwood, *Roosevelt and Hopkins* (New York, 1950), p. 243.

criticisms now on display in various archives and in his private papers)
and the attention-getting activities of other members of this directorate
have dominated the historiography of Anglo-American wartime diplomacy, and done much to give it an East/West cast.[27]

All this needs some radical qualification. It is of course true that
Churchill was the dominating figure in Britain's wartime affairs. But he
was decidedly more "European" than "Anglo-American" in his approach
to the war's international politics. It is also true that he made a great show
throughout the war of fidelity to the ideal of Anglo-American fraternity. It
is not at all clear, however, how deeply felt or sincere this was. It is often
overlooked that Churchill had throughout his long public life exhibited a
lively apprehension of American hegemonial ambitions. And, as we have
just seen, he saw Europe as his "primary concern." It seems likely, on the
whole, that the taproot of his wartime commitment to the Anglo-American
alliance was British necessity and self-interest rather than the transatlantic
romanticism that often bubbles effervescently in World War II's memoir
literature. The fact is that British necessity during the war required the
United States for survival and then for the maintenance of its war effort. It
also needed the Soviet Union for victory and postwar political tranquility.
Churchill behaved accordingly.[28]

It is easy to be distracted by the energy the British were putting into the
vital ties with the United States. But this was essentially a war-making relationship. The emphasis there came from the top – from Churchill, above
all, and also from the service chiefs and the financial and supply experts
concerned with the Anglo-American war machine. By contrast, the wider
British political establishment – comprising the War Cabinet, the House of
Commons, the Foreign Office, and many of the other policy-making institutions as well as the press and the general public – were, in practice and emotionally, more inclined to focus on, and take their opinions from, events in
Europe, and to see their future as well as their past there. And while it is true
that the 1941 decision to locate the strategic headquarters of the war effort
in Washington marked a certain American primacy in that sphere, the fact
that London remained home to the numerous European exile governments
registered its central importance in the continent's politics.

---

[27] Harriman to Roosevelt, Mar. 7, 1941, President's Secretary's File, Box 50, Roosevelt
MSS; Thorne, *Allies of a Kind: The United States, Britain, and the War against Japan*
(New York, 1978), pp. 116, 119; Harbutt, *Iron Curtain*, pp. 21–22.
[28] See Churchill to Law, Feb. 16, 1944, PREM 4.27/10, for a representative scold to an associate for ignoring the "majestic" Anglo-American concept.

The War Cabinet, whose work was at least to some degree a barometer of what the British establishment regarded as basic national interests, rarely discussed Anglo-American relations or reviewed Britain's American diplomacy, or looked into events or issues where Anglo-American interests clashed. Churchill kept much of this to himself, occasionally reporting on major developments. But the War Cabinet (whose work in the political realm, more than in the prosecution of the war, was shaped by several hands), and even more so the full Cabinet, were constitutionally and self-consciously the collective custodians of Britain's interests as a world power. The War Cabinet, especially, stimulated by Eden and sometimes by other ministers, spent a good deal of time dealing with the politics of Europe and engaging in a kind of high-level dialogue with the Foreign Office, which showered it with reviews and information about continental events and future prospects. Here, allowing a few overlaps and ambiguities, is the number of formal agenda items per country considered by the War Cabinet in 1944:[29]

Poland	40
France	25
Greece	24
Italy	21
India	19
Argentina	11
Yugoslavia	11
Russia	11
United States	10

The Foreign Office was the heart, not only of British foreign policy thinking but also of British Eurocentrism. While Churchill was typically furthering the war effort by spending weekends entertaining United States Ambassador John Winant and other American visitors at Chequers, his country residence, Eden was just as vigorously trying to shape the future by lunching with and otherwise cultivating the leaders of the exile European governments.

Eden, who was generally loyal to Churchill but whose constitutional powers as His Majesty's Secretary of State for Foreign Affairs were much greater than those of the secretary of state within the American system, was committed to the notion of a full British involvement in European

[29] See War Cabinet (WM) deliberations for 1944. Bound volumes under CAB 65 in Public Record Office, Kew, England.

politics based on collaboration with the Soviet Union. Not everyone was
happy with this. One acerbic senior ambassador dismissed Soviet culture
as little more than "folk songs tempered by executions." In fact, Eden cultivated the European leaders assiduously, and his negotiation with the
Soviet leaders in 1941 and the ensuing Anglo-Soviet treaty provided a personal and institutional focus to which he and the Foreign Office remained
faithful throughout the war. Not that Eden was insensitive to American
susceptibilities. "I have been asked by all European leaders for closer relations with Great Britain," he remarked in July 1943, "but I have put them
off for fear of upsetting the United States."[30]

And in many respects it was Eden rather than Churchill who was the
principal British actor in the calibrated adjustments that we see on both
sides of the Anglo-Soviet alliance. These helped define a field of European
political action that in its systemic compulsions, diplomatic power-
oriented maneuveres, and complex navigation through problems old and
new was very different from the world scene as it appeared to the Roosevelt
administration. Thus early in the war, when the Soviets were in desperate
straits, the British government was appropriately assertive, quietly supporting the Polish-Czech and Greek-Yugoslav "confederation" plans.
Stalin and Molotov, for their part, openly accepted these prospective structures despite their obvious replication of the pre-war anti-Soviet *cordon
sanitaire*.[31] Similarly, Eden persuaded Molotov to agree to the self-denying
"gentlemen's agreement" by which the two powers promised not to compromise the eventual peacemaking by making binding wartime agreements affecting the future with any of the smaller European states. But
after the Katyn crisis brought the eclipse of Polish political influence, and
the Red Army's victory at Kursk-Orel opened the way to postwar political
expansion, the Soviets, with perfect political logic, became more demanding, now making clear their opposition to confederations and abrogating
the informal agreement against client seeking by making a deal and then
a political and territorial treaty with Czechoslovakia's Benes. Now it was
Eden's turn to adjust, which he promptly did, with equal logic, accepting the new reality and then, in step with the Soviet advance into Eastern
Europe during 1944, presiding with Churchill over the further retreat by
stages of British influence, first in the Balkans and then in Central Europe.

---

[30] Eden memorandum, July 19, 1943, F.O. 954/22. The ambassador was Sir Reader Bullard,
      wartime British representative in Iran.
[31] Roberts note, Oct. 1, 1942, N4192/G, F.O. 371.32918; Eden to Churchill, July 12, 1943,
      F.O. 954/24.

These were all logical, nonconfrontational political moves, not heroic or even principled in most cases, but very much in the tradition of classical European diplomacy.

The diplomatic establishment in London was only rarely distracted from its intensely Eurocentric concentration. The Northern Department, which dealt with the Soviet Union and Eastern Europe, was the most dynamic section in the Foreign Office. The leading figures like Cadogan and Under-Secretary Orme Sargent, as well as the main political appointees and Eden himself, regularly added their own minutes and comments to the various ambassadorial dispatches, internal memoranda, and position papers that came up for review in this crucial department, giving the researcher some excellent insight into evolving thought and action. Other European sections also seem, judging by the length, vigor, and regularity of the minute writing, to have been busy and comparatively creative. The general view was that it would be unwise to ignore the virtual certainty of Soviet domination of Eastern and perhaps Central Europe, that this was acceptable though regrettable, and that Britain's fate, for better or worse, was tied up with that of Western Europe, the Mediterranean, and the Middle East, whose proper restoration and future stability, secured in some kind of concert with the Soviets, was the prime British interest. So pervasive was this thinking that by the end of 1943 we find leading figures in the pro-Polish Special Operations Executive (SOE) complaining of the "Russification" of Whitehall. But British officials now found it hard to envision an alternative. The Post-Hostilities Planners, a group dominated by the military authorities, advised in March 1944 that "FDR and the USCOS have given the opinion that American forces should be withdrawn as soon as possible." Sargent drew the obvious lesson. "I do not myself believe that the U.S. will stay long in Europe. ... we must therefore not count on the United States." Anglo-Soviet relations were "very difficult," and they would probably be very hard on the Germans, but "we should be unwise to falter in our support of Russia for such reasons."[32]

By contrast with the hum of activity in the Foreign Office's European departments, the North American section was small and unresourceful. This no doubt reflects Churchill's tendency to take most aspects of the American relationship under his wing and the influence of Lord Halifax, whose detailed weekly reports from Washington left little scope for the minute writers to do more than register the follies of the isolationists

---

[32] Perkins (SOE) to VCD, Aug. 13, 1943, HS4/144; memorandum, Mar. 7, 1944; PHP (43) 36A, Mar. 7, 1944.

and marvel at the extraordinary influence of Walter Lippmann and other pundits. These reports were mostly written by the Oxford philosopher Isaiah Berlin, famously confused by Churchill with the composer Irving Berlin. The head of the North American department, Neville Butler, when occasionally asked for an opinion about American attitudes, usually took the almost universally accepted line that it would be very unwise to expect any postwar political help from the United States.[33]

This was also the attitude taken by the opinion-shaping institutions in British society. The press was, by long tradition, Eurocentric and empire-conscious in outlook and tone. There was now more news from the American scene than in the pre-war. But, in general, much more attention was given to European issues. And here the press mirrored the views of both the establishment and public opinion. A strong Russophilia stands out during the period 1942–43, when the widely read Beaverbrook newspapers were campaigning energetically for a second front. A pro-Soviet line also permeated the always influential *The Times*, which consistently championed the Soviet Union and pressed the notion of the Anglo-Soviet treaty as Britain's postwar political lodestar. Here the supportive pro-Soviet dispatches from Moscow by its correspondent, Ralph Parker, long a Soviet stooge after being corrupted by the NKVD in the 1930s, worked neatly into the sympathetic editorial policies of Barrington-Ward, and were then further refined in the brilliant editorials of E. H. Carr, an ardent protagonist of Anglo-Soviet collaboration and later of the 1944 division of Europe into British and Soviet spheres of influence, later still an influential historian of Bolshevism. Other national daily and Sunday newspapers and most of the political journals echoed these sentiments to a greater or lesser degree. There was an occasional skeptical note in the Labour Party's *Daily Herald* and passionate criticism in the scarcely visible Polish émigré press, which spent much of the war fighting the equally vitriolic *Daily Worker* while trying to evade the Foreign Office's anxious monitors. But in general there was little questioning of the need for a strong European policy built around the Anglo-Soviet relationship, and little expectation of any significant political or economic help from the United States after the war.[34]

---

[33] See, for example, Butler note, May 23, 1944, F.O. 371.40740; H. G. Nicholas, ed., *Washington Dispatches, 1941–1945* (Chicago, 1981), passim.

[34] See Beaverbrook papers (*Daily Express* and *Evening Standard*) in late 1941 through 1942; *The Economist*, Sept. 13, 1941. Other London papers strongly supporting the second front included *The News Chronicle, The Tribune,* and the weekly *New Statesman.* See P. M. H. Bell, *John Bull and the Bear: British Public Opinion, Foreign Policy and the Soviet Union, 1941–1945* (London, 1990), pp. 58–66, 76–88. See also Alan Foster, "The

The increasing wartime solidity of the Soviet connection in British life, contrasting with the very thin Soviet presence in the United States, can be seen in various other institutional activities. One was the appearance of public groups like the Anglo-Soviet Public Relations Committee (ASPR), which promoted contacts between scientists and other distinguished people in various fields. The Labour Party, despite skepticism in some quarters, was broadly supportive. Its chairman, the political scientist Harold Laski, actively promoted contacts and proclaimed that "the Labour Party represented the interests of the working class in Britain just as the Communist Party of the Soviet Union did in Russia." He openly looked forward to the postwar reconstitution of the Socialist International. The British Communist Party was of course active in multivarious activities, and there was clearly a degree of communist influence and infiltration in certain public groups and a good deal of "second front" as well as class-sensitive action. But these were widely tolerated and even valued as expressions of solidarity with the indispensable fighting ally. Most significant in the long run was the joint formation in 1941 by the British Trade Union Council and the All-Union Central Council of Soviet Trade Unions of the Anglo-Soviet Trade Union Committee, an organization designed to nourish and strengthen solidarity at that important level. Here there were large ambitions from the outset, with numerous viewpoints looking to a postwar order organized along trade union rather than conventional political lines. There was also a range of politico-cultural activities. The Board of Education, as active here as in the promotion of American studies, set up in 1942 a Committee on Russian Studies, whose tasks included the publication of books on Russian and Soviet history and life for schoolchildren. Discussions of Russian literature on the BBC were organized, and there were careful observances of annual milestones such as Red Army Day, though Churchill drew the line at honoring the commemoration of the October Revolution.[35]

These elite susceptibilities appear to have faithfully mirrored the sentiments of the British people, who, though fully aware of and unmistakably grateful for the crucial aid, especially the food, flowing from the United States, appear to have been similarly Eurocentric rather than transatlantic in outlook during these years. They were relieved to find the United States

Times and Appeasement: The Second Phase," in Walter Laqueur (ed.), *The Second World War: Essays in Military and Political History* (London, 1982).

[35] For ASPR, see comment by A. V. Hill, N1457, F.O. 371.32896. H. J. Laski, "The Labour Party Delegation to Russia August, 1943" in File 2/11, E. Bevin MSS. Harbutt, *Iron Curtain*, p. 132. See Victor Silverman, *Imagining Internationalism in American and British Labor, 1939–1949* (Urbana and London, 2000), p. 4; and Foreign Office Press Bureau, Aug. 30, 1944, N12081, F.O. 371.47868.

in the war at their side in December 1941, and they approved Churchill's
vigorous effort to form a joint military command. Yet there was remarkably little gratitude toward, or even warm feeling about, the United States.
The writer George Orwell, a close observer of public attitudes, saw the
Soviet alliance as an unwelcome necessity, remarking privately of Stalin in
July 1941, "this disgusting murderer is temporarily on our side." Writing
in January 1942 for *Partisan Review*, however, Orwell noted "a tremen-
dous net increase of pro-Russian sentiment." He then went on to write
that he found "no corresponding increase in pro-American sentiment –
the contrary if anything. It is true that the entry of Japan and America
into the war was expected by everyone, whereas the German invasion of
Russia came as a surprise. But our new alliance has simply brought out
the immense amount of anti-American feeling that exists in the ordinary
lowbrow middle class." Orwell went on to discuss the more general British
hostility to America in cultural and political terms. "Cultivated people," he
declared, loathed the United States, which was regarded as the "vulgariser
of England and Europe." And, from a political point of view, "Americans
are supposed to be boastful, bad-mannered and worshippers of money,
and are also suspected of plotting to inherit the British Empire."[36]

While it is obviously important not to exaggerate the significance of
these attitudes, sentiments of this kind, with all their stereotypical thinking and defensive localism, were common in Britain during the war. They
are of course a mirror image of the well-documented Anglophobia that
historians have found at work in the United States after Pearl Harbor, and
a reminder of the chronic ill-feeling that has been just as significant in the
history of the Anglo-American relationship as the occasional bursts of fellowship. It may be objected that the available evidence of such thinking is
fatally selective and impressionistic. But more objective Home Intelligence
surveys by the British Ministry of Information tend to confirm Orwell's
diagnosis. They show profound, widespread admiration for the Russian
people in Britain through 1942 and into 1943. A report by political censorship officials in March 1942 noted, with an implied slap at the American
ally, "The majority of writers seem to pin their faith almost entirely on the
Russians – the chaps who don't talk but keep on killing Huns." And a special report in February 1942 on "Home Morale and Public Opinion" found

---

[36] For Orwell on Stalin, see *People on People: The Oxford Dictionary of Biographical
Quotations* (Oxford, 2001), p. 326. See also George Orwell, "Letter to *Partisan Review*,"
in Sonia Orwell and Ian Angus (eds.), *My Country Right or Wrong: The Collected Essays,
Journalism, and Letters of George Orwell* (London and New York, 1968), pp. 175–183.

that "[t]he gratitude and admiration for the great fight of the Russians far exceeds the feeling for any other foreign country."[37]

Various polls tell a similar story. Asked by the Gallup organization in May 1942 to name "the world's greatest living man," the British gave Churchill 42%, Stalin 24%, and Roosevelt 20%. Things hadn't changed very much by April 1943, when people responded to the pollster's question "Which country has so far made the greatest contribution towards winning the war?" by giving Russia 50%, Britain 42%, and the United States 3%. Not that the British were completely bowled over by the saga on the eastern front. In March 1943 twice as many correspondents felt it would be easier to get on with the United States than with Russia after the war. And by 46% to 32% they preferred an alliance with America to one with the Soviets. On the other hand, 31% thought the United States "would try to boss Britain after the war," while only 18% thought the Soviets would try to do so.[38]

These poll figures reveal something of the quite complex feelings of the British people about their two great allies in the middle of the war. At this time it was not really a matter of choosing one over the other. For the leadership, it was a matter of thinking and speculating about a future where fundamental British interests would clearly be at risk in a new way. Meanwhile, it was important to please both allies with a policy of calculated adjustments. Thus if Stalin was interested in some kind of de facto division of Europe, the government and the Foreign Office would play along but not so vigorously as to upset the United States or the small Eastern and Central European states. Similarly, when Hull and the State Department (and Roosevelt, less actively) began to press the need for a world organization, the British responded positively while watching closely to make sure that there would be room for a Council of Europe and that it didn't threaten their relations with Moscow. For the most part it was possible during this period to please both allies and balance their claims because the war was the main common preoccupation, and the spheres of strategic and political action were still distinct and separate. But events would soon push Britain more deeply into European affairs and toward its Soviet ally.

---

[37] Ministry of Information, Home Intelligence Reports 71 (February 2–9, 1942) and 76 (March 9–16, 1942), both in INF 1/292, Public Record Office, Kew, England. See also Bell, *John Bull and the Bear*, pp. 88–89.

[38] Gallup/BIPO Surveys 87 (March 1942), 89 (July 1942), and 98 (April 1943), all in Gallup Poll Archives, London, England. See also Bell, *John Bull and the Bear*, pp. 67–105.

THE RUSSIANS AND THEIR BRITISH ALLY

As a field of study, Soviet wartime and early Cold War foreign policy used to be a comparatively straightforward enterprise. It meant Stalin and his unappealing accomplice Molotov. It meant the dictatorship as a basic fact; the totalitarian model as an aspiration from which there was no apparent deviation; the Cold War mentality as a permanent reality; and the almost total absence of diplomatic documentation as a fatal bar to any further elucidation. The orthodox and entirely logical response by historians of World War II in the United States and Western Europe, and now in Russia, has been to do as Churchill and Roosevelt had done. This was to focus on Stalin, on his obvious power, his enigmatic personality, his system and supposed aims, so far as these could be judged from various historical, geopolitical, ideological, and psychological perspectives.[39]

There was contextual evidence of a kind. The monolithic, controlled press could be scrutinized for clues, and most of the diplomats serving in Moscow during World War II had spent much of their time reading these. The Soviet world occasionally produced a spirited, more open personality – Maxim Litvinov was one – and sometimes a drunken Red Army colonel in some remote posting might mutter something indiscreet and set the cables humming. Then too, there were the apparently licensed "Westerners" – people like Litvinov, Ivan Maisky, and Lenin's old associate Alexandra Kollantai – who seemed able to talk with foreigners in order to get some official point or attitude into the Western mind-set without compromising the party line. But the insights that governments normally expect from the diplomatic round – the access to the bureaucracy, the carefully nourished contacts with political figures and area specialists, the judicious mingling with the people – were thin indeed. It is hardly surprising, then, that Soviet foreign policy during the war was hard to fathom, or that Soviet diplomatic history, as opposed to study of the marginally more accessible domestic subjects, was, and still is, comparatively undeveloped.

We now know more, though much less than was hoped for in the heady days of the early 1990s. In one crucial respect, however, the new evidence

---

[39] For various assessments of Stalin's diplomacy during and after the Cold War, see, for example, Adam Ulam, *Expansion and Coexistence: The History of Soviet Foreign Policy*, 2nd. edn. (New York, 1974); Dmitri Volkogonov, *Stalin: Triumph and Tragedy* (London, 1991); and Vladimir Zubok and Constantin Pleshakov, *Inside the Kremlin's Cold War: From Stalin to Khrushchev* (Cambridge, Mass., 1996); and Geoffrey Roberts, *Stalin's Wars: From World War to Cold War, 1939–1957* (London, 2006).

has confirmed the old stereotype. Stalin was, it now seems clear, the sole decisive figure, at least in the high-level summit diplomacy with which we are mainly concerned here. The terror machine run by Lavrenti Beria under Stalin's watchful eye left no room for genuine independent action or thought. Molotov, the only other figure of real significance, assiduously deferred to Stalin's wishes.[40]

Certain other things that puzzled Kremlinologists during the Cold War are also now much clearer. Was Stalin guided by mainly ideological or geopolitical impulses? Two recent Soviet historians call these the two "suns of empire and revolution" in Stalin's mental universe, plausibly adding as a major factor the impact of his complex personality. Most contemporary authorities, despite the historian Martin Malia's powerful recent restatement of the case for the primacy of ideology, seem inclined to stress the geopolitical aspect. Another interesting feature is the accumulating evidence of Stalin's obsessive caution during the war. Far from being the Hitler-like expansionist of early Cold War imagery, bent on world conquest, he appears to have been concerned to seek a basis for cooperation with the Western allies and also to rein in the expectant communist elements in Eastern Europe, repeatedly warning them not to provoke their peoples and even holding out on several occasions the possibility of different roads to socialism. This caution appears to have had some of its roots in Stalin's reading of the revolutionary prospect, others in his well-attested passion for control of overenthusiastic radicals. In this, at least, Eduard Benes's predictive powers receive some rare vindication, for as early as 1942 he was stressing that Stalin was fearful of the postwar because "the communists abroad are all Trotskyites rather than Stalinist." In short, recent evidence gives us a more variegated picture of Stalin's mind, one that not only helps explain his various objectives – which, so far as Eastern Europe was concerned, were transparently revealed to Eden in December 1941 – but also suggests that he was feeling his way with some flexibility toward their fulfillment.[41]

A brief moment registered in the British archives gives us a tantalizing glimpse into Stalin's character and thinking. Late in 1945 he received a delegation of Finnish trade unionists, one of whom had the temerity to ask

---

[40] For Molotov, see Albert Resis (ed.), *Molotov Remembers: Inside Kremlin Politics, Conversations with Felix Chuev* (Chicago, 1993). See also Terence Emmons, "Opening the Soviet Archives," *The Stanford Historian*, 16, (Summer 1992), pp. 12–13.
[41] Zubok and Pleshakov, *Kremlin's Cold War*, p. 5; Martin Malia, *The Soviet Tragedy: A History of Socialism in Russia* (New York, 1994); Eden to Nichols, F.O. 954/4.

him what the cultural and educational aims of the Soviet government were toward their own people. Stalin held up three fingers and said:

Three things: first to make the people more human and less like beasts by stilling their animal passions, their fears and lusts and by giving them a longer perspective; second, to spread literacy and technical education much wider among the masses, since the war had shown that these were not spread widely enough; and lastly, to teach the Soviet people to think internationally instead of thinking of the USSR as a world to itself.[42]

These presumably unrehearsed remarks capture perfectly in Stalin the ruthless social engineer beneath the cosmetic idealism, with his zookeeper contempt (reminiscent of Hitler in the last stages of the war) for the "beasts" who had just saved him and his regime from total defeat and humiliation. But they also show a desire to modernize and even internationalize old Russia. Whether this was inspired by a genuine desire for comity with his wartime allies, or by a feeling that "socialism in one country" should now give way to a broader conception, is not entirely clear.

Undoubtedly something of the old enigma remains. But his steady, purposeful wartime promotion of some kind of Anglo-Soviet condominium for Europe suggests, on balance, that Stalin did indeed wish to pursue a postwar policy of collaboration. Indeed, it is not entirely fanciful to see Stalin, if we shelve the moral dimension for a moment, in the unfamiliar posture of a classical European statesman. Three points can be made in support of this perhaps startling proposition. In the first place, as we have seen, Stalin joined the British in a kind of diplomatic "realism," orchestrated to the changes in their relative power as the war unfolded. Like Churchill and Eden, he conformed to a visible pattern of calculated adjustment: moderate and acquiescent in 1941–42; bolder and more demanding as Soviet fortunes improved. His comparatively sharp assertiveness early in December 1941 does not invalidate this theory, for it sprang from his faulty assumption (soon abandoned) that the Red Army had permanently gained the strategic initiative.

Secondly, it is also the case that Stalin set – and for the most part dominated – the basic political agenda for the victorious tripartite alliance. For it will become ever more apparent as we proceed that he not only pushed his geopolitical objectives upon the reluctant British beginning in December 1941 but then steadily bent them to his will on the basis of

---

[42] Roberts to Bevin, Oct. 19, 1945, N14171, F.O. 371.47870.

an Eastern Europe–Western Europe/Mediterranean division that in late 1944 he refined with a collusive Churchill into a geopolitical "bargain." Similarly, as the United States came more slowly into the postwar planning, he identified Roosevelt's primary objective as a new world organization and then worked systematically and successfully (at least until early 1946) to force another "bargain," this one from the United States, exchanging acceptance of the United Nations for an acknowledged Soviet primacy in Eastern Europe. And thirdly, as one might expect from so purposeful a political leader, Stalin was in his relations with the Western powers a stickler for old-fashioned diplomatic punctilio and conventional formality, always calling for pre-conference agendas and consistently showing his distaste for the loose and designedly vague procedures by means of which Churchill and Roosevelt contrived to keep the Soviets in the war while avoiding, so far as they judged possible, the price of embarrassing commitments.

The new evidence also allows us to see that, whatever Stalin's inner motivations and/or hidden agendas, he pursued two comparatively clear lines of policy. One looked to relations with Britain and the United States on a basis of mutual accommodation, the kind of "high diplomacy" we have observed thus far. The other, necessarily more elusive, laid out a political scenario for the postwar domination of Eastern Europe based not on immediate relentless "Sovietization" but on a more emollient, evolutionary approach. It is entirely possible that he genuinely expected that a turn toward socialistic change would be widely popular in Eastern Europe. It is likely that at the level of strategic calculation his two policies – the diplomatic and the political – were intimately related, both in the geopolitical sense that collaboration with the Allies (and especially Britain) was designed to create for the Soviet Union the large, legitimized sphere of political control in Eastern and southeastern Europe that could then be worked upon, and in local application because Stalin clearly understood that unduly provocative policies within Eastern Europe would jeopardize that legitimizing support. His problem then was that he wanted, as the historian Eduard Mark aptly puts it, "collaboration with aggrandizement." Understandably unsure of his ability to bring off this difficult double achievement, he chose in his personal exchanges with Churchill and Roosevelt to dissimulate rather than reveal his inner thoughts, even as he stuck with considerable success to a straightforward "bargain" diplomacy. The difficulty he faced in trying to bring his two objectives into harmonious relation is clearly reflected in his highly compartmentalized treatment of the distinct diplomatic (Allied) and political (Eastern

European) arenas – a compartmentalization that is also clearly visible in his planning.[43]

Let us consider Stalin's approach to each of these areas. The geopolitical diplomatic planning was entrusted to two principal commissions established by Molotov in 1943, undoubtedly on Stalin's instructions, under the leadership of Maisky and Litvinov. Their charge was to prepare for the postwar. The choice of these two men reinforces the notion that Stalin was bent on cooperation with Britain and the United States. It has long been thought that during this period they were little more than diplomatic functionaries. They had presumably been removed in 1943 from their key ambassadorial posts, in London and Washington, respectively, either as a mark of Stalin's displeasure at their inability to produce a second front, or as a message of some kind to the host country, or again as a display of the usual Soviet reluctance to let any diplomat stay too long in one potentially seductive post. It is clear now that none of this was true, that they were brought home to help make plans for the postwar, and that they enjoyed, in some significant if finally obscure sense, the confidence of their master. This was especially true of Maisky, whom Molotov treated, according to a watchful Clark Kerr, with great deference.[44]

Maisky is of particular interest as a guide to Soviet attitudes in the lead-up to the 1943 tripartite conferences. In March he had urged Eden to remain faithful to the Anglo-Soviet nexus while in the United States. In the summer he called the foreign secretary's attention to the long, historic association of Russia and the British Empire, the supposed similarity of their national development, and, somewhat more plausibly, the complementary

---

[43] Eduard Mark, "Revolution by Degrees: Stalin's National Front Strategy for Europe, 1941–1947," Working Paper No. 31, Cold War International History Project, Woodrow Wilson International Center for Scholars (Washington D.C., 2001), p. 12 and passim. A basic unresolved issue among historians is whether Stalin had anything resembling a master plan for the conversion to communism of the countries falling under his sway. For the view that he had no such plan, see Melvyn P. Leffler, *For the Soul of Mankind: The United States, the Soviet Union, and the Cold War* (New York, 2007), p. 29. Geoffrey Roberts offers a similar perspective, though partly endorsing Mark's "revolution by degrees" conception in stressing Stalin's confidence that communists would prevail, even in free elections, in Roberts, *Stalin's Wars*, p. 250. Most recent historians appear to believe that while there was no "blueprint," there was a settled aim to communize the subject countries on a "step by step" basis. See, for example, pp. 6–7 and 30–33 in the Mark article cited above, and the review in Marc Trachtenberg, "The United States and Eastern Europe in 1945: A Reassessment," *Journal of Cold War Studies*, 10, 4 (Fall 2008), pp. 94–96.

[44] Clark Kerr to Eden, July 15, 1944, F.O. 954/26. Both retained Stalin's confidence, at least up to Yalta, for which Litvinov paved the way with significant articles in *War and the Working Class* and where Maisky appeared as the Soviet specialist on reparations.

nature of their national interests. Both nations, he pointed out, were on the fringes of Europe. Neither wanted to dominate Europe, but both would always resist others who did.[45]

In the late summer Maisky raised a basic question. Should the three allies work toward spheres, or should each "play over the whole field"? Churchill's response was that all three should be entitled to work for their own interests "in every capital" but that "the British and Russians having signed a 20 year treaty would doubtless always be helping each other." Similarly, when in September Maisky urged the importance of "concrete decisions" on the Soviet frontier issue, Eden advised him not to expect too much, yet held out the hope that the powers "might agree on something fairly precise ... even though it had to be expressed in general terms." Responses of this kind, couched in noncommittal language that doubtless had American sensitivities in mind, no doubt irritated the arithmetician in the Kremlin, only now emerging from acrimonious exchanges with Churchill over the latter's failure to produce a second front in 1943. There were further Western evasions over the Soviet desire for a firm agenda for the projected foreign ministers conference in October. Churchill told Eden he had no wish to give the Soviets "a clear definition of our attitude." In the end, only minimal lists of topics were forwarded from London and Washington.[46]

Maisky is also a good guide to the persistent Soviet concerns about the United States in the lead-up to the 1943 tripartite conferences. As we have seen, Soviet suspicions were already visible during Eden's 1941 visit to Moscow. The moralistic American intrusions during the long treaty negotiations with Britain that followed were also resented. Then, in August 1942, we find the ambassador complaining in London about American plans for postwar relief. They would be dominated by Wall Street and the Republican Party, he insisted, and would create "a very potent weapon for American imperialists." Republican gains in the 1942 congressional elections aroused further concern. Now more than ever it was necessary, Maisky told Eden, for Britain and Russia "to work together." By February 1943 the specter of American expansionism was again uppermost, and we find him telling the British politician Robert Boothby that the United States was planning "to link up from North Africa with Spain and Italy in order to establish a Catholic and anti-Bolshevik bloc in southern Europe." By May

---

[45] Eden to Churchill, September 3, 1943, PREM 3.172/1.
[46] Churchill to Attlee and Eden, September 3, 1943; Eden to Churchill, September 8, 1943; Churchill to Eden, September 14, 1943, all ibid.

he was registering concern with the Foreign Office about rumors that the Americans were buying up shares in the Anglo-Persian Oil Company.[47]

While these two themes – the need for closer Anglo-Soviet collaboration, and the danger for Europe of American intrusion – course insistently and intriguingly through Maisky's last year in London, he was from September onward clearly instructed to operate as a kind of preliminary point man for the now imminent conferences. In his last meetings with Eden he was full of resentment over the disproportionate war burden the Soviet Union was carrying. He pressed hard for an advance agenda so that the three powers could define their positions more clearly.[48]

The ambassador's trip home upon his recall in mid-1943 was marked by a series of complaints and veiled threats. In Cairo, he warned that Moscow wanted not communist but "progressive" postwar governments in Italy, Yugoslavia, and Greece. In Damascus, he complained again about the "unsatisfactory" handling of the looming foreign ministers conference, particularly the lack of "a positive agenda." The winter offensive, he noted pointedly, would bring the Red Army to the German frontier. Germany would likely be reduced to "a state of deliquescence." If the second front occurred only then, "the Russians would conclude that the Anglo-Americans were trying to capitalize on Soviet victories for their own advantages." They would think the Western powers had "only a small part in winning the war and were therefore only entitled to a small part in the peace." But even now he still clearly favored the British connection. Noting that American tendencies in Europe were "ultra-conservative," he predicted that after a few unpleasant surprises the United States would "lose out" in Europe. Then it would be for Britain and Russia to settle the fate of Europe between them. A British diplomatic report from the Levant noted that "it is because Russia and Britain have so much to do together that Maisky is so concerned at the estrangement between our two countries today."[49]

The fact that Stalin and Molotov chose as prospective architects of the peace settlement the two most Westernized people available to them, the two men with the most intimate personal connections with Churchill and Roosevelt, respectively, shows a degree of practicality and sophistication on Stalin's part. For these were most untypical Soviet diplomats. Litvinov was socially active in Washington and quite often at the White House, though

---

[47] Eden to Clark Kerr, August 12, 1942; Eden to Clark Kerr, January 5, 1943, both in F.O. 954/24; Boothby to Eden, February 25, 1943, F.O. 954/26.
[48] Eden to Churchill, September 1, 1943, ibid
[49] Cairo to Foreign Office, October 11, 1943; Spears to Foreign Office, October 7, 1943, both ibid.

temporarily out of favor in Moscow. Maisky was similarly well-connected in London, frequently meeting with Eden, quite often with Churchill. He had the habit of calling personally at the Foreign Office every day to get the latest news. The favor now shown to both of these men also qualifies, at least to some extent, the notion of an obscurantist or impotent diplomatic establishment. Maisky appears to have been especially influential from the time of his return to Moscow (the British Embassy reporting in July 1944 that Molotov treated him "as a distinguished person" and "with an air of affection"). This perhaps reflected the higher value the Kremlin appears to have placed on collaboration with Britain.[50]

Roosevelt was painfully aware of this, complaining to Eden in March 1943 that Litvinov, whom he had cultivated, seemed less in the confidence of the Soviet government than Maisky, and that American representatives in Moscow were also having problems. But Litvinov, the pre-war commissar for foreign affairs whose failed Western-oriented Popular Front policies had led to his replacement by Molotov in 1939, appears to have recovered his position somewhat by late 1943, and he too was seen by British observers as being "treated with distinction" in public. He was then given a most sensitive task in postwar planning. But as Maisky's group was quicker off the mark, working through late 1943 and producing its first major document in early January 1944, we will employ it here as a kind of register of the persistence and basic continuity of Soviet policy from December 1941 to February 1945 – and especially of its commitment to an Anglo-Soviet concert for hegemony in postwar Europe.[51]

In view of these developments, so favorable to Soviet prospects, it is not surprising to find that Maisky's vision enlarged faithfully upon that which Stalin had presented to Eden over two years earlier. After an introductory statement of general purpose, "to create a situation which will guarantee for a long period the security of the USSR and the maintenance of peace, at least in Europe and Asia," Maisky went on, "it is above all necessary that the USSR should emerge from the war with favorable strategic frontiers." This encompassed the Curzon Line, of course, but also a much wider orbit

---

[50] Clark Kerr to Eden, July 15, 1944, F.O. 954/26. Ivan Maisky, *Memoirs of a Soviet Ambassador* (London, 1967).
[51] I have drawn here on the analysis by Alexei Filitov of the "Maisky Commission Files in Archive of the Foreign Policy of the Russian Federation, Moscow" in "Problems of Postwar Construction in Foreign Policy Conceptions during World War II," in F. Gori and S. Pons (eds.), *The Soviet Union and Europe in the Cold War, 1943–1953* (London, 1996), pp. 3–22. For Litvinov's role, see Geoffrey Roberts, "Litvinov's Lost Peace, 1941–1946," *Journal of Cold War Studies*, 4, 2 (Spring 2002), pp. 39–45.

than the 1941 frontier, for it now added such accretions as the Petsamo region of Finland and South Sakhalin and the Kurile Islands in the Far East, a common frontier with Czechoslovakia, mutual assistance pacts with Finland and Romania permitting Soviet bases, and free transit across Iran to the Persian Gulf.

But this is not a call for unbridled expansion. Maisky envisioned the dismemberment and long Soviet occupation of Germany, its disarmament and de-Nazification, the severe punishment of war criminals, and the enforced labor in the Soviet Union of millions of Germans. On the whole, though, the document has an air of rationality and moderation. Poland is obviously a special case, with the frontier to be fixed on 1941 lines but with compensation in East Prussia and part of Silesia. Poland must not become "too strong," but "the USSR's aims must be to create an independent and viable Poland," a formulation suggesting a disinclination, not just among British and American politicians but within high Soviet circles as well, to probe for a close definition of sensitive terms that might have usefully (but embarrassingly) have clarified basic problems. Czechoslovakia, as Benes had proposed, "can be an important transmitter of our influence in Central and South-eastern Europe." France and Italy are not seen as great powers in the new European arena, but there is no hint of intended political molestation or any plan for a communist takeover. Hungary must be internationally isolated. Remarkably, the hope is expressed that all these settlements can be achieved through treaties and alliances. There is no suggestion of coercion. Soviet power is implied but not stated or elaborated. The tacit assumption is that the tools of conventional international diplomacy can be employed to achieve Soviet aims effectively, presumably in association with Britain, as in fact happened, more or less, a year later.

For basic to all this, and presumably obviating the need for a more openly coercive approach, was Maisky's call for some kind of facilitating partnership with Britain in creating and maintaining the postwar concert of Europe. His central proposition was expressed as follows: "What would be most to our advantage would be that in postwar Europe there should be only one strong land power, the USSR, and only one strong sea power, Britain." Along with this, from a British viewpoint, alarming echo of 1940–41, we do find here and there a touch of malice, such as the suggestion that the Soviet Union should "leave the honor of defeating Japan to the British and Americans. ... This would also be our revenge for the Anglo-Americans' position on the second front question." On the whole, though, Maisky showed respect for British interests in Western Europe and the Mediterranean, urging acceptance, for instance, of British bases on the continent and its mutual assistance pacts with Belgium and Holland as well as recognition of British interests in Greece.[52]

Where does the United States fit in here? Maisky had some fascinating comments on Anglo-American relations and on the superiority of Britain as the key political ally. He sensed a deep American ideological hostility to the Soviet Union, especially in the State Department and among Roman Catholics. He then went on to distinguish between American "dynamic imperialism" and Britain's more "conservative" variety, which would make the latter a force for stability and order in the postwar world. One begins to see why Roosevelt never got far with his strictures to Stalin on the sins of the British imperialists.

Maisky expressed a general desire for good relations with the United States. But he believed that such relations would be difficult to achieve and showed a lively apprehension of danger from that source. Thus, looking to "the more distant future," he predicted that American long-range aircraft would eliminate the Soviet invulnerability from attack and expressed fears that the United States might form a bloc with defeated Germany, or Japan, or France and China – but not, surprisingly, with Britain. For in line with classic Marxist-Leninist doctrine, Maisky anticipated, as we know Stalin did, a confrontation between the two capitalist-imperialistic powers. Thus:

The logic of things must press Britain closer to the USSR, because its fundamental struggle in the postwar period will be against the USA. ... I am also ... inclined to think that in this period it will be to the USSR's interest to keep Britain as a strong power: in particular, it will be interested in Britain's retention of a strong navy, for such a Britain can be needed by us to counter the USA's imperialist expansion.

In addition to the geopolitical logic and ideological precepts that, as we have seen, had been at the heart of the Soviet desire for collaboration with Britain since Stalin's 1941 discussions with Eden, Maisky stressed the very practical incentive of dealing with a pragmatic partner fully experienced in European politics. For Britain

... has from the outset manoevered on these questions more flexibly and cunningly than the USA. Eden told me more than once that he envisioned creating in the countries of post-war Europe "national front" governments which should

---

[52] Ibid. pp. 7–11. See also Chapman to Andrew, March 9, 1944, C3671/G, F.O. 371.43375; and Foreign Office memorandum (undated), N1530, F.O. 371.43375. In short, Maisky's elaborated notion of a postwar Anglo-Soviet condominium in Europe was a staple of Soviet thinking by late 1943, whether we look back to its origins with Stalin in December 1941 or ahead to the like prescriptions of Litvinov (of which more later) in the run-up to Yalta in early 1945.

include all the major progressive parties in each state. He appreciated that to wager on the reactionary elements would be a bad and quite unrealistic policy. The British, knowing Europe better and having more political experience, have made substantially fewer mistakes than their allies in European affairs. The main thing is that they have known how to take account of the facts, regardless of whether they like them or not.[53]

So much for Anglo-Soviet concord. What then of Stalin's aims in Eastern Europe? Here the picture is less focused and harder to get at but can best be seen in the execution of his various formal and informal directives to the Comintern and the agency that carried on its activities (the Department of International Information) virtually unchanged after the former's sham dissolution in May 1943. The object of the policy was "control." This was to be achieved not through revolution or coercive dictation but through support for the small communist parties that were to form broad coalitions with other left-wing parties and groups in a "national front" strategy reminiscent of the pre-war "popular front" approach. These pro-Soviet coalitions would, it was hoped, gain the goodwill of the people, even win free elections and guide their countries to socialism under the watchful but benevolent eye of the Soviet hegemon.

When notions of this kind were put forward in the mid-1940s by sympathizers with the Soviet Union in order to scold an allegedly impetuous Truman administration bent on confrontation, and again by later revisionists during the Vietnam era, they were widely greeted as fanciful. Today we can see that what some of these observers saw as an essentially moral commitment was actually a shrewd political strategy. During the period 1939–41, in alliance with Hitler, the Soviets had imposed themselves on eastern Poland and the incorporated Baltic states with a coercive brutality of executions and mass deportations. Now, in alliance with Britain and the United States, Stalin was apparently inclined to try a more liberal line. He appears to have been confirmed in this by the reinforcing assumption that in the wake of the destructive German occupation there was a long-suppressed desire in Eastern Europe for egalitarian, left-wing solutions (above all land reform) providing they were introduced with some sensitivity and sophistication. He therefore designed an initial, noncoercive approach even as the ultimate goal of socialism and some degree of overarching Soviet control was clearly affirmed. The new, less abrasive approach can be traced, as the historian Eduard Mark has shown, to Stalin's directive to Georgi Dimitrov, the head of the Comintern, on

---

[53] Filitov, "Problems of Postwar," pp. 10–12; Eden to Clark Kerr, Aug 12, 1942, F.O. 954/24.

June 22, 1941 – that is long before any likely alliance with Britain or the United States may have counseled an ingratiating gesture – instructing him to stress the general threat of fascism to all people rather than the prospect of socialist revolution. This was doubtless a tactical move made under severe stress. But Dimitrov elaborated the policy, calling for movements of national liberation that would include intellectuals, the petite bourgeoisie, and peasants as well as workers. It was this kind of thinking that issued logically in a "national front" strategy for the postwar.[54]

This strategy emerged more clearly in mid-1943 as the Soviet Union grasped the opportunities successively opened up in Polish affairs by the Katyn crisis, by the Red Army's apparently decisive victory at Kursk-Orel, and by Benes's sudden determination to place postwar Czechoslovakia's destiny in the Kremlin's hands. We see it first in Dimitrov's angry response to the radical proclamations issued by the tiny Polish communist group. You should focus, he instructed them, on "a democratic and not a Soviet order." Reproofs of this kind continued through 1944, stressing the importance of "a government supported by the majority of the people."[55]

It was apparently much the same elsewhere in Eastern Europe. The somewhat more amenable Rumanian communists were pressed to form a large, broad-based coalition that they could unostentatiously guide. In Bulgaria too the communists created a broad partisan movement, but in late 1944 they incurred the Kremlin's wrath for the vengeful excesses and political impatience that were said to be upsetting the British and Americans. Hungary turned out to be the real test and eventually became the graveyard of the illusion that communists under Soviet patronage would attract popular support.[56] They were badly defeated in free elections there in late 1945, by which time the international situation was

---

[54] For the Stalin directive, see Institute of General History, Russian Academy of Sciences, *Komintern I Vtoraya Mirovaya Voina*, Vol. 2 (Moscow, 1998), p. 4. For Dmitrov's elaboration, see ibid., pp. 93–95. For the Comintern directive, see ibid., pp. 114–115. See also Mark, "Revolution by Degrees," p. 15. It appears likely, however, though evidence before 1946 is inconclusive, that Dimitrov was, like Stalin, committed throughout at least to the long-term aim of a communized Eastern and Central Europe. See Stalin's reference, in September 1946, to a broad "peoples party" being "a convenient mask for the present period" and looking to a later "maximal program," cited in Ivo Banac, ed., *The Diary of Georgi Dimitrov, 1933–1939* (New Haven, 2003), pp. 413–414.

[55] British code interceptions of Soviet directives to European communist parties are in the Public Record Office, Kew, England, under code name ISCOT and reference "HW." This directive is in HW/61.

[56] See Mark, "Revolution by Degrees," pp. 23–33. Charles Gati, *Hungary and the Soviet Bloc* (Durham, S.C., 1986), pp. 33–37.

changing and the three Great Powers were already at odds. The Hungarian party leader, Matyas Rakosi, later revealed what he notoriously called the "salami tactics" by means of which the communists had from the outset planned a stage-by-stage march to full power. The suggestion that Stalin was carefully calibrating his moves rather than foreclosing an unwanted communization in Eastern Europe is confirmed by his remarks to Hungarian party leaders in late 1944 that they might have to share political power with other parties for ten or fifteen years in order to distract Western attention from the comparatively rapid sovietization of Poland.

Time and again, however, historians have found Stalin and Dimitrov, especially during the crucial 1944–45 period, justifying their reproaches to excitable comrades in Eastern Europe in terms of the need for good relations with the Allies. Thus the Polish communists were warned in July 1944 that their radicalism "would make Poland a bone of contention between the Teheran powers." In September of that year Dimitrov chastised the Bulgarians for "creating many difficulties for us with our Allies." And even as late as August 1945 we see Stalin advising the Bulgarian zealots of the need for good relations with the United States and Britain. "You must never ignore England and America," he told them. "You must have normal relations with them – I am absolutely serious about that. You must not shout too much about your eternal friendship with the USSR."[57]

What this seems to add up to is that in 1943 Stalin was pursuing two general but still independently managed lines of policy: on the one hand, the geopolitical concerns, which included rising concern over the growing scope of American power, looking to limited expansion and the geopolitical collaboration with Britain that lay at the heart of Maisky's report; and, on the other, the effort through Dimitrov to maintain control of the evolving, unprovocative socio-political transformation he desired in the liberated countries. The fuller implications of these political impulses will appear more clearly as we see their interaction and the difficulties this caused for all the principal Allied powers through 1944–45. First, however, it seems desirable, having focused thus far on the principal British and Soviet architects of the evolving European political order, to give the subject a little more density by throwing some light on the neglected exile governments cloistered in London.

---

[57] Mark, "Revolution by Degrees," p. 22; ISCOT, Oct. 28, 1944, HW 17/41; Vasselin Dimitrov, "Revolution Released: Stalin, the Bulgarian Communist Party and the Founding of the Cominform," in Gori and Pons, (eds.), *The Soviet Union and Europe in the Cold War*, p. 280.

THE "OTHER" EUROPEANS

The reader who is used to "high politics" interpretations may reasonably expect that now, having examined the basis of Soviet policy, we will move directly to the great tripartite summit conferences at the end of 1943. But a main purpose here is to present some sense of the neglected wartime views of the Europeans, both of their wartime experience and of their future prospect. I have therefore tried to interweave some reference to a wider political and public sentiment in an effort to bring a little evidential density to the story. We have looked at the broader British outlook. Let us now consider, with similar brevity, the continental Europeans. Here too there has been some neglect, especially among that legion of European scholars who, writing copiously about the foundations of postwar continental solidarity leading eventually to the Treaty of Rome, like to start their investigation in 1945 (or "Year Zero," as it is often called), as if nothing of real significance had occurred before that.

The Europeans washed up in Britain by the cyclonic dislocations of Hitler's war would not have accepted that dismissive view. They had concerns and attitudes that illustrate and to some degree substantiate the Eurocentric, geopolitically oriented theme we are uncovering – for, as the war turned against Germany, they shared the increasingly widespread belief that Europe's future was likely to be decided on the basis of new imperatives dominated by some kind of Anglo-Soviet association. It is true that in continental Europe during the war we find a further wide range of perspectives and nationally oriented outlooks. We also see a variety of claimants to the European heritage, extending from the German-Italian "New Order" through a Roman Catholic conservative strain to the more left-wing thinking found in many of the resistance/partisan groups. It is, however, among the exile governments in London that we may reasonably expect to find the most sensitive register of the Anglo-Soviet conception.

The exile governments in London were far more than an echo chamber or Greek chorus to the Great Powers – though they sometimes appeared in that light. They have often been overlooked in the understandable preoccupation with the Big Three. Yet several of these figures had a significant impact. Their existence reminds us that while Roosevelt had successfully established Washington as the nerve center of the Anglo-American war effort, the British had preserved London as the center of European Allied politics and the heart of the European anti-Nazi coalition, with its growing focus on the Anglo-Soviet nexus. Here the exiled leaders enjoyed varying degrees of influence. Some, like Sikorski and de Gaulle, were influential in London because they represented at least the shadow of substantial European states and because they were energetic and brought tangible assets under British command. Benes was cherished early in the war by the Churchillians as the martyr of Munich, from which disaster they tended to take their moral legitimacy in British politics as the vindicated anti-appeasers, and also because he supposedly directed a sophisticated intelligence network and was believed to be an authority on Soviet policy and attitudes. The Dutch Premier Van Kleffens and the Belgian Foreign Minister Paul-Henri Spaak enjoyed considerable respect. Lesser personalities eked out a wasting existence of speculation, paperwork, and intrigue memorably captured in Anthony Powell's lively, sympathetic portrait of Polish officers in wartime London in his 1968 novel, *The Military Philosophers*. All these Europeans had their own problems: with their home populations, with partisan groups, with each other, and with the British government that maintained them and uneasily monitored their activities, which variously included not just the provision of shipping and fighting personnel but the maintenance of intelligence services and outspoken newspapers.[58]

The exile governments were stranded regimes, vestigial residues of 1930s Europe emerging from a harsh, chronically insecure international arena. Their leaders, now situated in London amid all the bustle of the Anglo-American war effort, were, like the British themselves, increasingly aware of the rising power of the United States and eager to associate themselves with it. Yet they were deeply European in their outlook and skeptical as to the degree of American commitment. Anthony Eden was given a glimpse of this in October 1942 at one of the social evenings he periodically spent with the exile leaders. Sikorski electrified the meeting by announcing that the Germans were killing 10,000 Polish Jews every day. He called for a policy of reprisals. The Greek prime minister asked what he had in mind. Sikorski pointed out that there were many Germans in the United States and urged that they should be treated there as his compatriots were being treated in Poland. No objections were raised to this. Someone then pointed out that the Americans were unlikely to acquiesce as they had recently and without consultation with any allies begun releasing hitherto interned Italians. Eden noted in his account that "this was viewed with great astonishment and some resentment by the allies present." He also remarked upon the anger expressed by those present at

[58] Anthony Powell, *The Military Philosophers* (London, 1968). See also, generally, Terry, *Poland's Place in Europe*; and Francis Kersaudy, *Churchill and De Gaulle* (London, 1981).

current tendencies in American propaganda to emphasize the existence of a "good Germany" behind the bad Nazi front.[59]

Nevertheless, the exile politicians, like Churchill and most British leaders, often cast a hungry look at the United States. There had been a flurry of excitement among the Latvians and some of the Western Europeans at Roosevelt's intervention during the 1942 Anglo-Soviet treaty negotiations. Van Kleffens, in particular, was an advocate of a postwar Anglo-American strategic collaboration that would view the Low Countries as a permanent bridgehead, nominally against a German revival but implicitly as a barrier to Soviet expansion. But hopes invested in American participation in Europe's security after the war were generally short-lived. Visits to the United States were of course eagerly sought, and nearly all the political and royal leaders took advantage of the opportunities presented. These trips tended to follow a familiar pattern – a warm welcome and plentiful good food in captivatingly prosperous Washington; a ready invitation to voice concerns, which invariably drew sympathetic comment and uplifting but vague promises from the charmer in the White House; emotionally heartening encounters with emigrant communities from the old country in the hinterland; a gentle let-down on practical matters from Harry Hopkins or State Department officials before departure; a sudden return to war-ravaged London with warm memories and empty hands; and finally the consoling balm of notes compared with other exiled Europeans about American naivete and transatlantic "provincialism." Sometimes these postmortems were patronizing. The ubiquitous Benes, for instance, after a 1943 trip told Eden that "the attitude of the State Department was developing along the right lines and I thought I had taught them something during my last visit."[60]

It is hardly surprising, then, that nearly all the exile governments (even the Poles, who hoped for some future British protection, and de Gaulle's French administration, which looked suspiciously at Churchill's motivations) took a positive view of the Anglo-Soviet treaty and of the prospect it seemed to offer of a solid postwar security system led by these two powers in some sort of concert. Spaak and Benes – one representing the Western Europeans, the other the anxious Central Europeans – were particularly ardent in the cause.

---

[59] Eden memorandum, October 5, 1942, F.O. 954/4.
[60] Van Kleffens, broadcast to Netherlands, Dec. 28, 1943, in C183, F.O. 371.39325; Eden to Nichols, June 16, 1943, F.O. 954/3.

Spaak pressed the British throughout the war to take a more active leadership role in creating and consolidating a strong Western grouping that would secure the future. He had much support among the exiles, including van Kleffens, who told Eden late in 1943 that he was very anxious to discuss the possibility of an Anglo-Dutch defensive zone after the war. The Scandinavians were also eager to join a British-led Western bloc, as were the much-maligned Spanish and Portuguese rightist dictatorships later in the war as they assessed its likely outcome. Salazar, the Portuguese leader, envisaged "a West European bloc under British leadership including the Peninsula, France, Italy and the Low Countries." Talking about postwar Belgium, Spaak affirmed, as all the exiles ritually did, the importance of friendship with the United States. But this, he stressed, "could never be based on the same community of interests, political, cultural, historical and economic, as was Anglo-Belgian friendship." Belgium, he declared, must look primarily to the United Kingdom.[61]

If Spaak was the most energetic protagonist of what later came to be called a "Western bloc" under British auspices, Benes, once the Katyn crisis had destroyed the Czech-Polish confederation option, became the active, self-described architect of a solution for Central Europe that proclaimed his country's special role as a "bridge" between East and West, a conception that eventually led to his deposition at the hands of Czech communists and the establishment of his country as the western outpost of a Soviet-dominated Eastern bloc. Benes, despite his pre-war reputation as a shrewd politician, thus appears before history as a naïve statesman, one of Stalin's dupes. And here the British records are unkindly corroborative. During 1942–43 he was frequently and flatteringly consulted by Eden and Foreign Office leaders as a kind of oracle on occupied Europe and international politics generally, delivering a remarkable series of dogmatic but wildly errant predictions: that Japan would attack the Soviet Union in the spring of 1943; that the Germans would not defend Italy below the Po River basin or perhaps the Alps; that a Bolshevik-style "bloodbath" in liberated France was "inevitable"; that Stalin was not a dictator but simply the embodiment of a benevolent "group idea."[62]

Often wrong but never in doubt, Benes consistently expressed confidence in Stalin's and Molotov's support as he moved with the certainty

---

[61] Memo by Wilson, Dec. 25, 1943, C181, F.O. 371.39323 (van Kleffens). For Spaak, see WP (44) 181. For Lie broadcast, Jan. 15, 1944, see N379, F.O. 371.43234. Alexander memo (undated), F.O. 371.39030; *El Espanol*, January 1, 1944.

[62] Eden to Nicholls, Jan 21, 1942, March 23, 1942, April 22, 1943, all in F.O. 954/4.

of a sleep walker toward the Czech-Soviet treaty of December 1943, which, once its implications emerged, gave the Soviets the province of Ruthenia and thus a shared border with Czechoslovakia and a valuable entry point into Central Europe. Benes was therefore an influential actor in wartime politics. Well in advance of the Red Army's heavy confirming tread he brought Soviet political power and influence deeply into the heart of the continent. The activities of Spaak and Benes, then, are a corrective to the idea that Churchill and Stalin – or Britain and the Soviet Union, for that matter – were the exclusive progenitors of non-Nazi wartime Europeanism. They reflect the wider ambit of European autonomy and self-consciousness that gives the developing Anglo-Soviet concert a certain political and historical density.

One need only think of de Gaulle, of course, to qualify the notion of a universally favored Anglo-Soviet concert as the only sustainable way forward. The French leader was often critical of the Soviets, hated communism, and was by the end of the war quite eager to join a Western bloc of some kind, provided it was on terms of equality with Britain. His prickly behavior, his confrontational feuding with Churchill over French colonial possessions in Africa and the Levant, as well as their recurring arguments over the degree of deference to be shown to the United States have been widely attributed to a psychological need for self-assertion after the national shame of 1940, and were sympathetically viewed as such by many British leaders. Insofar as Churchill experienced de Gaulle's hostility, this seems to have been a superficial explanation. The defeat of 1940 certainly rankled, but the real hurt seems to have been the verdict of 1763, when Britain, victorious in the Seven Years' War, had stripped France of most of its overseas empire (the African and Near Eastern remnants or replacements of which de Gaulle now suspected Churchill of trying to steal) and had consigned it to a continental and, as it turned out, a revolutionary destiny.[63]

In general, however, it seems clear that behind the slow but steady evolution of the Anglo-Soviet geopolitical framework for postwar Europe (which will be our principal subject in the following chapter) there was a strong measure of political reinforcement from other Europeans. It is true that the Anglo-Soviet nexus was essentially a structural, geopolitical creation, and – however widespread its natural appeal to a deeply shaken continent that was looking for security above all else – it might be argued

---

[63] Anglo-French and Churchill–de Gaulle tensions may be studied in Kersaudy, *Churchill and De Gaulle*, passim.

that there was, despite a growing stream of intellectual, trade unionist, and cultural exchanges between the two during the war, little in the way of a philosophical or cultural bond. Yet we see in the epidemic speeches and declarations emanating from London during the war years a constant invocation of the need for a purified, better Europe.

Moreover, the idea of "Europe" – that is, of a continental solidarity that was self-conscious, autonomous, and inspired by some notion of a common political destiny – was very much alive during the war years. One can identify several variants. However morally repugnant it may be, it would be ahistorical to deny an Axis claim to some kind of European vision. Mussolini's Italy had proclaimed itself during the interwar years to be the bearer of a European *nuova civilita* that was bravely resisting economic, cultural, and political challenges from the United States and the Soviet Union. The loudly professed ideal here was "community," touched up with talk of an integrating politico-economic "corporatism." The reality, of course, was a totalitarian state ruled by a passionate but inefficient, sometimes brutal elite. Nevertheless, publicists like Guiseppe Bottai tried to put the best light on all this as the expression of a European sensibility, and given the ubiquity of fascist regimes in this era it would be idle to deny that these ideas had some appeal. It is not surprising to find the Italians in early 1943 insisting to their more exclusivist and there-fore much less enthusiastic but finally acquiescent German ally upon the need for a "European Charter," essentially a joint statement of war aims focusing on "the mortal danger of the Bolshevization of Europe." This only too obviously self-interested Italo-German campaign late in the war was, needless to say, only very marginally successful. Nevertheless, about 50,000 non-German Europeans volunteered for service in *Wehrmacht*-affiliated units, and many millions more served at one time or another in the armed forces aligned with Hitler.[64]

The British historian M. L. Smith suggests that, given the widespread pre-war distaste for communism, the perception of the failure of liberal-democratic capitalism, the challenge of American cultural domination, and the increasingly desperate desire for "order" and "continuity" – given all these representative themes in pre-1939 European life, the German wartime economic integration and late-blooming emphasis on "unity" and continental autonomy was, at least to some extent, in line with widely

[64] P. J. Morgan, "The Italian Fascist New Order in Europe," in M. L. Smith and Peter M. R. Stirk (eds.), *Making the New Europe: European Unity and the Second World War* (London and New York, 1990), pp. 30, 34–36, 39.

perceived concerns. Smith also believes, rather more controversially, that the German assertion of European leadership stimulated some new thinking about a continent-wide future – not, to be sure, with the British and Soviets, who treated all Nazi pretensions to European leadership with complete contempt, but among Resistance elements in the various occupied countries. There we do find, in addition to vigorous communist assertions of their collectivist, egalitarian model, a variety of more moderate left-wing alternative bases for the construction of a new Europe. In occupied Western Europe, notably in France and the Low Countries, this took the prevalent form of concerns for justice and human rights; in Eastern Europe, the emphasis was more typically upon national independence as the precondition of a better society.[65]

The gathering collapse of Nazi Germany exposed another strain of wartime European thinking – that associated with the Catholic Church. In recent years a powerful critique of the Vatican and the church's conduct has emerged, asserting various levels of complicity with or appeasement of the Axis. But this appears to involve mainly leading elites at an earlier stage of the war. The historian Michael Burgess finds evidence that the Nazis had by 1943 alienated both the Vatican leadership and general Catholic opinion as well as other Christian sentiment by their anticlerical approach and violent excesses. Another student of this issue, J. D. Wilkinson, stresses "the essentially Christian inspiration" that drove German Resistance impulses. Much the same was true in Italy, where a commitment to democracy inspired the formation of Democrazia Christiana in 1943 and then, just as the danger of a Soviet/communist takeover of Europe began to many to seem acute, the drift of at least a significant part of Catholic opinion toward liberal democracy rather than toward the now discredited authoritarian alternative. A significant number of European leaders in the early postwar years – de Gasperi in Italy, Konrad Adenauer in Germany, Robert Schuman in France – came out of this Catholic tradition, which did much to fill the conservative/rightist political vacuum left by the Nazi/fascist defeat.

Another significant stream of wartime thinking about European unity and autonomy can be traced back to the interest in a federalized continent in the years after World War I, when visionaries like Aristide Briand and Count Coudenove-Kalergi pressed the cause. From 1939 on, British thinkers (variously self-styled idealists and realists) like Lord Lothian,

---

[65] M. L. Smith, "The Anti-Bolshevik Crusade and Europe," in ibid., pp. 46–65.

Sir William Beveridge, and E. H. Carr contributed to what the historian Peter Wilson has called "The New Europe Debate in Wartime Britain." The connection here with the Anglo-Soviet political alignment we are following was tenuous, though Carr was an influential supporter. It was similarly thin in Italy, where the antifascist Altiero Spinelli and his comrades produced in 1941 the Ventotene Manifesto calling for a democratic, supra-national European state. Yet these activities, and even the incubatory thinking of exiles like Jean Monnet, lend some support to our broad theme – the persistence of European political and intellectual vitality. And these promoters were variously aware that London and Moscow were working together in some way and were the necessary magnetic poles for the future, and that, as Spinelli himself noted, only Britain and the Soviet Union now remained as viable, strong nation-states.[66]

It is tempting, then, to suggest by way of summary that under the sheltering promise of the evolving Anglo-Soviet concert a congeries of more or less wholesome integrationist impulses was developing in Europe as some counter to the Nazi blight. But that is perhaps to overstate the coherence of what was really a much more informal, largely uncoordinated drift of fragmented action and only slowly coalescing attitudes that would, however, have significant postwar outcomes. During the war many of these visions came to grief – the fascist ones because they lacked broad moral sanction and were steadily discredited by events; some of the more visionary, better-life ones because they lacked any practical connection to power. At this point, though, only the geopolitical variant – the Anglo-Soviet concert – seemed, in its developing habit of collaboration, its supposed commitment to security, and even for some its vague promise of some kind of convergence between Soviet collectivism and British liberal pragmatism, to offer at least a framework within which more visionary or at least ameliorative impulses might flourish.

The Anglo-Soviet association would go on, as will be seen, to consolidate and crystallize through the dramatic events of 1944. London and Moscow, the two poles of attraction for millions of Europeans caught in the intensifying violence of the war's final stages, would continue to develop, sometimes haltingly and in sudden lurches rather than through steady evolution, their partnership. But this is to look ahead prematurely. For they would first have to take account of the most significant American

---

[66] Michael Burgess, "Political Catholicism, European Unity and the Rise of Christian Democracy," in ibid., p. 142. Christopher Booker and Richard North, *The Great Deception: A Secret History of the European Union* (London, 2003), pp. 29–30.

political intrusion of the war so far, pressed upon them through the new medium of dramatic Big Three summitry.

THE SECOND AMERICAN INTERVENTION: MOSCOW AND TEHERAN

Did the Moscow foreign ministers conference, and the quickly following Teheran summit meeting at the end of 1943, break down the barriers between the European and American political arenas? Thus far I have emphasized a much higher degree of European self-consciousness and solidarity than conventional historiography allows. But now, it must be acknowledged, the "Big Three" conception comes irresistibly to the front of the stage, elaborated for posterity by Churchill and many other historians who have chosen to dramatize the summit meetings and play down the much less vivid continuum of European politics. These tripartite conferences were indeed highly significant. Yet we would do well to remember that by the time Roosevelt finally sat down face to face with Stalin, the war in Europe was well into its fifth year and had but eighteen months to run. Europe's future had seemed to most concerned observers to be in the hands of Europeans. The question here is whether the Moscow and Teheran conferences changed this.

Roosevelt's presence and the course he followed at Teheran certainly had a crucial impact on strategy that in some degree affected the future of Europe and the standing of the three leaders among themselves – strengthening Stalin, weakening Churchill, and creating at last a more substantial Roosevelt-Stalin connection. But it is questionable whether any of this materially altered the underlying persistence of a very traditional, practical European diplomacy. It seems more likely that by virtue of the manifest indifference to Europe's future they showed at these meetings, FDR and his secretary of state, Cordell Hull, actually spurred the already developing Anglo-Soviet collaboration on to the more dynamic, functionally oriented phase we will see emerging more clearly in 1944.

Cordell Hull, an old Progressive with a deep commitment to free trade and a hold on the mind of Congress that kept him in office despite Roosevelt's preference for the advice and company of others, came to the Moscow meeting of foreign ministers eager to put his European colleagues on the path to virtue. In March 1943, it will be recalled, he had presented Eden with the rudiments of a National Declaration of Independence, which seemed to oblige the British to grant self-determination to their various dependencies. Eden had recoiled in horror. Now it was Molotov's turn to take a pledge. The proffered regenerative instrument Hull brought to Moscow was again a declaration, this one binding the powers to accept not only the notion of a postwar international organization, which they were willing to do, but also an undertaking, somewhat in the now venerable Kellogg-Briand spirit, not to use their armed forces without consultation with others. Molotov refused the latter commitment point blank, advising Hull that it was bound to interfere with defense arrangements between the great powers and other states. He more than made up for this rebuff, however, by accepting the American's Four Power Declaration embodying the idea of an institutional successor to the League of Nations and, showing an uncharacteristic eagerness to please, even suggested the establishment of a tripartite commission to draw up plans for it. But this helpful gesture induced a kind of panic in the secretary of state. Soviet participation in the drafting of the wholesome Wilsonian formulas he had in contemplation was the last thing Hull wanted. Such a commission, he explained, would "stir up agitation" in the United States. The reader will recall that in May 1942 Molotov had similarly bristled at and quickly rejected Roosevelt's offer to mediate Soviet problems with Iran and Turkey. In each case the ostensibly well-meaning offer appears to have been received as a visitation from another planet. It would be difficult to invent two more revealing illustrations of the gulf between American and European thinking about the postwar at this juncture, and of the determination of leaders in each country (including Britain) to maintain control and resist the intervention of its allies on these most sensitive issues. On this occasion Hull was clearly intent, and surely this was realistic for an American statesman in 1943, on the struggle at home for the institutional realization of an American ideal, not on the creation of a geopolitical framework for peace in postwar Europe.[67]

Hull's only major European proposal, that envisaging the decentralization of Germany, was not vigorously pursued, in part because a difference between the president's preference for partition and the State

---

[67] For minutes of the Moscow conference between October 20 and 24, 1943, see FRUS, 1943, I (Washington, D.C., 1963), pp. 589–669. For Hull statements, see ibid., pp. 589–590, 592–595, 602–604, 640–642, 656–659, 669. For British records, see "Record of the Proceedings of the Foreign Ministers Conference Held in Moscow from 19th. October to 30th. October, 1943," N6971, F.O. 371.37031. For general treatments, see Dallek, *Roosevelt and American Foreign Policy*, pp. 418–424; Feis, *Churchill-Roosevelt-Stalin*, Chapters 22 and 24; and Harbutt, *Iron Curtain*, pp. 53–54. For a monographic account, see Keith Sainsbury, *The Turning Point: Roosevelt, Stalin, Churchill and Chiang Kai Shek, 1943: The Moscow, Cairo and Teheran Conferences* (Oxford, 1985).

Department's inclination to resist it had produced a kind of stalemate. The British, who put up an institutional plan for the study of the peacemaking with a defeated Germany, and the Soviets, who professed to have no plan at all, were even more cautious. This was not out of indifference. Germany was always potentially the most profound issue in Anglo-Soviet relations. They had up to this point carefully avoided it while they flattered each other's geopolitical traditions and addressed more immediate, peripheral, and solvable issues. The last thing they wanted was a premature self-exposure over Germany. Thus Molotov smoothly sidetracked the secretary, declaring that the Soviet government was "somewhat behind" in studying the problem.[68]

Hull, it seems fair to say, had little sense of "Europe" as it was experienced by its inhabitants, that is, as an intricate system, criss-crossed with interrelated issues. Political nuances, historical sensitivities, emotional proclivities had no discernible place in his particular version of American expeditionary diplomacy, which, as we see it in operation here, drew its strength from moral fervor, rationalism, and a strong linear approach. The combination of American political fastidiousness and straight-arrow thinking led to two very different levels of conference activity: a rarified strata of compliments and expressions of general understanding between the Americans and the Europeans (who were very solicitous of the elderly, dignified Tennessean), and a lower but more substantive level where, in traditional and practical fashion, Eden and Molotov debated and grappled with essentially European issues while Hull sat silently listening, sometimes with ill-concealed impatience.

In their very conventional encounter, Eden and Molotov seemed determined to demonstrate for the listening Americans the inevitability of a postwar Europe characterized by spheres of influence. They tackled a number of contentious issues. Eden predictably raised the "confederations" problem and the embarrassingly imminent Soviet-Czech treaty, as well as the Soviet violation of the delicate "gentlemen's agreement" not to seek small-state clients in Europe that Molotov had accepted earlier. But for all his express or implied reproaches, he accepted the Molotov-Benes fait accompli, softened no doubt by Molotov's pointing out that the treaty called for Polish adherence later (which was not likely to appeal to the exile government in London), and perhaps more so by his promise to participate in the

---

[68] See "Proposal with Regard to the Treatment of Germany," n. d., FRUS, 1943, I, pp. 720–723; "Summary of Proceedings of the 6th Meeting of Tripartite Conference, October 24, 1943," ibid., pp. 631–632.

Foreign Office's pet project – a European Advisory Commission (EAC) to
plan the peacemaking. It was all very European. Hull kept away from these
potentially compromising exchanges. He showed some respect for the
Europeans by accepting the EAC, though he and Roosevelt steadily subverted it by studied indifference through 1944. Eden and Molotov carried
on their European business as best they could. They discussed the possibility of getting Turkey and Sweden into the war. Here too Hull avoided
comment, though he did cable home for instructions. He sat silently during discussions over the appropriate Allied policy toward the Yugoslav
factions and refused Eden's plea for some support in a demonstration of
"keen concern for Poland's future." When Eden brought up the question
of future policy toward Iran, he scotched the initiative by urging reference
to a special committee.[69]

One is constantly struck, reading the transcripts, by the divergent interests and even mutual incomprehension of the participants. At one point
Eden, while the EAC was under discussion, passed a note to Hull: "Behind
this lies a big issue. One Europe or two." One might have expected this to
inspire a question or two from the self-declared mortal enemy of European
spheres of influence, perhaps an urgent corridor discussion, some expression of concern. None came.[70] Hull had not come to Moscow to debate
political arrangements or to have dangerously compromising intimate
discussions. He had very strong views, but they ran in different channels
from those he was now encountering. He did impress the conference with
the importance America attached to postwar economic plans. But he was
not interested in negotiation or indeed in bargaining of any sort, and he
came with no particular instructions from the president. His posture at
the meeting suggests the discomfort of an old-fashioned equity lawyer
stuck with a watching brief at a disreputable political trial in some dusty,
remote capital. This was his only wartime trip abroad. He preferred to
work at home, at arm's length through correspondence, or by lecturing
vulnerable European visitors to the State Department. His principal aim

---

[69] "Record of 2nd. Meeting of Tripartite Conference, October 20, 1943," ibid., pp. 583–
586; "Summary of Proceedings of 5th Meeting of Tripartite Conference, October 23,
1943," ibid., pp. 617–618; "Summary of Proceedings of 6th Meeting of Tripartite
Conference, October 24, 1943," ibid., pp. 624–627. Eden to Foreign Office, October 24,
1943, C12467/525/12, and Cadogan to Churchill, October 25, 1943, C12505/525/12,
both in F.O. 371.34340.

[70] Sainsbury, *Turning Point*, pp. 69–79. For Roosevelt's indifference to the Moscow conference, see Dallek, *Roosevelt and American Foreign Policy*, p. 418. Eden to Foreign Officè,
October 24, 1943, C12467, F.O. 371.34340.

in Moscow was simply to get European signatures on his wholesome declaration looking to a new League of Nations, the character of which, as events soon showed, he intended to define congenially and unilaterally as an instrument of international political and moral transformation when he got home. He achieved this, and then registered another success when Stalin told him informally at a banquet that the Soviet Union would come into the Pacific war once Germany had been defeated. He was now able to tell Congress upon his return to Washington that there would "no longer be need for spheres of influence, for alliances for balance of power, or any other of the special arrangements through which in the unhappy past the nations strove to safeguard their security or to promote their interests."[71]

Hull's conference minimalism, contrasting with his utopian overselling of the supposed accomplishment, must have left the Soviet leaders, who had wanted the foreign ministers conference simply as a means of divining Anglo-American intentions before the principal leaders met, rather puzzled. Roosevelt, who had only reluctantly approved Hull's mission (he would have preferred to send the more sophisticated Welles, who had been forced by scandal to resign just before the meeting), immediately showed a very different style at the Teheran meeting a few weeks later, demonstrating to Stalin in numerous ways that his diplomatic stock-in-trade was not watchful suspicion or abstract rationality but personal intimacy (he accepted Stalin's invitation to lodge in the Soviet embassy) and a desire to be helpful.[72]

On the surface, at least, there was some continuity. Like Hull, FDR pressed two particular causes: Allied agreement to a postwar United Nations, and Soviet participation in the Pacific war. Here Hull had apparently blazed a trail effectively, but Roosevelt, with a deeper level of awareness, seems to have understood (what was undoubtedly correct) that the encouraging Soviet references at the earlier meeting were more in the nature of an "invitation to treat" than the acceptance of a solid contractual commitment. He wanted, in any event, to consolidate the achievement. Many historians have also emphasized his fundamental desire to keep the Soviets fighting and also to form some sort of personal bond with

---

[71] Ibid., p. 117. Hull, *Memoirs*, II, pp. 1314–1315. John Lewis Gaddis, *The United States and the Origins of the Cold War* (New York and London, 1972), p. 22. For U.S. press comment on Hull's address, see *New York Times*, Nov. 20, 1943, and *Washington Post*, Nov. 4, 1943.

[72] The documentary record of the Teheran conference is in FRUS, *Cairo and Teheran, 1943* (Washington, D.C., 1971). For British records, see "Records of the Anglo-American-Russian Conversations in Teheran and of the Anglo-American-Turkish Conversations in Cairo," January 7, 1944, C181, F.O. 371.39323.

Stalin, with whom, at a brief private introductory meeting, Roosevelt set a tone by criticizing the British and French and signaling his hopes for a Soviet reaffirmation of willingness to enter the war with Japan. Stalin was not drawn, clearly waiting for more specific assurances.[73]

These came at the immediately following plenary session. The president opened by describing for Stalin the various Mediterranean options he and Churchill had been considering for 1944 and alarmed his military advisers with a show of interest in the Adriatic operation then favored by the British. The problem, he stressed, rather unnecessarily, was that by this move they might delay Overlord, which he would regret. He asked Stalin for his views. Stalin began with the pleasing announcement that the Soviet Union would indeed enter the war against Japan once Germany was beaten. His views on Overlord now emerged with, to Churchill at least, disconcerting clarity and emphasis. The important thing, the Soviet leader stressed, was to attack Germany through northern France with a supporting operation near Marseilles. He saw no value in any Adriatic activity or in the various wasting, diversionary operations through Turkey and the Balkans so much cherished by Churchill. As for the Italian front, the center of British strategic activity, it should be closed down as soon as possible.

Churchill immediately debated the wisdom of this striking conception, carefully avoiding the unmistakable geopolitical implications. He stressed the potential benefits of a campaign that would bring Turkey into the war. But Stalin was unmoved. Then, to Churchill's astonishment and consternation, Roosevelt immediately stated his complete agreement with Stalin's strategic formulation. He declared himself adamantly against any delay in Overlord, "which might be necessary if any operation in the Eastern Mediterranean were contemplated," and called for an immediate staff plan for the supporting operation in southern France that Stalin had suggested, an operation that would inevitably draw its resources from the British-dominated Italian theater that Stalin wanted closed down and that had never been seriously considered thus far by Anglo-American planners, who had not even bothered to bring to the conference the very provisional formulations that had been drawn up on the subject. Thus the whole laboriously plotted strategic approach of the Western allies was now subjected to sudden changes – in effect confining the Anglo-American war effort to the west – which, as it turned out, would indeed

---

[73] Bohlen minutes, Roosevelt-Stalin meeting, November 28, 1943, FRUS, *Cairo and Teheran*, pp. 482–486.

take the form Stalin desired despite passionate and continuing British protest through most of 1944.[74]

Here was a series of shocks for Churchill, setbacks that cannot be assessed simply in diplomatic or geopolitical terms as a blow to British interests. Once again the British were caught unprepared. Eden had been taken by surprise in December 1941 by Stalin's elaborate plans for post-war Europe. Now Churchill was taken aback by what he considered to be Roosevelt's strategic volte-face. In fact, there had been ample prior warning in each case. Churchill had certainly been thinking about the future. He had told an associate on the way to Teheran that "the real problem now is Russia. I can't get the Americans to see it." Before Teheran he appears to have believed that Stalin, for his own reasons, was genuinely interested in securing Allied military help in the eastern Mediterranean region. Now it seemed clear that Stalin was after all thinking in terms of future Soviet expansionism at the expense of long-term and traditional British interests in that sphere.

More personally, Churchill's dismay was intensified by a sense of loss and even betrayal at the hands of the president. His two years of remarkable domination of Anglo-American strategy was now clearly over. He had been lulled into complacency by the warm reception he had received from the Americans in a pre-Teheran Anglo-American meeting at Quebec only a few weeks earlier. There he thought he had secured Roosevelt's support for the idea of an eastern strategy, despite the known hostility of the American Joint Chiefs of Staff. Though Hopkins had warned the British beforehand that FDR was now determined to line up with Stalin on the second-front issue, the prime minister had come to Teheran expecting a solid Anglo-American front. He had exaggerated his hold on the president. Moreover, Roosevelt seemed now to have gone out of his way to humiliate him personally. It was all very disillusioning. His doctor, Lord Moran, observing Churchill's conference depression, noted in his diary, "Now he sees he cannot rely on the President's support. What matters more he realizes that the Russians see it too. ... The P.M. is appalled by his own impotence." To any politician all this would have been a heavy blow. To a statesman of Churchill's temperament – imaginative, impressionable, and acutely sensitive to power – the exposure must have been almost insupportable.[75]

---

[74] Bohlen minutes, first plenary meeting, November 28, 1943, ibid., pp. 487–497.
[75] Moran, *Churchill*, p. 151; Churchill note, April 1943, PREM 4.30/3; Wheeler-Bennet and Nicholls, *Semblance of Peace*, pp. 134–142, 290.

It is tempting, especially with Cold War hindsight, to see Roosevelt's approach as simply an expression of his limitations as an international statesman. But then it is always easy to find evidence of Roosevelt's superficiality. And we can see plausible explanations that put his performance in a clearer light. The first proceeds from political logic and assumes a degree of rational calculation. Facing a difficult reelection campaign, burdened with a truly global war, and deeply concerned to secure optimum conditions for the hazardous invasion of France, FDR was willing, at least in the short term, to subordinate Western Europe's political interests (as Churchill and other Europeans must have seen them) to the primary need to keep Stalin in the war at all costs. He was also eager to lay the ground, politically and emotionally, for future United States–Soviet collaboration. To this end, FDR at Teheran appears to have worked along two distinct lines. One was to deliver a solid promise that the long-delayed second front would take place in the spring of 1944. He was even willing to make this more credible by accepting Stalin's politico-strategic conception of the operation itself. The other line was to offer geopolitical reassurances to Stalin by exhibiting American contempt for and indifference to the fate of virtually all the European states to the west of the Soviet Union. Roosevelt consequently labored to create in Stalin's mind a lively expectation of American support for Soviet ambitions when it was all over. To this end he was ready, in this single personal opportunity with Stalin, to act on Casablanca principles (where "unconditional surrender" had been intended to serve the same cause of reassurance earlier in 1943) and say almost anything to please his host.[76]

Here then is a calculated motive to set alongside the notion that the president's disparaging remarks about the Europeans at Teheran were simply an expression of what the historian John Harper has characterized as a visceral hostility. Both strains seem to have been in play. Roosevelt made it very plain to everyone at the conference that he wanted to dismember Germany, cheerfully agreeing, despite Churchill's consternation, to Stalin's proposal to execute 50,000 leading Nazis at the end of the war. He looked to the break-up of the French empire and condemned the French elite. He had no kind words for the Poles or other European allies. And he blithely proposed the opening of the Kiel Canal and the Dardanelles to international (and especially Soviet) traffic, rational proposals in the abstract but intensely controversial in Europe. When to this we add his lack of respect

---

[76] See, for a critical interpretation, Voytech Mastny, *Russia's Road to the Cold War* (New York, 1979), pp. 122–133; and for a more positive account, Dallek, *Roosevelt and American Foreign Policy*, pp. 430–441.

for a Europe that, in its imperial manifestations, had seemingly closed off much of the world's productive resources (thus helping to prolong the Depression) and had twice in his lifetime grievously disrupted the world's and America's peace, we might well conclude with a degree of sympathetic understanding that FDR was, in his attitudes if not in his social background, a representative American of his time.[77]

The implications of all this, however, were disturbing to the British delegation. Roosevelt had now committed them to a second front in May 1944 and allowed Stalin to shape its character in a way that seemed likely to leave not just Eastern but much of Central and southern Europe and perhaps the eastern Mediterranean openly exposed to Soviet domination. No compensating balance of power was contemplated for Western Europe. In his private discussions with Stalin, Roosevelt made critical and dismissive references to British policy. In the plenary sessions he expressed disdain for France and an intention to strip the French of several of their colonies and generally reduce the country to second-class status. Germany was to be broken and broken up. The well-known summary of the president's scenario by Charles Bohlen, the State Department's expert on Soviet affairs, has never been bettered:

Germany is to be broken up and kept broken up. The states of eastern, southeastern and central Europe will not be permitted to group themselves into any federations or associations. France is to be stripped of her colonies and strategic bases beyond her borders and will not be permitted to maintain any appreciable military establishment. Poland and Italy will remain approximately their present territorial size, but it is doubtful if either will be permitted to maintain any appreciable armed force. The result would be that the Soviet Union would be the only important military and political force on the continent of Europe. The rest of Europe would be reduced to military and political impotence.[78]

This does, especially in hindsight, seem irresponsible. Certainly Churchill, like Bohlen, thought so. And indeed, insofar as the Soviet Union was concerned, it must have seemed dangerously invitational. It is hard to imagine a Woodrow Wilson, for instance, allowing himself to ventilate on profound subjects in this fashion at a major conference. One is bound to think that, whether or not it can fairly be said that Roosevelt devoted himself at Yalta to setting the table for Stalin (a question we will shortly come to), he was certainly going some way toward doing that at Teheran.

---

[77] For Roosevelt's remarks and his visceral dislike of Europe in general and of Germany in particular, see Harper, *American Visions of Europe*, pp. 7–131.

[78] Bohlen memorandum, December 15, 1943, FRUS, *Cairo and Teheran*, p. 846.

What then of Eastern Europe and the old problem of the Soviet Union's 1941 frontiers? Here too Roosevelt came to Teheran determined to give satisfaction, though here he had a price. It is often pointed out, correctly, that much of the president's prejudicial talk about Europe was casual. But he conducted a more substantial negotiation on this crucial topic in two private meetings with Stalin. In the first, Roosevelt broached the subject, central for him, of a postwar peacekeeping organization, asserting the need for a universalistic conception and scope for small-power participation. Stalin, in response, declared a strong preference for a purely regional European Council, thus tacitly inviting the logical American inducement. It came at their second encounter. FDR now told the Soviet leader that he agreed to the Polish eastern frontier being moved to the west, with compensation at German expense. But he could not say this publicly (nor did he tell Churchill) because of the domestic political problem created in an election year by the existence of numerous Americans of Polish descent. Stalin, no sluggard when it came to cynical politics, expressed complete understanding. The president then turned to the Baltic states, whose fate had inspired some American diplomatic vexation some eighteen months earlier. In this case also, he pointed out, there were many interested American voters. But FDR acknowledged the historical ties between these states and Russia and assured Stalin genially that he did not intend to go to war over the issue. It would be helpful, though, if Stalin could arrange for some sort of expression of the popular will. Perhaps a referendum? This led Stalin to try and explain the political problem. But he was cut short by Roosevelt, who pointed out that "the public neither knew nor understood." To this Stalin made a revealing response. "They should be informed and some propaganda work should be done." Roosevelt then, having made his basic geopolitical concession, adroitly brought the conversation back to his own quid pro quo, the prospective United Nations. Stalin immediately grasped the point and, according to the American record, "said that after thinking over the question of the world organization as outlined by the President, he had come to agree with the President that it should be world-wide and not regional."[79]

These exchanges, which in retrospect seem to have been a defining moment in United States–Soviet (or at least Roosevelt-Stalin) relations, call for some brief comment. For what we see here, I believe, are the foundational

---

[79] Bohlen minutes, Roosevelt-Stalin meeting, November 29, 1943, ibid., pp. 529–533; and Roosevelt-Stalin meeting, December 1, 1943, ibid., pp. 594–596. See also, for comment, Charles Bohlen, *Witness to History 1929–1969* (New York, 1973), pp. 151–153.

rudiments of a "bargain," involving some as yet only partially defined but unmistakable American support for Stalin's aspirations in Eastern Europe in return for the Soviet promise to participate in an as yet only partially focused but potentially influential postwar United Nations. We will see this bargain – henceforth an enduring element in United States–Soviet relations but almost completely overlooked in the historiography of American diplomacy, perhaps because Roosevelt never acknowledged it and always claimed to be operating on equitable and rational principles – in spasmodic operation through 1944 and into 1945. It is a factor of primary importance in United States–Soviet relations, particularly in its repeated invocation by Stalin, even after Roosevelt's death in early 1945.

The Roosevelt-Stalin understanding was of course confidential, though not casual. One wonders if it was recorded on a Soviet tape. But there can be little doubt that both men realized that everything would in the last analysis depend on events and the future tenor of their relations. Moreover, so far as the delicate Eastern European issue was concerned, each man was quick to make a crucial qualifying point. For when Roosevelt asked Stalin to allow some future expressions of public opinion in the Baltic states and Poland, as well as freedom to emigrate, he was surely identifying the essential condition for postwar collaboration between their two states – a Soviet sphere in Eastern Europe might be acceptable, but it must be one governed with a light hand that would not provoke confrontation. Similarly, when Stalin explained his position and asked Roosevelt to "inform" the American people, he was pointing to what he saw as the essential educative function that must be the Roosevelt administration's contribution to this supposedly desirable process. In the light of subsequent history, there is a considerable poignancy in this exchange. For if the Soviets had indeed behaved more generously and tolerantly in Eastern Europe (as Maisky's report recommended and the ever-cautious Stalin himself seems to have wanted at this stage), and if the American people had indeed been led by the Roosevelt government to understand, while the war was still on, something more of the European historical and political context and the Soviet obsession with security and postwar justice, then – it might be argued – the postwar gap in understanding might have been narrowed and the Cold War averted. But that, of course, is speculation. For the moment the point is that FDR and Stalin had, in this one moment of illumination, come close to some understanding of the predicament that in a sense they shared. Would they take each other's advice in the crucial year ahead?

One further point should be made about this "tacit" understanding at Teheran. It was not intended to bring the United States into European affairs, and it did not envision any executive role for the United States in Eastern Europe, something Stalin did not want and certainly would not have tolerated. As in early 1942, so now, what he wanted was American "acquiescence." Nor did this brief meeting of minds look to any Soviet influence in American planning, as Hull's abrupt refusal of Soviet help with the United Nations project makes clear. Quite the contrary. The "bargain" was intended to reconcile and reinforce, not to remove, the basic distinction we have been tracing between an autonomous European political arena (where Stalin could rely for practical cooperation upon his preferred association with Britain) and the very different American polity, with its introspective and effusively moralistic political culture.

Stalin then, at least on the face of things, had much to be pleased about so far as Roosevelt's various initiatives were concerned. Domination in continental Europe now lay before him if he could defeat Germany. Yet he showed little euphoria. Doubtless he was shrewd enough to wonder why Roosevelt's private commitments had to be kept from the public and to see this as some real limitation on the president's power. And as the historian Keith Sainsbury has aptly commented, "Stalin's whole life and character – and beliefs – would have predisposed him to suspicion of someone who purported to be as frank and unreserved as Roosevelt."[80] His most visible response is what one might expect from a leader with paranoic tendencies. It was to test the depth of Roosevelt's sincerity and ostentatious Anglophobia by attacking Churchill. To some extent this may also be taken as a vengeful response to the now open confirmation from the Americans that the British had always been the inhibiting element on the second-front issue. But Stalin's anger took a significantly European geopolitical form. He persistently needled Churchill, at dinner on November 29, on the subject of Germany, suggesting that the prime minister had a secret liking for the Germans and wanted a "soft" peace. Implying that Churchill saw German power as an alternative to the now rapidly receding vision of Anglo-American postwar cooperation in Europe, Stalin declared, "We Russians are not blind." He then went on to make his celebrated proposal for the liquidation of the whole German general staff.[81]

Churchill, on the wrong foot throughout a conference dominated by Roosevelt and Stalin, nevertheless responded robustly. He said angrily

---

[80] Sainsbury, *Turning Point*, p. 300.
[81] Bohlen minutes, tripartite dinner meeting, November 29, 1943, FRUS, *Cairo and Teheran*, pp. 552–554.

that he would never agree to cold-blooded murder or "barbarous acts," and when this inspired some crude joshing he left the room in disgust, returning only after peacemaking persuasion from Stalin and Molotov. Toward the end of the conference he assumed the defense of traditional Europe and questioned the radical dismemberment of Germany, point-edly asking Stalin whether he "contemplated a Europe composed of little states, disjoined, separate and weak." But it would be wrong to charac-terize Churchill's general response to these disturbing developments as morally vigorous. It is clear that he felt deeply humiliated by Roosevelt's betrayals and alarmed by his political recklessness. Thanks to the presi-dent, his personal and political standing with Stalin was now, he appears to have concluded, much diminished. Acutely conscious of this, and prob-ably anxious to restore himself in Stalin's eyes, he seized upon a subject he knew to be a prime Soviet interest – the future of Poland. Thus, after dinner on November 28, just a few hours after the embarrassing strategic denouement and in the absence of FDR, who had retired for the night, he sat down with Stalin and launched the Polish issue on a new and danger-ous course by declaring that the Great Powers should reach an agreement among themselves and impose it on the Poles. Using three matchsticks, he illustrated his plan to move the Polish state bodily to the west. The Soviets would advance to the so-called Curzon Line; the Poles would correspond-ingly advance west at German expense.[82]

This appears to have been done on impulse, like much else at Teheran and certainly like Roosevelt's dramatic strategic commitment to a May 1944 landing in France, which he had made that afternoon without dis-cussion or even notice to Churchill. Throughout 1943, it should be re-membered here, Churchill had repeatedly declared his desire to postpone territorial issues until the end of the war. Further, Churchill and Eden had reassured the Poles before departing from London that their interests would not be compromised. Indeed, they were already bound by treaty not to enter into unauthorized negotiations with the Soviets over Polish issues. Moreover, Stalin was not at this point seeking any decision on the Curzon Line. Finally, the notion of British acceptance of the Curzon Line with compensation for Poland in the west was only one side of preexisting British policy. The other side, which Churchill completely failed to present, was the obvious quid pro quo – not simply the territorial compensation

---

[82] Gilbert, *Churchill*, VII, pp. 570–593; minutes of Churchill-Stalin conversation, November 28, 1943, in "Records of Anglo-American-Russian Conversations," January 7, 1944, WP (44), 8.

in the west, which should surely have been a given, but something in the way of a solid Soviet guarantee of Polish postwar independence. Instead, not only by suggesting a solution that he knew would be unacceptable to the London Poles (and indeed to any Poles who were not Soviet stooges), but also by other retreats and damaging comments about the Polish character, Churchill on this occasion gave a powerful impression to Stalin of his eagerness to satisfy Soviet desires and of the British government's fundamental indifference to Poland's future. At one point later in the conference, he asked Stalin to allow the Polish-dominated city of Lvov, which lay behind the Soviet side of the Curzon Line, to remain within postwar Poland. Stalin refused. Churchill immediately responded that this "would not break my heart." He closed the "discussion," to which the gift-laden Stalin made virtually no positive contribution, with an unsolicited promise to present the proposed territorial settlement to the London Poles as a reasonable solution and then, if the Poles rejected the proposal, to wash his hands of it. They were, he added gratuitously of Britain's most enduring European wartime ally, "the sort of people who would never be satisfied anyway."[83]

Thus were the Poles made to pay the price for this great man's deep humiliation a few hours before. For what else can one conclude but that by responding in this way so soon after his put-down by Roosevelt at the plenary session, Churchill was seeking a compensating bond with Stalin at Poland's expense. This notion may seem fanciful to those who believe the notion that democratic statesmen are concerned only with "honorable" solutions and assume that these summit meetings were preoccupied with the search for justice and equity. In fact, at the wartime summit conferences the personal dynamics were crucial, both at Teheran and, as we will see, at Yalta. Churchill was an intelligent statesman, but he was also a politician with an unusually acute sensitivity to power. The notion that his Polish initiative may have been inspired less by a desire to settle a serious problem than by an emotional need to restore himself to the decision-making center of Big Three deliberations gets some reinforcement from a similar pattern of events later in the conference, this time at the expense of Turkey. It came after the dinner exchange on November 29, when Stalin had again attacked Churchill, accusing him of a soft attitude toward the Germans. At their next meeting, at lunch the following day, Churchill came back with another unsolicited offer, this time to revise the Montreux Convention

---

[83] Minutes of meeting, December 1, 1943, ibid. For a more truncated account, see Bohlen minutes, plenary meeting of December 1, 1943, FRUS, *Cairo and Teheran*, pp. 596–604.

governing passage through the Dardanelles in ways favoring the Soviet Union. It seems not to have mattered at all that Turkey, like the London Poles, had earlier received assurances from the British that there would be no potentially prejudicial discussion of their difficulties with the Soviets.[84]

Thus Churchill energetically scrambled back to the summit at the expense of two allies – Poland and Turkey – for whom Britain had accepted fiduciary and treaty obligations. This, as will appear, heralded a burst of sustained British appeasement of its Soviet partner in early 1944 that seems to have had as one of its causes, at least, this sudden sense of demotion and dispossession within the tight circle of the three Great Powers at Teheran. As Churchill himself acknowledged in homely terms later, the diminutive British donkey that was "the only one who knew the way home" now found itself somewhat encumbered between the Russian bear and the American buffalo. The way home for Churchill henceforth was to play the part not only of "the President's lieutenant," as he sometimes described (without apparent embarrassment) his relation to the United States, but also to make himself Stalin's accommodating partner in the postwar shaping of Europe.

Ironically, in taking this line, so destructive to any surviving Polish hopes, which can only have been based on the possibility of strong British or possibly American diplomatic support, Churchill was in fact exaggerating his value in Stalin's eyes. For the prime minister knew nothing of the compromising undertakings already secretly given to Stalin by Roosevelt. Moreover, Stalin was not, finally, dependent on either partner. The Red Army was already clearing the way efficiently. And then, waiting to grease the wheels, there was the ubiquitous figure of Benes. Stalin had scarcely returned to Moscow before the Soviets were rolling out the red carpet for the self-appointed Czech facilitator of Soviet expansion into Central Europe. The Czech-Soviet treaty, carefully nursed along by Moscow, was now complete. It left open, as promised, the subsequent joinder of a postwar Poland that in practice was likely to join only if it had a communist government. It seemed to Western observers to open the possibility that the Ruthenian Ukraine, formerly part of Czechoslovakia, would later be transferred to the Soviet Union (as in fact soon occurred), giving the two treaty states a common frontier. Benes thought this new ability to call on effective Russian support would prevent any future Munichs. Time would show that he was fighting the last war (or pre-war) and simply exchanging one

[84] Bohlen minutes, Roosevelt-Churchill-Stalin luncheon meeting, November 30, 1943, ibid., pp. 565–568.

tyrant for another. More to the point, the Soviets now had their opening wedge into Central Europe. Poland, and indeed the rest of Eastern Europe, were already outflanked.

Yet all this was rather deceptive. Despite the ingratiating Anglo-American performance at Teheran, Stalin, at the end of 1943, still had far to go. The Germans remained at the end of 1943 a formidable enemy, with more than 200 divisions still in the field in the east. Stalin could not be sure the Allies would follow through on Overlord. And if they did, who could say how far east they might go? Perhaps they would make a deal with Hitler, who could be relied upon to raise the specter of continent-wide communism as the Red Army moved west, or with a post-Hitler German government after a military coup. Meanwhile, there would be vexing problems in the liberated countries, notably in Poland but also in Hungary and throughout the Balkans, a region already pulsing with dangerously Trotskyite expectancies.

Roosevelt's cometlike appearance in this oriental capital offered a range of encouragements. Moreover, he appears to have made a genuinely favorable impression upon Stalin, who preferred him personally to a Churchill he seems never to have trusted.[85] But FDR was quickly gone, not to reappear personally until February 1945. He was preoccupied with his reelection campaign and with other important distractions, including Overlord and the Pacific War. His major diplomatic initiative in 1944 was the Dumbarton Oaks conference held in August–September to set the stage for a prospective United Nations whose likely impact on European politics remained for the moment obscure. It is not very surprising, then, to find Stalin in the aftermath of Teheran turning again to Churchill as his primary partner, and to the only briefly shelved Anglo-Soviet framework for postwar Europe.

[85] See, for instance, Simon Sebag Montefiore, *Stalin: The Court of the Red Tsar* (London, 2003), p. 475.

4

The Making of the Moscow Order

The Teheran summit reminds us that Allied diplomacy always worked on two levels. On one plane we see the three leaders working with and watching each other, each seemingly the source and embodiment of national power. This is the "Big Three" approach, the one that we have been schooled to view as decisive in virtually all that mattered. On another, much less obvious level one can observe the persistent thrust of national interests, always subject to variations in homage to power, tempered sometimes by ideological impulses, but essentially rooted in history and always the natural element of the foreign policy establishment in each state. This is the deeper, more enduring aspect of diplomacy where one looks to find logic and patterns rather than emotion and improvisation. It governed official thinking about Europe's future before Teheran. It quickly reasserted itself after "the Great Men" (as Eden once semiderisively called them) had gone home, ushering in, amid a year of extraordinary military drama, a period of spasmodic but increasingly purposeful Anglo-Soviet collaboration as the two European allies worked their way toward a mutually satisfactory postwar order.[1]

What we will see in the fifteen months between Teheran and Yalta, so far as Europe's future is concerned, is a process of growing and eventually definitional Anglo-Soviet understanding that developed in three distinct parts. First, at the beginning of 1944, Churchill and Stalin engaged unsuccessfully in an apparent effort to address the Polish issue, a problem then complicated by the suddenly more compelling

[1] Eden to Churchill, January 5, 1945, F.O. 954/22.

logic of an Anglo-Soviet geopolitical deal involving the Balkans and the Mediterranean. In the second phase, between August and October, there was a reassertion of Big Three diplomacy in three related conferences. These meetings, more politically substantive than the Moscow and Teheran conferences, brought the United States into the postwar political scenario for Europe, but still in a distinctively tentative and detached way that carefully maintained the transatlantic separation we have been following. They culminated, therefore, not in some harmonious tripartite consensus but in what may be called the "Moscow Order," after the location of the Anglo-Soviet conference in October that in large measure fulfilled the promise of the 1942 treaty negotiations and defined the concert of power – separating Eastern-Central Europe and a distinct Western European–Mediterranean arena – the two ringmasters had long envisioned for the postwar. In the third phase, the subject of the following chapter, we will see how this European concert was consolidated during the three and a half months leading up to the Yalta conference in February 1945.

CLEARING THE WAY

The drama and promise of the Teheran summit lingered in the minds of all the Allied peoples, and the meeting has enjoyed a robust historiographical afterlife. But the reassertion of traditional interests and modes of national diplomacy within a Europe/America rather than an East/West framework is clearly visible in the conduct of all three Allies after Teheran. In December the Soviet and Czech governments signed their long-anticipated treaty of alliance in Moscow. The Czechs got, so they thought, a promise of future protection from the most powerful European state. The Soviets got much more, for they now staked a claim, subsequently fulfilled, to a small slice of Czechoslovakia known as sub-Carpathian Ruthenia, which connected them directly with both that strategic country and Hungary, a geopolitical wedge into Central Europe, greatly advancing the Soviets' potential reach well beyond their borders and creating what the London Polish newspaper *Dziennik Polski* gloomily called "a machine for the USSR." Eduard Benes then returned to London and justified his action, both to the skeptical British government and in broadcasts to his own people in occupied Europe, as the culmination of Czech foreign policy. Czechoslovakia, he promised, would henceforth be a "bridge" between East and West in Europe. Full of references to the European balance of power, Benes's explanations made no significant mention of a United States he clearly did not expect to play any politically influential future role.[2]

In its response to the treaty the United States government made clear its displeasure at the reappearance of traditional European politics so soon after the ostensibly wholesome Moscow and Teheran conferences. The columnist Anne Hare McCormick, in the *New York Times*, reported widespread regret in Washington that the more universalistic idea of general security apparently accepted at the Moscow meeting had been abandoned in favor of power politics. This in turn inspired the Foreign Office (which quickly resigned itself pragmatically to the Soviet-Czech treaty) to voice several very traditional British comments on American moralism. One senior official, Frank Roberts, noted that "the United States has given the world no assurance that such a general security system will be forthcoming or that American practical support can be counted on." Cadogan noted tartly that the League of Nations had not worked. Anthony Eden summed up: "The Americans don't help themselves but are always ready to criticize the efforts of others."[3]

These events and exchanges help put Teheran into a proper perspective. It had indeed brought the crucial strategic decision of the war in Europe; it had produced a tonic effect on public opinion; and Roosevelt and Stalin had privately engaged in an enigmatic but potentially significant meeting of minds. There were of course political implications to all this, but so far as planning for Europe's future is concerned little seems to have changed despite all the casual talk. For here now were the three powers behaving exactly as they had done at the time of the Anglo-Soviet treaty in 1942: the Soviets pressing ahead politically; the British adjusting to accommodate them (though as little as possible consistent with the need to please Stalin and keep the Soviet Union in the war); the Americans lamenting the ethical imperfections inevitably involved, only to find the British turning on them for their naivete and hypocrisy. Above all, the distinction between the European and American outlooks is still abundantly clear.

What about the principal actors themselves? They were still largely preoccupied with the war. Roosevelt and Churchill in early 1944 were intensely and often argumentatively involved with strategic issues (especially the

---

[2] *Dziennik Polskie*, December 15, 1943. For the Soviet-Czech treaty, see Mastny, *Russia's Road*, pp. 133–144. For the Benes broadcast, see C510, F.O. 371.38920. See also Eduard Benes, *Six Years of Exile and the Second World War* (Prague, 1947), p. 227.

[3] For the McCormick article and comment, see Roberts memorandum, January 12, 1944; Cadogan note, January 15, 1944; Eden note, January 17, 1944, all in C268, F.O. 371.38920. For the Polish press, see Gatehouse memorandum, January 29, 1944, C941, F.O. 371.38937.

proposed landings in southern France that would diminish the importance of Churchill's cherished Italian campaign) and with all the complications of the run-up to D-Day. But in the diplomatic realm we find a rapid reversion to customary pre-Teheran behavior, with the two European powers showing a sharpened concern for their own political relationship and the diverging Americans more interested, when they turned to the postwar prospect, in the economic architecture of the postwar system. In three days at Teheran Roosevelt had suddenly burst enthusiastically into the European arena, seemingly confirming the prospective second front in France, reassuring his Allies that Europe-first was still basic American strategic policy, and making a great show of bringing Stalin in on the big strategic decisions for 1944 in the west, even as he showed a marked lack of respect for time-honored perceptions that, for better or worse, had guided European conduct in the past. Then, just as suddenly, he was gone. There was little political residue. The appointment of Averell Harriman as ambassador in Moscow is often cited as a major presidential gambit. It had little discernible impact until the autumn and not a great deal then. The United Nations plans, sketched out only vaguely at Moscow and Teheran, did not emerge in any formal sense until Roosevelt announced them in early June, and even then created surprisingly little stir in Europe.

The war forced some American political action in France and Italy, and stern warnings were issued spasmodically to the neutral powers. Roosevelt was sometimes active behind the scenes, working mainly through Churchill to constrain de Gaulle and occasionally making contact with Stalin, sometimes manipulating the hapless London Poles in the service of his reelection. But there was no significant exploitation of the diplomatic opening FDR had briefly made at the summit; no follow-up that we can identify as a serious American intervention in a European system he clearly still wanted to avoid and increasingly recognized as an Anglo-Russian arena; no task forces or high-level presidential study committees of the kind Woodrow Wilson had established during the previous war; no sustained effort to follow up Stalin's urging to "educate" the American public about European realities. Only at the end of the year, when the more politically engaged Anglo-Soviet combination began to move ahead very aggressively on their own and events took a turn that evoked memories of 1918–19 and threatened to upset American public support for the United Nations and postwar internationalism generally, did Roosevelt intervene significantly.

Not that the Roosevelt administration was inactive. Behind this renewed policy of detachment from inherently treacherous European political issues, American diplomacy, pushed in this election year (itself a profound distraction) by a combination of public- and private-sector impulses, was increasingly focused on the establishment of an open multilateral economic system. Roosevelt's Teheran assault on the old political order in Europe was a minor rhetorical impulse compared to the shrewdly targeted and very specific campaign he unleashed against the British economic system in early 1944. In January, the State Department requested that Britain sever its ties with Argentina, the main source of its chronically thin meat supply. In February, Roosevelt pressed Churchill to approve a conference on Middle Eastern oil that could only result in a gain of American influence at British expense. He also demanded that Britain further reduce its small American gold and dollar reserves, thus foreclosing, at least for the moment, any chance for an early postwar economic rebound. And he urged Churchill to endorse a commercial/financial negotiation that inevitably betokened further submission to a United States–dominated postwar economy. The British quickly took up defensive positions. For the most part, however, they were forced to give way, which they did as slowly as possible, much as they were now beginning to do politically in Europe in the face of Soviet expansionism.[4]

What then of the European summiteers? They reverted quickly to their pre-Teheran political preoccupations. Both Stalin and Churchill were Clausewitzian to their fingertips and acutely sensitive to the evolving political implications of the war. During 1944 their geopolitical interests in and around the European arena began to converge as the compression of the Axis center brought them physically closer together, even as they began to confront the potentially discordant and often ideologically tinged struggles for local dominance in the European states they were liberating. It is not surprising, then, to find Stalin and Churchill engaged at the beginning of the year in an effort to settle, or at least to compromise, the crucially troublesome Polish issue. For if they could remove this impediment, the otherwise geopolitically logical vision of an Anglo-Soviet order for postwar Europe held out by Stalin since 1941 – juxtaposing a solid Soviet sphere in Eastern and Central Europe with an L-shaped, British-led bloc in Western Europe and the Mediterranean, all justified and rationalized by

---

[4] Halifax to Churchill and Eden, Dec. 13, 1944, PREM 4.17/16. Churchill to Roosevelt, January 23, 1944, in Kimball, *Correspondence*, II, pp. 678–679 (Argentina); Churchill to Roosevelt, February 20, 1944, FRUS, 1944, 3, pp. 100–103 (oil); Roosevelt to Churchill, February 22, 1944, ibid., p. 45 (reserves); and Roosevelt to Churchill, February 23, 1944, PREM 4, 14/11 (conferences). Dallek, *Roosevelt and American Foreign Policy*, pp. 422–423.

the need to contain the malignant Germanic center – was bound to emerge more clearly and persuasively, as in fact it did in the spring of 1944.

The negotiation on Poland began with Stalin using Benes, who was returning from his Moscow treaty making in December through Morocco (where Churchill was convalescing after a post-summit bout of pneumonia) to patch up relations with the prime minister by sending warm "fraternal" greetings. Setting the stage for negotiations, Benes brought a map of Poland personally marked by Stalin that reflected the "matchstick" realignment Churchill had presented at Teheran. Churchill immediately seized upon this as giving the Poles "a fine place to live." Benes also gave the eagerly receptive prime minister his impression that the Soviets were freeing themselves from their old suspicions and genuinely favored collaboration. They were, he judged, "supreme realists." Stalin would insist on the Curzon Line but had no plans to "bolshevise" Poland (which he had described, according to Benes, as "an idiotic plan"), and renewed political relations were possible if the existing Polish government were satisfactorily reconstituted. Poland could later join the Soviet-Czech alliance. Churchill responded enthusiastically. His mood, still affected by the humiliations he had endured at Teheran, had oscillated during his convalescence in Morocco between thoughts of robust resistance to Soviet expansion and a casting about for ways to please Stalin, in whom, in the aftermath of Benes's energizing visit, he now claimed to have developed "a new confidence" as well as a belief in "deep-seated changes in the character of the Russian state and government." The tendency to this kind of emotional/intellectual volatility would persist in Churchill through 1944. But however we characterize his outlook, one constant remains: he was determined to pursue a settlement of the Polish issue with Stalin within a Big Three context and no other.[5]

For the British, this preoccupation with summitry was a fateful emphasis whose repercussions still echo in British politics today. Churchill had now to take more account, even as he prepared for a new approach to Stalin, of wider impulses beyond the charmed summit triad, most notably the growing desire in British and Western European circles for a higher degree of regional solidarity, the genesis of what later came to be called a "Western bloc," designed to operate under some kind of British leadership. For in 1944 we become ever more aware of two distinct lines of British thought and policy: on the one hand, a robust, quite broad-based agitation for the formation of

---

[5] Killearn to Eden, December 31, 1943; and Churchill to Roosevelt, January 6, 1944, both in F.O. 954/4. Churchill to Eden, January 1, 1944, PREM 3.399/6. For the Benes visit, see Gilbert, *Churchill*, VII, pp. 635–636.

a vitalized London-led Western Group; and on the other, the beginning of an effort by Churchill and Eden, largely through systematic adjustment, to clear a path for the Soviet Union in Eastern and Central Europe.

These two impulses – an "integrationist" one looking first and primarily to the creation and shoring up of a strong, self-reliant postwar Western Europe, and an "accomodationist" one concentrated almost exclusively on easing through top-level diplomacy the acceptable expansion in Eastern and Central Europe of the seemingly indispensable Soviet ally – might seem in a clinical sense to be compatible, two sides of the same coin. Stalin seems to have taken this view of the situation, at least in the first half of 1944. In fact, powerful cross-currents – the exigencies of war; the complexities surrounding both the fate of Poland and the role of France; the unsettled disposition of Germany; a concern to allay both American and Soviet suspicions; and, above all, a certain insecurity and lack of cohesive leadership among the British themselves – persistently intervened to muddy the waters. The two approaches were often at odds in London, with the accommodationists, particularly Churchill and sometimes Eden, tending to discourage practical steps toward a Western European unity that they feared would upset both Washington (always watchful to discourage any "regional" impulse that might trench on the "worldwide" United Nations concept) and Moscow, where the as yet undetermined fate of Germany was understandably thought to be a persistent source of anxiety.

The wartime integrationist impulse – resisted and later obscured by Churchill and often ignored by modern writers about European unity who view 1945 as a kind of "Year Zero" – deserves more attention. Its wartime saga had earlier roots, but its dynamic phase began in December 1943 with South African Prime Minister Jan Smuts calling, in a widely reported London speech, for the Western Europeans and the nations of the British Commonwealth to recognize the implications of growing Soviet power and gather round British leadership in the years ahead.[6] Eden, momentarily robust in the cause during Churchill's absence through illness in North Africa, lent support at this point, calling on a receptive Cabinet in January 1944 to endorse the principle of closer Anglo-French relations in general and specifically to support the restoration of French imperial power in Indochina. The theme was quickly taken up by the exile governments in London. Belgium's Paul-Henri Spaak, always a leading protagonist of Western European cohesion under British leadership, was again voluble in support. The Norwegian Trygve Lie and the Netherlands' van Kleffens

---

[6] Far Smuts' initiative, see *Sunday Times*, April 2, 1944.

had called for close future cooperation with Britain in year-end broadcasts. And there was approval in the Foreign Office, where resentment over the Soviet's agreement with Benes – a clear violation of the Eden-Molotov "gentlemen's agreement" – now inspired calls for a Western European bloc "to include Britain, Belgium, and the Netherlands with Norway and France perhaps thrown in."[7]

The Foreign Officer official directed to look closely into this issue found strong support for a British initiative of the type Smuts was recommending. The French looked to Britain for a lead. The Belgians and Dutch were especially enthusiastic, some even wanting fusion with the British Empire. Secret information suggested that public opinion in the Low Countries favored some kind of Western bloc. The Spanish and Portuguese also favored the notion, and Salazar, at the helm in Lisbon, was cited for a secret speech on February 8 to the Portuguese National Union in which "he envisaged a West European bloc under the leadership of Great Britain." Even the Italians, now suitably chastened, were thought to be "tired of politics" and at least potentially receptive. The official concluded that "the facts, as far as they can be discerned, point to an ardent wish on the part of the masses in Belgium, Holland, France, probably Switzerland, Spain, Portugal and Italy, for British leadership."[8]

French participation was seen as essential by most protagonists of a Western bloc. And de Gaulle himself, having now successfully withstood more than a year of American political subversion and hostility from Downing Street, was firmly in control of the French National Committee set up now in liberated Algeria. He reportedly favored closer ties, especially a closer economic association with several Western European states. Summing up the various public impulses on April 12, the London *Sunday Times* noted, "The impression created by all these utterances is a general call for Great Britain to take a lead in initial steps to build up firm and close relations with the smaller western states and France postwar." But the British government failed to seize the opportunity. By late March

---

[7] For van Kleffens's broadcast of December 28, 1943, see C183/183/25, F.O. 371.39325; for the Lie broadcast, January 15, 1944, see N379/379/30, F.O. 371.43234. Harrison minute, January 12, 1944, C181, F.O. 371.39323. *Sunday Times*, April 2, 1944. For Spaak, see Eden memorandum, February 11, 1944, WP (44) 11.

[8] Wilson memorandum, December 23, 1943, C181/181/G, F.O. 371.39323. Alexander memorandum, March 22, 1944, C3771, F.O. 371.39030. Eden memorandum, February 11, 1944, WP (44) 11. Harrison minute, January 12, 1944, C181, F.O. 371.39323. Gilbert, *Churchill*, VII, pp. 644–647. For Spaak, see Eden memorandum, April 3, 1944, WP (44) 181. For Churchill and de Gaulle in North Africa after Teheran, see Gilbert, *Churchill*, VII, pp. 644–647 and generally Chapter 37. *El Espanol*, January 1, 1944.

the Foreign Office had noticed charges among the European exiles that Britain had "sold out" to the communists and had "forfeited the leadership of Europe." Spaak was increasingly depressed. "It was," he declared at the beginning of April, "time for Great Britain to lead or lose prestige." This exasperated cry from the leading protagonist of a British-led postwar Europe echoes hauntingly through the postwar decades. Was there a missed opportunity here? Might not Churchill, drawing sensible conclusions from his humiliations at Teheran, have reached out in reconciliatory fashion during his long sojourn in North Africa to de Gaulle, now solidly entrenched in Algeria and seemingly in a mood to respond? But Churchill was not looking for open water. Instead, he became the chief impediment to the integrationist cause, refusing any leadership or encouragement to the as yet uncoordinated but potentially cohering impulses bubbling up in early 1944. He (and increasingly Eden too, though the foreign secretary wavered between the two approaches) committed himself to the Big Three approach, specifically seizing this new opportunity to find some satisfactory accommodation of Stalin's desires on the Polish issue. [9]

A range of ingratiating preliminary gestures convey something of the spirit in which Churchill and Eden approached their task. Shortly after his return from Teheran, Eden went before the War Cabinet to argue that the British government should now assert some supervisory control over the Polish government's radio connections with their compatriots at home – a preliminary gift he apparently intended to lay at Stalin's feet, though in the event he backed away temporarily from this gratuitous humiliation. Meanwhile, Churchill was also offering a more substantive preliminary sacrifice, notifying the Yugoslav partisan leader, Josip Broz Tito, "that the British Government will give no further support to Mihailovic and will only give help to you." This move, casting aside the noncommunist resistance in Yugoslavia and gravely compromising the future of that country, and specifically the return of King Peter after the war, was a purely British decision, seemingly taken without any prompting from Moscow. It appears to have been done mainly to please Stalin. The sacrificial instinct was still active when Churchill returned to London in January and refused to receive Jan Nowak, an emissary from the Polish Home Army whom even Eden had urged him to meet. Nowak had come to testify to the Poles' "deep distrust" of the Soviets and the pervasive skepticism in the country

---

[9] *Sunday Times*, April 2, 1944; Eden paper, April 3, 1944, WP (44) 181; Gilbert, *Churchill*, VII, pp. 644–647 and Chapter 37.

over the prospect of postwar independence. "This," Nowak insisted, "and not the frontier question, was the real issue."[10]

The British leaders, self-consciously "realistic" themselves after hearing Benes's characterization of Stalin as "a realist," saw themselves as determined to face facts, however unpalatable. As Churchill told Eden, referring to Eastern Europe, "we shall never attempt to turn them out." The foreign secretary agreed and went further in his January 5 reply. "I am convinced, as I was in 1943, that we should agree to all these claims." He explained that he wanted to avoid any public declaration until the end of the war for fear of seeming to violate the Atlantic Charter and upsetting the Roosevelt administration. At the same time, he wished to pass word confidentially to Stalin that the British "approved" and had "no intent to dispute" Soviet claims, explaining to him however that "we must go on saying wait for the postwar for a final settlement."[11]

In these propitiatory gestures and covert abdications we may reasonably detect, even before the start of serious negotiations with the hapless Poles (who had been invited to put their faith in the "good offices" of their British ally), the death rattle of earlier hopes – slim, perhaps, in view of the military realities – for any sustainable system of independent states in Eastern Europe. Yet the British leaders appear to have believed sincerely in early 1944 that they could achieve a workable compromise with Stalin. The actual effort to force the necessary concessions from the Polish government was initiated by Eden in late December, when he told the Polish foreign minister that the Curzon Line seemed the best solution in light of the Soviet willingness to offer territorial compensation in the west at German expense. "This," one watching diplomat drily observed, "is asking a great deal of the Poles."[12]

The Polish leaders knew nothing of what had transpired at Teheran. They had not been informed of Churchill's (and Roosevelt's) commitments to Stalin on the territorial issue. Nor were they told now of the declared Soviet plan to take Konigsberg for themselves, a move that, coming so soon after the Soviet-Czech treaty, was bound to arouse Polish fears of encirclement. In the event, nothing came of this early Foreign Office initiative. But then, in late

---

[10] For Cabinet see WM (44) 1st. Conclusions; Churchill to Tito, January 8, 1944, PREM 3.511/12. Stalin promptly acknowledged the "great significance" of Churchill's message to Tito – Gilbert, *Churchill*, VII, p. 641. Eden to Churchill, January 25, 1944, PREM 352/14A.

[11] Churchill to Eden, January 1, 1944; and Eden to Churchill, January 25, 1944, both in PREM 3.399/6.

[12] Douglas, *From War to Cold War*, pp. 28–29; Eden memorandum, January 23, 1944, WP (44) 48; Dixon diary, January 13, 1944.

January, Churchill weighed in against Prime Minister Stanislaw Mikolajczyk, urging him to accept the Curzon Line and justifying the amputation in terms of Russia's great sacrifices in two wars, its legitimate concerns about the western frontiers, its indispensable future role in restoring "a strong and independent Poland," and the noble mission awaiting the Poles in keeping Germany down in the east. Mikolajczyk tried to push the analysis to a deeper level. He noted, without any provoking reference to the invasion and deportations of 1939–40 or the Katyn massacres, a persistent Soviet desire to interfere in Polish internal affairs. From this he deduced that "the Soviets really wished to incorporate Poland into the Soviet Union." Churchill did not dissent, simply saying that this was an argument for settling now.[13]

A series of bruising encounters followed. The tone of Churchill's effort and his overriding determination to please Stalin is exhibited in his message to Clark Kerr on February 5 declaring his intention to press Mikolajczyk to both accept the Curzon Line and remodel his government. "We would make the best bargain we could for our unreasonable clients," he said, "and let the clients know that if at the proper time they do not accept it we would withdraw from the case." By late February Churchill had made some progress and was able to tell Stalin that the Polish government was ready to declare that the pre-war Russo-Polish frontier (the so-called Riga Line) "no longer corresponds to realities," and was willing, with British participation, to discuss, as part of a general settlement, new eastern and western frontiers. The final arrangement, it was stressed, must be part of a general European settlement. The Poles refused to accept any foreign intervention as regards the composition of their government, but sent assurances that by the time Polish-Soviet relations were restored only those committed to friendship with the Soviet Union would be included. The final settlement would be sanctioned by an Anglo-Soviet agreement confirming "the sovereignty, independence and territorial integrity of reconstituted Poland." Churchill further sweetened the deal with a public declaration in the House of Commons that the British government would support Soviet claims to the Curzon Line at the peace conference. Ironically, this coincided with the arrival of a study by the Foreign Office Research Department concluding that Soviet claims to the lands east of the Curzon Line had little if any more validity than those of the Poles.[14]

---

[13] Woodward, *British Foreign Policy*, III, pp. 161–165.
[14] Churchill to Stalin, February 20, 1944; and Churchill to Clark Kerr, March 5, 1944, both in PREM 3.355/9. See also Eden memorandum, January 23, 1944, WP (44) 48. *Parliamentary Debates* (Commons), 5th. series, Vol. 397 (1944), pp. 697–699.

Churchill's effort was all for nothing. Stalin now wanted complete submission. He took his time replying, and then on March 3 simply declared himself more convinced than ever "that the Polish leaders were incapable of establishing normal relations with the USSR." Here one sees the unfortunate consequences of the secret and unconditional commitments to the Curzon Line made by Churchill and Roosevelt at Teheran and their failure to balance the concessions by insisting on solid, functional, and reasonably watertight guarantees of Poland's genuine future independence. Stalin now had no real need to press the frontier issue. His allies would assure that for him – as indeed they did. He could now press on to his next objective, the creation of conditions for a subservient Polish government. Otherwise, he threatened in his message to Churchill, "a new government would emerge."

The effect of this escalation was to kill any chance for a negotiated solution. For now the Poles knew that if they gave way on the frontier issue, they would immediately be confronted with what Churchill himself called, speaking later of Soviet diplomatic practice, "a second series of demands." Understandably loath to function as the gravediggers of a proud nation's patrimony, something they would never be able to explain to their Home Army compatriots in Poland, who looked on them as the legitimate political authority, the London Poles decided to avoid the slippery slope and take their stand at the first hurdle in opposition to the Curzon Line, that they were prone to call the "Ribbentrop-Molotov Line" (which it almost exactly paralleled). On this they refused to budge, steadily alienating their British hosts, who were becoming ever more committed to close relations with Moscow and who, against all appearances (invasion, deportations, Katyn, later on the Warsaw tragedy of 1944) continued to take the view that the Soviets were well-intentioned in their approach to Poland. Privately, many British officials were realistic. Eden's private secretary, Oliver Harvey, predicted in late February that the Soviets would eventually establish their own regime in Poland, "and we shall have to recognize it." On March 7, Churchill made one more effort with the Soviet leader, stressing British support for the Curzon Line at the postwar conference and closing with the remark, "Force can achieve much but force supported by the goodwill of the world could achieve more." Stalin was a practiced purveyor of homilies. But he did not like to receive them. On March 27 he sent a fierce, contentious reply, warning that while he still wanted collaboration, "the method of intimidation and defamation, if continued, will not benefit our cooperation."[15]

---

[15] Stalin to Churchill, March 3, 1944; and Churchill to Stalin, March 7, 1944, both in SCCA, pp. 207–208. Stalin to Churchill, March 23, 1944, ibid., pp. 212–213; Harvey diary, February 29, 1944, Harvey, *War Diaries*, p. 334.

Churchill was now fed up with Stalin's stalling. The bulldog spirit reappeared. He stopped his personal correspondence with the Kremlin's master for about six weeks, consoling himself with a somewhat hypocritical blast to Eden about Clark Kerr ("He would give up anything to appease Stalin"), who had been urging him to please Stalin by endorsing "the new forces" in Europe. "Appeasement has had a good run," the prime minister piously declared on March 10. At the end of the month he was greatly encouraged in this new posture by a timely message from Cordell Hull complaining of Soviet "one-sided behavior" and observing "that the tide of Moscow-Teheran has now ebbed, that the British and Americans should now act in unity and talk plainly to the Soviets." Declaring that he now had "no confidence" in the Soviets and that the proper tactic was to lapse into "a moody silence," Churchill told Eden he would try and work from a closer Anglo-American basis. "Every effort must now be made to reach complete understandings with the United States," he declared. Moreover, Poland, so far as American public opinion was concerned, was "an extremely good hook." So far as Soviet expansionism was concerned, "any division between Britain and the United States will make us powerless in this matter. Together we can probably control the situation." His renewed hope of collaboration with Washington, signified by the reappearance of the familiar "hook" metaphor, is immediately visible too in Churchill's sudden anxiety about public reaction to what he now, in a sudden accession of transatlantic sensibility, conceded to have been his and Eden's "weak departures from the Atlantic Charter" on behalf of Russia.[16]

In fact, though, despite Churchill's tendency to clutch at these occasional intimations of American disenchantment with the Soviets, cooler heads in London had little faith in significant postwar help from the United States. The Foreign Office representative on the European Advisory Council, for example, had predicted in late February that the Americans would want to confine their occupation role to their northwest German zone and "leave the rest of Europe severely alone." In early March the British military made known their view that the president and American service chiefs would "withdraw United States troops as soon as possible from Europe" and in any case would be careful to avoid any role in southeastern Europe. Halifax reinforced this opinion on March 19, predicting that FDR would

---

[16] Churchill minute, March 2, 1944; Clark Kerr to Churchill, March 8, 1944; Churchill to Clark Kerr, March 10, 1944; all in PREM 3.355/9. Churchill to Eden, March 31, 1944, PREM 3.485/8.

avoid the Balkans and would want his troops diverted to the Pacific war "as soon as possible." A similarly authoritative warning from the head of the Foreign Office's North American Department, reminding colleagues that Britain would be very unwise to rely on any American help against the Soviet Union, reflected the prevailing view.[17]

Given these bleak predictions it is not surprising to find that the break in the continuity of the Anglo-Soviet collaboration was brief. As so often, it fell to the Foreign Office – always more attentive to geopolitical alignments than to personalized summitry and ideological abstractions – to apply the corrective. Eden, still eager to reassure the Kremlin of his commitment to the relationship, found it necessary to remind the volatile prime minister that "we have, either in public or private, already acquiesced in the strength of their claims to the Baltic States and Bessarabia which, like eastern Poland, go beyond their 1939 frontiers." Sargent made a broader point. Acknowledging the persistence of irritating "incidents" with the Soviets, but nevertheless endorsing the opinion of the Foreign Office's Soviet expert, Geoffrey Wilson, that Moscow was "cooperating rather than otherwise," the influential deputy undersecretary continued, "I hope we shall be able to persuade Mr. Hull not to jump to the conclusion that the policy of cooperation with the Soviet government has broken down." Sargent put Hull's intervention down to "inexperience of international cooperation because by and large they have followed a policy of international isolation." It was all very well for the United States to take a tough line on these European questions. It had "the luxury of abandoning the policy of cooperation with Russia if it proves troublesome to work, but it would be disastrous for this country if it were to do so unless absolutely forced to it." Britain had no leverage and little choice in its relations with Moscow, he concluded, for Soviet intentions remained the primary concern. And here, Sargent insisted, there were grounds for continuing optimism.[18]

Churchill soon saw the force of the argument. As he told the Dominion prime ministers at the beginning of May, "Russia must be associated with the postwar reconstruction." The problem had not been faced at Versailles,

---

[17] Strang note, February 28, 1944; and Halifax to Eden, March 19, 1944, both in U1386, F.O. 371.40733; Butler minute, May 23, 1944, N4424/748/G, F.O. 371.40740.
[18] Eden to Churchill, March 26, 1944; and Eden to Churchill, April 5, 1944, both in PREM 3.485/8. Wilson memorandum, March 31, 1944, N1908, F.O. 371.43304. Sargent review, April 29, 1944, N108, F.O. 371.43335. Kitchen, *British Foreign Policy*, p. 194.

and if the West did not take the Soviet position into account now, "We should be laying the foundation of another world war in a generation's time." But the sharpest spur to Churchill's second thoughts was the sudden perception in the spring of 1944 of a Soviet challenge, as the Red Army moved toward the Balkans, to the British position in the Mediterranean. "I confess to growing apprehension," Eden had warned in March, "that Russia has vast aims and that these may include domination of Eastern Europe and the Mediterranean and of much that remains." Churchill now plunged back into the arena of European geopolitics. On May 4 he asked Eden for a short paper on "the brute issues between us and the Soviet Union which are developing in Rumania, in Bulgaria, in Yugoslavia and in Greece. He himself defined the issue in apocalyptic terms. "Are we going to acquiesce in the communization of the Balkans and perhaps of Italy ... we ought to come to a definite conclusion about it." He began to talk now about "a showdown" with the Russians over their "communist intrigues" in Italy, Yugoslavia, and Greece." He told Eden of his fear that "great evil may come upon the world. ... the Russians are drunk with victory and there is no length they may not go." The upshot to all this anxiety in London was a British initiative that led Molotov to agree to a three-month Balkan arrangement whereby the Soviet Union would assume primary responsibility in Rumania and the British in Greece.[19]

This was a momentous development. British and Soviet interests were now about to come up against each other in a much more direct way than had yet occurred. In their diplomacy they would inevitably be much more attentive henceforth to each other's national preoccupations. This meant a much closer focus on the geopolitical implications of diplomacy, and a fuller solicitude for each other's spheres – in short, some significant movement toward a division of Europe. It meant too that Stalin, the political architect of the Red Army's seemingly irresistible southward push, would now have much more leverage on British policy. The losers were bound to be the Polish government in London, whose sadly placed homeland fell awkwardly and inconveniently outside the parameters of an otherwise geopolitically logical Anglo-Soviet accord and whose influence, therefore, already eroding significantly, would from now on be further diminished.

---

[19] PMM (44) 12th. meeting, May 11, 1944. Eden to Churchill, March 26, 1944, PREM 3.485/8; Churchill to Eden, May 4, 1944, PREM 3.66/7; Churchill, *Triumph and Tragedy*, pp. 61–66. For Eden's fear of "having the Russians on the Aegean," see Eden to Churchill, May 12, 1944, PREM 3.66/8.

Indeed, it would now increasingly come to be seen as a kind of pariah element, bent on frustrating the primary British interest in a logical, desirable, finally necessary deal with the advancing Soviets.

Once again, as in 1942, the Anglo-Soviet drift toward a European concert of power encountered a transatlantic hurdle. To the chagrin of the British, Molotov chose to inform the State Department of the new Balkan arrangements, which Churchill had not cleared in advance with the Americans. This prompted a predictably angry protest from Hull, and a more temperate one by Roosevelt, which Churchill fended off with reassurances that the arrangements were only a temporary practical response to local problems and certainly did not foreshadow any "sphere of influence" deal.[20]

This revived Soviet interest in American "legitimation" (for that presumably was Molotov's primary motive, though he may also have been interested in testing the character and solidarity of Anglo-American relations), along with Churchill's renewed interest in using "hooks" to attach the United States to British interests, testifies to the ever-increasing appreciation in Europe of the dimensions and potential of American power. But there seems to have been no evident Soviet intention to constrain the British initiative, which, even when modified to meet Washington's objections to a trial period of three months, they clearly welcomed.

For in fact all the signs at this point were that the two European powers were again strengthening their relationship. Molotov gave a lunch in late May to mark the second anniversary of the Anglo-Soviet treaty, which the Soviet press was observed to be celebrating "much more enthusiastically" than in 1943. The occasion, according to Clark Kerr, "glowed with brotherhood." Molotov toasted Churchill warmly and celebrated the treaty as "the cornerstone of the entire anti-Hitler coalition," an event, he declared, that Stalin had "welcomed with both hands." In the general euphoria following D-Day, a gratified Eden was able to draw the Cabinet's attention to an editorial in *Pravda* hailing the "community of basic interests" and noting that "[t]he Soviet-British Treaty of Alliance has been concluded for twenty years. This fact in itself means that both parties to the Treaty regard it as a basis for prolonged postwar collaboration."[21]

[20] Churchill to Roosevelt, May 31, 1944, in *Correspondence*, III, pp. 153–154. See also Dallek, *Roosevelt and American Foreign Policy*, pp. 455–456.

[21] Clark Kerr to Eden, May 29, 1944, N3244, F.O. 371.43414; *Pravda*, May 27, June 11, 1944; Eden memorandum, June 14, 1944, WP (44) 323.

The midyear euphoria inspired by the successful D-Day landings on June 6 revived the integrationists in London: the protagonists and supporters of a British-led Western Europe. Earlier in the year their hopes, focused on a consolidated regional bloc, had foundered for lack of leadership from Churchill and Eden, who had been diverted into the fruitless negotiation with Stalin over Poland. Now, in its second buoyant phase, the integrationists' campaign was driven by a growing sense of the need for a core Anglo-French relationship. The cause had by now reached into the Cabinet and was stimulated in wider government circles by outrage over the humiliating treatment meted out to de Gaulle and the French National Committee, who, largely at American insistence, had been denied any role in the planning for the invasion and the subsequent civil administration of liberated France. The ultra-sensitive general, kept out of Britain until the last moment, arrived in London from Algiers on June 3 in an aggrieved mood. He had a bitter confrontation with an unrepentant Churchill, who told the Frenchman that he should work to improve his relations with Roosevelt and also declared gratuitously, "Anytime I have to choose between you and Roosevelt I will always choose Roosevelt." Eden, a deeply embarrassed witness, recalled, "I did not like this pronouncement, nor did Mr. Bevin who said so in a booming aside. The meeting was a failure."[22]

Churchill's posture on this issue, widely criticized in London's political circles as kowtowing to the Americans and putting Britain's European future at risk, was a lonely one in mid-1944, though there was some support from the Foreign Office's North American Department and to some extent from Eden, who, with the presidential election pending and Roosevelt's commitment to a universalizing United Nations now out in the open, was characteristically anxious not to offend the watchful Washington establishment. The opposition, gathering round the cause of postwar Anglo-French solidarity, was more robust. On the political left, Attlee, the deputy prime minister and Labour leader, encouraged by Bevin, wrote to Eden on the eve of D-Day, pointing out, "We have a much bigger stake in France than the USA. ... I am sensible how much we owe the President but this should not lead us to agree to a mistaken policy." From the other end of the political spectrum, Churchill's Conservative friend and minister of information, Brendan Bracken, urged similarly that Britain "should go ahead alone" in support of de Gaulle, and the Tory colonial secretary, Lord Cranborne, called on Eden for an independent British policy on Europe based on the

---

[22] Eden, *The Reckoning*, p. 452; Gilbert, *Churchill*, VII, pp. 788–790.

French connection, declaring, "We cannot continue to wobble to and fro from day to day according to what telegrams arrive from the President." The Americans would respect Britain more, he declared, if the British followed "our own line."[23]

Robert Vansittart, former head of the Foreign Office, was particularly critical of Roosevelt. He told Eden, "I cannot stand by and watch not only Anglo-French relations but the whole future of Europe irremediably bedeviled by the folly and obstinacy of one man." At the ambassadorial level, Duff Cooper, now British representative with the French National Committee, warned against the danger of American domination. Sentiment was moving strongly toward a closer Anglo-French nexus in the Foreign Office, where Piers Dixon lamented "the P.M.'s pathological hatred of de Gaulle." Frank Roberts, soon to be chargé in Moscow, was now calling enthusiastically, in Spaakian fashion, for "a close connection with the West European countries." There was even support from Washington, where Secretary of War Stimson also urged a more pro–French National Council line, and from Australia, where the outspoken external affairs minister, H. V. Evatt, was openly critical of the Churchill approach. But once again, as with the earlier impulses after Teheran, the cause of Western European solidarity was squelched at the top. Here the authority was Churchill's, but the executor was Cadogan, who wrenched attention back to the Big Three and insisted, at the end of July, that the proper focus should be on political cooperation with the United States and the Soviet Union and the promising new world organization. "Lets review the issue in December," he concluded.[24]

Thus, while the first post-Teheran enthusiasm for a British-led Western Europe, inspired by Smuts as well as by Spaak and the exile governments, had withered from Churchill's neglect, Eden's passivity, and the spell of Big Three summitry, the second mid-1944 resurgence, which was moved by a widespread feeling that Britain's postwar relations with France were going to be crucial to any viable postwar Western Group, was sacrificed by Churchill, in the view of many, to the overriding demands of the link with Roosevelt. The integrationist cause did not die. If we look ahead for a

[23] Attlee to Eden, May 31, 1944; and Bracken to Eden, June 6, 1944, both in F.O. 954/9. Bevin to Churchill, June 6, 1944, PREM 3,177/4; Cranborne to Eden, June 12, 1944, N4956, F.O. 371.43335; Dixon diary, June 9, 1944, Dixon MSS.

[24] Vansittart to Eden, June 12, 1944, in F.O. 954/9; Cooper to Eden, June 6, 1944, PREM 3.177/4; Dixon diary, June 9, 1944. For Stimson, see Halifax to Eden, June 16, 1944; see also Australian Foreign Minister to Dominions Office, June 5, 1944, both in PREM 3.182/8. Cadogan memorandum, June 28, 1944, V6254, F.O. 371.40741.

moment we can also identify a third effort later in the year and into 1945, harder to pin down but characterized particularly by the passionate advocacy of Duff Cooper (first British ambassador to the post-liberation French government) and others in the diplomatic and intelligence establishments who we will find calling persistently for a cohesive Anglo-French treaty. This third phase was fatally undermined in late 1944 by the provoking intrusion of the British Chiefs of Staff and their Post-Hostilities Planning associates (both answerable to Churchill as minister of defence, though his involvement in these machinations is not fully apparent), who, while they made it clear throughout Whitehall in the autumn that they were sufficiently concerned about a postwar Soviet threat to want a strong, British-led "Western bloc," insisted that it should include the western industrialized parts of the defeated Germany.[25]

This blunt initiative shocked the diplomats. Impossible to hide, its effect was to prompt acute suspicion in Moscow and lead to a Soviet media campaign later in the year against what had been referred to in genteel terms as "the Western group" or "the Western union" but was now coming to be described in the world's communist media in a dangerously more metallic, confrontational way as "the Western bloc." All this prompted expressions of dismay in the Foreign Office. Eden, who had proclaimed receptively in May that "Western Europe looks to us," now began again to back away from the integrationist project, fearful of upsetting the Soviets, anxious too about both the American hostility to any manifestation of European "regionalism" and the opposition of the Dominion prime ministers, who (apart from Smuts) were already inclined to invest their hopes in the Washington-inspired world organization and were similarly disposed to dislike the notion of distinct European power centers. Sargent explained the growing dilemma. "We liked the idea of a Western Bloc and its possible value against a hostile Russia as well as against Germany. But we also grasped the point that we must not talk about its possible use against Russia." Unfortunately, he acknowledged, the German aspect is "already becoming known."[26]

We can therefore identify three rebuffs during 1944 that undermined the integrationist side of British diplomacy and, more specifically, the cause of a British-led Western Europe. Each setback seemed at the time to knock

---

[25] For examples of the Cooper campaign, see numerous letters from Cooper to Eden in F.O. 954/9. For samples of support of this third integrationist campaign, see Hollis to Jebb, July 27, 1944 (military); Roberts memorandum, July 10, 1944 (Foreign Officer), both in F.O. 371.40741. For the Post-Hostilities Planners' tensions with the Foreign Office, see Folly, *Churchill, Whitehall and the Soviet Union*, pp. 123–130.

[26] Sargent memorandum, September 21, 1944, F.O. 371.40741.

down an indispensable foundation. The first, at the beginning of the year, had depressed the smaller states whose hopes had centered on a British lead. The second midyear imbroglio had alienated the emergent Gaullists in France and their London supporters. The third, tainted by the military's call for the harnessing of German resources, upset the hitherto support-ive Soviets, who had initiated the whole notion of an Anglo-Soviet order in Europe back in 1941. The way was now open for Churchill, looking back on these shattered visions at the beginning of 1945, to declare that Britain could hardly make itself responsible for what he called dismissively "a cluster of feeble states." Yet he, more that anyone, had by his preoccupa-tion with Big Three summitry and a posture of neglect and active discour-agement toward the cause of Western European unity, foreclosed any such option.[27]

Still, ironies abound in this story. As it turned out, these setbacks were not fatal. The notion of Western European solidarity would persist into the postwar years and become a staple feature of Labour Foreign Secretary Ernest Bevin's foreign policy. Meanwhile, a further opportunity for an Anglo-Soviet balance in Europe would open up toward the end of 1944. And remarkably it was the accommodationists, Churchill with Eden following along, who in high-level negotiations with Stalin brought the long-developing Anglo-Soviet collaboration to its most impressive point, creating indeed the framework of a potential postwar "order" in Europe founded on the principle, pressed by Stalin since 1941, of a British-led West and a Soviet-dominated East. To explain this we need first to swing attention back to the Big Three, and to the fresh paths opened up by three crucial, related negotiations, all landmarks on the way to the Yalta denouement.

THREE CRUCIAL CONFERENCES

In the second half of 1944 the Anglo-Soviet relationship, in its application to Europe, began to acquire a more solid, functional character. This was largely due to the accelerating advance of the Allies upon the Nazi center from both east and west and their growing confidence that victory was now close. At the same time the United States, now successfully lodged on French soil but still skittish about assuming any political responsibilities in Europe, began to act more forcefully in the international arena. Here

---

[27] Churchill to Eden, February 8, 1945, U1900, F.O. 371.50826.

D-Day was the primary catalyst. For Roosevelt, still a master of political timing, chose this dramatically successful moment to announce to the American people and the world the structure and character of the proposed United Nations organization that was to become the new League and the centerpiece of a prospective United States–shaped postwar order that was likely, it was immediately apparent to sophisticated observers, to challenge the more traditional European conceptions we have been following. The initiative was well received in the United States and greeted with polite if somewhat skeptical approval in Europe. It encouraged Roosevelt to push things along by calling a meeting at Dumbarton Oaks in the Georgetown suburb of Washington.

There can be few more telling contrasts between the war as it was experienced in the United States and in Europe than that we can get by setting the bucolic surroundings at Dumbarton Oaks, where the State Department revealed its wholesome plans for a universalistic postwar order, and the brutal fighting between the Poles and the Germans in Warsaw, observed at a distance by a shocked world and very closely by suspiciously passive Soviet forces concurrently entrenching themselves on or very close to the eastern bank of the Vistula River. Churchill, deeply disturbed by Stalin's refusal to respond favorably to his requests to facilitate British and American air drops over the tormented city, referred to the "strange and sinister" Soviet stance. British newspapers, deeply attuned now to the compulsions of the lifesaving Anglo-Soviet alliance, tended to avoid the issue, drawing from George Orwell, in his *Tribune* column, a blistering reference to "the mean and cowardly attitude adopted by the British press towards the recent rising in Warsaw."[28]

Dumbarton Oaks certainly held the promise of better things. Roosevelt's call brought representatives of the Big Three and China to Washington in late August, charged to consider the State Department's proposals for a world organization more fully. It was a meeting that had a distinct bearing on the partly overlapping Roosevelt-Churchill conference in September at Quebec. And both these negotiations in North America had in turn a significant impact on the genesis and character of the Churchill-Stalin meeting at Moscow in October, which finally brought the Anglo-Soviet political and geopolitical relationship to a definitional point. We will examine the Dumbarton Oaks meeting more fully in a later chapter, for a grasp of its significance in the

---

[28] Churchill to Bracken, August 23, 1944, cited in Gilbert, *Churchill*, VII, p. 926. *Tribune*, September 1, 1944. For the Cabinet reaction see Churchill, *Triumph and Tragedy*, p. 124. Woodward, *British Foreign Policy*, III, pp. 202–221.

shaping of the Yalta conference and the subsequent political engagement of the United States with Europe is crucial to our story. Meanwhile, it will suffice to register here both the highly significant emergence of the United Nations concept as the central feature of the American postwar political scenario, and the fact that the Dumbarton Oaks conference failed to bridge the gap with a Europe that was now moving in another direction, toward a more traditional, essentially geopolitical solution to anticipated postwar problems.

The United States and the Soviet Union particularly, after Dumbarton Oaks, began to see themselves moving along diverging paths, even as the compression of the Axis center was bringing them closer together strategically and shortening the time available for some kind of mutual understanding. The Soviets had earlier made it clear that they were not opposed in principle to another world organization, but they were determined that it should be very different from the League of Nations, which had ended up expelling them, and that it should serve the interests of the Great Powers rather than the smaller nations. Notice of this critical difference had been given. The official instructions to the Soviet delegation stressed the importance of "centralized decision-making" and Big Three unanimity. Litvinov had published an important article on the subject, entitled "The International Organization of Security," in April 1944. A few weeks later the Soviets had again stressed, this time in a *War and the Working Class* article headed "On the Atlantic Charter," their concerns about the undue American preoccupation with "general principles" rather than actual "problems." These essays recalled the inadequacies of the League and were no doubt intended as an attempt to get the attention of the State Department's planners. But there seems to have been very little anticipation in Washington of the difficulties that the Soviet delegation raised at Dumbarton Oaks. They shocked the American officials by insisting on multiple memberships for the Soviet Union and also on the necessity for an absolute veto power for the Great Powers on both action and discussion. President Roosevelt appears to have drawn the conclusion from these crucial setbacks (for neither claim was then thought to be acceptable to American congressional or public opinion) and also perhaps from the apparent ruthlessness of the Soviet refusal to help the insurgent Poles, who were now fighting to liberate Warsaw from the Germans, that he must begin to address the practical issues of Soviet expansion and the associated implications, now increasingly visible to the administration's leaders, of Britain's declining power.[29]

---

[29] For Dumbarton Oaks, see documentary record in FRUS, 1944, I (Washington, D.C., 1966), pp. 713ff. M. Litvinov, "The International Organization of Security," *Leningrad*

This is the primary significance of the second conference in this phase, that held by Roosevelt and Churchill at Quebec beginning on September 11 and known by the code name "Octagon." This meeting has been seriously underrated. It has been argued that Roosevelt "insisted that Octagon limit itself to military matters" and that no important political decisions were made. In fact, Octagon was one of the most important politically oriented conferences of World War II. Churchill certainly viewed it in this light. His preliminary cable and telephone exchanges with Harry Hopkins set the stage. Hopkins urged that the British party be kept small and intimated that Roosevelt was now thinking less about strategy than about the political and economic issues of the supposedly imminent peace. Without going into detail, Hopkins sent word to Churchill that the president was ready to make "major decisions." Much the same urgency came from Smuts, who cabled in August warning Churchill that "the real issue on which the future of the world for generations will depend" is "the future settlement of Europe." Smuts urged: "Please let strategy not absorb all your attention to the damage of the greater issue now looming up."[30]

As in all the major Anglo-American encounters up to this point, there was, to be sure, a strong military-strategic aspect to the deliberations. Indeed, these were more important than ever now, for the string of victories in France since the accelerating breakout from Normandy in July had led Allied leaders to believe that the war would end in 1944. As Churchill declared at the opening session of what one British publication, in a burst of premature euphoria, hailed as "the Victory Conference," "Everything we had touched had turned to gold." Several formerly contentious military-strategic issues were now resolved. "The conference has opened in a blaze of friendship," the persistent summiteer cabled home. Roosevelt,

Zvezda, no. 4 (April 1944). Boris Stein, "On the Atlantic Charter," *War and the Working Class*, May 1, 1944. See also Geoffrey Roberts, "Litvinov's Lost Peace, 1941–1946," *Journal of Cold War Studies*, 4, 2 (Spring, 2002), pp. 40–41; and Robert Hilderbrand, *Dumbarton Oaks: The Origins of the United Nations and the Search for Postwar Security* (Chapel Hill and London, 1990). On the Soviet membership and veto issues, see Stettinius to Roosevelt, September 24, 1944, MRP, Roosevelt Library; and *Stettinius Diaries 1943–1946*, pp. 111–114. See also Dallek, *Roosevelt and American Foreign Policy*, pp. 446–467.

30 Warren Kimball, "The Two-sided Octagon: Roosevelt and Churchill at Quebec, September, 1944," in David B. Woolner (ed.), *The Second Quebec Conference Revisited* (New York, 1998), pp. 3–15. Hopkins to Churchill, August 21 and August 24, 1944, both in PREM 3.329/1. Smuts to Churchill, August 30, 1944, PREM 3.271/4. Halifax to Churchill, August 21, 1944, PREM 3.329/1.

still intent on minimizing any postwar American engagement in European political problems, accepted the British desire for the northern zone of occupied Germany, while the Americans took the southern area with an agreed exit corridor through Bremen. Roosevelt also accepted Churchill's passionately expressed desire for a larger British role in the Pacific, brushing aside the opposition of the United States Navy chief, Admiral Ernest King. FDR also endorsed Churchill's plan, if military success in the forthcoming British-led campaign allowed, for a strategic push through northeast Italy toward Vienna that, if successful, was recognized as having the political virtue of limiting the Soviet advance into Central Europe. In fact, all these moves obviously now had, with the accelerating pace of the war, a high degree of political significance.[31]

And indeed, when we turn to the conference as a whole, it is the political implications that seem most important, especially the question of Britain's role in a Europe that suddenly seemed acutely vulnerable to Soviet and communist expansion. For the first time Roosevelt showed a serious interest in this problem. A number of factors prompted this new attention. The growing public concern and even revulsion over Soviet conduct toward the Warsaw uprising must have been one of them. Cables from Harriman in Moscow during August and September warned of the Kremlin's "ruthless political consideration" in Poland and criticized its refusal to provide landing facilities for American planes at Soviet airfields in Eastern Europe, or in the Far East in preparation for operations against Japan from Siberia. Harriman's depressing cables spoke of "a startling turn" in United States–Soviet relations. OSS reports were similarly downbeat. Given this new and dangerous political drift and his own unwillingness or continuing inability, for political reasons, to take a direct stand against Stalin, it is not surprising that Roosevelt's thoughts turned to Churchill. Britain suddenly seemed less the self-aggrandizing, imperialistic menace of congenial American imagery than a politico-military partner that needed shoring up, one that suddenly seemed an increasingly overburdened, rickety power on the verge of bankruptcy.[32]

---

[31] Gilbert, *Churchill*, VII, pp. 954–70. Churchill to Hopkins, August 23, 1944, PREM 3.329/1. Dallek, *Roosevelt and American Foreign Policy*, pp. 467–478. The American documentary record is in FRUS, *The Conference at Quebec, 1944* (Washington, D.C., 1972). The British records are in PREM 3.329/4.

[32] Harriman and Abel, *Special Envoy*, pp. 340–341. See also Hull to Harriman, September 18, 1944, FRUS, 1944, IV, p. 991. Dallek, *Roosevelt and American Foreign Policy*, pp. 468–470.

Given this alarming context it is not surprising then that Churchill now felt emboldened to raise openly with the newly sympathetic Americans his own rising concern about the expanding Soviet power in Europe. He talked openly of "the dangerous spread of Russian influence" and found Roosevelt receptive. He raised the prospect of "the rapid encroachment of the Russians into the Balkans and the consequent dangerous spread of Russian influence in this area" and warned of the likely emergence, if no resistance were offered, of "a tyrannical communist government" in Greece. Churchill secured the president's promise of American planes to fly British troops to Athens to prevent that. FDR's new interest in Churchill's proposed military "right-hand move," from Italy toward Vienna, reflected a new American sensitivity to the fate of southeastern Europe. Most important, Roosevelt promised, in a follow-up meeting at Hyde Park, a full and exclusive sharing of all atomic research and development information. These agreements clearly had a political connotation and looked to the strengthening of the British position in Europe, with a view to providing some balance to Soviet power. The two leaders also contemplated a strike across Stalin's bow, a joint letter warning of "certain anxieties which are in our minds" about political developments in Europe. In the end, Roosevelt backed away and settled for provisional approval of Churchill's proposed cable to Stalin warning of "the political dangers of divergencies between Russia and the Western Allies in respect of Poland, Greece and Yugoslavia."[33]

All this has a premonitory Cold War feel to it. And indeed, there is no doubt that the two leaders were now concerned about growing Soviet power. But – and this point is crucial – their concerns were all expressed in an understood context (which the Octagon decisions clearly reflected) of the continuing separation of the two distinct European and American political arenas and of the persisting determination of the Roosevelt administration to avoid any European entanglements beyond the war effort. Churchill, anxious about Soviet expansionism and always eager to harness American power, was clearly bent on getting as many assurances of help as he could. However, he can have had few illusions that this would extend to anything resembling the credible, postwar Anglo-American political front, backed by the promise of direct American military assistance, that he would have preferred and would later bend his back to bring about after the Yalta dislocations had opened up an inviting path. We are still far from that in

---

[33] Ibid., pp. 467–477.

September 1944. Roosevelt's primary concern at this juncture, after all, was undoubtedly his reelection campaign. Otherwise, much of his thought was already revolving around the prospect of massive troop redeployments. Halifax, writing of Roosevelt's intentions even before D-Day, had plausibly warned that "his plain intention was to get as many troops out of Europe as soon as possible and into the war against Japan." Again, in November, just weeks after the Octagon conference, the president, concerned to dispel any illusions in London, told Churchill, "You know, of course, that after Germany's collapse I must bring American troops home as soon as rapidly as transportation problems will permit." And yet again, at the first plenary meeting of the Yalta conference in February 1945, he announced that he did not expect American troops to remain long in Europe.

Was FDR now seriously concerned about Europe's future course? He told one adviser that he was now convinced of the necessity for "keeping the British Empire strong," and "went far" in expressing his desire for postwar collaboration. Hopkins later elaborated Roosevelt's thinking to a British official. "He believes there is going to be another war," Hopkins told the startled diplomat, "and he has made up his mind that in that war there will be a strong Britain on the side of the United States. He wants you strong and he will help you to be so." But intimations of this kind constituted a rather ambiguous commitment with some familiar overtones. As the historian Martin J. Sherwin has aptly remarked, Britain's postwar role at this stage of American thinking was to be "America's outpost on the European frontier, the sentinel for the New World." To Churchill, the supportive atmosphere at Octagon probably revived memories of 1940–41 rather than the intimacy of post-Pearl Harbor partnership. Britain alone again on the ramparts, a new would-be European hegemon dangerously moving westward, and vaguely supportive offstage noises wafting across the Atlantic, hardly an enticing prospect.[34]

Roosevelt's strategic and military encouragements at Octagon were nevertheless significant and the product of genuine concern. The point is strengthened and illustrated by the many signs that after nearly a year of sustained assault on the financial and commercial foundations of British imperial power, he was now eager to try to restore Britain economically, pumping vitality back into the old empire, its past services in shielding

---

[34] Halifax to Eden, March 19, 1944, U3385G, F.O. 371.40733; Blum (ed.), *Morgenthau Diaries, Years of War*, pp. 306–314; Wright to Broadhead, November 14, 1944, PREM 4 27/7; Roosevelt to Churchill, November 18, 1944, FRUS, *Malta and Yalta*, p. 286. Sherwin, *A World Destroyed: The Atomic Bomb and the Grand Alliance* (New York, 1975), p. 113.

the United States from uncongenial threats and realities perhaps suddenly recalled. To this end he undertook to modify Lend-Lease policy to provide for its continuation during the period between the defeat of Germany and that of Japan, meanwhile allowing the British to divert some domestic resources to home and export production. He indicated that he would ask Congress for a postwar British loan. He also had a less orthodox plan for British reconstruction. This was the famous Morgenthau Plan, whose author, Treasury Secretary Henry Morgenthau, pressed the conception of a postwar Germany without industry, a "pastoral" country broken up into small states and small farms. This appealed to FDR, who wanted the Germans to end the war feeling "defeated," with just enough food from Army soup kitchens to keep body and soul together. At the same time Morgenthau stressed a number of other benefits that Roosevelt, always susceptible in his improvising way to multipurpose solutions, initially found irresistible. These included the incapacity of Germany to make war again, the sense of security the Russians would consequently feel (thus diminishing their desire for expansion), and the opportunity the de-industrialization of the German Reich afforded to help restore British prosperity without the United States having to give up the continuing campaign against world-girdling imperial preferences. For Britain, pushed into Europe even as its world role was diminished, would be richly compensated by succeeding to a virtual monopoly of the postwar European steel market well into the future. As the treasury secretary unveiled his plan, Churchill at first reacted violently, calling it "unnatural, unchristian and unnecessary," and declining to participate in such a "vindictive" policy of "vengeance." But when he saw the economic advantages the plan seemed to hold for Britain, he changed his mind quickly and became an ardent protagonist of the approach. As he told a protesting Anthony Eden, "he was going to prefer the interests of his own citizens to those of the enemy."[35]

Morgenthau's success was short-lived. When FDR returned to Washington he was immediately confronted by an outraged Stimson and Hull, who pointed out the many problems a policy of this sort would bring. FDR was obliged to agree. Henry Morgenthau "pulled a boner," he ruefully acknowledged. The initiative was indeed the product of emotion rather than careful analysis. There was no planning; there were no projections, no sense of all the likely practical consequences. Analysis suggested that the plan's effect on Europe generally would be devastating. It would

---

[35] Moran, *Churchill*, pp. 191–193; Dallek, *Roosevelt and American Foreign Policy*, pp. 468–469, 472–478; Churchill, *Triumph and Tragedy*, pp. 156–157; Carlton, *Eden*, p. 243.

inhibit recovery everywhere; it would intensify the refugee problem; it would lead to shortages, create unemployment, and prolong postwar suffering for millions of innocent people far beyond Germany. It would also be difficult for Britain, the intended beneficiary, to assert moral or political leadership in such an atmosphere, for, as one skeptical Foreign Office commentator drily observed, "we may have some exceedingly awkward moments with the European allies."[36]

Roosevelt's initial enthusiasm for the Morgenthau Plan suggests that his insight into the consequences of American actions still had limits. He now professed to be worried about the Soviets in Europe. Yet by crushing Germany and its economy he was weakening Eastern and Central Europe to the point where no sort of resistance to Soviet ambition, even from an economically reinvigorated Britain, was likely to be effective. He still refused to recognize de Gaulle's regime in France. Thus something of the spirit of Teheran – of tabula rasa in Europe – was still very much alive in the White House, tempered only, in some recognition of rising Soviet power, by the setting up of Britain as America's sentry in Europe, somewhat on the 1941 lines of material help without full commitment, complete with the comparatively tangible benisons of continuing Lend-Lease, help in getting a postwar loan from Congress, the zone of choice in Germany, and shared knowledge of the atom.

This view of the Octagon conference, emphasizing the president's efforts to encourage Churchill's Eurocentrism and use him as a kind of active agent of broad American purposes, gives us a suggestive context in which to ponder the next dramatic development, Churchill's departure for Moscow only three weeks after his return from Washington. Hitherto, as he had explained to Eden in October 1943, he had been anxious not to make premature and probably compromising territorial deals with Stalin for fear of a controversial storm in the House of Commons and adverse reactions in the United States. But now the Red Army's rapid southward advance through the Balkans was bringing matters to a head. Having taken full control of Rumania, Soviet forces reached the Bulgarian border on September 1 and entered Sofia on September 15. The specter of a Soviet-sponsored communist bloc (Yugoslavia, Rumania, and Bulgaria) aimed directly at a very vulnerable Greece, the Straits, and the Mediterranean generally now presented itself to the British, just as the accelerating German

---

[36] For the Morgenthau denouement, see Dallek, *Roosevelt and American Foreign Policy*, p. 477; Blum, *Morgenthau Diaries, Years of War*, pp. 375–383. Memorandum by Coulson, September 14, 1944, C12073/G, F.O. 371.39080.

withdrawal from Greece, leaving a vacuum where well-armed communist and monarchist factions seemed ready to fight for supremacy, suggested the need for a decisive British intervention. Greece was after all a key to Britain's position in the Mediterranean generally, and the geopolitically sensitive Eden was already sounding the alarm about the threat of a large expansionary Slav federation uniting Yugoslavia and Bulgaria.[37]

But the tendency to explain Churchill's trip to Moscow in October 1944 more or less exclusively in terms of the sudden threat to Greece is very questionable. There were now broader considerations. The war seemed to be moving rapidly toward its climax. Churchill had, largely in deference to American wishes, taken the view that controversial issues should be put off until the postwar peace conference. He had earlier noted, thinking of possible diplomatic clashes with the Soviets, "We will need the United States position clearly defined before we move in advance of the twenty-year treaty." But now the Americans had made their position clear. Roosevelt had, in effect, licensed Churchill to act in Europe even as he had clarified the limits of America's postwar engagement. It was logical, therefore, that Britain and the Soviet Union should come together at this moment to address large issues and try to crystallize at least some of the geopolitical arrangements they had been moving toward since 1941. And given that the Soviets for their part had continued to put out encouraging reminders through 1944 of the common Anglo-Soviet interest in the peace of Europe, it is not surprising that when the prime minister proposed his visit, he found a ready invitation from Stalin.[38]

Three other considerations beyond the Greek situation should be factored into any attempt to understand British thinking on the eve of the Moscow conference, which was given the code name "Tolstoy." The first is the almost unanimous conviction one now finds in the British political establishment both that Britain must come to terms in some fashion with Stalin's state if the European peace was to be sound, and that this was an achievable enterprise. "The peace of Europe depends," the right-wing *Spectator* insisted, in a widely representative comment, "more on the maintenance, or rather the increased development of good understanding

---

[37] Churchill to Eden, October 6, 1943, and October 10, 1944, both in PREM 3.399/6. Eden to Churchill, August 10, 1944, PREM 3.79/2, on earlier Balkan anxieties.

[38] For the immediate origins of the Moscow meeting, see Churchill to Stalin, September 27, 1944; and Stalin to Churchill, September 30, 1944, both in SCCA, pp. 257–258. See also Churchill, *Triumph and Tragedy*, pp. 206–225. See also Colville, *Diary*, October 8, 1944; and Chapman to Andrews, March 9, 1944, C3671, F.O. 371.43394. Sherwin, *A World Destroyed*, p. 113.

between this country and Russia than any other single factor." The bedrock assumptions that appear in nearly all the numerous Foreign Office reviews and surveys of the situation, and in most of the ambassadorial dispatches received from Moscow, were that Stalin was a statist rather than a revolutionary; that, while he would certainly want to expand Soviet power quite deeply into Eastern and Central Europe, his fundamental motive was security; and that he would be preoccupied long after the war with domestic recovery.[39]

From a review of all the stage-setting diplomatic papers of this period, the historian Martin Folly very reasonably selects as "the definitive Foreign Office view on Soviet policy" in 1944 two major papers, one on "Soviet Policy in the Balkans" produced for the Cabinet on June 7, the other on "Soviet Policy in Europe," dated August 9. Both acknowledged the inevitably speculative foundations of the analysis and were alive to a range of difficulties and uncertainties. Yet both were essentially optimistic, the broader "European" one especially so. It was noted that "before and during the war the emphasis in Russia has entirely and necessarily been on efficiency, discipline and achievement, not on political theories." The Soviets could be expected to try to implement a cooperative policy for five years at least, focusing on reconstruction in the short term and German revival later. Thus they would be inclined to respect British interests. This was the basic proposition Churchill and Eden would test in Moscow.[40]

Eden's August 9 Cabinet paper is of particular significance on a number of counts. First, there was some debate in the Foreign Office over whether or not there should be some reference in it to the United States, if only "to get her politically and economically interested." The conclusion, however, was that as the likely extent of her interest was "quite uncertain," the scope of the paper should be confined to the subject of Soviet influence in postwar Europe. Secondly, the paper puts British policy in unusually sharp focus and foreshadows in clear outline the understanding over the division of postwar Europe that Churchill and Stalin would consummate in Moscow some two months later, showing that what came to be seen in the United States as a notorious "spheres" deal, and by many historians as a hasty improvisation, was something more rooted and substantial.

---

[39] See, for representative sentiments, Willgress to Department of External Afairs (Ottawa), March 9, 1944; and Warner minute, May 5, 1944, both in N2652, F.O. 371.43335. *Spectator*, September 15, 1944.

[40] Eden memorandum, "Soviet Policy in the Balkans," June 7, 1944, WP (44) 304; Eden memorandum, "Soviet Policy in Europe," August 9, 1944, WP (44) 436. See also Folly, *Churchill, Whitehall and the Soviet Union*, pp. 121–123.

Noting that "the foundations of our postwar European policy must be the Anglo-Soviet alliance," Eden could see "no reason why within this framework we should not work to consolidate our position in three groups of European countries with which our relations have been traditionally close and intimate." These, he noted, were "France, the Low Countries and the Iberian Peninsula, especially Portugal; the Scandinavian countries; and the Mediterranean Group, comprising Turkey, Greece and, eventually, Italy." Then, having clearly identified the prospective "Western bloc," Eden went on to specify the balancing Soviet inheritance in states where Britain "should avoid any challenge to Soviet interests." These included "the Central European countries adjacent to the Soviet Union," which he listed as Poland, Czechoslovakia, Yugoslavia, Hungary, Rumania, and Austria – countries where the Foreign Office hoped to be able "to spread British influence" but was clearly prepared to acknowledge as falling within the Soviet sphere. Churchill's subsequent "sphere of influence" deal with Stalin, which substantially followed this line of geopolitical thought and marked out a division of Europe, was in fact a faithful expression of British policy.[41]

A second looming problem was the disposition and loyalty of postwar Germany. Should it fall into the British or Soviet orbit? Both governments had so far discreetly danced around this crucial issue, essentially shelving it while talking ambiguously of "dismemberment" or "punishment." They would continue in this watchfully passive posture at their approaching Moscow conference. But, as we have seen, the German problem had been carelessly (from a Foreign Office viewpoint) brought into the open by the British Chiefs of Staff, who, sharing the general skepticism in London about the willingness of the United States to play any useful role in defending postwar Europe, had reached the, as they saw it, logical conclusion that the vital western industrial part of Germany must be drawn into the postwar British defensive orbit as a necessary counter to any potential Soviet aggression, which they were known to consider a serious possibility. This was also, as we have seen, a view periodically voiced by Churchill. To the outraged Foreign Office, however, any show of British interest in using German power would immediately destroy any chance for postwar collaboration with the Soviets, bringing about the very evil the Chiefs of Staff professed to fear – a Soviet campaign against Britain. And indeed, by October the fully aware Soviets (briefed by the spy Donald McLean,

---

[41] Eden memorandum, "Soviet Policy in Europe," August 9, 1944, WP (44) 436.

among others) were already well launched into a sustained media blitz against the "Western bloc." This chilled those integrationist British leaders who, without any overt desire to incorporate German power, had been agitating for a postwar Western European group. As we have seen, it also led Eden to suspend further Foreign Office work on the subject. And it seems likely that it encouraged Churchill to extend his accommodative approach to Stalin from the purely Balkan deal that had been in operation since May, and to make the much wider concessions to the Soviets in Central and Eastern Europe that Eden had looked to in his August 9 Cabinet paper. It was clearly a card to play now.[42]

Thirdly, Churchill was determined to try once again to settle the festering Polish issue, now flaring up again with reinforced intensity as the world watched the tragic last phase of the uprising in Warsaw. The importance of this problem was widely recognized in London, but in a self-interested way. As one commentator explained, the "rift" over Poland is important because "the effect on Russo-British relations is more important in the long run than the effect on Russo-Polish relations." This is not quite how the situation was seen by the increasingly anguished London Polish government, now engaged in a series of bitter struggles with the Foreign Office.

There was, for instance, a battle of the treaties. In 1939 the far-seeing Colonel Beck had extracted from the British government various undertakings that it would "safeguard" Poland's territorial integrity. The main Anglo-Polish treaty, which Eden had confirmed in 1942, at General Sikorski's request, as the price of Polish acquiescence in the prospective Anglo-Soviet treaty, was now being openly violated by the British thanks to Churchill's public commitment to the Curzon Line. Nevertheless, the Polish government celebrated it vigorously in London each year (along with the Polish National Day, the anniversary of Sikorski's death, and a variety of other opportunities) with elegant invitations and elaborate ceremonies attended by a steadily diminishing corps of reluctant if not shame-faced British ministers and officials. The sharp specificity of the Anglo-Polish clauses contrasted with the more amorphous undertakings of the 1942 Anglo-Soviet accord, which the Foreign Office, in its turn, liked to play up annually with plenty of fanfare. The British efforts to

---

[42] For Chiefs of Staff and Post-Hostilities Planners views, see PHP (44) 15 (o), Final, August 25, 1944; and Ismay to Churchill, October 4, 1944, both in PREM 3.192/2. Sargent memorandum, October 4, 1944, C13518, F.O. 371.39080. Joint Intelligence Committee, "Russian Capabilities in Relation to the Strategic Interests of the British Commonwealth," CAB 81/124. See also, on this controversy, Folly, *Churchill, Whitehall, and the Soviet Union*, pp. 123–130.

drain the inescapably concrete Polish agreement of political relevance, even as they worked strenuously to fill the vague clauses of their Soviet treaty with rich, significant meaning, might, if the implications were not so tragic, be said to have had a comic side. Politically, this manifestation of the age-old struggle between law and power reflected an acute sense of embarrassment.[43]

For the Foreign Office, as it tried to fend off the Poles, was now putting a great deal of energy into improving general British understanding of the Soviet partner. As we saw earlier, there had been little study of Russia or the Russian language in Britain since 1917. Oxford University had ignored it. Even now there were initial stumbles. A leading British historian of Russia, Sir Bernard Pares, was brought into the Foreign Office but soon alienated senior officials and was discreetly pushed aside. Maisky, invited by the Board of Education to become patron of a supportive society, promptly showed a flair for clubland etiquette by blackballing several seemingly worthy officeholders. The Soviets were quick to put the transcultural emphasis in the correct place. The Lenin Library offered 500,000 volumes, crowned by the shelf-stretching works of the world's best-selling author, Joseph Stalin. And, after an awkward start, several educational and cultural programs were set up. As Sargent noted in mid-1944, the Foreign Office was interested in these improvements because "British postwar security would be largely based on the 20 year treaty of alliance with Russia."[44]

There were then serious concerns here, though one sometimes has the impression, observing these gestural pyrotechnics (which included proposals for a book of popular British songs for Soviet soldiers), that British diplomacy was being orchestrated by Mr. Punch rather than the descendants of Lord Palmerston. Practicality often veered off into sentiment and Benes-style illusionism. Here, for example, alongside such howlers as the Czech leaders's insistence that Stalin was "not a dictator, more the expression of a group idea," we might place the explanation of

---

[43] Churchill to Bracken, August 23, 1944, PREM 3.352/12. Churchill, Eden, Mikolajczyk, Romer meeting, June 22, 1944, PREM 3.352/14A. The Warsaw uprising is fully examined in Norman Davies, *Rising '44: The Battle for Warsaw* (London, 2003). For British and American responses, see Folly, *Churchill, Whitehall and the Soviet Union*, p. 136; Dallek, *Roosevelt and American Foreign Policy*, pp. 463–465. See also Gilbert, *Churchill*, VII, pp. 870–873. For key clauses of the 1939 treaty pledging British assistance in resisting and undermining of the "independence" of Poland by "a European Power," see Z. C. Szkopiak (ed.), *The Yalta Agreements: Documents Prior to, During and After the Crimea Conference, 1945* (London, 1956), p. 33 and passim. *Spectator,* September 22, 1944.

[44] Sargent minute, June 7, 1944, N3616, F.O. 371.43375.

the Foreign Office's leading Soviet expert that the ideology transmitted to young Soviet Communist Party members had "the same effect our teaching of Shakespeare to young people had in this country." After all, he continued, "The Party is the people." As for "the covert bitterness against the regime" scrupulously reported by hard-working British observers in Moscow, this was quickly domesticated for British consumption as "normal grumbling."[45]

The facts of life would soon play havoc with the various well-intentioned efforts to reinvent the Soviet Union as a socialized projection of the Home Counties. Meanwhile, the Foreign Office found itself waging a kind of political trench warfare with the illusion-free Polish press in England. This press was lively, amounting at one point to as many as forty publications that were often critical (not least of their own government) but were also dependent to a large extent on financial subsidies and allocations of scarce paper by a British government that monitored their activities in a state of rising, finally chronic irritation. Champions of free speech can only be impressed by the openness of the London wartime press generally. The Poles took full advantage. Themselves under almost constant attack from the Soviet embassy as well as from the London *Daily Worker* and other left-wing papers, the Polish publications frequently raked the BBC, the Reuters press agency, and Bracken's largely unsympathetic Ministry of Information over the coals for repeating uncritically what they saw as Soviet propaganda and playing down the Polish viewpoint. Amid the controversies one gets many glimpses of a growing anguish. At the end of August, as the fighting in Warsaw intensified and hopes for any help began to disappear, the Catholic journal *Sprawa* contrasted the wholehearted Polish commitment to the British cause from the beginning of the war with the current disloyalty of the British and Americans, who were "doing their best to disinterest themselves in the Polish question" and were in effect, it declared, consigning the country to the Russian sphere. Meanwhile, the writer continued, in Poland "former Communists and godless agitators" were being set up as a Soviet satellite regime. "Everyone of us is asking what we are fighting for. For what ideals? Is it possible that we are fighting only to satisfy the aims of the Big Three? Should this be the case every drop of Polish blood and every Polish life would have been shed in vain."[46]

---

[45] Lott memorandum, May 22, 1944; and Wilson minute (undated), both in N22958. F.O. 371.43386.

[46] For representative Foreign Office attitudes, see Gatehouse memorandum, August 24, 1944, C10949, F.O. 371.39442. See also WM (44) 122 and *Sprawa*, August 31, 1944. Polish attitudes can be sampled further in *Mysl Polska*, July 20, 1944; and *Listy*

Undoubtedly the Polish commentators were sometimes provocative, and they played relentlessly on the uneasy consciences in Whitehall. There was, though, a degree of mean-spiritedness at work on the other side. We have already noted Eden's eagerness after Teheran to please Stalin by stripping the London Poles (whose countrymen had made several basic components of the valuable Ultra intelligence system available to the British before the war) of their private radio communications with the strong resistance movement in the homeland that acknowledged their political leadership. In April 1944, to cite another instance, a group of private British citizens wanted to petition the Soviet government to allow the emigration of the children of those Polish soldiers who had been permitted to leave the Soviet Union earlier and were now serving with the British. The Foreign Office refused any help and told the petitioners that the issue "could not be divorced from the question of the general relations between the USSR and the Poles." The group then planned an approach to Maisky on the issue. But the Foreign Office quickly discouraged this on the ground that the British Government had "no locus standi."[47] Another embarrassing matter came up in September 1944 when the Polish government asked for help in bringing to Britain several members of the ill-fated Polish Cabinet of 1939 – Britain's original allies against Hitler – who had just been liberated in Rumania. The British Cabinet now wanted nothing to do with these former associates, again fearing repercussions from the Soviets. The British authorities would not help them to get out of Rumania, the Cabinet decided, but if they did manage it, Eden was authorized to resettle them "some place" in the empire, but expressly not in the United Kingdom.[48]

Churchill had his own solution for the more than 150,000 Poles fighting under British military command, a policy perhaps best described as "transcendence through trauma." This was to ensure that they were very rarely away from the front line. He appears to have been puzzled by the less than rapturous response with which the Polish ministers, representing people he persistently referred to as "a warrior race," greeted his repeated

---

z Londynu, July 25, 1944. For criticism of the *Daily Worker* campaign, see *Dziennik Polskie*, August 9, 1944.

[47] Marley to Eden, April 1, 1944; Randall minute, April 5, 1944; Wilson minute, April 10, 1944, all in N1682, F.O. 371.43404. Elma Dangerfield was the prime mover in this campaign to bring some of the children from the Soviet Union, survivors from among the approximately one and a half million Poles deported during 1939–41. For her press campaign, see the *Manchester Guardian*, December 23, 1943; *The Scotsman*, February 16, 1944; *Glasgow Herald*, February 18, 1944.

[48] WM (44) 122.

assurances that they would find ample solace for the territorial amputation of half their country by taking up the heroic role of Europe's (essentially Russia's) military guardians in the east against any resurgence by Germany. Meanwhile, their soldiers would be kept busy. Churchill instructed the Chiefs of Staff, "Please do not on any account let the Polish Division be kept out of the battlefront." His papers are studded with reminders to various generals to keep the Poles ("a magnificent fighting force") from worrying about their miseries by putting them more or less permanently on the front line, where, he counseled – thinking perhaps, to take a charitable view, of the strenuous athletics traditionally imposed upon British schoolboys to ward off unhealthy thoughts – they would have less time to agonize over their country's "tragic" affairs.[49]

These British attitudes, which may seem dispensably peripheral to our main Europe/America theme, are in fact central to it. For the extreme emotionalism on display, so uncharacteristic of British officialdom, shows the depth of the concern felt in London for a closer understanding with the Soviets, both for victory in the war and, just as importantly, for peace in Europe afterward rather than another great war, which, as everyone recognized, Britain would be in no position to contemplate after her exertions in the current crisis. The strongest spasms of acute anxiety and anti-Polish sentiment invariably surfaced when that understanding with Moscow seemed most at risk. Much that seems out of character in a proud tradition can therefore be explained by reference to profound and understandable anxieties.

At the same time, a degree of political opportunism at the expense of the Poles must be acknowledged. Of this Churchill was a frequent exemplar, flaunting a calculated disdain for the Poles as an easy way to strengthen his personal bond with Stalin. Thus we find him seated once again in Stalin's Kremlin office on October 9, after another laborious journey around Hitler's contracting but still extensive periphery. Intent as always on breaking the ice and establishing a comradely spirit, he suggested to his formidable host that they begin "with the most tiresome question – Poland." As at Teheran, he found himself again unable in Stalin's presence to rise to a principled level of statesmanship on this issue, going out of his way to convey the impression that he saw the Polish issue not as the profound problem it really was, but as a pestilential nuisance to which he and the

---

[49] Prime minister's memorandum, January 23, 1944, WP (44) 48; Churchill to Brooke, May 21 and May 27, 1944, PREM 3.352/14A; Churchill to Ismay, July 13, 1944, PREM 3.354/10.

Soviet leader must reluctantly descend from the contemplation of more elevated matters. Churchill was painfully ingratiating and showed virtually no sympathy with Polish sentiment. After Katyn he had been quick to condemn the Polish complaints about the Kremlin's murderers, which he knew were accurate, and to assure Stalin that no one in Britain believed in Soviet culpability. So now he accepted "absolutely" Stalin's explanations of the highly dubious Soviet conduct over the Warsaw crisis. He emphasized Soviet rights over the Curzon Line as "right, fair and necessary for the safety and future of Russia." He ridiculed the London Poles, especially their anti-Soviet defense minister, Sosnkowski. "He and Mr. Eden had for months been trying to get Sosnkowski sacked," he declared. As for his first replacement, General Bor-Komorowski of Warsaw Uprising fame, "the Germans were taking care of him." The new commander in chief was "some colourless man" whose name he could not remember. The political leaders, Mikolajczyk and Romer, were referred to in similarly dismissive fashion. "He had them tied up in an aircraft and it would take only 36 hours to Moscow" if Stalin deemed it "worthwhile" to send for them. If they came, "they could, with British and Russian agreement, be forced to settle." At Teheran, despite contrary reassurances to both governments, he had gone out of his way to demonstrate to Stalin his intention to force not only the Poles but also the Turks to make crucial concessions of sovereignty to Soviet ambition. So again here. Russia had "a right and moral claim," he now declared, to full, unimpeded access through the Straits. He did not want Turkey "to abuse her sovereignty and to grip Russian trade by the throat." Russia, he added expansively, should have "free access to the Mediterranean for her merchant ships and ships of war."[50]

Having signaled his intention to please Stalin over the fate of Poland and to support Soviet demands against Turkey, Churchill moved to clarify his thoughts about a fuller European settlement. He may have hoped to give the impression of American support, but Roosevelt, after initially raising no objection to Churchill's Moscow trip, had on Hopkins's advice, probably prompted by the now imminent American election, informed Stalin that while he approved Churchill's proposal to include Harriman in some (but pointedly not in all) the talks, he felt obliged to reserve his options because "the solution of still unresolved questions can be found only by the three of us." This American reservation actually had little effect

---

[50] For Churchill-Stalin meeting, October 9, 1944, and the full British documentary record of the Moscow conference, see PREM 3.434/2. See also Churchill, *Triumph and Tragedy*, pp. 226–243; Douglas, *From War to Cold War*, pp. 37–49.

on the two Europeans. Indeed, it seems to have strengthened their sense of European mutuality. Churchill's response was to exclude Harriman from the most sensitive private meetings with Stalin. And the Soviet leader, after expressing some initial irritation upon finding that Churchill was not able to speak for Roosevelt, also responded in classic European style by telling Churchill he noticed "signs of alarm" in the president's letter and on the whole did not like it. It seemed to demand too many rights for the United States and left too little for the Soviet Union and Britain, who after all, he emphasized, had a treaty.

By the time Churchill left Moscow ten days later they had much more than a vaguely harmonious treaty. The crucial exchanges began with a somewhat garish scene engraved on the memories of all modern diplomatic historians. Churchill, thinking the moment "apt for business," pushed a piece of paper across the table to Stalin. It contained certain percentages reflecting the actual or projected degree of British or Soviet influence in each Balkan state: Britain to have 90:10 in Greece; the Soviet Union to have 90:10 in Rumania; Bulgaria, Yugoslavia, and Hungary to be shared 50:50. Stalin, according to Churchill, examined the document for a moment, placed a large blue tick upon it and returned it to Churchill. The prime minister appears to have been somewhat awed by this casual display of power. Seized by a sudden scrupulosity, he said, "Let us burn the paper." "No, you keep it," replied Stalin. Churchill later eased his conscience by cabling the War Cabinet that these were, of course, only convenient wartime arrangements. They were in fact the logical culmination of the long process inaugurated in the Eden-Stalin talks of December 1941 and developed thereafter in thought and action on both sides. Moreover, the "percentages," for all their crudity, almost exactly mirrored Eden's geopolitical designations of the two spheres in his August 9 Cabinet paper, simply registering in the various minority quotients the Foreign Office's hopeful gloss that the principal proprietor in each case would not insist on exclusive control.[51]

This was, nonetheless, power politics (or rather "power geopolitics") in form and content. Thus Churchill said, just to make it crystal clear, "Britain must be the leading Mediterranean power." Stalin did not demur, simply asserting with equal logic that Russia must have primacy in the Black Sea, a position he then held to justify the higher Soviet superiority in Bulgaria. These percentages then underwent some revision by Eden and

---

[51] Churchill-Stalin meeting, October 9, 1944, PREM 3.434/2; Gilbert, *Churchill*, VII, pp. 989–1033.

Molotov in later sessions. These were haggling sessions in which Molotov, in true Soviet style, worked to improve his take, demanding 80:10 in both Bulgaria and Hungary in return for a vague promise of British participation in the future Allied Control Councils there. Eden accepted the retreat in Hungary but continued to claim a more substantial role in Bulgaria, which he feared as the springboard for any future pressure against Turkey, Greece, and Yugoslavia. All this ended inconclusively but with the British clearly acknowledging that they would have little influence anywhere in Central or southeastern Europe.[52]

It is noticeable that, despite the minority percentages, neither party, except for perfunctory British noises about Bulgaria and Rumania, sought from the other any undertakings about the actual treatment of areas given up or about the practical character of the "access" they would receive. No one wanted to open up new lines of controversy. The British were conscious of their weak hand, conscious too that they were laying themselves open to criticism at home and perhaps around the world. Hence, Churchill's squeamish wish to burn the incriminating paper. Thus, his messages to London and Washington denying anything more than a temporary wartime expedient, an explanation repeated in his memoirs. So too Eden's fey attempts to cover himself with a critical Foreign Office. Cadogan and Sargent (who reminded Eden unavailingly that it was functions rather than "percentages" that really counted) had expected him to claim a substantial role in Bulgarian affairs, seen in London as vital to Britain's Mediterranean interests. In the event, he conceded almost exclusive Soviet wartime control in return for vague undertakings of an enhanced Anglo-American participation in the Allied Control Council's functions later on. Eden was hard put to explain all this to his skeptical Foreign Office staff. He characteristically resorted again to psychology, saying that he had not realized how strong the Russians' "feelings" were about these issues.[53]

We come then to a question of fundamental importance. Was this a division of Europe, as some historians, notably Albert Resis, have argued? Or at least so large an advance toward it as to make such a division at some future point virtually certain or probable? This bears heavily on the valuation we put on the full significance of the subsequent meeting at Yalta. Is it here, rather than at Yalta, that the division of Europe occurred? If

---

[52] Churchill-Stalin meeting, October 9, 1944; and Eden-Molotov meetings, October 10, 11, 1944, all in PREM 3.434/2.

[53] Churchill to Attlee, October 9, 1944, PREM 3.434/2. Sargent to Eden, October 12, 1944; Eden to Foreign Office, October, 16, 1944, both in C14111, F.O. 371.39255.

so, it becomes at least questionable whether the United States can be held responsible.[54]

On the face of it, this was not a full and certainly not a formal division of Europe. Germany remained an open, delicately avoided question; and despite much effort, the Polish issues were not, as we will see, put to rest. Nevertheless, the widespread public assumption at the time that the Moscow conference addressed only the continent's southeastern corner was misplaced. For both by explicit agreement and natural political implication it endorsed the Soviet grip upon virtually all the parts of Eastern and Central Europe that later came under its full sway. Bulgaria and Rumania would be run by the Soviets almost exclusively, with some minimal, face-saving British presence. Yugoslavia, hitherto seen in London as a British preserve, would now be shared, but with the Soviets clearly having, as Tito's recent visit to Moscow suggested, the political momentum – so much so that the British half-share there, which included the coastline, was apparently a geopolitical gesture to Churchill, a signal from Stalin of his support for a clear-cut distinction between a Soviet Eastern Europe and a British-dominated Mediterranean.

So far, with the Yugoslav addition, we may think we are seeing little more than a logical extension and crystallization of the May 1944 Balkans/southern Europe arrangement. But now we find ourselves on a "staircase" moving north toward the Baltic Sea. The significant British concession in this northward progress from the Balkans was in Hungary. This was the key to the developing political (and military?) situation in Central Europe. One might have expected some political self-assertion on the British side given Hungary's western orientation, its strategic position, and the manifest desire of its desperate leaders to align with Britain rather than with Russia. But Churchill and Eden conformed to the logic they had been following since the Anglo-Soviet treaty. The Soviets would obviously occupy Hungary. It was therefore written off. "It is useless to argue," as one diplomat conceded. This left Czechoslovakia, the next step northward. But this was already, thanks to Benes's dubious diplomacy, firmly in the Soviet sphere and recognized as such by all interested parties. Indeed, the Benes government was already feeling the force of what Soviet primacy meant – disappointment over Hungarian reparations; Ruthenia, destined for the Soviets, already pulsing with pro-Soviet agitation; criticism in the

---

[54] Albert Resis, "The Churchill-Stalin Secret 'Percentages' Agreement on the Balkans: Moscow, October, 1944," *American Historical Review*, 83 (April 1978), pp. 368–387. See, however, Mastny, *Russia's Road*, pp. 207–212.

Soviet media for insufficiently active resistance to the Germans. This left, to complete the creation of a Soviet domain running from Bulgaria in the south to the Baltic in the north, only Poland and the three Baltic republics. But the latter were already incorporated into the Soviet Union and regarded in London as beyond challenge.[55]

Thus in the end, if we focus on the issue of a divided Europe, only the still unsettled question of Poland remained. Churchill had no intention of leaving the gap unclosed. As soon as he had given up all British rights to a significant voice in all these states, he summoned Mikolajczyk from London for what he manifestly intended to be a final settlement of this vexing, European problem. Had he been successful in settling the Polish issue on terms satisfactory to the Soviets, we would, in contemplating Churchill's seemingly impressionistic nation shifting, be aware that we are looking both at the political origins of the line "from Stettin in the Baltic to Trieste in the Adriatic" that Churchill self-righteously used to such potent effect to describe the division of Europe in his famous "Iron Curtain" speech in March 1946, and also, more generally, except for the as yet unresolved question of Germany's destiny, at something that very closely resembles the map of a divided Europe as it actually existed from 1945 to 1989, a "political" map (for the military outcomes were not yet complete) agreed upon in anticipation of conquest by Churchill and Stalin, and later presided over in mutual animosity but remarkably strict cartographical respect by two mighty coalitions, the American-led West and the Soviet Union's East. In other words, while the military historians cannot be faulted for putting conquest at the center of their causation, the political division of Europe was settled in advance of this by Stalin and Churchill. This work in Moscow was a serious, thought-out business with very deep, at least partially recognized implications and not, as it has sometimes been caricatured, the antics of an unrepentant imperialist.[56]

But the Polish issue was not settled, and in this area the business was neither thought-out nor realistic. At their first meeting, in Stalin's presence, Churchill told Mikolajczyk that the Soviet Union's wartime "sacrifices" and its efforts to liberate Poland entitled it to the acquisition of the latter's territories behind the Curzon Line. When Mikolajczyk refused to accept this rationale, Churchill threatened the withdrawal of British support. The British, he said, having themselves been "a hair's breadth from defeat," had

[55] Sargent to Eden, October 12, 1944, C14111, F.O. 371.39255. Allen minute, October 4, 1944, C13223, F.O. 371.39254.
[56] *Vital Speeches*, March 15, 1946, pp. 329–332.

"the right to ask the Poles for a great gesture in the interest of European peace." When Stalin, who harshly and intimidatingly interceded on several occasions to debate points with the Polish leader, subsequently refused to accept any compromises (such as the Polish retention of Lvov), Churchill again raised the pressure in an agitated way, accusing the Polish leaders of again turning to the "Liberum Veto," which had shattered their independence in the eighteenth century and opened the way to partition and lost independence. When Mikolajcyck tried to bring some realism to this talk of Soviet and British "rights" by remarking that unilaterally giving up the disputed territories would mean "I sign a death sentence against myself," Churchill's frustration erupted. "We will tell the world how unreasonable you are. You will start another war in which 25 million lives will be lost. But you don't care."[57]

Mikolajczyk had no cards to play. At the outset he had to endure Molotov's revelation, which Churchill rather sheepishly confirmed, that Roosevelt had accepted and "strongly endorsed" the Curzon Line nearly a year earlier at Teheran. As a leading historian of this episode notes, thinking no doubt of Churchill's manipulations and Roosevelt's cynical cosseting of the visiting Mikolajczyk in the run-up to the American election a few months earlier, "the Polish premier had been well and truly conned, not so much by the Soviets, who had been brutally direct, but by the Western allies." The Polish leader pointed out that he was being asked to give up 40% of Poland and to compromise its independence in forced association with the Lublin group – all in return for a vaguely described compensation in the west that could not be published. He then asked a pointed question. "Would it not be possible to proclaim that the Great Powers have decided on the frontiers of Poland without our presence?" To this direct invitation to assume some public responsibility for the problem, and for the unauthorized arrangements he had been cultivating privately with Stalin over the past year, Churchill was only able to offer, according to the British official record, the following response: "We will be sick and tired of you if you go on arguing."[58]

The hapless London Poles were not even given the courtesy of a reasoned explanation, much less an apology. They were expected to take

---

[57] Davies, *Rising '44*, p. 444. For Polish aspects at Moscow, see ibid., pp. 444–445; Kitchen, *British Policy*, Chapter 10; and Gilbert, *Churchill*, VII, pp. 1011–1024. For the Polish account, see *Documents on Polish-Soviet Relations, 1939–1945*, Vol. 2 (London, 1961), pp. 239–241, 416–424.

[58] Davies, *Rising '44*, p. 445.

the odium by themselves. Churchill was at no stage willing to give them any meaningful political cover for the amputational sacrifices he was demanding. The later meetings went no better, with Churchill castigating the London Poles as "callous people who wanted to wreck Europe" and accusing Mikolajczyk personally of "cowardice." Of the discussions about Poland at Moscow, the historian Norman Davies aptly says that "they provided one of the most heart-breaking moments in modern diplomacy." The observant Dixon noted, "We are all sympathizing deeply with Mikolajczyk." In the end, the Polish leader, perhaps thankful to get away personally unscathed (he had asked in an emotional moment to be parachuted into Poland so that he could share his compatriots' fate) undertook to return to London to consult his colleagues.[59]

We see in these exchanges a dimension of Churchill's diplomacy that is often overlooked. He was, in many ways, an impressively self-conscious practitioner of the diplomatic arts seemingly called for in a British prime minister trying to maintain himself and his country's fundamental interests in a difficult coalition with two more powerful partners. Doubtless he meant well. But his tactical approach seems seriously open to question. He often relied excessively on personal charm. He could deploy an impressive knowledge embellished with historical precedent and was, despite his well-known orotundity, a skilled debater. But at the highest level it is impossible to read deeply into the record of his dealings with Roosevelt and Stalin, for instance, without recognizing the extent to which, having identified their respective primary aversions, he associated himself vigorously with them and in a very personal way reinforced (making full use of his stimulating flair for inventive, ingratiating, and often unpleasant characterizations) their dominant prejudices.

Thus he systematically forged a bond with Roosevelt in personal hostility to de Gaulle. With the cantankerous Frenchman, certainly, he had his own problems, but the record, especially of 1944, makes it clear that it was the American animus to the Free French leader that sharpened and prolonged the confrontation and did much to turn Churchill away from rational compromises, arguably at some cost to Britain's and perhaps to Europe's postwar prospect. He took the same line with Stalin. When Soviet prospects were low, as they seemed to be in December 1941, Churchill had treated Stalin's expansionist ambitions with disdain. But as Soviet power grew, so Churchill began, notably at Teheran and systematically thereafter,

[59] Ibid., p. 444. Dixon diary, October 14, 1944, Dixon MSS.

to present himself to Stalin as a useful partner who shared his supposed dislike for the "irresponsible" Poles and had the ability to force them and the recalcitrant Turks to make fundamental compromises of their sovereignty and security in the Soviet interest. The fact that France and Poland had been Britain's first and most durable allies in World War II (and that Turkey also was a long-standing British ally) seems to have been steadily subordinated to the prime minister's overarching personal need to please Roosevelt and Stalin. Churchill's rationale, to the very limited extent that he acknowledged any of these tendencies, was that "humbling submissions" were needed to keep the Soviet Union in the war and its inevitable postwar expansion within reasonable bounds. Perhaps so. Whether this line of diplomacy was necessary or desirable to the extent that Churchill indulged it will always be one of the great historical questions of this era.

In any event, by October 1944 the creation of a Soviet-ruled, or at least Soviet-dominated, Eastern Europe was now clearly in contemplation, and the prize of Britain's legitimizing endorsement was now safely in Stalin's hand. The British would take the lead in Western Europe and the Mediterranean. We must still ask, nonetheless, how the two principals to this agreement actually put it into practice in the following months before satisfying ourselves that it was a fully functioning bargain.

5

Consolidation

The arrangements made by Churchill and Stalin at Moscow in October 1944 were, it has been argued, a culmination of visible trends and relationships, not a sudden improvisation. The ongoing discussion consequently resolves itself into two main tasks. The first, the subject of this chapter, is to substantiate the claim that the so-called Moscow Order was a significant, developing political reality during the period between the Moscow conference and the meeting at Yalta three and a half months later. The second, which will be the focus of subsequent chapters, will be to show not so much how and why it failed – for in its territorial framework it did not fail; indeed, it lasted for nearly half a century – but rather how its political character was transformed by the sudden entry of the United States into the equation in early 1945, signifying the first stages, at least, of an East/West confrontation that shortly led to the Cold War and, arguably, to something we might call the Cold War Order.

Two other preliminary issues present themselves. The first addresses a semantic point. Is it justifiable here to use the term "order" rather than the phrase "wartime expedient," which Churchill used at the time, or the pejorative "sphere of influence," the characterization with which many suspicious American commentators greeted this questionable transaction? Eden spoke of it in terms familiar to all Europeans as "a concert." As we have found with the post-1945 treatment of Yalta, there is a high degree of emotional freight in the words used, often with manipulative intent, to describe controversial events. It can hardly be denied that the Moscow conference contemplated "two spheres." But surely two adjoining spheres created – politically speaking, at least – by mutual agreement and intended by both parties to be elements in a general system of security may be said to constitute some kind of "order."

There has been some theoretical discussion of "order," mainly by international lawyers. One eminent academic authority, the late Hedley Bull, suggested in *The Anarchical Society* that the term presupposed a system where two or more states are in regular contact with each other to the extent that they "make the behaviour of each a necessary element in the calculations of the other." British and Soviet conduct in this case seems to conform to the standard. Another criterion favored by some writers is the existence of some "expectancy" on the part of the participating states. By this test too the arrangements made at Moscow seem to justify the idea of "order," for, as the following review will show, each side appears to have left the meeting with a clear sense of what it was now licensed to do, and how it should respond to its partner. The best test is doubtless to be found in the practical consequences of the Moscow arrangements, to which we will turn in a moment.[1]

Second, an informed reader who has shown the stamina to keep up with some of the debates about World War II diplomacy may reasonably ask why, if this Moscow Order was important, it has received less than its due as a significant event. This is only partly because of its association with "spheres of influence" and other dismissive descriptive terms. Even at the time it was obscured by a number of more tangible factors. For one thing, it was a secret agreement, though its main thrust was the subject of much speculation in Europe at the time. And it coincided, in its working out, with a dramatic phase of the war in Europe, so that many understandably distracted contemporaries were scarcely aware of it. Further, it was misunderstood at the time in the United States, where a deeply rooted conviction that nothing constructive could emerge from the vicious cat's cradle of European diplomacy tended to cast doubt upon the notion of a genuine Anglo-Soviet collaboration. Even leading figures in the Roosevelt administration who knew something of the event interpreted the Tolstoy arrangements as a kind of temporary "devil's bargain" between mutually antagonistic Tories and Reds, united only in chauvinism and greed. It was conveniently put to service in that sense as a welcome stage setting for the president's mediatory peacemaking at Yalta.[2] Then too, the Moscow deal was not comprehensive in its continental reach, failing to bring about a

---

[1] Hedley Bull, *The Anarchical Society* (London, 1977), p. 10. See also Steve Smith, "Is the Truth Out There? Eight Questions about International Order," in T. V. Paul and John T. Hall (eds.), *International Order and the Future of World Politics* (Cambridge, England, 1999).

[2] The president's "Briefing Papers" in FRUS, *Malta and Yalta*, pp. 237–305, contain several references to Anglo-Soviet rivalry.

Polish settlement and obviously excluding the fate of postwar Germany. And, most obviously, perhaps the simplest and most plausible explanation, it was soon overshadowed by the quickly following Yalta conference and its aftermath, which, whatever view one took of it then or later, soon became the new touchstone of Big Three politics and later the primary historiographical reference point.

These contemporary distractions might not have thrown historians off the scent but for three later developments. One was the combination of social dislocation and economic devastation in Europe that had become increasingly obvious by the spring of 1945. The notion of an independent role for the forlorn inhabitants of the old continent must already have seemed a lost cause. Another was the Americocentrism of much postwar historiography, which consequently tended to overlook or downgrade the importance of autonomous European initiatives, including those between Britain and the Soviet Union. And a third, amply reinforcing that tendency, was Churchill's misleading characterization of his Moscow encounter with Stalin as nothing more than a wartime "expedient." It is true that this is how he justified it to the War Cabinet and to Roosevelt at the time. But here too, as in his account of Yalta and its aftermath, Churchill was evasive and self-protective. Writing in his *Triumph and Tragedy* at the height of the early Cold War, in a climate where books about "the rape of Poland" and the "betrayal of Eastern Europe" were agitating Western minds, he had no more wish to be branded as Stalin's partner in the 1944 division of Europe at Moscow than to be accused of giving Eastern Europe away at the ensuing Crimean conference. The latter role was, by the time Churchill published his memoir account, already conveniently occupied by the supposedly naïve Franklin D. Roosevelt, whose conduct became for many the centerpiece of the "tragedy."[3]

Still, many contemporary observers in Europe – Axis and neutral as well as Allied – had little doubt that the main business at Moscow represented some kind of agreement about the future of Europe, a future that could be imagined at this stage only in the shape of some kind of sphere-of-influence arrangement. Security had of course been tight, and nothing was known

[3] See Churchill, *Triumph and Tragedy*, pp. 226–243. Churchill told Moran long after the war that the "percentages" agreement with Stalin had been transacted "on the spot in a few minutes. You see, the people at the top can do these things, others can't do." Moran, *Churchill*, p. 481. See also David Reynolds's analysis in *In Command of History*, pp. 457–461, though I differ from his judgment that the percentages deal "came from nowhere" and that Eden was "surprised," for it had all been foreshadowed in the foreign secretary's memorandum "Soviet Policy in Europe," August 9, 1944, WP (44) 346.

for sure. Nevertheless, Churchill was impatient for news of the European reaction when he arrived home. "Are there no BJ's?" he inquired, referring to the Ultra and other European intelligence that he had been receiving throughout the war. "Surely the Jap Embassy at Moscow talked?" By this time commentaries were appearing, and sure enough the observant Japanese diplomat led the way, telling his masters in Tokyo of the "friction" over Poland, but warning that the Big Three were "closing ranks" to finish Germany first. The general line in the Axis countries was that Stalin was the winner and that the British and Americans had "saved face" but had "virtually given in to the USSR" and in doing so had given a spur, as the German Ministry of Foreign Affairs put it, to "the spread of communism in Europe." The Turks, on the other hand, according to several diplomats in Ankara, were well satisfied with the talks, apparently fully aware of the geopolitical implications whereby the Mediterranean was to be preserved from Soviet expansion and British interests secured. And certainly the principals themselves seemed pleased. Stalin, in a November 6 speech, referred to "the spirit of complete unanimity" animating the talks with Churchill. The Soviet press and radio were enthusiastic, with *Pravda* connecting the talks to the 1942 Anglo-Soviet treaty, still seen as "a cornerstone, not only of the joint struggle against Hitlerite Germany, but also of the future stable peace in Europe." This was also, naturally enough, the Foreign Office line in London, where Wilson similarly described the proceedings as "a putting into practice of the Anglo-Soviet treaty." And *The Times* registered general press approval by congratulating Churchill and Stalin on "their brilliant and far-reaching success."[4]

Actions tell the fuller story.

THE SOVIET SPHERE

Almost immediately after Tolstoy the Soviets began to clamp down on their now "legitimated" fiefs in Rumania and Bulgaria. Here, as in other areas of Central Europe, the British had had hopes earlier in the war of postwar influence. But they had given way slowly as Soviet power increased. Their retreat began, it will be recalled, with the post-Stalingrad collapse of the

---

[4] *Pravda*, October 21, 1944. Wilson memorandum, November 7, 1944. Reactions to the Moscow conference are in Churchill to C, October 23, 1944, HW1/3284 and HW1/3376. See also note by C, October 3, 1944; and C to prime minister, October 34, 1944, both in HW1/3284. For German reaction, see C to prime minister, October 25, 1944, HW1/3286; and for Turkish response, C to prime minister, October 28, 1944, HW1/3294. *Pravda*, November 7, 1944. *The Times*, November 6, 1944.

"confederation" schemes and the Soviet repudiation of the "gentlemen's agreement" following the grave-digging activities of Benes. During 1944, Hitler's disillusioned and desperate satellite regimes in Hungary, Rumania, and Bulgaria had all put out secret feelers to the British (and even tentatively, in some cases, to the Americans) in vain hopes of a safe landing. But the August 1944 coup led by King Michael against the pro-Nazi Rumanian strongman Marshal Antonescu had led to the rapid Soviet occupation of that country and the Red Army's quickly following move into Bulgaria at the beginning of September. The ensuing armistices with these two states had therefore been orchestrated by Moscow with reluctant but clear-eyed acquiescence on the part of the British. Now, following Churchill's Moscow arrangements with Stalin, Britain had only a nominal toehold in each country. The Soviets, using their domination of the Allied Control Councils (reluctantly conceded in the talks by Churchill and Eden) quickly assumed full control, freezing out the various Allied missions, whose members were confined to selected areas, denied communications facilities, and fobbed off with reminders of the Red Army's security and supply needs in a still-dangerous region and vague promises of a fuller role after the war.[5]

The Foreign Office, which had hoped the minority percentages in the upper really meant something, was upset by these exclusionary tactics and contemplated some kind of protest, especially over Bulgaria, where Britain had received a higher recognition of acknowledged interest than in the more remote Rumania. In December Eden embarrassed Churchill by raising the issue with the War Cabinet. But the prime minister deflected the challenge by persuading his colleagues that communism was rife in the Balkans even without Soviet patronage. In truth, the British were mostly resigned to the situation. Churchill defended the Soviet deportations of "Saxon" elements now taking place in Rumania on the ground that it was "understood" that they would "work their will in this sphere." As he put it, when confronted with protests from British agents on the spot, "I don't think our people out there have the slightest idea of the very small stake we have elected to take in the affairs of Rumania." Earlier in 1944 the Post Hostilities Planners had produced a paper stressing the powerful influence the Soviets were bound to have in the postwar Balkans. It was in this context that the main consideration in London soon came to be the shoring up of Greece and, more generally, keeping the Soviets out of the Mediterranean. The Soviets seemed to understand. As Churchill told Eden

[5] Rothwell, *Britain and the Cold War*, pp. 212–216; and Mastny, *Russia's Road*, pp. 195–207.

in December, "Considering the way the Russians have so far backed us up over what is happening in Greece, which must throw great strain on their sentiments and organization, we really must not press our hand too far in Rumania." Still, even Churchill had occasional qualms. As the volume of protests from British representatives in Bucharest mounted, we find him asking Eden anxiously, "Will any of this ever become public?"[6]

Hungary and Czechoslovakia, though still firmly in German hands, were also during the period between Moscow and Yalta abandoned politically by London to the virtual certainty of Soviet conquest and dictatorial postwar control. Here, as with the two Balkan states, Eden had been diverted by Molotov's promises that while the Soviets would dominate the Allied Control Councils in these Central European countries until hostilities ended, there would be some unspecified tripartite participation afterward. Here too there were understandable doubts and qualms in the Foreign Office. This was a disappointing conclusion to the secret British negotiations with Admiral Horthy's emissaries as the Budapest government tried unsuccessfully to slip out of the war. The watchful Germans had then intervened decisively, handing over power to fascistic bitter-enders. This ensured a fight to the finish there and ultimate power to the Soviets, who had themselves been in negotiations with elements of the Horthy regime. In the end there was an almost complete British capitulation, extending even to support for the Soviets against American pressure for larger reparations for the Czechs and others, a gesture of solidarity that, one official noted hopefully, "may earn us a good mark with the Soviet Government." A Foreign Office diplomat pronounced the appropriate epitaph on London's Hungarian connections: "We have done what we could and can do no more." British representations to Moscow thereafter were largely limited, as with almost all the states now coming into the Soviet orbit, to laborious efforts to get basic facilities for their harassed diplomatic officials.[7]

---

[6] For Bulgaria, see Churchill to Eden, October 14, 1944, PREM 3.79/5; and Michael Boll, *Cold War in the Balkans: American Foreign Policy and the Emergence of Communist Bulgaria, 1943–1947* (Lexington, Ky., 1984), Chapters 2 and 3. For Rumania, see Churchill to Eden, November 4, 7, December 11, 1944, and January 18 and 25, 1945, all in PREM 3.374/13A. See also WM (44) 164; and Liliana Saiu, *The Great Powers and Rumania, 1944–1946: A Study of the Early Cold War Era* (New York, 1992), pp. 43–53.

[7] For the British view of the Hungarian armistice, see Eden to Sargent, October 11, 1944, C14105, F.O. 371.39255. Chaplin minute, December 2, 1944, C16437; and Harrison note, December 22, 1944, C14645, both in F.O. 371.39256. For dashed British hopes, see Kitchen, *British Policy*, p. 202.

There was a similarly abdicatory tone to British efforts to keep up a relationship with Benes's reconstituted Czech government. Benes's faith in his chosen Soviet mentors had by the end of 1944 been sorely shaken. Within weeks of the Soviet-Czech treaty in December 1943 he found his government being severely criticized in *Pravda* for not inspiring more vigorous resistance to the occupying Germans. The ingenous Czech leader was now, a Foreign Office member noted, learning "the sad truth." Further indignities followed, and when the Czech minister of finance appealed to British ministries for help, he found many doors closed. The attitude in Whitehall, where there were still resentful memories of Benes's destructively opportunistic unilateralism in 1943, was that the Czechs had made themselves a Soviet "protectorate" in order to get "special favours." Emotions cooled later in the year, but, as with Hungary, it became clear that the self-designated "bridge" between East and West was going to find itself enclosed inside the Soviet sphere, well beyond the reach of British political or diplomatic assistance. At the end of 1944 the Special Operations Executive operations in the country were shut down, and it was made clear that the country was henceforth to be regarded as within the Soviet sphere. All future requests from the Czech underground were to be channeled through Moscow. Thus the Foreign Office's calculated retreat in the face of rising Soviet power continued, its interest now coming to focus on holding the line with an agreed tripartite occupation in Austria.[8]

The British were also backing away ever more decisively on the still unresolved Polish issues. Churchill had made it clear to Stalin in Moscow that he had no intention of sustaining Polish hopes or ambitions. The British government continued to recognize the London Poles, but when Mikolajczyk resigned in November, having predictably failed to rally any support for concessions to Stalin, relations deteriorated sharply, and the new government's communications with Poland were at last cut. Churchill maintained a personal connection with Mikolajczyk, whom he still hoped to push into a significant role in Poland, whether out of a genuine belief (or at least a hope) that this patriotic figure would be able to share in the power with Lublin or simply as a kind of face-saving gesture to show that he was still trying to help, is unclear. After months of frustration at the hands of the Foreign Office during which virtually no independent information was obtained about actual conditions in Soviet-occupied Poland,

---

[8] *Pravda*, January 16, 1944. Roberts note, February 4, 1944, C1346; and Andrews to Jebb, March 13, 1944, C3276, both in F.O. 371.38920. See also Kitchen, *British Policy*, p. 189.

the Strategic Operations Executive was authorized by the uneasy prime minister to send a six-man team – the so-called Freston Mission – into the country. It departed for Poland on October 13, only to endure a series of fruitless encounters with partisans in the forests and then incarceration in a Red Army prison before repatriation in March. No serious complaints were ever lodged. Meanwhile, the accommodationist diplomatic line was being played out at the political level. When word came from another SOE source inside Poland that most Poles were adjusting themselves to Soviet control, Churchill wrote "Good" on the informing document. The British government registered little more than a formal protest when in January the Soviets announced their recognition of the Lublin group as Poland's government, though Churchill typically began now to think about the possibilities of a discreet back-up role to the unmistakably more alarmed Roosevelt administration, if indeed it could be persuaded to act.[9]

Stalin's long-anticipated imperium was now, with a high degree of British legitimation, beginning to take a more definite shape. It was, as military historians are quick to remind us, essentially the product of conquest rather than Allied license. It was certainly not the consequence of any significant invitational impulse from the region's inhabitants, despite a widespread hatred of the Germans and the presence of active but tiny communist parties in the various countries. But these early regimes were not yet the communist police state elites of later Cold War reality. What is striking at this stage is how closely Soviet policy appears to have followed the scenario set out by the Maisky commission in 1943. Brutalities and atrocities certainly occurred. But Maisky, it will be recalled, had envisioned the possibility of opposition in the various countries and had looked to an evolutionary solution that allowed a pluralistic, political approach. During 1944 defeated Finland got off lightly and was granted virtual autonomy in domestic matters. Perhaps a model for Poland? No one knew, but it seemed possible. In a review at the beginning of 1945, the *New Statesman and Nation* judged Soviet policy to be "flexible," with broad-based coalitions and "land reform" the only radical domestic policy, though complete loyalty to the Soviet Union was required. Certainly at the end of 1944 the Popular Front model, in various forms tailored to local situations, seemed to be making some sort of reappearance in Rumania and Bulgaria and

---

[9] A further fruitless meeting between Churchill and Mikolajczyk took place in London after the Moscow conference – Gilbert, *Churchill*, VII, pp. 1043–1045. Allen minute, December 5, 1944; and Roberts minute, December 5, 1944, both in C16712, F.O. 371.39436. For the "Freston" mission, see Davies, *Rising '44*, pp. 449–453, 465–466, 535, 635.

especially in Hungary, though it left the local communists in key positions and the Red Army and NKVD operatives were never far away. In general, though, Stalin's concern for control and practical arrangements rather than ideological purity was in evidence. He particularly disapproved of left-wing radicalism in the Balkans, especially in Bulgaria, where by late 1944 left-wing extremists were actively pursuing an orgy of violent score settling.[10]

The early Soviet emphasis on state control and Popular Front models rather than radical change and ideological purity is vital to any understanding of the now evolving Moscow Order. It was a consistent source of moral reassurance to British observers who had devised and then clung to the view that Stalin was inspired above all by the desire for the geopolitical security the Soviet Union had lacked before 1941. This was the line repeatedly pressed by the British diplomats in their reports from Moscow and accepted by their colleagues in London. There were, of course, occasional dissenting voices throughout the war and a tempering caution even in the most optimistic assessments. But a determination to look on the bright side is persistently evident through 1944, even in the War Cabinet, where the response to Eden's steady stream of carefully balanced but upbeat predictions was nearly always positive.

Recently available Soviet evidence tends to confirm the accuracy of the hopeful British diagnosis. We have already noted Maisky's late 1943 stress on Soviet security and on the value of a long-term Anglo-Soviet alliance with adjoining spheres of influence that could be expected to ensure up to fifty years of peace, creating a framework for what Stalin and his associates appear to have expected: the evolutionary transformation toward socialism of the territories under Soviet control. Now we can cite Litvinov, who made a very similar argument in his "On the Prospects and Possible Basis of Soviet-British Cooperation," a paper drawn up for Molotov on November 15, 1944. The subject and conclusions of this paper appear to confirm the significance, in Soviet eyes, of the Moscow conference. Indeed, much of it could have been written in the Foreign Office. The Soviet and British partners, Litvinov stressed, would contain Germany and preserve peace on the continent generally. He sketched out a Soviet sphere encompassing all the Moscow-dominated territories from the Baltic to Bulgaria (adding Sweden, Finland, and Turkey, but not Greece). The British zone

---

[10] *New Statesman and Nation*, January 6, 1945. For a recent review based on Soviet records, see Geoffrey Roberts, *Stalin's Wars: From World War to Cold War, 1939–1953* (New Haven and London, 2006), pp. 228–253.

was to take in Western Europe, including France. A novelty here was a proposed neutral zone comprising Norway, Denmark, Germany, and Italy. But the principle of a divided Anglo-Soviet Europe was clearly affirmed here, and again in another paper on January 11, 1945, where Litvinov downplayed the possibility of any American involvement "in light of the widespread public opposition ... to blocs and spheres of influence."[11]

The Anglo-Soviet relationship was not all sweetness and light, and it was never intimate. The European diplomatic system in 1944, if we probe beneath the continuing Nazi overlay that inevitably distorts our view and focus only on the developing Soviet and British spheres, was still very much what Americans had traditionally claimed it to be: an insecure, power-oriented arena where the political impulse was never still and sentiment was only rarely a match for ambition, intrigue, and violence. Illustrations from the 1940s to support that thesis are hardly necessary. But the point can be substantiated, and the transatlantic divergence further exposed, by reference to a less dramatic European habit that had no American counterpart. This was the tendency of political allies to reinsure. Of this Bismarck, with his famous Reinsurance Treaty, is the classic exemplar. This manifestation of chronic doubt had persistently functioned as an irritating but accepted descant to the orchestration of an otherwise logical if power-dominated European diplomacy ever since. Thus when Molotov came to London to complete the May 1942 treaty, he annoyed his British hosts by spending considerable time with de Gaulle and Benes, a pointed reminder that the Soviet government had other options. Benes was quick to exploit the opening, choosing to align with Moscow largely for geopolitical reasons but also, many felt, in some congenial retribution for the British betrayal at Munich. De Gaulle was a habitual reinsurer (early in the war he even attempted, unprofitably, to cultivate the Americans at British expense) who frequently and ostentatiously flattered "dear and beloved Russia" in ways calculated to anger what he liked to call "the Anglo-Saxons." Churchill played this game against the Soviets on numerous occasions by stressing Britain's American ties. At Tolstoy, for instance, he warned Stalin that "[t]he Americans may return." And he responded to the apparition of Franco-Soviet intimacy in December 1944 by telling Stalin, contrary to his actual preference at the time, that the

[11] Maxim Litvinov, "On the Prospect and Possible Basis of Soviet-British Co-operation," cited in Roberts, *Stalin's Wars*, pp. 230–231 and p. 409, n.5. See also, for both papers, Roberts, "Litvinov's Lost Peace, 1941–1946," *Journal of Cold War Studies*, 4, 2 (Spring, 2002), pp. 41–43.

"World Organization" (with its implied intimation of American power) must be superior to all "regional" European arrangements.[12]

Another feature of the Anglo-Soviet concert that qualifies the general impression of political solidarity – a step away from the line that Maisky had put to Eden in 1943 contemplating the possibility that the Big Three should "work with each other" in all capitals – was the Soviet insistence now on a "closed" conception of the two spheres rather than the "open" version that had been endorsed by Churchill in 1943 and would be revived in a late-blooming American variant after the war by Charles Bohlen. Thus, as we have seen, the Foreign Office was upset to find after the apparent amity at Tolstoy that Britain was essentially shut out in Bulgaria and Rumania. There was also disappointment at the Soviet refusal to consider plans for the international administration of the Danube. Meanwhile, the Americans, already upset at but reluctantly accepting the exclusionary Soviet policy over the direction of the Allied Control Councils, were facing a similar disillusionment on what they considered larger matters. For a frustrated Harriman and his staff were now finding obstructions in Moscow as they sought entry for various American missions charged, with Stalin's earlier approval, to carry out various inspections and to set up facilities for the Soviet entry into the Pacific war. This determination to keep their allies at arms length was an ominous development, telling us that, for the Soviets at least, the Moscow Order was rooted in respect for sharply drawn boundaries rather than in trust and practical interaction.[13]

But none of this seems to have worried Churchill. Unlike the diplomats, he appears now to have been perfectly content with the notion of closed spheres. There are several possible explanations. A fundamental one was the unchallengeable fact of Soviet power, which he repeatedly acknowledged. Another was his personal faith in Stalin as a realist and statist. Associated with this, it seems reasonable to assume, was a perception that while the Soviets were, as expected, taking full and exclusive control of their hard-won postwar inheritance, they were also at the same time, by accepting an adjoining British-led system, fashioning for themselves a kind of self-chosen "containment." And containment – a word we properly associate with its

---

[12] Scaife memorandum, October 12, 1942, N5414, F.O. 371.32918; *Daily Telegraph*, May 8, 1944; Churchill to Stalin, November 25, December 5, 1944, SCCA, pp. 273–274.

[13] An undercurrent of resentment over the exclusionary character of Soviet policy in Bulgaria and Rumania persisted into 1945 in the Foreign Office. See Eden to Churchill, March 24, 1945, F.O. 954/26C. See, similarly, Gilbert, *Churchill*, VII, p. 1042, on Lublin and the conference on Danube transport. See also correspondence in Boxes 175 and 176, Harriman MSS.

author, the American diplomat George F. Kennan, but which in its practical manifestations has a long European lineage dating back to 1917 – had been at the heart of Churchill's policy toward the Soviets (and that of many other conservative European leaders as well) since the Bolshevik regime had established itself after World War I. Later he would condemn the barrier the Soviets were now erecting as an "Iron Curtain." In 1944, however, he was somewhat complicit in helping to create it. The quid pro quo was, of course, a similar exclusivity in the West. This meant the elimination or at least the subjection of communist or left-radical impulses in the non-Soviet sphere, a cause to which Churchill devoted himself during the post-Tolstoy period. Occasionally in this season of Anglo-Soviet cordiality he produced a more ecumenical conception. "I think it is like breeding pestilence," he told Eden, "to try to keep a nation like Russia from free access to the broad waters." But such departures from the containment principle were rare. And even here there was some security insurance behind the sentiment. "We have no need to fear the movement of a Russian fleet through the Straits. Even if it were to join de Gaulle a British fleet and air bases in the Mediterranean will be capable of dealing with either or both."[14]

There was another, more positive dimension to the Churchill-Stalin partnership during this phase, one that also had roots in the World War I era. This was the rocklike faith they shared in the desirability of a directing role for the Great Powers over the importunate small states of Europe. Stalin never tired of urging the "unity" of the Great Powers, counterpointing the mischievous tendencies of the smaller ones. Here too Churchill sometimes spoke up in contrary fashion, as he memorably did at Yalta when he declared that "the eagle should let the small birds sing." But his general outlook and practice was closer to Stalin's. He had long lamented the disappearance of the great pre-1914 empires and the fatal emergence, as he saw it, of Wilsonian self-determination – a memory that goes far to explain his spasmodic suspicions of both Rooseveltian "meddling" in European affairs during World War II and the prospect of a Washington-designed world organization for the postwar. Now in Stalin he seems to have felt that he had, at least for the moment, a somewhat like-minded collaborator in the geopolitical reshaping of a postwar Europe that would reproduce at least some of the supposed structural solidity of the pre-1914

[14] Churchill to Eden, October 10, 1944, PREM 3.412A; Churchill to Ismay, October 17, 1944, PREM 3.397/3. For Churchill's post-1917 actively confrontational approach to the Soviet Union, see Harbutt, *Iron Curtain*, pp. 10–13. See also, for Churchill's faith in British air and naval power, Churchill to Eden, November 25, 1944, PREM 4.30/8.

era. In this attitude he reflected most "establishment" thinking in London. Thus, acknowledging that the Soviets would "play the major part in the postwar settlement and future ordering of Eastern Europe," one influential journal went on to conclude, "If the alliance is to survive we must accept these things as the perfectly natural acts of a Great Power."

The contrast here with Eden and the Foreign Office – a matter of degree only, for the diplomats were also solidly committed to some kind of Anglo-Soviet diarchy – is instructive. The diplomatic establishment wanted some Soviet recognition of British residual rights in Bulgaria and Rumania. Churchill cared nothing for these states and urged a free hand for the Soviets. "Would it not be better to let them adjust their political differences in their own way and without our being involved?" he asked Eden on November 28. He often spoke disparagingly of smaller states, even of allies like Greece and Turkey. Contrary to the impression given by his later activism, Churchill was at times erratically inclined to wash his hands of the Greek affair. When Eden showed some solicitude for the Turks and wanted a harder line with Moscow taken on their behalf, Churchill's cool response was, "I should think your assurances to the Turks ... were more than voided by their refusal to give us any help last January." As we have seen, without any prior consultation with the Turks he promised Stalin at Teheran, and again at Tolstoy, full support for a transformation of the Montreux Convention. Churchill thought habitually in Great Power terms. Smaller powers could be assets or liabilities, but were mostly the latter. In May 1944 he predicted "a litter of broken states" between Britain and Russia. In December he was talking of Europe's "helpless nations." At Yalta he would dismissively describe "the cluster of small states" supposedly interested in a British-led Western bloc as a prospective burden. And when the Foreign Office urged acceptance of the State Department's revised formula for a limited United Nations veto that would bestow more rights upon the smaller powers, Churchill, declaring himself "in entire agreement with the Russians," refused to comply, pointedly asking the foreign secretary, "Are you also wise to proceed upon a line which alienates you so markedly from Russia?" It was much the same story in the Far East when Eden expressed similar concern about Soviet ambitions at Chinese expense. Here too Churchill wanted to give the Soviets free rein, conscious that this might help protect British interests in Hong Kong against the twin threats of Chinese revisionism and American commercialism and/or moralism. Against this background we can hardly be surprised to find that, by the end of 1944, Churchill, in characteristically domineering style, had taken over from Eden as the most vigorous champion of Soviet ambitions as they seemed to be crystallizing in Europe, the Near East, and the Far East, and was also siding with the Soviets over the unresolved problems surrounding the prospective world organization forum.[15]

The various political moves by each party during this phase of the Anglo-Soviet relationship also reflect a surprising like-mindedness, especially over the need to subdue the politically dislocative elements each found in the areas coming under its control. Practicality invariably trumped ideology, producing some remarkable juxtapositions. Thus Stalin the communist actively curbed the radical leftists in his sphere, and Churchill the conservative monarchist showed little compunction in consigning the kings of Greece, Italy, Yugoslavia, and Albania to what seemed to many contemporary observers a kind of terminal limbo. As this shedding of old loyalties might suggest, the notion of some sort of "convergence" was a staple of wartime discussion in Britain. Churchill himself penned an unsent letter to Stalin at the Tolstoy conference in Moscow referring to "the narrowing differences" in their respective spheres and expressing "the feeling that, viewed from afar and on a grand scale, the differences between our systems will tend to get smaller and the great common ground which we share of making life richer and happier for the mass of the people is growing every year."[16]

The burgeoning Anglo-Soviet relationship was further eased in these months by the unmistakable post-Moscow warmth that the Soviets, despite their insistence on a closed sphere, were now showing at various levels of political significance toward the British partner. The British representative on the European Advisory Commission reported "better" Anglo-Soviet cooperation after the Tolstoy meeting. A British Broadcasting Corporation representative was, after months of fruitless application, suddenly accepted in Moscow. In November, the head of the Press Section of the Foreign Affairs Commissariat in Moscow gave a convivial dinner party for members of the British embassy. It was announced that Soviet historians were preparing a lecture series on Britain's past. Much publicity

---

[15] Churchill to Eden, January 25, 1945, PREM 4.31/1. For expressions of Churchill's pro-Soviet and anti–small power approach, see Churchill to Eden, November 28, 1944, PREM 3.212/10, and December 11, 1944, PREM 3.374/13A (Balkans); Churchill to Eden, January 28, 1944, PREM 3.412A (Turkey and China); and Churchill to Eden, December 6, 1944, PREM 4.30/10 (U.N.). See also PMM (44), 12th meeting, May 11, 1944; and Eden to Churchill, October 10, 1944; and Churchill to Eden, October 10, 1944, both in PREM 3.412A. *Spectator*, September 22, 1944.

[16] Stalin's approach was signaled in Maisky's survey and adhered to in the main by Dmitrov. Churchill to Stalin, October 20, 1944, PREM 3.397/3 (unsent). The journalist-historian E. H. Carr was a leading proponent of convergence in his editorials in *The Times*.

was given in the Soviet press to a meeting in the London Coliseum of the Congress of Friendship and Collaboration with the Soviet Union, a group pressing for closer Anglo-Soviet unity. And the Soviet propaganda bite, traditionally nagging and harsh, was now found on close examination to be noticeably less critical than before. All the principal Soviet media now began to publish Churchill's speeches regularly and fully, and in December even went so far as to present their doubtless puzzled readers with the annual "King's Speech from the Throne." Stalin would brook no interference in his Balkan accessions, and he was not responsive to calls for reparations on behalf of the Greeks, who had suffered grievously from their Bulgarian occupiers during the war. But he pleased the British by fencing in the expansion-minded politicians in Sofia, who wanted access to the Mediterranean and appeared to be the principal proponents of the vast Slavic federation with Tito's Yugoslavia that agitated the Foreign Office. The Soviet expansionary impulse was not entirely damped down by the new warmth. In November, Molotov's claim for Bear Island and Spitzbergen from Norway caused a momentary chill, as did an expressed Soviet desire to administer one or more of Italy's Mediterranean colonies. But these probes were very tentative and not pressed with any vigor at this point. On the whole, indeed, Stalin showed no inclination to move beyond the demarcations agreed upon with his British partner.[17]

It was entirely in keeping with his affirming view of Anglo-Soviet solidarity that Stalin was also now more sensitive about his relations with the United States, whose rising power during 1944 he obviously respected. The dismissive attitudes of 1941–42 were now very much a thing of the past. Indeed, no sooner had he waved goodbye to Churchill in Moscow than we find Stalin cabling Roosevelt agreeing to another tripartite summit. But the significance of this should not be misunderstood. The key point is that Stalin continued to keep his relations with the two Western powers anchored in the two "bargains" we have identified as central to his diplomacy, each in a separate compartment. He did not want the United States in postwar Europe. Observers in Moscow during October noticed signs of this. The British chargé cabled his belief that the Russians would be more worried about the United States than Great Britain after the war.

---

[17] Strang to Eden, November 7, 1944, PREM 3.137/1. Clark Kerr to Eden, November 10, 1944, N7465; and Balfour to Warner, November 21, 1944, N7884, both in F.O. 371.43307. For the Soviet press, see Clark Kerr to Eden, December 1, 1944; and Warner note, December 5, 1944, both in N7579, F.O. 371.43303. *Pravda*, November 7, 1944. See also Mastny, *Russia's Road*, pp. 229–232; and Harbutt, *Iron Curtain*, p. 108.

And in November his respected Canadian counterpart, Dana Willgress, reported continued Soviet hopes that "[t]he United States would not take too great an interest in European affairs"[18]

Here again we see Stalin's consistency. Far back in December 1941, as he began to build his regional association with the British, he had made clear his desire to keep the moralistic and potentially intrusive Americans out of his Eastern European sphere. What he had wanted then, and by all appearances now again in late 1944, was simply American "acquiescence" in the geopolitical arrangements he was working toward systematically with the British. Meanwhile, he was careful to signal Roosevelt that the Eastern Europe/United Nations negotiating nexus was still at the heart of his policy toward the United States. On October 15 *Pravda* referred ostentatiously to "the great work carried out in Dumbarton Oaks ... an important step towards the organization of the postwar world." And in his November 6 speech Stalin himself expressly praised the Dumbarton Oaks meeting and declared that only an international security organization could prevent a recurrence of aggression. But this too should be seen for what it was: not a capitulation on the unresolved membership and veto issues, but what lawyers call an "invitation to treat." For at the same time, clearly intent on retaining his leverage for the forthcoming summit conference, he continued to insist that real security depended on a close Big Three collaboration, a position that seemed to foreclose any prospect of a receptive United Nations forum for small power grievances. The clear "bargain" intimation, first clearly signaled at Teheran and now being clarified and reinforced by articles Litvinov was publishing in *Voina i rabochii klass,* an anthoritative journal conveying Soviet views on international affairs, was that Roosevelt would have to "acquiesce" in the new Soviet sphere if he wanted the kind of United Nations he seemed to need in order to establish postwar internationalism in the United States.[19]

Thus far we have focused attention on the Soviet consolidation in their sphere, a process eased by pragmatic British acceptance and undisturbed by any overt interference from Washington. But if the Moscow arrangements are to be seen as constituting an authentic European "order," one

---

[18] Stalin to Roosevelt, October 19, 1944, SCRT, p. 165; Balfour to Warner, October 9, 1944, N6565/G, F.O. 371.47860; Willgress to secretary of state (Ottawa), November 9, 1944, N20/20/38, ibid.

[19] *Pravda*, November 7, 1944; *New York Times*, November 7, 1944; *Izvestia*, November 16, 1944. For the Litvinov articles, see *Voina i rabochii klass*, July 15, 1944, and December 15, 1944. This journal's content "was closely controlled by Stalin and Molotov"– Geoffrey Roberts, "Litvinov's Lost Peace," pp. 23–54.

must be able to identify something comparable in the way of a balance in the West. The Soviets expected it. As Dana Willgress wrote from Moscow, the Kremlin hoped the Anglo-Soviet agreements at Moscow would mean "the regulation of Europe by the United Kingdom and the Soviet Union."[20] And indeed, we do find a purposeful process of development, consolidation, and political mobilization emerging, albeit in a much more complicated and fitful fashion, in the vast Western Europe/Mediterranean sphere on the British side of the prospective European fence.

THE BRITISH SPHERE

There is a widespread perception in the historical literature that the British "sphere" after the Tolstoy conference was confined to a precarious foothold in Greece that Stalin, having received some totally disproportionate kind of political title to much of continental Europe in return, was able to tweak repeatedly in order to keep Churchill in line when questions arose over Soviet policy elsewhere. On the face of it, a very poor bargain: a small consideration for a gigantic giveaway, one moreover that the British would have to pay for again and again.

Actually, this is a misleading perspective. It is certainly true that Greece was Churchill's principal Balkan/Mediterranean focus at the turn of the year. Here there had been historic ties and pre-war associations as well as complex, entangling legacies from the failed British effort to defend the country in 1941. After years of bitter wrangling among the Greek exiles in London and Egypt, British troops finally returned to Athens in October 1944 on the heels of the retreating *Wehrmacht*. Political clashes between left and right soon led to a break-up of the fragile governing coalition and then to violence in December as Churchill, very much the focused personal director of events here, notoriously ordered his commanding general to treat Athens as a "conquered city" and put down leftist-inspired demonstrations with "bloodshed" if necessary. "Having paid the price we have to Russia for freedom of action in Greece," he told Eden on November 7, the British must be "forceful." One close observer in the prime minister's entourage was struck by his "bloodthirsty" determination to prevail. To those old enough to remember it may have reawakened memories of Churchill's attempted "defence" of Antwerp in 1914. To many in the wider world of 1944 the whole episode seemed uncomfortably reminiscent of a discredited imperial arrogance. Churchill's commands were leaked to

---

[20] Willgress to secretary of state (Ottawa), November 9, 1944, N20/20/38, F.O. 371.47860.

the American press and upset opinion in the United States and indeed in Britain as well. This led to a serious crisis in Anglo-American relations and some acrimonious transatlantic cables. But Stalin proved a loyal collaborator. His military mission to the communist or leftist-radical groups in the ravaged countryside was credited in London as a genuine effort to pacify the insurgents. In late November, British officials in Greece found "no evidence" of a Soviet political role. "Good," Churchill commented. "It shows how Stalin is playing the game." Stalin seemed pleasingly alert to the geopolitical implications. True, he had been conceded most of southeastern, Eastern, and much of Central Europe. But Britain should have the Mediterranean and, by long-standing implication, the lead in Western Europe, and there would be no territorial Soviet intrusion.[21]

For Greece was really only part of the post-Tolstoy British focus. Churchill's intense personal engagement there (both in fact and later in his memoir account) has obscured the wider scope and coherence of Britain's energized post-Tolstoy conduct throughout the Mediterranean and Western Europe. Greece was indeed the principal focus of British interest and action. But it was also a kind of pivot from which, in the aftermath of the Tolstoy conference, a new, more engaged British diplomacy, largely directed by the prime minister, began to ripple east and west along the north Mediterranean littoral and on into the Near East, even as it also began to act more forcefully to create a more coherent solidarity in Western Europe. The initiatives and commitments varied in intensity and from place to place, and the developing British constellation never achieved the kind of solid, power-based cohesion one sees in the now complementary Soviet bloc. It was – as one might expect from any prolonged contemplation of British imperial practice, and indeed from the divisions and inhibitions we have already seen in wartime Whitehall – heterogeneous and improvisational in character. There was little in the way of political coordination, either at the level of government action or in the British political establishment itself, where old divisions, including that between integrationists and accommodationists, persisted. The attention of many of the ardent protagonists of a British-led Western bloc, for instance, was still focused on Western Europe, while Churchill directed most of his attention, as he had done throughout the war, to the Mediterranean theater. There were differences between Churchill and Eden and in the Foreign Office itself, as well as a

[21] Dixon diary, December 4, 1944; John O. Iatrides, *Revolt in Athens: The Greek Communist "Second Round" 1944–1945* (Princeton, N.J., 1972), pp. 287–292, 307–325. For Soviet support, see Churchill, *Triumph and Tragedy*, pp. 287–292, 307–325.

chorus of discordant voices in Fleet Street and in the provincial press. It was in essence a project begun but, in the short time between Tolstoy and Yalta, only marginally developed. And, finally, it was overshadowed in the minds of contemporaries by the more eye-catching, gathering climax of the war and perhaps later in the minds of some historians by the approach to renewed Big Three summitry. Nevertheless, haltingly and spasmodically the British were now, with Soviet encouragement, at last beginning to act like the Great Power they still believed themselves to be and that the Soviets seemingly wanted them to be.

We get a clearer sense of this if we get away from the Greek imbroglio and look at the Turkish view of the post-Moscow situation. The politicians in Ankara, mostly pro-German in sympathy, had long been worried about Soviet designs on the Straits and their insistence on a revision of the Montreux Convention, which in effect barred them from easy access to the Mediterranean. The Turks, instinctively suspicious of any Kremlin policy, clung to Montreux as the essential condition of their independence. As in the aftermath of the Teheran conference, so now after the Tolstoy meeting, they were told nothing of Churchill's Moscow open-handedness over the Straits. But they did receive significant reassurances of their protected position within the British sphere, first from Molotov, who told the Turkish ambassador in Moscow that he was sure that a fair, nonviolent solution could be found, and then from Clark Kerr, who made the crucial point that the Straits issue could not be solved "unilaterally." British support was now taken for granted. The Japanese ambassador, who had previously characterized the country's American connection as "merely of a platonic nature," reported in December that "the keynote of Turkish foreign policy continued to be, of course, the Anglo-Turkish alliance."[22]

A fuller insight into the scope and geopolitical particularity of the British view of the rapidly developing Anglo-Soviet concert can be seen in similar reassurances that Eden gave the Turkish ambassador in London in November. After expressing his satisfaction with the Tolstoy arrangements and his appreciation of the "intelligent" treatment of them by the Turkish press, Eden reassured his guest that he had told the Soviets that the Mediterranean basin and surrounding area was "one of our vital interests," and that Britain "wouldn't welcome any external influence or intervention." The Russians had agreed with this, Eden said, and had stated that they would not interfere in this sphere. The Soviets wanted a primary position in the Black Sea but had given "explicit assurances"

---

[22] Turkish ambassador (Moscow) to Ankara, November 29, 1944, HW1/3362.

that they would not come into the Mediterranean. There was no cause for concern about Montreux. The Soviets had not raised the issue (Churchill had done that), and their earlier press agitation had died down. The overall impression the foreign secretary gave was of unconditional British support within a constructive context of increasing Anglo-Soviet collaboration.[23]

The Mediterranean, then, and not Greece alone, was the principal stake (along with Western Europe) for Britain in the Moscow Order. Indeed, the British hoped to extend their eastward collaboration with the Soviets beyond Turkey to the old Anglo-Russian arena in Iran. Here they failed, leaving what turned out to be a fatal gap in the new geopolitical framework. Eden had tried in Moscow to interest Molotov in mutual military withdrawals from Iran before the deadline they had earlier accepted of six months from the end of the war in Europe. But Molotov refused to consider or even discuss the issue, still smarting, perhaps, from the Iranian government's refusal earlier in 1944 – under pressure from the United States, in one of its rare political initiatives in this area – to grant the Soviets oil exploration and development rights in the north of the country. Immediately after the Tolstoy conference, Soviet propaganda began to speak ominously of "fascism" in Iran and to ratchet up political pressure against its fragile government. The British remained fearful, as they had since the nineteenth century, of Russian expansion through Iran to the wider Middle East and even to India, whose politically inflammable masses were now increasingly at odds with British rule and potentially susceptible – both the Post-Hostilities Planners and the India Office persistently warned – to Moscow-inspired subversion. Eden's private secretary noted anxiously on November 16, "Persia is clearly going to be what the Straits have been for the past two centuries in Anglo-Russian relations." The foreign secretary would try again to ward off the danger at Yalta, at Potsdam, and on other occasions. His successor, Ernest Bevin, would try yet again as late as December 1945. But the British found little interest in Washington and got no satisfactory response from Stalin or Molotov on any of these occasions. The consequences of this failure were profound, for while nearly all the attention was focused on Soviet action in Eastern Europe, the neglected Iranian issue was allowed to fester dangerously. At the beginning of 1946 it suddenly erupted, taking the Truman administration by

---

[23] Turkish ambassador (London) to Ankara, November 30, 1944, HW1/3362. WM (45) CA, also in CAB/65/45.

surprise and leading to the dramatic United States–Soviet confrontation which arguably launched the Cold War.[24]

But none of this seemed likely in late 1944 as, notwithstanding the exceptional standoff in Iran, the British and Soviets consolidated the new European framework. As the historian Roy Douglas remarks of this period, "matters were beginning to fall into place in much of South-eastern Europe at the beginning of 1945, well before the famous Yalta conference." For the rapidly maturing Anglo-Soviet sensitivity to the geopolitical dimension was also evident now in the central Mediterranean, and with seemingly better results. In Yugoslavia, the 50:50 ratio designed by Eden and Molotov distinguished a Soviet-dominated interior from a British-run coastline. Stalin was helpful here too, taking the opportunity of a visit to Moscow by a high-level Yugoslav delegation in January 1945 to urge Tito's territorially ambitious regime to exercise restraint and cooperate with the British and to consult with Moscow before taking potentially destabilizing steps. As in Greece, however, there were many local complications. Marshal Tito's Partisans, communist but stubbornly independent of the Soviets, already looked destined in 1944 to inherit the country. But the competing pro-monarchist Cetniks still enjoyed American support and even had contacts with Soviet missions. Here too Churchill himself was deeply involved, trying to rebuild in late 1944 a personal relationship with Tito, who, despite British backing earlier, had angered him by flirting provocatively with the Soviets. Churchill forced the young King Peter to accept a state of virtual abdication and managed to stitch together a shaky coalition of dominant Partisans and moderate monarchists under the so-called Tito-Subasic agreement. The local politics was complex and exhausting to those trying to influence it. But Churchill, like Stalin, was focused on two principal objectives: control of disruptive local radicals, and a clean geopolitical division between the domains of the two cooperating Great Powers.[25]

It is remarkable then that as the British worked to strengthen their position in the eastern Mediterranean, they found the Soviets willing partners in curbing the radical impulse in these devastated lands, especially in Greece and Yugoslavia, and helpful too in reassuring the Turks. But as

---

[24] "British Strategic Interests in the Eastern Mediterranean and Middle East," PHP (44), 16, (o), November 18, 1944. Dixon diary, November 16, 1944, Dixon MSS. Roberts, *Stalin's Wars*, pp. 234–237. For British concerns, see also Bullard to Eden, October 15, 23, 1944, PREM 3.237/5.

[25] Roberts, *Stalin's Wars*, pp. 234–235. WM (45) CA also in CAB 65/45. See also Douglas, *From War to Cold War*, pp. 37–40, 49 and generally.

the consolidating impulse moved westward along the northern littoral, fresh complications appeared. In Italy, where the internal divisions were almost as difficult as in Greece and Yugoslavia, American sentiments had to be considered. This was a British-led military theater, and, as we saw earlier, Churchill and the Foreign Office took a proprietary view, fighting hard to obtain and keep an edge over their American colleagues in political matters. On the whole, they were successful. Here again Stalin was helpful, as he had promised Churchill he would be at Tolstoy. Thus the communist leader, Togliatti, loyally supported and sustained the London-backed Badoglio. But Roosevelt, deeply concerned about the Italian vote in the forthcoming election, and always inclined to a soft peace for Italy anyway, looked favorably on the mainly liberal opposition. With the fall of Rome in June there was a political shakeout. The king abdicated, Badoglio resigned, and a moderate named Bonomi took over as prime minister. Liberals like Count Sforza and the historian Bernadetto Croce now sought office. At the end of 1944 Churchill in effect tried to veto the appointment of Sforza, a man he distrusted largely on personal grounds, as foreign minister. But Sforza, who had influential political and media connections in the United States, where he had spent the war, fought back. This helped produce the Anglo-American crisis of December 1944. But Stalin did not exploit the situation. He took no advantage of the drift to the left, and Foreign Office researchers could find no explicit support for the Italian Communist Party in the Soviet media.[26]

What then of Western Europe? We have already noticed Churchill's reluctance to take the lead politically in Western Europe. Nor had his government shown much interest in the political future of East Asia or the Pacific. In geopolitics as in strategy, Churchill was inclined to focus obsessively on the Mediterranean, the corridor to an empire already showing signs of incipient fragmentation. Some in the Foreign Office were inclined to follow his lead. Eden himself was always especially alert to threats to British interests in the Mediterranean region and the Near East, increasingly so as the end of the war approached and Churchill began to dominate foreign policy. In August the Foreign Office's Geoffrey Wilson had urged the importance of "making abundantly clear to the Russians our

---

[26] For Churchill's evolving approach to the Italian situation, see Churchill to Macmillan, November 3, 1943, PREM 3.243/8; Churchill to Eden, June 10 and 20, 1944, PREM 3.243/12; and Douglas, *From War to Cold War*, pp. 57–59. For U.S. policy, see Dallek, *Roosevelt and American Foreign Policy*, pp. 412–414, 504. See also Gilbert, *Churchill*, VII, Chapter 57 and passim.

vital interests in Middle East oil and the security of our communications in the Eastern Mediterranean." His paper drew much approving comment.[27]

But as American and British forces advanced toward Germany, the future political complexion of Western Europe came more insistently into prominence. Encouraged by the new Soviet indulgence, Churchill was now increasingly active here as well. In November he established a strong British military presence in Brussels to support the shaky returning exile government against massive, communist-led demonstrations. There was a brief flurry of criticism in the Soviet media, which soon faded as the British prevailed and the leftist surge subsided. Indeed, an apology of sorts soon arrived in the form of an article just a few weeks later in the authoritative *War and the Working Class,* pouring scorn on the notion that any reasonable person could object if the British, to secure their positions in Belgium and the Netherlands, made special agreements with the governments of those countries. The Churchill government was in fact already doing that (and doing so in Norway also). Thus in Western Europe as in the Mediterranean, Great Power politics trumped the radical impulse.[28]

As they tried in various ways, adapting to different contexts in individual countries, to impose order or foster solidarity, the British kept a weather eye on the Soviet press and radio, looking especially for expressions of support for leftist and/or resistance clients and for criticism of British actions. And here there was encouragement. The Foreign Office Research Department's survey in mid-December found that, apart from occasional outbursts in response to local episodes like the Belgian crisis, "there has been a rather conspicuous absence of comment to which exception could be taken."[29]

The Soviet media were less generous about British links with Spain, which (like Portugal) was eager to shelter under the British umbrella. Bitter memories from the civil war, and from the excesses of the volunteer "Blue Division" Franco had sent to fight with Germany on the eastern front, understandably cut across neat geopolitical solutions. There was also much opposition in Britain to any ties with Franco. But Churchill, wanted to sustain the Caudillo and bring the Iberian states – the geopolitical hinge in the Western Europe–Mediterranean "system" – into the British

[27] Eden memorandum, March 31, 1944, F.O. 371.43304. Wilson memorandum, August 10, 1944, N5792, F.O. 371.43306.
[28] Mastny, *Russia's Road*, pp. 230–231; *War and the Working Class*, December 15, 1944.
[29] Foreign Office Research Department, survey, December 13, 1944, N8063, F.O. 371.43303. See also Warner to Sargent, December 4, 1944, N8059, F.O. 371.43303.

(or at least non-Soviet) orbit. Otherwise, he told Eden, Spain could easily go communist, whereupon "we must expect the infection to spread very fast through both Italy and France." Noting that all the liberated countries were "seething with communism," Churchill warned that "only our influence with Russia prevents their actively stimulating this movement, deadly as I conceive it to peace and also to the freedom of mankind."[30]

What then of France? Here was the basic problem for any viable British blueprint for Western Europe. At once we are reminded – even as we may grasp the logic (if not necessarily the morality) of the geopolitical arrangements the British and Soviets were now trying to impose upon a Europe that was still only partly liberated from Hitler and pulsing with radicalism and discordant emotions – of the two basic difficulties in the developing Anglo-Soviet concert. In the east it was Poland: the awkward element in an otherwise rational geopolitical line-up. In the west it was France, now under the dubious control (Churchill and some others felt) of General de Gaulle. But if there was to be anything like a power balance between East and West in postwar Europe, France was an indispensable element. Churchill acknowledged this. As he told the Dominion prime ministers in May 1944, "We could not be responsible for defending large areas of the Continent, as we should have to, were they to be taken into our British system. To do so we would have to condemn our people to the maintenance of a vast standing army, which they would never be prepared to contemplate."[31]

Manpower, and a standing army, of course, along with all the resources and experience of an advanced industrial state, were precisely what France could bring to a united Western Europe. But Churchill, though he conceded as early as June that de Gaulle had the support of "most of the elements" in France that supported the Allies, could not bring himself to take any serious initiative in that direction. In the crisis of 1940 he had offered Prime Minister Reynaud full Anglo-French union. Now he would not offer Gaullist France a minimal partnership in Europe, let alone the treaty so many British (and French) officials wanted.[32]

But as the Anglo-Soviet consolidation developed, Churchill, though still prone to intemperate characterizations of the general ("a marplot" and "this menacing and hostile man" are but two examples) began to make

---

[30] Churchill to Eden, November 10, 18, 1944; and Eden to Churchill, November 17, 1944, both in PREM 8/106. See also Douglas, *From War to Cold War*, pp. 60–61.
[31] Prime ministers meeting, May 11, 1944, 12th. meeting, PMM (44), in PREM 4.38/7.
[32] Churchill to Roosevelt, June 20, 1944, PREM 3.177/4.

the logical overtures, and there was a steady drift toward Anglo-French collaboration. Closer dealings with the Soviets, and the promise they repeatedly held out of a mutually acceptable division of Europe, invariably stimulated the Anglo-French impulse in Eden and even in Churchill. Thus the foreign secretary cut across American policy immediately after Teheran by offering support for a French return to Indochina. Now, within days of his return from the Tolstoy conference, we find Churchill authorizing the dispatch of de Gaulle's Blaizot Mission to that region while cautiously passing word that there was no need to inform Roosevelt, who was known to oppose any French restoration there. De Gaulle himself now seemed to want a closer link with London, provided French interests were respected. And even Churchill softened when, on his first official visit to liberated Paris in November, he found de Gaulle a gracious host. In moving scenes on Armistice Day, November 11, the two leaders engaged in various ceremonies including a walk together down the Champs Elysees to a reviewing stand, greeted by enormous, rapturous crowds. In a public speech Churchill at last rose to the occasion, hailing de Gaulle as "the incontestable leader" of France. The private talks were also amicable. The two men agreed on the need for Anglo-French cooperation and held discussions that reflected their common interest in controlling postwar Germany and their similar outlooks as traditional imperial powers vis-à-vis the United States and the Soviet Union. Churchill was glad to find de Gaulle concerned about left-wing eruptions in the capital and quickly arranged for shipments of arms for the Paris police.[33]

In this changing political context, the two leaders were now rediscovering some common interests. Both were essentially conservative, empire-minded statesmen, hostile to communism and radicalism generally. Both, moreover, were already thinking about ways to harness German postwar resources. De Gaulle's desire to assert French political control in Germany's provinces west of the Rhine was already known. He also hoped for economic benefits in the form of reparations, while Churchill was tantalized by the possible acquisition of Germany's export markets. Thus German power would in various ways come under Anglo-French control. Churchill's increasingly frequent private references to the possible harnessing of German power reflect the Chiefs of Staff's plans for a

---

[33] Churchill to Eden, January 19, 1944, PREM 185/4; Churchill to Jacob, September 4, 1944, PREM 185/8; "Record of Churchill–de Gaulle Meeting, Paris," November 11, 1944, PREM 3.188/4; Churchill to Roosevelt, November 27, 1944, *Correspondence*, III, p. 416.

German component in future European security. The Germans could be put to use if Soviet expansion threatened. This was reinsurance on a grand scale. Similarly, we find de Gaulle, in a review of the Foreign Legion early in 1945, turning to a confidant and remarking that this famous French force would be a future home for German youth.[34]

A strong reconciliatory instinct consequently appears in the prime minister's report to Roosevelt recording that "I reestablished friendly relations" with de Gaulle. Now at last Churchill was thinking in practical terms about links with France. He told FDR that he now wanted France to participate in the forthcoming summit conference and be brought more fully into the general political picture, "knowing well," he continued, "that there will be a time not many years distant when the American armies will go home and the British will have great difficulty in maintaining large forces overseas." Five days later, the cause of France, and of a politically cohesive Western Europe, received a significant impetus when Stalin, acting very much in the spirit of the consolidating Moscow Order, notified Churchill on November 20 that he had no objection to de Gaulle's participation in the forthcoming summit meeting, providing Roosevelt agreed. The ground seemed prepared for a further huge step toward the consolidation of the Moscow Order.[35]

But Roosevelt did not agree. Churchill, again shrinking from a challenge to the president, backed away while expressing to Stalin, in a face-saving gesture, his hope that de Gaulle could "come in later" when issues directly affecting France were discussed. De Gaulle was again humiliated, with large consequences appearing in early 1945 after the Yalta conference. But cold water from Roosevelt was not the only problem. Churchill and de Gaulle fell out, as they had before, over French aspirations in the Levant, where de Gaulle's desire to reconstitute French power clashed with British commitments to Syria and Lebanon. Churchill was ambivalent. "We are not committed to recognize France's dominant position in Syria and Lebanon. ... If she gains it we do not oppose it; if she does not, we cannot work for it." De Gaulle's renewed flirtation with the Soviet Union was also provoking. The occasion was the Frenchman's visit to Moscow in December, where he hoped to obtain a boost in domestic and international

[34] Anthony Beevor, *Paris after the Liberation* (London, 1987), p. 56. Arthur L. Smith, *Churchill's German Army: Wartime Strategy and Cold War Politics: 1943–1947* (Beverly Hills and London, 1977), passim.
[35] Churchill to Roosevelt, November 15, 1944, PREM 3.185/3; Stalin to Churchill, November 20, 1944, SCCA, p. 272.

prestige in the form of a treaty like that Stalin had made with the British years before. Eden had no objection to this, nor to the alternative of a tripartite agreement linking all three major European states. But this too was promptly knocked down by Roosevelt, who, asserting "the very highest importance" of the Dumbarton Oaks project, made clear his desire to avoid "a competitor to a future world organization." Churchill told an inquiring Stalin, who was again clearly anxious not to offend British sensitivities, that he, unlike the president, would not stand in the way of Soviet treaty arrangements with France. Privately he seems to have been outraged at what he saw as the Frenchman's clear attempt to usurp his primacy as Stalin's European partner, telling Eden, "as I have frequently pointed out de Gaulle will be a great danger to peace and to Britain in the future."

At the same time Churchill recognized the deeper British interests at stake and subdued his personal antipathy to the French leader sufficiently to press the French cause with the Soviets and Americans, notably at Yalta, where he worked hard and successfully, against the initial opposition of both Roosevelt and Stalin, to bring France into the leadership group both in the anticipated control of postwar Germany and in the prospective United Nations. At the same time, though, even as he raised no impediment to the Franco-Soviet treaty, he set himself against an Anglo-French treaty or any further intimacy with the Paris authorities while de Gaulle remained in charge.[36]

The importance of France in the Anglo-Soviet equation was, at bottom, its potential role in consolidating a more equal balance of power in Western Europe. Churchill, for all his resistance to de Gaulle (but not to France), was instinctively sensitive to the underlying realities here. He was also fully aware that while power in the east would be massive, coherent, and tightly concentrated under Soviet control, its western counterpart would be heterogeneous, vulnerable, and extremely hard to maintain. Even the robust Churchill occasionally shrank from the task. But he continued to draw some confidence from Roosevelt's promises at Quebec, which

---

[36] Roosevelt to Churchill, November 16, 1944. *Correspondence*, III, pp. 393–394. Stalin to Churchill, November 20, 1944; and Churchill to Stalin, December 5, 1944, both in PREM 3.173/1. Churchill to Eden, January 11, 1945, PREM 4.30/11. See also Churchill to Eden, December 31, 1944, and February 5, 1945, both in PREM 3.173/1. Mastny, *Russia's Road*, pp. 229–232, suggests that Stalin wanted a pact with France in order to keep the French out of the Western bloc. For Churchill's later efforts on behalf of France, see Chapter 7, this volume; and for Eden's optimism, see Kitchen, *British Policy*, p. 201. For Roosevelt's negative on the tripartite treaty, see Roosevelt to Churchill, December 6, 1944, *Correspondence*, III, pp. 444–445.

were designed, as we have seen, to strengthen Britain so that it could take the politico-military lead in Europe that FDR did not expect (or perhaps want) the United States to assume.

EUROPE AND AMERICA AT ODDS

A European geopolitical framework for the postwar was then, though far from complete, already in a state of advanced development by the end of 1944. It was reinforced at the level of attitudes and emotions by a concurrent sense, felt on both sides of the Atlantic, of a growing divergence between the character and aims of the European and American allies, who now began, in historically conditioned fashion, to define themselves and their objectives ever more sharply in terms of the other's bad behavior.

Much of this can be traced to the American design for the United Nations at Dumbarton Oaks, which the two European powers had felt obliged to endorse in principle if not in detail, but were in fact inclined to view with suspicion. The British, already under pressure from the Roosevelt administration over civil aviation routes, oil rights, and much else, tended to see its scope – especially its potentially expansible trusteeship dimension, giving the world organization extensive supervisory powers – as a direct threat to the integrity of the British Empire and potentially a cloak for American commercial intrusion and even some degree of political hegemony. Roosevelt's persistent criticism of British imperialism did much to strengthen this impression. There was also concern in London (and in Moscow) about the kind of "meddling" and moralistic criticism to be expected from a United States–led United Nations organization poking its nose into European affairs, especially as Anglo-American tensions over British conduct in Greece, Italy, and Yugoslavia developed at the end of 1944.

Even before Dumbarton Oaks, Churchill had given only qualified approval to the idea of a United Nations, declaring that it should be limited to the prevention of war. Now in December 1944, referring to Stalin's refusal to accept the American conceptions of both the veto power and membership, he told Eden, "I am in entire agreement with the Russians." Instinctively hostile to the prospect of any American political or economic interference, he continued to campaign for a self-protective European "autonomy" in the form of "regionalism" – a term expressing British and Soviet concerns about American intrusions – at the very moment that American official opinion was beginning to coalesce around the notion of "trusteeship" and the limited veto, concepts that Soviet communists and European imperialists had ample reason to believe would expose them to the world's complaints. On the eve of Yalta, increasingly aware of Roosevelt's investment in the issue, Churchill modified his position. If the Russians agree on the American compromise over the United Nations, he told Eden, "I will accept it. I cannot undertake, however, to fight a stiff battle with them on the subject."[37]

The Soviets were also worried about the Americans. They were, like the British, protective of their putative "empire" in Eastern and Central Europe. It is a measure of rising Soviet anxiety – sometimes expressed in a call for European "regionalism," more often in an insistence upon central Great Power control – that Litvinov was again called in to register and publicize rising concerns about American intentions in three articles published during 1944 in *Voina i rabochii klass*. The first, in July, was a call for Big Three "unity," the supreme value in Soviet eyes and a necessary check on the anticipated importunities and harassments of smaller powers under the American model of a world organization. The second, more specifically focused essay reflected serious concern over Dumbarton Oaks, especially the supervisory functions and widely shared powers envisaged in the American proposals. Here Litvinov, echoing Churchill's familiar reservation, stressed the superiority of the "regional" approach, whereby local Great Powers (obviously Britain and the Soviet Union in Europe) would give each other "mutual aid" while the carefully subordinated smaller powers would contribute by providing bases. In the third article, published on the eve of the Yalta conference, Litvinov again stressed several of these themes, asserting explicitly that the crucial peacekeeping powers should be wielded "only by those in the continent concerned." The clear implication of the whole sequence was that the Soviet Union and its British partner would exercise full control in Europe in the postwar era, each in its own sphere. The United States would be kept out. The smaller powers would be kept down.[38]

Even as they defined, in this way; quite separately, a certain common interest against various kinds of anticipated American intrusion, the two European powers were thinking as usual in very concrete, geopolitical terms. Some illustration of how this was already working out in practice can be seen when we look at their respective visions for the postwar Pacific,

---

[37] Churchill to Eden, December 6, 1944, PREM 4.30/10; Churchill to Eden, January 25, 1945, PREM 4.31/1.

[38] *Voina i rabochii klass,* July 15, December 15, 1944. Memorandum by Eden, August 9, 1944, F.O. 371.43336.

the region where all three allies had historic but potentially conflicting interests. Since their disastrous defeats in early 1942, the British had left most of the political running in China and the Pacific to the United States. As one Foreign Office diplomat put it early in 1945, "If, as I suspect, we can really do very little, the less we say about it the better." The pervading view, expressed by Cavendish-Bentinck, was that "China is not vital to the maintenance of our Empire and we can do without Chinese trade." But, as he showed at the Octagon conference, Churchill was eager to restore a significant British presence in the Pacific and was determined above all to reclaim and protect Hong Kong. Churchill and the military planners expected to feel American pressure most heavily there and consequently made it clear to the Foreign Office that they favored the territorial and strategic gains Stalin wanted at China's expense in Manchuria, including the use of Dairen and Port Arthur. For these would not compromise, it was felt – indeed, they would strengthen – the British position to the south in Hong Kong, otherwise vulnerable to American and Chinese political and moral pressure. The Soviets were believed – in their approach to this region, at least – to take a tolerant view of the British Empire. This was shown to be correct at Yalta, where Stalin rejected Roosevelt's plan to exclude Britain from the postwar governance of Korea and also showed little interest in the exclusive Pacific partnership that the president seemed to be holding out to him. One is driven to the conclusion, the more so when one recalls Stalin's refusal to countenance any but the most minimal American presence in the Soviet Pacific provinces during the war, that neither he nor Churchill wanted to be left alone in the Pacific with the Americans.[39]

As we cross the Atlantic we find a mirror image to these expressions of European solidarity. For in the weeks before Yalta the American political establishment, including key elements of the Roosevelt administration, Congress, the press, and public opinion, feeling now that the war was soon to end, were similarly engaged in a process of reinvigorated self-definition, seeing themselves not just as the righteous hammer of Hitler and Hirohito but as coming together also in disapproval of their misbehaving and unreliable European allies, who appeared to be imposing themselves, with little regard for the principles of the Atlantic Charter or the sensitivities of American opinion, upon such liberated countries of deep ancestral significance to Americans as Greece, Italy, and Poland.

---

[39] Churchill to Eden and Ismay, October 23, 1944, PREM 3.397/3; Cavendish-Bentinck minute, March 13, 1945, F1331, FO. 371.46232. See also, for British hopes of recovery in China, Hall-Patch memorandum, March 10, 1945, F1331, F.O. 371.46232. For British thinking generally, see Kitchen, *British Policy*, pp. 200, 207.

The stage was clearly set for some kind of political eruption. In late November an increasingly aroused American public found itself contemplating an ugly burst of realpolitik in the conduct of both its European allies (for memories of the Warsaw Uprising were still fresh, and the Greek crisis was intensifying) just as the great, redemptive Wilson revival – another unifying theme in the United States – was coming to full flood, pushed along by a compounding surge of books and articles celebrating liberty, democracy, and American values. When it came, the fire was ignited by the improbable figure of Edward R. Stettinius, Jr., one of the most Anglophile of Roosevelt's aides, now secretary of state upon Hull's retirement. Advised that the British interference in the formation of a new Italian government was attracting "widespread critical comment in press and radio," and pressed by his leading adviser on European affairs, H. Freeman Matthews, to issue some response registering American concern, Stettinius came out on December 5 with a public statement declaring that "the composition of the Italian government is purely an Italian affair." He went on to say, in obvious reference to Greece, "that the policy would apply to an even more pronounced degree with regard to governments of the United Nations in their liberated territories."[40]

This statement may seem comparatively inoffensive given the turbulent politics of the time. But as the *Manchester Guardian* noted, "It is a rude statement and it is meant to be rude." Stettinius's political broadside was greatly praised at home, setting off a storm of American press and public dissatisfaction with both Britain (especially) and the Soviet Union. The historian Robert Hathaway describes the sentiments of average Americans, who, viewing the apparent British efforts to restore imperial power and discredited conservative elites, believed themselves to be watching a traditional politics of self-interest. "All they saw," he writes, "was that British troops, quite possibly using American lend-lease weapons, were coercing Belgians and gunning down Greeks who, until recently, had been gallantly resisting the German foe." The influential radio commentator Raymond Gram Swing declared that the British were "giving an ugly twist to the word liberation." The columnist Drew Pearson thought that the issue "boils down to whether the Allies are going to champion kings or republicans in Europe under the Atlantic Charter."[41]

[40] See Robert Hathaway, *Ambiguous Partnership: Britain and America, 1944–1947* (New York, 1981), pp. 89–111. Matthews memorandum, December 1, 1944, Box 222, Stettinius MSS; Department of State, *Bulletin*, 2 (December 1944), p. 722.
[41] Hathaway, *Ambiguous Alliance*, pp. 91–94.

The Stettinius initiative led with stunning speed to the most dangerous Anglo-American public argument of World War II. American criticisms drew in return a fiercely combative rejoinder from London, including protests from Churchill to Roosevelt and a barrage of Fleet Street complaints centered around the old charges of American hypocrisy, self-righteousness, and irresponsibility. Roosevelt was not altogether unsympathetic, but when Churchill sent a bitter message implicitly charging him with disloyalty, FDR put the blame squarely on the London authorities for not consulting Washington before their seemingly high-handed and certainly unilateral actions.[42]

The most pointed British rejoinder came in an *Economist* editorial that was almost unanimously approved in Britain and widely read in the United States. It castigated what it characterized as the injustice and hypocrisy of the American criticisms. These only made the average Briton "one degree more cynical about America's real intentions of active collaboration, and one degree more ready to believe that the only reliable helping hand is in Soviet Russia." This influential publication drew the lesson that Britain should, if its interests required, side unhesitatingly with the Soviet Union in the game of European power politics. "And, if Americans find this attitude too cynical or suspicious, they should draw the conclusion that they have twisted the tail of the lion just once too often."[43]

For President Roosevelt, however, the most significant and alarming feature of this "transatlantic cacophony" (to use Robert Hathaway's apt characterization) lay elsewhere. It was not the sharp rift between the two governments, or the discreditable bond between America's European allies, or even the accompanying press war, serious though all these were. It was the chilling demonstration the crisis gave to FDR and his advisers that their careful postwar strategy of engaged internationalism – focused on building domestic support for the establishment of a United Nations organization built along American lines and eased into full acceptance as a fruitful peacekeeping institution by the cooperation of well-behaved, congenial allies – was now in dire jeopardy. British actions in the Greek theater, the historian Robert Dallek writes, "in themselves concerned Roosevelt less that the demoralizing effect they would have on internationalist opinion in the United States." During the crisis FDR complained to Halifax that the

---

[42] Churchill to Roosevelt, December 6, 1944; *Correspondence*, III, pp. 437–439; Roosevelt to Churchill, ibid., pp. 433–444; Halifax to Eden, January 6, 1945, PREM 3.356/16; *The Economist*, December 30, 1944; *The Times*, December 30, 1944.
[43] *The Economist*, December 30, 1944.

London critics "did not realize his difficulties in bringing American opinion along." There was ample cause for concern. Public opinion polls now told a grim story, with large majorities expressing disillusionment with America's allies and an increase of over 60% since the summer of those who thought other nations were taking advantage of the United States. The respected *Christian Century*, thinking of 1919, warned its highly principled readers that "another great betrayal is under way." This was, much evidence suggests, a widely held view. Isolationist sentiment suddenly again seemed a formidable threat.[44]

Then there came, into this already combustible atmosphere, the shocking Soviet recognition on January 1, 1945, of the Lublin Polish regime as the provisional government of Poland. The Soviets were already receiving considerable press criticism for their heavy-handed approach in Eastern Europe. Now this apparent prelude to the complete takeover and likely communization of Poland was deeply alarming. As we will see in later chapters, this event had a profound impact upon Roosevelt's approach to and conduct at the Yalta conference. The president, forewarned of this alarming development, had protested with unusual vigor to Stalin in mid-December, asking him to defer a decision until the now imminent summit conference. But Stalin, consistent with his clear determination to put all his demands and wishes on the table well before what was obviously going to be the last wartime conference (he also conveyed to Washington in advance his desire for large economic credits and acceptance of large-scale territorial and political accessions in the Far East), refused the request. The Soviet demarche over Lublin, however, was in a different category, one of urgent concern. It would prove in the long run to be as significant a catalyst to change as the American commitment to a United Nations conception months before, for it set up with unmistakable clarity two incompatible future scenarios and also reintroduced (though no one seems to have recognized in Washington that Stalin was working on this basis) the "bargain" Stalin clearly intended to press with FDR once he got to the Crimea. Meanwhile, Roosevelt was obliged to take all these alarming events seriously, because beneath the surface issues in United States–Soviet relations (the United Nations, Eastern Europe, Far Eastern matters, Germany's fate) lay a darker, unacknowledged reality. He had so far failed to resolve the dilemma he had created for himself: the fact that he had held

[44] Hathaway, *Ambiguous Alliance*, p. 97 and Chapter 6; Stettinius memorandum, December 30, 1944, Box 231, Stettinius MSS; *Christian Century* cited in Divine, *Second Chance*, p. 259; Dallek, *Roosevelt and American Foreign Policy*, pp. 503–504.

out to Americans the attainable goal of a postwar shaped by the ideals of the Atlantic Charter even as he had implicitly promised Stalin a virtual free hand in Eastern Europe. He would now have to face this apparent contradiction, now refined – thanks to the incompatibility of the Dumbarton Oaks vision and the recognition of Lublin – to a sharp point, or find some way around it.[45]

There was a significant difference, meantime, in the British and American responses to Stalin's Lublin shock. The British were philosophic. The Foreign Office's Oliver Harvey expressed a sense of resignation now familiar to us after the recent retreats over Bulgaria, Hungary, and Czechoslovakia. "As regards Stalin recognizing the Lublin Committee ... I doubt if there is any more we can do." The historian Michael Kitchen speaks of "a growing conviction by the end of December that Britain would have to recognize the Lublin government." On January 8, Sargent remarked that Lublin "will, I am certain, attract to its banner large numbers who have hitherto been indifferent or hesitating." Cadogan wrote that Mikolajczyk had "missed the bus." And on the very eve of Yalta, Eden, who had already cast an indulgent eye on reports that the French government had discreetly bowed to Soviet pressure and extended a form of recognition to Lublin, simply counseled the Czechs, now believed to be contemplating a similar step, to make the move in discreet stages rather than all at once. At the same time there was widespread recognition in London's official and press circles that the United States was taking the Lublin issue more seriously because, coming on top of all the seemingly provocative European realpolitik of late 1944, it threatened the modest internationalism congenially woven into the United Nations prospect. Thus the *New Statesman and Nation*, reflecting leftist intellectual thinking, took the news calmly, finding Lublin's advent "inevitable" owing to the London Poles "intransigence." But, it significantly predicted, as did many British commentators, that the decision "would create something of a political storm in the United States."[46]

Stalin's sudden elevation of the Lublin Poles would materially shape the form, character, and historical significance of the Yalta conference, now only five weeks away. Up to this point all three governments appear to

---

[45] Roosevelt to Stalin, December 20, 1944; Stalin to Roosevelt, December 27, 1944, both in SCRT, pp. 175, 180–181.

[46] Harvey note, December 24, 1944, F.O. 371.39421; Sargent note, January 8, 1945, F.O. 371.47575; Eden to Churchill, January 18, 1945, F.O. 954/4; Kitchen, *British Policy*, pp. 243–244; *New Statesman and Nation*, January 6, 1945.

have been expecting, or at least hoping, to bypass the exhausting Polish issue and focus attention on Germany. This seems to have been Eden's wish. The first Foreign Office attempt at an agenda, a week after the Lublin shock, was headed by eight German topics. Poland was included further down the list, but only the problem of her future western frontier. There was, Geoffrey Wilson noted, "little advantage in raising the united government issue." The Soviets too had earlier expressed a desire to concentrate on German issues, though having promoted Lublin so provocatively they must have anticipated a defensive struggle there. Roosevelt typically presented no agenda, simply declaring his usual wish for informal discussion. He too had wanted to avoid Poland, and indeed most other European problems. "I want to focus on Germany alone," he had told Harriman in October. Stalin's demarche confounded all these hopes. Poland's tragedies and tribulations, so long a potent presence in European politics and so carefully fended off by Roosevelt up to this point, were now suddenly and insistently reaching out across the Atlantic, reinforcing the already powerful disenchantment created in the United States by Soviet and British actions in many parts of Europe, and claiming at last the full attention of the Western Allies.[47]

Let us simply take stock here – as we register without further elaboration at this point the appearance, in the form of Stalin's recognition of Lublin, of the central issue that would shortly transform relationships among the Big Three – of the unacknowledged substantiality of the Anglo-Soviet scenario for postwar Europe that was in its political character, though not in its enduring territorial residue, about to pass away. This had been a purposeful development. We have seen, first, its long and spasmodic but increasingly concerted evolution – its inauguration in the Eden-Stalin talks in December 1941; its quasi-institutionalization in the Anglo-Soviet treaty of May 1942; its more precise delineation by the Foreign Office in Eden's Cabinet-approved paper on August 9; its culminating definition, amounting to the recognition of a division of Europe, at the Churchill/Stalin Tolstoy conference at Moscow in October 1944; and its subsequent consolidation as the two powers, in apparent harmony, began to entrench themselves in their respective parts of a Europe now shaking off the German blight.

We have also noted, in a contextual sense, the development – rudimentary and limited, to be sure – of a more or less common European outlook, sharpened by concerns over the counterpointing American Dumbarton

---

[47] Wilson memorandum, January 7, 1945, N390, F.O. 371.47881; Eden to Churchill, January 28, 1945, F.O. 954/7.

Oaks model, and expressing itself in a desire to constrain the American political role in postwar Europe, even as an indispensable American economic role in reconstruction was increasingly acknowledged to be desirable if not indispensable. And we have seen, behind all these developments and tendencies, the way in which both Europeans and Americans were by the end of 1944 beginning, as the prospect of imminent victory over Hitler's Germany started to loosen their wartime bonds, to define themselves in very traditional terms of the "other," a logical outcome given that their peacetime scenarios – after Dumbarton Oaks and more recently the emergence of a reinvigorated British political activism and a Soviet-sponsored regime in Poland – did indeed seem increasingly to diverge, not only in political and functional ways, but also along moral-cultural lines long entrenched by historical experience.

To these foundational elements we can add, as an indication of the historical significance of these developments in the minds of contemporaries, and as a kind of capstone to the case for closer historiographical attention to the so-called Moscow Order, the widespread assumption among world leaders at the time that after a postwar shake-out of some as yet unpredictable character, Europe and the United States were, even as they participated in some form of world organization, likely to maintain their historical separation. There were, of course, other voices, including those of optimists who still believed in the possibility of a harmonious Wilsonian makeover of the international system as the Dumbarton Oaks vision took a material form. And, though no one appears to have predicted the actual course of later events with precise accuracy, one must also acknowledge the prescience of the pundit Walter Lippmann, who, in his 1944 book, *War Aims,* forecast the emergence of a transatlantic bond between the North American and Western European states in (hopefully) harmonious relations with a separate Soviet-dominated Eastern Europe.

The list of statesmen who expected the establishment of some kind of Anglo-Soviet system in postwar Europe juxtaposed to a detached America is more formidable. So far as the Soviets and their worldwide leftist supporters are concerned, it starts with Stalin and his initiative in December 1941, steadily embroidered by Litvinov, Maisky, and others until the leader put the capstone on it himself in October 1944. For the British, faith in this outcome runs consistently through Eden and most of the British establishment, taking its cue from the Anglo-Soviet treaty of 1942 and eventually receiving an energizing charge from Churchill in the months before Yalta. In the United States it includes Roosevelt, who consistently proclaimed, with a sincerity amply borne out by private documentation, his personal aversion to any direct American postwar role in European political affairs and who therefore, very logically, gave Churchill the green light (and a considerable "golden handshake") at the Octagon conference to go ahead and develop a satisfactory European solution. Certainly the United States offered no creative alternative to the Anglo-Soviet framework for postwar Europe. To these dominating leaders, moreover, we can add a host of surrounding political figures, from Europeans like Spaak and Benes to empire leaders like Smuts, and attach also a considerable tally of supportive press and public sentiment in Britain and elsewhere in favor of some kind of Anglo-Soviet–led postwar Europe. Even Orwell, who hated Stalin, envisioned a democratic postwar Britain as "the political leader of Western Europe" and urged in September 1944 that "Nothing is more important in the worled today than Anglo-Russian friendship and cooperation.[48]

Events, as we know, took a very different turn. Quite suddenly, in February 1945, the whole situation among the three allies began to undergo a transformation. After Yalta an unmistakable East/West orientation appeared, with the British and Americans collborating and the Soviets now the odd man out. The European option, with its Anglo-Soviet dynamic, faded. Political leaders, commentators, and other observers quickly adjusted to a new dispensation in which the United States, politically masterful as it brought the United Nations to life and economically crucial to the revival of a liberated Western Europe that was rapidly losing confidence in itself, was suddenly seen to be playing the leading hand. And very soon, as people looked back and tried to understand their current predicaments and their disappointments by tracing earlier lines of causation, they found the tripartite drama of Yalta and its aftermath standing invitingly in the way, completely overshadowing the little-known and mostly unacknowledged decisions, actions, and intrigues of the Tolstoy period in Europe. Historians, focused largely on American thought and action, were led on this vein by Churchill, whose post-Yalta conduct did everything possible to foster the new Americanizing trend, and whose memoirs skillfully played up the warnings he had given in various contexts about Soviet power and played down his actual collaboration with Stalin, thus obscuring further the full meaning and intent of what was now inevitably seen as a morally dubious attempt to promote the division of Europe in which Churchill had in fact, insofar as it was a political event, participated.

---

[48] Walter Lippmann, *War Aims* (New York, 1944), Chapter 6. For Orwell, see *Tribune*, September 1, 1944, and John Carey, ed., *George Orwell: Essays* (New York, 2002), pp. 640, 733.

A historian attempting to restore the full reality of the late 1944 European dimension in Allied diplomacy in general, and the significance of the Tolstoy conference specifically – as well as the fundamental problem all this created for President Roosevelt on the eve of Yalta and in the more universalizing context of public American diplomacy – has therefore to confront not only the skepticism of professional colleagues who have put the emphasis elsewhere, but also the understandable doubts of today's informed lay readers. Might not such a reader, armed with some knowledge of the aftermath of World War II, noting the apparent absence of an economic dimension in the Anglo-Soviet relationship and with the photographs of ruined cities imprinted on his mind, very reasonably assume that the sheer devastation of Europe's social and economic resources toward the end of the war must make the wartime pretensions of British leaders to a grand postwar role for the continent in association with the Soviet Union appear, to the historian if not to the possibly deluded statesmen of the day, fanciful in the extreme?

Two points might be made in response. The first is that there were in fact recurrent efforts during the war to bring an economic dimension to the relationship. The Foreign Office contemplated the possibility of a wide-ranging commercial agreement as early as 1942, before shelving the proposal as premature. In June 1944 we find Sargent publicly talking up the point that "the British postwar economy required that trade between Great Britain and Russia should be increased in every way possible." The problem was always credit. In August, Eden produced a paper for the War Cabinet emphasizing the virtual disappearance of Britain's financial power, a message already being spread through Whitehall by the leading economist John Maynard Keynes. A Soviet request for long-term credits nevertheless prompted a strong feeling that some gesture must be made. The Foreign Office consulted the Treasury. The cupboards were vigorously scoured, and the financial experts came up with an offer of 30 million pounds for 5 years at 2.25% interest. This was immediately rejected by Moscow, where it was perhaps taken as an expression of the famous British sense of humor. Negotiations came to an abrupt halt. The Soviets now focused on the much more promising United States, seeking a $6 billion credit that dwarfed the British offer. From then on, the British announced to the Soviets, trade would have to be on strictly commercial terms.[49]

---

[49] Eden memorandum, "Soviet Policy in Europe," August 9, 1944, WP (44) 436; Kitchen, *British Policy*, pp. 200–209.

The acknowledgment of threadbare resources was chastening for the Foreign Office. There had been hopes for reciprocal trade, especially for the exchange of British manufactures and machine tools for Russian timber. It was the Soviet demand for credits that exposed the grim realities. Eden was irate. "They are much richer than we are," he declared, "and are fully able to pay cash for what they buy." Sargent pronounced a suitable epitaph. "For the last 200 years," he informed his colleagues, "we have displayed in our foreign relations the rich man's complex, and this has become so much a matter of course that we do not realise how far we have relied in our diplomacy on the *cavaliere de St. Georges* in order to maintain and assert our influence in foreign countries."[50]

But the setback on the financial front – and this is the second point – was far from fatal to the Anglo-Soviet concert. For this there were two reasons. First, both governments seem to have felt that they had viable alternatives. Both expected in late 1944 – that is to say, well before the full collapse of the German economy in the spring of 1945 – to benefit in some way from Germany's political eclipse, either in the form of succession to the Reich's markets in the case of Britain (a vision by no means confined to Morgenthau), or in the shape of the massive reparations envisioned by the Soviets. Moreover, both countries had high hopes for postwar assistance from a United States that was expected to be helpful in that area even as it maintained its traditional political detachment. This was particularly true of the British, who were steadily becoming more aware of their parlous situation but had not yet seen the fuller implications, partly because they nursed certain illusions about the empire's willingness to forgive debt and partly because they continued, despite mounting evidence to the the contrary, to believe that London's control of the sterling area would be an effective bargaining element in negotiations with the United States. Thus, as late as December 1944, we find a prominent left-wing publication, responding to doubts about the financial practicability of the socially reforming Beveridge Plan, coming out with a ressuring analysis headed "We Can Afford It." The Soviets also had perceived alternatives in the form of the anticipated reparations and bounty from the non-German territories coming under their sway, while the lack of accountability in their political system doubtless sustained a degree of detachment about the suffering of their people that would have been unacceptable in more open polities.

---

[50] Eden memorandum, August 18, 1944, N4975, F.O. 371.43353; Sargent memorandum, June 1, 1944, N2996/302/38, F.O. 371.43351.

A second and perhaps decisive reason why the undeveloped economic dimension was not, at least up to the time of the Yalta conference, as limiting a factor as one might have thought, is that the Anglo-Soviet wartime concert was from the start driven much less by economic considerations than by politics and geopolitics, essentially by the drive for future security and political stability. The Kremlin was not put off by the commercial and financial setbacks it encountered in Whitehall. The economic ruin of Germany was not yet clearly evident. By the end of November, indeed, the tone of Anglo-Soviet relations was probably better than it had ever been. The framework of a viable European postwar order was emerging sharply enough for contemporaries to notice it and comment on its prospects. Eden's secretary, Piers Dixon, noted in his diary at this time that the Tolstoy deliberations had "cleared the air." Relations were so satisfactory that "Anglo-Russian problems don't loom large. Our chief irritations are with the Americans, alas." Timing is a large part of the explanation here. After the apparently harmonious meeting at Yalta, the emphasis in European thinking about the postwar did indeed turn from politics to economics – from essentially speculative concerns about security, now somewhat allayed, to the suddenly more urgent practical problems of relief and reconstruction – and this consideration must be factored into any account of the decline of the Anglo-Soviet bond and the transformations that then occurred. Politics and geopolitics, nonetheless, are the best key to understanding the course of events that led not just to the consolidation of the Anglo-Soviet concert after October 1944 but also to its quite sudden decline and fall early in 1945, a political process in which the Yalta conference was the pivotal event.[51]

Our informed reader, however persuaded that the apparent lack of economic substance in the wartime Anglo-Soviet concert was not seen as a bar to their effective political collaboration, might reasonably raise another objection. Assuming there was some kind of genuine European system developing up to February 1945, surely any respect for historical proportion and significance should, as one tries to frame a compelling master narrative of the Grand Alliance, oblige the historian to give more emphasis to the American role. The United States was, after all, an increasingly dominating wartime actor not only in its global reach but also in its massive military contribution in Europe from late 1942 onward; in its unique sponsorship and organization of refugee relief, shipping supply systems,

[51] Dixon diary, November 22, 1944; Wilson minute, January 7, 1945, N390/G, F.O. 371.47881; *New Statesman and Nation*, December 9, 1944.

and much else that addressed immediate practical problems the Europeans were unable to handle on their own; and as the architect of plans and institutions (Bretton Woods, Dumbarton Oaks, etc.) that looked constructively to the postwar. Surely then European contemporaries were, or should have been, more alive to the likely implications of all this. Surely too, it might be thought, a historian excavating the morally dubious and, as it turned out, short-lived arrangements devised by the Europeans should defer to the dominant historiographical tendency by putting the spotlight more fully upon the American scene and the context of a supposedly looming East-West confrontation, the United States' contribution being both so obviously influential at the time and so profoundly portentous for the future.

The basic flaw in this view is not only that it perpetuates a misperception but also that it is unduly retrospective and gets the timing wrong. Europeans struggling to understand events in the months before February 1945 seem almost universally to have assumed (as most Americans did) that United States forces would, very soon after the European war was over, be returning home or redeployed to the Pacific theater. The United States would therefore be in no position, even if it wanted to, to address the fundamental rationale underpinning the Anglo-Soviet concert, namely, the felt need for order and political security in postwar Europe. For one striking feature of the transatlantic "divergence" we have been looking at in the months before Yalta is that just as the Europeans had put forward no clear postwar economic plan to compete with the remarkable American Bretton Woods proposals, so the Americans had offered no significant politico-military alternatives or realistic solutions (other than the seemingly rarified Dumbarton Oaks scenario, which Europeans viewed with some skepticism) to the chronic security dilemmas of an old continent schooled by hard experience to value certainty over promise. In this situation, a haunting fear in European government circles was that the pre-war transatlantic separation would return, alleviated perhaps by some form of American economic help for reconstruction but essentially reproducing, unless the British and Soviets were able to build a strong, mutually acceptable framework, much of the structural, political, and ideological stress of the 1920s and 1930s.

The argument for more attention to the American economic plans as a direct factor in European socioeconomic calculations before February 1945 may seem better based. But it was never clear to most European leaders – neither to Churchill, buffeted by the Roosevelt administration's relentless economic pressures and demands through 1944, nor to the deeply suspicious collectivists in the Kremlin – whether the transformative nostrums that issued freely from Washington were basically designed to effect a mutually beneficial postwar recovery or were simply the opening wedge for an American capitalism that was beginning to seem very much on the move in 1944 and that looked to observers in each of the European states to be bent on breaking down British imperial solidarity and/or creating intolerable mischief in the totalitarian/communist Soviet Union.

The final answer on the issue of historiographical emphasis, then, is one that puts the stress on accurate reconstruction and respect for context and timing. The key point is that most official and informed European and much American thinking in the months before Yalta was largely governed by a widespread conviction that the historic separation of Europe and the United States would continue. As Walter Lippmann wrote on December 21, "The fact of the matter is that the main structure of a European settlement has now taken shape. ... Far from deploring this development we should regard it as fulfilling our cheif war aims. "For, he continued, "it is our best way of not having to intervene again." The theologian Reinhold Niebuhr similarly gives us a sense of the felt gulf between the two arenas. Writing on the eve of Yalta, Niebuhr noted the failure of the United States to offer "creative solutions" to Europe's security problems. "But America is unable to make such proposals, even if she had statesmen capable of elaborating them," he continued, "because her relations to Europe are not intimate enough, and her continued cooperation in a European settlement not sufficiently certain, to give her the vantage point from which to make such proposals." Not only did America have "no political counter in Europe with which to play the political game," but even if it did have some kind of "sphere of influence" there, this would be ineffectual because "there are no historic presuppositions for such an American policy and not sufficient geographic contiguity to make it effective."[52]

This lucid register of fundamental realities, in its emphasis on enduring constraints as well as visible problems, helps explain both the persisting gulf between the European powers and the United States in the months before Yalta, and the difficulties that later delayed the full engagement of the two arenas even after the unforeseen repercussions of that extraordinary Crimean conference had narrowed the transatlantic gap and brought the United States and the Soviet Union into the more abrasive relationship that led finally to the Cold War.

---

[52] *New York Herald Tribune*, December 21, 1994; Reinhold Niebuhr, *Spectator*, February 14, 1945.

6

Roosevelt's America

A World Apart

The notion of two spheres – America and Europe – was fully recognized and deeply felt by the World War II generation. Europeans fortunate enough to make the wartime trip to the United States were forcibly struck by the contrast. As if in a badly organized art gallery, the typical visitor appears to have felt himself abruptly moved, with only the mediating pause of a nightmare transatlantic journey, from the Hieronymus Bosch collection to the sunlit world of the French Impressionists. A striking symbol of the bright vitality of wartime America was the joyous Rodgers and Hammerstein musical *Oklahoma*, which opened to acclaim on Broadway in 1943. The all-too-understandable nesting tendency of British officials once they reached the U.S. irritated Churchill even more than the similar Anglo-clustering in Cairo.[1] In fact, though, Churchill himself – the personification of restless high-level statesmanship, the father of modern peripatetic diplomacy – never showed any desire to bring his numerous North American visits to an early conclusion.

Of course, there was serious political business beyond the human frailty and cultural dissonance on show in these transatlantic exchanges. But here too, once they adjusted to the Washington ambiance, European visitors found themselves confronting a distinctively different environment. The British, for instance, found that instead of guidance from an authoritative Foreign Ministry they had to deal with a multivoiced State Department that was itself constantly struggling for position among a myriad of competing agencies. And at the highest levels they found, even after they had

---

[1] Churchill to Eden, July 20, 1943, F.O. 954/6.

mastered the constitutional and organizational complexities, that they faced not the obsessively power-gathering and monitoring prime minister they had grown accustomed to in London but an elusive president who encouraged his acolytes to compete with each other in a bewildering political arena. The exasperated British wartime ambassador, Lord Halifax, likened governmental business in Washington to dealing with "a disorderly line of beaters" on a rabbit-shooting expedition.

Such views remind us of the deep contrasts between Britain (and Europe) and the U.S. and their chronic capacity for mutual irritation. It will be worth probing a little more deeply into these differences at this point, for we are now at a crucial point in our inquiry. Thus far we have focused on the steady if not smooth development of a European scenario for the continent's postwar centered on an increasingly collaborative Anglo-Soviet association that by the beginning of 1945 had acquired an enhanced density and momentum. But we know that this did not last, that at some point around the time of the Yalta conference early in 1945 the European partners fell out, and that more or less simultaneously the United States emerged from a self-imposed detachment on the sidelines of Europe's political affairs to assume an increasingly dominant role in a new East/West configuration. It seems sensible, therefore, before examining this transformation, to pause for a moment and focus briefly upon the United States and its enigmatic leader as they stood on the threshold of a remarkable volte-face.

The discussion will consider in turn three American lines of approach to the postwar. The first may be roughly characterized as the liberal multilateral internationalist outlook captured in Arthur M. Schlesinger, Jr.'s, conception of the Roosevelt administration's "universalism." This is the image (and to some degree the substance) the United States presented to much of the world during World War II. The second is a looser set of impulses emanating from various political and private sources that also looked to a full American participation in the postwar world but was more nationalistic, unilateralist, and self-interested, as well as somewhat harsher in tone. These two approaches obviously intersected and overlapped at times, especially in official actions and attitudes. But they were distinct. Together they may be seen as two sides of a growing American international presence in the year or so before Yalta that was self-consciously detached from the alternative, Anglo-Soviet system we have been following so far, but that in retrospect appears to have been laying pincer-like foundations for the sudden envelopment of that system that came early in 1945. The third takes us to President Roosevelt's preparations for the Crimean conference that launched the transformation.[2]

ROOSEVELTIAN APPROACHES

Since the early days of the republic – up to World War II, at least – Americans had a clear sense of their distinctive diplomatic tradition. Geographical and historical conditions were naturally determinative. Centuries of virtual immunity from European interference, except briefly during the revolutionary and Napoleonic eras, produced the powerfully influential notion of "two spheres" and a diplomatic tradition memorably proclaimed and inaugurated in President Washington's Farewell Address and enshrined later in innumerable declarations and policy statements that urged the merits of active commercial relations but no "entangling alliances." Succeeding generations were easily persuaded. For a long time this happy combination of material fact and congenial philosophy was sanctified by what was, on the whole, a successful historical experience.

During the twentieth century, however, two transforming developments put all this in question. From within came the conversion of the U.S. from a widely dispersed, predominantly agricultural/pastoral society into an increasingly centralized industrial state. From Europe came trouble in the form of the two world crises of 1914–18 and 1939–45, which drew the U.S. into the center of world politics. The new involvement in Europe meant that the U.S. had to deal with at least the threat of foreign intrusion, if not invasion, and to accept a degree of reciprocity in its diplomacy as the external milieu began to act on American society more directly than before, forcing unwelcome choices, narrowing options, claiming blood and treasure, and bringing a variety of changes that raised high emotions and sharpened political attitudes.

Through all these changes the American people maintained a remarkable self-preoccupation. The United States seemed to its citizens to be the primary actor in any relationship it took on. America projected power outward. It was invariably the subject – acting on, or sometimes with, more or less acquiescent objects. So far as the exercise of power was concerned its modus operandi was not the desperate defense of threatened national

---

[2] For Halifax, see Warren Kimball, *The Juggler: Franklin Roosevelt as Wartime Statesman* (Princeton, N. J., 1991); p. 21; Arthur M. Schlesinger, Jr., "Origins of the Cold War," *Foreign Affairs*, 46 (October 1967), pp. 22–52; and idem, *Wall Street Journal*, June 21, 1990.

interests that tended to characterize the European experience, but the dispatch from an immune homeland of an expeditionary force. In such circumstances the world's political arena presented itself to Americans not as a realm of necessity but as a range of choices. It was a comfortably insulated posture that brought the advantage of time for debate and reflection before action and allowed a wide margin for error if initial moves were unprofitable. It was a situation that naturally encouraged introspection rather than a feeling for international reciprocity or a sophisticated awareness of the sensibilities of other states.

The effect of all this was to heighten the sense of distinction vis-à-vis Europe. It led the United States away from any resigned acceptance of power politics or meaningful compromises with the European states that were habitually seen as the cause of all the world's troubles. It encouraged, rather, a certain moral censoriousness and a sense of superiority toward Europe along with an easy faith in permanent solutions on an American model that emphasized reason, law, and the supposedly problem-solving primacy of economics over politics.

So far, a familiar story. But if we look more closely at Americans of the World War II generation, we find that in thought and action they were nevertheless drawing, not simply on bitter memories of the rejection by European realpolitikers and backward-looking senators of Wilson's universalist scenario of 1919, but, more constructively, on a homegrown mode of thought and action that may fairly be characterized as "managerial."[3] Actually, a tradition of that kind emerged with the nation's first appearance as a great power. For we can recognize the managerial tendency, to take only its twentieth-century manifestations, in the active American promotion of international law in the early 1900s; later in the powerful governmental and business impulse toward international organization; in campaigns for the establishment of regular procedures and predictability in international commerce during and after both world wars; in a receptive and indeed promotional attitude toward all technological innovation; in a willingness to shape and lead collective economic and political institutions; and in an interest in the creation of legal and arbitral regimes – all arguably culminating, as will be seen, in an increasingly integrated, evolving complex of initiatives during World War II. These managerial approaches, hallmarks of pre-1945 American thinking, are sometimes overlooked or discounted by historians drawn to more

---

[3] For a critical elaboration of the managerial thesis, see Richard J. Barnet, *Root of War: The Men and Institutions Behind U.S. Foreign Policy* (Baltimore, 1973).

personalized or politically oriented formulations. "Expansion," to take the most energetically explored rival conception, can certainly be traced in its origins to a gleam in the eye of any driven statesman or corporate chieftain. But in its modern form, it presents itself to us most clearly as an outcome rather than a motive – as a consequence, especially in the case of a complex industrial society like FDR's America, of some degree of systematic thought and behavior that when laid out for inspection can reasonably be characterized as managerial. This is after all, the natural line of thought and action in a commercially oriented society trying to maintain or advance its core values in the midst of vast unanticipated dislocations.[4]

Is this managerial outlook, the Halifax critique not withstanding, a key to understanding Roosevelt's wartime diplomacy? As all historians know, it is very difficult to force Roosevelt into any clear explanatory framework. One starts with a promising hypothesis, finds a certain amount of initial reinforcement, soon runs into a world of political complexity and labyrinthine mental processes, and emerges ruefully into the daylight thinking sympathetically of the unfinished multivolume enterprises of Frank Freidel and Arthur M. Schlesinger, Jr., and understanding only too well why they ran onto the sand as the subject of World War II loomed up.[5]

Indeed, the inability of so many gifted scholars to pin Roosevelt down is daunting. As we saw in the discussion of Yalta's imagery in Chapter 1, politics intruded from the start. The tendency to blame FDR personally for the imperfections of American wartime diplomacy developed quickly once he had departed from the scene. Celebrated memoirists like Churchill and de Gaulle found much to criticize, and European-oriented writers like Chester Wilmot in Britain and Artur Conte in France amplified a general charge of incompetence and naivete. Not all the European historians have been hostile. The British scholar Donald Cameron Watt, for instance, acknowledged Roosevelt to have been "a great statesman" but found him "grotesquely ill-informed" and suggested that he had little control over his administration or events. American conservatives of the 1950s like Felix Wittmer and James Crocker, who charged Roosevelt with various forms of

---

[4] See Alfred Chandler, Jr., *The Visible Hand: The Managerial Revolution in American Business* (Cambridge, UK, 1977); and Oliver Zunz, *Why the American Century?* (Chicago and London, 1998).

[5] Frank Freidel, *Franklin D. Roosevelt*, 4 vols. (Boston, 1952–73); and Arthur M. Schlesinger, Jr., *The Crisis of the Old Order, 1919–1933* (Boston, 1957), *The Coming of the New Deal* (Boston, 1959), and *The Politics of Upheaval* (Boston, 1960).

betrayal at Yalta, were able to draw some moral support from respectable historians like Charles Beard and Charles Tansill, both of whom accused Roosevelt of having deviously manipulated the U.S. into World War II. In more recent times the negative tradition has been revived by Frederick Marks III in *Wind Over Sand*, a remarkably full compendium of all FDR's alleged sins and shortcomings.[6]

The roll call of more sympathetic scholars is of course far longer, at least in the United States But here too, despite an enormous range of archival material, it has been difficult to bring Roosevelt into clear focus. The titles of the solidly documented favorable accounts of Roosevelt's wartime diplomacy convey an impression of their subject's ambivalent, dualistic character, and complexity. Thus James McGregor Burns's study of the war period is entitled *The Lion and the Fox*. Robert Dallek's account of FDR's diplomacy has four parts, three of them titled, in order: "The Internationalist as Nationalist," "The Nationalist as Internationalist," and "The Idealist as Realist." The impression of unresolvable frustration also seems immanent in Warren Kimball's aptly titled recent book, *The Juggler*, where he notes in Roosevelt an inability or refusal "to think about problems in a structured way."[7]

One explanatory strategy is to follow Geoffrey C. Ward, who traces Roosevelt's elusive persona to a mask assumed in childhood to hide deep, genuine feelings. Another plausible approach, notably in John Harper's *American Visions of Europe*, stresses the emotional/visceral side of Roosevelt's performance. FDR himself set this trap. He liked to describe himself as "a Christian, an American and a Democrat." Less guardedly, he said in May 1942, "You know I am a juggler, and I never let my right hand know what my left hand does … . I may be entirely inconsistent, and furthermore I am perfectly willing to mislead and tell untruths if it will help win the war."[8]

Many historians have followed this clue into explorations of Roosevelt's personality and motivations rather than his actions, emphasizing the well-documented manipulative, improvisational, always optimistic character

---

[6] D. Cameron Watt, *Times Literary Supplement*, July 3, 1992; Frederick Marks III, *Wind Over Sand: The Diplomacy of Franklin Roosevelt* (Athens, Ga., 1988). See also the discussion in Chapter 1 of this volume.

[7] James McGregor Burns, *The Lion and the Fox* (New York, 1956); Dallek, *Roosevelt and American Foreign Policy*; Warren Kimball, *The Juggler*, p. 8.

[8] Kimball, *The Juggler*, p. 7; Geoffrey C. Ward, *A First Class Temperament* (New York, 1989); John Lamberton Harper, *American Visions of Europe: Franklin D. Roosevelt, George F. Kennan, and Dean G. Acheson* (New York, 1994).

of his leadership. And indeed, if there is any kind of common denominator in the Roosevelt literature, it is the belief that, in one way or another, he was a political artist. Vastly experienced by 1941, he both radiated self-confidence and conveyed an inspirational sense of purpose to his own associates. He was generally nonconfrontational and evolutionary in his thinking, preferring to work with events and, where possible, letting the recognizable play of power further his causes with foreign leaders. Roosevelt was a patient statesman. Noticeably, he did not, except in the "destroyers for bases" deal of 1940, where domestic skepticism dictated a hard bargain, press the British too strongly in the early days of the war, choosing to wait until 1944 before imposing almost irresistible pressure to effect important economic transformations. And his acute sense of timing – another visible trait – came out quite often during the war, most dramatically in his withholding public release of his potentially controversial proposals for a postwar United Nations organization until the success on D-Day, whereupon they were launched on a tide of approbation.

Even his shortcomings were those of the lonely artist in politics. Roosevelt, familiar to us in his improvisations, his manipulative skills and playful dissimulations, did not like to plan or to work from the plans of others. The carefully prepared blueprints sent up by the State Department or other governmental agencies received little attention in the Oval Office. His approach was instinctive and visceral, most famously in his attempts to effect a constructive personal relationship with Stalin. And even where he felt hedged in by structural constraints and policy considerations, he loved to intervene personally in ways that were sometimes seen (in Britain, at any rate) as "meddling." He was, by his own admission, only too ready to deceive.

Where, then, is the managerial dimension? Not, assuredly, in any discernible sense of a hands-on, rigorously scrutinizing, detail-oriented administrator. We find it rather in Roosevelt's efforts to meet some of the tough challenges he faced: the need to harness American resources for the war effort; the struggle to keep on top of an articulate press and a volatile public opinion; the problems presented by two very different European allies, whose interests often cut across American expectations and whose political importunities had to be met with a careful combination of practical encouragement and political detachment. Here there seems to have been both a fair measure of success and, by necessary implication if not by some more material register, a passion for control and a degree of managerial skill. One concludes, provisionally, that Roosevelt was both artist and manager, thus succumbing like other pathfinders to the dualistic temptation.

Consider, among many possible illustrations, three significant roles Roosevelt chose to play during the war. First, he both saw himself (as he had often done in domestic politics during the 1930s) and actually acted as a kind of "broker," notably in managing Britain's (and often other countries') relations with Congress and American public opinion. This is a constant theme in his correspondence with Churchill.[9] Secondly, he liked, especially from late 1944 on, when he was looking for an acceptable definition of the suddenly enlarging American political presence in Europe, to see himself as a "mediator" trying to bring some harmony to supposedly tense if not acrimonious Anglo-Soviet relations.[10] This may well have been a sham aimed at the American public's supposed preference for a detached posture in transatlantic diplomacy, for the two European powers were in fact collaborating harmoniously. But here, at least, we see Roosevelt acting the part of a manager rather than the directionless statesman.

Thirdly, Roosevelt saw himself as a decision maker. As was the case in domestic matters, he rarely involved himself in detailed diplomatic negotiations or planning. He functioned effectively as the final authority on major issues and then, less efficiently, as the expediter of those decisions, a crucial dimension in which he relied largely on close aides like Harry Hopkins, whose monitoring and energizing talents were applied far and wide throughout the governmental bureaucracy and on the multiple boards and commissions that were conceived, often on very short notice, to fill unanticipated gaps and discharge urgent critical tasks. FDR also relied a great deal on the energetic Churchill (who in turn relied on Roosevelt for much of his own authority at home) in European and international matters, binding him as tightly as he could on political issues as a useful corollary to their necessary unity in military/strategic matters. There were many well-known differences, over such matters as de Gaulle's role and British policy toward India, and finally over basic strategy. And in relations with the Soviet Union, Roosevelt upset Churchill by falling self-indulgently into the posture of a disinterested mediator. They continued to the end, however, to work together.

In all three roles FDR, always deeply sensitive to the play of power, appears to have relished his responsibility as the ultimate authority. Indeed, much of his claim to greatness as a war leader must rest on the

---

[9] Kimball, *The Juggler*, pp. 99–100. See, for instance, Roosevelt to Churchill, October 10, 1944, *Correspondence*, III, pp. 346–347; and editor's notes in ibid., pp. 34, 36.

[10] The mediatory posture is pronounced in governmental and media comment in the United States in the weeks before Yalta.

judgment he showed in making crucial, often controversial wartime politico-strategic decisions against significant opposition. Thus in 1940 he made the "destroyers for bases" deal with the British in the face of sharp criticism from the navy, from much of Congress, and from many skeptical Americans. In early 1941 he pushed Lend-Lease through Congress in the teeth of powerful isolationist opposition. In 1942, he sided with Churchill against his own top military advisers in choosing an invasion of North Africa rather than landings in France. In 1943, he overrode Churchill's passionate opposition and endorsed General George Marshall's pleas for a commitment to landings in 1944. In 1944, he publicly endorsed Secretary Hull's conception looking to the early establishment of a postwar United Nations against the arguments of people like Secretary of War Henry Stimson, who urged that the political groundwork be laid first. On the whole, each of these decisions holds up well in historical retrospect.[11]

It must be conceded that, so far as Europe and its future are concerned, the managerial thesis looks at first sight much less convincing. The historian John Harper has pressed the view that Roosevelt in his whole attitude to Europe during the war was guided by a powerfully emotional Europhobia and that his "personal political motives in Europe were too brutal to be proclaimed." They involved nothing less, Harper claims, than Europe's "indefinite retirement from the international scene." Harper builds his case largely from Roosevelt's many statements, mainly to political associates, expressing his frustration and disgust with European politics. And as we have seen, FDR was a persistent advocate of breaking up rather than uniting European political combinations.[12]

Thus in the spring of 1942 he had tried to ward off the Anglo-Soviet deal with meretricious promises to the Soviets of an imminent second front. Meanwhile, he carefully refrained from encouraging the British-sponsored confederations in Central and Eastern Europe. The various schemes for European regionalism, such as Churchill's Council of Europe, were also coldly received. The whole animus against de Gaulle, though certainly inspired in part by personal hostility, reflected a well-documented sense of disdain for France and its pre-war elites. To this seemingly destructive approach to Western Europe's various aspirations we may add Roosevelt's hands-off approach to Eastern Europe (well described in the Norwegian

---

[11] Dallek, *Roosevelt and American Foreign Policy*, pp. 243–248 (destroyers for bases); 252–260 (Lend-Lease); 321–322 (North Africa); 430–454 (Overlord); and 466–467, 506–525 (U.N.).

[12] Harper, *American Visions*, pp. 89, 131, and passion.

historian Geir Lundestad's aptly titled book, *The American Non-Policy Towards Eastern Europe*), manifest in the lukewarm support extended to the London Poles and the many marks in Roosevelt's personal conversation of his indifference to the postwar fate of that region, which he seems to have consigned in his own mind to the postwar Soviet sphere. All this calls to mind again Bohlen's epitaph on the president's scenario of European political dismantlement at Teheran.[13]

Through most of 1944, moreover, these negative attitudes appear, if anything, to have intensified. The United States failed to cooperate with Anthony Eden's European Advisory Council, apparently reluctant to encourage European solutions for Germany's future. And the whole Morgenthau Plan affair, as we have just seen, reflected the President's remarkably casual approach to, and lack of understanding of, what might be necessary for the recovery of Europe. As we have seen, these attitudes underwent some revision around the time of the Octagon conference, when, upon the surge of Soviet power, the administration was forced to recognize the need for and even encourage British political activism in European affairs. But this was soon overtaken by a further series of anti-European actions by the United States before and during the Yalta conference. All in all, it is not difficult to understand the widespread feeling in Western Europe after the war that Roosevelt had betrayed vital interests.

There were, at the time and since, similar resentments in London as Roosevelt campaigned at various levels against the British empire. Here there is a dense critical literature inaugurated by Churchill himself and carried forward in the detailed work of historians like Wm. Roger Louis, Christopher Thorne, and Randall Woods. The principal Rooseveltian target was always the imperial preference system, seen by many Americans as a root cause of the economic miseries of the 1930s and even, in Cordell Hull's conflation of politics and economics, of the run-up to the war itself. Ancillary to this was a constant sniping over the continuing subjection of India, and a more spasmodic but alarmingly invitational approach to the white Dominions, which the war was drawing ever more fully into the American orbit.[14]

---

[13] Julian G. Hurstfield, *America and the French Nation, 1939–1945* (Chapel Hill, N.C., 1986), Chapter 7 and pp. 221–240; Geir Lundestad, *The American Non-Policy Towards Eastern Europe, 1943–1947* (New York, 1978).

[14] For EAC, see Kitchen, *British Policy*, pp. 167–168. For Morgenthau, see Warren F. Kimball, *Swords or Plowshares: The Morgenthau Plan for Defeated Nazi Germany, 1943–1945* (Philadelphia, 1976). Wm. Roger Louis, *Imperialism at Bay: The United States and the Decolonization of the British Empire* (New York, 1978); Christopher Thorne, *Allies of a Kind: The United States, Britain and the War Against Japan* (London,

Within the confines of a divided historiography in the United States we are inclined to see the two great manifestations of what might fairly be called the "American alternative" – the Bretton Woods system and the projected United Nations organization – as expressions of either a deeply rooted idealism or an aggressive expansionism. In fact, each institution seems to combine both elements. Bretton Woods, for all its well-meaning rationality, was intended to destroy British imperial protection. And the United Nations, garlanded with altruism, was very directly targeted at the staple practices of traditional European diplomacy. At the same time, both were – in their conception, organization, and purpose – unmistakable products of a managerial outlook.

Moreover, there is perhaps another, more constructive explanation of this apparent hostility. For what Harper puts down to the president's Europhobia can also be seen as an attempt to clear the ground for a positive alternative American scenario for Europe's future that was simply incompatible with the return of traditional politics, which the growing Anglo-Soviet collaboration seemed certain to reestablish. The obvious manifestation of such an American alternative was of course the United Nations project. Roosevelt came relatively late to this cause, but, after some rhetorical flirting with the "Four Policemen" and other power-oriented nostrums, he committed himself to the updated Wilsonian solution in 1943. From that moment on we cannot characterize FDR's solution for Europe in entirely negative terms. For the various strategems that signified a continuing American desire to avoid entanglement with Europe's politics during the war (and to prevent the continent's own leaders from reverting to traditional practices) were now juxtaposed to a highly purposeful American effort to entangle the Europeans in a very different system of America's own devising.

Further, there was much more to this "universalism" than the proposed United Nations. If we are to understand the full dimensions of Roosevelt's unacknowledged and only slowly developing scenario for the postwar, and for Europe especially, we should see the prospective international organization as only the most visible part of an evolving congeries of declarations, conferences, and institutions, in effect a web of American initiatives, each part of which has its own genesis and history, but which together in the retrospect of over half a century appear to be the harbingers of the United States' final emergence as a dominating world power, and even of what we

1978); Randall Bennett Woods, *A Changing of the Guard: Anglo-American Relations, 1941–1946* (Chapel Hill, 1990).

have come to think of as its drive toward international interdependence
and globalization.[15]

The emergence of this web, clearly recognizable in three distinctive sets
of initiatives appearing at different stages of the war, stands out clearly
against the backdrop of war and alliance politics. It begins when the
detached United States, not yet fully involved in the war, commits first
to Roosevelt's Four Freedoms in 1940 and then to the Atlantic Charter
of August 1941 with its fulsome, visionary promises of freedom, prosperity, and respect among nations. More declarations appeared to mark
American entry into the war, such as the Declaration of the United
Nations in December 1941 and then, to register American concern for the
world's oppressed, the still-born Declaration on National Independence
in the spring of 1943, which had brought such grief to Anthony Eden.
The primary function of all this rhetoric, which the more down-to-earth
Europeans were inclined to treat dismissively, was to meet the need, at this
early stage of American belligerency, for inspiration and the mobilization
of a united citizenry.

By 1943 a second class of American initiatives – representing a move
from moral exhortation to practical responses to more functional
demands – was beginning to appear. These were essentially organizational initiatives, the hallmark of the managerial mind-set. They included
the Food Conference of 1943 to organize relief in liberated areas and,
developing from the Bermuda Conference of 1942, the United Nations
Relief and Rehabilitaion Administration, which was also established in
that year.[16] Here we see the United States taking up morally necessary
international tasks that the European powers are either too distracted or
unwilling to deal with themselves. By 1944 this functional second phase
of American international leadership was becoming habitual, as we see
in the convening of the Civil Aviation Conference in Chicago and the
International Labor Organization conference in Philadelphia, both on
American initiative.[17]

Finally, in the more familiar third stage during 1944, we see the two great
American politico-economic initiatives looking to the future: the appearance of the U.N. proposal in June, followed by the validating Dumbarton
Oaks conference in September, and the Bretton Woods meeting in July to
establish facilitating financial institutions – later the World Bank and the

---

[15] Schlesinger, *Wall Street Journal*, June 21, 1990.
[16] Woods, *A Changing of the Guard*, p. 90.
[17] Gilbert, *Churchill*, VII, p. 1074.

International Monetary Fund – as foundations of a postwar international economic order.[18]

There appears to be a high measure of evolutionary logic in the unfolding of these coherent American initiatives. They clearly reflect a practical "managerial" tendency and, unless we subscribe to the view of him as a habitual improviser with no sense of political coherence, they seem to identify Roosevelt as the hidden impressario of a steadily developing functional internationalism. The effect was to propel the United States into wartime issues and postwar planning very much on its own terms – that is, by steadily drawing its allies, Britain and the Soviet Union as well as many other countries, into a web of cooperative activities while still managing to maintain a basic detachment from the more traditional, security-oriented European politics that, as many Americans saw it, were distracting its two allies.

For on the eve of Yalta we are still looking at two distinct systems of behavior and styles of diplomacy as the two great political arenas, non-Nazi Europe and the United States, moved uneasily together toward victory. During the war up to the Yalta conference they had remained, in their postwar planning, substantially apart, reflecting their distinctively different historical experiences and geopolitical objectives. With the advantage of hindsight we can see that the two were, however slowly and tentatively, getting ever more entangled in each other's affairs even before the transformative events of early 1945. Thus the United States was now inescapably more involved in Europe by virtue of its military surge as well as the other activities just mentioned; and Britain and the Soviet Union were beginning to come at least marginally into the American orbit through their participation in many of the planning conferences orchestrated in Washington and looking in various ways toward a radically different world order.

But the general outlook in the months before Yalta was all the other way. Indeed, it is in the differences between the two arenas, and the divergent ways in which their leaders expressed their hopes for the future – the Americans fashioning a rational system of structured liberal internationalism, the European powers defining and settling upon a more traditional framework focused on politics and security – that we find a primary source not just of the misunderstandings that cropped up during the war (and most alarmingly just before the Crimean conference), but more fundamentally of the widespread belief on both sides

[18] See Hilderbrand, *Dumbarton Oaks*, Chapter 2 and passim; Woods, *Changing of the Guard*, pp. 133–148, 229–240.

of the Atlantic that each arena was destined, with whatever ameliatory nostrums the political leaders could conjure up, to revert to historical experience and go its own way.

Still, supportive elements, as yet largely uncoordinated, for a more cohesive, interdependent international order did exist in the United States, carrying the potential for a fuller engagement, so long as the feat could be managed on American terms.

PRELUDE TO ENVELOPMENT

In October 1943 the relatively calm course of Anglo-American collaboration was violently disrupted by claims from five United States senators who had been touring the various fronts that the British were up to their old tricks. They were slackening their fighting effort, passing off Lend-Lease materials directed to other states as their own, and working vigorously to reclaim and prolong their imperial grip well into the future. This immediately set off a transatlantic crisis of confidence. The senators found a good deal of support in Congress and the American press. The British defended themselves vigorously. Churchill made a scathing rejoinder in the House of Commons. *The Economist* launched a counterattack. More temperately, the *New York Herald Tribune*, looking back a few week later on this spasm of mudslinging, noted that, after nearly two years of unusual decorum, "the wartime taboo" on criticism had been lifted.[19]

This particular storm passed, but it serves to make a point. It is not enough, if we are to grasp the full intent and impact of American wartime diplomacy, to confine ourselves, as we have done so far, to "high diplomacy." Schlesinger's "universalist" characterization, with the managerial gloss given it here, conveys a valid sense of the liberal multilateralist internationalist "policy" orientation of the Roosevelt administration. But to complete the picture (as we must do if we are to understand the surprisingly rapid consolidation of a practical American leadership after high-level diplomacy produced the catalytic crisis at Yalta) we must also take some account of elements that reflect a more nationalistic or unilateralist approach and a harsher tone in pressing it on America's allies. The more down-to-earth advocates of American interests, to whom Roosevelt was just as attentive as he was to the protagonists of high-minded liberal initiatives like Dumbarton Oaks and Bretton Woods, included members

---

[19] Ibid., pp. 90–91; *New York Herald Tribune*, October 26, 1943.

of his own administration, the Congress, the military leadership, and (much less cohesively) a range of corporate heads, newspaper magnates, columnists, and other shapers of public opinion.

If isolationists are properly seen as the natural foil to the internationalists during the wartime years, these expansion-minded nationalists, inspired by varying degrees of patriotic emotion and self-interest, might be viewed as the shock troops who brought some teeth to Roosevelt's visionary policy making. Here too we find some of the features of a web, or at least of a collection of interrelated impulses responding to various managerial stimuli. For a strong managerial bias is also present, though it is one that is much more hard-boiled and less prone to compromise than the presidential variety. Taking the nationalists together, we do in fact see the building blocks of a strong, emerging system of power working toward a leading place for the United States in the postwar world.[20]

Roosevelt himself exhibits the pitfalls of too exclusive a focus on high diplomacy. He was inevitably both internationalist and nationalist. His overall postwar politico-economic aims were "liberal" in a Wilsonian sense. And he vigorously supported the British war effort, even as he plotted the destruction of the British imperial system, which he viewed as standing in the way of the open financial/commercial system needed to avoid a postwar return to depression.[21] But FDR was no Anglophile. The documentary records at Hyde Park, New York, and elsewhere are full of adverse private comments he made about many British notables from Churchill down. He cheerfully agreed with the similar remarks of others in his entourage and commented on more than one occasion that he expected more trouble with the British than with the Soviets after the war. "What a wonderful old Tory to have on our side," he had exclaimed while hosting Churchill in the first days of the alliance. Churchill remained an admired figure, though even his allure was fading by the end of 1943. But neither Roosevelt nor his associates liked "Tories," and nearly all the British emissaries the prime minister sent over during the war (Halifax, Beaverbrook, and Stanley among them) seemed to come from that side of British political life. Attlee, Bevin, Herbert Morrison, and other Labour leaders were kept at home, and Eden, a comparatively

---

[20] See, for premonitions of this, W. T. Stead, *The Americanisation of the World* (London, 1901).

[21] Anglo-American economic relations were always tense. For Churchill's reliance on "the power of the debater" but impression that "[a]s far as I can make out we are not only to be skinned but flayed to the bone," see Churchill to Wood, March 12, 1941, PREM 4.17/1.

progressive Conservative, made no appearance before March 1943. Moreover, while he portrayed himself as, and did in fact act as, Britain's honest broker in the Washington jungle, Roosevelt tended to give unstinting support to those like Morgenthau, Stimson, Hull, and others who, even as they collaborated loyally in the prosecution of the war effort, were engaged in various ways in the permanent reduction of British political and economic power in the world.[22]

It is worth stressing here that the spirit of the World War II New Dealers, as seen from London, was still remarkably militant. It is easy to accept the conventional portrait of Roosevelt's wartime administration as a jumble of feuding, uncoordinated bureaucratic satraps, intent only on their own advancement. Certainly the diaries and memoirs of people like Vice President Henry Wallace, Treasury Secretary Henry Morgenthau, Cordell Hull, Harold Ickes, and others tend to suggest a remarkable self-preoccupation. The diaries of Henry Wallace, in particular, are a strong corrective to anyone in thrall to the romantic conception of statesmanship. The well-intentioned vice president, almost totally obsessed with Washington intrigue and his own declining political prospects, appears, like Jane Austen during the Napoleonic Wars, but with considerably less justification, almost unaware of the great world events through which he was passing. He certainly seems an improbable candidate for the demanding role of Soviet spy fastened on him by some recent historians. In this respect he was perhaps similar to the otherwise very different Harry Dexter White, under secretary of the Treasury, who fits the espionage profile more plausibly but who, in the characterization of John Maynard Keynes's biographer, Robert Skidelsky, "saw in the march of history a coming together of the Soviet experience in Russia with the New Deal programmes of the United States." Such attitudes are perhaps not so surprising in post-Depression America, where even the impeccable liberal icon John Kenneth Galbraith can be found telling a colleague that

---

[22] Kimball, *Forged in War: Roosevelt, Churchill and the Second World War* (New York, 1997), pp. 13, 14. While it is true that Roosevelt and his associates disliked the Tory mentality and found some of Churchill's colleagues (Brooke, Beaverbrook, and even the well-intentioned Halifax on occasion) condescending, they were determinedly collegial, and Roosevelt willingly collaborated with Churchill in frustrating a trip to the United States by Harold Laski, the Labour Party chairman, at the invitation of Eleanor Roosevelt. See Fraser J. Harbutt, "Churchill, Hopkins and the 'Other' Americans: An Alternative Perspective on Anglo-American Relations, 1941–1945," *International History Review*, 7, 2 (May 1986), pp. 236–262.

Russia should be permitted to absorb Poland, the Balkans and the whole of Eastern Europe in order to spread the benefits of Communism."[23]

But it would be very wrong to write these people off as dreamy radicals. The New Deal, for all its well-documented internal divisions, was still a tough, intensely focused, and highly successful political movement. It had triumphed over the Republicans and conservatives in 1932 and had kept them firmly underfoot thereafter. It had fended off the surge from the left in 1935–36. It was now steadily overcoming both the Nazis and fascists in Europe and the Japanese imperialists in the Pacific. And at the same time it was engaging, at various levels and with a strong sense of unity and commitment, in a last campaign against its ultimate antagonist – the growth-inhibiting, manipulative, Tory-dominated British Empire. "Leftwingers in the New Deal," Robert Skidelsky remarks, "much preferred the idea of American partnership with progressive Soviet Russia to one with reactionary, imperialist Britain." To which one might add that, from varied intellectual and emotional perspectives but with a similar intensity, a great many more moderate and conservative Americans were also eager to bring the old empire to its knees.[24]

The cutting edge of this campaign to break down the British Empire was the effort, conducted largely by Morgenthau and White from the Treasury, to commit Britain to practical economic arrangements facilitating Roosevelt's postwar multilateral conception, increasingly feared by the British as the likely instrument of their eclipse. The ultimate aim was to pave the way for postwar American hegemony by breaking down the imperial preference system established by the Macdonald-Baldwin government at Ottawa in 1931, and then to force Britain and its sterling area associates into a United States–dominated economic arena. The strategy in pursuit of this aim was both to bind the British, while they were in a position of wartime dependency, to agreements giving effect to that purpose – treaties mandating currency convertibility and establishing rules of multilateral trading and financial order – and to prevent any premature wartime recovery on the part of the British (by a successful effort to build up their dollar reserves, for instance, or by starting an export drive before Germany was defeated) that might allow them to escape the new American dispensation. The leverage behind the strategy came first from the British dependence on Lend-Lease (which came up for review in Congress every six months) and

---

[23] Woods, *Changing of the Guard*; Blum (ed.), *Wallace Diaries*, passim; Robert Skidelsky, *John Maynard Keynes: Fighting for Freedom, 1937–1946* (London, 2002), p. 242.

[24] Ibid., p. 242 and passim.

later from the many indications that Churchill's government was going to need further help, in the form of loans or other support, during the immediate postwar transitional period.[25]

The negotiations began in 1942 with talks on methods of postwar currency stabilization. The British hopefully advocated a clearinghouse system that, somewhat in anticipation of later International Monetary Fund procedures, would allow states to draw funds on an overdraft basis while retaining a wide field of sovereign autonomy. The proposals envisaged the United States using its vast surpluses as a general creditor, more or less on conventional banking principles. The American negotiators quickly saw through this and insisted on more rigid controls (in effect imposed by the United States) and a substantial up-front subscription of capital by member states that was, it quickly became apparent, far beyond their likely postwar capacity. These unproductive initial talks highlighted the differing approaches to full currency convertibility, which Morgenthau and his associates saw as a primary instrument in the destruction of the enclosed sterling area. Meanwhile, they made it clear that Imperial Preference would have to go and quickly closed another potential escape hatch by successfully resisting British efforts to build some small dollar balances that would permit a modest renewal of commerce in preparation for postwar competition. Morgenthau threatened a congressional curtailment of further Lend-Lease. These tactics were deeply resented in London because the Roosevelt administration, by contrast, was permitting Soviet dollar balances to grow without question.[26]

Confronted with the prospect of coercive measures, the British cast about desperately for alternatives. There was throughout and after the war a body of influential empire loyalists who urged that there should be no postwar cooperation with the United States and that Imperial Preference should be upheld and strengthened. This hope, pressed most vigorously by the economist Hubert Henderson, the Federation of British Industries, and assorted Bank of England officials, turned out to be as illusory as the clearinghouse proposals. It assumed that the British Dominions as well as India and other sterling bloc countries – which, by virtue of their substantial material contributions to Britain during the war, were building up very large, nonconvertible sterling balances in London – would be content once the war was over to let Britain continue to shape their future and direct their

---

[25] For Treasury Department policies, see Woods, *A Changing of the Guard*, passim. For the British perspective, see Skidelsky, *Keynes: Fighting for Freedom*, especially Chapter 6.
[26] Woods, *A Changing of the Guard*, pp. 81, pp. 91–94.

postwar trade predominantly toward the purchase of British manufactures, thus bringing about the desired recovery and warding off the importunate Americans. As the war dragged on, however, and the British reliance on the United States grew to enormous proportions, the likelihood of any British recovery unassisted by American largesse of some kind steadily diminished. Worse, officials in London were forced to realize that Canada, Australia, New Zealand, and even South Africa had during the crisis years attached themselves much more closely to the United States out of strategic and political necessity. They were not likely, once the crisis had passed, to deny themselves the benefits of access to American capital and markets. Consequently, the notion of a renewed Imperial Preference system came to seem increasingly far-fetched.[27] The leading economist John Maynard Keynes pointed to the flaw. The members of the sterling bloc, however loyal in war, would want new horizons. "They would be able to and would wish to buy American goods with their large London sterling balances." Keynes did not think there was enough "solidarity" within the sterling system to allow the "forced loans" Britain would wish to impose upon its members.[28]

In the midst of all these complexities, carefully anatomized by the historians Randall Woods and Robert Skidelsky in recent work, the intellectually capacious Keynes, who led the British negotiators in all the important wartime meetings with the American officials, was pursuing two basic objectives. The first was a determination that Britain should emerge from the war as a Great Power. The second was, whatever sacrifice he had to make in his Washington negotiations, to yoke the United States firmly to Britain so that their future collaboration, when present inequities would hopefully be ironed out, could be assured. Keynes was in fact pursuing in the economic arena the permanent Anglo-American association that Churchill, fitfully during the war but strenuously and without deviation after Yalta, was attempting in the political realm. Together they were, among all the personalities on both sides of the Atlantic, the primary bridge builders who, in the great transitional era between the middle of World War II and the onset of the Cold War, worked self-consciously to bring this about. In their belief that intimate association with the United States would allow Britain to remain a first-rank power they were, in retrospect, unduly optimistic.[29]

[27] Skidelsky, *Keynes: Fighting for Freedom*, pp. 210–211 and Chapter 6 generally.
[28] Ibid., pp. 210–211.
[29] Ibid., p. 474, where Skidelsky writes, "In the world of economics and finance Keynes had come to occupy the same position as Churchill in the world of politics. ..."

The recognition of American economic power and the conviction that Britain must be associated with it condemned Keynes to a laborious search for compromises with the relentless Morgenthau/White combination (and sometimes with other administration figures as well). As a negotiator he was endlessly fertile in argument and in fashioning quasi-solutions. The Bretton Woods system, preeminently, was his final achievement, one that went on to play a large, constructive role in postwar international economics. But at the time it seemed to be an unsatisfactory solution both to the pressing general problems of reconstruction (for only the United States could afford to subscribe capital) and to the immediate problem for the British of insufficient liquidity to permit the recovery that they were trying unavailingly to jump-start during the latter stages of the war.[30]

In the end, nevertheless, there was a continuing and eventually augmented flow of funds from the United States to Britain. This was inspired, not by Keynes's negotiating magic, but by a combination of economic and political impulses. Administration leaders visiting Britain in August 1944, including a suddenly chastened Morgenthau, returned with chilling predictions of impending bankruptcy.[31] And this came just as Roosevelt, Hopkins, and others were becoming more fully aware of the political implications of the now looming Soviet presence in Eastern and Central Europe. If the United States was not, as the president appears genuinely to have thought, going to be able to maintain armed forces in postwar Europe, the British partner must be revived and supported. This, as we have already seen, was the politico-economic inspiration for the Octagon conference at Quebec in September, which saw Morgenthau, still bent on breaking up Britain's imperial system but obsessed now with his plans for German pastoralization, willing at last to fall in with FDR's wish to give Britain the needed reassurances of continuing American economic support. This meant Lend-Lease help until the end of the Pacific war, a transitional loan, and the prospect of enlarged commercial opportunities in postwar Europe following the destruction of German industry. But this was not really an American retreat. The hard-won structural changes would be vigorously pursued. Britain was to be revived commercially at the expense of a pastoralized Germany, not by abandoning the

---

[30] For Bretton Woods, see Woods, *A Changing of the Guard*, pp. 133–148, 229–240. See also Thomas W. Zeiler and Alfred E. Eckes, *Globalization and the American Century* (New York, 2003), p. 124.

[31] Halifax to Foreign Office, August 14, 1944, PREM 4.18/6; Woods, *A Changing of the Guard*, pp. 167–168.

great prize of imperial economic dismantlement. The primary politico-economic objective of the Roosevelt administration during World War II, the break-up of British Imperial Preference and its replacement by a United States–dominated multilateral system, would, it was now confidently expected, be achieved.[32]

Long before this, in the autumn of 1943, the nationalistic impulse had begun to emerge in Congress. Up to this point the post–Pearl Harbor feeling of solidarity as well as the exigencies of war had muted criticism both of presidential activism and of the British ally. But the remarkable Republican gains in the 1942 elections, the unexpected survival of many congressional isolationists, and the clear vision of victory that came with the military successes of 1943 led to a revived partisanship, especially in the Senate. It was into this atmosphere that in October 1943 the five angry members of the Senate Military Affairs Committee had returned from their battlefront tour. They complained bitterly about British misappropriation of Lend-Lease and various practices in the Middle East and Asia, where the old imperial system was, they alleged, being stealthily revived. The senators were loudly critical. One of them, Senator Butler (Republican of Nebraska) called Lend-Lease "the most colossal dole of all time." And Senator Brewster (Republican of Maine) called for a thorough investigation of Lend-Lease administration.[33]

These charges played into a growing sense, well beyond the administration and the Senate, that the time had come to grasp the well-earned opportunity for the United States to insist on a suitable recompense for Lend-Lease. This in turn stimulated all sorts of expansionary sentiments. From naval circles came intimations that the United States should become a dominant maritime nation, with or without British cooperation. The president of United Airlines urged collaboration among all American airlines for "maximum strength for competition with other powers." This line of thought was inspired largely by the huge airfields being built by the United States government in various parts of the world, including North Africa, the Middle East, and the Pacific. American interests, it was argued, required postwar rights of access that would promote the furtherance of American commercial aviation. This led in 1944 to the tortuous and acrimonious international discussions at Chicago over postwar aviation. Meanwhile, the U.S. Chamber of Commerce was proposing that American

[32] For the Quebec conference, see Chapter 4 of this volume. David Rees, *Harry Dexter White: A Study in Paradox* (New York, 1973), pp. 266–288.
[33] Woods, *A Changing of the Guard*, pp. 90–91. *New York Times*, October 11, 1943.

businessmen be allowed to go into the war zones to establish themselves before the peace.[34]

All this agitation aroused the Senate Committee to Investigate the National Defense Program, chaired by the Democratic Senator Harry S. Truman of Missouri. Here too the sense of violated innocence at the hands of the crafty British was palpable. The Truman committee quickly produced a report pointedly reminding the administration and the American people that, so far as Britain was concerned, "Lend-Lease was never intended as a device to shift a portion of their war costs to us but only as a realistic recognition that they do not have the means with which to pay for materials they needed." Implicitly acknowledging that monetary repayment was impossible, the Truman report noted bleakly that Lend-Lease recipients should be using their own resources fully before asking for the aid and then went on to suggest other means of compensation. Britain, it was stressed, should show its appreciation by transferring ownership of some of its valuable oil resources to American ownership.[35]

The committee's focus was not on Britain alone. The Anglo-Dutch rubber monopoly should be broken up. But London was the main target. Americans should not again be made the "victims" of British politicians as they had been in the 1920s, when, according to Truman, "we were forced to pay exorbitant prices for rubber at the same time as we were being called Shylocks in the British press for requesting payment of our war loans." Further, the United States should be given "rights in British owned resources of nickel, copper and tin and iron in countries outside the British Isles, and the right to receive manganese from Russia after the war in return for Lend-Lease articles furnished to it now." If this firm approach were adopted, the U.S. could look forward to "the greatest and soundest era of prosperity this nation has ever enjoyed." But this would not occur automatically. The Truman report warned, "Our foreign trade will depend on the policy we adopt concerning Lend-Lease and rehabilitation, and every effort should be made to reduce the cost to our taxpayers to the minimum."[36] These claims were supported by Senator Richard Russell (Democrat of Georgia), a strong protagonist of American commercial aviation. He urged the Roosevelt administration to negotiate now rather than after the war. He lauded Britain as a "splendid" ally, but wanted the ninety-nine-year Caribbean base leases made permanent,

---

[34] *New York Times,* October 11, 1943; Campbell to Foreign Office, October 8, 1943, T160/1154.

[35] *New York Times,* November 6, 1943.

[36] Ibid.

future defense facilities given in Iceland, reassurances that Dakar in Africa would be secure, and base rights given in New Caledonia.[37]

Universalism or unilateralism? The Schlesinger formulation put a pleasing gloss on these demands. The British, taking in these threatening effusions, which were all amplified and dramatized in the American press, thought they saw a familiar grasping Yankee trader mentality at work. Keynes, who happened to be in Washington at the time of the Five Senators crisis, was in despair. He wrote to a London associate on October 11:

At breakfast this morning I was much depressed by reading nothing but a long string of articles to the effect that Great Britain, having removed the labels off various packages in order to represent American Lend-Lease goods as her own, was so untrustworthy that any question of postwar collaboration must be out of the question, and other articles that the whole of Lend-Lease must be wound up as soon as possible, seeing how grossly it was abused. All this without a word of denial from ourselves.[38]

The denials and recriminations from across the Atlantic came soon enough. Churchill made a stout defense of British conduct and policy in the House of Commons, emphasizing the British contribution to the partnership and asserting the increasingly dubious notion – in the United States, at any rate – of Lend-Lease as "a pooling of resources." The London newspapers also replied in spirited fashion, some arguing the moral superiority of Britain's long war effort and stressing the fact that there were still at this point more British than American troops in battle with the Axis. But here too bitter memories came quickly to the surface, and with them gloomy premonitions. Thus *The Economist* noted "an explosion of economic nationalism in the United States" and continued, "In political matters the tide in the United States is flowing toward Wilson, but in those questions of economic cooperation which are the lifeblood of an enduring settlement there are signs of a return to the big stick and the ideology of McKinley."[39]

Gradually the storm abated, thanks in part to the apparent success of the helpfully distracting Moscow foreign ministers conference in late October 1943 and the Teheran summit meeting at the end of November. If anything, the crisis reinvigorated British faith in President Roosevelt as it demonstrated the truth of the difficulties, which some in London thought

[37] *New York Times*, October 29, 1943.
[38] Keynes to Eady, October 11, 1943, T160/1154. This was viewed by Treasury officials as "nasty reading" – Lee to Harmer, November 8, 1943, ibid.
[39] *The Economist*, October 8, 1943.

he had hitherto exaggerated, that he faced in supporting the British war effort at such high levels of expenditure and supply. As Keynes put it on November 1, "the so-called anti-British feeling is very largely a version of anti-Roosevelt feeling. Everything from now onwards is pure politics. Roosevelt is associated with the Prime Minister. Any attack on us, therefore, if it has a popular success, pricks the President."[40]

It is interesting here to see a tendency in both the British figures I have identified as the leading bridge builders to a postwar Anglo-American economic and political collaboration to assume that American suspicions of Britain in wartime America were simply a product of partisan politics rather than deeply felt and widely shared emotions. For, like Keynes, Churchill (who was also prone to separate Stalin from presumably more sinister Soviet power centers) greeted the various American economic challenges to the British postwar scenario in early 1944 as purely political causes pushed upon the president while he was distracted. These illusions would be cruelly exposed in due course.

Nonetheless, these tensions were soon overtaken by the positive images associated with the Moscow and Teheran conferences. There was, moreover, a notable closing of ranks among the Eastern establishment, who were always sensitive to the introspectively strident nationalism of the *Chicago Tribune* and the supposed opportunism of the Midwestern senators, who were vocal and well represented among the critics. James Reston of the *New York Times,* in a sympathetic review of the British reactions to some of the more provoking statements by representatives of the American private sector, suggested that they had led to the conclusion in Britain "that for domestic reasons the Yankee horse-trader was being revived as the ideal in U.S. foreign affairs."[41] Similarly, in the *New York Herald Tribune* we find calls for an end to "petty criticism."[42] And toward the end of October the top military leaders, Stimson and Marshall, found it desirable to warn members of Congress that the war was far from being over and that the United States could not "indulge in the luxury of petty criticism and narrowly nationalistic wrist-slapping."[43]

Yet the American military establishment itself was also thinking of postwar expansion. And it was rife with the same range of highly charged emotions we see in the administration and the Congress – a basic acceptance

---

[40] Keynes to Eady, November 1, 1943, T160/1154.
[41] *New York Times*, October 11, 1943.
[42] *New York Herald Tribune*, October 11, 1943 (G. F. Elliott).
[43] Ibid., October 22, 1943.

of the need for the intimate alliance with Britain but a chronic tendency toward suspicion and mistrust. For Stimson and Marshall these impulses went back to the early days of the war when they were laboring, during a breathing space of neutrality they fully expected to be brief, to build a serviceable military capacity almost from scratch. In 1939 the United States Army was the world's nineteenth largest. The growing commitment of resources to Britain's war effort after the shocking fall of France in mid-1940, while accepted as to some degree desirable or even necessary, was a severe drag on an American mobilization that was predicated from the start on the assumption that the U.S. might at very short notice have to confront direct two-front threats from both a Nazi-dominated Europe and imperial Japan.[44]

These tensions, briefly allayed after Pearl Harbor and Churchill's apparent acceptance of American leadership in the military management of the Anglo-American alliance at the ensuing Washington conference, quickly flared up again early in 1942 over the strategic issue of whether the first major coalition effort should come with landings in France, as the American Joint Chiefs of Staff wished, or in North Africa, as favored by the British. Behind this lay old arguments over the primacy of the European over the Pacific theater of action, the latter being the persisting preference of the U.S. Navy. Marshall periodically threatened the anxious British with a diversion to the Pacific. In the event, as we have seen, Roosevelt decided both these issues in ways that favored Churchill, who was thus able to dominate Anglo-American strategy until the Teheran conference at the end of 1943, when, as we have seen, he was somewhat rudely unhorsed. A cross-Channel invasion was then settled for summer 1944, and Marshall was given the governing role in overall war management in Europe that he held with a tight grip until the end of the conflict.

Well before that, however, fresh sources of tension associated with the approaching postwar were appearing within the military as well as in political circles of the Anglo-American coalition. And here too one is struck by the expansionary instinct of the American leadership and its preoccupation not only with international order and a secure peace but also, more specifically, with American national interests. Here the navy was in certain respects the pacesetter, as indeed it had been in pressing American expansionism since the palmy days of Admiral Mahan and the Spanish-American War. Throughout World War II, but with increasing

---

[44] Mark Stoler, *Allies and Adversaries: The Joint Chiefs of Staff, the Grand Alliance, and United States Strategy in World War II* (Chapel Hill, N.C., 2000), pp. 41–45.

intensity in 1943 and 1944, the navy urged the importance of securing and retaining mostly permanent bases in the Pacific and elsewhere for its postwar global role.

But the immediate instigator of the developing interest in a global strategic reach was the president himself. As early as December 1942 he notified the Joint Chiefs of Staff that he foresaw the need for some kind of international police force and asked for a study directed to the provision of "air facilities," a plan that was to be made "without regard to current sovereignty." The historian Mark Stoler has shown how, over the initial objections of the president's representative on the Joint Chiefs of Staff, Admiral Leahy (who reminded his colleagues of FDR's express "internationalist" focus), the military leaders redirected the thrust of the ensuing studies from "international" to "national" requirements.[45] Leahy soon backed off, and by March 1943 the Joint Chiefs had produced what historian Wm. Roger Louis has called "the genesis of the Joint Chiefs 'master plan' for a global security network," a design that stressed national rather than international interests.[46] For these plans emphasized, very much in the Mahanian spirit, the connection between American military and commercial interests, with a stress on United States–led aviation as a decisively reinforcing reality. In much the same way we find Roosevelt in June ordering an investigation by the navy of Pacific islands that could serve not only security but also civil aviation needs, thus looking to a fully integrated American presence in this vast arena.[47]

The president's expansionary impulse in the Pacific quickened again toward the end of 1943. More wary of sovereignty issues than the military chiefs, he focused on international trusteeship as the appropriate political cover for the coveted island archipelago of American bases. But he was scarcely less determined to gain the necessary control. Moreover, his approach was global. As always, he wanted American control of Dakar and other northwest African sites as well as several islands in the Pacific. The Joint Chiefs' planners responded to this encouragement with a seminal document calling for further enlarged plans, building on their March scenario and looking now to a total of seventy-two potential bases – thirty-three in the Atlantic theater, thirty-nine in the Pacific. They called for a broad-based consideration of postwar military issues and for Joint

---

[45] Ibid., p. 138.
[46] Ibid., pp. 138–139. Wm. Roger Louis, *Imperialism at Bay*, pp. 261, 267.
[47] Stoler, *Allies and Adversaries*, pp. 152–153.

Chiefs' representation on other postwar planning groups so that, as Mark Stoler puts it, "military consideration may be integrated with political and economic considerations."[48]

The impression one gets here of an increasingly purposeful and expansionary American state is reinforced by Roosevelt's more explicit endorsement of this scenario in late 1943. As he prepared to confront Churchill at Teheran on the second-front issue, all FDR's deep suspicion of British motives reemerged. During the crossing on the USS *Iowa*, he regaled the receptive Joint Chiefs with a variety of aphoristic criticism of the leading American ally. He castigated Britain's European policies, especially over France and Italy, where, as we have seen, he had recently received some rebuffs. The British wanted, Roosevelt said, "to build up France as a first-class power which would be on the British side." This, he emphasized, was undesirable. The British also wanted to restore the monarchy in Italy – another black mark. He then moved on to attack British and French colonialism, saying he would not support the restoration of France in Indochina, New Caledonia, or elsewhere in the Pacific, or indeed at Dakar, which should come under American control. He intended, he advised his delighted listeners, to oppose the British push for command in the Mediterranean and to insist, contrary to British wishes, on an occupation zone in the north of Germany rather than in the southwest. Above all, he declared, "we should not get roped into accepting any European sphere of influence." The felt danger here was again British manipulation, the fear that the London government would find a way to upset United States–Soviet relations or even bring the two countries into confrontation. His subsequent Teheran experience with a deeply upset Churchill only intensified the president's rising Anglophobia. In December, buoyed by the belief that he had formed a bond with Stalin at Teheran, Roosevelt said that "he thought he would have more trouble in the postwar world with the English than with the Russians."[49]

A striking feature of this expansionary assertiveness on display during the middle period of American belligerency is that it came largely from the state, not from the private sector and business community so often portrayed in revisionist accounts as the driving force pushing the United States into full engagement with the world. True, much of the congressional and some of the executive activism was prompted by private interests, oil and communication/transportation corporations prominent among them, but

[48] Ibid., p. 159.
[49] Ibid., pp. 161–164.

on the whole it is the government that we see taking the primary initiatives and clearing the way.

We get some idea of the sheer weight of governmental influence during the war, and of its primacy in promoting American commercial and other activities overseas, when we see that between March 1941 and V-J Day in August 1945 the U.S. spent nearly $50 billion on Lend-Lease (about $27 billion to Britain and $10 billion to the Soviet Union). This is more than six and a half times the book value of all U.S. direct foreign investment at the war's end.[50] Moreover, the Roosevelt administration took an active leadership role in many areas, especially where the procurement of scarce raw materials was at issue. Thus the Reconstruction Finance Corporation created both the Metals Reserve Corporation, which organized and/or financed the purchase of copper, nickel, tungsten, and other ferro alloys in fifty-one countries, and also the Rubber Reserves Corporation, which was similarly active in promoting crucial imports of natural rubber and then working with Firestone, Goodyear, and other companies to create and stockpile artificial rubber.[51]

Oil was of course a primary concern. Most oil imports during the war came from the Western Hemisphere (especially Venezuela), and the U.S. government was active in facilitating negotiations between the major oil companies and Mexico and Venezuela. Increasingly, however, attention was focused on the vast Middle Eastern reserves. Saudi Arabia was gradually lured into the American fold (and away from the British) by hastily arranged infusions of direct Lend-Lease. The Petroleum Reserve Corporation was formed in 1943 to ease governmental participation in all oil negotiations. In this latter instance, state dynamism received a setback because public control upset the private interests (who also deflected an Anglo-American Petroleum Agreement between the two governments in 1944) and was later abandoned. Later that year, however, the Roosevelt administration encouraged and helped two private American companies that sought concessions in Iran, hitherto an exclusive Anglo-Soviet preserve, leading to considerable tension with both European allies and eventually to an Iranian decision to postpone all negotiations until the end of the war.[52]

---

[50] See Mira Wilkins, *The Maturing of Multinational Enteprise: American Business Abroad from 1914 to 1970* (Cambridge, Mass., 1974), p. 282.

[51] Zeiler and Eckes, *Globalization and the American Century*, p. 112 and Chapter 5 generally.

[52] Ibid., pp. 112–115; Wilkins, *Multinational Enterprise*, p. 279. For Venezuela, see Stephen G. Rabe, *The Road to OPEC: United States Relations with Venezuela, 1919–1976* (Austin, Tex., 1982), p. 351.

However, apart from these special, internationally oriented industries (and a few others, such as aviation companies like Pan-American Airways and various shipping and communications firms), corporate America during the war was markedly ambivalent about, if not openly reluctant to involve itself in, postwar commerce overseas. This was particularly true of large manufacturing corporations that had blazed a trail internationally between the wars but remembered chastening experiences during the 1930s and early 1940s, often at the hands of European governments, as overseas plants were seized or destroyed, patents were taken, market channels disrupted, and profit repatriation blocked by currency controls or other impediments. Additionally, there was widespread distaste for the looming revival of New Deal regulatory harassment that seemed implicit in the government's elaborate postwar planning, and also a feeling that the domestic market, primed by vast wartime savings, would be much more reliable and profitable.[53]

Thus far we have focused on large institutional components of the developing American system. But what of public opinion – supposedly the final determinant in foreign policy as well as, more obviously, in the realm of market consumption? Was there a sustainable basis in the public primordium for all this intensive international activism by the Roosevelt administration? Here the picture is more difficult to read clearly. Polls and surveys were still comparatively unsophisticated. Regional differences remained. And while radio was steadily creating a stronger sense of national community, most people still took their news from the local newspapers, whose long-rooted hegemony seemed as strong as ever.[54]

There were important press chains with large readerships (the Hearst group has been estimated to have had 72 million daily readers in the mid-1940s), and there was a large number of influential syndicated columnists, mostly stationed in the East Coast's urban centers. The numerous New York daily newspapers covered a spectrum ranging from the *Wall Street Journal* and Hearst's *Journal-American* on the conservative right through the variously moderate *New York Times* and *New York Herald Tribune* to the left-wing *PM*. They were mostly internationalist in outlook (whether from a national or more "universal" perspective), as were the popular Luce magazines, *Time* and *Life*, and other newsmagazines like *Newsweek* and *U.S. News and World Report*. Certain well-known pundits like Walter Lippmann

---

[53] Wilkins, *Multinational Enterprise*, p. 283.

[54] For a brief survey of the American media during World War II, see James Baughman, *The Republic of Mass Culture: Journalism, Filmmaking, and Broadcasting in America since 1941* (Baltimore, 1997), pp. 1–29.

and Anne Hare McCormick, as well as radio commentators like Raymond Gram Swing, had large audiences. Further west, local influences supervened. Here exclusively nationalist or isolationist tendencies (which had an East Coast foothold in the *New York Daily News* and a handful of other papers) were more prominent in the small towns of the old Midwest and more noisily voiced in the regionally dominant *Chicago Tribune*. The West Coast presented a kaleidoscope of news and opinion with a natural Pacific emphasis.[55]

The full significance of all these American impulses – the universalist scenarios of Roosevelt and his associates and the more down-to-earth interests and projections emanating from the wider American society – can hardly be summed up in a brief generalization. They convey an impression that the American state, notwithstanding a degree of uncertainty in the public realm, was steadily developing, so far as Europe and much of the rest of the world was concerned, a capacity for economic if not political envelopment. This was hardly a new idea. Historians often cite the British writer W. T. Stead's *The Americanization of the World*, published in 1901, as an early bellwether of what soon developed into a very widespread expectancy. American economic power, however mishandled during the interwar years, was now underpinning most of the Allied war effort (though perhaps only about 10% or so in the Soviet Union) and would, it was becoming very clear by early 1945, be crucial in any broad reconstructive effort. People could see that the United States had already taken the primary initiative in planning for refugees, supply, and shipping; that the American military, fully engaged in the Pacific and now furnishing more than two-thirds of the Allied forces in Western Europe, was preparing for a remarkable global expansion; and that America was also taking the lead in the establishment of a new international political authority.[56]

But the really significant step, to a full postwar politico-economic engagement with Europe, was by no means foreordained. The old barriers – geographic separation and historic detachment – still stood in the way. And few observers in late 1944 were ready to assume some inevitable American

---

[55] In the absence of a fully satisfactory overview, the following general studies are useful: Richard W. Steele, *Propaganda in an Open Society: The Roosevelt Administration and the Media, 1933–1941* (Westport, Conn., 1985); Paul Fussell, *Wartime: Understanding and Behavior in the Second World War* (New York, 1989). See also W. A. Swanberg's two books: *Citizen Hearst* (New York, 1961) and *Luce and His Empire* (New York, 1972). Mitchel V. Charnley, *News by Radio* (New York, 1948), and Ronald Steel, *Walter Lippmann*, are also useful.

[56] For American public attitudes toward the proposed United Nations, see Robert Divine, *Second Chance*, passim; and toward the Soviet Union, see Ralph Levering, *American Opinion and the Russian Alliance, 1939–1945* (Chapel Hill, N.C., 1976).

postwar political hegemony. Many Americans seem, at this pre-Yalta juncture, to have been aware of the apparent Anglo-Soviet determination to preserve European political autonomy under their own aegis and, on the part of the Western European powers, of a widely expressed intention to regain their imperial possessions. They saw too, as we can today, Roosevelt's studied detachment up to this point from wartime European politics, and especially from developments in Eastern Europe. They were doubtless aware as well of the continuing disinclination of the American people (committed to the war effort, certainly, but still substantially preoccupied with domestic affairs and suspicious of foreign entanglements) to take on anything more than the rarified international organization (whether destined to be an effective instrument of international safety or simply a convenient distancing mechanism from the world's real problems was not yet clear) that Roosevelt was now presenting to his countrymen as a general political framework for the future.

With hindsight, of course, we know that all this changed and that after Yalta assertive American impulses finally came to the fore politically as well as in other fields and began to take on a more cohesive aspect. In 1944, however, it was not at all clear that public opinion in the United States was ready to move from support for the expeditionary projection of American military power to approval of the more generally expansionary attitudes and actions whose wartime roots we have been examining. But fundamental change was on the way, and the obvious question for the historian is when and how this occurred. The broad answer we are working toward – superficially demonstrable on a simple before-and-after comparison, but calling for a fuller explanation – is that the Yalta conference and its aftermath produced the catalytic events that led to a reorientation and then to a fundamental transformation in the relationships of the three victorious powers.

It is necessary then, having now paid tribute to two of the primary elements in play – the consolidating but not entirely stable Anglo-Soviet concert, on the one hand, and the powerful multifunctional American impulses developing in the wings and imperceptibly coalescing into a potential alternative system, on the other – to consider the acts and thoughts of President Roosevelt as he prepared for his last summit meeting with America's European allies.

PREPARING FOR YALTA

We have now seen something of the purpose and power of the wartime United States. It is easy enough in hindsight to sense the future hegemon emerging from the mists of war. The increasingly looming U.S. was stronger, the frazzled security-obsessed Europeans weaker, than our focus on wartime Europe has allowed. But for the historian trying to understand the thinking of the war generation, a retrospective assessment of that sort would yield a distorted perspective. As late as February 1945 most contemporary observers expected the pre-war separation of America and Europe to reappear: modified perhaps, the old gulf somewhat narrowed, but still substantially two different arenas. For the transformative dynamic, the catalyst that would reshuffle all the elements stirred into turbulent confusion by World War II into the now familiar East/West relationships, had not yet appeared.

In the arena of high-level diplomacy, however, we can, again with the advantage of hindsight, clearly see the two fundamentally incompatible elements that identify late 1944 as a period of approaching United States–Soviet confrontation. One was the wholehearted, exclusive American commitment, clearly registered at the Dumbarton Oaks conference, to the concept and institution of a United Nations organization. The other was the Soviet determination, exhibited most ominously in the recognition on January 1, 1945, of the Lublin regime as the provisional government of Poland, to dominate the future of Eastern and Central Europe, an objective seemingly endorsed already by Churchill and Eden in October 1944. Dumbarton Oaks and Lublin are the two poles of growing U.S.–Soviet tension, registering sharply divergent visions of the postwar order. And this was ominous in the months before Yalta because President Roosevelt, intent on Allied unity but distracted by his reelection campaign, had never addressed the now widening gap between his public assurances that victory would bring a wholesome peace along Atlantic Charter lines and his private intimations to Stalin of some significant degree of support for Soviet aspirations in Eastern Europe.

Certainly there is little evidence that Roosevelt, so often credited with political clairvoyance, foresaw the basic realignments that emerged from the Yalta meeting in early 1945. He had earlier talked a good deal about the hegemony of the "Four Policemen." But by late 1944 the direct leadership role he envisioned for the United States in postwar continental Europe was mainly economic and organizational, and political only in the leverage that it would bring, in the eradication of Nazism, and in the realm of moral suasion associated with the projected United Nations. As he told Churchill just before D-Day, "Do please don't ask me to keep any American forces in France. I just cannot do it. I would have to bring them all back home. As I suggested before, I denounce and protest the paternity of Belgium, France and Italy." He then went on to pin the parental responsibility upon the British. "You really ought to bring up and discipline your own children. In view of the fact that they may be your bulwark in future days, you should at last pay for their schooling now." FDR was personally content, though other Americans were not, to see Churchill moving toward the geopolitical arrangements with Stalin that we have seen culminating in the Moscow order. Indeed, at critical moments, though not consistently and sometimes pulled back by his associates, he appears, as this cable suggests, to have actively encouraged them.[57]

Right up to Yalta Roosevelt was true to his basic twofold policy: keeping the Soviet Union in the wartime alliance, which meant a stream of encouragement and no complaints in his relations with Stalin; and maintaining unity at home, which similarly mandated a constantly upbeat approach. These lines of thought and action were also temperamentally congenial, playing to FDR's optimistic and nonconfrontational style and to his conception of himself as the indispensable "broker." On substantive matters he generally chose evasion or procrastination, only rarely reaching out to grasp the various nettles presented in 1944. And when faced with unavoidable problems, he was still, as the record from the New Deal "experimentation" of the 1930s to the wartime Morgenthau Plan illustrates well, a habitual improviser. Thus he dealt with the growing Soviet problem in Eastern Europe and the Balkans by encouraging a hitherto strategy-distracted Churchill to plunge deeply into the European geopolitical maelstrom of late 1944. But now he was getting into deeper water. He had done little to address the basic dilemma that the bustle of global war had allowed him to shelve but that was now increasingly urgent: how to fashion a peace in and around Europe that would satisfy both the ambitions of Joseph Stalin and the hopes of the American people.

The key to understanding the evolution of this dilemma is that during 1944, and indeed right up to the Yalta conference in February 1945, Roosevelt's attention was focused primarily on his own domestic front. Here he had two imperatives that were more important to him than a deeper involvement in the disagreeable European milieu. The first was to establish the United Nations – first the idea, then the creation of the institution itself – in the hearts and minds of the American people. The second was to win reelection to an unprecedented fourth term. These were intimately related objectives. For Roosevelt, therefore, the proposed world

---

[57] Dallek, *Roosevelt and American Foreign Policy*, p. 476.

organization was the focal point of both domestic and foreign policy in the year between Teheran and Yalta.

Roosevelt had come rather late to the United Nations campaign. Earlier in the war, conscious both of persisting post-1914 American suspicions of a world political authority, and of the confirming failures of the League of Nations, he had privately advocated the Great Power–oriented "Four Policemen" concept. He pressed this for a time upon Churchill, Molotov, and later Stalin. It had obvious appeal to the disillusioned generation of the 1930s and early 1940s. Roosevelt remained faithful to it in spirit even as in late 1943 he felt obliged to adopt Cordell Hull's more democratic and egalitarian United Nations model. Sentiment favoring that more widely inclusive kind of institution made itself felt soon after the U.S. entered the war. The pollster George Gallup announced in July 1942 "a profound change in viewpoint on international affairs." Of his sample, 50% wanted the United States to join a new international "league" after the war, with only 22% opposed. Gallup then eliminated the "no opinion" category and concluded that about 73% overall favored such a commitment, a big jump from 50% in July 1941 and 33% in 1937. A similar result during the same period came from the National Opinion Research Center, which found 72% giving an affirmative answer to the question, "Should the U.S. join a union of nations if one is formed after the war?" Even Republicans, hitherto mostly isolationist, were undergoing a conversion. In the summer of 1942 Gallup found that 70% of that political group were willing to join a postwar league compared to only 23% in 1937.[58]

In March 1943 guidance and leadership came in the form of a Senate resolution inspired by Senator Joseph Ball (Republican of Minnesota) and three others calling on the U.S. to ask its allies to create a permanent international organization during the war that would carry on the war, administer relief, resolve disputes, and establish a postwar police force to frustrate "military aggression by any nation." This produced a remarkable surge of public enthusiasm. The historian Robert Divine remarks, "By the end of March it was clear that the Ball resolution had aroused the whole nation and provided the internationalist movement with the focus it had lacked."[59]

---

[58] For the evolution of Roosevelt's "Four Policemen" idea, see Dallek, *Roosevelt and American Foreign Policy*, pp. 342, 389–390, 434, 482. For his adherence to the Hullian concept, see Divine, *Second Chance*, pp. 184–213. *New York Times*, July 5, 1942; "Survey of Opinion and Ideas on International Post-War Problems," July 15, 1942, Box 82, Hull MSS. See also *Public Opinion Quarterly*, 6 (Fall 1942), p. 491.

[59] *Congressional Record* (March 16, 1943), p. 2030; Divine, *Second Chance*, p. 96.

Momentum gathered quickly. The House of Representatives passed Congressman William Fulbright's June 1943 resolution asking Congress to go on record favoring the creation of "appropriate international machinery" to establish and maintain a just peace and American participation therein.[60] Internationalist organizations began to appear everywhere.[61] All this activity, of which the United Nations quickly came to be seen as both symbol and prospective political instrument, was reinforced by significant developments: the increasingly global reach of America militarily and strategically in both the Atlantic and Pacific theaters; the leadership the United States was giving in a variety of nonmilitary ways such as relief, food supply, and help for refugees; and the dramatic summitry at the Moscow and Teheran conferences.[62] Internationalist sentiments were stimulated too by publicists like the *Time/Life* proprietor Henry Luce, whose summer 1941 article lauding "the American Century" touched off an enthusiastic response, and by Vice President Henry Wallace's influential book *The Century of the Common Man*, where the author, in a brief step away from the Washington political arena that was his chief preoccupations, modestly urged America's humanitarian mission. Wendell Willkie's *One World* (April 1943) appealed to Americans to see their destiny as linked with that of other peoples and nations. Behind these well-known authors a growing phalanx of academics and pundits, such as the geopolitical specialist Nicholas Spykman and the influential columnist Walter Lippmann, gave some intellectual substance to the cause. There were, of course, wide differences in emphasis and detail. Conservatives tended to want a more autonomous approach with minimal foreign constraints, an echo of 1919 and the conflict between Senator Henry Cabot Lodge and President Wilson. Realists wanted a peace founded on a recognition of America's power and interests, but also on a sense of its limitations. Liberals looked to a strong but more egalitarian organization, with respect shown for the sovereignty of all nations and with an internationally controlled police force to keep the peace.[63]

---

[60] *Congressional Record* (June 16, 1943), pp. 5943–5944.
[61] For a study of the many internationalist groups during this period, see Divine, *Second Chance*, Chapter 5.
[62] For the sharply positive impact of the Moscow and Teheran conferences on public confidence in Soviet postwar cooperation, see Levering, *American Opinion and the Russian Alliance*, p. 205.
[63] *Life*, February 17, 1941; Henry A. Wallace, *The Century of the Common Man* (Washington, D.C., 1942); Wendell Willkie, *One World* (New York, 1943); Nicholas Spykman, *America's Strategy in World Politics* (New York, 1942). See also Lippmann's regular columns originating in the *New York Herald Tribune*.

Roosevelt appears to have observed all this with mixed feelings. There were obviously many unresolved issues that he would have to address. He made numerous supportive but carefully noncommittal public comments, but usually only when forced to do so by events or zealous pressure groups. A convinced internationalist himself, he was, as we have seen, a "realist" at heart who was deeply skeptical about the visionary scenarios he was accustomed to use as a mode of communication with the American public. He was also inhibited by persisting anxieties. He worried that all the activism and high emotion associated with the internationalists' desire for premature commitments might produce an isolationist backlash that would imperil the national unity he had carefully nourished for the war and endanger his reelection prospects by reinvigorating a Republican Party that had been tamed by wartime prosperity and the presidential candidate Wendell Willkie's passionate internationalism.

Nonetheless, once converted, Roosevelt bent himself to the cause, showing his characteristic good timing by announcing the administration's intentions on the morrow of the successful D-Day landings. The momentum then accelerated as delegates from the Soviet Union, Britain, and China convened on August 21, 1944, at Dumbarton Oaks in Washington for the inaugural four-power conference (the Chinese necessarily arriving only after the Soviets, who were not at war with Japan, had left) to discuss and plan the prospective United Nations organization. This meeting was intended, as Hull put it publicly, to allow "informal conversations and exchanges of views on the general subject of an international security organization." There was some optimism in the State Department. British and Soviet cooperation was expected, though this was tempered by an alarming Soviet preliminary draft plan requiring, among other conditions, an absolute veto power for the Big Four. The State Department plan, based largely on classic American constitutional principles, was published beforehand to general domestic approval. Its Madisonian schema envisioned a Council with peacekeeping powers, a General Assembly, and a World Court. The four convening powers (plus France, which was also to be given a permanent Council seat) would dominate the Council and have an as yet undetermined veto power, but the inevitable impression of a Great Power "superstate" was strenuously denied by official spokesmen, who tried to please the more zealous internationalists with assurances that all participating states would earmark military forces that would be available for peacekeeping action.[64]

---

[64] The most comprehensive study of Dumbarton Oaks is Robert C. Hilderbrand, *Dumbarton Oaks: The Origins of the United Nations and the Search for Postwar*

The conference, held in secret to avoid public scrutiny and embarrassing speculation, was intended to lay foundations for the other prospective U.N. members to consider and approve subsequently. Had this happened, the United Nations would not have been an issue at Yalta, and indeed that conference might not have taken place. But although an ostensibly large measure of agreement was found – on some membership issues and on the institutional framework, for instance – the closed character of the deliberations (many of which were in fact leaked to James Reston of the *New York Times* and published, thus becoming the subject of feverish media debate) was irritating and bred public suspicion about the administration's real intentions. This also meant, as the historian Robert Divine notes, that the Roosevelt administration missed an opportunity to educate the American people about the differences among the leading powers.[65]

For the conference foundered on potentially fatal arguments over two primary Soviet demands. One was their call for separate memberships in the General Assembly for the sixteen Soviet republics. This drew attention to the facts of life as seen from Moscow, notably that in the new organization, as in the old League of Nations, the British Dominions constituted a substantial bloc and that the numerous Latin American members would vote in lockstep with the United States. The consternation aroused by this Soviet demand (Stettinius recalled that it burst upon the British and Americans "like a bombshell") is a telling illustration of the State Department's lack of imagination and foresight in this area. One might have expected better of President Roosevelt, who, urging American membership in the League of Nations while campaigning for vice president in 1920, was reported to have noted "that because of the number of South American nations who would almost certainly vote with the United States on matters of importance, membership in the League would greatly enhance American power." No one seems to have had any significant historical memory or understanding of the unhappy Soviet experience with the League of Nations (they had been expelled earlier in the war), or to have considered the sense of isolation the Soviets might legitimately feel in any international organization of this kind. A worried Roosevelt, concerned about the effect of these developments on American public opinion, cabled Stalin asking him to reconsider. Stalin refused to budge, but

---

Security (Chapel Hill, N.C., 1990). For concerns about a possible "superstate," see ibid., pp. 105, 85–107.

[65] Ibid., pp. 75–76, 78–79, 97; Divine, *Second Chance*, p. 222.

replied suggesting that they shelve the issue for consideration at a future summit meeting.[66]

The other Soviet demand was even more upsetting. This was their insistence upon an absolute veto power – on all matters, procedures, and actions, as well as discussion – for the proposed five Great Powers who were to be permanent Security Council members. This too might well have been anticipated. Indeed, the American position on the veto was itself far from clear at the beginning of the meeting, and the State Department delegates took no initial position. Several of its members thought the veto power should apply automatically where military enforcement was at issue; others in Washington thought the Senate might require this kind of ultimate American control. Ultimately, however, probably in deference to press and public sentiment, the self-consciously progressive American and British delegations argued that all member states should be put on an equal footing. Accordingly, they opposed the absolute veto and took the view that a party to a dispute, even a Great Power, should not be able to vote on its resolution. But the Soviet delegation, led by their ambassador to Washington, Andrei Gromyko, rejected this argument. Roosevelt invited him to the White House and argued that allowing a party to sit in judgment on its own cause violated the American sense of "fair play," which, he explained, had its roots in the days of the Founding Fathers. Any break with this tradition would cause difficulties for him in the Senate. Then, moving with characteristic ease from the profound to the mundane, FDR observed that husbands and wives in matrimonial difficulties were never permitted to vote in their own case, though they were always given a chance to testify. It should be the same, he thought, with the family of nations. Gromyko, not the most humorous of statesmen, promised to convey the president's thought to Moscow.

Roosevelt again addressed Stalin directly, emphasizing that American opinion would "neither understand nor support" a plan that violated the principle that an interested party could not vote in his own case, urging too the point that the small nations would resent any attempt by the Great Powers to "set themselves up above the law." But Stalin continued to insist on the protection of the absolute veto.[67]

---

[66] Hilderbrand, *Dumbarton Oaks*, pp. 95–96. Roosevelt to Stalin, August 31, 1944, FRUS, 1944, I, p. 760; Stalin to Roosevelt, September 7, 1944, ibid., pp. 782–783.
[67] The veto issue is discussed in Divine, *Second Chance*, pp. 216, 225–258, 255–256, 294–296, and in Hilderbrand, *Dumbarton Oaks*, pp. 183–208. For Roosevelt and Gromyko,

In the end, therefore, the Dumbarton Oaks conference concluded, from the administration's viewpoint, unsatisfactorily. Roosevelt himself ordered it terminated after the failure of various compromise attempts, telling Stettinius that he would take the disputes up with Stalin later. He and other officials put on a brave public face, insisting, as the president put it, that "ninety percent agreement" had been achieved. Because of this, and because much of the contention had been hidden from public view, the general response was favorable. The Republican presidential candidate, Governor Thomas Dewey of New York, declared himself "very happy" at the result. Even Herbert Hoover showed enthusiasm. The press was generally supportive. But many questions were raised. Conservatives, remembering Henry Cabot Lodge's campaign in 1919, worried about congressional prerogatives; liberals lamented the absence of an international police force and of any provision for economic reform as well as the apparent undermining of the principle of sovereign equality promised at the Moscow conference of 1943.[68]

In retrospect, Dumbarton Oaks was a mixed bag. In a positive sense, it went some way toward recognizing the reality of power politics, now enshrined in the privileges accorded the five permanent members of the projected council. The basic flaw in the League of Nations, it was widely thought, had been the failure of its architects to acknowledge and allow for the primitive character of international society. They had exalted rights rather than order, forgetting that only the Great Powers, working together, could provide real security. Some now thought Dumbarton Oaks had done better. In London *The Times*, for instance, looked back approvingly on the conference as "practical peacemaking" that represented a sensible advance on the "juridical league." It was admittedly an "idealistic" conception, but because it was "honest" and offered no guarantees it offered the hope of averting catastrophe by creating "a common interest and a common responsibility in making the system work."[69] In retrospect, however, we may think today that there was a dangerous unreality about these deliberations. The secrecy was unfortunate. It aroused public and political suspicion, and the vigorous "spin" put on its apparently only limited success created, as the historian Robert Divine comments, "a very

---

see Stettinius, diary, September 8, 1944, Stettinius MSS. See also Roosevelt to Harriman, September 8, 1944, Roosevelt MSS; Stettinius to Roosevelt, September 14, 1944, FRUS, 1944, I, pp. 806–807; and Stettinius, *Roosevelt and the Russians*, pp. 20–22.

[68] *New York Times*, October 10, 1944; Dulles to Hull, October 13, 1944, Box 191, Long MSS.

[69] *The Times* (London), March 13, 1945.

misleading impression of agreement among the Big Four and between the administration and Congress. The basic issues on which the League had foundered had yet to be faced."[70]

Perhaps the most striking feature here from a diplomatic perspective is the confidence of President Roosevelt and others that the Soviets would be willing to be drawn without serious reservations into a powerful, postwar international organization that it could not hope to control or perhaps even materially influence, where their conduct would be exposed to constant (and in all likelihood hostile) scrutiny and perhaps to economic and even military sanctions, and where the "rules of the game" would rest securely in the hands of the inevitable majorities that could be marshaled by the dominating bourgeois states, to whom the Kremlin had been reluctantly yoked only by the unanticipated and by all accounts much-regretted betrayal of Adolf Hitler in 1941.

Given all this it is remarkable that we do not find among contemporary American or British statesmen any serious attempt to analyze and understand the Soviet perspective on this now looming institution. The American hosts at Dumbarton Oaks had shown exquisite sensitivity in small things. The portrait of the famous Polish pianist and statesman Ignacy Paderewski was temporarily removed from its habitual place in the main conference room for the duration to avoid putting the Soviet delegates off their game.[71] There was less imagination on the larger matters. We observe, as is so often the case in American diplomacy, a great deal of faith in goodwill and human rationality. The prevailing view in American government circles on the eve of the Dumbarton meetings seems to have been that, in the midst of so much international misery, no sensible person could object to the establishment of a high-toned institution of this kind and that everyone would or should be glad to find the U.S. government again taking up the onerous burden of trying to establish one. It appears to have been assumed that the Europeans understood (many did) that the establishment of such an organization was a vital condition for any postwar continuation of the American internationalism that was now saving Europe from Hitler and might well be needed again. Thus Hull, ignoring or perhaps not even aware of the Roosevelt-Stalin discussions at Teheran juxtaposing Eastern Europe and the United Nations, saw fit to instruct Harriman in early 1944 to make the Soviets understand that American support for

---

[70] Divine, *Second Chance*, p. 228.
[71] Hilderbrand, *Dumbarton Oaks*, pp. 69–70.

such an international organization would depend upon the Kremlin's willingness to abandon "unilateralism."[72]

This was a well-meaning initiative. But the notion that Stalin could be induced to give up his plans for postwar domination in Eastern Europe for fear of losing the chance to participate in a United Nations shaped by the Roosevelt administration seems dubious indeed. The idea that some Europeans may not have wanted what Churchill had called American "governance," or had mixed feeling about such an American commitment, or perhaps had other plans altogether, surfaced only very occasionally in a Washington diplomatic establishment that was not always working at the highest level of sophistication. For the stronger belief in Foggy Bottom was that the Europeans, having been through the furnace of war twice in thirty years, must want, or at least needed, American models to set them straight. Such thinking rested finally on a deep Enlightenment faith in reason, law, and the kind of productive managerial procedures that the directors of United States foreign policy, with their own great eighteenth-century constitutional legacy always in mind, now felt willing and able to bestow upon the irritatingly troublesome but obviously desperate outside world. And, reinforcing this kind of self-confident thinking, lay the public emotions stirred in the United States itself by the great Wilson revival of 1943–44, which redemptively celebrated the true architect and champion of American internationalism. Surely the world would not fail to grasp the proffered "second chance."[73]

Yet the Soviets appear to have felt they had good reason to be fearful of these developments. Thus, in his reply to Roosevelt's September cable asking him to break the deadlock on the veto issue, Stalin replied that he believed the Big Three at Teheran had accepted the need for coordination and unanimity among the Great Powers. What had happened to that proviso? He felt obliged to insist on this protection in the proposed Council voting. Drawing attention to the initial American proposal at the conference for "special procedures" in cases where a permanent member was party to a dispute, he urged the point that among those powers "there is no room for mutual suspicions." In justification he cited the persistence of "certain absurd prejudices" that often worked to hinder "an actually objective attitude towards the USSR."[74]

[72] Hull to Harriman, January 25, 1944, FRUS, 1944, III, pp. 1234–1235.
[73] For the Wilson revival, see Divine, *Second Chance*, pp. 168–174.
[74] Stalin to Roosevelt, September 14, 1944, FRUS, 1944, I, pp. 806–807.

There would appear, in the unfortunate absence of clear guidance from the Soviet archives, to be four possible ways to interpret Stalin's refusal to end the impasse on the veto. The first, quite common in American and British postmortems on Dumbarton Oaks, is that the Soviets simply did not understand the various implications and explanations. Stalin and his associates occasionally adopted this tactical pose, but given both their practical experience of the League and the sharp political consciousness habitual to the communist mentality, this view of their conduct seems implausible. A second view is that they were committed from the start to a "unilateral" course and were therefore deliberately destructive at Dumbarton Oaks and bent on frustrating the evolution of this potentially inhibiting institution. This interpretation (common on the conservative right) conflicts with the abundant evidence we now have that Stalin was prepared to join the United Nations (if the terms were satisfactory) and that he preferred a policy of cooperation with the Western powers.

A third view – that Stalin may or may not have been sincere in his voiced objections but was thinking in terms of what we have already identified as the "bargain of Teheran," which saw him withholding full participation in the proposed United Nations until assured of supportive American understanding of Soviet aspirations in Eastern Europe – is much more plausible. It is very easy, once the existence of this "bargain" approach in Stalin's diplomacy is accepted as in some way habitual (and it stands out, as we have already seen, in his relations with Britain as well as with the United States), to see him setting up, in his insistence at Dumbarton Oaks on multiple Soviet memberships and an absolute veto, the negotiating counters he would later use at Yalta to extract from Roosevelt the freedom of action he desired in Eastern Europe.

But is this the whole story? Can Soviet churlishness at Dumbarton Oaks be reduced to a calculated gambit in the suddenly accelerating push for position in the now imminent postwar arena? Perhaps. But there is another, deeper dimension, perhaps a fourth explanation of Soviet conduct here, where we can sense genuine anxiety in Moscow. For we can, surely, see two more or less understandable Soviet concerns. At the emotional level, they must have been mindful throughout of their experience only a few years before, with the Anglo-French–dominated League, an organization they viewed as a failure, so far as their own protection in the 1930s was concerned, and from which they had been brusquely expelled on the initiative of Britain and France during their association with Nazi Germany. The second, more practical concern must have been the anticipated membership-stacking activities of the U.S., which would not only enhance American power but expose the Soviet Union to the future sniping of many unsympathetic small states. Gromyko's initial position was that membership should be confined to the twenty-six states that had signed the United Nations Declaration in 1941. But the new, more open dispensation, taking in all states that had declared war on Germany before March 1945, set off a vigorous and ill-concealed recruitment drive by the United States, which, in the months leading up to Yalta, marshaled the numerous Latin American countries into what can only have been seen in Moscow as a well-disciplined American voting bloc. The British had some means to protect themselves, for they too could supposedly still rely, as they had in the League, on their numerous empire and Western European associates to back them up. The Soviets, by contrast, had no friends and no apparent legal safeguards. Their insistence on multiple memberships and on the absolute veto was in this sense logical, realistic, and, one would have thought, predictable.

This lack of sensitivity to historically founded Soviet concerns can be seen not only in exchanges over the general membership of the United Nations but also in American attitudes toward the makeup of the crucially central Security Council. With France now added at Dumbarton Oaks, the "West" had four of the five votes. The United States then asked that Brazil also be made a permanent member. Here the Soviets and even the bemused British both balked at what they clearly saw as a self-interested, aggrandizing American initiative. It was immediately following the American claim for Brazilian elevation that the Soviet delegation first insisted on the sixteen extra memberships and the absolute veto. The historian Gabriel Kolko sees this as "an obvious Russian warning" to the Americans "not to press domination of the new organization too far."[75]

To understand the Soviet anxiety over the full implications of Dumbarton Oaks and of this postwar system building (as we need to do in order to understand some of the background to the Yalta conference), we might usefully look ahead to two later United States–Soviet confrontations for which Stalin has been much maligned both at the time and since, and which, with more foresight, might have been tempered if not wholly avoided. The first occurred at the United Nations conference at San Francisco in the spring of 1945. There, as we will see later on, the generally

---

[75] Gabriel Kolko, *The Politics of War: The World and United States Foreign Policy, 1943–1945* (New York, 1968), p. 273. See also, for a fuller discussion of the Brazil issue, Hilderbrand, *Dumbarton Oaks*, pp. 123–127.

well-intentioned American delegation, even as they tried to some degree to accommodate Soviet concerns, was consistently able to organize large majorities to achieve its various objectives, often against solitary or minimally supported Soviet opposition. In other words, the organization from the outset began to function, with plenty of behind-the-scenes politicking and mobilization activity, as the smooth, Washington-dominated political system the Soviets had clearly anticipated.[76] It is hardly surprising, then, that membership was from the start a contentious issue at Dumbarton Oaks. More remarkable is the fact that the admittedly provocative Soviet claims for their constituent republics, which had now been set up with obviously bogus foreign ministries of their own, were not more widely anticipated.

Nor is it surprising that Stalin wanted the full veto protection to institutionalize his constant calls for three-power unanimity and unity. He doubtless feared future U.N. "interference," either by the United States and/or Britain, who could mobilize large majorities to justify various forms of "enforcement," or through the manipulative activities of the numerous smaller states around the Soviet periphery who might summon up the courage to take advantage of the "discussion" power to appear to the Security Council and frustrate Soviet interests in Eastern Europe and elsewhere. For if we ask why Stalin was not willing at this point to allow "discussion" of grievances, part of the answer may lie in his apparent preference for "accepted" rather than "coerced" Soviet control over these peripheral states. There was some awareness of this possibility in the Foreign Office, where Eden's secretary, Oliver Harvey, speculating about future Soviet aggression against such neighboring states as Poland, Iran and Afghanistan, thought the latter might appeal to the United Nations. "This," he suggested, "may explain the Soviet thesis at Dumbarton Oaks."

One must assume that Stalin foresaw that without the protection of an absolute veto he might well be obliged to impose "total" rather than "partial" control upon those states in order to forestall appeals to the U.S.-dominated world body by only loosely controlled, rather than fully subordinated, regimes in or around the Soviet Union. Ironically then, the only answer to the mixture of embarassing moral scrutiny and potential political interference implicit in an American-dominated U.N., he may have reasoned, was total control: a political technique Stalin himself

---

[76] See discussion in Chapter 8 of this volume.

had already brought to near-perfection.[77] Were such concerns, assuming they existed, fanciful? Here again the forward look is instructive. The Iran crisis of early 1946 – when a seemingly Moscow-dominated but, as it turned out, insufficiently intimidated Teheran government did in fact successfully appeal, with American backroom prompting and overt political support, to the United Nations Security Council against the continuing Soviet military occupation of their country, an act that arguably did much to bring on the Cold War – developed in precisely that way. In all these respects the Dumbarton Oaks skirmishes appear to have cast a long shadow.[78]

The effect of the Dumbarton Oaks conference, then, was to bring the United States, at least tentatively, into everyone's postwar scenario. But it also, more alarmingly, brought it into a potentially confrontational relationship with the Soviet Union. A clue to the perceived significance of this as a source of United States–Soviet tension is that just as the Soviets registered more concern over the implications of Dumbarton Oaks than the British, so the United States showed more anxiety than the Churchill government over the developing Soviet clamp-down in Eastern Europe, especially upon the Soviet recognition of the Lublin regime as the provisional government of Poland. The two emerging superpowers were now beginning to focus more sharply on each other. Despite these ominous portents, we find in the months leading up to the Yalta conference in February 1945 an obsessive American focus simply on shoring up the United Nations concept, both with the American public, to whom Stettinius dispatched high-level teams of well-briefed officials to cities and towns throughout the nation, and in Latin America, where a State Department recruitment campaign worked vigorously to enlarge the prospective American voting bloc.[79] There were also fitful, fruitless efforts to work out a compromise on voting rights with Gromyko in Washington.

Similarly, the Soviets concentrated most of their political effort in the months between Dumbarton Oaks and Yalta on consolidating and extending their hold on the states falling under their control in Eastern and southeastern Europe. There was only a very limited effort by either side to find common ground or a compromise, so that the issue steadily sharpened as the anticipated summit approached. Roosevelt certainly

[77] Mark, "Revolution by Degrees" passim.
[78] See for Iran crisis, see Harbutt, *Iron Curtain*, Chapters 8 and 9.
[79] For State Department diplomacy toward Latin America, see Stettinius to Roosevelt, November 15, 1944, FRUS, *Yalta*, 52; and ibid., pp. 49, 91.

understood what was at stake in Europe. Indeed, his insight about Soviet expansionism, stimulated by the tragedy of Warsaw and by the counsels of Churchill and Harriman, as we saw in Chapter 4, led him to encourage the British leader to take the lead in doing something about it while he focused on his reelection campaign.

The trouble here was that Churchill succeeded too well, going on to create along with Stalin an image of Europe's likely postwar character that by the end of 1944 was undermining American faith in Dumbarton Oaks, the United Nations idea, and many other international impulses. FDR had offered no objection to the "sphere of influence" arrangements made by the Europeans at Moscow in October. In fact, he had tacitly approved them. But as the fuller implications of the Moscow Order revealed themselves in the last weeks of 1944, with both the Soviets and the British imposing their power in increasingly ostentatious fashion on a congeries of small states, the political vision of United States–Soviet collaboration registered in American public opinion at Dumbarton Oaks was steadily overshadowed by the return of an all-too-familiar U.S.–European tension. For the effect of Anglo-Soviet actions was to inflame American press and public opinion, reawakening transatlantic memories of World War I's aftermath and appearing to many to mock American efforts and hopes. All this ushered in a prolonged U.S.–European crisis that pulsed along disconcertingly in the weeks before Yalta, reaching its highest point of tension in the provocative Soviet recognition of the Lublin regime at the turn of the year. Roosevelt immediately recognized this as a fundamental threat to the fragile public approval on which his whole postwar scenario rested. He pleaded with Stalin to defer the move until they had had a chance to meet and talk about it. But Stalin refused, implausibly citing the implacable processes of the Soviet Presidium. Recognition was formally announced on January 1, 1945. The effect was inevitably to sharpen FDR's dilemma and force him toward the difficult choices he would face at Yalta.

A brief recitation of the principal actions and reactions during this dangerous United States–European crisis will demonstrate the serious character of Roosevelt's growing predicament. One might well start with the pollster Hadley Cantril, who advised FDR in early November that American opinion was "unusually sensitive" to overseas events. In the wake of the Warsaw tragedy, trust in future cooperation from the Soviets had already fallen from 56% to 47%. At this point the Soviets seemed the principal offenders, operating in Poland, together with their Lublin associates, with considerable ruthlessness. But, as we have seen, it was British behavior that attracted the most vigorous public and press criticism, beginning with Churchill's declaration, when the Bonomi government in Italy collapsed on November 26, that Count Sforza, a liberal with American connections, would be unacceptable in any future high position. This "interference" attracted "widespread critical comment" in the United States and, taken together with the earlier controversial British actions in Greece and Belgium, led Stettinius to issue on December 5 his public statement scolding the British government. The cumulative effect of all these events was to bring great pressure upon Roosevelt to come more forcefully into the public arena with some sort of plan or other practical definition of American purposes.[80]

The fragile state of American public support for postwar international engagement had been a primary concern for the president during the protracted election season and a compelling reason to focus attention on the United Nations and away from the dangerous distractions of European politics. Alarmed by European developments in the fall, he had in effect helped push Churchill into the arena and had then tacitly registered his discreet support for the geopolitical arrangements he had reached with Stalin. When Harriman came home in late October to report on the Tolstoy meeting in Moscow, he found Roosevelt showing very little concern for the small states of liberated Europe "except as they affect sentiment in America." A few days later, FDR spoke to Harriman about his plans for Yalta, saying that "he wanted to have a lot to say about the settlement in the Pacific but that he considered the European questions were so impossible that he wanted to stay out of them as far as practicable, except for the problems involving Germany." One can certainly sense in these declarations the exhaustion of an already ailing statesman (Harriman commented after his White House visit on Roosevelt's deteriorating physical and mental condition), but in general they are all authentic representations of Rooseveltian internationalism at this juncture: a puristic commitment to the idea and constitutional substance of a Washington-conceived United Nations; a hope for productive personal diplomacy with Stalin in February to address a narrow range of outstanding issues; and a desire to avoid all unnecessary entanglements with Europe's congenitally difficult problems. As late as November 5 we see him brushing off the future ambassador to Poland Arthur Bliss Lane, who

---

[80] Cantrill to Tully, November 10, 1944, OF 857, Box 3, Roosevelt MSS; State Department, *Bulletin*, II (December, 1944), p. 722. See also discussion in Chapter 5 of this volume.

had urged him to seek Stalin's acceptance of Polish independence, with the comment, "Do you want me to go to war with Russia?" And just days before Yalta he told a group of leading senators that the United States could not break with the Soviets and must simply try "to ameliorate" the situation.[81]

The growing sense of concern in American political circles about Soviet intentions was just part of a more general atmosphere of declining optimism and policy disintegration in the weeks before Yalta. The Dewey campaign complaint that "nobody knows what our policy is" was echoed by Lippmann, who by late December was writing scathingly about "the collapse of a policy" based on "postponement" that had created an "impossible" situation for the anxious Europeans. There were a number of damaging confrontations with the financially ailing British, notoriously over their conduct in Greece and Italy, but also about Argentinean meat, Middle Eastern oil, and other socioeconomic issues that put in question the postwar economic arrangements that had been the administration's principal field of political action. A leading State Department Europeanist wrote, "The combination of all these things may bring about an uproar which will result in a situation that will make U.S.-U.K. relations after World War I (and God knows they were bad then) look like a love feast by comparison." There was also now a somewhat similar deterioration in relations with the Chinese government, hitherto the chosen American partner in postwar Asia. None of these disappointments appears to have generated a significantly creative response. There was no serious effort to formulate a coherent approach to the fate of Germany, the one European issue Roosevelt professed to care about. The State Department took one line, the War Department another, while FDR's thinking, to the extent it was discoverable, seemed to vary from day to day.[82]

It is not surprising, given these attitudes, and given the impression one gains of FDR's passivity and detachment from foreign policy issues into November and beyond, to find that there was very little formal planning for the Yalta conference. Roosevelt's reassurances that he would fix

[81] Harriman, "Memorandum of Conversations with the President," October 21 to November 19, 1945, Box 175, Harriman MSS. Dallek, *Roosevelt and American Foreign Policy*, p. 503.

[82] *New York Herald Tribune*, October 15, 21, December 21, 1994. Hickerson memorandum, November, 1944, FRUS, III, p. 72; Kolko, *Politics of War*, p. 291; PPA, 1944–1945, pp. 511–514. For China, see Dallek, *Roosevelt and American Foreign Policy*, pp. 485–502. For various policies for Germany, see Eisenberg, *Drawing the Line*, pp. 14–70.

outstanding issues in personal discussions with Stalin discouraged further exploration. There were no Cabinet discussions, not much brainstorming analysis, no blueprints apart from the half-finished Dumbarton Oaks model. What little planning there was took place in the State Department rather than in the White House.

And here, to judge by the various papers in the Department's briefing book presented to the president, there was much more spirit and focused aspiration. The general impression they give is that the United States should take a much more active part in trying to shape the postwar politics of Europe in a just, rational way. On the central Polish issue the aim was expressed to be "truly democratic government," and the more general point was made that "it would appear highly desirable ... if the influence of the U.S. is to be felt and if the types of truly democratic governments the American people hope to see established in Europe are to be set up, for the United States government now to take an active part in seeing that in each liberated country liberal democratic groups are given a full opportunity to participate in the activities of their internal regimes." Other papers amplified the point. The United States, like Britain, should work to build up France. But on many issues the State Department went well beyond the compromises associated with the Anglo-Soviet Moscow Order. It sought a real American role in the Balkans. It advocated a challenge to Soviet hegemony in Hungary; it scorned the British effort in Yugoslavia, seeing the Tito-Subasic deal as leaving virtually all power to the communists; it called for more support for Turkey in defending itself against Soviet pressure, a protest against Soviet actions in Iran, and in general expressed a solicitude for the democratic future of Europe that went far beyond Roosevelt's persisting detachment.[83]

FDR's response, both before and at Yalta, was in essence to ignore all this advice, fascinating as it is as a reflection of the path envisioned by the nation's professional foreign policy elite but systematically shunned. Two particular illustrations of Roosevelt's indifference are striking. On November 10, 1944, Stettinius brought him a memorandum on policy toward Germany. Roosevelt said he would send it for their comments to the War, Navy, and Treasury Departments. Apparently no action of any kind followed, and the file was returned from the White House to the State Department on March 6, 1945. Similarly, on January 17, Stettinius submitted a suggested reply from Roosevelt to Churchill on "the Iranian

---

[83] See Briefing Book, FRUS, *Yalta*, pp. 230–234, 245, 256, 292, 331.

question." A White House status sheet records that it "was taken to Yalta by the President but not read by him until his return to U.S. when he read it at Hyde Park and sent it to file without action."[84]

Stettinius, who succeeded Hull in November, seems to have been part of the problem. He focused almost exclusively on the United Nations issue, the principal point of interest for the president. He appears to have had two main concerns. One was to rally and please the Latin American states, whose expected role as a tail for the United States worried the Soviets. To this end, Stettinius promised to attend a proposed Pan-American meeting in Mexico immediately after Yalta. The secretary's other principal objective was to find a compromise on voting procedures. Here a modified formula was hammered out. Its essence, distilled from what one historian has justly called "extremely complex veto procedures," was that the five permanent powers in the council would have an absolute veto power on any kind of "action," but not on "discussion." This was a compromise between the Soviet approach confining virtually all power and initiative to the Great Powers, and the Anglo-American view that small states with grievances must have some recourse to the United Nations organization. On December 5, Roosevelt hopefully set this out for Stalin who, however, again rejected any conditions or qualifications on the desired absolute veto and again urged the paramount importance of tripartite unanimity and "unity."[85]

Stettinius persisted doggedly in his preoccupation with the United Nations issues. The point man, as before, was Leo Pasvolsky, who met twice with Gromyko (at the latter's request) in the weeks just before Yalta in an effort to explain the American position and especially the crucial modifications preserving the veto on action but allowing discussion. Gromyko professed to be confused but undertook to pass the word to Moscow. He then came to what appears to have been his main point. As Pasvolsky reported, "He thought that we were emphasizing too much moral, judicial and organizational issues and paying too little attention to the political side of the question." The Soviet ambassador made it clear that his government preferred to have the political settlement clarified before the United Nations terms were finally accepted.[86]

---

[84] Ibid., pp. 171–172, 338–339.
[85] Kolko, *Politics of War*, p. 277. Roosevelt to Stalin December 5, 1944; Stalin to Roosevelt, December 27, 1944. Feis, *Churchill, Roosevelt, Stalin*, pp. 551–552.
[86] Pasvolsky to Stettinius, January 11, 15, 1945, FRUS, *Yalta*, pp. 68–76. Notter, *PostwarForeign Policy Preparation*, p. 384.

The imminence of the summit was pushing the Soviets to link these two crucial issues more explicitly than in the past. Stalin, pressing the "invitation to treat" aspect of his "bargain" diplomacy while carefully holding his United Nations concessions in reserve, plainly wanted the Americans to know in advance of the approaching summit conference that he wished to be satisfied about Eastern Europe (and especially Poland) first. He was by no means alone in his desire to tackle political issues in advance of the institutionalization of the United Nations. The State Department itself went some distance in this direction, taking up the suggestion of John D. Hickerson, a leading figure in the Division of European Affairs, for an Emergency High Commission for Liberated Europe designed to "assist in establishing popular governments and in facilitating the solution of emerging economic problems in the former occupied and satellite states of Europe." When he submitted this proposal to Roosevelt on January 18, Stettinius found the president alarmingly noncommittal, though it remained in the Yalta briefing book. Others were pressing more directly for an approach that settled political issues first. At Dumbarton Oaks, Cadogan had made it clear that Britain would prefer to see four-power agreements on major issues before a final vote on the Charter. The British were inclined to be critical of the American concept of an imposed top-down "universality." The better view, according to the London parliamentarian and diplomat Harold Nicolson, was that "an expanded internationalism should start from an inner nucleus of cohesion and thereafter move outwards." At home, Stimson and the influential Michigan Republican Senator Arthur Vandenberg took a similar view, professing a general skepticism about the ability of a highly formalized organization to solve serious problems effectively. Politics should come first.[87]

This, of course, is precisely what Roosevelt did not want, especially while Stalin was pushing relentlessly the political quid pro quos he wanted settled before the desired Yalta settlement. FDR, focused on domestic opinion, wanted the United Nations set up first, and certainly before the messy politics of the postwar (foreshadowed by the ugly Anglo-Soviet curtain raisers currently on view in Europe) showed up to undermine it with the American people. But politics was already intervening. Stalin, for his part, was bent on pressing his side of the bargain while the U.N. arrangements were still

---

[87] Kolko, *Politics of War*, p. 274. For Stimson, see Gaddis, *United States and the Origins*, pp. 158, 203. For Vandenberg, see *Congressional Record*, January 10, 1945, pp. 164–167. *Spectator*, October 5, 1945.

comparatively fluid and unresolved. Thus FDR was confronted with an increasingly dense stream of events and then more precise demands from Moscow. He gave no hint that he was framing his preparations for Yalta in terms of the large United Nations/Eastern Europe deal that Stalin was now persistently hinting at in his provocative actions. The real pressure lay elsewhere, in the domestic arena that mattered most to Roosevelt. In mid-December, Hopkins had warned Churchill that American public opinion was "deteriorating rapidly" because of the Greek situation. And through December and January there was indeed ample and mounting evidence of the public's ebbing confidence in America's allies. This produced a sense of rising desperation among leading American officials. Thus in January, on the eve of the Yalta conference, a series of polls from Hadley Cantril and the State Department recorded "increased public skepticism" over the prospects of the Atlantic Charter and the United Nations. Stettinius's analysis noted "a significant decline" in public confidence during the preceding six months. Both European allies, each now vigorously consolidating its own agreed sphere, were attracting deep suspicion. Interestingly, more opprobrium attached to the British than to the Soviets.

A State Department survey similarly found 54% blaming Britain, while 18% blamed the Soviet Union, for the evident decline in Big Three cooperation. Roosevelt tried to arrest the drift. In his State of the Union address on January 6, and in a subsequent radio speech to the American people, he bleakly set out the political problems with the Allies, resolutely and uncharacteristically refusing to sugarcoat the difficulties but trying to put them on a more elevated plane by urging understanding and rejecting "perfectionism." He tried also to shift the focus to the United Nations project, emphasizing the importance of not allowing "the many specific and immediate problems of adjustment connected with the liberation of Europe to delay the establishment of permanent machinery for the maintenance of peace." In other words, let a solidly established United Nations be set up under American auspices so that it could deal with the inevitable, drawn-out postwar difficulties.[88]

By late January, however, the danger of a breakdown seemed even more acute. This aroused concern in Britain, where the *New Statesman and Nation* commented on "the disillusionment which is now darkening the American view of the political future." Pasvolsky recommended the

[88] Cantril to Tully, January 11, 1945, OF 857, Box 3, Roosevelt MSS; "American Opinion on Recent European Developments," in Stettinius to Roosevelt, December 30, 1944, Roosevelt MSS; *PPA, 1944–1945*, pp. 511–514; *New York Times*, January 7, 1945.

practical, politics-oriented Emergency High Commission plan as "the most powerful antidote that we can devise" for the collapsing optimism and on January 23 pointed out to Stettinius (who hardly needed the warning) "the rapidly crystallizing opposition in this country to the whole Dumbarton Oaks idea on the score that the future organization would merely under-write a system of unilateral grabbing." Similarly, Archibald McLeish, assis-tant secretary of state for public and cultural relations, warned on January 24 of "the wave of disillusionment which has distressed us in the last several weeks," which, he predicted, would increase if the American people got the impression that "potentially totalitarian provisional governments were being established in liberated Europe."[89] Fires of this kind were already being stoked in Congress and in the press. A significant intervention dur-ing this period came from Senator Vandenberg, whose numerous constitu-ents of Polish descent inspired him to an influential speech on January 10. The speech is often seen, with some reason, as a positive development because this prominent former isolationist now proclaimed his conversion to internationalism and went so far as to suggest a solution to Soviet inse-curity in postwar Europe in the form of permanent German disarmament under Big Three supervison. But it did not really help Roosevelt with his immediate predicament. For Vandenberg emphasized that Soviet "sphere of influence" actions in Eastern Europe were "contrary to our conceptions of what we thought we were fighting for." The speech was in fact an unmis-takable warning to the president that a "just" solution of the Polish issues was a precondition for Republican support for the United Nations and perhaps for other initiatives.[90]

On the whole, therefore, FDR's predicament – how to bring Stalin and American opinion into a more harmonious relation – intensified during January. He struck a modestly hopeful but responsible note in his meeting with an anxious group of leading senators on January 11. When one sena-tor ventured the thought that the best procedure might be to press ahead with the Dumbarton Oaks proposals, Roosevelt responded enthusiasti-cally: "this is exactly the course ... the administration is following." But what would happen, another senator asked, if the Soviets simply settled everything "by force of arms"? Roosevelt responded that much could be

---

[89] Stettinius to Roosevelt, January 18, 1945, FRUS, *Yalta*, pp. 97–98; Pasvolsky to Stettinius, January 23, 1945, ibid., pp. 81–85; McLeish to Grew, January 24, 1945, ibid., pp. 101–102. Gaddis, *United States and the Origins*, p. 159. *New Statesman and Nation*, January 13, 1945.

[90] *Congressional Record*, January 10, 1945, pp. 164–167.

done by "readjustment" provided that the machinery could be set up and "if the Russians could be brought in and could acquire confidence in it." Here we seem to catch a Wilsonian echo, a tendency in the president, as his control of political events seemed to be slipping away, to rest his hopes on the possibility that the unsavory exhibitions of European *machtpolitik* now on display could be redeemed or adjusted in some as yet unexplained way by a functioning United Nations enjoying the support of American and world opinion. What is clear is that Roosevelt's foreign policy was now tied closely to the early establishment of a United Nations institution whose fate now looked very problematic.[91]

If Roosevelt the manager was on the eve of Yalta losing some of his grip – in Europe, in China (where a succession of disappointments had further darkened postwar hopes in late 1944), and among influential sections of American opinion – the political artist was still functioning. His lack of interest in the purely diplomatic preparations for Yalta, whether one puts this down to a characteristic insouciance or declining health, was counterpointed by a systematic set of initiatives designed to ensure a positive public reception of what he must have anticipated would be a potentially dangerous, unpredictable encounter. Thus he insisted on a stringent censorship with no journalists. A single government photographer would be taken. No publicity was to be given to the preliminary meeting with the British at Malta, and no report on Yalta was to be released until two days after the conference. Most significantly, he included in the party two rather improbable political figures. One was the so-called "assistant president," James F. Byrnes, whose task it would be to return as soon as the conference was over (or even before, as actually happened) to give the appropriate spin to the proceedings while Roosevelt cruised home in more leisurely fashion. The other was a New York politician, Ed Flynn, who was to visit the Vatican and Moscow and ask the Pope to help square American Catholics (and especially Polish Americans) with the notion of a collaborating, more tolerant Soviet Union. Meanwhile, Harry Hopkins, again at the center of events, was dispatched to London, Paris, and Rome on a mission of conciliation and reassurance that was also designed to sound out Western European opinion. Hopkins was unusually guarded and reticent on this trip. At his last stop in Rome, he told American journalists that the United States had wanted to postpone its political involvement in

---

[91] Thomas M. Campbell and George C. Herring, eds., *The Diaries of Edward R. Stettinius, Jr., 1943–1946* (New York, 1975), pp. 213–215; Dallek, *Roosevelt and American Foreign Policy*, p. 508.

Europe's affairs until victory had been won. But it was now seen that this was impossible. Just what these enigmatic comments portended would lie with President Roosevelt, now trying to renew his flagging energy on the transatlantic crossing on the USS *Quincy*. [92]

Yet the evidence we have seen strongly suggests that the arrangements he wanted to make with Stalin and Churchill were going to be, in Roosevelt's mind, subordinate to the overarching demands of the American political arena. Almost certainly he would have agreed with Archibald MacLeish who, in a lecture at Cambridge University in 1942, told his perhaps bemused listeners:

The principal battleground of this war is not the South Pacific, or the Middle East; it is not England or Norway or the Russian Steppes. It is American opinion. Specifically, it is the individual opinion of individual Americans. [93]

[92] Robert L. Messer, *End of an Alliance: James F. Byrnes, Roosevelt, Truman and the Origins of the Cold War* (Chapel Hill, 1982), pp. 39–52; George Q. Flynn, *Roosevelt and Romanism: Catholics and American Diplomacy, 1937–1945* (Westport, Conn., 1976), pp. 221–222; Charles to Foreign Office, February 1, 1945, F.O. 371.4981.

[93] Cited in Hurstfield, *America and the French*, p. 139.

7

The Yalta Disorder

We come now to the fateful conference that changed the relationships we have been following thus far and opened the way to the postwar world. This assertion challenges the recent judgment of an influential historian, Tony Judt, who states, "Yalta actually mattered little."[1] This, however, as we saw in Chapter 1, is only one of the many highly generalized epitaphs on the meeting. Clearly the road from hypothesis to acceptable thesis about Yalta is always hard and complex.

In this it bears a metaphorical resemblance to the obstacle-strewn paths traced by the American and British participants as they made their way laboriously to the Crimea. The remote physical setting of the conference was extraordinary. The suggestion for a Black Sea rendezvous came originally in October 1944 from Harry Hopkins, to whom Churchill later unkindly remarked, "We could not have found a worse place for this meeting if we had spent ten years looking for it." But this was a desperate initiative after Stalin had declined a series of suggestions from President Roosevelt. FDR first proposed an autumn 1944 meeting in northern Scotland, a location that may have generated in Stalin and Molotov much the same combination of foreboding and mordant humor with which Roosevelt and Churchill finally brought themselves to accept the Crimea. The president did better with a second try, urging a Mediterranean location in November. But Stalin, variously pleading operational priorities and poor health, was not to be drawn by temptations of that sort. The presidential election then intervened, Churchill and Stalin having met

---

[1] Tony Judt, *Postwar: A History of Europe since 1945* (New York, 2005), pp. 101–102.

meantime in Moscow and established a basis for their essentially European postwar concert of power. At last Yalta was chosen. Now it was the turn of Roosevelt and Churchill to worry about their health and all the perils of the reputedly unsanitary Black Sea region. But they went ahead with elaborate plans, which for FDR meant a nearly 6,000-mile journey.[2]

The Crimea, and especially Yalta, had a certain social cachet as a summer home for the tsars and the nobility. Chekhov had had a house there, now a shrine. Hitler too dreamed expansively of possessing "the beauties of the Crimea which ... will be our Riviera." He envisioned an autobahn from Germany to the region. Instead, his scorched-earth retreat had by February 1945 left Yalta a ruined town except for a few despoiled palaces that the Russians restored for the three delegations with totalitarian speed. It was still a far-from-perfect environment. Bathroom facilities were minimal. All but the top-level people had to share accommodations, eleven colonels in one room in one case. There was plenty to complain about: bedbugs in the mattresses; mechanical bugs in the ceilings. The latter were useful, not only in keeping Stalin closely in touch with what his guests were saying, but socially as well. A casual comment on the absence of lemon peel for cocktails quickly produced a lemon tree in the hall of one of the residential palaces. The Russians were relentlessly hospitable. Chefs had been imported from the best Moscow hotels. The sea views were beautiful, and vodka was regularly served with breakfast.

Simply getting to Yalta and making the social and organizational arrangements occupied appreciably more of the Roosevelt-Churchill correspondence than the rare stab at some preliminary canvas of the political issues one finds in the documents there. Advance parties were sent to scout the route. Their reports were bleak, discouraging, and, as it turned out, accurate. Roosevelt traveled comfortably enough by sea to an Anglo-American preliminary meeting at Malta, where he spent some of his flagging energy warding off Churchill's predictable efforts to modify existing strategic arrangements and line up a common negotiating front over Poland and other issues. Meanwhile, one of the two planes carrying the large British delegation (over 600 British and American officials set off for Yalta, which was a full-dress affair, unlike Teheran) crashed in the Pelagian Islands, killing all on board. After their brief meeting at Malta, where Eden and Stettinius managed to review some of the issues and agreed in vague terms to stand up to Soviet demands on the Lublin problems, Roosevelt and

---

[2] For the arrangements, see FRUS, *Yalta*, 1945, pp. 3–40; and Gilbert, *Churchill*, VII, Chapter 59. For the conference's antecedents, see Clemens, *Yalta*, pp. 107–117.

Churchill flew separately to Simferapol in the Crimea – a long, wearying journey. There they were met by Molotov (Stalin not attending, though he was already in the Crimea) and were revived with prodigious quantities of vodka, meat, and fish before being bundled into cars for the eight-hour drive over winding mountain roads to Yalta, a route guarded by Russian soldiers at ten-yard intervals.[3]

The three statesmen, coming together without a preliminary agenda, soon found themselves engaged in a very unusual, fast-moving kind of negotiation. Both Roosevelt, by pressing the United Nations concept upon his allies at Dumbarton Oaks, and Stalin, who had forced the Polish issue by installing the Lublin government, share the responsibility for the conversion of Yalta into what might arguably be called a premature peace conference. It was in part, no doubt, the memory of the Versailles conference and the dismal aftermath following World War I that led the three powers to rush their fences in this way rather than waiting for a calmer postwar deliberation. But that is remote causation. In fact, the statesmen of Yalta were driven by pressing immediate concerns. All three appear, to some degree, to have wished in principle to prolong their collaboration into the postwar. Behind this lay a darker concern that all three appear to have shared, that their wartime bond might not outlive the imminent defeat of Nazi Germany. Moreover, these were not simply fears of a falling out after the war. There were more immediate anxieties. The British, for instance, were well aware from their ULTRA intercepts that top Nazi leaders (including Hitler, Goebbels, and Ribbentrop) were now desperately hoping to make a deal with Stalin, perhaps through the Japanese. On the other side, Stalin's chronic paranoia about British and American intrigues with the Germans, which had already surfaced several times during the war and would again flare up immediately after the Yalta conference, had not abated, and he was patently anxious to make further reassuringly binding agreements with London and Washington that would ensure (and proclaim to the world) the continuing unity of the Big Three.[4]

At the same time, there were more positive motivations. Insofar as there were particular issues to settle the three powers had already exposed their

[3] For British preparations, see Bright to Ismay, January 31, 1945, PREM 4.77/1B. See also Hannen Swaffer, *Daily Herald*, February 28, 1945. For Hitler, see Mark Mazower, *Dark Continent: Europe's 20th. Century* (London, 1998), p. 146.

[4] For awareness of past conferences, see Charles Webster, *The Congress of Vienna, 1814–1815* (London, 1920), p. 148; and Margaret Macmillan, *Paris, 1919* (New York, 2003), passim. For examples of Nazi hope, see British intercepts in Files 3546, 3620, 3641, and 3645 in HW/1, Public Record Office, Kew, England.

main desiderata during 1944 and needed a decisive meeting to clear up the various qualifications and objections that had emerged and were causing difficulties. Most of the various aspirations were known, or should have been. The United States, for example, still showed little appetite for close political encounters with Europe, though it needed a decent solution over the Polish issues. More particularly, it wanted a settled basis for the proposed United Nations with the Dumbarton Oaks lacunae cleared up; and it wanted confirmation of Soviet participation in the war against Japan along lines already set out. The Europeans had already determined much of their business. Since October 1944 they had been consolidating their respective spheres for the postwar in a remarkably cooperative spirit. So far as Poland was concerned, the Soviets had also received from Churchill an endorsement of their desired enlargement to the Curzon Line and preeminent interests elsewhere, much as Stalin had set out his ambitions for Eden back in 1941 and affirmed them in Moscow in 1944. They now wanted some degree of American acquiescence in their "sphere" in Eastern Europe, already agreed upon with the British, and acceptance of their ambitions in the Far East. The British, for their part, wanted to avoid any threat to their primacy in the Mediterranean and to bring about some meaningful restoration of their French ally in Western Europe. In many respects, therefore, one might have assumed that rational solutions were possible.[5]

And it is indeed possible to write an upbeat account of Yalta from a "rational" perspective of this kind. Yalta's most influential historian, Diane S. Clemens, did just that in her 1970 book, *Yalta*. By focusing on the basic issues and the bargaining styles and maneuvers of the participants, she was able, in an admirably analytic study, to clarify the aims of the conferees and to portray a Yalta where each of the three statesmen was able, in a context of compromise and adjustment, to gain his principal objective. Yalta was therefore, on this reading, a constructive encounter in which Roosevelt, Churchill, and Stalin "prized agreement by traditional negotiation as preferable to unilateral action which might undermine international stability."[6]

---

[5] For an omnibus treatment of American aims, see "Negotiations and Recommendations on Principal Subjects," in FRUS, *Yalta*, pp. 41–428. See also Dallek, *Roosevelt and American Foreign Policy*, pp. 506–508. For British objectives, see Eden to Churchill January 4 and 26, and February 5, 1945, all in PREM 3.51/3.

[6] Clemens, *Yalta*, p. 288. Clemens was arguing against the standard conservative interpretation that Stalin had prevailed against a naïve Roosevelt and a helpless Churchill. See, for other representative views, John Snell (ed.), *The Meaning of Yalta;* and Russell

There are, however, general and specific problems with that interpretation. It is an approach that tends to exalt reason, exaggerate the level of understanding among the parties, and ignore or downplay the elements of fear and mistrust on display or under the surface at Yalta. These ripple through nearly all the recorded discussions and go far to explain the extraordinary range of qualifications, conditions, and ambiguities attached to the various "agreements" as well as the large issues left unaddressed. Most of the difficulties were skillfully obscured at the post-conference moment of public presentation by a diverting array of astute window dressing. Associated with these positive attitudes is the fact, sometimes ignored by historians who emphasize the harmony of the Yalta encounter, that within little more than two weeks of the conference relations between the Soviets and the Western powers were moving rapidly to a point of crisis, which is hard to explain if one assumes a genuine meeting of minds. A tendency among revisionist historians has been to gloss over that crisis and move straight from the conference to the death of Roosevelt in early April and to blame the post-Yalta chill largely on the impetuousity of his successor, Harry S. Truman. More orthodox historians typically explain the unanticipated breakdown by arguing that, for reasons remaining unclear, it was Stalin who deceitfully violated his Yalta undertakings, thus paving the way for the Cold War.[7]

A better explanation – one that throws light on the conference and also on its turbulent, unanticipated aftermath – derives from a recognition of the deeper impulses at work: Stalin's anxious preoccupation with preserving the unity of the coalition as the war neared its end; Churchill's wavering path as he tried to balance between his "European" relationship with Stalin and the tantalizing prospect at last presented by Roosevelt's surprisingly lively response to the unwelcome advent of the Lublin regime and the president's consequent newfound interest, as it seemed after the promising pre-Yalta talks with Stettinius at Malta, in Europe's future; and, most importantly, the deep political dilemma of Roosevelt himself. The president's predicament – developing in a diplomatic sense from the divergent conceptions deriving

---

Buhite, *Decisions at Yalta*, which is strongly anti-Soviet. For representative European views, see Chester Wilmot, *Struggle for Europe;* Pierre de Senarclens, *Yalta;* and Jean Laloy, *Yalta: Yesterday, Today and Tomorrow.* See generally the discussion in Chapter I of this volume.

7 Compare, for instance, the orthodox view stressing Stalin's accountability in Gaddis, *The United States and the Origins*, pp. 360–361, with revisionist accounts urging Truman's responsibility in Clemens, *Yalta*, pp. 288–291, and Yergin, *Shattered Peace*, pp. 275–302.

from the American commitments at Dumbarton Oaks and the Soviet recognition of the Lublin regime in Poland, and politically from the impact at home of these contrasting scenarios and, more generally, of provocative European behavior – was that he had throughout the war encouraged the American people to expect that their allies would behave well, and that victory would bring about the rational, congenial world order portrayed in the Atlantic Charter and dozens of other similarly visionary proclamations and now prospectively institutionalized in the United Nations, while at the same time he had promised Stalin "friendly governments" in Eastern Europe even though, as his private remarks show, he was well aware of the scope if not the full character of Soviet ambitions in the area. He had never, before Yalta, faced up to the incompatibility of these commitments. The drama of Yalta is that, having put himself in a summit conference situation at a delicate juncture in the war, Roosevelt would now have to make some kind of choice between his public protestations and his private assurances, choosing not simply between Stalin and Vandenberg but between Stalin and the American people. He would have to confront Stalin aggressively on his plans for Poland and Eastern Europe or find some other way to finesse the situation. In the event, as will be seen, and indeed as might have been foreseen by any close student of his political career, Roosevelt chose finesse and deception, with consequences that would contribute to the breakdown of the Grand Alliance.[8]

It appears to have been a strategy he formed and kept to himself, understandably, since any opportunity to resolve or fend off this basic dilemma – by warning the Soviets, or by educating the American public, as Stalin had urged him to do at Teheran – had by the beginning of 1945 long since passed. It is often said, with justice, that Roosevelt did not adequately study his briefs or otherwise prepare suitably for Yalta. But in one area he did prepare, not for the negotiation itself but for the image of it he was determined to create. His strategy for Yalta, therefore, did not center upon specific issues, though these must have been somewhere in his mind. It focused, rather, on three steps toward the image he felt obliged to create: the careful pre-conference stage setting we have already noted; a concentration at the conference itself on securing the constituent elements of a

---

[8] For Roosevelt's awareness that he would now have to face this dilemma, see Hopkins's pre-Yalta remark that political solutions were now "necessary" in *News Chronicle*, January 31, 1945. Similarly, in conversation with Eden at Malta on February 1, Stettinius stressed "the extreme importance" of early political solutions from the viewpoint of the establishment of the world organization. PREM 3.51/6.

carefully contrived vision of success; and a vigorous presentation of that vision to an expectant America.

The two European leaders, preparing for the second substantial American diplomatic infusion of the war period, approached Yalta in a very different, more defensive spirit. Churchill and Stalin had already agreed on a postwar framework far Europe, and both seemingly wished to protect and preserve it. They had continued, as we have seen in earlier chapters, to consolidate their respective spheres in a cooperative spirit. There were persisting difficulties over exclusionist Soviet policies in Bulgaria that prejudiced Greek stability, and in the weeks before Yalta a Soviet press agitation against the "Western Bloc" registered the Kremlin's concern to discourage any pre-summit Anglo-American solidarity. It is also true that they had shelved German issues and had been unable to resolve the Polish problems completely. But Churchill had long since accepted the Curzon Line's territorial settlement, and it was well understood in London that the Polish problems were not going to be allowed to frustrate the two allies' broader collaboration. The Soviet establishment of the Lublin regime was upsetting and provocative. It revived an old temptation, leading Churchill and Eden to move discreetly toward a closer understanding with the Americans as Yalta approached. But the British still hoped to get Stalin to allow representatives from the London government to participate in Polish politics. As we have seen the various Foreign Office agendas for Yalta had initially placed Poland well down the list. Like the Soviets, the British wanted to move on now to discuss the German settlement.[9]

Stalin's basic concern at Yalta, like Roosevelt's, lay beneath the surface issues that have naturally captured attention. Just as FDR appears to have been preoccupied at Yalta with the search for a medley of decisions, declarations, and images that could be fused into a pleasing, reassuring vision of common purpose and values, so Stalin wanted the meeting to produce a powerful impression of unity to ensure and proclaim (not least to the increasingly desperate Germans, who were correctly presumed to be watching intently for a possible deal with one of their enemies) that there would be no last-minute betrayal as the war's dangerous climax approached. Thus in essence the Americans and the Soviets wanted much the same kind of general outcome – a reassuringly harmonius image of the meeting – though for very different reasons. And this meant that, even as

---

[9] Eden to Churchill, January 26, 1945, PREM 3.51/3.

they addressed specific issues, they treated each other with notable consideration and carefully avoided probing discussions that might have exposed their differences and put the public image of Big Three unity at risk.

"Unity," then, appears to have been the predominating Soviet concern at Yalta. A staple of Soviet media commentary throughout the war, even when specific American and British elements were under press attack, it was the centerpiece of Stalin's important November 7 speech. The *Manchester Guardian* commented, "The most significant note of the speech was the emphasis on the need for Allied Unity." Gromyko repeatedly made the same point in Washington, urging the importance of avoiding even an appearance of disagreement among the Great Powers. "Unity" was stressed repeatedly by Stalin at Yalta as a supreme value. He too had precise political objectives, but, despite the manifest assertiveness of his pre-Yalta demands, he seems to have realized that after his Lublin demarche he would be on the defensive at the Crimea meeting. In the longer run he faced a dilemma of his own, wanting some kind of large postwar imperium in Eastern Europe, but also eager (all the available evidence suggests) for continuing cooperation with Britain and the United States. This meant a degree of circumspection. True, the Western allies had swallowed Katyn; they had seemingly accepted his explanations of the Warsaw Uprising; and they had failed to challenge his crudely unilateral administrations in Rumania and Bulgaria. "Bargain" diplomacy had already brought about the desired geopolitical arrangements with Britain. Now, facing the more mysterious Americans, he was looking to the maturation of a similar deal with Roosevelt on the basis of a United Nations/Eastern Europe nexus.[10]

Stalin was encouraged by his geopolitical concert with Churchill, and he appears to have hoped for some support from the prime minister in the face of anticipated American pressure. Stalin's preparations for Yalta, however, suggest a clear anticipation that the Americans, if not the British, would be in a revisionary mood. This concern was doubtless the inspiration of the last of Litvinov's pre-Yalta articles in *War and the Working Class* urging the value of "regionalism." This was a reiteration of the Anglo-Soviet thesis that regional groups (Churchill too had been thinking of an autonomous Europe) should be permitted under the United Nations

---

[10] Edouard Mark, "Revolution by Degrees," p. 12 and passim. *Manchester Canadian*, November 8, 1944.

framework. In this sense, the collaborative spirit of the Moscow Order was still very much alive in the Kremlin.[11]

But Yalta caught Churchill in a divided mood. He had, following his Moscow meeting with Stalin, taken up the two-Europe idea with considerable vigor, and, like Stalin, he does not appear to have come to Yalta with any intention to go back on the Anglo-Soviet agreement in any fundamental way. Pushed variously by Stalin, Roosevelt, Smuts, and a host of others, he had emerged in the autumn of 1944 as the active champion of a British-led Western Europe, even going so far as to patch up relations with de Gaulle. But three considerations now seem to have been pushing him in a different direction. The first was a renewed concern about Soviet and communist expansion as the Red Army's plunge into Central Europe accelerated to the point that it had reached within forty miles of Berlin as the conference assembled, while the Allies had still not broken into German territory. The second was a growing doubt, doubtless reinforced by the storm of protest in America, about Britain's capacity to lead and consolidate, without American help, the balancing Western bloc that had until now been on offer from Moscow and that still seemed to many Europeans in 1942–45 to suggest Britain's postwar destiny. And the third, following logically, was the welcome reappearance of the Americans, suggesting hopes of a compensatory Anglo-American political solidarity following Stalin's Lublin shock and its adverse reception in the United States. His aim then, as his pre-Yalta comments show, was to push Roosevelt forward and support him discreetly while trying not to alienate Stalin. With this strategic outlook he approached Yalta in a watchful, opportunistic frame of mind. In the end, this too would have a profound effect on the future.[12]

This Big Three summitry again posed a threat to European solidarity. The political ripples of Moscow and Teheran had not, in 1944, thrown the British and Soviets off their collaborative course. This time it would be different.

---

[11] *Voina i rabochii klass,* December 15, 1944. See also Geoffrey Roberts, "Litvinov's Lost Peace, 1941–1946," p. 41 et seq.

[12] For Churchill's post-Tolstoy focus, see Chapter 4 of this volume. For expressions of his anxieties, see Churchill to Eden, October 23, 1944, PREM 3.397/3; and Churchill to Eden, December 6, 1944, PREM 4.30/10. For the Malta discussions, where Eden tried with some success to invigorate Stettinius for a confrontation with the Soviets over Poland, see FRUS, *Yalta*, pp. 463–546.

YALTA: TRADITIONAL DIPLOMACY

On the first morning of the conference, February 4, there was a flurry of introductory meetings. Roosevelt, seeking an initial meeting with Stalin, found that the Soviet leader intended to visit Churchill first – perhaps a gesture, gratifying to the British, of continuing Soviet commitment to the Moscow Order. This meeting was cordial, the discussion confined to reassuring generalities. Molotov, in a simultaneous exchange with Eden, was especially ingratiating, assuring the foreign secretary that the British-sponsored European Advisory Council (largely avoided until recently by the Soviets) had "unlimited potential."[13]

Meanwhile, the Americans were having preliminary meetings among themselves. The first words in the State Department's voluminous record of Yalta come from a meeting of the Joint Chiefs of Staff. "Admiral Leahy said there had not been time to study the papers and asked for a summary." A somewhat disconcerting start. A few minutes later, Leahy moved on to another meeting where Stettinius was briefing President Roosevelt. By this time the State Department's briefing book, which FDR may or may not have looked at during his long sea trip, had been boiled down to a one-page summary of seven topics.[14]

Whether Roosevelt had done his homework on the long sea voyage is still an unresolved question. In any event he was, as usual, plotting his own course. When he met Stalin privately just before the first plenary meeting (which was, like all the others, held in the president's residence at the Livadia Palace), he captured the social initiative with flattering tributes to the Red Army, reassurances that he wanted tough measures against postwar Germany, and complaints at some length about British avarice and shrewd practice. Clearly, he signaled, there was no Anglo-American political linkage and no intimacy with the prime minister. Roosevelt's determination to please his host, often at Churchill's expense, is a recurrent theme in the ten days of the Yalta meeting. If – as most Americans, perhaps including Roosevelt himself, believed – the British and Soviets were implacably antagonistic (their occasional liaisons typically being seen as simply temporary tactical adjustments), then the president clearly intended to side with Stalin. Stalin, enigmatically unresponsive, could be forgiven for thinking he was back in Teheran.[15]

---

[13] Meeting between the prime minister and Stalin, February 4, 1945, PREM 3.51/4. For the Eden-Molotov meeting, see PREM 3.51/6
[14] Meeting of the Joint Chiefs of Staff, February 4, 1945, FRUS, *Yalta*, pp. 562, 564–567.
[15] Bohlen minutes, Roosevelt-Stalin meeting, February 4, 1945, ibid., pp. 570–573.

Despite these mostly emollient beginnings, the first two days were tense. The initial plenary session on February 4 was devoted to the military situation. The Soviet and American Chiefs of Staff reviewed the two theaters. At this point, we now know, Stalin was considering postponing the final drive on Berlin, now only about fifty miles away, which had been planned to start in early February. He was anxious not to alarm his allies, whose operations in the west lagged behind. Marshall had conceded that the Rhine could not be forced until March at the earliest. A dramatic show of Soviet power might, Stalin supposedly thought, tempt the Western powers to a last-minute accommodation with Hitler or some post-Hitler group. Such concerns go some way to explain his repeated, obsessive emphasis at Yalta on the close unity of the three Great Powers, a condition he was also openly eager to promote for the postwar order as well. There were other subtle intimations beneath the polite if rather stiff exchanges. Stalin cultivated a sense of obligation by reminding everyone of past Soviet sacrifices made to help the Allies in quickly adjusted offensives launched before D-Day and again during the recently concluded Battle of the Bulge. He showed his primary anxieties by asking sharp questions, tinged with suspicion, about the substantial shift of resources by the Germans from west to east, and about the Allied will and ability to frustrate *Wehrmacht* deployments to the eastern front from Italy and Norway.[16]

The conference was by now sorting out its organizational pattern. The foreign ministers, who, as the process developed, became the workhorses of Yalta, met each morning before attending the afternoon plenary sessions with their leaders. The military delegates also met regularly during the early stages. There relations were cool and sometimes difficult. The Soviet generals refused to accept a shifting bombline that would allow deeper Allied air penetration from the west. Always resistant to fraternization and to any kind of intrusion beyond what they considered strictly necessary, they agreed only reluctantly to anything suggesting closer coordination, except to some limited extent in the Far East. Some collaborative visits by American bomb inspection and surveying groups to sites behind the Red Army's lines were accepted at Yalta. Most of them were quickly cancelled or otherwise sidetracked after the conference. The Americans were now learning, just as the British had come to accept in the geopolitical sphere, that the Soviets, for all their diplomatic and media emphasis

---

[16] Bohlen minutes, first plenary meeting, February 4, 1945, ibid., pp. 573–580.

on unity and a strong front both against Hitler and in opposition to small-power assertions, would brook no interference in their own sphere.[17]

The first full day concluded with a dinner hosted by Roosevelt at the Livadia Palace. It was on this occasion that FDR, trying to break the ice, told Stalin that he and Churchill called him "Uncle Joe." The attempted camaraderie fell flat as Stalin expressed resentment and, perhaps recalling Churchill's similar gesture of disgust at Moscow in 1942, made as if to get up from the table and leave. Molotov hastened to explain, rather unconvincingly, that it was all a pretense. Churchill tried to calm the waters with a toast to "the Great Powers." This proved the perfect curative, for it launched Stalin on one of his favorite subjects, a long discourse on the indispensable unity of the three Great Powers and the need to keep the mischievous small powers under strict control. Churchill's eloquent riposte – "The eagle should permit the small birds to sing and care not wherefore they sing" – cut no ice with the Soviet leader, whose preoccupation with Big Three unity would prove to be the central theme in Soviet diplomacy at Yalta.[18] Eden's epitaph on the dinner is revealing:

Dinner with the Americans; a terrible party I thought. President vague and loose and ineffective. W. understanding that business was flagging made desperate efforts and too long speeches to get things going again. Stalin's attitude to small countries struck me as grim, not to say sinister. We were too many and there was no steady flow and brisk exchanges as at Teheran. I was greatly relieved when the whole business was over.[19]

The tone was not much better on the second day as the conference took up the fate of Germany. This profound subject, it will be recalled, had originally been the anticipated central feature of the conference before the Lublin shock. Even after the Soviet demarche the British Foreign Office and the Soviets, eager to avoid further unproductive debate over Poland, had initially put it at the head of their topic lists; Molotov did so again on February 3. And Roosevelt himself had declared his intention to focus, among European topics, on Germany alone. But with Stalin's Lublin gambit and its detrimental effect on American opinion the Polish issue inevitably supervened. The three statesmen consequently continued at Yalta, as they had in the past, to dance awkwardly around the German issue, pausing only to endorse the earlier decisions of the European Advisory Council, reached shortly before Yalta, on the surrender terms and

---

[17] Minutes, first tripartite military meeting, February 5, 1945, ibid., pp. 595–608.
[18] Bohlen minutes, tripartite dinner meeting, February 4, 1945, ibid., pp. 589–591.
[19] Eden, *The Reckoning*, p. 593.

the tripartite zonal arrangements, one of the few concrete achievements of the conference.[20]

Nevertheless, three important subjects emerged during the discussions on Germany. One was the role of France, which Churchill championed as a restored Great Power. Roosevelt conceded France a small zone but, citing her poor war record, refused her the crucial prize of a seat on the Control Commission for Germany. This gave Stalin a useful diplomatic opening. Once FDR had shown his hand on the issue, Stalin could expect to ensure British cooperation on Poland and other controversial matters by siding with the Francophobic President, which he promptly did. The Soviet leader, always a skilled negotiator, could now juxtapose Britain's need for France with the Soviet Union's need for a "friendly" Poland. Here, after all, was Britain's indispensable partner in the West, a foundational element in the evolving European future fully acknowledged by the Soviets since 1941, and all the more now after FDR's statement on the first day of the conference (at which Churchill later professed to be shocked, but which had in fact been clearly signaled earlier), saying that he did not envision American troops staying in Europe more that two years after the war. Stalin's resistance now was probably tactical. He quickly changed his mind without any fuss or question at the end of the conference when Roosevelt relented in the face of Churchill's protests and decided that France should after all have a seat on the commission. By that time Stalin had achieved his goals on Poland and Eastern Europe. Meanwhile, much of Churchill's energy had been wastefully spent in an uphill effort to enhance France's part in the postwar system.[21]

Stalin's deft negotiating skill can also be seen in his insistence on the inclusion of a vaguely phrased dismemberment clause in the surrender terms. He was transparently concerned to chill any possible German peace overtures to the Western powers, perhaps from right-wing military circles, a development he dreaded and probably expected. He was successful there. However, he expressed displeasure when Roosevelt and Churchill refused to make a commitment to permanent dismemberment and called for further study of the matter. One can understand Stalin's concern. It has been suggested that he had hoped to get agreement to large-scale reparations

---

[20] Bohlen minutes, second plenary meeting, February 5, 1945, FRUS, *Yalta*, pp. 611–623. For the European Advisory Commission's agreed surrender terms and zone allocations, see FRUS, *Yalta*, pp. 110–127.

[21] Bohlen minutes, second plenary meeting, February 5, 1945, FRUS, *Yalta*, pp. 611–623; Bohlen minutes, seventh plenary meeting, February 10, 1945, ibid., pp. 897–906.

by making a show of falling in with the supposed Anglo-American desire for dismemberment. Both Roosevelt and Churchill had earlier given the impression that they favored some degree of dismemberment. But second thoughts, as yet uncrystallized in policy, had begun through 1944 to raise questions in the United States about Europe's economic recovery in the absence of a German dynamic, and to produce rising anxiety in Britain about the continent's political stability in the face of the Red Army's advance. The three powers, intent on more immediate concerns and eager to avoid this dangerous topic while the war continued, understandably decided once again not to confront the dismemberment issue fully at Yalta. Molotov quickly reassured Stettinius and Eden that the Soviets also wished to study the problem more fully.[22]

Reparations was another touchy subject. Here the Soviets were determined to nail down some kind of agreement. Here again, however, as was often the case at Yalta, the Western powers had failed to anticipate Soviet concerns and were woefully unprepared and unwilling to make commitments. They had not explored the reparations problem at home, nor had they bothered to discuss it at Malta. The issue did not even feature in Stettinius's abbreviated note for the president. They were therefore taken aback when Stalin asked Maisky to unveil what turned out to be a very thoroughly worked out plan. Reparations were to be "in kind" rather than monetary, thus avoiding the post–World War I financial fiasco. Large withdrawals of German wealth together with annual payment in goods for ten years would yield $20 billion, of which the Soviets would claim $10 billion.

Here too Stalin found a disappointing response. Roosevelt was outwardly sympathetic but made it clear that the United States would under no circumstances pay Europe's reparations bill. He pointedly asked if labor services were envisaged, and Stettinius repeated the inquiry later in a foreign ministers meeting. Was this intended to register a human rights caveat, or was it a tacit invitation to Stalin to make up his reparations in this fashion? Almost certainly the latter. Better German slave labor than American charity. The Soviets gave no answer. In the end, Roosevelt agreed to accept the $10 billion claim as "a basis for discussion," but the British refused to commit to any sum. Once again "more study" was the outcome, and a tripartite commission was designated to study the issue in Moscow. The reparations issue forced Churchill into an acrimonious confrontation

---

[22] Bohlen minutes, second plenary meeting, February 5, 1945, ibid., pp. 611–623.

with Stalin. The prime minister's dismissive response to Maisky's figures, which he considered far beyond any realistic assessment of Germany's capacity to pay, angered Stalin, who later, as at Teheran, responded with insinuations that Churchill was pro-German. But as the prime minister pointed out, the British wanted to know how Germany's starving people were to be fed, a practical concern because they would be responsible for the crowded northwest zone, including the industrial Ruhr – a zone, moreover, that was likely to be inundated with refugees as the Poles were ceded a large part of east German territory.[23]

After two days of probing and fencing over these two dangerous subjects – the strategy of ending the war militarily without losing the tenuous bond that only Hitler's aggression had created, and the problems involved in settling the future of Germany in a mutually acceptable way – each of the three leaders must have gained a more distinct impression of the others' main concerns. It was clear to all that Roosevelt was seriously ill. His participation in the early debates was brief, and he was dependent on Hopkins, whose advisory notes (he handed four to the president at the February 5 meeting) seem to have kept him on course. Generally, however, the relationships seem to have been resolving into a Teheran-like mode. FDR, eager to please Stalin, and apparently indifferent to European geopolitics, again showed his enduring animus against the old continent. France was to be kept down. Germany should be severely punished. There would be no Anglo-American intimacy. American troops would be withdrawn within two years. The effect of this and of Roosevelt's passivity in debate, as at Teheran, was to put Anglo-Soviet collaboration at risk by pushing Churchill, who had come to Yalta hoping to work in behind American initiatives, into a series of characteristically spirited defenses of broad European interests. This led to unwanted confrontations with Stalin. For the unsatisfactory discussions of German dismemberment and reparations inevitably indicated a certain solicitude for Germany's future. And this, together with the failure of the Western visitors to enthuse over Stalin's call for a tight Big Three directorate at the expense of the world's smaller powers, can only have suggested to the suspicious Soviets that they could not take their allies for granted. In any event, with the anticipated challenges over Poland still to come, Stalin was anxious enough to telephone Marshal Zhukov and call off the pending assault on Berlin. "You are wasting your time," Stalin told him. "We must consolidate on the Oder

[23] Ibid., pp. 620–623.

and turn all possible forces north." The unity of the alliance was now seen to be more important (and perhaps more problematic) than a provocative coup de theatre over Berlin.[24]

On the third day, February 6, the Teheran echoes were left behind as the conference focused more narrowly and directly on the two immediate political issues they could not now avoid. Roosevelt, as chairman, announced at the outset that the day would be given over to the United Nations voting rights question and the Polish issues, an ostentatious linkage that was presumably meant to signal that he recognized some nexus between the two. The American voting rights proposal, centered on the scope of the veto power, was taken up first. It had from Dumbarton Oaks on been presented, mainly by Stettinius and his staff, in unnecessarily obscure, ambiguous terms, with strained illustrations of its practical working that tended to confuse rather than enlighten. Stalin professed a lack of understanding, almost certainly a deceptive pose, since the formula had finally and painstakingly been clarified for Gromyko long before. When Stalin put on his show of ignorance, Stettinius tried to simplify the formula but again got tangled up in hypothetical scenarios. Stalin soon revealed his real concern, pointing out that between the Great Powers' veto on action and the small powers' right to air their grievances lay a gray area where "recommendations" (a form of "action," after all) could be voted on. The effect, he pointed out, might well be to mobilize opinion against one country, a consideration the rational State Department planners had not considered seriously. Stalin reminded his listeners of the unhappy Soviet experience with the League of Nations. He again stressed the danger that the small powers presented to Great Power unity, his constant preoccupation at Yalta. Having made these points with some force, he again reserved his position and asked for time to consider the matter. In this "invitation to treat" approach he was following his Teheran ploy of an initially noncommittal response to Roosevelt's opening gambit, in effect inviting the president to enlarge the inducement on Eastern European issues before offering any concession over the United Nations.

The discussion then turned to the Polish issues. At first Stalin must have felt encouraged. Roosevelt's opening in this area was strained: confirming his acceptance of the Curzon Line; announcing that as a non-European he took "a distant view" of the Polish difficulties; asking Stalin only to reconsider the absorption of the overwhelmingly Polish city of Lvov on

---

[24] For Hopkins's notes, see FRUS, *Yalta*, pp. 633–634. Vassili I. Chuikov, *The Fall of Berlin* (New York, 1967), p. 120.

the Soviet side but saying weakly he "would not insist on it." He capped all this by remarking that the Poles were concerned only "to save face" – a remark that has been excoriated by many writers. At the end, however, he suddenly showed some spirit, surprising his British listeners by coming up with Mikolajczyk's idea of a broadly representative Presidential Council charged to create a provisional government that would replace the unacceptable Lublin regime.

This stimulated a flurry of British support for the Poles. Churchill, seizing the chance to move in vigorously behind the president, was emboldened to champion Polish "sovereignty" and to declare, with a vehemence he had never before shown in Stalin's presence, that "he could never be satisfied with a settlement that did not leave Poland free and independent." Having accepted the Curzon Line, he now said that he must insist on "guarantees" that would let Poland "be mistress in her own house and captain of her soul." This sounds robustly progressive and was certainly a stiffer approach than Churchill had shown in his Tolstoy talks. But here too one sees the importance of the more subtle signals the three conferees were sending each other in these early days of the meeting. Roosevelt had done so bluntly in registering with Stalin his mistrust of Churchill, rather more subtly in conveying his understanding of the United Nations/Eastern Europe nexus. In Churchill's case, the eye is caught here by the phrase "mistress in her own house," which belies the impression of feisty resistance by suggesting a willingness to accept internal autonomy for Poland rather than full sovereignty, leaving ultimate control to the Soviets. This, after all, must be the inevitable consequence of the earlier promises Churchill and Eden had made to Stalin of their support only for East European regimes "friendly" to the Soviet Union. Eden's repetition of exactly the same phrase later in the conference strengthens the suspicion that this was the final compromise the British were aiming at. At the very least it appears to have been, like much else at Yalta, a calculated ambiguity.[25]

How can a country or state be "free and independent" (a phrase much heard at Yalta) if its government's authority is confined to domestic, internal affairs? No one inquired. No one addressed the question. A state, a province, a municipality? The fact is that the British and Americans had long been determined to leave contradictions, confusions, and ambiguities of this kind unexplored, even as they hung intently on Stalin's periodic gnomic utterances concerning Poland's fate. The Soviets had shrewdly

---

[25] Bohlen minutes, third plenary meeting, February 6, 1945, FRUS, *Yalta*, pp. 660–671. See, for a recent analysis, Gardner, *Spheres of Influence*, p. 237.

inaugurated this game of Fudge the Issue with articles published before and after Yalta suggesting that both the Western powers and the Soviet Union (and, by implication, the future governments of those states now coming under their wing) were full-fledged "democracies," simply of a different kind. But "free and independent" suggests something more basic to the human sensibility, and here the studied ambiguities of Yalta would cause profound difficulties later on. Meanwhile, in the failure of Roosevelt and Churchill to ask the Soviet leaders for some elucidation of what the phrase really meant in practice we find another example of that calculated complicity in unreality that had undeniably helped the alliance to maintain its coherence successfully through the war but, persisted in now during this last wartime opportunity to reach a genuine meeting of minds, allowed each of the Big Three to go home and put a dangerously self-interested (and sharply divergent) public stamp on what had been done at the conference.

Stalin nevertheless felt obliged, in the face of Roosevelt's initiative, to make some kind of a case on the unavoidable and controversial Polish issue. Now, as always in wartime diplomacy, he proved himself an effective, resourceful debater. Speaking with passion, he noted that the Curzon Line had been settled at the Paris Peace Conference in 1919 by Western statesmen. He could hardly be less Russian than Curzon and Clemenceau. Lvov was a just reward for the Ukrainians, who had suffered greatly and whom he could not betray. He moved on to defend the Lublin regime and even offered to bring its leaders to Yalta for consultation. He emphasized, however, that the governmental issue was an internal Polish matter that should be settled without intervention from outside. With this thorny issue openly joined at last – Polish problems would feature at all subsequent plenary sessions – the conferees wisely decided to adjourn for the day.[26]

Stalin now received another shock. His defense of the Polish status quo – a characteristic combination of grim realism, hard logic, dubious assumptions, and self-interested assertion, all delivered with the sophistication of an experienced debater – provoked a stronger American response than the Soviets must have expected from Roosevelt's tentative start and their memories of his performance at Teheran. That evening Hopkins, Bohlen, and some of the State Department officials sat down to try and put a little backbone into the American proposals. They drafted a presidential letter for FDR to send to Stalin. "In so far as the Polish government is

---

[26] For a Soviet definition of "democracy," see Zaslavsky article, *Pravda*, February 17, 1945.

concerned," it began, "I am greatly disturbed that the three great powers do not have a meeting of minds about the political set-up in Poland. ... Surely there is a way to reconcile our differences." Then taking up and extending Stalin's offer to bring some Lublin leaders to Yalta, Roosevelt called on him to extend an invitation to "representatives of other elements of the Polish people," whom he named. The draft was then taken to the British, who, delighted to be consulted, stiffened it further by adding three names from the London government, including Mikolajczyk. It was then delivered to the Soviet headquarters that evening.[27]

Stalin was again thrown on the defensive but again responded adroitly. At the next plenary meeting, on the afternoon of February 7, he announced implausibly that he had received the Roosevelt letter only an hour before. He had tried unsuccessfully to contact the Lublin Poles. Alas, there would not be time for the other Poles to reach Yalta. However, he quickly reassured the disappointed Americans, the typists were even now preparing a proposal on Poland that would please them. Meanwhile, he suggested, let us return to the Dumbarton Oaks voting issue. Then, as the American delegates pricked up their ears attentively, he announced that the Soviet Union would after all accept the American formula, essentially confining the veto power to action. Furthermore, the Soviets would no longer insist, as they had until now, upon membership for all the Soviet republics and would be content with two or three. At this point the attention of the now visibly enthused American delegation was directed to Molotov, who in Father Christmas fashion came forward again to announce a modified Soviet proposal for Poland. There would be some minor changes in the Curzon Line in favor of Poland. More importantly, the Soviets now agreed to "enlarge" the Lublin government by bringing in "democratic" leaders from Polish émigré circles. Molotov, Harriman, and Clark Kerr in Moscow were to be "entrusted with the discussion of enlarging the Polish Provisional Government and submitting their proposals to the consideration of the three governments." All these pleasingly material easements in the hitherto tough approach of the Soviets (who also agreed now to attend the proposed founding conference of the United Nations in San Francisco in April) were thus introduced ostentatiously in the context of the United Nations/Eastern Europe "bargain." They produced a brief euphoria. Roosevelt, clearly gratified, acknowledged that progress had been made. "He felt that this was a great step forward which would be

[27] Roosevelt to Stalin, February 6, 1945, FRUS, *Yalta*, pp. 727–728.

welcomed by all the peoples of the world." Churchill also expressed his "heartfelt thanks to Marshal Stalin and Mr. Molotov for the great step forward."[28]

This was a remarkable moment. Stalin had on February 6 characteristically withheld agreement on Stettinius's United Nations formulas in clear anticipation of concessions on the Polish issues. Instead, on February 7 he found himself confronting unexpected American resistance. Roosevelt seemed seriously committed to the creation of a new regime in Poland. One assumes it was therefore with some anxiety that Stalin had now played all his principal cards at once in a bold attempt to ward this off. He may well have been encouraged by a short private meeting with Roosevelt just before the plenary session, where he got substantial approval (with a few details ironed out with Harriman later) of his political price for entering the Pacific war. FDR had been abundantly forthcoming over the Chinese ports, the territorial acquisitions from Japan, and control of the Manchurian railways, asking only that Chiang Kai Shek be consulted. The terms were recorded, after some haggling over detail that on balance strengthened the Soviet hold on the region, in a written agreement completed at subsequent meetings on February 10. There was scant concern for the Chinese, despite provision for the "concurrence" of the Generalissimo. The Societ accessions were described as the "former rights of Russia," and the agreement concluded, "The Heads of the three Great Powers have agreed that these claims of the Soviet Union shall be unquestionably fulfilled after Japan has been defeated." Churchill, brought into the picture only at the last moment, also signed it. Diane S. Clemens has plausibly suggested that on this showing Roosevelt envisioned the Soviet Union as a future "junior partner" in the Pacific at the expense not only of China and Japan but also of Britain, France, and the other European colonial powers. Stalin might well have gained that impression, especially as the president used their February 8 meeting as another opportunity to get off a few more shots at the British. Declaring that he wanted to "transfer" surplus American and British shipping to the Soviet Union on credit and free of interest, he remarked, according to the transcript, "the British had never sold anything without commercial interest, but he had different ideas." Later, as the discussion turned to trusteeship for Korea, he revealed his desire to exclude the British. Stalin said he thought they should be included.

---

[28] Bohlen minutes, fourth plenary meeting, February 7, 1945, ibid., pp. 708–718.

As Roosevelt and Stalin moved from this remarkable conversation to the immediately following plenary session, the Soviet leader must have felt some degree of reassurance. But because FDR had always carefully refrained from any explicit commitment to the two "bargains" Stalin had been persistently working on in his diplomacy with the United States – the United Nations/Eastern Europe nexus; the promise of belligerency in the Pacific war in return for political/territorial accession in the Far East – the Soviet leader cannot yet have been sure whether Roosevelt may have viewed these concessions to the Soviets at the expense of China and Japan as a sufficient price for the treatment of Poland that, to this point of the Yalta conference at least, he seemed to be looking for.[29]

On the other hand, it must have seemed to Stalin that, at least on the crucial Polish problems, he still had some way to go. As the Big Three met on the afternoon of February 8, FDR's Presidential Council proposal was still on the table. Further, a British paper was now presented accepting the Molotov/ambassadors commission but charging it with the "establishment" of a new provisional government rather than the "enlargement" of Lublin. As Roosevelt sat passively by, Churchill and the Soviet leaders debated that issue. Molotov advanced the now usual, increasingly meretricious objections, claiming that any outside representation would "insult" the Poles, who had stayed home during the war. Churchill disdainfully ignored this, pointing out that the Western powers had been given no access to Poland, and moved the discussion quickly to the likely consequences of a failure to resolve the issue satisfactorily. "It was stamping the conference with a seal of failure, and nothing else we did here would overcome it. ... If the British Government brushed aside the London government and went over to the Lublin Government there would be an angry outcry in Great Britain." It would be seen as a betrayal of the approximately 150,000 Poles now fighting bravely with the British. "It would be said," he continued, "that we did not know what was going on in Poland and that the British Government, having given way completely on the frontiers, had accepted the Soviet view and had championed it." The debates in Parliament, he emphasized, would be "most painful" and "dangerous to Allied unity." There must, therefore, be a new start on equal terms, looking to an unimpeachable election.

This blast of compressed realism, together with Roosevelt's silence during the argument, appears to have disconcerted Stalin. He countered

---

[29] Bohlen minutes, Roosevelt-Stalin meeting, February 8, 1945, ibid., pp. 766–771; Clemens, *Yalta*, pp. 244–252.

Churchill with the French parallel, professing to see little difference between the position of the unelected but accepted de Gaulle and that of the Lublin group. He then insisted that the Lublin leaders were popular because they had spent the war in Poland. Indeed, he continued, "the Red Army had been received by the Poles in the light of a great national holiday. The people had been surprised that the Polish government in London had not participated in the celebrations." Precisely why the Poles – having endured the Red Army's invasion and brutal occupation of 1939–41; the forced deportation of one and a half million citizens to the eastern reaches of the Soviet Union, where many died in backbreaking labor and harsh conditions; the Katyn massacres by Soviet functionaries of the nation's elite; and the notoriously spectatorial role of the Soviet forces outside Warsaw in 1944 – might now greet Soviet troops with this kind of rapture was not explained. Neither Churchill, whose sources of intelligence already spoke of widespread police roundups and executions in Lublin-run Poland, nor the studiously self-effacing Roosevelt had the bad taste to question their host's festive scenario. Stalin then moved on to criticize British policies toward France and Yugoslavia and, while disclaiming any intention to intervene there, put a little twist in the knife by pointedly asking what was going on in Greece. At this juncture all pleasantries seemed to be vanishing. Yalta was turning into something ominously resembling the American stereotype of a classic European diplomatic exchange.

Roosevelt – highly allergic, like all his closest associates, to this kind of European bickering – had by this stage apparently seen enough. "We are all agreed on the necessity of free elections," he declared, "the only problem is how Poland is to be governed in the interval." He asked how long it would be before elections could be held. Possibly in a month, came Stalin's quick reply. These would prove in the end to be the talismanic assurances upon which the Polish government issue turned at Yalta. From this moment on, so far as the Americans were concerned, the future of Poland, a central concern up to this point, began to slip into the shadows as the prospect of early elections became the focus of attention. It was now the Soviets' turn to experience a touch of euphoria. The suddenly changed emotional context was palpably obvious as the three statesmen met for dinner that night at Stalin's headquarters in the Yusopov Palace.[30]

The mood at this February 8 party was decidedly upbeat, even among the British, who still knew nothing about the United States–Soviet Far

[30] Bohlen minutes, fifth plenary meeting, February 8, 1945, ibid., pp. 771–782.

Eastern deal and who still appear to have harbored the illusion that some broad-based Presidential Council along the lines of Roosevelt's proposals might yet be formed to organize the projected Polish elections. Optimistic sentiments were accordingly expressed in characteristic fashion first by Churchill, who looked to "the broad, sunlit plains of peace and happiness," and also by Roosevelt, who wished "every woman and child on this earth the possibility of security and well-being." The most jovial figure was the hitherto dour Stalin, who now suddenly went out of his way to please Churchill, whom he called "the bravest governmental figure in the world." He recalled Churchill's "courage and staunchness" when Britain stood alone and said he knew of few examples in history "where the courage of one man had been so important to the future of the world." The explanation of this extraordinary encomium, coming on the heels of their bitter exchanges only hours before, is not far to seek. Having just seen the pleasing impact upon the president of his early election offer, Stalin appears to have sensed that he had after all succeeded in deflecting the anticipated American challenge over Poland, and perhaps over Eastern Europe generally. Now, always insuring in the classic European mode, he was turning back to reassure Churchill that the Anglo-Soviet concert – the basis since 1941 of his projected geopolitical framework for postwar Europe – was still intact and valued.[31]

Stalin's optimism about the developing American volte-face was fully justified. The following morning, February 9, saw the beginning of a rapid American retreat over the hitherto contested interim arrangements for Poland. At the meeting of the foreign ministers, Stettinius announced that the United States was dropping the Presidential Council idea. This was the end, so far as the United States was concerned, of the "new" government conception. Stettinius also accepted Molotov's ambassadors commission proposal looking to the "reorganization" of the present government. The secretary of state, always honest despite his other limitations, did not attempt to justify these concessions on political or moral grounds. Significantly, he linked them not with any concern for Poland's interests, much less for Europe's political future, but with the damage the various European problems, including Poland, were causing to the prospects for American postwar internationalism. "From the standpoint of psychology and public opinion," the secretary of state declared, "the Polish situation was of great importance at this time to the United States." He therefore

---

[31] Gilbert, *Churchill*, VII, pp. 1194–1196; Gardner, *Spheres of Influence*, p. 235; Bohlen minutes, tripartite dinner meeting, February 8, 1945, FRUS, *Yalta*, pp. 797–799.

hoped "with all his heart" that the Polish question could be settled before the Crimean conference broke up.[32]

The British now felt the ground falling away beneath them. Eden continued to press for a "new" government and a place in it for Mikolajczyk. During the first few days at Yalta the British strategy had been to tuck in supportively behind the prospect, raised temptingly at the preliminary Malta talks, of a potentially strong American determination to force the Soviets to agree to a new regime to replace Lublin. Because of Roosevelt's passivity in debate, however, Churchill had become the chief protagonist for this view in the plenary debates. Now, in the face of what appeared to be an American retreat, he and Eden suddenly found themselves abandoned and exposed. They had followed FDR up the hill, even pushing him at times. Now, obedient to the play of power, they got in behind the Americans on the downhill trajectory, though with a braking show of regret and reluctance. Thus, after the February 9 foreign ministers session, Eden tamely presented an amended proposal accepting a "reorganized" Polish government rather than the "newly established" one he had called for earlier.

That afternoon Churchill had to listen to Roosevelt declaring, after listening to Molotov's proposals, that "we are now very near agreement and it is only a matter of drafting." It was, he repeated, "only a matter of words and details." FDR then said he agreed with Stalin's characterization of the Poles as "a quarrelsome people" but "would like to have some assurance for the six million Poles in the United States that these elections would be freely held." The prime minister at this point tried to establish a new defensive position, stressing the need for observers in Poland, especially for the projected elections. But when Stalin proved resistant, he too quickly retreated to a simple request that Mikolajczyk be allowed to participate. The British still saw a ray of hope. At the end of the February 9 plenary session there still seemed a chance that the Americans could be rallied for an insistence on election observers. Churchill struck a more optimistic note in a cable to Attlee that evening, noting that Eden's "good draft" was still alive. He stressed that the main objective was supervised elections and "informing ourselves properly about what is going on in Poland. All the reality in this business depends on this point which will be fought out today."[33]

---

[32] Page minutes, foreign ministers meeting, February 9, 1945, FRUS, *Yalta*, pp. 802–807.

[33] For British concerns, see Record of Foreign Secretaries Meeting, February 9, 1945; Record of Plenary Meeting, February 9, 1945; and Churchill to Attlee, February 9, 1945, all in WP (45) 157, CAB66/63. See also Clemens, *Yalta*, pp. 210–211.

Once again the British were to be disappointed. The American back-off became a headlong retreat on February 10. Stettinius told the other foreign ministers that the president was now dropping the call for election observers. He would of course "receive reports" from his representatives, and the secretary went on to warn that "the President would be free to make any statement he felt necessary on Poland." No one seems to have taken this very seriously. Stettinius was again disarmingly frank. He stated that he personally preferred to keep the provision for observations. "The President, however, is so anxious to reach agreement that he is willing to make this concession."[34] Thus on February 9 the United States had abandoned the Presidential Council and the "new" government conception because it needed a settlement over Poland to shore up public sentiment for the United Nations at home. Now on February 10 it dropped the election observers provision because the president was "so anxious to reach agreement." Yet another accommodation to the Soviets followed, this time bestowed by FDR himself. At the plenary session on February 9 Roosevelt had submitted the Declaration of Liberated Europe, looking to free elections on the continent and charging the Big Three to "immediately establish appropriate machinery" to carry out their responsibilities. Now, a day later, Molotov successfully gutted this initiative and got the obligation reduced to an undertaking that "they will immediately take measures for the carrying out of mutual consultation."[35]

To the increasingly disquieted British these successive steps toward the abandonment of Poland to the discretion of the Soviet Union seemed irresponsible. Churchill had pleaded with Roosevelt to stay longer, but without success. The president made it clear that he was eager to wrap things up.[36] Churchill and Eden, now highly concerned as the Americans seemed to be moving back to an all-too-familiar detachment, made an effort to restore the now frayed Anglo-Soviet nexus. In a February 10 private meeting with Stalin on the Polish issue, Churchill explained again to the Soviet leader that he would find it difficult to reassure Parliament and the British people that the unsupervised elections would be fair. The British knew from their own intelligence services, he went on, as well as from arguably more suspect Polish sources, that the Lublin regime was not popular and that under the

[34] Page minutes of foreign ministers meeting, February 10, 1945, ibid., pp. 802–807, 871–877.
[35] Bohlen minutes of seventh plenary meeting, February 10, 1945, ibid., pp. 897–906.
[36] For British criticisms of Roosevelt's conduct, see Wilmot, *Struggle for Europe*, p. 405. Historian Michael Howard described Roosevelt as "ludicrously naïve about Stalin" in *The Eagle and the Bear*, A&E network, April 3, 1988. Churchill more delicately conveyed a more muted but similar opinion in *Triumph and Tragedy*, pp. 346–402.

protection of the Red Army a widespread political purging operation was already being violently pressed. Stalin, with the American challenge now defused, was in no mood to be helpful. The British should recognize the reorganized Lublin government, he said, and then make arrangements for the desired "observations" with them. The effect of this was to place the entire emphasis upon the anticipated Moscow "consultations," where, it became apparent within two weeks of Yalta, the Soviets intended to interpret the "reorganized" formula to exclude anyone they mistrusted.[37]

The British delegation was increasingly disoriented. The Americans had led them into a dangerous argument with Stalin over Poland only to back away at the "crucial moment." The British diaries and memoirs bristle with complaints, especially about the president's performance. Lord Moran records several of Churchill's anguished protests over Roosevelt's inattentiveness. Moran himself noted that "the President's opinions flutter in the wind." Cadogan commented that "the President is very wooly and wobbly."[38]

The truth, of course, is that FDR was now seriously ill. Everyone at Yalta watched him closely, fully aware of his physical decline. Did this affect his performance? Harry Hopkins, who was closest to him, thought that he heard only half of what was said at the conference table. Moran rightly suspected cerebral problems and was sure he was looking at "a very sick man." Churchill was also struck by Roosevelt's decline since their last meeting in September 1944. So was Eden. The foreign secretary was disgusted with Yalta generally and particularly with Roosevelt (whose performance he described in his diary as "vague, loose and ineffective"). But Eden did not think the president's malaise affected his performance at Yalta. He was inclined to see here again, as at Teheran, a persistent spirit of careless indifference to the issue of Europe's future security and general prospect. Alger Hiss, then a senior State Department official, similarly thought Roosevelt was robust and in command at the conference. And Harriman's daughter Kathleen, upon meeting the president, wrote to a friend, "He's absolutely charming – easy to talk to with a lovely sense of humor. He's in fine form, very happy about accomodations and all set for the Best."[39]

---

[37] Record of conversation between Churchill and Stalin, February 10, 1945, WP (45), CAB 66/63. See also Churchill, *Triumph and Tragedy*, p. 385.

[38] Moran, *Churchill*, pp. 243, 247; Cadogan diary, February 11, 1945, Dilks, ed., *Cadogan Diaries*, p. 709.

[39] For Hopkins, see Eden to Churchill, March 10, 1945, PREM 3.51/3. See also Moran, *Churchill*, p. 242. Robert Rhodes James, *Anthony Eden* (London, 1986), p. 290; *New York Times*, March 12, 1988. Kathleen Harriman letters, February 10, 16, 1945, Box 176, Harriman MSS.

One finds expressions of sympathy for the president in the British records. But they were preoccupied with the larger issues. Roosevelt's conduct of the Polish issues was unnerving. Even worse, his whole attitude toward Europe's future seemed, as it had at Teheran, shot through with disdain. FDR did not appear to have thought much about the very basic problem of Germany's future. His rhetoric had earlier seemed to favor dismemberment and harsh treatment. But in the backwash of the now discredited Morgenthau Plan there seemed to be no systematic American thinking. A similarly casual approach seemed to characterize FDR's reparations policy, which, by fastening postwar Germany with what the British regarded as unrealizable exactions, was bound to jeopardize the European recovery and exacerbate the looming refugee problem. Then there was France, again consigned to a humiliating postwar role without any consideration of her importance to a Britain that Roosevelt had himself charged, in the more realistic deliberations at the Octagon conference, with the future security of Western Europe in some kind of balance with Soviet power. To British observers at Yalta, the headlong American retreat on the Polish issue after Stalin's simple promise of early elections suggested an all-too-familiar gullibility. In the last few days at Yalta, therefore, the British found themselves wondering yet again whether and to what degree they could rely on Roosevelt as an effective partner in European politics. "The President is behaving very badly," Churchill told Moran. "He won't take any interest in what we are trying to do."[40]

This raises a question. What were the British trying to do? They appear to have come to Yalta, not with any intention of abandoning the Anglo-Soviet nexus (or the Moscow Order it had produced) but with the notion, inspired by the provocative Soviet recognition of the Lublin regime, that they could push the Americans forward on the Polish issues. Now, thanks to FDR's erratic course (as Churchill and Eden saw it), they found themselves exposed to Stalin's wrath. Toward the end of the conference, Eden made an effort to convert Yalta into a pragmatic Anglo-Soviet encounter, reminiscent of the 1943 foreign ministers conference at Moscow. To this end he presented several papers on Balkan issues, on the Austrian zonal arrangements, and on the desirability of a closer Anglo-Soviet understanding over oil and troop withdrawals from Iran. But Molotov was either totally negative or grudging in his responses. Similarly, the personal exchanges between Churchill and Stalin were often hard and anything

[40] Moran, *Churchill*, p. 247.

but comradely. Stalin repeatedly nagged Churchill over British policies in Greece, Yugoslavia, and Western Europe as he looked without much success for British cooperation on the Polish issues. He appears to have particularly resented the British refusal to accept Maisky's reparations plan. "If the British do not want the Soviets to receive any reparations they should say so," he declared at their last social meeting. There were several similar echoes of Stalin's earlier taunts at Teheran that Churchill was pro-German.[41]

Yalta, then, put Anglo-Soviet collaboration to a severe test. Disturbing events elsewhere raised doubts about the durability of the Anglo-Soviet concert and even of the Moscow Order itself. Cables coming into Yalta from London told of concern in Athens that ELAS (the left-communist militia) was again active, and concurrently expressed concern that the London-sponsored Tito-Subasic agreement in Belgrade was breaking up under communist pressure. There were also renewed anxieties about Soviet noncooperation over the delineation of Allied zones in Austria.

Most alarmingly, a message arrived on February 9 from Sargent and Richard Law in the Foreign Office registering concern that France (already receiving dismissive treatment from Roosevelt and Stalin) was, owing to American and Soviet resistance, to be denied any participation on the projected German Disarmament and Reparation Committee. The Foreign Office urged Churchill and Eden to show more support for France. They blamed Roosevelt. "To declare that United States troops will not stay in Europe longer than two years," they wrote, "and at one and the same time to veto the participation of France in the settlement of Germany is to upset the balance between East and West to Russia's advantage." Even more "worrisome" were the intimations of an apparent Soviet volte-face. "It almost looks as though it might be part of a considered policy of weakening Western Europe both politically and militarily." The cable concluded ominously that "[t]he future of Europe for some time to come may therefore turn on the treatment of France at the present conference."[42]

One should not exaggerate these anxieties. The British and Soviet conferees at Yalta were hard-bitten European politicians who seem in many ways to have felt they understood each other. Both sides made it clear that even if the Anglo-Soviet concert was fraying at the personal

---

[41] Foreign secretaries meetings, February 9, 10, 1945, CAB 66/63; Page minutes, foreign ministers meeting, February 10, 1945, FRUS, *Yalta*, p. 877; Matthews minutes, seventh plenary meeting, February 10, 1945, ibid., p. 909.

[42] Law and Sargent to Eden, February 9, 1945, PREM 4.78/1.

level they wanted to preserve the Moscow Order they had earlier created. It was in this spirit, in all probability, that Stalin had showered compliments upon Churchill at the February 8 dinner and also in the end extended an olive branch by agreeing to give France a seat on the Allied Control Council for Germany. There were other flashes of solidarity as the Europeans joined forces in ways that showed some continuing reservations about the rise of American power. This was especially true on United Nations issues. Churchill irritated Roosevelt by supporting Stalin early on in his doubts about the voting rights formula. When Churchill expressed support for seats in the United Nations for two or three Soviet republics, Stalin gratefully responded with support for Turkish membership, notwithstanding the already tense character of Turco-Soviet relations. And Stalin again refused, as at Teheran, to join Roosevelt in personal criticism of Churchill behind his back. Nor did he show any enthusiasm for the president's anti-empire rhetoric. When FDR tried to exclude Britain from a postwar role in Korea, Stalin argued that it should be included.[43]

Further, the British were inclined to blame Roosevelt rather than Stalin for the evident difficulties at Yalta. Undoubtedly, leaving aside his physical ailments for a moment, some of Roosevelt's limitations were visibly on display at Yalta. He had not prepared carefully. None of his various proposals on the Polish issues were his own. The plan to bring the Poles to Yalta originated with Stalin. The Presidential Council notion came from Mikolajczyk and later Cadogan; the Declaration on Liberated Europe was a State Department creation; and while the prospect he laid before Stalin of a politically devitalized postwar Europe may be more truly seen as an original, if dubious, contribution, it was a repeat of his Teheran performance and an obvious link with Vandenberg's pre-Yalta scenario of a Soviet Union that was more likely to collaborate with the United States if it saw no threat from the West. Then too, Roosevelt's participation in the debates was thin and often not well focused. Forceful American action, when it occurred, seems to have sprung from Hopkins, from the inexperienced but hard-working Stettinius, from certain State Department officials, and from Harriman, who negotiated the final terms of the Far Eastern agreement with Stalin in a businesslike encounter involving some Soviet concessions.[44]

[43] See references in FRUS, *Yalta*, pp. 714, 770, 774.
[44] Harriman, memorandum of conversations, February 10, 1945, FRUS, *Yalta*, pp. 894–897.

At the social events, the president's characteristic jocularity sometimes grated. Unabashed by his "Uncle Joe" mishap on February 4, he resumed his assault on Stalin's dignity on February 8 with a story about Eleanor Roosevelt's visit to a country school. A young child had asked her what was the great blank space that dominated the schoolroom map of Eurasia. It was of course Russia. This cartographical neglect, Roosevelt now told Stalin, had been the event that led him to recognize the Soviet Union in 1933. Stalin's response to this somewhat patronizing anecdote from the Hudson Valley squire is not recorded. But one does begin to see in the proliferation of such moments something of the problem that the two European leaders – highly focused men of business for all their vices and personal idiosyncracies – had in getting through to the elusive American president, and also perhaps why Churchill and Roosevelt began to irritate each other during the last phase of their great wartime partnership: too much highly charged gravitas about mundane things from the Englishman, on the one hand; too much frivolity about serious matters from the American, on the other.[45]

Nevertheless, the image of an ailing, "irresponsible" Roosevelt blundering through his last great crisis is misleading. Roosevelt was actually far from being a "passenger" at Yalta, to cite the critical but unperceptive description used by one of the British party. Indeed, he was the central figure. To some extent this was clearly apparent. The president chaired the plenary sessions and determined much of the agenda as it developed. It was he, after all, who introduced the United Nations and Polish issues together on February 6. For three days he focused the meeting's attention on Poland as he tried to get a satisfactory deal from Stalin. It was almost certainly his persistence, rather than Churchill's eloquence, that obliged Stalin to make successive concessions – of a "reorganized" rather than a simply "enlarged" provisional government, of a tripartite Moscow commission, and finally of "early elections" – none of which the Soviets can have wanted. And – more substantively, from an American viewpoint – FDR secured the crucial quid pro quos from the Soviet leader of full acceptance of his voting rights formula (as well as a commitment to attend the founding United Nations conference in San Francisco) and a reaffirmed promise to come into the Pacific war. Once these were in the bag, Roosevelt quickly gave up the Presidential Council, the election observers, and the "machinery" aspect of the Declaration on Liberated Europe. The British saw all this as a disastrous retreat. Roosevelt doubtless

---

[45] Bohlen minutes, tripartite dinner meeting, February 8, 1945, ibid., pp. 797–99.

saw it as a necessary adjustment on issues where he knew he could not prevail, after he had won the greater prizes.

Moreover, this is by no means the full or even the main story of FDR's efforts and influence at Yalta. Both at the time and since, participants and commentators and historians have tended to view Yalta as an exercise (a failed one, many have thought) in compromise and traditional diplomacy. But this is to miss a vital dimension of the meeting. Making political arrangements with Stalin in the Crimea was one thing. But in the broader sense, taking in his preparations for Yalta, the conference itself, and its public presentation, we can see that Roosevelt's primary objective – one that in the end was more important to him than relations with the Soviets, though the two were now obviously linked – was to get himself into a position where he could effect the transformation of American public opinion. And here he appears to have been thinking less of the tangible commitments he was finding it difficult to get from Stalin and more of the images, attitudes, and visions he needed from Yalta in order to reassure increasingly skeptical Americans that the war had not been fought in vain and that they could profitably and constructively engage with Europe in the postwar world. The specific political decisions we have seen explored and settled at Yalta, even those affecting the United Nations project, were not enough. Something more was needed. To get at this we need a fresh perspective, one that explains why, even as he was apparently settling with Stalin on February 9 in more or less conventional diplomatic terms for what he later resignedly called "the best he could get for Poland," Roosevelt was actually shifting gears and moving quickly to a more radical diplomatic strategy that would create an irresistibly positive vision of Yalta that he could use at home to reignite the forward-looking American internationalism he had come to Yalta to save.[46]

RADICAL DIPLOMACY

The Making of the "Fraudulent Prospectus"

Franklin Roosevelt was the radical statesman of the Grand Alliance. Churchill and Stalin, for all their particularities, can fairly be seen as more or less recognizable exemplars of the European tradition, steeped in political realism, attentive to history, geopolitically aware, and acutely sensitive to the play of power. Here it is useful to remember the distinction between

[46] Moran, *Churchill*, p. 247. William Leaky, *I Was There* (New York, 1950), pp. 315–316.

the American and European modes of diplomacy. While the British certainly, and perhaps even the Soviets to some very limited extent, had always to take some account of public feeling – and especially so in early 1945 as the end of the war began to seem imminent and impulses generated by the wider political world were beginning to break into the hitherto closed circle of elite diplomacy – they were still able to practice a more or less traditional foreign policy of interests, alliances, and territorial adjustment. For the United States, however, with its uniquely open and articulate polity and its future political engagement with the world now tentatively tied to a prospective United Nations organization that was not yet firmly anchored in public acceptance, the crucial issue was whether President Roosevelt could persuade his impressionable countrymen (always a kind of invisible but potent "fourth party" in American summit diplomacy during World War II) that this was a viable and worthwhile enterprise. With that in view, he went to Yalta hoping certainly to achieve concrete objectives (agreement on a United Nations conference, a satisfactory veto formula, and Soviet reassurances about their plans to enter the war against Japan) but also believing he had to create for his domestic constituency the public image, if not the full reality, of a transformatively successful conference with the European allies.

The Soviets and Americans had approached the Yalta conference in very different ways. Stalin had presented his allies during the war with some embarrassing situations (Katyn, Warsaw, Eastern Europe's looming subjugation) but also with rather straightforward central bargaining propositions: a geopolitical division with Churchill, an Eastern Europe/United Nations nexus with Roosevelt. He prepared for Yalta in a traditional way, too, suggesting an agenda and setting out his objectives clearly in advance. He was critical of the poor American preparation. He and Molotov worked hard at the conference, debated vigorously, and negotiated closely on every issue as they worked systematically toward tight agreements and tangible results. They showed much less interest than the Americans in the public presentation of the conference results. Two comments are illuminating. On February 10, Molotov suddenly asked his colleagues if any thought had been given to the communiqué. Indeed it had, replied Stettinius reassuringly, the American delegation was preparing one. Later Stalin also showed some casual interest, asking who was taking down the various decisions. He received similar American reassurances.[47]

---

[47] Page minutes, foreign ministers meeting, February 10, 1945, FRUS, *Yalta*, p. 875; Bohlen minutes, seventh plenary meeting, February 10, 1945, ibid., p. 905.

The American approach was markedly different: flexible and nonconfrontational on substantive matters before and at Yalta; acutely focused, however, on the presentational aspects all the way from initial planning in Washington to Roosevelt's report to Congress and the American people on March 1. This sensitivity to American public opinion had an impact on the rhythm of the conference. For it is one of the ironies of Yalta that while Stalin and Molotov may appear to have been piling up points in their seemingly successful efforts to resist intrusion and to secure legitimation from the Western powers of their Polish and by extension Eastern European policies, so as the various decisions were transfigured into written agreements for the world audience they were conceding marks to the image-conscious, media-sensitive Americans, who were from the start bent on fixing a liberal imprint upon the whole proceedings. This was radical diplomacy of a new kind, inaugurated at Yalta with profound results by a dying man who, according to his closest associate, "only heard half of what went on" at the meeting, and perhaps felt he had insufficient time left to achieve his central goal in any other way.

These distinctions become clearer if, for the purpose of analysis, we think of Yalta as a meeting operating at two distinct levels, related obviously, and overlapping to a point, but different in ways that mattered. At the first level, the one we have been examining so far, the assembled leaders might be seen as engaged in a more or less conventional diplomatic exchange, moving through a familiar continuum of preparation, announcement, conference debate and negotiation on the issues, and culminating in a communiqué of decisions reached. The second level, a kind of subdued, unacknowledged presence in that earlier phase, cropping up occasionally in debates and references, came fully into its own only in the last days of the conference after most of the main issues had been settled or talked out and the crucial bargain had been struck between Roosevelt's United Nations concerns and Stalin's persisting hold on Poland. It too was of course "political," but in a fundamentally different way. For its constituent parts comprised, not the visible tangible political issues around which debate overtly flowed, but rather all those elements – the references to the Atlantic Charter and the prospective United Nations, the Declaration on Liberated Europe with its expansive democratic promises that neither the Soviets nor the British understood properly or took sufficiently seriously, the liberal undertakings in the Polish agreement, the communiqué as a whole – that could be gathered in and used by Roosevelt and his aides upon their return home to convey an attractively congenial image of Yalta's real meaning. The value of this "two-level" conception lies in the clarity it brings to the divergent approaches of the two major powers and the way in which it highlights the fact that the political character of the first traditional phase of Yalta (and especially the decisions on Poland and the carefully avoided nondecisions on Eastern Europe generally) was markedly at variance with the words and liberal phrases used by Roosevelt to ornament and characterize the conference later on, creating the unreal vision that Winston Churchill later called "a fraudulent prospectus."

What then is the case for this supposed "second-level" interpretation of Yalta? Its substance is found in two documents in the final communiqué: the agreement on Poland and the Declaration on Liberated Europe. The Polish document seems almost surreal in retrospect. It recorded the Allies' "common desire to see established a strong, free, independent and democratic Poland." It described the agreed-upon procedures (notably the projected ambassadors commission) and looked to "the holding of free and unfettered elections as soon as possible on the basis of universal suffrage and secret ballot." The broader Declaration also looked to "free elections of governments responsive to the will of the people" and recorded the intention of the three powers to assist both the liberated countries and the former Axis satellites "to solve by democratic means their pressing political and economic problems." It twice affirmed their faith in "the principles of the Atlantic Charter," and referred abundantly to such concepts as "democracy" and "democratic means" as well as to "sovereignty and self-government" and "the Declaration of the United Nations." Taken together, all these expressions obviously convey an illusory image of Yalta that contrasts dramatically with the hard political realities that, especially in the case of Poland, we have seen shaping the debates and decisions at the conference.[48]

President Roosevelt, presumably aware of the discordance, was carefully nonprovocative. It will be remembered that the Declaration in its original form also contemplated a tripartite Emergency High Commission to carry out and oversee this attractive reconstruction of political Europe. But Roosevelt dropped this idea. He must have calculated that Stalin would not accept this kind of tripartite institutionalization in postwar Europe. Nor did FDR want American entanglements of this kind. It was the Declaration itself – a statement of moral values and intentions looking to a broken Europe that was to

---

[48] For the Declaration in its Yalta form, see FRUS, *Yalta*, pp. 971–973. For its State Department genesis, see Stettinius, *Roosevelt and the Russians*, pp. 88–89. For more on its origins and development, see Bohlen, *Witness to History*, p. 193. For a British view of its potential value, see Law and Sargent to Eden, January 31, 1945, PREM 4.30/9.

be transformed by the collaborating Allies, at some indeterminate later date, into something closely resembling free American-style democracies – that really mattered. Conveyed to the president in the pre-Yalta briefing book, this pleasingly fashioned compendium of basic American values received little attention until Roosevelt introduced it at the conference on February 9. It then became the primary feature of the fresh diplomatic strategy – essentially a move from private to public diplomacy – and a key element in his presentation of Yalta to the American people and the world, establishing in the eyes of millions a code of correct conduct in Eastern Europe that the Soviets, to their cost, proved unwilling or unable to meet.

Why, it might be asked, was this potentially subversive declaration necessary when Roosevelt now already had Soviet agreement to the projected United Nations conference in San Francisco, acceptance of the American voting formula, and a seemingly reasonable deal on memberships? The answer, we must assume, was a lively appreciation in the president's mind that, given the disillusioned atmosphere in pre-Yalta America, conventional commitments of this kind were not enough. Here too there was a Wilsonian caution. President Wilson had brought home a fully developed League of Nations blueprint from Paris in 1919. But this had failed to stem the tide of postwar disenchantment. Roosevelt consequently felt the need, as he had told the British Labour politician, Harold Laski, to put matters "on a somewhat higher level." The situation therefore called not only for a new world organization but also for something more inspirational, capable both of clearing away the existing sour mood and, more positively, of functioning, much as the Atlantic Charter had done for the war years, as a beacon of hopeful aspiration, but now with the additional, more specific focus appropriate to a mass constituency looking now for tangible proofs of the better world it had fought and sacrificed for.[49]

The second question is somewhat more problematic. Why, given the obvious revisionary potential of the Declaration in its application to the future of Poland and Eastern Europe, did Stalin accept it? The discussion following its introduction at the plenary meeting on February 9 suggests that initially its potential significance as some kind of revisionary instrument was lost on the two European leaders, perhaps because it was introduced just as Roosevelt and Stettinius were backing down on the Polish issue. The retreat was visible to all, both to the gratified Soviets and to the shaken British. They saw the retreat and missed the significance of the new, seemingly only rhetorical front being opened by the Americans. Yet there

[49] Roosevelt to Laski, January 16, 1945, cited in Hathaway, *Ambiguous Partnership*, p. 117.

had been earlier, if rather delicate and obscure, warnings. At the foreign ministers meeting that morning Stettinius, even as he abandoned the short-lived American campaign for a Presidential Council in Poland and retreated to the notion of a "reorganized government," had told the Soviets that the president would feel "perfectly free" to make any statement he wished to the American people upon receiving reports from the American ambassador in Warsaw. This, in retrospect, appears to have been intended as a hint to the Soviets that, notwithstanding their unassailable, politico-military domination of Poland (and, by extension, of Eastern Europe) and their negotiating successes at Yalta, their conduct would – in the United States, at least – be expected to conform to some kind of as yet unspecified moral standard. And even as he tacitly acknowledged the carefully cultivated link between the Polish issues and the United Nations that lay at the heart of Stalin's "bargain" diplomacy, the secretary of state warned that the political decisions now being made should be considered "from the standpoint of psychology and public relations." He was in effect giving the Eastern Europe/United Nations "bargain" a new twist by warning that once the conference record emerged from the closed Big Three summit milieu it would confront an American and world opinion that would have strongly democratic expectations.[50]

These delicate reminders to the European foreign ministers that the Yalta decisions would have an unavoidable public dimension later on were then given a more explicit and dramatic airing at the February 9 plenary meeting a few hours later. Roosevelt had circulated the Declaration on liberated Europe earlier. Stalin reacted quietly, even referring approvingly to the document, though he immediately tried to turn its focus into more congenial channels by urging the addition of a phrase recommending support to political leaders "who have taken an active part in the struggle against the German invaders." Roosevelt ignored this suggestion but, stressing his desire to promote democratic values, made it clear that the Declaration "would of course apply to any areas or countries where needed as well as to Poland." He hoped that the Polish election would be the first practical implementation of the Declaration. In this, given what had gone before, Roosevelt may seem to have been disingenuous, even naïve. But his principal purpose, as he made clear, was simply to help win support for the various Yalta conclusions in the United States. To that end he emphasized the European-wide character of the document by abandoning at the last minute a plan for a

---

[50] Page minutes, foreign ministers meeting, February 9, 1945, FRUS, *Yalta*, p. 803. See also Page minutes, foreign ministers meeting, February 10, 1945, ibid., p. 872.

separate, potentially distracting "Declaration on Poland." There is no reason to believe that FDR was trying to lure the Soviets into some kind of
confrontation or trap on the basis of the divergent views on the Polish and
Eastern European issues that the Yalta conference (and previous events) had
unmistakably revealed. Indeed, the Declaration was primarily intended to
avoid any such clash by distracting American public attention from the realities of Yalta and by putting a pleasing gloss on these controversial matters that would enable Roosevelt to reanimate enthusiasm at home for the
United Nations and postwar internationalism generally.

Nevertheless, this precise targeting of the Declaration to the areas of highest Soviet concern, encourages one to speculate that Roosevelt wanted to put
the Soviets on notice first that he was not as naïve as he may have appeared,
and more tangibly that the Declaration, designed to function in the first
instance as a kind of reassuring coloration to decisions made earlier in the
conference that he knew would be controversial at home, could in its potential character of a violated treaty be quickly transformed in the tumultuous
arena of American public life into an instrument of political mobilization at
the option of the president, if matters went badly in Poland or elsewhere in
Eastern Europe. This is more or less what actually happened, as we will see.

It is not surprising, then, that the Soviets quickly came to see the
Declaration, at least potentially, had some sharp teeth. Molotov soon characterized it as the potentially revisionary political instrument that it in fact
was, one that might be used by the Western powers to justify interventions
in the Soviet sphere of influence. He consequently began a serious and sophisticated assault upon it. The document, he claimed, "amounted to interference in the affairs of liberated Europe." He raised numerous objections
and, following Stalin's lead, submitted amendments at the foreign ministers
meeting that were designed to convert the document into an instrument focused exclusively on preventing "fascists" taking power in postwar Europe.
Unobjectionable on its face, this was immediately seen by Eden not simply
as an attempt to favor leftist regimes but as a potential springboard to Soviet
hegemony not just in Eastern Europe (long since written off by the British)
but further west as well. It was indeed open to that interpretation and was
actually seen in that light later by several insecure Western European regimes
who feared Soviet intrusions on behalf of local leftists. Stettinius joined the
foreign secretary in opposing the inclusion of these antifascist maxims,
and, in the event, Molotov backed down. Always tenacious, however, he
then insisted, this time successfully, on converting the Declaration's original
charge to "immediately establish appropriate machinery for the carrying out
of the joint responsibilities set forth in this declaration" into an apparently

anodyne obligation "to take measures for the carrying out of mutual consultation" – in other words, to hold talks about talks.[51]

If the Soviet leaders were slow to see any danger in the now truncated Declaration on Liberated Europe it may have been because Churchill, supposedly alert at all times to any opportunity that might lead to American involvement in Europe and especially to an Anglo-American "front" against Soviet expansion, completely misunderstood its meaning. He saw the American formula, coming so soon after his similar misunderstanding over the supposed application to the British Empire of the trusteeship proposals for the projected United Nations, as another potential weapon in the arsenal of America's war against the British Empire. In a heated exchange with the president, he made it clear that he would accept the Declaration only "as long as it was clear that the reference to the Atlantic Charter did not apply to the British Empire." When he went on to say that he had explained his attitude to the late Wendell Willkie on the latter's visit to London, Roosevelt cryptically remarked, "Was that what killed him?"[52]

We might register in passing here that Churchill's response to the Declaration is a corrective to the view that the Yalta conference was an exclusively East/West political negotiation, or indeed a perceived preliminary to the Cold War. There were in retrospect tendencies in that direction, especially on the Polish issues. But the British had additional concerns, and Churchill's instinctive and passionate resistance to the Declaration reveals again the complex political currents now shaping relations among the Big Three. It illustrates the depth of resentment in Britain over their looming economic dependency upon an increasingly demanding America; their worries over the restoration of the empire and Britain's traditional status as a Great Power; and, more immediately, the persisting bad feeling over the Anglo-American confrontation only a few weeks before. Churchill's suspicions were far from fanciful. Only a few weeks earlier Stettinius had circulated in the State Department an endorsement of the idea that the proposed United Nations "trusteeship" responsibility should indeed include "all colonies."[53]

These two defensive European responses to the Declaration are significant. They demonstrate the varying sensitivities of the Europeans – the

---

[51] Ibid., p. 873. Early to Daniels, February 11, 1945, FRUS, *Yalta*, p. 976. Record of foreign secretaries meeting, February 9, 1945, WP (45) 157, CAB 66/63. Bohlen minutes of sixth plenary meeting, February 9, 1945, FRUS, *Yalta*, p. 848. One historian characterizes Molotius's intervention as a "Soviet intention to rig the vote" in Poland and elsewhere. Mastny, *Russia's Road*, p. 251.

[52] Bohlen Minutes, sixth plenary meeting, February 9, 1945, FRUS, *Yalta*, pp. 848–849.

[53] State Department, Paper on Dependent Territories n.d. Briefing Book, FRUS, *Yalta*, pp. 92–93.

tenacious British custodians of an old empire; the aspiring Soviet masters of a new Eastern European constellation that was rapidly becoming an empire in all but name – to the rising power of the United States and the uses to which they thought the Roosevelt administration, in communion with its supposedly malleable public opinion, might put that power. They reflect too the persisting gulf in understanding between the Europeans and the Americans. Moreover, these concerns were rooted in realistic perceptions. Rooseveltian America did indeed have certain designs on the British Empire and also hoped for at least the appearance of satisfactory solutions in Soviet-dominated Eastern Europe that were very different from the blueprints circulating in the Kremlin. Stalin and Molotov cannot, therefore, have seen the Declaration as quite the innocent instrument the president was making it out to be.

We return, then, to the nagging question. Why did the Soviets accept the Declaration, as they did after Molotov had effectively gutted it of any automatic executive functions? Perhaps we should look more broadly at Stalin's overall situation as the conference drew to a close. The claim of his recent biographer, Simon Sebag Montefiore, that "Stalin had won virtually all he wanted from the Allies" may sound excessive given all the qualifications and conditions with which many of his gains were now hedged. Yet it is true that Stalin had successfully resisted repeated attempts by Roosevelt and Churchill in the three days from February 6 to 9 to break down the Lublin regime and open up power in Poland to a wider constituency. Also, Eastern Europe, already largely under Soviet control, was never discussed – a diplomatic triumph of sorts, albeit for Stalin a negative one. The region had of course already been tacitly consigned to the Soviets by the British in conformity with the Moscow Order of October 1944, but the men in the Kremlin must have anticipated the possibility of complaints from the Americans, who were not previously bound. They were undoubtedly pleased to notice that FDR had focused obsessively on Poland alone and carefully ignored the wider region. Stalin also secured large gains in the Far East and various other welcome undertakings. It is not surprising, then, to find support for Montefiore's conclusion from another British historian, Geoffrey Roberts, whose recent study based on Soviet sources concludes that "Stalin had every reason to be pleased with the results of Yalta. On almost every policy issue the Soviet position had prevailed. ... The only major concession to western wishes was the Declaration on Liberated Europe."[54]

---

[54] Montefiore, *Stalin,* p. 494. Roberts, *Stalin's Wars,* p. 242.

But this "major concession" had, as it turned out, a profound impact on future events. Stalin can hardly be faulted for not seeing – as, with hindsight, we can today – the full consequences of his decision to accept the Declaration (and also the liberal wording in which the Polish part of the communiqué was deceptively couched), which began to reveal themselves only after the conferees had returned home. What did slowly emerge over the next year or so is that by giving his imprimatur to two fundamental elements in Roosevelt's diplomacy at Yalta, Stalin had done much to create conditions that in the end came together to propel the hither to politically detached United States into nearly half a century of confrontation with his country. The first was the agreement of the three powers to participate, largely on American terms, in the founding conference of the United Nations at San Francisco. Out of this would come the institution – in effect a kind of Court – within which future Soviet actions (most notably their military occupation of northern Iran, which brought on the transformative United States–Soviet clash in the Security Council in March 1946) would soon come to be judged by American and world opinion. The second was the president's high-principled Declaration on Liberated Europe – in effect a Code – by whose standards, largely derived from the Atlantic Charter, those actions would in the end be judged.

In retrospect one might well conclude that it was not Roosevelt but Stalin and Molotov who fell into the notorious "words" trap at Yalta. The charge that a naïve Roosevelt was systematically deceived by the Soviet resort to linguistic ambiguity at the conference is a familiar one. One can, to be sure, find evidence of that here and there in the record, for this was an international meeting where the participants often talked past each other and were prone to conceal their differences in diffuse language. But in surrendering crucial definitional authority to Roosevelt in this way – and this was clearly the designated function of the Declaration on Liberated Europe – Stalin was giving, whether he knew it or not, a dangerous hostage to fortune.

The truth is that he had little choice. For now the shoe was on the other foot. Stalin could hardly deny Roosevelt over the Declaration after all his own earlier protestations of commitment to "democracy" and "elections" and sovereign "independence" during the awkward discussions over Poland. Had he done so, all the masks would have fallen to the ground and the conference, in the success of which both of the two emerging superpowers clearly felt they had a vital and immediate stake, might well have broken up in failure. Stalin would then have lost not only the qualified but impressive gains he had achieved in the conventional phase of the conference, but also his more urgent objective: the projection to the world of that image of Allied "unity" he felt he needed to guide the Soviet Union through the potentially treacherous finale of the war with Germany, a cause that was probably as fundamentally important to him as the fashioning of a striking image of success at Yalta was to Roosevelt. Nevertheless, one is bound to assume that Stalin and Molotov saw some danger that the Declaration and the equally deceptive Polish agreement might, in the unpredictable hands of the Americans, become a rogue element in the developing post-Yalta scenario. And that, indeed, is precisely what happened.

As to Soviet motives, we have some authoritative Soviet evidence in a 1975 recollection by an aging Molotov:

> We signed a very important declaration at the Yalta conference in 1945, on the liberation of the peoples of Europe. A magnificent declaration. Stalin treated it warily from the outset. The Americans submitted a draft. I brought it to Stalin and said, "This is going too far!" "Don't worry," he said, "work it out. We can deal with it in our own way later. The point is the correlation of forces." It was to our benefit to stay allied to America. It was important.[55]

The Presentation

Having secured the Declaration on Liberated Europe and the extensive liberal moralizing in the communiqué and the texts of the published agreements promising freedom, independence, and democracy for Poland, Roosevelt moved to the next stage of what appears to have been a carefully planned design, which was to send a high-ranking official home from Yalta early enough to put the president's definitional stamp on the conference for Congress and the American people.

This was James F. Byrnes's moment. A former United States senator, Supreme Court justice, and the man widely known for his wartime services in Washington (he was now director of the Office of War Mobilization) as FDR's "assistant president," Byrnes had little diplomatic experience, but he was intelligent and influential in Washington. The historian Robert Messer has persuasively traced his Yalta experience. This adept communicator was taken to the Crimea, given a very selective view of the proceedings there, and then sent home early, on February 10, so that his arrival in Washington would closely coincide with the publication of the conference communiqué. He immediately called a press conference that was packed with news-starved reporters eager to get the unique first-hand account.

---

[55] Resis (ed.), *Molotov Remembers*, p. 51.

Byrnes gave a bravura performance, which Messer has aptly called "his very personalized and often inaccurate version of the meaning of Yalta."[56]

Byrnes focused on the president's outstanding leadership and what he portrayed as Roosevelt's two great Yalta achievements. One, understandably, was the United Nations voting rights formula and the anticipated founding conference. This was crucial given the need for congressional acceptance of American membership in the world organization. Byrnes, with his strong congressional associations, was the perfect agent in this respect. The other was the Declaration on Liberated Europe, which he characterized as "of the greatest importance." He presented it, not as an inspired statement of good intentions, but rather as a concrete decision and commitment by the three powers to establish by "free and unfettered elections" independent governments throughout liberated Europe, clearly including Poland and all the Soviet-held areas. The Polish settlement, which Stalin had shaped skillfully to his advantage in the traditional negotiating phase of Yalta, was now fundamentally distorted by being firmly harnessed to this universalistic scenario. Citing what he called Roosevelt's "personal solution," Byrnes said the Polish agreement would be the first specific application of the Declaration's general progressive principles. Moreover, "the three powers are going to preserve order until the provisional government is established and elections held."

There was to be no turbulence or revolutionary activity in the face of this tripartite unanimity. The new agreements also spelled out, Byrnes stressed, both the elimination of the exclusive spheres of influence in Europe that had agitated American opinion to this point and the satisfying vindication of the Wilsonian principle of self-determination and the application of American principles to the rest of the world. And presiding over it all, he declared triumphantly, would be the new United States–designed world organization, soon to be launched on a tide of Great Power influence and goodwill.[57]

Unfortunately, this image making was for the most part an exercise in wish fulfillment. Churchill later called the Declaration on which it was largely based "a fraudulent prospectus." Roosevelt had indeed got the United Nations voting rights agreement he wanted. But in return he had basically conceded not just the Curzon Line but also the governmental issue in Poland to Stalin, accepting a "reorganized" Lublin regime that

---

[56] For Byrnes's projected and actual role, see Messer, *End of an Alliance*, pp. 39–52. For Roosevelt's preparations, see FRUS, *Yalta*, pp. 3–40, and Chapter 5 of this volume.

[57] For the press conference, see *New York Times*, February 14, 1945.

would soon hold unsupervised elections. He had at no point confronted Stalin over Eastern Europe, which was never even discussed at Yalta. No Allied "action" was contemplated in the region under the Declaration, only "consultations," and those only in the unlikely event that all three powers thought them necessary. Further, for all its generalizing rhetoric the Declaration had nothing to do with the contrasting detail of the Polish agreement, which had been substantially settled before the Declaration was even introduced. It is true that FDR had received Stalin's assurances about Soviet entry into the Pacific war, but only on what were almost certainly unnecessarily humbling terms that would have seriously undermined Byrnes's rosy account had they been publicly revealed. But none of this seems to have mattered to Byrnes or Roosevelt. Both were fully focused on creating the desired impression. Carefully monitoring Byrnes's efforts as he traveled home by sea in leisurely fashion, the president cabled his congratulations on Byrnes's "magnificent" performance, noting that "your press conferences have been grand."[58]

They undoubtedly produced the desired effect. Byrnes spent the first few days after his arrival energetically lobbying a very receptive Congress, addressing an estimated two-thirds of the membership. Meanwhile, the American press erupted in a collective hosanna to Roosevelt's apparent success. Approval rippled across the ideological spectrum – from the communist *Daily Worker,* to the leftist New York daily *PM*, and on further through the liberal *New York Times* to the *New York Herald Tribune* and *Time* on the moderate internationalist right. Herbert Hoover saw in Byrnes's version of Yalta "a strong foundation from which to rebuild the world." A chorus of bipartisan enthusiasm emerged from Congress, with the Senate majority leader, Alben Barkley, viewing the conference as "a source of great gratification," and his Republican counterpart declaring that "a great work has been done." Even Vandenberg, unhappy for his Polish constituents, seemed receptive to Byrnes's private explanations. The enthusiasm was immediately reflected in general opinion. A poll on February 20 showed only 9% viewing Yalta's results as "unfavorable" to American interests.[59]

---

[58] Memorandum for the president from Byrnes, February 17, 1945, Folder 92, and memorandum from the president to Byrnes, February 26, 1945, Folder 622, Byrnes MSS, Clemson University, Clemson, North Carolina.

[59] See *New York Times, New York Herald Tribune,* and *Daily Worker*, all February 14, 1945. See also *The Nation*, 175 (February 17, 1945), pp. 169–170; *The New Republic*, 112 (February 19, 1945), pp. 243–244; and *Time*, February 19, 1945. Messer, *End of an Alliance*, pp. 61–64.

Meanwhile, Roosevelt, having brought the conference to an abrupt conclusion – both Churchill and Stain had wanted to extend it – was finding the return from the Crimea almost as arduous as the inward journey. There were now two badly planned drives to his exit point, where his fighter escort began by escorting the wrong plane. Harry Hopkins had been promised a special train but was unable to identify himself at the station and had to spend the night in a squalid baggage car with a handful of sunflower seeds for dinner. Stettinius, on a quick and apparently inconsequential trip to Moscow, found his sleep at the American embassy interrupted by an exploding water boiler. Things looked up for FDR when he reached Cairo, where, very much the rising potentate, he bestowed gifts and received flattering tributes from three kings (Farouk, Ibn Saud, and Haile Selassie) among other Middle Eastern leaders. Churchill then arrived to bear anxious witness to the changing allegiances now on display in this traditionally British sphere. But as the USS *Quincy* swept triumphantly westward, the president met the political equivalent of a leveling wind. De Gaulle ostentatiously refused his invitation to meet on French soil. Hopkins, relied on for help in drafting the report to Congress, fell ill again and left the ship. A cherished presidential aide, "Pa" Watson, died suddenly. There may also have been a narrow escape. According to British news reports, police in Ceuta, across from Gibraltar, discovered in timely fashion a German U-boat lookout post supposedly on watch for the ship as it passed through the Straits.[60]

Once home, however, with Byrnes having so adeptly set the stage, Roosevelt was able to make a triumphant appearance before Congress on March 1. In the two-week gap between Byrnes's press conference in mid-February and Roosevelt's long-delayed arrival by sea on February 28, State Department concern that the enthusiasm would get out of hand led Acting Secretary of State Joseph Grew to warn, in a statement released on February 18, "We must seek what is desirable within the realm of the attainable," remembering "the almost insuperable difficulties and controversies attendant upon the framing and adoption of our own Constitution." And indeed, by the end of the month some second thoughts had inevitably begun to temper the general enthusiasm. Leading Polish figures in Britain and the United States had from the outset condemned the Yalta settlement, taking their lead from the London exile government, which had immediately declared that it would have no part of the "reorganized" regime.

[60] Kathleen Harriman letter, February 16, 1945, Box 176, Harriman MSS. Kimball, *Forged in War*, pp. 318–319.

But while these reactions attracted sympathetic comment in Britain, they had comparatively little impact in the United States, where Byrnes's carefully contrived optimism was still holding up well in American opinion. Nevertheless, doubts were creeping in, and Churchill's report to Parliament on February 27, a day before Roosevelt's address, was generally hopeful but far from euphoric in the Byrnes mode and pointedly expressed continuing anxiety over Poland's fate.[61]

Roosevelt received an ovation and, despite concern aroused by his haggard appearance and his apology for having to deliver his speech sitting down, his presentation was politically successful. For the most part he followed the path of unqualified optimism first set out by Hull and himself in 1943 after the first tripartite conferences and now – as he must have hoped – in its post-Yalta application swept free of intervening doubts by Byrnes's unvarnished triumphalism. The conference, he declared, "ought to spell the end of the system of unilateral action, the exclusive alliances, the spheres of influence, the balances of power and all the other expedients that have been tried for centuries – and have always failed." He stressed the United Nations achievement, with all its hopeful portents. What Yalta had achieved, he said, was the foundation for a lasting peace settlement based on Atlantic Charter principles. The Declaration on Liberated Europe had arrested the dangerous trend toward spheres of influence, which, "if allowed to go unchecked … might have tragic results." The Polish agreement was also characterized in rosy terms as "the most hopeful agreement possible for a free, independent and prosperous Polish state." However dubious in its political judgments, the president's association of Big Three political unity, the prospective United Nations as world problem solver, and the animating ideals of a vindicated Atlantic Charter was irresistibly attractive. He enjoyed a considerable media and public success, manifest in a crop of positive polls reflecting general approval.

At the same time there was a significant tempering, even philosophic note in Roosevelt's generally upbeat speech that reflects a concern to moderate the dangerous excitement Byrnes had stirred up and perhaps hints tantalizingly at deeper personal sentiments. We know Roosevelt had realistic political concerns over Poland and other issues at the time. Now he emphasized the need for the American people and Congress to actively support the peace arrangements. He again counseled against "perfectionism" and echoed Grew's stress on the evolutionary character of

---

[61] *New York Times*, February 18, 19 and March 1, 1945.

the peacemaking process, referring to the travails of the Founding Fathers as they had moved uncertainly, but with eventual fulfilment, toward the American Constitution. In all this he was able, without deflating the public optimism, to catch the note of more sober hopefulness now beginning to characterize the columns of the nation's more reflective editorialists and pundits. Yalta was still, at least for the moment, a great public success in the United States.[62]

We are not yet at the end of "Yalta" as we have defined it here – that is, as a three-stage, politically transformative event encompassing the preparation for the meeting, the conference itself, and finally the aftermath of crisis to which we will now turn. But we have already seen enough, perhaps, to question the charge that this was not a significant event. The historian examining the record today is perhaps more likely to think that Yalta's loose ends, numerous qualified undertakings, and ambiguous semantics were bound to cause trouble. This would have mattered less if the Big Three had not treated Yalta as a "peace conference" – that is, as an attempt to solve prematurely problems best left for calmer postwar deliberation. It might have mattered less, too, if the United States had remained, as it did after the much more general discussions of the 1943 Teheran conference, essentially detached from European politics. But the expansive margins of time and space in which loose commitments could be made without serious consequences had now passed.

How then do we explain Yalta? One strategy is to emphasize the more or less successful settlement of outstanding issues – the United Nations and the fate of Lublin prominent among them. But the almost immediate post-Yalta breakdown puts that in question and inclines one to look for deeper impulses. We find them in the shared concern of the American and Soviet delegates to bring about, at almost any cost, a harmonious outcome that could be exhibited to an expectant world. Roosevelt needed something inspirational to revive support for international engagement and the United Nations project in the United States; Stalin wanted a convincing display of continuing unity to discourage the Germans and head off the danger of Allied betrayal. They therefore refrained from any deep probing of the sensitive United Nations and Polish issues, putting Churchill's feistier performance in sharp relief. Roosevelt and Stalin knew they had not settled these basic problems, which resurfaced in a more dangerous

---

[62] For the speech, see FDR, *Public Papers*, XIII: pp. 570–586. Dallek, *Roosevelt and American Foreign Policy*, p. 520. For a recording, see Henry Steele Commager (ed.), *FDR Speaks* (Washington, D.C., 1960), side 12.

form within days of the conference. As FDR told Admiral Leahy, when the latter pointed out the elasticity of a Polish agreement that could be interpreted in different ways, "I know it, Bill. I know it. But it's the best I can do for Poland at this time." Similarly, one thinks of Stalin's calmly dismissive response to Molotov's concerns about the destructive potential of the Declaration on Liberated Europe for Soviet aims in Eastern Europe. "The point is the correlation of forces."[63]

We have still to examine the politico-diplomatic aftermath of Yalta. Only then can we hope to gain a fuller understanding of the event's significance and specifically of its relation to the Cold War's origins. But a few comments seem appropriate here. It is immediately apparent, for instance, that in trying to solve his pre-Yalta dilemma – essentially by playing up to the public opinion upon which American postwar internationalism depended – Roosevelt had in effect created a predicament for Stalin. The Soviet leader, focused on the negotiation, appears to have hoped by means of his "bargain" approach to their relationship to get from Roosevelt something of the same collaborative support, or at least understanding, that he had received from Churchill. As we will see, he would twice in the weeks after Yalta disrupt American United Nations plans when challenged on the Polish governmental issue. Meanwhile, thanks to the political embroidery now being spread around the world from Washington, he was now presented with a hard choice. He could try to live up to the liberal image for which FDR's distortions had improbably cast him – the benign architect of a progressive arena in Eastern and Central Europe – or, by continuing on his existing path, he could tell the world he was rejecting that role, running the risk that this would bring the Soviet Union into international opprobrium and at some point into a serious confrontation with the United States. His behaviour in the weeks after Yalta, when he carefully made known his resentment over the Anglo-American interpretations of the conference results while at the same time maintaining the minimal commitment to cooperation he needed in order to navigate the war's dangerous final stages, suggests some recognition on his part that the Soviet Union and the United States had not yet stepped far away from the looming collision course that had brought them to Yalta.

When that collision came – in March–April 1946 – it was indeed due in some large degree to the public disenchantment that had grown in the United States over the intervening year, as the refusal or inability of the

---

[63] Leahy, *I Was There,* pp. 315–316. Resis (ed.), *Molotov Remembers,* p. 51.

Soviet government to live up to anything resembling the Rooseveltian vision had become ever more evident. When we look for more specific causation, however, we find much of it in three structural changes in the relationship of the three powers. Each of these can be traced directly to the Yalta conference and its immediate aftermath.

First, the United States, looking ahead to the coming peace, had engaged itself at Yalta very substantially with Europe's future. This was a repudiation, not only of George Washington's formidable injunction against "entanglements," but also of the detachment FDR himself had carefully maintained up to this point from the European postwar scenario that had long been developing in the hands of the custodial Anglo-Soviet partnership we have been following. The reorientation came very quickly. Just weeks before Yalta, Roosevelt had reaffirmed his commitment to that traditional, hands-off approach, making it clear that he was determined to confine himself at the forthcoming meeting to the treatment of postwar Germany, which he envisioned as some degree of enforced impoverishment. When domestic pressures aroused by violent Anglo-Soviet action and the Lublin imbroglio subsequently obliged him to contemplate a broader and more energized diplomacy in the Crimea, he did not reach out for guidance but kept his own counsel, simply assuring his aides that he would settle everything with Stalin. Once he was at Yalta, however, FDR made sweeping connections, perhaps far beyond his original intentions. By virtue of his now clearly expressed intention to participate fully in the postwar treatment of Germany; his sponsorship of the Declaration on Liberated Europe, with that document's proclaimed responsibilities for the whole continent; and his public commitment to Polish independence and to participation in the ambassadorial commission that seemed to have been set up to bring this about, Roosevelt took the historic step at Yalta of attaching the United States to Europe's political, economic, and social future, boldly taking in some of the most dangerous and potentially controversial issues now presenting themselves.

Second, the Soviets also moved forward at Yalta. Their projection was made with similar reluctance, reflecting the high price each government was willing to pay to extend some semblance of a cooperative relationship into the postwar era. There was, however, a major difference in the Soviets' move. For the new arena they were entering was not territorial like the American projection into Europe, but rather intangible, though deeply political and judicial. Specifically, the Soviet Union, thanks to its apparent public compromises on the loosely framed Polish settlement and its commitment to the liberal Declaration and, at least prospectively, to the developing United Nations, was now well on the way to its own entanglement, not in conventional American politics, certainly, but in an American-shaped web of moral codes and opinion-molding institutions that, in one way or another, could be mobilized with world opinion to pass judgment upon its conduct in the regions under its control. For behind the moral imperatives of the Atlantic Charter there now lay the more tangible commitments of the Declaration on Liberated Europe. And behind the Declaration there now stood the institutional promise of a functioning United Nations and Security Council. In effect, the liberal international community, under American leadership, was now arming itself with both a Court and a Code. Within fourteen months, this seemingly innocent judicial-political mechanism – the epitome of Enlightenment rationalism – would be instrumental in turning United States–Soviet relations into a full confrontation.

This interpenetration of each other's cherished political arenas, tentative and embryonic though it clearly was in February 1945, and hedged about on both sides with protective qualifications, opened up a new political context that was bound over time to become more intimate and probably more dangerous. United States–Soviet relations would now be more, not less, focused upon the working out of the still largely unresolved and ill-defined United Nations–Eastern Europe dichotomy and its immediately pressing Polish flash point. And in general the two emerging hegemonic powers, no longer operating at arm's length, would naturally became more aware of each other. They were now bound, especially during the agonizingly slow unravelling of the ambiguities of Yalta, to watch each other much more closely than before, and in all probability they were likely, given the slow but steady reappearance of ideological differences that had been carefully submerged during the war against Germany, to work on each other abrasively. For Yalta's abundant misunderstandings, and especially the contrast between the political reality and the public image of what had happened there, had left many hostages to the immediate future. These were likely, especially in the context of the war's last, dangerous stages and the ever-closer scrutiny of the American and world press, to cause trouble for the three Great Powers.

Nevertheless, a United States–Soviet confrontation on the Cold War scale was by no means inevitable in early 1945. The tensions associated with the Dumbarton Oaks formulas and the emergence of Lublin – reflecting the supposed incompatibility between "universalism" and a "spheres" approach – were still only embryonic at that point and in the succeeding months were overshadowed, in the public domain at least, by the war's exciting last stages. And although there were difficult moments and some frank official discussions later as Europe began its difficult transition to peacetime order, there was no really dangerous bilateral confrontation between the two emerging powers before the decisive one that occurred in early 1946, almost exactly a year later. Neither government – nor American opinion, for that matter – appears to have wanted a Cold War. The convention of public cordiality was carefully maintained at the official level. And, most importantly, the two countries had no actual or historical clash of interests or point of sensitive contact to argue over. As the chief American military representative in Moscow said, in a harsh critique of Soviet conduct he sent home before Yalta, "We have few conflicting interests and there is little reason why we should not be friendly now and in the foreseeable future." How is it, then, that these two countries fell out so decisively only a year after the Yalta conference?[64]

As we turn to grapple briefly with that profound issue we will find ourselves looking back, not only to the new currents initiated at Yalta by the American engagement with Europe and the looming Soviet encounter with the coils of Dumbarton internationalism, but also to the third and more immediately destabilizing of Yalta's main outcomes. This was the breakdown of the long-anticipated political framework for postwar Europe: the Anglo-Soviet collaboration that had been built up since December 1941, achieving some quasi-institutional form in the Anglo-Soviet treaty negotiations of 1942, and consolidated in the Moscow Order of October 1944. That settlement, it will be recalled, had two aspects. One was a territorial division of Europe that was never seriously discussed at Yalta and, in tribute to the power realities, was destined to outlast all disruptions for nearly half a century. The other, much more vulnerable dimension of the Moscow Order was the directing Anglo-Soviet political partnership. This we have already seen beginning, with the return of the Americans to Europe in the lead-up to Yalta and at the conference itself, to show some fraying at the edges, though it remained substantially intact as the delegates departed. But then, as Americans (and some, but by no means all, Europeans) continued to celebrate the apparent successes of Yalta, the British leadership, particularly Churchill but also some leading Foreign Office figures, began to take a more transatlantic and less European view of what they saw as the new realities, and gradually aligned themselves with the Rooseveltian rather than the Soviet version of the Crimean decisions,

---

[64] Deane to Marshall, December 2, 1944, FRUS, *Yalta*, p. 447–449.

a step that was quickly registered in Moscow and led two British governments into a rapidly escalating confrontation with the Soviet Union that
soon spilled over into the Mediterranean and the Near East, creating by
early 1946 what we may reasonably call "a first Cold War."

The effect of this new Anglo-Soviet confrontation, and of this whole
post-Yalta reorientation, was therefore to stimulate and elevate the hitherto subordinated East/West dimension of Big Three diplomacy. And in
proportion as this occurred (though it was hastened along too by a sudden decline in Western European self-confidence and solidarity, which
will require a separate explanation) we see the almost complete eclipse of
the Europe/American conception that, so far as Europe's future was concerned, had up to this moment guided the expectations of all three powers
and their numerous allies.

Britain then would not, after all, be the effective American shield or
surrogate in postwar Europe envisaged by Roosevelt at the Octagon conference in September 1944. Instead, caught in the confusing backwash of
the Yalta Disorder, alarmed by the rising strength and militance of their
erstwhile European partner, unsure that the Western bloc could be turned
into a viable balance to Soviet power, and tempted now to seek deliverance in the unanticipated but welcome American commitment at Yalta
to a more "responsible" role in Europe, the British reverted after Yalta
to a familiar role. They began again to see themselves and to function as
the corridor through which, now for a third time in three decades, the
United States might be invited to move forward to confront what its own
citizens – themselves now launched by Roosevelt on a year-long journey
from confusion to a degree of crystallized conviction – were slowly coming to view as the stricken continent's new hegemonic threat.

8

Aftermath

The great significant fact of the moment – the really big result of the Crimea – is that the Americans are committed, on paper at all events, to playing their part in Europe.

Piers Dixon, secretary to Anthony Eden, London, 1945

In Hungary, I am Yalta!

Kliment Voroshilov, chairman, Allied Control Commission, Budapest, 1945

President Roosevelt won his post-Yalta battle for American public support, and though the initial enthusiasm soon waned, it was enough to carry through to the San Francisco conference and the establishment of the United Nations in June 1945. In general, though, the divided Yalta he had created ushered in a year of dislocation and confusion among the Big Three, greatly exacerbated, unsurprisingly, by the turbulent last passages of the war. So far as Europe's postwar structure is concerned, we can justly frame this period by recalling that in January 1945 it seemed solidly set and accepted as being largely in the hands of a collaborating Britain and the Soviet Union, with a benevolent but still detached United States on the sideline. If we then jump ahead to, say, April 1946, we find the discernible if still somewhat embryonic foundations of another coherent line-up, with an Anglo-American nexus now confronting an alienated Soviet Union on a continent still divided along the lines established at Moscow in October 1944, an element of continuity. The challenge here, then, is to understand the complex intervening year (if we can have "long" and "short" centuries, we can surely have a "long" year), which began with the first consequences of Yalta's "disorder" and ended with the beginning of the Cold War.

It will help, in considering this transitional year, to keep one's eye on three distinct sets of political relations. The first is the United States–Soviet association, increasingly the central dynamic in international politics. This was, during the whole 1943–46 period, guided largely by sporadic attempts and finally by the failure of these two powers to fully reconcile their post-war preoccupations: the Rooseveltian United Nations project and Stalin's determination to control Eastern and Central Europe and the Northern Tier. The tensions generated by these ultimately incompatible polarities – mild enough before Yalta, but steadily more problematic thereafter – finally erupted with transformative political and geopolitical results in early 1946.

But this was still a three-power arena. For these rising difficulties between the emergent superpowers should not be seen in isolation from the other two relationships with which they were at almost every stage interwoven and interrelated. The second association to watch, then, is the Anglo-Soviet nexus, which began to break down in the new context created by Yalta and its aftermath, and had by the end of 1945 turned into a sharp-edged confrontation over the fate of Europe and its environs. The third is the Anglo-American relation, characterized on the British side after Yalta by the varied efforts of Churchill, and later of the Labour government that took office in the summer of 1945, to draw the United States to its aid in that developing geopolitical struggle, and on the American side by what was, on the whole, a traditional and continuing reluctance to let that happen.

Many people at the time experienced 1945 as a series of military triumphs tempered by a growing sense of political disillusionment. At the level of high politics and decision making, however, the transition from war to Cold War is marked recognizably by two crises. The first, arising out of the tensions between the Western powers and the Soviet Union that followed the Yalta conference, was mainly diplomatic and largely shrouded in wartime secrecy. It ran roughly from February through May 1945. It arose directly from the two incompatible versions of what Yalta meant. At a practical level, it registered the entry of the United States into European affairs made explicit at Yalta; its unprecedented, though brief, collaboration with Britain against the Soviet Union; and the end of the Anglo-Soviet concert in Europe. This crisis was not the beginning of the Cold War, but it did bring about the sharp waning, if not the collapse, of the Grand Alliance as a cooperative enterprise.

By the beginning of June a degree of revived United States–Soviet collaboration is evident, manifest most obviously in the third great summit of the era, the Potsdam conference, that followed in July. Nevertheless, the post-Yalta crisis gave rise to the conditions through which the Cold War would come about. The conclusive denouement came during a second burst of acute tension early in 1946, when, after a comparative lull, another crisis erupted. This one, initially geopolitical and much more public in character, was engendered by a perceived Soviet expansionary thrust toward Iran, Greece, and Turkey, then intensified by Churchill's "Iron Curtain" speech in March, and finally crystallized by the ensuing United Nations Security Council confrontation between the United States and the Soviet Union over the latter's persisting occupation of northern Iran. That second confrontation, with its sudden and fateful convergence of European geopolitics and American universalism, established the United Nations as a functioning instrument of American power and had from the start a much more sharply defined East/West character. It brought on the Cold War.

THE BREAKDOWN OF THE GRAND ALLIANCE: THE POST-YALTA CRISIS

None of this seemed likely in Yalta's immediate aftermath. The apparent reality of a harmonious summit conference, conjured up by the artful image making of James F. Byrnes and then of President Roosevelt, briefly created a widespread sense of euphoria. This is hardly surprising. Many pre-Yalta anxieties – in Europe about the commitment to international cooperation of the United States, and in America about the ability of the Europeans to behave decently – were now allayed if not entirely dissolved. More surprisingly, perhaps, the three leaders themselves, in their private remarks, expressed some initial, apparently genuine optimism. Roosevelt gave an upbeat assessment to his associates. Churchill was more guarded but was similarly positive about Stalin, famously saying, "Neville Chamberlain was wrong about Hitler, but I don't think I am wrong about Stalin." And Stalin himself, asked by Marshal Zhukov how the conference had gone, expressed satisfaction and remarked that Roosevelt had been "very friendly."[1]

It may seem logical now to follow the conventional course and, having reviewed the American reaction, move without interruption to the Soviet response to Yalta and its presentational aftermath. But that would be to fall prematurely into the familiar bilateral conception of the period, which focuses almost exclusively on United States–Soviet relations. In fact, the

---

[1] Dallek, *Roosevelt and American Foreign Policy*, p. 521; Moran, *Churchill*, p. 280; Dalton diary, February 23, 1945; *The Memoirs of Marshal Zhukov* (New York, 1971), p. 582.

full Soviet reaction took some time to show itself and was preceded, and appears to some extent to have been prompted, by a significant but often overlooked Churchillian initiative. It therefore seems best to approach that reaction, which was of course crucial, from a broader perspective and consider it in the context not only of Rooseveltian manipulation but also of a European response to Yalta that was by no means as upbeat as the contrived optimism in the United States.

The development that really pleased the British for instance, was not the specific tally of decisions, much less the vision of postwar harmony conjured up in the United States. It was the apparent reality that the United States had, for the first time, committed itself to a promisingly extensive role in European affairs. As Churchill told the House of Commons, "The United States has entered deeply and constructively into the life and salvation of Europe." It was this that inspired Piers Dixon to call the apparent American commitment "the really big result of the Crimea."[2] Such sentiments were widespread in diplomatic circles. Another Foreign Office commentator noted, "Our most optimistic expectations as to the outlook for American cooperation in the political sphere have been more that realized." Ambassador Halifax cabled similarly from Washington, "To have the American public believe that Yalta was 'an American success' would be a cheap price to pay for acceptance of American participation in the settlement of European problems."[3]

Yet, despite all these positive reactions, trouble came. As so often during the war, Churchill's responses offer a good guide to the developing problems. He continued, in the days after Yalta, to receive a steady stream of intelligence reports telling of Soviet and Lublin excesses in Poland, and of persisting European and Mediterranean anxieties, which he shared, about the danger of Soviet expansionism and the character of the enigmatic Yalta agreements. Always much more sensitive to these impulses than Roosevelt, he was also aware, as he prepared his speech to Parliament scheduled for February 27, that European views of the conference were by no means as upbeat as the contrived optimism in the United States.

The press and public reaction in Britain was rather mixed. Here too there was praise, or at least satisfaction, from *The Times*, the *Daily Express*, and most of the other daily newspapers, especially those that had consistently

---

[2] Parliamentary debates (Commons), 5th. series, Vol. 408 (1944–45), pp. 1283–84. Dixon diary, March 3, 1945; Dixon MSS.

[3] Halifax to Eden, February 17, 1945, F.O. 371.50838. Donnelly memorandum, February, 24, 1945, U1247, F.O. 371.50838.

championed the Anglo-Soviet relationship. As usual, Churchill received accolades from his inner circle. Beaverbrook sent word that the British people now regarded him as a great, creative statesman. Bracken, the minister of information, wrote to him, "The whole British press acclaim the results." This was not strictly true. There was some skepticism in liberal papers like the *Manchester Guardian*. The leftist *Tribune* suggested that Churchill, for all his "romantic strutting and political exhibitionism," was no longer "influential." There was serious criticism in Scotland, where Polish troops had been based and were popular, and in the Conservative Party. This last consideration doubtless weighed with Churchill, who had now to think about the likelihood of a general election. He was soon to be jolted too by criticism from the Dominion prime ministers, who came to London for a conference in the early spring. The New Zealand prime minister, Peter Fraser, raised serious doubts about the efficacy of the pledges given to Poland. Churchill conceded that "the force" of these criticisms was "inescapable" but pointed out, as he regularly did after Yalta, that "we cannot go further in helping Poland than the United States is willing or is prepared to go."[4]

British observers, monitoring a wide range of foreign radio and press, found little rejoicing in continental Europe. The increasingly desperate Germans inevitably played up what they portrayed vigorously as Stalin's victory over the Western Allies, who were seen as having "swallowed Lublin whole." Churchill was blamed for betraying Europe to Bolshevism. Ribbentrop told the Japanese ambassador in Berlin that he could understand American policy, "for if she let Europe be trampled down … American capitalism could swagger about the world like a lord, but what future Britain saw for herself in a situation which was merely bolshevizing Europe and increasing her own dependence on America he could not for the life of him understand." These were quite representative right-wing sentiments. The Spanish media regretfully noted "concessions" to Stalin, and a diplomatic observer in Lisbon found Portuguese opinion believing that "Great Britian has abandoned all the European countries to Russian influence." Meanwhile, there was acute anxiety around the vast non-European Soviet periphery. The Turks were deeply worried again. The Chinese, acutely suspicious, were now comparing notes with hapless Polish officials. And the observant Japanese missions in their European outposts – Berlin,

---

[4] Bracken to Churchill, February, 14, 1945, PREM 3.385; Beaverbrook to Churchill, February 14, 1945, ibid.; *The Times, Daily Express,* and *Tribune,* all February 15, 1945; *Manchester Guardian,* February 28, 1945.

Moscow, Bern, Madrid, and Stockholm – sent home a stream of messages describing public concern in Europe about rising Soviet political as well as military power.[5]

The Western Europeans, confused in the wake of Yalta, were now beginning to have doubts about a British-led "Western bloc." There was concern in Italy and the Benelux countries that the Declaration on Liberated Europe was not the commitment to the establishment of liberal democracies in Eastern Europe that Roosevelt had celebrated but actually a license for Soviet/communist interference in their affairs and for political and perhaps even military intervention in Western Europe. Thus, on February 19, a Dutch official informed the Foreign Office of his fear that the Soviets would use the Declaration to force communist representatives into his government. Similar inquiries came on February 22 from Italian officials, also fearful of domestic communist pressure. On the other hand, the French ambassador in London, M. Massigli, somewhat more insightfully interpreting the Declaration as a potential instrument of Western diplomacy, called at the Foreign Office to ask the more congenial question: "Would the Declaration apply to Poland?"[6]

There was now, after this American political intrusion into Europe, a certain turn to transatlantic thinking that naturally fostered these second thoughts. The new American undertakings (there were now well over three million American soldiers in Europe) and Roosevelt's enthusiastic sponsorship of a United Nations were perhaps bound to undermine the earlier faith in purely European solutions. Other factors contributed to post-Yalta reconsiderations. One was the erosion of effective leadership. Even before Yalta, Churchill had begun to turn away from his late 1944 European activism toward the renewed Anglo-American possibilities opened up by the provoking Soviet sponsorship of the Lublin regime. Disappointed by the American performance in the Crimea, Churchill did not respond, as he had after Teheran, by turning back toward Europe. Instead, he came quickly to see in Yalta's Rooseveltian commitments a fresh opportunity to effect a meaningful fusion with the United States. De Gaulle was also turning away from the late 1944 solidarity that had drawn the Western European states together. He delivered a highly publicized radio broadcast during the Yalta conference proclaiming that France, having been

---

[5] British intelligence files, HW1/3559 (Germany); HW1/3651 (Spain); HW1/3542 (Portugal); HW1/3711 (Turkey); HW1/3586 (China); and HW1/3641, 3674, 3678, 3682, 3683, and 3713 (Japan).

[6] Ward memorandum, February 18, 1945, U1331; Cadogan minute, February 22, 1945, U1396; Harvey minute, February 19, 1945, U1332, all in F.O. 371.50835.

excluded, would not be bound by its decisions and would follow an independent line. His resentful unilateralism raised general concern about the future course of the French government, whose partnership with Britain in any credible Western European grouping was recognized by nearly all observers as essential to its success. De Gaulle's conduct, ostentatiously devoted to France's "own interests," predictably infuriated Churchill and, notwithstanding his earlier efforts at Yalta on behalf of the French, inspired him now to resist all calls by Duff Cooper and other Francophiles in the Foreign Office and elsewhere for an alliance or indeed any liaison with de Gaulle's government.[7]

Meanwhile, the lesser Western European states were drifting away, exasperated with the Anglo-French quarrels and now attracted, as all the Western European chancelleries were after Yalta, by the new American alternative centered on the forthcoming San Francisco conference and the proposed world organization. Not all this diminishing geopolitical solidarity can be traced to political calculations, or even to Yalta itself. Indeed, the most compelling factor in liberated Western Europe early in 1945 was the specter of starvation, mass illness, and irremediable unemployment. But here too it was the United States, with its control of shipping and much of the needed supplies, that gave the only real hope of relief. The French, Italian, Dutch, and Belgian governments were now desperately preoccupied with inadequate food supplies, internal and regional transportation problems, refugee issues, and all the only partially anticipated socioeconomic dislocations brought on by the war's climactic miseries. All these regimes were confronted with severe problems of reconstruction and almost complete industrial breakdown. For the moment, at least, survival trumped geopolitical security. Many still worried about communist fifth columns and internal subversion generally. But the Soviet Union and the Red Army seemed, at least for the moment, much less threatening after the Yalta meeting. There was, therefore, neither the time nor the inclination now for the contemplation or creation of elaborate security scenarios.[8]

Churchill, however, was still focused on the Soviet threat. As he prepared his speech for Parliament he must have been conscious of several divergent but ominous impulses. He was bound, of course, as one of the Yalta principals, to put an optimistic face on the conference. On the whole he did so, drawing the attention of the House of Commons on February 27 to the solidarity of the three Allied powers, their continuing collaboration

---

[7] HW1/3528 (France). Churchill to Eden, April 5, 1945, FO 954/9.
[8] Normanbrook notes, Cabinet meeting, March 22, 1945, WM (45) 35th conclusions.

toward military victory, and the plans they had formed for the reduction of German power, including industrial dismantlement (though not of anything like Morgenthau proportions), de-Nazification, punishment of war crimes, and reparations. And there were references to other harmonious agreements and warm tributes to the American and Soviet allies. But the focus of Churchill's remarks (which were all the more resonant with the world audience because they were delivered two days in advance of Roosevelt's speech) and of his genuine concern, as we can see from his private conversations during this period, was the future Soviet attitude toward Europe in general and Poland in particular. He defended the Curzon Line decision, while acknowledging the understandable anguish of the Poles. He then came to the point:

The home of the Poles is settled. Are they to be masters in their own house? Are they to be free, as we in Britain and the United States are free? Are their sovereignty and their independence to be untrammeled, or are they to become a mere projection of the Soviet state, forced against their will by an armed minority to adopt a Communist or totalitarian system. I am putting the case in all its bluntness.[9]

Indeed he was. True, Churchill went on to express his faith in Stalin's "solemn declarations" and in the Soviet government, "which stands to its own obligations even in its own despite." But behind the warm saving phrases the meaning was clear. Churchill was doing three potentially disruptive things. First, he was reminding the world that the Soviet Union was a "communist" and "totalitarian" state, breaking a wartime taboo on such references. Second, he was declaring that the Polish issue had not been resolved, contrary to the general impression now prevailing. And third, he was telling everyone that Stalin should be held strictly to account for the performance of the undertakings he had accepted, explicitly in the Polish agreement, but also implicitly in the Declaration on Liberated Europe. His definitional precision on this must have seemed to his summit partners to be bent on exposing publicly the profound differences rather than the illusory commonalities of Yalta. It may be premature to identify this as the first expression from an Allied leader of what we might call "Cold War rhetoric." But certainly there is a great contrast here with Roosevelt's soft optimism. By linking Stalin personally to the demanding liberal obligations and responsibilities of Yalta, Churchill was entrenching, in unmistakably dichotomous fashion, a contractually oriented commitment that he must have suspected would

---

[9] Parliamentary debates (Commons), 5th series, Vol. 408 (1944–45), pp. 1283–1284. For the full speech, see ibid., pp. 1267–1295.

not be, and perhaps could not be, honored by the architect of the Polish deportations and the Katyn massacres. For the effect of his starkly drawn polarities can only have been to register and finally lodge in people's minds, far more deeply than Roosevelt's evolutionary scenario, the two poles – freedom and "totalitarian" tyranny – around which tensions were likely to develop unless the Soviets demonstrated a genuine change of heart.

One must not, of course, ascribe excessively Machievellian motives to the prime minister. He now confronted genuine problems at home. He was himself, after all, one of the historically accountable "Men of Yalta." Soviet misconduct in Poland and elsewhere (of which he already had extensive private knowledge) was bound to lead to difficulties not only with the London Poles and their sympathizers (he was prepared for that) but also with many in the Conservative Party and the country at large, which was now looking forward to a post-war general election. He doubtless felt he needed some political cover for the domestic storm he saw on the horizon. But it was also a bold gambit in the high politics of Yalta's aftermath, one that must have been seen in the Kremlin as conveying a sharp warning, if not a threat. There is no evidence to suggest that Churchill was at this stage playing for a break with Stalin or wanted to start a "Cold War." But increasingly after Yalta, and with the enhanced prospect of support from a United States now explicitly committed to "freedom" throughout Europe, he was looking for some kind of "showdown" that would bring about a better postwar settlement.[10]

It would therefore be naïve to see this as a purely self-defensive initiative. Churchill wanted, as he had since the establishment of the Lublin regime in January, to bring some Anglo-American pressure to bear against the Soviets, in the hope of saving some independence for Poland and/ or keeping the final lodgment of Soviet "barbarism" as far to the east as possible. He had tried the diplomatic road, calling unsuccessfully for a preliminary week-long foreign ministers meeting in the lead-up to Yalta, pressing the Polish case at the conference, and urging Roosevelt to stay longer at Yalta in the hope of a settlement with Stalin. None of this had worked. Now the negotiating moment had passed, and he seems to have been thinking in terms of a stronger Anglo-American political front that might be founded on the chastened public support he may well have anticipated as the "realities" became more apparent. He could then press for

---

[10] For an illustration of Churchill's sincerity in urging Clark Kerr to accept Molotov's "friendly offer" to allow British representatives to visit Poland, see Churchill to Clark Kerr, February 28, 1945, PREM 3.356/9.

a "showdown" (a word that crops up often in his post-Yalta talk) that would force some amelioration from the Soviets.

One also senses, in his distinctively bleak formulation of the Polish issue, the forward-looking opportunism that would steadily come to characterize Churchill's high-stakes diplomatic strategy during the next several weeks. He must have realized that his provocative anatomization of the problem would, as in fact it did, anger the Soviets. He perhaps hoped, without much confidence, that they would respond with better conduct in Poland. But his deepest aim, by framing the issue in such strong dichotomous terms, seems to have been to bind the United States ever more tightly and securely to its new international role—to the defense of its appealing but improbable missionary ideals, now embodied explicitly in the Yalta language and Byrnes's enthusiastic propagations, and prospectively also to the Anglo-American nexus that would be realizable if and when, as must have seemed likely, the Soviets refused or were unable to live up to their apparent commitments.

Associated with this thinking, in all probability, was a concern that the United States might back away from its remarkable and unprecedented undertakings. Even the State Department, in its Briefing Book, had couched its comparatively positive recommendations to the president with ominous references to America's "observer" status. And amid the loudly proclaimed promises of Byrnes's euphoric presentation we find less-noticed, contradictory references to FDR's skill in preserving America's right to avoid, if desired, any unwelcome entanglement in future European crises. From 1919 onward Churchill's generation of British statesmen had been deeply sensitive to this American tendency to want to have it both ways (not so different, perhaps, from the chronic European habit of diplomatic reinsurance) and to promise and then retreat from firm international action. Roosevelt's performance during the first phase of the Yalta conference had been a recent reminder. Churchill's effort to take advantage of the opening Roosevelt had presented to entrench the American engagement even more strongly on the inviting Polish issue was in this sense a logical move.[11]

Sifting motivations of this kind must always be a somewhat speculative venture. But when we come to examine the impact of Churchill's initiative we find firmer ground. The speech was reported throughout the United States and widely cited and discussed in a press still waiting for Roosevelt's report. It was a commonplace saying during the war that Americans looked to Churchill for inside information rather than to Roosevelt, who rarely

---

[11] FRUS, *Yalta*, p. 103. *Baltimore Sun*, February 14, 1945.

spoke of postwar plans and had not addressed Congress for two years before his Yalta speech. Embassy officials frequently noted, perhaps with some exaggeration, Churchill's hold on American opinion. As Halifax put it, "Americans really listen to Mr. Churchill." Byrnes and Roosevelt certainly held the floor in these first weeks, but Churchill's tough-minded reference to the Polish issue was widely approved and now lodged in an American mind-set that by the beginning of April was highly critical of Soviet policy there.[12]

It is, however, in the Soviet response that we find the most direct reaction to Churchill's comments. The early Soviet public reaction to the conference had, it is true, been reassuringly calm and optimistic. The definitional imprint here, however, was significantly different. In the West, thanks largely to the energetic American stage setting, the emphasis was on a glowing postwar vision organized on Atlantic Charter lines. The Soviets, by contrast, were thinking in more immediate, practical terms. *Pravda* led the Soviet media in stressing the reaffirmed "unity" of the Big Three in the continuing war effort, tacitly acknowledging pre-Yalta anxieties that Roosevelt and Churchill might yet strike a deal with Hitler (fears that dangerously erupted again a few weeks later). The Soviets also, as they had throughout the war, hailed a strengthened Great Power solidarity in maintaining a stable postwar order against the anticipated intrigues of unnamed lesser states.[13]

Despite what must have seemed to them a dangerously misdirected emphasis developing in the West, the Soviets maintained a positive outlook until the end of February. Molotov, in his opening session with the Western ambassadors in Moscow on the Polish government issue, was cordial and cooperative, even undertaking as late as February 23 to facilitate the entry of Anglo-American observers into Poland without forcing a politically compromising application to the Lublin regime. And behind the scenes there was a significant change in the Kremlin's approach to Germany's future. The hitherto constant calls for a "people's uprising" ended on February 17. It appears that a joint Allied administration in Germany was now envisaged. At the same time the German communists' "Action Program for the Bloc of Militant Democracy" was also scrapped, having been, in the words of one of their leaders, Wilhelm Pieck, "overtaken by events." Eden's impression,

---

[12] Halifax to Eden, March 3, 1945, AN 791, F.O. 371.44536. *New York Times*, March 1, 1945.

[13] Radio Moscow, February 14, 15, 16, 1945, *BBC Digest*, Files 2035, 2036, 2037, and 2038. *Pravda*, February 13, 1945. *Izvestia*, February 13, 1945.

conveyed to Benes on February 23, was that the Russians "were anxious to work with us." The historian Vojtech Mastny suggests that "the thrust of the changes was to promote a solution in the spirit of Allied solidarity."[14]

There were from the start, however, significant signs of Soviet concern. Within a few days of the conference *The War and the Working Class* (the former *Voina i rabochii klass*, now published in an English edition) presented a relatively ecumenical front-page editorial approving the work at Yalta and, presumably with the German terms in mind, celebrating "the fact that the stern and emphatic language of the Crimean decisions is as far from the pompous and diffuse language of Wilson's Fourteen Points as heaven is from earth." In truth, as we have seen, the Yalta documents were full of loose, so-called Wilsonian phrases compared to which the Fourteen Points stands out as a model of political precision. But when the historian Daniel Yergin characterizes Byrnes's exposition as "pure in its Wilsonianism," one easily grasps his meaning, so firmly had Woodrow Wilson's reputation now been bound to both the cause of visionary idealism in the United States and the image of American naivete in Europe.[15] Two days later, on February 17, amid the world's enthusiastic reception of Yalta, the Soviets showed a sophisticated concern about the political consequences of misrepresentations associated with language in a *Pravda* review by the authoritative commentator David Zaslavsky. He noted Yalta's positive results but emphasized the different meanings attached to words like "democracy." Each of the three Allies had a different view of democracy, he pointed out, and the people of liberated Europe would "have the possibility of creating democratic institutions according to their own choice." Despite this and other early hints of concern, however, the Soviet government was intensely focused at this point on the image of Allied "unity" – even if it meant playing down for the moment what it doubtless regarded as the distorting talk about "democracy" in Eastern Europe that was raising hopes in the West and especially in the United States. The BBC's transcripts of Soviet broadcasts, eagerly pored over by British officials, reflect a constant refrain: that Yalta had shown the indissoluble unity of the three Allies, who were determined to confound by their solidarity the last hopes of the "Hitlerites" and their desperate friends.[16]

---

[14] Clark Kerr to Eden, February 28, 1945, F.O. 371.47866; Mastny, *Russia's Road to Cold War*, p. 254; V. Laschitza, *Lampferische Demokratie gegen Faschismus*, pp. 136–138. In another emollient gesture the Soviet authorities gave orders to the Red Army to curb its troops violence against German civilians. Donovan to Roosevelt, March 6, 1945, OSS (March 1945), Box 171, PSF, Roosevelt Library.

[15] *War and the Working Class*, February 15, 1945; Yergin, *Shattered Peace*, p. 66.

[16] *Pravda*, February 17, 1945.

Then, quite suddenly at the end of February, these tempered concerns gave way to a much harder Soviet line, most ominously in Poland and Rumania. By then it had become clear to observers in London that the Red Army and Soviet authorities were taking harsh measures in liberated Poland. On February 28, Churchill described to Roosevelt the dangers posed by the "liquidations and forced deportations" of anti-Lublin elements. This came on the heels of riots in Bucharest on February 24, followed by the arrival of Vyshinsky, who harangued King Michael in bullying fashion on February 27 on the need for a new government dominated by local communists. He arrogantly dismissed the king's objections and then departed, notoriously slamming the door so hard that the plaster cracked. A coup quickly followed, placing a pro-Soviet communist regime in power. These Romanian events preceded Churchill's speech and, though Vishinsky's ostentatious involvement suggests a Soviet desire, in the face of Byrnes's dangerously diversionary scenario, to show the world who was master in Eastern Europe, the crisis there seems to have developed largely out of local political tensions.[17]

Where, then, do we find a significant response to Churchill? Not, certainly in the public arena, where the warm afterglow of Yalta continued for several weeks. Rather, we find it is the "high politics" milieu. The key date is March 6. Up to this point Molotov had shown a pleasing goodwill toward his fellow commissioners in the ambassadorial group set up in Moscow. He had even promised, among other things, to arrange the dispatch of Western observers to Poland. But at the March 6 meeting he suddenly changed his tune, informing a dismayed Clark Kerr that he was withdrawing his undertaking. Application for entry to Poland must be made directly to the Warsaw regime (now relocated from Lublin). He gave two explanations. One was that the Western ambassadors had refused to invite the Warsaw Poles for consultation. This was patently incorrect, as Clark Kerr pointed out. The second and seemingly real reason, referring to the Soviet protégés in Poland, was that "Churchill had recently made some contemptuous remarks about them in the House of Commons." The ambassador reported that Molotov spoke with a smirk on his face but "left me in no doubt about his intention to withdraw his undertaking." At the same time the Soviets, in their habitual pay-back fashion, responded to the embarrassing British

[17] Churchill to Roosevelt, February 28, 1945, *Correspondence*, III, p. 539. Schuyler to Department of War, January 20, 1945, Rumania file, U.S. Military Mission, Moscow, RG 334, National Archives. Henry L. Roberts, *Rumania* (New Haven, Conn., 1951), pp. 262–263. Stephen Fischer-Galati, *The New Rumania* (Cambridge, Mass., 1967), pp. 28–29.

challenge to their role in Poland by launching a punitive strike against the Churchill government's most sensitive current theater. Clark Kerr's report on March 7 noted "the abandonment by the Soviet press of the previously ostentatiously neutral attitude about Greece."[18]

The post-Yalta crisis was thus set in motion. Against a background of suspected Soviet oppression in Poland, it appears to have started with Churchill's initiating emphasis on the governmental problem, acquired a focus with the Soviets' calculated response in the central institution set up to solve that problem, and was subsequently prolonged as Churchill embarked on a systematic campaign to press Roosevelt (and later Truman) to join him in an increasingly generalized confrontation with Stalin and Molotov. From this moment the ambassadorial commission became a contentious, stalemated arena, with Clark Kerr and Harriman (the American being somewhat less assertive as the State Department tried spasmodically to calm the waters) insisting on their right to invite Mickolajczyk and other moderate noncommunists for consultation, and sparring with the obdurate Molotov, who rejected most of these figures and demanded prior consultation with the Warsaw Poles and their associates.[19]

Yet remarkably, neither the United States nor the Soviet Union wanted this crisis. Indeed, they shared an interest in avoiding it. From their common though unacknowledged perspective, Churchill – whose promotional tenacity in succeeding weeks irritated the Americans and angered the Soviets – was doing two unwelcome things. First, he was exposing the as yet unresolved realities behind the delicate Polish situation that both Roosevelt and Stalin were trying in their different ways to put aside with their political embroidery. And second, he was forcing this issue prematurely. For both the emergent major powers needed more time to achieve their principal post-Yalta objectives.

This was certainly true of the United States government, where Roosevelt, focused on clearing a smooth path to San Francisco, seems in the weeks after Yalta to have been completely preoccupied with his domestic constituency. In his March 1 address, it will be recalled, he gave a white-washed view of the Polish prospect and ignored Romania altogether, much as he had passed over the real issues of Eastern and Central Europe at the summit conference. He was careful to warn against "perfectionism" but

---

[18] Clark Kerr to Eden, March 6, 1945, PREM 3.356/9.
[19] For a British overview of the commission and this period, see Harbutt, *Iron Curtain*, pp. 93–99.

was otherwise intent on accenting the positive and the hopeful. The effect was to place an authenticating seal on the preceding two weeks of image making that – in the United States, at least – had created a pleasing mix of Wilsonian triumphalism and Rooseveltian pragmatism. True, Roosevelt's sharp focus on San Francisco was in marked contrast to the Soviets' similarly selective emphasis on Big Three unity and the supposedly joyful liberation of Eastern Europe. But these were still separate political orbits, and each of the two governments was now pushing ahead with its primary objective and seemingly not worrying overmuch about the other emergent superpower's actions.

For the Soviets also needed time, a point made obliquely by Molotov who, encountering Harriman just after Roosevelt's death, missed the opportunity to display some unsuspected emotional depth and simply expressed his regrets at the loss by muttering "Time, time, time."[20] As his constant reiteration of deeply felt concern at Yalta suggests, Stalin was anxious to preserve at least the appearance of Allied unity until the end of the war and perhaps into the postwar period, though this is less certain. And he also needed time to establish effective control over the European states now falling into his sphere. It is not surprising, then, that he had, with only a modest show of reluctance, accepted Roosevelt's deceptive, liberal formulations at Yalta, or even that he did not react aggressively to the provoking visions, which must have stirred some resentment, conjured up by Byrnes and American commentators in February. Only Churchill – always suspect in Moscow because of his past and his persistent promotion of the Anglo-American collaboration that Roosevelt repeatedly dramatized for Stalin by his ostentatious repudiations – led the Soviets to rise to the obvious challenge.[21]

They did so with some sophistication by choosing to make their resentment felt in the ambassadorial commission rather than through direct action such as a display of overt coercion in Poland or a strident propaganda campaign complaining about the American gloss on Yalta, either of which would have encouraged the Germans, upset the Americans, and undermined Allied unity. The Soviets chose instead this more cloistered forum where they could take their stand effectively in what was really a guarded process rather than an attention-getting event, and as such was open to various remonstrances and delaying techniques (including

[20] Harriman memorandum, April 13, 1945, FRUS, 1945, 5, pp. 826–829.
[21] For Soviet views of Churchill, see Resis (ed.), *Molotov Remembers*, pp. 17, 45.

time-wasting debate about Yalta's ambiguities) that could be drawn out over time with the Americans, who, as they must have perceived, were focused on clearing an untroubled path to San Francisco and therefore shared their desire to avoid an open confrontation.[22]

It would have been much easier for Churchill to rally Roosevelt for a joint front on the Polish issue if the Soviets had opted for a more militant strategy. As it was, he had to struggle first to get the president's attention, and then to get some kind of effective action from the diplomatic establishment in Washington that was now drafting most of Roosevelt's correspondence. That he was able to inspire a significant response was in the deepest sense due to the Soviets' refusal or inability to live up to the perhaps impossibly high standard of conduct in Poland and Eastern Europe that Roosevelt had set for them at Yalta and then tried to fix in the public mind through Byrnes's energetic showcasing. But the crisis was also due, at least in the immediate sense, to Churchill. For it was he who lit the spark and tried to further his own Anglo-American cause by publicly embracing that standard, even though he knew (or should have known) that it was a misleadingly optimistic gloss on the actual summit negotiation. His provocative February 27 reference to Poland alone might not have served his purpose, and if unsupported might have condemned him to a lonely battle with Stalin while trying to fight off "warmonger" charges from a variety of critics. But on March 1 Roosevelt came to his aid in his report to Congress by similarly ignoring both the diplomatic realities of the Crimea (Lublin in charge, unsupervised elections pending, Soviet rule in Eastern Europe unquestioned) as well as the oppressive measures the Soviets were known or at least suspected to be taking in Poland and elsewhere. Instead, he essentially endorsed the idealized version of the fateful transaction that Byrnes had presented to a briefly credulous world. FDR certainly had his reasons, but in hindsight it seems that he was now falling into a trap of his own making.

For the flaw in FDR's approach, the one that was most immediately significant, both as a generative force politically and as a matter of positioning within the Anglo-American relationship, was that by engaging the United States in Europe's problems as he had done at Yalta, and then exaggerating publicly the ease with which those problems could now be resolved by the Wilsonian moral codes and Atlantic Charter precepts (independence, self-determination, a new kind of League) now enshrined in the Yalta documents and apparently accepted by the Soviets, FDR had exposed himself to

---

[22] Churchill to Roosevelt, March 8 and March 13, 1945, *Correspondence*, III, pp. 547–551.

the manipulations of his European partners. Stalin, most obviously, could at any time confute him with discordant actions that would demand public explanation and perhaps some forceful reaction. But he had also given an opening to Churchill, who, if Stalin did not adhere to the publicized Rooseveltian vision (and he was hardly likely to do so in the long run), could now hope to forge a closer Anglo-American association by pressing FDR to live up to and defend, in the face of a predictable Soviet backsliding, his triumphant public vision of the Yalta achievement. Here was a great irony. Anxious to avoid a confrontation with the Soviets, Roosevelt had now, out of a felt necessity as he saw domestic support turning away from international engagements, created conditions that were likely to bring it about: suspicion in Moscow, which by the end of February was already inspiring harsh Soviet actions in Eastern Europe, and temptation in London, which within two weeks of the conference was producing a Churchillian campaign to press the United States ever more strongly into an Anglo-American political front in defense of what the prime minister feared would be seen, if it were not defended, as "a fraudulent prospectus."[23]

In all this there is a deeper irony. Roosevelt, as obedient as modern conditions allowed to George Washington's famous injunction against "entangling alliances" with the Europeans, had gone to great lengths throughout the war to preserve American freedom of political action and to avoid, so far as possible, any compromising engagements with the European allies, especially the British. At Yalta, however, he had found it necessary, in order to safeguard the prospective United Nations in American affections, to commit himself far beyond his wishes. Moreover, he had gone far toward the violation, not only of a cardinal tenet of American diplomacy, but also of a classic rule of statesmanship: that a Great Power should never place its destiny in the hands of a lesser, self-interested partner. There is an echo here of Neville Chamberlain's volte-face in 1939, when – acting, like Roosevelt, under great domestic pressure – he had given an unconditional guarantee to Poland and thus delivered Britain's fate into the overconfident hands of Colonel Beck.[24] The parallel is certainly not exact, given, among other distinctions, the fact of American power and the absence as yet of a mobilized public opinion in the United States. But something of this sort, at least within the circle of the three Yalta statesmen, did occur here, with Churchill now at last able to begin an increasingly systematic campaign to press Roosevelt into an Anglo-American front protesting

[23] Churchill to Roosevelt, March 8, 1945, ibid., pp. 547–551.
[24] A. J. P. Taylor, *The Origins of the Second World War* (London, 1961), pp. 253–263.

against Stalin's refusal to play the implausible role Roosevelt had cast him for, the role of a benevolently progressive champion of Western liberalism in Eastern Europe.

Churchill clearly came to see the opportunity as the gap between the Rooseveltian vision and the Stalinist reality of international diplomacy became more evident through February and into March. So did his advisers. The Foreign Office's Orme Sargent, discussing the Polish problem in a February 19 minute, wrote, "In any case surely we can invoke the Declaration." Cadogan replied, "In actual fact the arrangement over Poland was made separately and without reference to the Declaration. But if the Soviet Government proves difficult in the matter of Poland and shows signs of going back on the arrangement it will, I think, be possible to invoke the Declaration." These intriguing possibilities prompted a meeting of the engaged diplomats which concluded that in view of the Romania/ Greece understanding with Moscow in 1944 it would be better to "let sleeping dogs lie." To this, however, they attached a significant qualification. Britain would not invoke the Declaration "except for the specific purposes of inducing the Americans to accept responsibility for any line of policy which might be agreed with them in the areas of Europe in which we have a major interest." Thus the Foreign Office was from the outset ready to take advantage of the welcome American opening. And Churchill himself, in as clear an expression of European realpolitik as one could wish for, told the Cabinet on March 6, "It would be for consideration whether the Yalta Declaration on Liberated territories could be construed as superseding previous arrangements such as that in respect of Rumania and Greece which had been made at a time when we could not rely on United States assistance."[25]

It was from this revisionary posture that Churchill now began a systematic effort to press Roosevelt into some kind of joint demarche against Soviet conduct. In a strong cable on February 28, he had drawn attention to the now proliferating reports of "liquidations" and "deportations" in Poland. Perhaps hoping to influence the president's speech scheduled for delivery to Congress the next day, he emphasized the deteriorating public

---

[25] Sargent minute, February 19, 1945, Cadogan minute, February 20, 1945, both U1332/G in F.O. 371.50835. WM (45) 26th Conclusions, CAB 65/51. Churchill cabled Roosevelt raising the prospect that the Declaration on Liberated Europe would be seen by world opinion as a "fraudulent prospectus" – Churchill to Roosevelt, March 8, 1945, *Correspondence*, III, pp. 547–551. For Eden's desire to use the Declaration against the Soviets in Romania, see Eden to Churchill, March 5, 1945, PREM 3.374/9. For the Soviet desire to use it in the aggressive manner envisaged by Molotov, see *Pravda*, May 26, 1945.

climate in Britain, where "there is a good deal of uneasiness in both parties that we are letting the Poles down." This brought no response from the White House. The president was clearly in no mood to be rushed off his feet at this point. On March 8, Churchill tried again, focusing this time on Rumania. He accused Stalin of following a course in Rumania and Bulgaria "which is absolutely contrary to all democratic ideas." Citing the long-tolerated submergence of the Allied Control Commissions in those countries, he now urged the need for American resistance. Given Britain's Moscow commitment to Soviet supremacy in the Balkans, Churchill some-what lamely concluded by urging the United States to take the lead. "We will, of course," he added, "give you every support."[26]

The improbable notion here that the United States might take the lead on such a sensitive European matter (Eden was also instructing a British representative in the Balkans "to follow the U.S. lead as far as possible instead of taking the initiative yourself") was doubtless inspired in part by Churchill's reluctance (even as he was turning his energies to the creation of an Anglo-American front) to put the Tolstoy deal with Stalin and Greece's protection at undue risk. This inhibition remained through March, and even beyond, a subtheme in the prime minister's policy. He was prepared to risk a rupture with Stalin if he could forge the more-than-compensating tie with the Americans, but, always eager to insure, he still hoped to keep some sort of line out to Stalin. With this in mind, he tried to push the Americans to act unilaterally in Rumania (a vain effort, as it turned out) and worked to damp down Foreign Office and ambassadorial complaints about the treatment of British personnel and property in Rumania and Bulgaria. He even urged the dismissal of the right-wing Greek prime minister, Plastiras, whom he pronounced himself willing to "market" to the Soviets: an expression of Churchill's well-developed tendency, shared with Stalin, to subordinate the interests of small countries to a transcending Great Power rationale. At the same time, considerations of honor still had some salience. Thus he directed that the deposed Rumanian prime minister, Radescu, should be defended by force if he sought asylum in the British embassy in Bucharest. And he urged the minister of information to give widespread publicity in Britain to the leftist atrocities now disfiguring the liberation of Rumania and Bulgaria under Soviet protection. But all this was subordinate to the now primary Anglo-American emphasis in Churchill's post-Yalta activism. On March 13 he was on the

[26] Churchill to Roosevelt, March 8, 1945, *Correspondence*, III, pp. 547–551.

president's tail again, sending him a long evidentiary list of Soviet excesses in Poland, all directly confuting the image of popular support for Lublin still being pressed by the Moscow media.[27]

But Churchill found Roosevelt a most elusive quarry. FDR fended off the importunate prime minister, urging the importance of working for "a political truce" between Lublin and the Home Army units beholden to the London government, and of doing nothing to inhibit Lublin's "land reforms." He conceded that a "whitewash" of Lublin could not be accepted but preferred to work through the ambassadors, now engaged in their increasingly tense "consultations" with Molotov, rather than address Stalin until "every other possibility of bringing the Soviet government into line has been exhausted." He declined to intervene over Rumania, which he described as "not a good test case," in part because it lay athwart the Red Army's communications line.[28]

Roosevelt's reluctance to act, and his habitual turn to avoidance when faced with British initiatives of this kind, were entirely representative of most official opinion in Washington. When the Foreign Office inquired about the real meaning of the Declaration on Liberated Europe, the State Department, from which the document had originally emanated just before Yalta, professed not to know and resolutely resisted any suggestion that it might be invoked against the Soviets. Halifax cabled on March 8 that the State Department did not want a joint note to Moscow and took a "softer" view of the post-Yalta developments than the British, whose approach seemed to them "too unconditional and shows too great a distrust of Soviet intentions in Poland." Bohlen was sent to explain personally to the ambassador that the president wanted to avoid the "heavy artillery" of a joint Anglo-American protest and preferred "to give the matter time."[29]

But Churchill, doubtless aware that he now had both the high ground and the ability to appeal to American public opinion, was not to be deterred. In another message, on March 13, he laid it on the line in a reprise of his February 27 statement. "Poland has lost her frontier. Is she now to lose her freedom? That is the question which will undoubtedly have to be fought out in Parliament and in public here." He went on to talk of

---

[27] Churchill to Eden, March 5, 1945, PREM 3.374/9; Churchill to Eden, March 17, 1945, PREM 3.374/11; Eden to Stevenson, March 8, 1945, PREM 3.374/9; Churchill to Roosevelt, March 13, 1945, *Correspondence*, III, pp. 564–566.

[28] Roosevelt to Churchill, March 11, 1945, ibid., pp. 561–562.

[29] Halifax to Eden, March 8, 1945, and Sargent note, March 12, 1945, both in U1692/G, F.O. 371.50835.

"divergence" between the British and American governments and warned that he would soon have to declare publicly that "we are in the presence of a great failure and an utter breakdown of what was agreed at Yalta, but that we British have not the necessary strength to carry the matter further and that the limits of our capacity to act have been reached." This powerful declaration, foreshadowing the profound British geopolitical abdications of 1947 that would lead to the Truman Doctrine, urged Roosevelt to focus on the deteriorating situation in Poland and the increasing frustration of Harriman and Clark Kerr in Moscow as they met with Molotov, who was still insisting on a Soviet veto of any Polish candidate for office. It was clearly intended to bring about some kind of Anglo-American alignment. But Roosevelt was still determined to avoid a confrontation with Stalin. He responded calmly on March 15, simply expressing agreement and concern and promising some unspecified coordination in a stiff note to Moscow.[30]

While these initiatives were in an uncertain state of transatlantic gestation, Stalin suddenly raised the stakes for the president. He shared with Roosevelt, I have suggested, a desire for time to allow his policies to work out. Neither had any interest in a destabilizing confrontation. But the ostentatious triumphalism in the United States and growing signs of reluctance on the part of the British and Americans to accept the Soviet line in Eastern Europe led him back to the logic of "bargain" diplomacy. He tweaked the now fraying United States–Soviet understanding. When the Western powers refused to invite the as yet unreconstructed Warsaw/Lublin regime to San Francisco, he announced that Molotov would not attend. The message was clear. If Roosevelt continued to interfere over Poland, the Soviets would undermine his United Nations conference.[31]

Churchill quickly took advantage again. "It is as plain as a pikestaff," he cabled Roosevelt on the Polish issue, "that Molotov's tactics are to drag the business out while the Lublin Committee consolidate their power." He reminded Roosevelt yet again that "if we fail altogether to get a satisfactory solution on Poland and are in fact defrauded by Russia," he and Eden were pledged to report this to the House of Commons. He continued:

There I advised critics of the Yalta settlement to trust Stalin. If I have to make a statement of facts to the House the whole world will draw the deduction that such advice was wrong ... surely we must not be manoevered into becoming parties

---

[30] Churchill to Roosevelt, March 13, 1945, *Correspondence*, III, pp. 564–566; Roosevelt to Churchill, March 15, 1945, ibid., pp. 568–569.
[31] Stalin to Roosevelt, March 7, 1945, SCRT, pp. 199–200.

to imposing on Poland, and on how much more of Eastern Europe, the Russian version of democracy? There seems to be only one possible alternative to confessing our total failure. That alternative is to stand by our interpretation of the Yalta declaration.

At the same time, even as he pushed Roosevelt ever more strongly to defend his elevated view of Yalta, Churchill proceeded cautiously. As he told the Cabinet, "We can't go beyond the United States." But he now looked forward with more confidence to a joint protest. He also began to take a more optimistic view of what he had earlier referred to dismissively as "the world fair in San Francisco." He had not been enthusiastic about the proposed United Nations conference, he told Cranborne on April 3, but if the Soviets refused to come, then "in that event, I should become very keen upon it." The pro-Western world line-up would be "the best tactically and morally," and "nothing would show the Soviets where they got off more clearly." Here then was another of Churchill's famous "hooks." As he told Eden, Britain couldn't press beyond where it could carry the United States, but "nothing is more likely to bring them into line with us than any idea of the San Francisco conference being imperiled."[32]

The combined result of all these events was to force Roosevelt's hand, though he disappointed Churchill by insisting on parallel cables rather than a joint protest to Stalin. These went off on April 1, with Churchill complaining of obstructionism in Poland and threatening a statement to Parliament, and a more circumspect Roosevelt conceding the Yalta bias in favor of Lublin but insisting on a "new" government and warning that American opinion would not accept a "thinly disguised continuation of the present Warsaw regime."[33]

At the beginning of April another Soviet initiative, again ostensibly directed at the United States, roiled the waters. This was the famous "Bern Incident" that began with Stalin's passionate and understandable – given the growing contrast between stubborn, reinforced German resistance in the east and an apparently softening *Wehrmacht* presence in the west – protest to Roosevelt over the surrender negotiations allegedly being conducted by Allied intelligence operatives in Switzerland with high-ranking German officers from the Italian theater. Roosevelt defended himself

---

[32] Churchill to Roosevelt, March 27, 1945, *Correspondence*, III, pp. 587–588; Churchill to Eden, March 24, 1945, PREM 3.356/9; Churchill to Cranborne, April 3, 1945, PREM 4.31/7. For the "world fair" reference, see Churchill to Eden, April 8, 1945, PREM 3.173/3.

[33] Churchill to Stalin, April 1, 1945, cited in Churchill, *Triumph and Tragedy*, pp. 435–437; Roosevelt to Stalin, April 1, 1945, FRUS, 1945, 5, pp. 194–195.

vigorously, denying that the American authorities had acted in bad faith and expressing his resentment that "such vile representations" should be given credence. Stalin sent an emollient reply, and the crisis passed.

But there was a significant sting in this episode for the British. Historians tend to see the Bern Incident as a United States–Soviet confrontation. Stalin's refusal to address himself to Churchill directly has a punitive, perhaps relegatory aspect. For it seems clear that it was here that his real grievance lay. As he wrote to FDR, "Nor can I account for the reticence of the British who have left it to you to carry on a correspondence with me on this unpleasant matter, while they themselves maintain silence, although it is known that the initiative in the matter of the Bern negotiations belongs to the British." The unmistakable implication was that Churchill had cooked up the whole affair, manipulated the Americans, and was now deceitfully refusing to acknowledge his responsibility. Churchill promptly cabled Stalin setting out the facts in an exculpatory way and denying any "dishonorable thoughts." The crisis was soon subsumed by the general end-of-war confusions. But it is a striking illustration both of the sharp Soviet identification of Churchill rather than Roosevelt as the prime mover in the gathering Anglo-American front, and of the rapid decline not just of the Stalin-Churchill relationship but also, and more seriously, of the Anglo-Soviet concert that had seemed so promising just a few weeks earlier.[34]

Churchill himself was unfazed by the Bern affair, and downplayed it in his report to the Cabinet. He was encouraged by the developing military situation in the west, which was now increasingly favorable, while the Soviets seemed stuck in the approach to Berlin. He and Roosevelt seemed at this point to be closer on the Polish issue generally than they had ever been. Churchill put it in familiar language on April 1: "Every effort must be made to reach complete understandings with the United States, and Poland is an extremely good hook." In the Foreign Office, Sargent was similarly robust in an April 2 review. Until recently, he noted, the British had expected the Soviets to occupy the heart of Germany and had consequently set themselves to "propitiate" them. But with the sudden military breakthrough in the west "the situation has radically changed." Now was the time "to speak plainly to the Soviet Government, to show

---

[34] Stalin to Roosevelt, April 3, 1945; Roosevelt to Stalin, April 4, 1945, both in FRUS, 1945, Vol. 3, pp. 731–746. For background on United States wartime intelligence in Switzerland and the Bern Incident, see Allen Dulles, *The Secret Surrender* (New York, 1966). Churchill to Stalin, April 5, 1945, SCCA, pp. 311–313. For Churchill's attitude, see Gilbert, *Churchill*, VII, p. 1282.

our resentment, and to formulate what we consider our rights." Sargent called for "a showdown on the grounds that our respective positions in the European scene have altered." In the same spirit Churchill told Eden on April 8, "I think the time has come for a showdown on these points and the British and the United States are in complete alignment. We may go far and long before finding an equally good occasion."[35]

The prime minister may well have been right, for there is convincing evidence that the president was now turning sharply against the Soviets. According to his daughter he had burst out, upon receiving a cable from Harriman on March 24, "Averell is right, we can't do business with Stalin. He has broken every one of the promises he made at Yalta." He told the journalist Anne O'Hare McCormick a few days later that "Stalin was not a man of his word." On the other hand, he played down the Bern issue and continued to try and hold Churchill at bay. In his last cable from Warm Springs, Georgia, on April 11 he struck a temperate note, telling Churchill, "I would minimize the general Soviet problem as much as possible because these problems in one form or another seem to arise every day and most of them straighten out, as in the case of the Bern meeting. We must be firm, however, and our course so far is correct."[36]

Sadly for these hopes, Roosevelt died on April 12. The "showdown" never took place. But the fact that the Anglo-American front had reached this point of development by early April should surely caution us against a cavalier dismissal of the immediate post-Yalta period, sometimes brushed aside by historians who, looking for a crucial turning point, move too quickly from Roosevelt's supposedly sophisticated summit accommo-dationism to President Harry Truman's initial militance. For, focusing entirely on a "high politics" approach, we have seen a serious falling out among the Big Three since Yalta, due both to British and American concern about the stalemate in the Polish negotiations and to Soviet upset over the disjunction between the conference itself and the divergent presentation of it to an essentially captive world audience by the Western powers. The effects of this can be quickly summarized: a drift toward an East/West line-up, a trend exacerbated by Roosevelt's utopianism that, when chal-lenged, turned slowly but perceptibly to a show of resistance to Moscow;

[35] Churchill to Eden, April 1 and April 8, 1945, both in PREM 3.356/16. Sargent memoran-dum, April 2, 1945, N4281, F.O. 371.47881.
[36] Cited in Wilson D. Miscamble, C.S.C., *From Roosevelt to Truman: Potsdam, Hiroshima and the Cold War* (Cambridge, 2007), pp. 73–74. Roosevelt to Churchill, April 11, 1945, *Correspondence*, III, p. 630.

Stalin's harsh correctives in Poland and Eastern Europe; and Churchill's exploitation of the growing United States–Soviet divide in the hope of a fundamental reorientation. By April 12 this tendency – involving a fading Europe/America scenario and a growing East/West line of thought and action – was already well under way.[37]

But as we take stock of the situation upon Truman's accession we see that the new dispensation was still far from securely established. Roosevelt, while finally finding it necessary to register his remonstrance with Stalin on the Polish issue, had successfully avoided both a full confrontation with Stalin and an intimate collaboration with Churchill. The result was that while a new East/West association was slowly beginning to emerge, the Anglo-Soviet collaboration was breaking down as Churchill and Stalin contended ostensibly for the fate of Poland, but actually for the support of the now formally engaged but still skittishly reluctant United States.

The post-Yalta decline of British leadership in Western Europe was another consequence of this developing reorientation. Indeed, the post-Yalta breakdown of the Anglo-French partnership is just as striking as that we see occurring between London and Moscow. De Gaulle was certainly partly responsible. His surly attitude toward the Americans after his exclusion from the meeting spilled over into that large reservoir of hatred for the Anglo-American domination he had been forced to endure during the war. Not content with the promised occupation zone in Germany, he was now insisting on what amounted to French control of the Rhineland and even parts of the Ruhr. He frequently interfered with the disposition of the French troops under Eisenhower's command. And he was by April already clearly bent on forcing on the Syrians and Lebanese an unwelcome French military presence that was bound to inflame Arab hostility and create difficulties for the British.[38]

By mid-April the sense of impending breakdown and a growing disillusionment was seeping out into the wider world. It was becoming clear that Yalta was not, after all, the foundational postwar settlement so vigorously promoted in February. There was increasing criticism in the West of Soviet policies. Soviet concern about its allies' good faith was also coming into the open. While its domestic press maintained a reassuringly upbeat perspective, Soviet external broadcasts increasingly calibrated their message to specific audiences, emphasizing to the British, for example, "the

---

[37] The "continuity" thesis, from Roosevelt to Truman, is fully argued in Miscamble, *From Roosevelt to Truman*, pp. 34–127 and passim.
[38] Kolko, *Politics of War*, pp. 93–96.

insatiable greed of former American appeasers" and reminding their American listeners of the British tendency to avoid dangerous military actions and operate only in relatively safe theaters while their allies did the dirty work. Dissentient views about Yalta had of course been expressed by virtually all Poles in Britain and by various right-wing politicians and publicists, among other skeptics. By mid-March the leftist *Tribune* was also drawing attention to the "very uneasy compromises" made in the Crimea, and the Labour Party's *Daily Herald* was soon afterward pointing out that the wording was "so ambiguous and so ill-drafted" that there was "no real agreement at all." Early in April the Dominion prime ministers, meeting in London, confronted an embarrassed Churchill and Eden with their own misgivings about the shaky quality of the supposed agreements. In the United States also the imperfections of the Yalta agreements were becoming apparent. Anti–New Deal, conservative papers like the *Chicago Tribune* and the Hearst chain had been critical from the start. Now a host of other publications and columnists were raising questions, especially after Roosevelt was forced to acknowledge that he had agreed to the Soviet Union securing two extra seats in the proposed General Assembly of the United Nations. It was not just the ambiguous meanings in the accords that were coming under fire. There was also a growing awareness of their fragility, and of difficult issues too quickly skated over in order to get an agreement. The divergences over Poland's future were becoming only too apparent. The historian Ralph B. Levering notes that "by April almost all newspapers were criticizing Russia for dominating the Poles" And there was criticism of including the Soviet conduct in Rumania, Moscow's tardy processing of American prisoners of war, and the lack of access to Eastern Europe. The gathering disenchantment was reflected in Cantrill polls showing a decline from 54% to 45% between late February and mid-May of those Americans with faith in Soviet willingness to cooperate after the war. It was also becoming clear that the path to San Francisco was not as simple as had been suggested. And speculation was rife over the supposed Far East agreements, whose secrecy encouraged the general air of confusion and unresolved issues increasingly associated with the Yalta conference.[39]

If one asks why these developing tensions and disenchantments did not lead to a more direct East-West confrontation at this point, a large part of

---

[39] Radio Moscow, March 13, 16, 1945, *BBC Digest*, Files 2065, 2068. *Tribune*, March 9, 1945; *Daily Herald*, April 2, 1945. For American press, see Balfour to Foreign Office, March 6, 1945, F.O. 371.50835.

the answer lies in the preoccupation of all the Great Powers with the practical problems of liberated Europe. A sense of the multiple contradictions and loose ends left by the Yalta disorder had already emerged by March 22, when the British Cabinet looked into the agreements over Germany's future. The chancellor of the exchequer, Sir John Anderson, a voice of bleak financial accountability, pointed out again, as he had on earlier occasions, that large-scale reparations and dismemberment, which the Soviets seemed to want, were "incompatible."

The ensuing discussion makes it clear that the relationships between reparations, dismemberment, and deindustrialization had not been thought out. Eden argued that if the Russians took machinery from the British zone in the populous Ruhr, they should provide compensating food from the eastern zone. This would later be part of the deal that arguably saved the Potsdam conference. But nothing of this kind had been discussed at Yalta, and the reaction of one Cabinet member was that the Soviet plans for the expulsion of the Germans in the east would turn the British zone into "a vast soup kitchen." Could Britain support a destitute population? What were the alternatives? One was to hand the British zone over to the Russians, who, after all, had the food. Another looked to the old interwar solution – "Back to the Dawes Plan and loans." None of these options seemed very attractive. The Labour ministers, with their sharper social sensitivities, seem to have taken a more practical line and backed up the anxious chancellor. Thus Hugh Dalton posed the question, "If industry is destroyed can 80 million live on the agriculture that is left?" Churchill was still reluctant to abandon the Morgenthau scenario. If the Soviets took all the machinery, "at least that would remove German competition and leave the way open to us."[40]

Beneath these surface manifestations of post-Yalta unease we see that the architects of the Crimea accords were also now deeply at odds. Roosevelt's failure to get a satisfactory deal from Stalin over Poland and Eastern Europe at Yalta during the first phase of the conference had led him to the dangerous dramatization we have been following. This produced a renewed optimism in the United States. The high politics context, however, became increasingly acrimonious as Stalin and Molotov found their negotiating achievement subordinated to the specter of a Jeffersonian Eastern Europe, which a deluded world had been led to think they had endorsed. Stalin could of course expose the illusion at any moment with an ostentatious show of power, but only by sacrificing much Western goodwill.

---

[40] Normanbrook notes, March 22, 1945, WM (45) 35th Conclusions.

It is sometimes claimed that Stalin felt some warmth for Roosevelt. This seems unlikely. FDR's post-Yalta distortions may well have stirred memories of his unfulfilled promises of a Second Front in 1942. Stalin's famous appraisal of the two Western leaders, reflecting his well-attested paranoia, is probably a better guide. "Churchill is the kind who, if you don't watch him, will slip a kopeck out of your pocket. ... Roosevelt is not like that. He dips his hand in only for bigger coins." Molotov contributed a touch of doctrinal analysis, characterizing FDR as "an imperialist who would grab anyone by the throat." He was "wilier" than Churchill, who, according to the Russian diplomat, was a "100% imperialist." But Churchill was "the strongest, the smartest among them." At the same time, having observed Roosevelt's failing health at Yalta the Soviet leaders appear still to have viewed Churchill as their principal antagonist, perhaps functioning as a shrewd Iago to FDR's disoriented Othello. Meanwhile, the Western leaders were having their own difficulties. Just as Churchill was frustrated by the president's calculated evasions and passivity on the Polish problem, so Roosevelt appears to have been irritated by the way Churchill persistently forced this sensitive issue with its implicit threat to his United Nations project. Finally, to complete this circle of comprehensive alienation, FDR appears to have turned bitterly against Stalin in his final days.[41]

Most of these upsets and reorientations can be attributed in one way or another to the transformative effects of the bifurcated Crimean conference. So can Yalta's two significant structural changes. The first of these was the eclipse of virtually all the assumptions, arrangements, and agreements associated with the idea of and planning for an autonomous postwar Europe. By April 1945 the Churchill/Stalin relationship, the Anglo-Soviet nexus, and the "Western bloc" were all, except in vigorous Soviet press fulminations against the "bloc," fading from the scene. This European project had from December 1941 to 1945 been dependent on the establishment of some kind of Western group to balance Soviet power. But Yalta's temptations had led Churchill to desert the cause for the alluring prospect of an Anglo-American front. Meanwhile, de Gaulle's resentful unilateralism, and the ebbing commitment of the smaller powers as they grappled with the midwinter problems of their broken societies, were now stretching the bonds of solidarity almost to the breaking point.

The falling away of Western European solidarity and activism led naturally to the other crucial structural consequence of Yalta: the direct

---

[41] Djilas, *Conversations with Stalin*, p. 73; Resis (ed.), *Molotov Remembers*, pp. 17, 45, 51; Miscamble, *From Roosevelt to Truman*, pp. 74, 78.

political exposure of the United States and the Soviet Union to each other, unmediated and unobscured now by a British or Western European political "buffer" and with only fading American illusions about an arbitral role in settling Anglo-Soviet disputes. During 1944, United States–Soviet relations, regulated by their divergent but as yet only potentially trouble-some postwar preoccupations – the establishment of a functioning United Nations and the mastery of Eastern and Central Europe, respectively – had been comfortably conducted at arm's length. But now the differences between these ultimately incompatible systems were sharpening. The mirage of a British-led group as the vital Western constituent of an auton-omous Europe from which the United States could remain comfortably detached was now falling away. And as the two stronger powers began in this clarified environment to look at each other more closely, the persisting argument over the supposed Soviet promise at Yalta to allow "freedom" and "independence" in its provocatively inaccessible eastern sphere, pro-moted by Churchill and others, was steadily becoming the touchstone of American official and public thinking.

If we knew nothing of events after January 1945 we might be tempted to ascribe the decline in Western European solidarity to calculated Rooseveltian policy. He had, after all, systematically opposed or under-mined such cohesive initiatives as the European Advisory Commission, the notion of "regionalism" within the United Nations framework, and any move toward Anglo-French collaboration. This was not necessar-ily mindless negativism. The reader may recall that in Chapter 6 it was suggested that FDR saw the reduction of Western European power as an essential precondition to the multilateral order he envisioned and had indeed laid some foundations for as a politico-economic framework for the postwar era.

The flaw in Roosevelt's approach was that he never addressed himself in any insightful way to the means by which the political dimensions of that vision could be brought to practical realization. Politically, his hopes were invested in the early establishment of the United Nations and the postpone-ment of divisive issues until Germany had been defeated. Consequently, when European power politics erupted suddenly in late 1944, he had no ready response. He reacted, much as any close observer of his public career might have expected, with a series of improvisations. Thus, as Soviet expansion began to concern him in September, he shelved his Europhobia briefly and encouraged Churchill to take a larger, leading role. That turned out badly as robust British and Soviet actions in the liberated areas upset Americans and suddenly endangered the United Nations prospect. FDR then looked to restore domestic confidence through personal diplomacy with Stalin during the first phase of the Yalta meeting, hopefully raising the various nostrums that had emerged in American, British, and Polish official thinking. When that failed to convert Stalin, the president turned to manipulation and presented Yalta to the world as a success. That brought a short-lived euphoria, but the emerging truths inspired public criticism and forced him into an unwanted anti-Soviet front with Churchill, something he had struggled to avoid throughout the war. The outcome of these final missteps was that the American road to the postwar years would not in this crucial, transitional year be shaped by the "universalism" of Hull and Roosevelt – though the institutional foundations of their multilateral order would survive and become a principal source of political cohesion and economic growth in the postwar West – but by the political "realism" of Churchill and Truman.

The point here seems to be that virtually all the ostensibly "practical" agreements made in the Crimea were, by the time of Roosevelt's death, being steadily revealed as unreal or unsatisfactory or irremediably ambiguous. What then, on April 12, remained of Yalta? Not surely the much ballyhooed "spirit" that Byrnes and Roosevelt had proclaimed. One of Yalta's many productions, however, was now flourishing. This was the Declaration on Liberated Europe, steadily coming forward both in the diplomatic exchanges and in the public imagination as a kind of register of broken agreements and blighted hopes. For this was not the Rooseveltion Declaration made so much of in the days immediately after Yalta as a heartfelt affirmation of values and intentions. Rather, it was the Churchillian Declaration viewed as a solemn Soviet commitment to the "freedom" and "independence" of Eastern Europe made, it now seemed, in return for the Curzon Line and generous Western acceptance of the former Soviet pariah state as one of the Great Powers in the new international arena. And increasingly, it was seen that Stalin was breaking that basic commitment.

This brings us to President Harry Truman, long kept in the dark by Roosevelt over important issues, including the deliberations at Yalta. His take on the Declaration on Liberated Europe, as on the agreement over Poland, was straightforward and unqualified. They were treaties, he insisted, that Stalin was apparently violating.

This perception became a foundation of his whole approach to the Soviet Union. Though little has been made of it by historians, the Declaration functioned through 1945 both as an agent of political mobilization and as a rationale for action. It was, together with the Polish agreement, an integral part of the Byrnes/Roosevelt presentation of Yalta, and then served as a compelling spur to and justification of American diplomatic activism as hopes of Soviet cooperation faded. The British, as we saw earlier, had quickly recognized the Declaration's potential as they tried to associate the United States with their developing resistance to Soviet expansionism. It is not surprising, then, that one of the most accurate descriptions of how this worked in practice during the transitional year after Yalta came from a Foreign Office diplomat reflecting on the 1944 Moscow Order and writing about the Balkan states in July 1945.

We were before Yalta perfectly prepared to allow the Russians the predominance in the ex-satellite Balkan countries to which we agreed in Moscow, but it has unfortunately been quite impossible to persuade them to realize that the Yalta Declaration on Liberated Territories altered this and not only entitled us, but even obliged us, to interest ourselves in what the Russians were doing.[42]

Given this attitude it is not surprising that the accession of Truman gave the Anglo-American front some unexpected momentum. This was due in part to the predicament and personality of the new president. Suddenly cast into these international tensions without adequate preparation or experience, Truman calmed his inner anxieties with repeated displays of a bold decisiveness that Washington insiders found a refreshing change from the chronically procrastinating Roosevelt. In this Truman was supported and encouraged by old Roosevelt hands like Harriman, Leahy, and Forrestal, who had long wanted a firmer line with the Soviets, and by Churchill, to whom he turned in these early days for counsel. Now at last the prime minister got his long-sought Anglo-American united protest. Truman collaborated with Churchill on a joint message to Stalin, sent on April 15, complaining about the disappointing consultations in Moscow and calling explicitly for a "new" Polish government. This was to be formed, in a return to something like the old Presidential Council idea, by seven Polish leaders: three from Warsaw, three from London, and one neutral. Churchill, needless to say, was delighted with his new American partner, and after further optimistic reports from Eden, who was in Washington en route to San Francisco, he noted that "Truman is not to be bullied by the Soviets."[43]

---

[42] Stewart memorandum, July 12, 1945, N444909, F.O. 371.47883.

[43] Truman, *Year of Decisions*, pp. 1–27; Gaddis, *United States and the Origins*, pp. 198–200; Yergin, *Shattered Peace*, pp. 87–88. For Hopkins's assessment of Truman for the British, see Halifax to Churchill, April 15, 1945, PREM 4.27/10. For Truman's bitterness toward the Soviets, especially regarding the treatment of American prisoners of war and the lack of access to them, see Eden to Churchill, May 15, 1945 PREM 3.430/1. See also Churchill and Truman to Stalin, April 15, 1945, FRUS, 1945, 5, p. 219; Churchill, *Triumph and*

Truman did indeed impart a significant charge to the now fast-cohering Anglo-American "front" against what were now increasingly seen as dangerous Soviet expansionary ambitions. The particular expressions of his sudden belligerence are well known: the harsh interviews with Molotov (also now on the way to San Francisco as Stalin's gesture of respect for Roosevelt), who, according to some but not all accounts, was told in unvarnished language to "carry out your treaties"; the abrupt termination of Lend-Lease shipments; the new tough line on reparations; and the close collaboration with Churchill.[44]

The Soviets clearly felt the American pressure through April. They reacted in a characteristically European way by turning back to a brief reconciliation with the British. This actually began just before Roosevelt's death. Clark Kerr received reassurances from Kollantai, and also from Maisky, who told him that Anglo-Soviet relations were still "fundamentally sound." On April 14, Ilya Ehrenburg, who had been writing sarcastic columns sniping at the Western powers, was reproved by *Pravda*. And then Stalin himself moved forward, replying cordially to a message from Churchill, who had asked him to facilitate Mikolajczyk's inclusion in the Polish political leadership. Stalin agreed to this and also urged Churchill once again to understand the Soviet need for security as an aspect of the Polish situation. The Soviets had not, he pointed out in his habitual bargaining mode, interfered in Belgium or Greece, both so important to Britain.[45]

Churchill replied in a conciliatory spirit. This seems to have been genuine. He still hoped for a general understanding with Stalin, provided it was based not only on the mutual respect and consideration he thought he had created in the Anglo-Soviet Moscow order in October 1944, but also on a power balance that now meant an Anglo-American entity in the West. He did not make this last point explicitly here but wrote a long letter reviewing the post-Yalta difficulties, replying calmly to Stalin's charges, and appealing to him not to underrate "the divergencies which are opening about matters which you may think are small but which are symbolic of the way the English-speaking democracies look at life."[46]

Tragedy, pp. 486–488; ibid., p. 492. See also Terry Anderson, *The United States, Great Britain and the Cold War, 1944–1947* (Columbia, Mo., 1981), pp. 56–60.

[44] Miscamble, *From Roosevelt to Truman*, pp. 91–103; Harbutt, *Iron Curtain*, pp. 100–101.

[45] Stalin to Churchill, April 24, 1945, SCCA, pp. 330–331. Clark Kerr to Eden, April 17, 1945, N4902, F.O. 371.47881; *Pravda*, April 14, 1945 (cf. *Izvestia*, April 12).

[46] Churchill to Stalin, April 28, 1945, SCCA, pp. 338–344.

But Churchill, though still ready to correspond with Stalin, was not to be distracted from his main objective. Encouraged by Truman's militance, as well as by the unexpectedly rapid advance of the Allied forces in the West, he was now returning in late April and early May to the politico-military activism that had characterized his efforts in late 1944. His purpose was still to check Soviet expansion by consolidating Western power wherever possible. Thus in early April he warned the Chiefs of Staff that "the changes in the Russian attitude and atmosphere since Yalta are grave" and instructed them to do more to help Turkey, which "may be of service to us in the future." By mid-May we find him calling for Turkish rearmament and capitalizing on the Anglo-American success over the Trieste issue by urging Truman to let American troops join British forces in occupying the strategically placed Greek island of Rhodes. Meanwhile, he was emphasizing the importance he attached to frustrating communism in Italy, noting that "the United States Government is very fond of Italy." Most of this was almost certainly known to the Soviets, either from simple observation or from their spies in the British governmental labyrinth. In early May all pretences to amity were dropped, at least for the moment, in the scramble for position in the middle of the continent. Churchill successfully urged Eisenhower to reach Lubeck in time to secure the capture of about a half-million German troops in the Baltic/Scandinavian theater.[47]

On May 14 the prime minister made another of his aggressive public statements in a broadcast marking the fifth anniversary of his appointment to the office. In an obvious reference to the Soviets, he declared that there was no place in postwar Europe for "totalitarian" or "police" regimes. This was widely reported and drew approving comment from the *New York Times* and other newspapers in the United States, which saw it as an accurate portrait of the situation in the Soviet sphere. Walter Lippmann and the influential broadcaster Raymond Swing admonished Churchill for what the former called his "unnecessarily provoking approach" to the Soviet Union. But a columnist in the *New York Herald Tribune* noted, in

[47] For the Trieste episode, see Gilbert, *Churchill*, VII, pp. 1303–1327, 1334. Churchill to Eisenhower, March 31, 1945, PREM 3.341/5; Churchill to Roosevelt, April 1, 1945, *Correspondence*, III, pp. 603–605; Churchill to Roosevelt, April 5/6, 1945, ibid., pp 613–614; Roosevelt to Churchill, April 6, 1945, ibid., p. 617; Stephen E. Ambrose, *Eisenhower and Berlin, 1945: The Decision to Halt at the Elbe* (Garden City, N.Y., 1967), pp. 84–98; Churchill, *Triumph and Tragedy*, pp. 515–516; Chiefs of Staff to Joint Staff Mission (Washington), May 30, 1945, PREM 3.398/10; Sargent to Churchill, May 9, 1945, PREM 3.123/2.

a more representative remark, that "the extent of Soviet backsliding upon its Yalta engagements seems by now fairly clear to the general public."[48]

But by the beginning of May the British were worried again. For one thing, Truman's general feistiness was counterpointed, as Churchill saw it, by a lack of political sophistication in the conduct of the European war's concluding military operations. He did show considerable resolution in resisting Tito's near takeover of Trieste (which Churchill called "this Muscovite tentacle"), but this was not a direct confrontation with the Soviets. The really important issue now, as the British saw it, was the question of where the two sides would end up in Central Europe at the moment of victory. Even earlier, Churchill had been shocked when on March 28 Eisenhower had unilaterally notified Stalin of his intention, despite the bridgehead he had established across the Rhine three weeks before, to drive toward central Germany rather than toward a Berlin that suddenly seemed within his grasp. Roosevelt had then rejected Churchill's protest that Berlin had "political significance." In late April there was another disappointment as Eisenhower (prompted by Marshall, who resolutely refused to allow political considerations to affect strategy) again refused to move vigorously toward Berlin as he could have done after his forces had crossed the Elbe on April 11. Truman upheld his military commanders, who saw little point in wasting lives when the zonal arrangements had already been settled. The Red Army consequently took Prague as well as Berlin. The prime minister's purpose in all this was to press on as far as possible into the areas already designated by agreement for postwar Soviet occupation in order to obtain by subsequent leverage the desired political easements in Poland and elsewhere. It was also becoming clear that, as Roosevelt had repeatedly warned, the United States was not planning to maintain forces in Europe any longer than was strictly necessary. More seriously, in mid-May Marshall informed Eden that the approximately 3.5 million American troops in Europe would be repatriated or sent to the Pacific at a proposed rate of 230,000 in June rising to about 400,000 in August.[49]

Meanwhile, tensions at the San Francisco United Nations conference, which opened on April 25, were dramatizing the emerging East/West confrontation. Here, to be sure, we do need a bilateral United States/Soviet frame of reference. To this point we have viewed the post-Yalta tensions as

---

[48] *New York Times*, May 14, 15, 1945; *New York Herald Tribune*, May 14, 15, 1945.

[49] Churchill to Eden, May 11, 1945, PREM 3.495/1. Ismay to Churchill, May 17, 1945; Churchill to Ismay, June 9, 1945, both in PREM 3.484. Halifax to Eden, cited in Anderson, *United States, Great Britain*, pp. 206–207, n. 47. See ibid., pp. 72–74, for an overview.

essentially an Anglo-Soviet struggle for the support of successive American administrations, with Churchill bent on a political attachment and Stalin on making Washington see the manipulative British hand at work behind every problematic issue. But now we are addressing the primary American postwar objective, and Soviet anxieties about its potential isolation, first announced at the 1944 Dumbarton Oaks conference, come again prominently into view. The very extensive coverage of the proceedings by the American and world media shows a series of United States–Soviet confrontations over such issues as the organization of the conference, the scope of the Charter, memberships for such states as Argentina, Poland, and the Ukraine, and finally, once again, vexing questions about the extent of the veto power. The feeble "European" presence was widely noticed. The British for the most part supported the American delegation and were comparatively passive, viewed by many American commentators as the representatives of a secondary power. Yet the Soviets continued their now persistent practice of blaming the Churchill government for their difficulties. *Izvestia*, for instance, declared bluntly on May 19 that the difficulties the Soviets were facing in San Francisco were due to the machinations of the British delegation.[50]

Even more alarmingly, Moscow launched a "war of nerves" through May against Turkey and Greece, the two vulnerable British client states in the Mediterranean. This was characterized by the British ambassador as "part of a Russian campaign to work on Turkish nerves." On May 7 word came of 400,000 Soviet troops massing on the Greek-Macedonian frontier. Over the next year or so these would be persistent politico-military flashpoints in an Anglo-Soviet relationship that was now decomposing rapidly.

There was, accordingly, considerable concern once more in London over the danger of Soviet geopolitical threats, with their clear repudiation of the Moscow Order. Meanwhile, the British were harassed in their European policies by a rising propaganda campaign by Stalin's regime against the so-called Western bloc. This was all the more worrying for the British because they were themselves losing control in the West. Domestically, the problem was that while the Foreign Office was still committed to a leadership role in this sphere, Churchill had virtually

---

[50] *Izvestia*, May 19, 1945. Divine, *Second Chance*, pp. 279–298. *New York Times*, May 24, 1945. *Izvestia*, May 25, 1945, again discussing the San Francisco conference, charged that "in particular the delegation of England" had not yet done everything in its power "to dispel all undesirable reservations and misunderstandings."

abandoned it after Yalta as he began to chase the grail of Anglo-American intimacy. The Western Europeans themselves were beginning to lose enthusiasm. The three Benelux states and Norway remained keen, as did the only half-welcome Iberian dictatorships. But the Swedes preferred a more universalistic system. The real sticking point was, as always, France. The pre-Yalta reconciliation had now worn out. Churchill and de Gaulle were still feuding over French aspirations in the Levant. An Anglo-French treaty, seen by most contemporaries as the precondition for a successful Western group, now seemed a distant prospect. "The problem is what to do next in view of the Prime Minister's reluctance to support the idea of a Western Group," lamented a leading Foreign Office diplomat, noting the prime minister's determination to avoid any intimacy with de Gaulle's government.[51]

By May all these dispiriting events were inducing in Churchill a mood of heavy despondency. Here we find talk of "a great catastrophe" and descriptions of the Soviet advance as "one of the most melancholy events in history." "What are we to do?" he lamented to Eden on May 11 as he watched the Anglo-American armies "melting" while hundreds of Red Army divisions remained. Pressured by the Soviets, disenchanted with France, no longer sure of American resolve (yet telling Eden that it was vital to settle with the Soviets "before the U.S. withdrawal"), Churchill retreated again, as he had done in late 1944, to thoughts of the last and certainly the least respectable option: the idea of collaboration with the German military. At the beginning of May his race for Lubeck was intended to ensure that the half-million or so German troops in Scandinavia would surrender to the British rather than to the Russians. The Soviets soon caught on to this and began to charge in their media that the British were setting up a secret German army.[52]

---

[51] Churchill to Peterson, June 17, 1945; PREM 3.447/4A. Harbutt, *Iron Curtain*, pp. 108–109. Radio Moscow, June 5, 1945, *BBC Digest*, File 2149. Churchill to Eden, February 8, 1945; minute by Ward, January 11, 1945, both in F.O. 371.50826. Hood minute, April 2, 1945; Ward minute, January 11, 1945, both ibid. For a journalistic champion of the Western bloc, see *The Economist*, June 2, 9, 23, 1945.

[52] Churchill to Eden, May 4, 11, 1945, PREM 3.495/1; Ambrose, *Eisenhower and Berlin*, pp. 84–98. Churchill, *Triumph and Tragedy*, pp. 515–516; Radio Moscow, July 18, 1945, August 3, 1945, *BBC Digest*, Files 2192 and 2208. For postwar confirmations of Churchill's wartime thoughts of enlisting German assistance, see Halifax, *Diary*, September 15, 1952, and Parliamentary debates (Commons), Vol. 535 (1954–55), pp. 170–171. For Churchill's plans to establish a Polish "Foreign Legion" in Germany, see Churchill to Grigg, May 31, 1945, PREM 3.352/13. See also Smith, *Churchill's German Army*, pp. 11–24 and passim.

It was then in a context of general policy disintegration that the British had from about mid-May to endure the consequences of Truman's second thoughts. It was perhaps inevitable that the new president would realize at some point how far he had drifted from Roosevelt's very public policy of accommodation and comity with the Soviet ally. Opinion polls in May suggested that about 75% of Americans favored continuing cooperation. Truman was now falling under the intellectual sway of Joseph P. Davies, former United States ambassador to Moscow and a persistent advocate of the Soviet viewpoint. He began, accordingly, to question his association with Churchill. Writing to Eleanor Roosevelt on May 10, he said, "The difficulties with Churchill are nearly as exasperating as they are with the Russians." Unsurprisingly, therefore, Truman responded to an idea generated by Harriman and Bohlen that he send Hopkins to Moscow to try and patch up relations with Stalin. The shallow character of his early aggressiveness, much of it rooted in personal insecurity, can be measured by the minimal instructions he gave Hopkins, simply asking him, in the course of a ten-minute conversation, to try to recapture the mood of Yalta and "put things right with Stalin."[53]

The Soviets, probably tipped off by Davies (whom Truman sent on a complementary, unwelcomed mission to Churchill), prepared the ground carefully. *Izvestia* remarked reproachfully on May 25 upon "an impression that the foreign policy of Roosevelt no longer reflects the true tendencies of the United States." *Pravda*, a few days later, declared that "if only Roosevelt had been alive everything would have been different." Gratifyingly, they found in Hopkins a virtual reincarnation of the dead president, different only in his more businesslike approach. Stalin put himself out and, according to Bohlen, who accompanied the emissary, made himself available at any time Hopkins desired. Stalin opened the talks with a series of bitter criticisms of British policy and of Churchill, whom he blamed for the difficulties that had appeared since Yalta. Hopkins attempted no defense. The agreement he reached with Stalin, which Truman soon endorsed, gave non-Lublin Poles (subject to Soviet approval) four or five of the projected eighteen of twenty ministries, all the others going to Lublin or its nominees. It was a triumphant moment for Stalin. Not only had he maintained his association with the Allies through the war's finale, but by standing firm since Yalta he had

---

[53] For polls, see memorandum by MacLeish, May 23, 1945, SD 711.61/5–2345. Letter cited in Robert Ferrell (ed.), *Off the Record: The Private Papers of Harry S. Truman* (New York, 1980), pp. 20–22. For Davies see Miscamble, *From Roosevelt to Truman*, pp. 135–153.

got what he wanted in Poland. Just as important, he had seemingly broken the Anglo-American political alignment, one that was unlikely to be renewed as the Truman administration accelerated its troop withdrawals from Europe.[54]

During these talks Stalin yet again resorted, during a rare moment of debate and uncertainty over the list on non-Lublin Poles to be invited, to his habitual "bargain" diplomacy. In San Francisco, Gromyko suddenly reversed course and insisted, once again upon the veto power over discussion in the Security Council, characterizing it on June 1 as his "final position." This last-minute reopening of the old argument produced consternation. Truman immediately cabled Stalin accepting the Soviet formula for Poland and instructing Hopkins to raise "the impasse that had come about at the San Francisco conference." Stalin immediately responded, after a charade of consultation with Molotov, by signifying his return to his Yalta promise. Remarkably, there still seems to have been no recognition in Washington of Stalin's tactics, the assumption apparently being that the Soviets treated these issues as entirely separate from each other. Yet Stalin was simply asserting again his now chronic yet scarcely noticed tendency to work his whole American policy on the United Nations/Eastern Europe basis.[55]

The Hopkins mission marks the conclusion of the post-Yalta crisis. That crisis was the consequence, at root, of Roosevelt's failure to resolve his Yalta dilemma – how to satisfy Stalin without losing control of American domestic sentiment – and his consequent resort to a dangerously false public vision of the meetings' outcome. But it was also due to Churchill, who, doubtless wanting to help Poland but also eager to create a working Anglo-American front, had publicly and politically entrenched Roosevelt's false version of Yalta and the improbably high standard of conduct this imposed upon the Soviets. This provoked the hard-line Soviet response in the Moscow ambassadorial commission, which in turn gave Churchill the opportunity to pressure Roosevelt to join in confronting the Soviets. From the Soviet viewpoint the whole affair must have been seen as the Western Allies' effort to win through public diplomacy (where they held all the high cards thanks to Stalin's signature on the compromising Yalta documents) what they had failed to win through negotiation at Yalta. But Stalin stood firm and, through a series of

---

[54] The full record of the Hopkins-Stalin talks is in FRUS, 1945, Vol. 1 (Washington, D.C., 1960), pp. 21–62. See also Sherwood, *Roosevelt and Hopkins*, pp. 887–912; and Forrestal, *Diary*, May 20, 1945. *Izvestia*, May 25, 1945; *Pravda*, May 27, 1945.

[55] Divine, *Second Chance*, pp. 294–296. For British perplexity, see Law to Churchill, June 4, 1945, and Churchill to Halifax, June 6, 1945, both in PREM 4.31/7.

encounters, prevailed in the end, achieving both a satisfying settlement over Poland and a breach in the Anglo-American alignment.

Looking beneath the surface charges and countercharges, we see too that the post-Yalta crisis was significant in being the first Anglo-Soviet struggle over the fate of Europe. For more than three years the two powers had moved, warily but steadily, toward the apparent crystallization manifest in the Moscow Order in October 1944. Now, in the new spectrum of possibilities opened up by the confusing backwash of the American engagement at Yalta, they were confronting each other, ostensibly over the fate of Poland, but really for the support of the United States. Thus, on three occasions (the "blunt" February 27 speech with its "totalitarian" references; the March 27 effort to commit Roosevelt to "our" interpretation; and the May 14 speech dramatizing the establishment of "totalitarian" and "police" regimes in Eastern Europe) Churchill had tried to strengthen the American commitment to the Yalta standard. And on at least three occasions Stalin had tried to expose, mainly for American edification, the manipulative British hand (by ostentatiously subverting British authority in Greece in early March after Churchill had tried, secretly and without success, to push FDR forward there; and then by blaming Britain, first for the Bern Incident and later for its supposed role in undermining Soviet diplomacy at the San Francisco conference). Here too it was Stalin who appeared to have prevailed.

A series of striking denouements soon followed. The United States and the Soviets now moved closer to each other. Stettinius proclaimed that strengthened collaboration with Moscow was the "primary" American objective. Stalin and Truman exchanged several cordial messages in June, including the former's warm acknowledgment of American aid during the war. Truman now took the initiative, over Churchill's protests, in withdrawing American troops from their forward positions in the east. Meanwhile, the Truman administration turned a colder shoulder to the British, rushing ahead of the embarrassed Foreign Office in recognizing the only lightly modified Polish government and publishing accelerated schedules of anticipated troop withdrawals from Europe. Churchill was able to dissuade Truman from his wish to meet alone with Stalin before the Potsdam conference. But Anglo-American relations were now cooler at every level.[56]

Within days of Hopkins's departure from Moscow, the Soviets, in a retributive mood, launched a propaganda campaign attacking London's imperial policies and recalling the sins of the "Men of Munich" and the City of London capitalists. More substantively, the threat to Britain's clients

---

[56] Harbutt, *Iron Curtain*, pp. 105–110.

and strategic interests, hitherto largely a "war of nerves," began in early June to assume a more ominous cast. Now the Soviets formally demanded a role in Norway's affairs. They then moved on Britain's Mediterranean sphere, announcing a desire to participate in the international administration of Tangier, facing Gibraltar. Systematic "splitting" techniques were now employed in the media to stir up the existing tensions between Britain and France over the fate of Syria and Lebanon.[57]

Meanwhile, a dangerous crisis was erupting over Turkey. The Soviet government had long wanted a revision of the Montreux Convention (which Churchill was prepared to accept) and a naval base on the Straits in Turkish territory. Now they insisted on the outright cession of the eastern provinces of Kars and Ardahan. The Turks resisted this fundamental threat to their independence stoutly and called on their British ally for help.

The British responded with promises of diplomatic support and more tangible aid if necessary. As Eden put it, "We must go ahead, basing ourselves primarily on our alliance with Turkey and our special interests in the Eastern Mediterranean." There were hopes for American support, but at this point none was forthcoming. Churchill faced up to the issue. "The Turks expect us to act even without U.S. support," he cabled an anxious Clark Kerr, "and we have told the U.S. government we will."[58]

The British accordingly registered a strong protest in Moscow and hoped to put off further Soviet pressure until the now imminent Potsdam summit conference, where some American diplomatic support might be found. But it was increasingly clear after the Hopkins mission that they were now isolated and that the fundamental geopolitical basis of the Moscow Order – the understanding that Soviet power in Eastern and Central Europe would be balanced by British predominance in Western Europe and the Mediterranean – was beginning to unravel.

The British felt their sudden isolation acutely. "We are alone again," lamented the Foreign Office's Orme Sargent. Churchill, surveying the new, bleak reality and now concerned also with an impending general election that had left him briefly at the head of a transitional all-Conservative government, felt powerless to resist. He composed tough-minded letters to both Truman and Stalin, lecturing the president on the superiority of Anglo-American values to the balance-of-power obsessions of the Soviets

---

[57] Radio Moscow, June 5, 6, 7, *BBC Digest*, Files 2149, 2150, 2151. Peterson to Eden, July 3, 1945, PREM 3.447/4A; Mastny, *Russia's Road*, p. 289; Harbutt, *Iron Curtain*, pp. 108–109.

[58] Eden to Halifax, June 12, 1945; and Churchill to Clark Kerr, June 17, 1945, both in PREM 3.495/10.

and warning him not to ignore the philosophical differences between the freedom-loving Anglo-Americans and the Soviet methods of "police government, which they are applying in every state which has fallen a victim to their liberating armies." He then drew up a blunt cable to Stalin drawing attention to the gathering political division of Europe and the dangers posed by power politics. "It seems to me," he wrote, "that a Russianised frontier running from Lubeck through Eisenach to Trieste and down to Albania is a matter which requires a very great deal of argument between good friends." But Churchill's self-confidence was now ebbing, and he did not send either of these messages.[59]

This was a particularly difficult moment for the British leader, reminiscent of the politico-military reverses and the sudden lurch in power and status that came in early 1942. Here he was in the spring of 1945 at the crowning point of his brilliant, unique career – "the man who won the war," as millions saw it – yet weighed down with foreboding. All Churchill's policies were now either discredited or in a state of near collapse. The laboriously constructed Anglo-American political front, for which he had put his relations with Stalin at risk, was now damaged if not completely broken. Moreover, the Americans seemed more committed than ever to a rapid liquidation of their responsibilities in Europe. The Anglo-Soviet nexus, in which so much had been invested, systematically by the Foreign Office and sporadically by Churchill himself, had now turned into a dangerously escalating confrontation. The solidarity of Western Europe had been badly compromised since Yalta by the continuing failure to work creatively with de Gaulle's France. And the loyalty of the empire was also in danger of unraveling as Indian independence became more certain and the Canadians moved ever closer to the United States. The Australian and New Zealand delegates at the San Francisco conference, whose countries had already moved into the strategic orbit of the United States, were now loudly proclaiming their independent outlook as leaders among the smaller powers. Meanwhile, his coalition at home was breaking up as the Labour ministers moved into formal opposition. Within a few weeks the downward spiral would be complete as Churchill lost both the postwar general election and the premiership.

Sargent, contemplating Britain's broader predicament in the face of Soviet hostility, found the new situation created by the Hopkins and Davies missions "too much like 1938 to be altogether pleasant." Most alarmingly,

---

[59] Churchill to Truman (draft), May 27, 1945, PREM 3.430/1. Churchill to Stalin (draft), June 23, 1945, PREM 3.495/10. Sargent memorandum, May 31, 1945, N6645, F.O. 371.47882.

he perceived in this unwelcome American activism "a certain restatement of what has always fundamentally been America's European policy." "She is not going to be dragged into a quarrel between Great Britain and the Soviet Union," he continued, "and she is not going to allow Great Britain to dictate to her European policy." Therefore, he concluded, "we should walk warily in our dealings with Russia." Eden noted on the memorandum "I am in entire agreement."[60]

In fact, after a further nine months of uncertainty, it all turned out very differently. Sargent was probably right in assuming that Truman's America still aspired to be a detached "independent" mediator, a posture it soon took, so far as European issues were concerned, at the Potsdam conference that opened in late July. And clearly Churchill's bid to create the desired Anglo-American line-up against the Soviets on the basis of the Polish issue had failed. But some of the more promising aspects of Yalta's legacy – the agreement on a United Nations structure that would give small countries access to a functioning institution; the more concrete if not yet conclusive entanglement of the United States in European affairs (significantly, Sargent had referred back to the woes of 1938, not 1919); the compromising Soviet commitments in the Declaration on Liberated Europe and other documents – would continue to shape attitudes and determine the course and character of events and eventually go on to produce a second decisive diplomatic confrontation with Stalin's state in early 1946. This would take place – not over a complex European issue where the British association was for the United States an inhibiting factor, where wartime considerations still operated, and where the Soviets were still widely believed to have a genuine interest and some degree of morality on their side – but in the pristine arena of the new Security Council and over what was widely recognized and easily portrayed as the clear and visible violation by a predatory Great Power of the sovereignty of an innocent small power. There, at last, American "universalism" and Soviet "expansionism" would come into a direct, conclusive confrontation.

THE COMING OF THE COLD WAR: THE MARCH–APRIL 1946 CRISIS

It took the second post-Yalta crisis in early 1946 to bring the United States and the Soviet Union face to face directly in what is habitually called the Cold War. Yalta was now a year distant, and there were, needless

---

[60] Sargent memorandum and Eden comment, May 22, 1945, ibid.

to say, significant intervening causative elements. But the lineage is still clearly discernible. Yalta had brought the United States more fully into the European political milieu. Its two most characteristically American features – the "Code and Court" values expressed in the Declaration on Liberated Europe and the practical arrangements for the United Nations, now institutionalized – are a fundamental context for any explanation of the March 1946 confrontation. That crisis brought about the crucial reorientation of the three World War II allies. For unlike the tensions immediately following Yalta, this event saw the fateful convergence of an American universalism now embodied in a working United Nations, and European geopolitics in the form of what was sometimes called an Anglo-Soviet "war of nerves" but was in actuality a first Cold War.

We certainly cannot ignore the momentous half-year from Potsdam to the United Nations/Iran crisis of early 1946. It was full of dramatic incident, much of it having a bearing on that crisis, though indirectly, and indeed on the course of the later Cold War. But it is very clear that after the Truman administration turned away from confrontation in late May 1945, a quieter period followed. There were innumerable distractions ranging from the apparent Big Three collaboration at Potsdam, through the shocks of Hiroshima and Nagasaki to victory over Japan, and then the turn of public attention to the agitations of demobilization and socioeconomic reconversion. The Soviets, for their part, were busy consolidating their position in Eastern Europe; the British turned during the summer to a domestically oriented Labour government. There were controversial issues, to be sure. The coming of the atomic age brought immediate complications. There were difficulties over the governance of Germany and Japan. And the first steps in the general peacemaking were disappointing and sometimes acrimonious.

But none of these issues, important as they seemed at the time or in retrospect, were inflamed enough in 1945 to drive the United States and the Soviet Union into a general political confrontation. Few scholars accept today, for instance, the revisionist argument that the atomic bomb was used against Japan primarily to intimidate the Soviets. It undoubtedly fostered anxiety and suspicion in Moscow and inspired Stalin to accelerate his own nuclear program. Truman, and especially Byrnes, privately viewed the American monopoly as a diplomatic asset, but they were studiously unprovocative in public and by November had committed the United States to the principle of international control, hardly the action of a state bent on intimidation.[61]

---

[61] Gaddis, *We Now Know,* Chapter 4; Holloway, *Stalin and the Bomb*, passim.

There were more overt tensions as the post-Potsdam administration of Germany took shape, but here again more or less predictable reactions were far from fatal. Germany was the principal business at the Big Three Potsdam summit in July and August. Roosevelt had originally intended to focus on Germany at Yalta and avoid other European issues. This is, on the whole, the line that Truman followed. As he openly declared, "I have not come here to judge each separate country in Europe or examine the disputes which should be settled by the world organization set up at San Francisco."

The arrangements made for Germany at Potsdam, however, were very much an American initiative. James F. Byrnes, now secretary of state, skillfully pushed through a formula that gave the Soviet Union a specific share plus a percentage of non-essential production from the western zones in return for needed food from their more agricultural zone. It has been argued that the failure to resolve the German issue conclusively at Potsdam led to partition and therefore made the Cold War likely, if not inevitable. Perhaps in the long run it did. But this is not how things looked at the time. For one thing, everyone appears to have recognized and understood at least some of the difficulties involved as well as the rights, in some form, of all the allies to be involved in the final postwar settlement. The familiar instinct to defer persisted here. Nevertheless, the Allied Control Council began to function, and rising suspicions over Soviet motives in London and Washington were tempered by irritation over the distracting French agitations for radical dismemberment in the western part of the country. Like the atomic bomb, the German issue was always a central and sometimes dramatic object of concern and political commentary. By mid-1946 it had become a dangerous flashpoint. But by then the Cold War had already received its initiating spark from other causes, as we will shortly see.[62]

There were also tense exchanges over the Far East as well as the Soviets pushed for a larger part in the administration of Japan. General MacArthur, a virtual sovereign there, was rigidly opposed. The Truman administration backed him up and showed an increasing determination to strengthen the Nationalist regime in China and to limit the growth of Soviet influence in the region generally. But for most of 1945 the Soviets seemed bent on honoring their pledge to support Chiang Kai Shek. Meanwhile, both the major powers appeared to favor a nationalist-communist compromise.

---

[62] See, for a study of American perspectives and policies, Eisenberg, *Drawing the Line*. pp. 72–120. For Truman at Potsdam, see Miscamble, *From Roosevelt to Truman*, pp. 188–200. See also FRUS, *Potsdam*, passim.

This was a chaotic, grievously damaged region in the aftermath of nearly fifteen years of war. The slowly developing United States–Soviet rivalry in East Asia was a relatively new factor among several deep-rooted themes working themselves out with varying degrees of tension and violence.[63]

The fourth theme in United States–Soviet relations during this interim period – the tensions engendered by the initial peace negotiations for peace treaties with Hitler's satellites – is not so easily put to one side, for it has a closer bearing on the early 1946 crisis. Here there were some difficult diplomatic encounters, though again no one expected postwar problems to be resolved easily, given the extraordinary dislocations of the war and the acknowledged differences in outlook among the victors. Still, the first postwar meeting of the foreign ministers in London in September 1945 was alarming to many, for it soon developed into angry exchanges between the Western powers and the Soviets over the status of France and China and the eligibility of the Rumanian and Bulgarian regimes for diplomatic recognition. Byrnes's decision to terminate the stalemated conference shocked a public used to the well-packaged illusions of wartime summitry.[64]

From this point on, there was a growing sense of irritation with the Soviets in the Truman administration and in the American media. When the notoriously flexible Byrnes returned from Moscow at the end of December, having made what now seemed to many in Washington dubious compromises with Stalin and Molotov, he ran into the displeasure of the president. Truman was now under rising pressure from Congress, from the Republican-oriented press, and from several influential members of his own administration and political circle to take a harder line with the increasingly uncooperative Kremlin. Truman is said to have told Byrnes, "I'm tired of babying the Soviets." And it seems clear that he reprimanded the secretary of state for exceeding his authority in Moscow and failing to clear matters with him. But the underlying concern now was Soviet conduct, and it seems fair to say that from this moment on the new reality in Washington was an administration that was suddenly receptive to the idea of a basic change in its Soviet policy. The problem – which reflects the still uncrystallized character of American postwar diplomacy – was finding a

---

[63] Michael Shaller, *Douglas MacArthur: The Far East General* (New York, 1989), pp. 120–157. See also, for Soviet reassurances to Chiang Kai Shek in mid-1945, Yawei Liu, "Mao and America" (Ph.D. dissertation, Emory University, 1990), p. 121. Despite the Yalta assurances the Soviets did, in July 1945, try to press the Chinese into further concessions – Clark Kerr to Eden, July 18, 1945, F.O. 371.54073.

[64] For the London foreign ministers conference see FRUS, 1945, 2, pp. 192–310; and Messer, *End of an Alliance*, pp. 115–136.

way to bring this about. No one seems to have had a clear sense of how to effect such a transformation.[65]

Where then, if not in these events, do we find the direct cause of the March 1946 crisis? We find it in the sudden convergence of the very different and thus far distinct American and Soviet working political arenas. The American one was of course the United Nations Security Council, hitherto little more than a blueprint but suddenly available at the beginning of 1946 as an active instrument of power. This now gave the United States a congenial forcing ground both for political activism and for an educative display that would strengthen the new internationalism. But like any legal institution the Security Council needed litigants. Here we find the deeply rooted geopolitical tension between the Soviet Union and Britain in and around Europe and especially along the so-called Northern Tier of Greece, Turkey, and Iran. The key to understanding the 1946 crisis is that these two arenas converged at the beginning of 1946 as the Anglo-Soviet struggle over Iran came into the orbit of the United Nations Security Council.[66]

The geopolitical dimension was crucial. As we have seen, Soviet pressure upon the British clients in the Northern Tier began soon after Yalta. The intensity of the Soviet outward thrust abated somewhat at the time of Potsdam as diplomatic concessions seemed possible. But it flared up more fiercely later in 1945 as the United States appeared, despite its new responsibilities in Europe, eager to return to a traditional detachment (at least so far as Britain's problems were concerned) and British policy fell into the hands of the domestically oriented Labour Party. By this time it was already clear to observers in London that the Soviets were determined to violate and move beyond the constrictions of the Moscow Order. Entrenched now in Eastern Europe, an inheritance they had always justified in terms of security, they seemed bent on expanding beyond it into the Mediterranean and Near East, where they apparently felt they could hope to advance their interests at British expense and without serious opposition from the United States.[67]

Why did the Soviets mount this inevitably destabilizing campaign against their erstwhile associate? It must be said first that despite a general

---

[65] Ibid., pp. 157–165.
[66] For the first Security Council sessions, see S.C. Official Records, 1st. year, 1st. series, no. 1.
[67] See, for this evolution, Harbutt, *Iron Curtain*, pp. 118–150. For British anxiety over Soviet moves, see Donaldson (India Office) to Warner, November 20, 1945, cited in Baxter minute, December 21, 1945, N16025, F.O. 371.47858.

fidelity, at least in the first half-year of its existence and fitfully for a time thereafter, to the Anglo-Soviet concert and the Moscow Order, the Soviets had throughout made clear their desire, first, to secure from Turkey a base at the Straits with its necessary implication of access to the Mediterranean, which Churchill had been willing to accept because he believed it could be controlled by British and associated power, and, second, to secure a dominant position in northern Iran. To some extent these aims blurred the 1944 distinction between a Soviet sphere in Eastern and Central Europe and the British Mediterranean arena. In neither case, however, does there appear to have been any desire to occupy the whole country, though the Turks and Iranians could hardly have been expected to believe that. The striking characteristic in each case is that these were enduring Soviet objectives, persisted in since the nineteenth century. Later on, during the Cold War itself, much of the Western analysis of Soviet motives interpreted this "new" expansionary thrust as part of a push toward world domination, variously inspired by state imperialism, communist ideology, or by Stalin's personal ambition or paranoia. But national interest, historically informed, seems to have been the governing Soviet impulse during the transitional period we are studying.

More generally, two primary interests seem to stand out from a review of Soviet conduct in these years. One, the need to secure Eastern Europe, was by now virtually achieved. The second, similarly geopolitical and also of long standing, was domination of the regions to the south – the Balkans, the Straits, and northern Iran. Molotov in his memoirs recalled Stalin contemplating a map of the Soviet Union's borders after the war and expressing general satisfaction with what had been achieved but worried about vulnerabilities in the south that needed to be addressed. But here, following the path set by the tsars, the Soviets, in the words of Bevin's secretary, "found us in the way." And it probably was the prospect of consequent difficulties with Britain that reinforced the logic of a third compelling concern for the Soviet leaders, a natural one for the distinctively separate state in what appeared to be developing into a three-power system, to ensure that the United States and Britain – or, more precisely, the marriage of American power and Britain's worldwide interests – did not combine against them.[68]

This perspective allows us to identify the great permissive cause of the post-Yalta Soviet campaign against Britain and her European,

---

[68] Ulam, *Rivals*, Chapter 4; Mastny, *Russia's Road*, pp. 6, 7; Resis (ed.), *Molotov Remembers*, p. 8; memorandum by Dixon, September 24, 1945, N13101/G, F.O. 371.47861.

Mediterranean, and Near Eastern associates and client states. It was the growing sense of license that must have come from the impression of detachment from British interests consistently given through 1945 by Roosevelt, Hopkins, Truman (except briefly in the spring of 1945) and Byrnes. There were, moreover, further reassurances in the actual repatriation of United States forces and the frequent declarations from American spokesmen of an intention to withdraw all but a few troops from Europe, suggesting a primary interest in the Western Hemisphere and the Pacific. Then too there was – for the moment at least, if not in the longer term – little to worry about in the constant identification by American leaders of the as yet untested United Nations Security Council as the exclusive forum for the solution of political problems. And behind these impulses again lay the fact, as the British embassy in Washington noted, that while there were now several serious socioeconomic Anglo-American tensions (food and transportation issues, oil rivalries, civil aviation disputes), the Soviet Union "rotating in its own orbit presents no comparable point of friction."69 Charles Bohlen drew a similar conclusion in a lecture on October 12:

> Between the Soviet Union and the United States there is no material concrete dispute of any character. There is no place where our material interests clash. There is no question of territorial dispute. There is no economic dispute or difference between the Soviet Union and the United States. So that objectively there is absolutely no reason why the two nations should not work out any problems they have between them. There is no need of war between the United States and Russia. The geopolitical location of the two countries does not provide places where the friction arises automatically.70

After Potsdam, then, the Soviet pressure against Britain and her associated states fell initially and most heavily on Turkey. But it now went far beyond the Straits issue. The demand for the cession of the eastern Kars and Ardahan provinces to the Soviet Union was a major escalation. The Turks sturdily refused to comply. The most significant event in the autumn, however, was an attempted left-wing coup in the northern Iranian province of Azerbaijan, still under Red Army occupation. This was put down but produced an ominously sharp Soviet media campaign in support both of the rebellion and of an autonomy for the region that could only bring it under Soviet domination.71

---

69 Halifax to Bevin, August 9, 1945, AM2560, F.O. 371.44557.
70 Bohlen lecture, October 12, 1945, Bohlen MSS, Box 3.
71 Harbutt, *Iron Curtain*, pp. 120, 124. The British sense of isolation as Soviet pressure intensified in late 1945 was palpable. Isaiah Berlin, stationed in Washington, remarked in

These were simply the flashpoints of what in late 1945 increasingly seemed to be a general, escalated Soviet push toward a dominant role in the Mediterranean and the Persian Gulf. In a clear departure from the Moscow Order, Stalin had laid claim at Potsdam to the postwar trusteeships of Cyrenaica in North Africa and the Dodecanese Islands. There were occasional temptations. At the London conference in September, Molotov raised the issue with Bevin and seemed willing to give up these new Soviet Mediterranean aspirations in return for the desired base in the Straits. But the British were in no position to betray the Turks, still very much a foundation of their influence in the region.[72]

Soviet press and radio attacks against the "reactionary regimes" in Turkey, Greece, and Iran intensified toward the end of the year amid reports of menacing Soviet troop movements on all the threatened frontiers. Other dangerous impulses were now developing into a general Soviet "war of nerves" against Britain and her numerous associations around the world. The *New Times,* as the English-language version of the bellwether *War and the Working Class* was now called, was seen in London as "going over to the offensive." In a long series of attacks on British "imperialism" and "colonialism," particular attention was paid to the British difficulties in India, the Far East, and Egypt. The British, blamed earlier by the Soviet media for the problems at the United Nations conference in San Francisco, were now accused of undermining the Allied Control Council in Germany and maintaining large *Luftwaffe* units in their zone, of showing excessive sympathy for the high-ranking Germans now on trial at the British-conducted Lüneburg trials, and, *inter alia*, of obstructing the international trade union conference in Paris. Meanwhile, there was a steady drumbeat of renewed agitation against the "Western bloc" supposedly taking shape under the aegis of British and French socialists (sometimes referred as "Mensheviks of the Second International"), and this was now counterpointed by effusive expressions of support for the large French and Italian communist parties. Britain was criticized also for its alleged close political ties with the fascist regimes of Spain and Portugal, both favored targets of Soviet hostility, and for trying to revive the economic power of the Ruhr in a British

October that "American/Soviet relations were better than Anglo-American." Roberts to Eden, October 30, 1945, N15507, F.O. 371.47858.
[72] Harbutt, *Iron Curtain*, pp. 118, 124–128; *New Times*, August 8, 1945; Clark Kerr, minutes of Bevin-Molotov meeting, September 23, 1945, N13784, F.O. 371.47883.

zone now, it was continually stressed, partially garrisoned by General
Anders's bitterly anti-Soviet Polish forces.[73]

What we see here, at the turn into 1946, is nothing less than an
Anglo-Soviet confrontation amounting to a first "Cold War," complete
with those basic characteristics – acute political tension not amounting
to actual violence between the two states, large geopolitical theaters of
contention, opposing systems of allies and client states, distinct ideological
differences, loud and virulent media polemics, all the while maintaining,
nonetheless, diplomatic representation and other contacts – that we recognize as marking the more familiar United States–Soviet Cold War that
grew out of this pre-existing struggle. This is not simply a semantic point.
For once this basic analogy is recognized, we find ourselves contemplating
a neglected feature of the mid-1940s, one that justifies a continuing attention to the gravitational pull of European politics, even after Yalta had
brought the United States somewhat more fully into the picture. This is the
fact that, with admitted differences in detail and context, the United States
was now poised to move, for the third time in three decades, largely again
because of its association with Britain and her interests but now through
a political instrument of its own making, to confront the latest would-be
European hegemon, joining once again a pre-existing struggle that had
already, as in the case of the two world wars, reached a significant point
of maturity. Whatever reservations one might have about a structural
approach to modern history, this is a remarkable recurrence that surely
deserves a deeper analysis.

But none of this was foreordained, though the situation in January 1946
was one of dangerous political uncertainty. The Truman administration
was frustrated by what it had come to regard as chronic Soviet obstructionism and eager to arrest with some forceful gesture the drift toward
accommodation signified by Byrnes's deals with Stalin in December. But it
was still unwilling to forge an anti-Soviet front with the British and unable,
in the absence of any traditional, territorial, or other point of contention
with Moscow, to see how the move to a harder line could be managed. On
the other hand, in a reconfiguration of the old European arena, we observe
a tense Anglo-Soviet relationship now seemingly on the verge of political
or even military confrontation. Unlike the Americans, however, the British
did see a clear way out. The best approach, Churchill recommended

---

[73] *New Times*, October 1, 15, 1945; Roberts to Bevin, October 31, 1945, N15702/G,
F.O. 371.47883. For Soviet media, see Radio Moscow, October 2–31, 1945, *BBC
Digest*, Files 2268–2297.

privately to Bevin in mid-November, was "to intertwine" the affairs of the British Commonwealth and the United States. This was also the view of the Foreign Office, of British and American diplomats in Moscow, and of several high-ranking officials in the Truman administration. But here too it was difficult to see how the trick could be turned. The gulf between the essentially practical, mostly administrative issues that agitated the surface of United States–Soviet relations, on the one hand, and the increasingly tense geopolitical antagonisms of the separate Anglo-Soviet Cold War, on the other, together with traditional official and public American suspicions of British diplomacy and the persisting personal tensions between Byrnes and Bevin, all worked to preclude a closer collaboration.[74]

At this point our thoughts turn to the second arena: the new world of the United Nations Security Council. It had been envisioned as, among other things, an outlet for the grievances of small as well as large powers. It seems fitting, then, that we begin with the unprompted action of the leader of a small power that set in motion the chain of events that would within two months bring the United States and the Soviet Union into a full political confrontation. This was the formal protest by Ebrahim Hakimi, the Persian prime minister, to the Security Council, scheduled to meet in January 1946 for its inaugural session in London. This initiative, pressed by the highly nationalistic Majlis in Teheran, sprang from the Soviet-supported coup in November in northern Iran that had led to the proclamation of both a national government of Persian Azerbaijan and the so-called Kurdish Peoples Republic, both now under the continuing protection of the Red Army.[75]

This invitation to crisis was avoidable. Neither Britain nor the United States promoted this initiative. Indeed, at the Moscow conference in late December Bevin had accused Stalin and Molotov of trying to force the incorporation of Azerbaijan into the Soviet Union, but he shrank from the prospect of a Security Council confrontation, urging instead the creation of a three-power commission to investigate the general situation. He warned Molotov of the danger of a Security Council crisis over Iran, noting that it would make trouble for all three powers. And Byrnes, declaring that he was "seriously disturbed," twice cautioned Stalin that Iran might complain to the Security Council, whereupon the United States would feel

---

[74] Churchill to Bevin, November 13, 1945, F.O. 800/512; Roberts to Bevin, October 23, 1945, N14346/G, F.O. 371.47883.

[75] For the situation in Iran, see Kirk, *Middle East*, pp. 64–65; Lenczowski, *Russia and the West*, p. 294.

obliged to support its right to be heard. Stalin, despite his own warnings at Yalta and later that the smaller powers might use the United Nations in this way to divide the Big Three, was strangely unworried. He promised Byrnes that the Soviets would withdraw as soon as they felt secure from the threat of Iranian sabotage to Soviet installations at Baku. He passed off the warning lightly, saying, according to Byrnes's recollection, "We will do nothing that will make you blush."[76]

Stalin's self-confidence seems to have come from a belief that the Iranian government of Hakimi, with the Red Army some thirty miles from Teheran and left-wing Tudeh Party agitators active in the streets of the capital, would back down. In the event, despite vigorous efforts by the British and Americans to dissuade him, Hakimi, pressed by the Majlis, went ahead with the protest and then, when the Soviets retaliated with a deadly campaign of economic strangulation, promptly resigned. The Soviets apparently suspected a British intrigue designed to create another Anglo-American front. But there is no evidence to substantiate this.[77]

The scene now moves to the January Security Council meeting in London. The Soviet delegate, the formidable Vishinsky, bristling with a resentment he did nothing to hide, immediately lodged a similar protest against alleged British excesses in Greece, while his Ukrainian delegate likewise complained about their conduct in Indonesia. The proceedings quickly degenerated into a series of angry Anglo-Soviet shouting matches. The Americans, who had also dreaded the confrontation but had felt obliged to tell the Iranians in principled fashion that they were "entirely free" to come to the United Nations, stood carefully aside. But the whole episode gave further impetus to anti-Soviet sentiment in the Truman administration and in the press. A week later, thanks largely to extreme economic pressure imposed on Iran by the Soviets, a more complaisant government came to power in Teheran, and Vishinsky was able to push the issue to bilateral Soviet-Iranian negotiations.[78]

This first Security Council debacle was disappointing to many observant Americans whose hopes were strongly invested in a United Nations that would curb violence, solve problems, and reflect the determination of the victorious powers to work together harmoniously and rationally to build

[76] For Bevin, see Bohlen, *Witness to History*, p. 250; for Byrnes's effort, see Byrnes, *Speaking Frankly*, pp. 118–120; cf. Memo of Conversation, December 23, 1945, FRUS, 1945, 2, pp. 750–752.

[77] Kirk, *Middle East*, pp. 64–65.

[78] SC Official Records, 1st. year, 1st. series, Supplement N.1, pp. 17–19; *New York Times*, January 21, 1945.

a better world. At the political level, however, its significance in the general move toward a full United States–Soviet confrontation lies in the fact that it was the first of several events that, coming one after another in late January and February, suddenly provoked a higher level of American governmental, press, and public antipathy to the Soviet Union. Another sensation was the shocking revelation on February 3 that a Soviet atomic spy ring had been active in the Manhattan Project. Then came the embarrassing exposure of Roosevelt's extensive Far Eastern concessions to Stalin at Yalta. This was followed by Stalin's famous February 9 "election" speech, asserting that communism and capitalism were "incompatible." It was widely perceived, at this sensitive juncture, as a declaration of postwar noncooperation. The cumulative effect of all these seemingly provocative Soviet actions – which together may be viewed as the first stage of a four-stage crisis – was to reinforce the Truman administration's desire to toughen up its Soviet policies, but still without offering a clear course of action. At the same time, in the absence of a clear lead from the nation's political leaders, who were still reluctant to openly confute the Rooseveltian Yalta vision of postwar collaboration with the Soviets, public opinion was now more alert and troubled but still confused rather than polarized.[79]

This brings us to the second stage of the 1946 crisis. The provocations – the first stage – were quickly followed by two authoritative definitions of the Soviet conduct that had produced them together with precise prescriptions for the appropriate response. The first to occur was the famous "long telegram" of February 22 from the United States' chargé-in Moscow, George F. Kennan. Asked by the puzzled State Department for his analysis of recent Soviet behavior, Kennan, respected by all foreign representatives in Moscow for his knowledge and insight into Soviet patterns of behavior, wrote that they viewed the world as divided between communist and capitalist camps that could not coexist. They saw themselves as engaged in a constant struggle for power and were devoted to the aggrandizement of the Soviet state, by covert as well as conventional means. The United States must mount a defensive resistance and wait for internal changes in the Soviet Union to ameliorate the situation. Kennan's intellectually cogent review was widely noted in the Truman administration and disseminated in Washington, though its impact on the course of events at this point is hard to evaluate.[80]

---

[79] Gaddis, *U.S. and the Origins*, pp. 299–301; De Santis, *Diplomacy of Silence*, pp. 172–175; Harbutt, *Iron Curtain*, pp. 158–159.

[80] Kennan to Byrnes, February 22, 1945, FRUS, 1946, 2, pp. 696–709. Author's interview with Sir Frank Roberts, March 1986.

This is in part because it coincided with – and, in a sense, competes with, as a foundational document in the ideological and political reorientation of United States policy during this tense period – Winston Churchill's "Iron Curtain" speech at Fulton, Missouri, on March 5, presented in the seemingly endorsing presence of President Truman. The available evidence suggests that the first intimations of a harder American line, which appeared on February 12, two days after Churchill met with Truman and Byrnes at the White House to discuss the forthcoming speech, were inspired in some way by that anticipated event. For Churchill made it clear to Truman and Byrnes that he intended to charge that the Soviets wanted, not war certainly, but the fruits of war, namely, "the indefinite expansion of their power and doctrines." The threat to Europe and beyond could only be met by what, in deference to American reservations about "empire," he intended to call "a fraternal association," but which would be universally recognized as a full Anglo-American political and military alliance on a global basis.[81]

This was a worldwide sensation, breaking completely with the convention of public cordiality toward the Soviets hitherto observed, despite rising misgivings, by other British and American public figures. The speech was a remarkably multidimensional political oration, containing within it a characteristically Churchillian blend of grand themes, resonant cultural associations, striking metaphors, and closely focused arguments. In essence it was a call to the American people to recognize and face up to a Soviet threat, which he spelled out in graphic detail:

From Stettin in the Baltic to Trieste in the Adriatic, an iron curtain has descended across the Continent. Behind that line lie all the capitals of the ancient states of Central and Eastern Europe ... and all are subject in one form or another, not only to Soviet influence but to a very high and increasing measure of control from Moscow ... the Communist parties, which were very small in all these eastern states of Europe, have been raised to preeminence and power far beyond their numbers and are seeking everywhere to obtain totalitarian control. Police governments are prevailing in nearly every case, and so far, except in Czechoslovakia, there is no true democracy.

Churchill went on to argue that this new would-be hegemon was very much on the move, advancing beyond Europe now and bent, he clearly implied, on Nazi-like world domination. He specifically drew attention to

---

[81] *Vital Speeches*, 12 (March 12, 1946), pp. 329–332. For background diplomacy, see Harbutt, *Iron Curtain*, pp. 159–182.

the vulnerability of the British sphere in the Mediterranean and the Near East and called for an Anglo-American "fraternal association," with full military cooperation and sharing of bases around the world, to lead the free nations in protecting "Christian civilization."[82]

It is important to recognize that Churchill's speech was much more than an exercise in political definition and public mobilization. It was also a key part of a fundamental American policy reorientation – fairly seen as a third stage in the course of the accelerating crisis – now being initiated by Truman and Byrnes. A look at the sequence of events between February 10 and March 5 illustrates the point. Before Churchill's visit to the White House on February 10 it is hard to find any trace of a "firm" American response to the unsettling Soviet behavior that was now agitating the American press and public. As late as February 4, for instance, Secretary Byrnes was still talking enthusiastically to reporters about the prospects of accommodation with the Soviet Union. On February 10, however, Truman and Churchill agreed, according to Admiral Leahy, who was present, that the subject of his far forthcoming speech would be "the necessity for full military collaboration between Great Britain and the United States." Leahy foresaw "forceful objection by the Soviets." But that seems to have been the point, for almost immediately Byrnes, moving quickly to associate himself with this new approach, sent an unprecedented volley of protests to Moscow. On February 12, he complained about Soviet conduct in Bulgaria, Rumania, and Austria, and also sent a formal reprimand to the communist regime in Albania. On February 15, he questioned the Soviet failure to honor the Potsdam agreement revising Allied Control Council procedures in the Balkans and in Hungary. On February 17, he ostentatiously created a public stir by flying to Florida for a visit with Churchill, clearly in connection with the now imminent speech, which was already attracting considerably press speculation about a new, tougher stance toward the Soviet Union. On February 22, Byrnes embarked on some delicate stage setting by sending secret word to Teheran encouraging the new Iranian prime minister (in a reversal of his earlier attempts to play the issue down) to return his protest over the Soviet occupation to the next Security Council meeting scheduled for New York in March, and clearly implying that the United States would be supportive.[83]

---

[82] For analysis of the speech and responses, see ibid., pp. 183–208.

[83] For the February 10 meeting, see Leahy diary, February 10, 1946, and Halifax diary, February 10, 1946. For diplomatic initiatives, see Byrnes to Cohen, February 12, 1946,

Then came the secretary's landmark February 28 speech to the Overseas Press Club announcing a new American approach to the Soviet Union based on "patience and firmness." The United States wanted "friendly relations" but would not accept "unilateralism." It intended to "defend the Charter" and would "resist aggression" (broadly defined to include political subversion) by force if necessary, for, he added, "if we are to be a great power we must act as a great power not only in order to secure our own security but in order to preserve the peace of the world." Finally, on the very day of Churchill's speech, March 5, Byrnes hammered the Anglo-American association home by sending three terse geopolitically far-reaching notes to Moscow. One, patently designed to cause embarrassment in Moscow, called for copies of the supposedly coercive bilateral economic agreements the Soviets had made with the Eastern European governments. This was reinforced by a critical aide-memoire lodged on the same day with the Bulgarians. The second protested against the recent Soviet economic demands upon China. A third complained strongly about Soviet conduct in Iran. The *New York Times*, which picked up the protests over China and Iran but missed the initiatives on Eastern European issues, commented, "One would have to go back far ... to find two United States protest notes to one power on two different issues on the same day."[84]

We see here the appropriation of a very willing Winston Churchill by Truman and Byrnes. They apparently saw the forthcoming Fulton speech, which they knew after February 10 would be an unprecedentedly harsh political attack upon the current course of Soviet policy, as an ostensibly individual initiative behind which they could, without the completely unambiguous commitment of support that might well stir Anglophobic and other criticism at home, make it clear to the Soviets that they agreed with Churchill. More substantively, they were telling the Kremlin, through

SD 874.00/2–946; Byrnes to Berry, February 12, 1946, FRUS, 1946, 6, p. 576; Byrnes to Eckhardt, February 12, FRUS, 1946, 5, p. 307. Byrnes to Kennan, February 15, 1946, FRUS, 1945, 6, pp. 74–75; Byrnes to Kennan, February 22, 1946, FRUS, 1946, 7, pp. 334–335. *New York Times*, February 18, 1946. *Daily Worker*, February 20, 1946.

[84] For the speech, see Department of State, *Bulletin* (March 10, 1946), pp. 355–358. For diplomatic initiatives, see Byrnes to Kennan, March 5, 1946, FRUS, 1946, 6, pp. 269–270 (economic); Department of State *Bulletin* (March 17, 1946), pp. 448–449 (China); and Byrnes to Kennan, March 5, 1946, FRUS, 1946, 7, pp. 340–342 (Iran). *New York Times*, March 5, 1946. For good measure the Senate hearings on the British loan opened on March 5 (no doubt coincidentally) with an encouraging flood of warm endorsements. Finally, to demonstrate the substance behind all this diplomatic action Byrnes made the official announcement on March 6 of the USS *Missouri*'s flag-showing visit to Turkey and the eastern Mediterranean.

Byrnes's aggressive diplomatic initiatives, that they were launched on a fundamental reorientation of their policy that went far beyond the ominous but still generalized language the secretary had used in public only a week earlier, and was even farther removed from the residual accommodationism Byrnes had exhibited in Moscow at the end of December. Instead, there would now be a sharply focused, more confrontational approach, challenging Soviet conduct in Eastern Europe, the Far East, and along the Northern Tier.

This kind of veiled, policy-changing strategy, with all its shadow-boxing menace, was a characteristic feature of both British and American diplomacy during this confusing, transitional year before the Western powers had fully concerted their lines of thought and action, and when the two fundamental forces we must always have in mind – the Soviet government (Stalin) and American public opinion – had yet to fully reveal themselves or to come into the more stable relation, as they eventually did, of a clearcut confrontation. The British, it will be recalled, had tried, around the time of the Yalta conference, to strengthen their position, while carefully avoiding a direct affront to Stalin, by endeavoring to push the reluctant Americans forward on the Polish and later the Rumanian issues. This had backfired. Now Truman and Byrnes, somewhat similarly, were happy to have an enthusiastic Churchill make the definitional running in public while they tucked in behind supportively – sending aggressive signals while they awaited the outcome of the Englishman's broadside – but not so ostentatiously as to burn their boats with Stalin prematurely, or to leave themselves without some line of retreat if the domestic reaction was unfavorable.

The aggressive strategy seemed to have failed in the immediate, confused aftermath of Churchill's speech. His clarion call drew an initially mixed reception in the United States. His strong identification with the defense of the British Empire, and a widespread suspicion of British diplomacy generally, worked against him, and Truman and Byrnes both found it politic to deny any prior association or future commitment. But within a few weeks a remarkable change occurred, and by the end of March it is clear that most Americans – administration, press, and public – were inclined to agree at least with the diagnosis of a Soviet threat, and increasingly as well with the prescription of a firm Anglo-American response.[85]

That portentous transformation was largely due to the impact which these second and third stages in the developing crisis – the Churchill

---

[85] For the hardening trend, see Harbutt, *Iron Curtain*, pp. 197–208.

definitional speech, and the associated American militance so fully displayed to the Soviets but only partially to the American public – had upon the suspicious observers in the Kremlin. It will be seen that Stalin and Molotov were so alarmed that, instead of a sensible retreat before the now imminent second Security Council meeting in New York, where they had reason to anticipate further hearings on the Iran issue, they chose to respond with a confused show of mixed resentment, unilateralism, and belligerence. This led them, after several miscalculations, onto a politico-judicial battlefield where, it is clear in retrospect, they were at a great disadvantage. The seemingly clumsy Soviet actions that followed – the fourth and conclusive stage of the early 1946 crisis – presented the watching world with what many saw as a striking confirmation of the accuracy of the Kennan-Churchill thesis of a dangerously expansionary Soviet state and, by the same token, lodged the new American harder line firmly in public approval.

This came when, on March 18, just two weeks after Churchill's speech, the new Iranian government, now led by an ostensibly pro-Soviet but actually patriotic landowner called Sultaneh al Qavam, frustrated by the continuing Soviet refusal to withdraw their troops until a one-sided pro-Soviet agreement on an oil concession and Azerbaijani autonomy had been signed, repeated Hakimi's brave gesture of January and filed a fresh complaint for the second Security Council meeting scheduled for New York on March 25. A tense week of politico-diplomatic maneuvering in and around Teheran followed. Once again Stalin used the carrot and the stick. As early as March 13 he had created a "war scare" with menacing Red Army reinforcements and threatening maneuvers in northern Iran even as he courted Qavam with vague promises and ambiguous conditions for the withdrawal agreement, all the while calling for a postponement of the issue in the Council. In the end Qavam's nerve held, and the Iranian complaint was the first order of business when the historic New York session opened on March 25 in an atmosphere characterized by extraordinary publicity, and with an estimated 200 journalists in attendance for each delegate.[86]

In this second Council meeting the political realities were very different. Now the Americans, not the British, took the lead. Moreover, the State Department was active from the time of Churchill's Washington visit on February 10 and Byrnes's new harder line on February 13 in effectively

---

[86] Ibid., pp. 231–241. See also Kuniholm, *Origins of Cold War*, Chapter 5; Lenczowski, *Russia and the West*, p. 298; Feis, *From Trust to Terror*, pp. 82–84.

stage managing the case. On February 22, Byrnes had instructed Kennan to inform Qavam, then negotiating in Moscow under intense pressure from Stalin and Molotov, of the American view:

That ample opportunity is afforded to the Iranian government to return the question to the Council, either on its own initiative, or through a third party in the event that the negotiations take a turn which the Iranian government regards as threatening the integrity of Iran. This government has publicly made clear its expectation that the results of the present negotiations agreed to by the Council will be in full conformity with the principles and purposes of the Charter of the United Nations.[87]

The contrast with the first Security Council meeting in London only a few weeks earlier is remarkable. Then the U.S. had either discouraged an Iranian initiative or expressed a bland neutrality. Now it was actively promoting, behind the scenes, a second initiative. Byrnes, eager to demonstrate his new "firm" policy in the congenial New York Security Council setting, and well aware that he had a morally appealing case, was now working actively to bring about a confrontation with the Soviets. As early as March 8 we find him trying to line up Bevin for a joint sponsorship of the Iranian cause and reminding Qavam, now returned to Teheran but still without a Soviet promise to withdraw, of the "seriousness" with which the United States viewed the 1943 Declaration regarding Iran, promising Big Three support for the postwar independence of the country. The American courtship continued right up to the opening of the March session with various kinds of backstage encouragement from the U.S. embassy in Teheran. The Iranian delegate in New York, who was guided by an American law firm, had his instructions forwarded from Teheran in the American diplomatic pouch, and also received constant advice from the State Department.[88]

Byrnes himself led the United States delegation when the session opened on March 26. The proceedings, fully reported and commented on throughout the United States and much of the world, quickly took on the character of a courtroom drama, complete with the usual compelling conflict of good and evil. The secretary of state acted throughout like a prosecutor. He immediately opposed Gromyko's opening demand that the complaint be removed from the agenda on the ground that an agreement had been completed and was in effect. This was a bluff easily called, for there was no such

---

[87] Byrnes to Kennan, February 22, 1945, FRUS, 1946, 7, pp. 334–335.

[88] Ibid., pp. 234–231; Byrnes to Winant, March 21, 1946, FRUS, 1946, 7, pp. 7, 33. Minor memorandum, March 21, 1946, SD 501 BC/3.1846. The law firm was Covington, Rublee & Co. For delegate and State Department, see FRUS, 1946, 7, p. 383 and passim.

agreement. Byrnes then, having embarrassed the Soviet delegation in this way, cited all the alleged Soviet violations. The removal application was then defeated by a vote of nine to two, with only the Soviets and their compliant Polish supporters (whose press agencies American journalists now called Tass and "demi-Tasse") dissenting. Gromyko then asked for a postponement. Again Byrnes led a successful opposition, winning by the same vote. The next morning, after failing once more to block a discussion of the Iranian issue, the frustrated Gromyko gathered his papers and, watched by a hushed audience, ostentatiously walked out of the chamber.[89]

This created a sensation, immediately arousing worldwide fears that the Soviets would leave the organization altogether. This was perhaps unlikely, given its probable conversion thereafter into some kind of political front institution against the Soviet Union. But it was clear that Stalin, overconfident that Qavam's supposedly weak government would not defy him, had overplayed his hand and had in some sense been outmaneuvered and embarrassed by the suddenly militant and masterful secretary of state.

The consequences were profound for all the Great Powers. The Soviets were initially resentful but also anxious. The Security Council setback was followed by a number of conciliatory gestures and reassurances that the Soviets would not withdraw from the UN. At the same time, they tried in early April to recapture the initiative by giving Qavam a much more liberal agreement, which he quickly accepted, and then, returning to the Council, declaring that this vindicated their earlier stand and that the issue should accordingly be removed from the agenda. But Byrnes now had the bit between his teeth. As the Red Army troops had not yet in fact been withdrawn, he again, wielding his firm nine to two majority, refused to comply. The Soviets then got Qavam himself, now eager to placate his formidable neighbor, to apply for a removal. Again Byrnes refused.

"The Council must satisfy itself that the Soviet troops ... have been withdrawn," he insisted. This was widely seen in the U.S. as a principled stand. Once seized of a dispute, the Security Council, not the parties, was master of its own agenda. The thrust of this move – with Byrnes acting like a latter-day John Marshall – was to enlarge the practical scope and

---

[89] Halifax to Bevin, March 30, 1946, AN 960/1/45, F/O. 371.51607. For a reconstruction of the Security Council proceedings from March 25, see Kuniholm, *Origins of the Cold War*, pp. 326–342; and for legal and procedural aspects, see Richard von Wagenen, *The Iranian Case, 1946* (New York, 1946). For a fuller record, S.C. Official Records, 1st. year, 1st series, no. 2, pp. 27–292. *New York Times*, March 27, 28, 1946.

power of the Council far beyond anything envisaged by the Roosevelt administration. "This was the purpose," sang an approving *New York Times* headline. Moreover, Byrnes was now drawing substantial support for these robust stands. Not only was he telling the Soviets where they got off, he was also shaping the new Security Council mechanism in what was widely perceived as a constructive way. Truman and virtually all the leading administration figures were delighted. Praise came from Republican as well as Democratic congressional leaders. "Firmness" was also paying off with most of the significant press and with public opinion.[90]

Byrnes's initial firm line in the Security Council on March 26/27 had been, apart from several left-liberal publications, almost unanimously approved. The favoring public climate for what was now seen as a principled policy was even more marked as the Soviets later made their unavailing efforts to get the Iran case off the agenda. A State Department survey of press and radio comment on the handling of the Iran issue since early April found three "generally held" views:

1. The U.S. position before the Security Council continues to receive general support.
2. Iran is generally thought to be acting "under pressure" – not as a free agent – in withdrawing her complaint.
3. It is frequently stressed that Russia's earlier pledge to withdraw her troops is too recent to be forgotten.[91]

Why had Stalin, so presciently concerned since Yalta, indeed since Dumbarton Oaks, to avoid this kind of disruption at the hands of "small powers," allowed a situation of this kind to occur? Various possibilities present themselves. The combination of a profound setback in the Security Council and the prospect of an Anglo-American challenge along the Northern Tier, all in the alarming context of Churchill's rhetorical aggression, seems to have thrown the Soviet diplomatic posture off balance. The direct clash in the Security Council should be seen as a further final expression of the persistent Soviet tendency to react to any American challenge in Eastern Europe (now in Iran) by some undermining initiative against the United Nations. This had worked well for Stalin with Roosevelt, and more recently as a spur in the talks with the even more

---

[90] See, for these developments, Harbutt, *Iron Curtain*, pp. 248–266.
[91] Department of State, "U.S. Public Opinion on Relations with Russia," April 17, 1946, SD501 (rest of citation faded).

accommodating Hopkins. But this was different. Now the United Nations was not simply an easily targeted project in the making but rather, in the form of its Security Council, a working American-led institution with teeth. It was unimaginative of Stalin to tackle the United States in its new formidable arena, with a watchful American public opinion very much at stake. In all probability Stalin was lulled by his success, both in the outcome of the post-Yalta gese's and at the earlier London Council meeting, where the Soviets had attacked the British and diverted the Iranian complaint while the Americans sat quietly by. The timing of the Iran hearings in New York, also, created a problem for Stalin. He seems to have been overconfident, first in assuming he could bend Qavam to his will, then in thinking a strong front in the Security Council might get the Americans to back down, much as Hopkins had conducted a retreat following strong Soviet resistance over Poland the previous May. Perhaps he prolonged the agony in the Security Council out of a genuine wish to demonstrate the danger – a Soviet preoccupation since Dumbarton Oaks – that small countries posed to the Great Powers. All this is largely speculation in the absence of that inner history we still seek.

But the crucial determinant for Stalin was almost certainly geopolitical. The Security Council argument, seen in a vacuum, might appear to be a straightforward clash between the emergent superpowers – bringing American universalism and Soviet expansionism into that conclusive confrontation our focus on the potential incompatibility of the United Nations and events in the Soviet sphere has led us to anticipate. But that is at best a half-truth. The fact is that this whole episode was permeated with geopolitical elements, including the fate of Iran and its neighbors, the Anglo-Soviet "Cold War," Byrnes's public undertaking to defend the Charter "by force if necessary," and Churchill's provoking "Iron Curtain" speech pressing for an Anglo-American "fraternal association." And behind the dramatics in New York lay the chronic Soviet fear of that union of American power and British interests and connections indelibly associated with Winston Churchill.

It is hardly surprising, then, that the Soviets blamed Churchill. In early April a resentful Stalin told the new United States ambassador to Moscow, Bedell Smith, that Churchill had committed "an unfriendly act ... an unwarranted attack upon the USSR." A few weeks later he repeated these accusations to the new British ambassador and insisted that the former prime minister had been speaking for the British government. In April, Molotov complained to Byrnes about "the unfriendly attitude of the United States in the Iranian case" and "denounced" the Fulton speech, declaring that "Churchill's call to action to contain the Soviet Union was resented by the Soviets." Many years later Nikita Khrushchev wrote:

One reason for Stalin's obsession with Eastern Europe was that the Cold War had already set in. Churchill had given his famous speech in Fulton urging the imperialistic forces of the world to mobilize against the Soviet Union. Our relations with England, France, the USA and the other countries who had cooperated with us in crushing Hitlerite Germany were, for all intents and purposes, ruined.[92]

It is noticeable that, Molotov's remarks notwithstanding, the Soviets were at this point still disinclined to hold the United States to account for this crisis. The full-throated animus against Churchill was probably sincere. His efforts to bring about a closer Anglo-American alignment, had been patently clear since Yalta. He had precipitated the post-Yalta crisis by the comparatively circumspect but provocative polarities he had employed in his February 27 speech to try to get a "showdown" on the Polish issue. Stalin and Molotov had reacted on that occasion in a shrewdly calibrated way that was eventually successful in warding off the challenge. Now, Kremlin observers could see him trying again, setting off the spring 1946 crisis with the much more threatening, uninhibited "Iron Curtain" speech calling openly for an Anglo-American "alliance" (though he was still careful not to use that word) against a vividly portrayed Soviet "threat." This time Stalin's response – taking place not in the safely cloistered Moscow ambassadorial commission but on the exposed world stage of the New York Security Council meeting – was blustering and comparatively clumsy. This is in part because the Fulton speech came at what a British diplomat accurately called "an awkward moment" for the Soviets, suddenly caught as they were in an illegal, morally compromising, seemingly predatory posture in Iran. Later George Kennan spoke aptly of Churchill's having "finessed" Stalin on that issue. And it seems fair to conclude that, after losing the first round in May, Churchill had finally defeated Stalin in their 1945–46 struggle to influence the future direction of American power and diplomacy.[93]

[92] Talbott, *Khrushchev Remembers*, pp. 361, 393; Isaac Deutscher, *Stalin*, rev. ed. (Middlesex, England, 1966), p. 565. For Stalin's reaction, see Bedell Smith, *My Three Years in Moscow* (New York, 1950), pp. 52–53; for Molotov's, see Bohlen, *Witness to History*, p. 253. Peterson to Bevin, May 28, 1946, PREM 8.349.

[93] Harbutt, *Iron Curtain*, pp. 197–208; Cantril and Strunk, *Public Opinion*, pp. 963, 1060; *U.S. News*, March 15, 1945.

These events play out rather like a Greek tragedy, with the Soviets, who did more that any power to win the war in Europe, now taking Britain's place as the odd man out, having dug themselves into a hole, mostly but not entirely of their own making. Character may indeed be destiny. A good deal of writing about the origins of the Cold War is fundamentally based on subjective premises of that kind. And indeed, all these leaders seem to have been stalked by a kind of nemesis that robbed them of power and control at crucial moments. Thus Roosevelt lost political traction with grievous results in his last months; Churchill left office in the spring of 1945 amid the collapse of all his political strategies; and now Stalin, paying for his misguided diplomacy in Iran and New York, was left to contemplate life in opposition to the Anglo-American combination he had long tried to avoid.

Reflections of this kind lead us back, not to classic visions of man as a plaything of the gods, but to a reinforced respect for the interplay of statesman and context we find at the heart of the structural perspective. For we see, in this last pre–Cold War crisis, not the consequences of one statesman's calculations, but a process developing through the actions of several hands in the four distinct stages we have identified – apparent Soviet provocations, influential clarifying definitions, a veiled but sharply pointed American policy reorientation, and a confirming, self-defeating Soviet response – each of which was indispensable to the final outcome.

That "final outcome" was the beginning of the Cold War. For the spring 1946 crisis produced in both Washington and Moscow a new and, as it turned out, permanent hard-line posture toward the other superpower. The establishment of the new American firmness toward the Soviets now became settled policy. Here too there is much evidence, far beyond our summary here, that the 1946 crisis was a turning point from a general posture of accommodation and detachment vis-à-vis the Soviets to a harder line from which the Truman administration did not subsequently deviate. The new line was clear to both the Soviets and the British as they saw Byrnes consolidate it with administration, congressional, and public approval in the numerous peacemaking conferences in Europe that followed.

The new policy was given a full airing in a remarkable State Department paper, prepared by Bohlen but drawing largely on Kennan's February 22 analysis, that Byrnes sent to the influential State-War-Navy Coordinating Committee in early April. Refuting the notion that Soviet actions were prompted by "security" considerations, it insisted that their motives were "expansionist" and "unlimited." The United States still wanted "peaceful coexistence," but it must "demonstrate to the Soviet government in the first instance by diplomatic means, and in the last instance by military force if necessary, that the present course of its foreign policy can only lead to disaster for the Soviet Union." For the moment, the paper went on to stress:

The Charter of the United Nations affords the best and most unassailable means through which the U.S. can implement its opposition to Soviet physical expansion. It not only offers the basis upon which the greatest degree of popular support can be obtained in the U.S., but it will also ensure the support and even assistance of other members of the United Nations. If, as may occur, the United Nations breaks down under the test of opposition to Soviet aggression, it will have served the purpose of clarifying before American and world public opinion, and thus make easier whatever future steps may be required by the U.S. and other like-minded nations in the face of a new threat of world aggression.

Thus the new dispensation celebrated the congenial American forum that had so far vindicated all the hopes invested in it. At the same time, it was recognized that while the 1946 crisis had demonstrated the value of the United Nations, it could be only one component of an active foreign policy. The necessary geopolitical dimension so carefully avoided up to this point now received a full endorsement:

If Soviet Russia is to be denied the hegemony of Europe the United Kingdom must continue in existence as the principal power in Western Europe economically and militarily. The U.S. should, therefore, explore its relationship with Great Britain and give all feasible political, economic and if necessary military support within the framework of the United Nations, to the United Kingdom and the communications of the British Commonwealth. This does not imply a blank check of American support throughout the world for every interest of the British Empire, but only in respect of areas and interests which are in the opinion of the U.S., vital to the maintenance of the United Kingdom and the British Commonwealth of Nations as a great power.[94]

There was a similarly conclusive stiffening in Soviet policy after the Fulton/Iran setbacks early in 1946. As the confrontation in the Security Council had intensified during March, the Soviet and world communist media began for the first time to concentrate their harsh spotlight rather more on American rather than British targets. A variety of anti-American themes – allegations of "atomic diplomacy," protests against diplomatic manipulations in the United Nations, abusive references to Wall Street "parasites," and played-up references to racial discrimination prominent

---

[94] H. Freeman Matthews, "Memorandum for the State-War-Navy Coordinating Committee from the Acting State Member," April 1, 1946, SD 711.61/3–1446.

among them – now issued regularly from *New Times* (as *War and the Working Class* was now called) as from well as Radio Moscow and standard Soviet publications. Stalin and his associates appear to have concluded by the end of April, if not before, that the reorientation of American policy that they had observed since mid-February was now settled policy. They now looked increasingly upon the United States as their principal antagonist and on the "Anglo-American bloc" as a new reality. Criticism of British policy continued, but in a lower register, and was tempered now by spasms of diplomatic warmth amid the usual "splitting" techniques directed to the apparent partners. By midsummer an energetic consolidation campaign could be observed in Eastern Europe, with "the unity of the Slavic peoples" now being juxtaposed with the West's German-sounding "Anglo-Saxon bloc." The Soviets refused Western appeals to settle arrangements for Vienna. A tightening up of policy was now evident in East Germany (where a degree of political experimentation had been tolerated) and elsewhere in the Soviet bloc as Stalin clamped down on the few remaining oases of pluralistic expression, in part probably to guard against any repeat of the Iranian embarrassment. At home, meanwhile, he launched the notorious *Zhdanovschina*, the anti-Western cultural campaign with which Stalin tried in the second part of 1946 to mobilize sentiment for the new comprehensive confrontation.[95]

The age of the competing superpowers was thus ushered in. With this reorientation and final shaking out of what was left of the wartime relationships, the East/West conception at last comes triumphantly into its own. The Europe/America conceptual framework that serves well to explain the course and conduct of Allied politics up to Yalta – and then reappears briefly between the two crises we have examined in truncated form as an Anglo-Soviet "Cold War" rather than the "concert" of the war years – was now at last eclipsed.

But not entirely dead. Consider finally the two principal elements of that fading European configuration. To be sure, the Anglo-Soviet relationship, though it survived and even showed some political animation from time to time, was henceforth a secondary factor in world politics as the British accepted, on the whole thankfully, a new role as America's junior partner. The territorial manifestation of the Moscow Order, on the other

---

[95] *New Times*, May 1, 15, June 1, 15, July 1, 15, 1946. For similar material, see Radio Moscow, March 28–June 4, 1946, *BBC Digest*, Files 2445–2513. For *Zhdanovschina*, see McCagg, *Stalin Embattled*, pp. 163–166, 390–391; and Gavriel Ra'anan, *International Policy Formation in the USSR* (Hamden, Conn., 1983), pp. 54–61.

hand, endured as the primary geopolitical and territorial foundation of the new Cold War system as the two superpowers organized their relationship to mutual advantage in the summer of 1946.

This becomes clear as we follow Byrnes from his Security Council success in New York to the long series of tripartite and later multilateral meetings in Paris that gave a firmer geopolitical basis to the postwar European system. At the first of these, the Council of Foreign Ministers meeting from April 25 to May 16, the atmosphere was, not surprisingly, strained and tense. There were charges and countercharges and much aggressive public diplomacy, not least from Byrnes, who carefully cultivated the now strongly anti-Soviet Senator Vandenberg, a key member of his delegation, and made regular reports of his difficulties with the Soviets to the now supportive president and the American people. Byrnes also authorized General Lucius Clay, the American military governor in Germany, to suspend on May 3 all further reparations shipments to the Soviets pending the creation of the unified institutions that Moscow was holding up. Unsurprisingly, in this atmosphere very little progress was made toward the peace settlements with Hitler's former satellites.[96]

But neither the Americans nor the Soviets really wanted confrontations of this kind. In a second foreign ministers meeting between June 15 and July the various logjams began to clear. The dangerous Italo-Yugoslav tussle over Trieste, which both sides claimed, was now resolved in favor of Italy in return for $100 million in reparations for the Soviet Union. The Soviets then made a basic concession, abandoning at last their Mediterranean claims to Cyrenaica and the Dodecanese Islands. This induced the Western powers to recognize the Soviet-installed Bulgarian and Rumanian governments.[97] Thus the Americans and British now conceded Soviet supremacy in Eastern Europe in return for a clear field in the Mediterranean and Western Europe. The Anglo-Soviet Moscow Order – thus reaffirmed territorially, but with the political proprietorship modified by the post-Yalta attachment in the West of the United States as Britain's partner, so that we might now call it the Cold War Order – became once more the accepted geopolitical foundation of a divided but now stabilized Europe, a condition that lasted without basic alteration until 1989.

---

[96] Yergin, *Shattered Peace*, pp. 191–192, 221, 232–233, 252–253, 257–258; Ward, *Threat of Peace*, pp. 78–171.
[97] Yergin, *Shattered Peace*, pp. 259–261.

9

Reflections

A venture that began simply as a search for the meaning of the Yalta conference, has turned into an attempt to explain the tripartite association of powers that triumphed in World War II, insofar as it related to the wartime politics and future configuration of Europe. It began by asking the reader to consider the reality of two explanatory paradigms – the familiar East/West one and a neglected Europe/America one – and it also urged the importance, if one is to grasp that reality, of a crucial distinction between the strategy of the Allied war effort, which did of course develop almost entirely on East/West lines, and the politics of the war as it affected Europe, which seems to need a very different conception, one that emphasizes both the collaboration of the two European powers in planning the future of their arena, and the detachment for almost the entire war period of the United States. This dichotomy persisted up to the time of the Yalta conference and its immediate aftermath, when, through a complex reorientation, it was transformed into the East/West dualism that then led into the Cold War.

This scenario – which brings Europe more fully into the picture and moves the United States from the center to the periphery in this crucial dimension of pre-Yalta wartime politics – emerges from a reconstructive and analytic approach that tends to play down personalities and emphasizes the more structural dimensions of Allied diplomacy. The word "structural" is not intended to be provocative or to announce another French assault on American academia. It has nothing to do with providential or ideological designs, or with immanent processes in the Hegelian fashion, much less with the schematic rigidities of doctrinaire Marxism. It comes, simply, from an appreciation of the constraints imposed on states and statesmen by the deep forces of geography and history and a sensitivity to the recurrences and patterns of behavior that present themselves to the historian who is willing to probe beyond the "actor" approach to an understanding of the past. We tend to gloss over or ignore the quasi-deterministic aspects of history. This is perhaps more true in the United States, where a happier experience and a progressive, linear view of the past encourages historians to see the movement of the republic in the world's affairs in terms of purposeful founders, Toqueville's predictions, Wilson's noble failures, and the redemptive satisfactions of a benign American expansionism. The European experience – fragile nation-states wedged into a tight combustible system marked by chafing constrictions and sharp temptations, by traditional flashpoints and recurrent crises, and above all by a constant oscillation between the urge to dominate and a desperate search for security – has been very different. This contrast lay at the heart of Allied diplomacy in World War II. It deserves, I believe, a more spacious airing in the historical literature.

From this mixed "free" and structural perspective, the story of the Grand Alliance takes on something of the character of a drama in three stages, each of which seems to set the scene for the next. During the period 1941–February 1945, as the United States became an increasingly masterful global actor, Britain and the Soviet Union moved in a series of balletic diplomatic interactions toward a mutually satisfactory division of Europe enshrined in what, in tribute to the 1944 conference that brought this denouement into fuller existence, I have called the Moscow Order. This was a significant event not least because the territorial arrangements made there, and consolidated in the months between the Moscow conference and Yalta, formed the geopolitical basis of what soon evolved into the Cold War Order that lasted for nearly a half-century.

Yalta – preparations, conference, aftermath – constitutes the second stage. It is inaccurate to suggest that it produced "a division of Europe." This already existed, both in the military sense as a consequence of the Red Army's success and politically as a result of the Anglo-Soviet concert we have followed in this account. Yalta is significant for other reasons. Above all, it brought the United States – permanently, as it turned out – into European politics. This was the unsought achievement of a reluctant President Roosevelt, whose hand had been forced shortly before the conference by the reaction of a shocked American public opinion to the unseemly vigor with which the British and Soviets had begun to consolidate their respective European spheres. American postwar internationalism, and the hitherto acceptable prospect of its United Nations institutionalization, were now placed in serious jeopardy. But as we saw earlier, FDR was more fortunate than Woodrow Wilson had been in 1919 because he was confronted with this problem before rather than after he came to grips with the Europeans. The imminence of Yalta gave him an opportunity to do something about the problem.

To succeed, however, Roosevelt needed Stalin's cooperation. At Yalta, consequently, Stalin was able to force the "bargain" he had long angled for, agreeing to the American plans for the United Nations in return for FDR's apparent acceptance of Soviet hegemony both in Poland and also, by implication (for the subject was discreetly avoided at Yalta), in the Eastern European sphere the Soviet leader had already settled with Churchill. But Roosevelt could not lay power politics of this kind before the American public. And in any case, he needed something more appealing than an agreement about voting rights. He therefore deemed it necessary to get Stalin and Molotov to endorse some high-sounding liberal flourishes in the Declaration on Liberated Europe and other Yalta documents, which he then used to create a falsely upbeat vision of the meeting for the American and world audience. He thus created two Yaltas – one bleakly realistic and diplomatic but, in key essentials, secret; the other attractively visionary and public. Stalin, after some initial hesitation, refused to go along once he saw that he was not going to get the license and legitimation he seems to have felt he had been granted at Yalta on the crucial Polish issues, and the post-Yalta crisis grew in large part out of these misunderstandings.

There are perhaps three distinct ways of looking at the Yalta conference. One is to follow the mainstream path, focus strictly on the meeting itself, and see it as a conference that produced agreement on a number of pressing issues: Poland, the United Nations, the peace terms for Germany, France's role, and the Far Eastern negotiation. At that level it seems entirely logical to view Yalta as a success. Another perspective, the one elaborated here, is less sanguine. It sees Roosevelt and Stalin only half-achieving an understanding of each other's basic dilemmas: the president's need not simply for acceptance of his voting rights proposal, or even for Stalin's undertaking to participate in the San Francisco conference, but more broadly for a better moral-political context in which to reanimate the United Nations project at home; and Stalin's need for some endorsement of his course in Poland and Eastern Europe and for reassurances of Great Power unity for the war's finale. Unfortunately, neither made their concerns fully explicit. There was no discussion or clear understanding as to how, in actual execution, they would resolve their problems. Roosevelt said nothing about the dangerously theatrical way in which he intended to use the Declaration on Liberated Europe and the Polish agreement. Stalin let the unresolved ambiguities in the Polish clauses pass without question (indeed, he inaugurated many of them) and said virtually nothing about his provocative actions and specific intentions in Eastern Europe. Neither challenged the other or probed sufficiently with a view to creating some basis for mutual anticipation in the short term or trust in the longer run. At this deeper level, therefore, Yalta was an unsuccessful negotiation that left too many dangerous loose ends.

A third perspective, which may well become the standard characterization a century or so from now, when the Cold War is only a distant memory, might dismiss the foregoing considerations as minor or episodic compared with the really profound consequence of Yalta: the full engagement at last of the historically detached United States with the political future of Europe. In the event, despite (or perhaps because of) FDR's efforts, there was in the weeks before Yalta a measure of American disenchantment with the Europeans that was alarmingly reminiscent of 1919–20. This time, however, the eventual outcome was engagement rather than rejection. The reasons have largely to do with developments at and after Yalta, but they also owe much to the absorbed "lessons" taught by the refusal to collaborate with Europe after the earlier conflict, and also to the elements we identified in Chapter 6 as some of the more tangible wartime sources of American international commitment: a coherent politico-economic blueprint for the postwar world; a more open business community and an ambitious military establishment; a more sophisticated press and public opinion; and, perhaps most importantly, the embedded character of American military power and the practice (despite the qualifications advanced here) of a deeper politico-diplomatic association with the European allies than had occurred in World War I.

To understand this transition properly, however, we need to move beyond these two phases – the European-focused 1941–45 period and the Yalta conference itself – to the third, more turbulent stage in the process that occurred after President Roosevelt's manipulation of the meeting's results. For that distortion opened up an opportunity for Churchill to align himself with Roosevelt's literal, overt vision of Yalta and then go a long way toward entrenching it in the minds of those who heard or read his report to the House of Commons (and later his "Iron Curtain" speech). In effect, he chose the suddenly beckoning chance for closer Anglo-American political solidarity over the prospect of prolonged relations with Stalin. And indeed, once the British, with apparent American support, began to push against his Polish plans, Stalin reacted bitterly. He blamed Churchill rather than Roosevelt for what he seems to have regarded as a betrayal over Poland, and as soon as he had achieved a reconciliation with the United States through the efforts of the Hopkins mission he turned against the London government, inaugurating a "war of nerves" against Britain and her clients that spelled the end of the Anglo-Soviet political concert. If we burrow vigorously enough beneath the surface of events, then, we see that the effect of this post-Yalta crisis was to replicate the familiar conditions of 1914–17 and 1939–41 – a potentially hegemonic continental power threatening the security of Britain and her client or associated states in and around Europe; a detached but watchful and increasingly sympathetic United States; sustained efforts by Britain and its American supporters to align the two English-speaking powers against the supposedly predatory power; and finally a transforming crisis that did in fact bring this about.

The structural perspective is also useful in drawing attention to the way in which Yalta and its aftermath opened up two very different paths through which the United States could move to consolidate its new engagement with Europe. One was the preferred Rooseveltian road to measured change and postwar adjustment through the United Nations, essentially a congenially judicial and pleasingly semi-detached mode of association. The other was the Churchillian option of passage through the familiar British corridor to confrontation with the latest would-be continental hegemon. For nearly a year after Roosevelt's death the Truman administration wobbled between these two paths – one wholesome and hopeful but of uncertain relevance and diminishing plausibility, the other bleak and unappealing but increasingly demanding and persuasive – as they developed along roughly parallel but separate lines. When, in early 1946, Soviet designs on Iran clumsily brought an essentially geopolitical Anglo-Soviet issue into the American orbit of the United Nations arena, these two lines converged to create a receptive setting for the second, decisive crisis that finally crystallized the American commitment and led directly to the policy reorientation that brought on the Cold War.

In drawing attention to these various individual actions and recurring contextual processes, I am not suggesting that the victorious Allied statesmen were operating in a closed frame of reference. These three notably strong-willed men enjoyed a large element of open choice in wartime, strategic decision-making. They indubitably "made" history. One need only think of the profound impact of Stalin's 1939 decision to make terms with Hitler, or of Roosevelt's choosing the European over the Pacific theater, or of Churchill's obsession with the Mediterranean strategy. But in the political realm of competing nation-states they were often more constricted.

It is striking, for instance, that when we try to identify decisive turning points in Allied diplomacy as it moved in its late stages from collaboration toward confrontation, we usually find a clear combination of free will and constrained behavior. During the crucial period between August 1944 and April 1945 each of the three leaders in turn took a unilateral decision that appears to have significantly determined the course of events yet was at the same time deeply rooted in historical thinking. The crucial sequence, setting in motion a kind of chain reaction of inter-related moves, begins with Roosevelt's decision, forced by the need for a clear American policy, to press the Wilsonian cause of a new world organization upon his allies. The Dumbarton Oaks initiative, in turn, together with the prospect of an imminent summit conference, led Stalin, very much in the spirit of tsarist expansionism, to respond in a characteristic bargaining mode with a decision of comparable significance, namely, the recognition of the Lublin regime as the provisional government of Poland. This, together with Soviet and British coercion in various parts of Europe, did much to provoke the sharp disquiet in the United States that shaped Roosevelt's strategy at Yalta, forcing him to try to obscure Stalin's refusal to back down on the Polish issue by the creation and propagation of a wholesome but false "American" vision of Yalta. Now it was the prime minister's turn. FDR's egregious overselling of Yalta's achievement produced Churchill's campaign (inspired by the now traditional determination to draw American power to Britain's aid against the continental threat) to press Roosevelt – and later, with more success, Truman – to live up to the wholesome vision rather than the diplomatic reality of Yalta. This turned out to be fateful. The Americans and the Soviets subsequently patched up their relations for a time. But the collapse of the last vestiges of the Anglo-Soviet concert shortly followed, together with Stalin's aggressive campaign against Britain and its associates in the Northern Tier, which in turn stimulated a trend toward the alignment of the two Western powers, now firmly committed to the vision rather than the reality of the Crimean conference. When the second crisis came, in March 1946, Stalin's uncharacteristically awkward diplomacy led to a conclusive reorientation. Overall, however, it seems that each of these statesmen had a hand in the step-by-step deterioration of tripartite collaboration.

None of the three important decisions I have mentioned made the Cold War inevitable. The United States and the Soviet Union had few, if any, dangerous points of connection. Roosevelt and Stalin both appear to have been willing to take an evolutionary view of developments up to and even for a short time after the Yalta conference. Both apparently hoped to maintain a degree of postwar cooperation, as FDR's tacit adherence to

Stalin's "bargain" diplomacy attests. Stalin's acceptance of the Washington-designed United Nations and the president's implicit acknowledgment of a certain Soviet hegemony in Eastern and Central Europe reinforce the point. What endangered the relationship was the combination of Roosevelt's dangerous public overselling of Yalta, Churchill's not entirely innocent effort to try and hold the president to a literal view of the attractive but distorted vision he had created, Stalin's harsh overreaction, and the impact of all this on the unsettled Polish governmental issue. These were the destabilizing elements that, moving into the wide gap that opened up after Yalta between public expectations and Soviet realities, aggravated the inevitable tensions of the war's last stages and laid a powder trail for the cold war.

Where then does the final responsibility lie? A moral perspective naturally simplifies the issue of accountability. The structural approach, with its focus on analysis, turning points, convergences, chain reaction diplomacy, and the like tends to complicate it. Today the accusing finger of mainstream thought still points to Stalin. In a way his historiographical fate was sealed from the start. It was obvious to many observers in June 1941 that his regime bore no resemblance to the fit partner for a "league of honor" celebrated in April 1917 by Woodrow Wilson in a fleeting moment of pre-Leninist optimism. But Churchill and Roosevelt, focusing tenaciously on victory over Germany, found it politic to pretend that it did, finally crowning the artifice for a world audience after Yalta with the false vision of a reformed Soviet Union bent on bringing democracy to Eastern Europe. The historian today may well look back and find this image-making understandable, though unfortunate in the fateful confusion it caused. But surely his real charge, especially now that the Cold War with all its partisan polemics is long over, is not to throw bouquets or brickbats at long-dead statesmen, but to be usefully objective and explore the lines of causation wherever they lead.

In that cause I have tried in this account to play down the retrospective look and show how matters appeared to the principal figures as they moved through the two distinct stages of the deterioration: first, the breakdown of the so-called Grand Alliance, and only then the coming of the Cold War. So far as the pre–Cold War decline in solidarity is concerned, a pertinent question might be: Which of the three leaders first stepped away from the collaborative principle? If a turn to unilateralism is the appropriate test, then Stalin seems to have a historiographical grievance. For his recognition of the Lublin regime in Poland on January 1, 1945, provocative and dangerously consequential as it undoubtedly was, had been signaled in advance, came as the culmination of a long process in which all three powers had been involved, and was bestowed in anticipation of an imminent summit conference that was expected, even by Stalin, to pass some kind of collective judgment on the decision. Far more unilateral, in the context of tripartite solidarity, were Roosevelt's public distortion of Yalta's main diplomatic outcome and Churchill's subsequent attempt to entrench that false vision as the standard by which future Soviet behavior should be judged. Both these initiatives were launched without any real prior notice to the Soviets. And each decision was taken strictly in the national interest of each power, with FDR intent above all on pleasing American opinion and Churchill focused tightly on the creation of an Anglo-American front. It in no way glosses over Stalin's murderous past or approves the practices of his sordid regime to point out that his resort to sustained unilateralism came after, not before, Roosevelt and Churchill wrong-footed him in Yalta's aftermath.

For the Cold War, however, we see a rather different set of circumstances. During 1945 one notices, in policy-making circles in the United States and Britain, a declining faith in closed diplomacy and a rising sensitivity to the emergence of an anxious and increasingly watchful public opinion. FDR's false vision of Yalta produced a diplomatic crisis, but in the short term its effect was to reassure American opinion and bring time for the war's successful conclusion and the establishment of the United Nations. Moreover, Roosevelt's gambit did not, as it turned out, preclude the United States–Soviet reconciliation that actually occurred in the late spring of 1945. The basic issues, however, centered on the acceptability in the West of the scope and character of Soviet expansionism, had not been resolved; indeed, they were aggravated by the inevitable disillusionment that developed as the real situation in the countries occupied by the Red Army became increasingly obvious. Tensions therefore persisted in oscillating fashion through the year and then, thanks largely to what was seen as a sharp Soviet turn away from cooperation, intensified at the beginning of 1946, creating in the United States the swelling tide of suspicion and foreboding clearly registered in the polls, newspapers, and political discourse of the moment.

This is the context in which the crisis that brought on the Cold War actually developed. For once unilateralism had been subvertingly introduced by the Western leaders early in 1945, Stalin outdid them both in the scope and vigor of his own self-assertion, resisting Anglo-American pressures over Poland and Eastern Europe, turning down diplomatic opportunities to restore trust (notably over access and prisoner of war repatriation), turning the first Security Council meeting in London into a bear pit, starting a multidimensional campaign against his erstwhile British partner, and threatening the fundamental security of Britain's vulnerable client states along the Northern Tier. Specifically, it seems to have been Stalin's expansionary thrust against Greece, Turkey, and Iran that began in a systematic way to convert this latent hostility into a reliable constituency, in the United States at least, for active confrontation. And here we see a familiar historical pattern. For just as the Western democracies in Europe had reluctantly endorsed Hitler's 1938 takeover of the Sudetenland, with its tincture of acceptability on the grounds of racial affinity, but had jibbed decisively at his subsequent occupation of the rest of Slavic Czechoslovakia, where no such justification could be advanced, so most opinion in Britain and the United States had by 1944–45 resigned itself to some form of domination by Stalin in Eastern Europe, with its touch of equity in the insistently proclaimed Soviet desire for security, but was now sharply upset by his subsequent threatening moves against Greece, Turkey, and Iran, where no such claim could be plausibly proclaimed. Increasingly there was talk of communism's messianic aspirations and a Soviet bid for "world supremacy."

Thus when Molotov insisted years later that in his persistent search for secure enlarged frontiers Stalin had known when and where to stop and had "kept well within the limits," he was astute in pinpointing the central importance of that Soviet expansionism as the geopolitical root cause both of the Big Three's wartime political tensions and finally of the Cold War itself, but at fault in his positive assessment of Stalin's performance in pursuit of it.[1] For Stalin, like Hitler before him, had gone "a step too far." Even now the Cold War was probably avoidable. But Stalin's relatively easy success in breaking down the Anglo-American front the previous year seems to have corrupted his judgment. At the Security Council's March 1946 meeting in New York he chose to challenge the United States openly on the Iranian issue. Here he paid the price, bringing himself into collision with what had always been, at least prospectively, the other elemental factor in the developing crisis: an American public opinion that had been increasingly troubled by earlier Soviet conduct and now showed itself, as the Iranian complaint came dramatically before it in the congenial "Court and Code" character of a peculiarly American institution, ready to support the new firm line the Truman administration was eager to establish. The outcome is easily traced in the historical record: the crystallization of an aroused American opinion; the careful stage-by-stage consolidation by the Truman administration through 1946 and into 1947 of the new hard-line American policy; and steadily thereafter, as political leadership and public

---

[1] Resis, ed., *Molotov Remembers*, p. 59.

sentiment interacted in a mutually reinforcing alignment, the development of an American national consensus.

One tantalizing question remains. Could the Anglo-Soviet concert – the long-anticipated scenario so suddenly subverted by Yalta – have avoided, had it survived the post-Yalta shakeout, the Cold War? Many during World War II had envisioned an ostensibly solid postwar structure, with Europe divided reasonably harmoniously between a Soviet-dominated East and a British-led West and a still-detached United States presiding benevolently in North America. The flaw in that design, increasingly obvious after the frenzy of destruction in Western Europe early in 1945, was the comparative weakness of the Western European grouping in relation to the Soviet bloc. There were, as we have seen, several personal and material causes for this. But much of the political responsibility lies with Winston Churchill. For despite a brief if vigorous effort in late 1944, his influence was on the whole destructive. His passionate response at Yalta to a paper from the British embassy in Moscow advocating support for a postwar Western bloc give us a clue to his deeper preoccupations. His reply was succinct: "to make Britain safe she must become responsible for the safety of a cluster of feeble states. We ought to think of something better than these."[2]

The "something better," it seems safe to speculate, was the preservation of Britain as a fully functioning Great Power, with its Empire intact and its worldwide interests restored. But here the United States presented a fundamental problem. It is hard to tell which of his two great allies Churchill worried about more. Most accounts understandably emphasize his anxiety, frequently expressed, about Soviet and communist expansion. But his concern over the looming American hegemony, and the "rulership" of which he had warned in 1943, may have had an even deeper resonance in the thinking of this most historically conscious British statesman. It is tempting to think, conjecturally, that his mind went back to 1763, when the British had in effect appropriated most of the French empire and pushed their old antagonist back into Europe. The French found themselves obliged to exchange their global ambitions for the continental mastery they achieved in the revolutionary and Napoleonic wars. France tormented the Germans in those days but in the process raised them up as a formidable foe. Later the Germans overcame the Russians but similarly found that they in turn had created a more impressive opponent in doing so. During all this time Britain, at the height of its imperial power

---

[2] Churchill minute, February 8, 1945, cited in Gilbert, *Churchill*, VII, p. 1196.

and in control of the seas, successfully boxed in the spasmodic attempts of those who presided over these turbulent power centers – Napoleon, Kaiser William II, and even Hitler – to break out of what in the twentieth century had become, from a continental viewpoint, a European cage to which the the British, with their similarly peripheral Russain and American alllies, held the key.

Now, as Churchill seems to have seen it, American leaders – Roosevelt, Morgenthau, and a host of others on into the Cold War era – ready and eager to inherit the blessings and the burdens of global hegemony on their own, seemed bent on pushing Britain into that very same European cage, even as they urged the independence of India, picked up the remnants of Britain's Far Eastern position, and began to harness Britain's anxious dependencies of Australia, New Zealand, and Canada. Churchill, reduced in early 1945 to begging the president for shipping to transport British troops from one imperial reclamation project to another, was determined to avoid the European trap whose miseries were constantly before him in the form of de Gaude's historically infused resentments. He preferred to take a chance on being able to re-create traditional British power, or at least to join the United States in a more or less equal worldwide partnership with the new Atlantic superpower. These hopes turned out to be as illusory as the now lost dream of a British-led balance to Soviet power in Europe. It would be the lavishly endowed Americans who, denied the services of the British surrogate they had hoped for, would themselves finally put things together in Western Europe, paving the way for a dominating Franco-German combination. The British, their pride intact, maintained a cherished independence, as they have to this day. But by early 1946, with their empire beginning to disintegrate and their economy facing bankruptcy, they were already moving slowly toward a dignified withdrawal from the center of the world's stage.

Select Bibliography

A. Primary Sources

1. Archival and Manuscript Collections

Acheson, Dean. Papers. Harry S. Truman Library, Independence, Missouri.
Allen, George V. Papers. Harry S. Truman Library, Independence, Missouri.
Alsop, Joseph and Stewart. Papers. Library of Congress, Washington, D.C.
Attlee, Clement. Papers. Bodleian Library, Oxford, England.
Baruch, Bernard. Papers. Princeton University Library, Princeton, New Jersey.
Bevin, Ernest. Papers. Public Record Office, Kew, England.
Bohlen, Charles E. Papers. National Archives, College Park, Maryland.
Byrnes, James F. Papers. Clemson University Library, Clemson, South Carolina.
Cadogan, Alexander. Papers. Churchill College, Cambridge, England.
Churchill, Winston L. S. Papers. Churchill College, Cambridge, England.
Clayton, William. Papers. Harry S. Truman Library, Independence, Missouri.
Clifford, Clark. Papers. Harry S. Truman Library, Independence, Missouri.
Dalton, Hugh. Papers. London School of Economics, London, England.
Davies, Joseph E. Papers. Library of Congress, Washington, D.C.
Dixon, Pierson. Papers. Piers Dixon, London, England.
Dulles, John Foster. Papers. Princeton University Library, Princeton, New Jersey.
Eden, Anthony. Papers. Public Record Office, Kew, England.
Elsey, George M. Papers. Harry S. Truman Library, Independence, Missouri.
Forrestal, James V. Papers. Princeton University Library, Princeton, New Jersey.
Halifax, Lord. Papers. University of York Library, York, England.
Harriman, Averell. Papers. Library of Congress, Washington, D.C.
Harvey, Oliver. Papers. British Library, London, England.
Hopkins, Harry. Papers. Franklin D. Roosevelt Library, Hyde Park, New York.
Hull, Cordell. Papers. Library of Congress, Washington, D.C.
Inverchapel, Lord. Papers. Public Record Office, Kew, England.
Ismay, Hastings. Papers. Kings College, London, England.
Kennan, George, F. Papers. Princeton University Library, Princeton, New Jersey.

Leahy, William D. Papers. Library of Congress, Washington, D.C.
Matthews, H. Freeman. Papers. National Archives, Washington, D.C.
Morgenthau, Henry M., Jr. Papers. Franklin D. Roosevelt Library, Hyde Park, New York.
Patterson, Robert B. Papers. Library of Congress, Washington, D.C.
Roosevelt, Franklin D. Papers. Franklin D. Roosevelt Library, Hyde Park, New York.
Rosenman, Samuel I. Papers. Harry S. Truman Library, Independence, Missouri.
Stettinius, Edward, R., Jr. Papers. University of Virginia Library, Charlottesville, Virginia.
Stimson, Henry L. Papers. Yale University Library, New Haven, Connecticut.
Swing, Raymond Gram. Papers. Library of Congress, Washington, D.C.
Truman, Harry S. Papers. Harry S. Truman Library, Independence, Missouri.
Wallace, Henry A. Papers. Franklin D. Roosevelt Library, Hyde Park, New York.

2. Documentary Collections: Official

a. United States

Public Papers of the Presidents: Harry S. Truman 1945–1950. Washington, D.C., 1961–65.
United States Congress. *Congressional Record*, 78th, 79th, and 80th Congresses, 1942–48.
    Senate Committee on Foreign Relations. *A Decade of American Foreign Policy: Basic Documents, 1941–1949.* Washington, D.C., 1950.
United States Department of State. Department of State *Bulletin*, 1945–46. Washington, D.C., 1941–46.
    General Records. Decimal Series, 1941–47, National Archives, Washington, D.C.
    Foreign Relations of the United States. Annual volumes, 1941–46, Washington, D.C., 1958–70.
    Foreign Relations of the United States: The Conference at Quebec, 1944. Washington, D.C., 1972.
    Foreign Relations of the United States: The Conferences at Cairo and Teheran, 1943. Washington, D.C., 1961.
    Foreign Relations of the United States: The Conferences at Malta and Yalta, 1945. Washington, D.C., 1955.
    Foreign Relations of the United States: The Conference of Berlin (The Potsdam Conference), 1945. 2 vols. Washington, D.C., 1960.

b. United Kingdom

Parliamentary Debates (Commons), 1941–46. London, England.
Prime Ministers Papers, 1940–47. National Archives, Kew, England.
Cabinet Papers, 1940–47. National Archives, Kew, England.
Ministry of Information Papers. National Archives, Kew, England.
Treasury Papers. National Archives, Kew, England.

British Broadcasting Corporation. *Daily Digest of World Broadcasts, 1943–1947*. Written Archives Center, Reading, England, and Library of Congress, Washington, D.C.

c. United Nations

United Nations Organization, Security Council, *Official Records*, 1st. Year, 1st. and 2nd Sessions, 1946. New York, 1947.

d. Soviet Union/Russia

Commission for the Publication of Diplomatic Documents, *Correspondence between the Chairman of the Council of Ministers of the USSR and the Presidents of the USA and the Prime Ministers of Great Britain during the Great Patriotic War of 1941–1945*. 2 vols. Moscow, 1947.
Foreign Policy Archives of the Russian Federation. Fonds 6 and 7. Moscow, Russia.
Russian State Archives. Fond 82. Moscow, Russia.
The Teheran, Yalta and Potsdam Conferences: Documents. Moscow, 1969.
Documents on Polish-Soviet Relations, 1939–1945. 2 vols. London, England, 1961–67.

3. Documentary Collections: Unofficial

Dallin, A., and F. I. Firsov, eds. *Dimitrov and Stalin, 1934–1943*. New Haven, CT: Yale University Press, 2000.
Degras, J., ed. *Soviet Documents on Foreign Policy. Vol. 3 (1933–1941)*. London: Oxford University Press, 1953.
Foreign and Commonwealth Office. *Churchill and Stalin: Documents from the British Archives*. London: FCO, 2002.
Kimball, Warren, ed. *Churchill and Roosevelt: The Complete Correspondence*. 3 vols. Princeton, NJ: Princeton University Press, 1984.
Polonsky, A., and B. Druckier, eds. *The Beginnings of Communist Rule in Poland*. London: Routledge and Kegan Paul, 1980.
Rosenman, Samuel, ed. *The Public Papers and Addresses of Franklin D. Roosevelt*, Vols. 9 to 13, 1940–45. New York: Macmillan, 1941–50.
Ross, G., ed., *The Foreign Office and the Kremlin: British Documents on Anglo-Soviet Relations, 1941–1945*. Cambridge: Cambridge University Press.
Rzheshevsky, O.A., ed. *War and Diplomacy: The Making of the Grand Alliance (Documents from Stalin's Archive)*. Amsterdam: Harwood Academic Publishers, 1996.

4. Newspapers and Periodicals

Bolshevik
Christian Science Monitor
Chicago Sun

Chicago Tribune
Daily Herald
Daily Worker
Dziennik Polski
Economist
Humanite
Izvestia
Life
Los Angeles Times
Manchester Guardian
Nation
New Republic
New Statesman and Nation
Newsweek
New Times
New York Herald-Tribune
New York News
New York Times
New York World-Telegram
New Yorker
PM
Pravda
Reader's Digest
San Francisco Examiner
Scotsman
Spectator
The Times
Time
U.S. News
Voina I Rabochii Klass (War and the Working Class)
Wall Street Journal
Washington Post
Washington Star

5. Memoirs, Diaries, and Papers

Acheson, Dean G. *Present at the Creation: My Years in the State Department*. New York: Norton, 1969.

Alliluyeva, Svetlana. *Twenty Letters to a Friend*. London: Penguin Books, 1968.

Attlee, Clement. *Twilight of Empire: Memoirs of Prime Minister Clement Attlee*. New York: A. S. Barnes, 1962.

Banac, I. *The Diary of Georgi Dimitrov, 1933–1949*. New Haven, CT: Yale University Press, 2003.

Baruch, Bernard. *The Public Years*. New York: Holt, 1960.

Berezhkov, V. *History in the Making: Memoirs of World War II Diplomacy*. Moscow: Progress Publishers, 1983.

Bidault, Georges. *Resistance: The Political Autobiography of Georges Bidault*. London: Weidenfeld and Nicolson, 1965.

Blum, John Morton, ed. *From the Morgenthau Diaries*. 3 vols. Boston: Houghton, Mifflin, 1959–67. Vol. 3: *Years of War, 1941–1945*, 1967.

 ed. *The Price of Vision: The Diary of Henry A. Wallace, 1942–1946*. Boston: Houghton, Mifflin, 1973.

Bohlen, Charles E. *Witness to History, 1929–1969*. New York: Norton, 1973.

Bullitt, Orville H., ed., *For the President: Personal and Secret. Correspondence between Franklin D. Roosevelt and William C. Bullitt*. Boston: Houghton, Mifflin, 1972.

Byrnes, James F. *Speaking Frankly*. New York: Harper & Bros., 1947.

 All in One Lifetime. New York: Harper & Bros., 1958.

Campbell, Thomas, and George Herring, eds. *The Diaries of Edward R. Stettinius, Jr., 1943–1946*. New York: New Viewpoints, 1975.

Carey, John, ed. *George Orwell: Essays*. New York: Knopf, 2002.

Churchill, Winston S. *The Second World War*. 6 vols. Boston: Houghton Mifflin, 1948–53.

Clay, Lucius D. *Decision in Germany*. New York: Doubleday, 1950.

Colville, John. *The Fringes of Power: 10 Downing Street Diaries, 1939–1955*. London: Hodder & Stoughton, 1985.

Dalton, Hugh. *Memoirs: Vol. 2, High Tide and After, 1945–1960*. London: Frederick Muller, 1962.

Daniels, Jonathan. *White House Witness, 1942–1945*. New York: Doubleday, 1975.

Deane, John R. *The Strange Alliance*. New York: Viking Press, 1947.

De Gaulle, Charles. *War Memoirs: Call to Honour, 1940–1942*. New York: Viking Press, 1955. *Unity, 1942–1944*. New York: Simon and Schuster, 1959. *Salvation, 1944–1946*. New York: Simon and Schuster, 1960.

Dilks, David, ed. *The Diaries of Sir Alexander Cadogan, O.M., 1938–1945*. London: Cassell, 1971.

Djilas, Milovan. *Conversations with Stalin*. New York: Harcourt, Brace and World, 1962.

Eden, Anthony. *Full Circle: The Memoirs of Anthony Eden*. Boston: Houghton, Mifflin, 1960.

 The Reckoning: The Eden Memoirs. Boston: Houghton, Mifflin, 1965.

Ehrenburg, Ilya. *The War, 1941–1945*. London: McGibbon & Kee, 1964.

Ferrell, Robert H., ed. *The Autobiography of Harry S. Truman*. Boulder, CO: Associated Press of Colorado, 1980.

 ed. *Off the Record: The Private Papers of Harry S. Truman*. New York: Harper & Row, 1980.

 ed. *Dear Bess: The Letters from Harry to Bess Truman, 1910–1959*. New York: Norton, 1983.

Galbraith, John Kenneth. *A Life in Our Times: Memoirs*. Boston: Houghton, Mifflin, 1981.

Grew, Joseph C. *Turbulent Era: A Diplomatic Record of Forty Years, 1904–1945*. Boston: Houghton, Mifflin, 1952.

Gromyko, Andrei. *Memories*. Trans. Harold Shukman. London: Hutchinson, 1989.

Harriman, Averell, and Elie Abel. *Special Envoy to Churchill and Stalin, 1941–1946*. New York: Random House, 1975.

Harvey, John, ed. *The War Diaries of Oliver Harvey, 1941–1945*. London: Collins, 1978.

Hull, Cordell. *The Memoirs of Cordell Hull*. 2 vols. New York: Macmillan, 1948.

Jebb, Gladwyn. *The Memoirs of Lord Gladwyn*. London: Weidenfeld and Nicolson, 1972.

Kennan, George F. *Memoirs, 1925–1950*. Boston: Little, Brown, 1967.

Khrushchev, Nikita S. *Khrushchev Remembers*. Trans. Strobe Talbott. Boston: Little, Brown, 1970.

Krock, Arthur. *Memoirs: Sixty Years on the Firing Line*. New York: Funk & Wagnalls, 1968.

Leahy, William D. *I Was There*. New York: McGraw, Hill, 1950.

Lilienthal, David E. *The Journals of David E. Lilienthal*, Vol. 1: *The TVA Years, 1939–1950*. New York: Harper & Row, 1964.

Maisky, Ivan. *Memoirs of a Soviet Ambassador*. London: Hutchinson, 1967.

Mikolajczyk, Stanislaw. *The Rape of Poland: The Pattern of Soviet Aggression*. New York: Whittlesey House, 1948.

Millis, Walter, ed. *The Forrestal Diaries*. New York: Viking, 1951.

Moran, Lord. *Winston Churchill: The Struggle for Survival, 1940–1965*. London: Constable, 1966.

Murphy, Robert D. *Diplomat among Warriors*. New York: Doubleday, 1964.

Perkins, Frances. *The Roosevelt I Knew*. New York: Viking Press, 1946.

Resis, Albert, ed. *Molotov Remembers: Inside Kremlin Politics*. Chicago: Ivan Dee, 1993.

Roosevelt, Elliott. *As He Saw It*. New York: Duell, Sloan and Pearce, 1946.

Smith, Walter Bedell. *My Three Years in Moscow*. Philadelphia: J. B. Lippincott, 1949.

Stettinius, Edward R., Jr. *Roosevelt and the Russians: The Yalta Conference*. New York: Doubleday, 1949.

Stimson, Henry L., and McGeorge Bundy. *On Active Service in Peace and War*. New York: Harper & Bros. 1947.

Strang, Lord. *Home and Abroad*. London: Andre Deutch, 1956.

Sulzberger, Cyrus L. *A Long Row of Candles: Memoirs and Diaries, 1934–1954*. New York: Macmillan, 1969.

Szwalbe, Stanislaw. *Swiadectwo Czasu*. Warsaw: Wydawnictwo Spoldzieleze, 1988.

Truman, Harry S. *Memoirs*, Vol. 1: *Year of Decisions*. New York: Doubleday, 1955.

Vandenberg, Arthur H., Jr. *The Private Papers of Senator Vandenberg*. Boston: Houghton, Mifflin, 1952.

B. Secondary Sources

Books

Alexander, G. M. *The Prelude to the Truman Doctrine: British Policy in Greece, 1944–1947*. Oxford: Clarendon Press, 1982.

Ambrose, Stephen. *Eisenhower and Berlin, 1945: The Decision to Halt at the Elbe*. New York: Norton, 1967.

Anderson, Terry H. *The United States, Great Britain and the Cold War, 1944–1947*. Columbia: University of Missouri Press, 1981.

Barker, Elisabeth. *British Policy in South-East Europe in the Second World War*. London: St. Martin's Press, 1976.

Churchill and Eden at War. New York: St. Martin's Press, 1978.

Becker, Josef, and Franz Knipping, eds. *Power in Europe? Great Britain, France, Italy and Germany in a Postwar World, 1945–1950*. Berlin and New York: Walter de Gruyter Co., 1986.

Beevor, Anthony. *Stalingrad*. London: Penguin Books, 1991.

Bell, P. M. H. *John Bull and the Bear: British Public Opinion, Foreign Policy and the Soviet Union*. London: Edward Arnold, 1990.

Bennett, Edward M. *Franklin D. Roosevelt and the Search for Victory: American-Soviet Relations 1939–1945*. Wilmington, DE: S R Books, 1990.

Bernstein, Barton J., ed. *Politics and Policies of the Truman Administration*. Chicago: Quadrangle Books, 1970.

Best, Geoffrey. *Churchill: A Study in Greatness*. London and New York: Hambledon & London Press, 2001.

Bird, Kai, and Martin Sherwin. *American Prometheus: The Triumph and Tragedy of J. Robert Oppenheimer*. New York: Simon and Schuster, 2005.

Blumenthal, Henry. *Illusions and Reality in Franco-American Diplomacy*. Baton Rouge: Louisiana State University Press, 1986.

Bohlen, Charles E. The *Transformation of American Foreign Policy*. New York: Norton, 1969

Witness to History, 1929–1969. New York: Norton, 1973.

Boll, Michael M. *Cold War in the Balkans: American Foreign Policy and the Emergence of Communist Bulgaria, 1943–1947*. Lexington: University of Kentucky Press, 1984.

Booker, Christopher, and Richard, North. *The Great Deception: A Secret History of the European Union*. London: Continuum, 2003.

Borhi, Laszlo. *Hungary in the Cold War, 1945–1956: Between the United States and the Soviet Union*. Budapest and New York: Central European University Press, 2004.

Boyer, Paul S. *By the Dawn's Early Light: American Thought and Culture at the Dawn of the Atomic Age*. Chapel Hill: University of North Carolina Press, 1994.

Buhite, Russell D. *Decisions at Yalta: An Appraisal of Summit Diplomacy*. Wilmington, DE: S R Books, 1976.

Bullock, Alan. *Ernest Bevin: Foreign Secretary, 1945–1951*. New York: Norton, 1983.

Stalin and Hitler. London: HarperCollins, 1991.

Burns, James MacGregor. *Roosevelt: The Lion and the Fox*. New York: Harcourt Brace, 1956.

Roosevelt: The Soldier of Freedom. New York: Harcourt Brace Jovanovich, 1979

Campbell, Thomas M. *Masquerade Peace: America's UN Policy, 1944–1945*. Tallahassee: Florida State University Press, 1973.

Carlton, David. *Anthony Eden: A Biography*. London: Allen Lane, 1981.

Churchill and the Soviet Union. Manchester: Manchester University Press, 2000.

Charlton, Michael. *The Eagle and the Small Birds: Crisis in the Soviet Empire: From Yalta to Solidarity*. London: British Broadcasting Corporation, 1984.

Ciechanowski, Jan. *Defeat in Victory*. New York: Doubleday, 1947.

Clarke, Peter. *The Last Thousand Days of the British Empire: The Demise of a Superpower*. London: Penguin Books, 2007.

Clemens, Diane S. *Yalta*. New York: Oxford University Press, 1970.

Charmley, John. *Churchill's Grand Alliance*. London: Hodder & Stoughton, 1996.

Coates, W. and Z. *The History of Anglo-Soviet Relations, 1917–1950*. London: Lawrence Wishart, 1944.

Conquest, Robert. *Stalin: Breaker of Nations*. New York: Penguin Books, 1991.

Costigliola, Frank. *Awkward Dominion: American Political, Economic and Cultural Relations with Europe, 1919–1933*. Ithaca and London: Cornell University Press, 1984.

France and the United States: The Cold Alliance since World War II. New York: Twayne Publishers, 1992.

Dallek, Robert. *Franklin D. Roosevelt and American Foreign Policy, 1932–1945*. New York: Oxford University Press, 1979.

Danchev, Alex. *Very Special Relationship: Field Marshal Sir John Dill and the Anglo-American Alliance, 1941–1944*. London: Brassey, 1986.

On Specialness: Essays in Anglo-American Relations. New York: St. Martin's Press, 1998.

Davies, Norman. *Rising '44: The Battle for Warsaw*. Basingstoke and Oxford: Macmillan, 2003.

Europe at War, 1939–1945. London: Macmillan, 2006.

Davis, Lynn Etheridge. *The Cold War Begins: Soviet-American Conflict over Eastern Europe*. Princeton, NJ: Princeton University Press, 1974.

Deighton, Anne, ed. *Britain and the First Cold War*. London: Macmillan, 1980.

De Senarclens, Pierre. *Yalta*. New Brunswick and Oxford: Transaction Books, 1988.

Deutcher, I. *Stalin: A Political Biography*. London: Pelican Books, 1966.

Dilks, D., ed. *Retreat from Power: Studies in Britain's Foreign Policy in the Twentieth Century*. Vol. 2. London: Macmillan, 1981.

Divine, Robert A. *Second Chance: The Triumph of Internationalism in American during World War II*. New York: Atheneum, 1967.

Roosevelt and World War II. Baltimore: Johns Hopkins University Press, 1969.

Douglas, Roy. *From War to Cold War, 1942–1948*. London: St. Martin's Press, 1981.

Draper, Theodore. *A Present of Things Past: Selected Essays*. New York: Hill and Wang, 1990.

Edmonds. *The Big Three*. London: Penguin Books, 1991.

Eisenberg, Carolyn. *Drawing the Line: The American Decision to Divide Germany, 1944–1949*. Cambridge and New York: Cambridge University Press, 1996.

Erickson, John. *The Road to Berlin*. London: Weidenfeld and Nicolson, 1983.

Eubank, Keith. *Summit at Teheran: The Untold Story*. New York: Morrow, 1985.

Feiling, Keith. *Neville Chamberlain*. London: Macmillan, 1946.

Feis, Herbert. *Churchill, Roosevelt, Stalin: The War They Waged and the Peace They Sought*. Princeton, NJ: Princeton University Press, 1957.

From Trust to Terror: The Onset of the Cold War. New York: Norton, 1970.

Fischer, Bernd. *Albania at War, 1939–1945*. West Lafayette, IN: Purdue University Press, 1999.

Folly, Martin H. *Churchill, Whitehall and the Soviet Union, 1940–1945*. London: Macmillan, 2000.

Fromkin, David. *In the Time of the Americans: FDR, Truman, Eisenhower, Marshall, MacArthur – The Generation That Changed America's Role in the World*. New York: Knopf, 1995.

Gardner, Lloyd. *Architects of Illusion: Men and Ideas in American Foreign Policy, 1941–1949*. Chicago: Quadrangle Books, 1970.

Spheres of Influence: The Great Powers Partition Europe, from Munich to Yalta. Chicago: Ivan Dee, 1993.

Economic Aspects of New Deal Diplomacy. Madison: University of Wisconsin Press, 1964.

Gardner, Richard. *Sterling-Dollar Diplomacy: The Origins and Prospects of Our International Economic Order*, rev. ed. New York: McGraw, Hill, 1969.

Gaddis, John Lewis. *The United States and the Origins of the Cold War, 1941–1947*. New York: Columbia University Press, 1972.

The Long Peace: Inquiries into the History of the Cold War. Oxford and New York: Oxford University Press, 1987.

We Now Know: Rethinking Cold War History. Oxford: Clarendon Press, 1997.

Gat, Moshe. *Britain and Italy, 1943–1949: The Decline of British Influence*. Brighton: Sussex Academic Press, 1956.

Gilbert, Martin. *Winston S. Churchill*, Vols. 7 and 8. Boston: Houghton, Mifflin, 1986–88.

Gori, Francesca, and Silvio, Pons, eds. *The Soviet Union and Europe in the Cold War, 1943–1953*. London: St. Martins Press, 1996.

Gormley, James. The *Collapse of the Grand Alliance, 1945–1948*. Baton Rouge: Louisiana State University Press, 1987.

Gorodetsky, G. *Stafford Cripps Mission to Moscow, 1940–1942*. Cambridge and New York: Cambridge University Press, 1984.

ed. *Soviet Foreign Policy, 1917–1991*. London: Frank Cass, 1994.

Gross, Jan T. *Revolution from Abroad: The Soviet Conquest of Poland's Western Ukraine and Western Belorussia*. Princeton, NJ: Princeton University Press, 1988.

Hamby, Alonzo. *Man of the People: A Life of Harry S. Truman*. New York: Oxford University Press, 1995.

Hammond, Thomas T., ed. *The Anatomy of Communist Takeovers*. New Haven, CT: Yale University Press, 1975.

ed. *Witnesses to the Origins of the Cold War*. Seattle: University of Washington Press, 1982.

Harbutt, Fraser J. *The Iron Curtain: Churchill. America and the Origins of the Cold War*. New York: Oxford University Press, 1986.

The Cold War Era. New York: Blackwell, 2002.

Harper, John L. *Visions of Europe: Franklin D. Roosevelt, George F. Kennan and Dean G. Acheson.* Cambridge and New York: Cambridge University Press, 1994.

Hathaway, Robert M. *Ambiguous Partnership: Britain and America, 1944–1947.* New York: Columbia University Press, 1981.

Haslam, Jonathan. *The Soviet Union and the Struggle for Collective Security in Europe, 1933–1939.* New York: St. Martins Press, 1984.

Healey, Denis. *The Curtain Falls: The Story of the Socialists in Eastern Europe.* London: Lincoln-Praeger, 1951.

Heinrichs, Waldo. *Threshold of War: Franklin D. Roosevelt and American Entry into World War II.* New York: Oxford University Press, 1988.

Herring, George C. *Aid to Russia, 1941–1946: Strategy, Diplomacy and the Origins of the Cold War.* New York: Columbia University Press, 1973.

Hilderbrand, Robert C. *Dumbarton Oaks: The Origins of the United Nations and the Search for Postwar Security.* Chapel Hill: University Of North Carolina Press, 1990.

Hinsley, F. H., et al. *British Intelligence in the Second World War.* London and New York: Cambridge University Press, 1979.

Hogan, Michael J. *A Cross of Iron: Harry S. Truman and the Origins of the National Security State, 1941–1954.* Cambridge and New York: Cambridge University Press, 1998.

ed. *America in the World: The Historiography of American Foreign Relations since 1941.* Cambridge and New York: Cambridge University Press, 1995.

Holloway, David. *Stalin and the Bomb: The Soviet Union and Atomic Energy, 1939–1956.* New Haven, CT: Yale University Press, 1994.

Hoopes, Townsend, and Douglas Brinkley. *FDR and the Creation of the UN.* New Haven, CT: Yale University Press, 1997.

Howard, Michael. *The Mediterranean Strategy in the Second World War.* London: Greenhill Books, 1993.

Hurstfield, Julian G. *America and the French Nation, 1939–1945.* Chapel Hill: University of North Carolina Press, 1986.

Iatrides, John O., ed. *Greece in the 1940s: A Nation in Crisis.* Hanover, NH: University Press of New England, 1981.

Ingram, Edward. Britain's *Persian Connection: Prelude to the Great Game in Asia.* Oxford: Oxford University Press, 1992.

Isaacson, Walter, and Evan Thomas. *The Wise Men: Six Friends and the World They Made.* New York: Simon and Schuster, 1986.

Jones, Howard. *"A New Kind of War": America's Global Strategy and the Truman Doctrine in Greece.* New York: Oxford University Press, 1989.

Jones, Matthew. *Britain, the United States and the Mediterranean War, 1942–1944.* Basingstoke and London: Macmillan, 1996.

Judt, Tony. *Postwar: A History of Europe since 1945.* New York: Penguin Books, 2005.

Reappraisals: Reflections on the Forgotten 20ᵗʰ Century. New York: Penguin Books, 2008.

Kennan, George F. *American Diplomacy, 1900–1950.* Boston: Little, Brown, 1951.

Kennedy-Pipe, C. *Stalin's Cold War: Soviet Strategies in Europe, 1943–1956.* Manchester: Manchester University Press, 1995.

Kersten, Krystyna. *Jalta w Polskiej Perspektywie.* London and Warsaw: Aneks, 1989.

   The Establishment of Communist Rule in Poland, 1943–1948. Berkeley: University of California Press, 1991.

Kimball, Warren F. *Forged in War: Roosevelt, Churchill and the Second World War.* New York: Morrow, 1997.

   The Juggler: Franklin Roosevelt as Wartime Statesman. Princeton, NJ: Princeton University Press, 1991.

Kitchen, Martin. *British Policy towards the Soviet Union during the Second World War.* London: Macmillan, 1986.

Kolko, Gabriel. *The Politics of War: The World and United States Foreign Policy, 1943–1945.* New York: Harper and Row, 1968.

   The Limits of Power: The World and United States Foreign Policy, 1945–1954. New York: Harper and Row, 1972.

Kuklick, Bruce. *American Policy and the Division of Germany: The Clash with Russia over Reparations.* Ithaca, NY: Cornell University Press, 1972.

Kuniholm, Bruce R. *The Origins of the Cold War in the Near East: Great Power Conflict and Diplomacy in Iran, Turkey and Greece.* Princeton, NJ: Princeton University Press, 1980.

Lacey, Michael J., ed. *The Truman Presidency.* Cambridge and New York: Cambridge University Press, 1989.

Laloy, Jean. *Yalta: Yesterday, Today, Tomorrow.* New York: Harper and Row, 1988.

Lane, A., and H. Temperley, eds. *The Rise and Fall of the Grand Alliance, 1941–1945.* London: Macmillan, 1995.

Larres, Klaus. *Churchill's Cold War: The Politics of Personal Diplomacy.* New Haven, CT: Yale University Press, 2002.

Larson, Deborah Welch. *Origins of Containment: A Psychological Explanation.* Princeton, NJ: Princeton University Press, 1985.

Leffler, Melvyn P. *A Preponderance of Power; National Security, the Truman Administration and the Cold War.* Stanford, CA: Stanford University Press, 1992.

   and D. S. Painter, eds. *Origins of the Cold War:* London: Routledge, 2005.

   For the Soul of Mankind: The United States, the Soviet Union, and the Cold War. New York: Hill and Wang, 2007.

Leuchtenberg, William. *In the Shadow of FDR: From Harry Truman to Bill Clinton.* Ithaca and London: Cornell University Press, 1983.

Levering, Ralph B. *American Opinion and the Russian Alliance: 1939–1945.* Chapel Hill: University of North Carolina Press, 1976.

Lippmann, Walter. *The Cold War: A Study in U.S. Foreign Policy.* New York: Harper, 1947.

Louis, Wm. Roger. *Imperialism at Bay: The United States and the Decolonization of the British Empire, 1941–1945.* New York: Oxford University Press, 1978.

   and Hedley Bull, eds. *The "Special Relationship": Anglo-American Relations since 1945.* Oxford: Oxford University Press, 1986.

Lukacs, John. *Churchill: Visionary. Statesman, Historian.* New Haven, CT: Yale University Press, 2002.

Lukas, Richard C. *The Strange Allies: The United States and Poland, 1941–1945.* Knoxville: University of Tennessee Press, 1978.

Lundestad, Geir. *The American Non-Policy towards Eastern Europe, 1943–1947: Universalism in an Area Not of Essential Interest to the United States.* Oslo and New York: Universitet (Tromso) and Humanities Press, 1975.

The American "Empire" and Other Studies of U.S. Foreign Policy in Comparative Perspective. New York and Oxford: Oxford University Press, 1990.

Maier, Charles, ed. *The Origins of the Cold War and Contemporary Europe.* New York and London: New Viewpoints/ Franklin Watts, 1978.

Malia, Martin. *The Soviet Tragedy: A History of Socialism in Russia, 1917–1991.* New York: Free Press, 1996.

Marks, Frederick W. *Wind over Sand: The Diplomacy of Franklin Roosevelt.* Athens: University of Georgia Press, 1988.

Mastny, Vojtech. *Russia's Road to the Cold War.* New York: Columbia University Press, 1979.

The Cold War and Soviet Insecurity: The Stalin Years. Oxford: Oxford University Press, 1996.

May, Ernest. *"Lessons" of the Past: The Use and Misuse of History in American Foreign Policy.* New York: Oxford University Press, 1973.

Mayers, David. *The Ambassadors and America's Soviet Policy.* New York: Oxford University Press, 1995.

George Kennan and the Dilemmas of U.S. Foreign Policy. New York: Oxford University Press, 1988.

Mazower, Mark. *Dark Continent: Europe's Twentieth Century.* London: Penguin Books, 1998.

Medvedev, R. and Z. *The Unknown Stalin.* New York: Overlook Press, 2004.

McCagg, William O., Jr. *Stalin Embattled, 1943–1948.* Detroit: Wayne State University Press, 1978.

McJimsey, George. *Harry Hopkins: Ally of the Poor and Defender of Democracy.* Cambridge, MA: Harvard University Press, 1987.

McNeill, William H. *America, Britain, and Russia: Their Cooperation and Conflict, 1941–1946.* London: Oxford University Press for the Royal Institute of International Affairs, 1953.

Meacham, Jon. *Franklin and Winston: An Intimate Portrait of an Epic Friendship.* New York: Random House, 2003.

Mead, Walter Russell. *"Special Providence": American Foreign Policy and How It Changed the World.* New York: Routledge, 2003.

Messer, Robert L. *The End of an Alliance: James F. Byrnes, Roosevelt, Truman and the Origins of the Cold War.* Chapel Hill: University of North Carolina Press, 1982.

Miller, James Edward. *The United States and Italy, 1940–1950: The Politics and Diplomacy of Stabilization.* Chapel Hill: University of North Carolina Press, 1986.

Milward, Alan S. *The Reconstruction of Western Europe, 1945–1951.* London: Methuen, 1984.

Miner, S. Merritt. *Between Churchill and Stalin: The Soviet Union, Great Britain, and the Origins of the Grand Alliance.* Chapel Hill: University of North Carolina Press, 1988.

Stalin's Holy War: Religion, Nationalism and Alliance Politics, 1941–1945. Chapel Hill: University of North Carolina Press, 2003.

Miscamble, Wilson D. *From Roosevelt to Truman: Potsdam, Hiroshima and the Cold War.* Cambridge and New York: Cambridge University Press, 2007.

Murray, Philomena, and Paul, Rich. *Visions of European Unity.* Boulder, CO: Westview Press, 1996.

Nadeau, Remi. *Stalin, Churchill, and Roosevelt Divide Europe.* New York: Praeger, 1990.

Nagai, Yonosuke, and Akira Iriye, eds. *The Origins of the Cold War in Asia.* New York: Columbia University Press, 1977.

Naimark, Norman. *The Russians in Germany: A History of the Soviet Zone of Occupation, 1945–1949.* Cambridge, MA: Harvard University Press, 1995.

and Leonid Gibianskii, eds. *The Establishment of Communist Regimes in Eastern Europe, 1944–1949.* Boulder, CO: Westview Press, 1997.

Neilson, Keith. *Britain, Soviet Russia and the Collapse of the Versailles Order, 1919–1939.* Cambridge: Cambridge University Press, 2006.

Nisbet, R. *Roosevelt and Stalin.* Washington, DC: Regnery, 1988.

Northedge, F. S., and Audrey Wells. *Britain and Soviet Communism: The Impact of a Revolution.* London: Macmillan, 1982.

Notter, Harley A. *Postwar Foreign Policy Preparation, 1939–1945.* Washington, DC: U.S. Government Printing Office, 1949.

Nove, Alec, ed. *The Stalin Phenomenon.* London: Weidenfeld and Nicolson, 1993.

Offner, Arnold A. *Another Such Victory: President Truman and the Cold War, 1945–1953.* Stanford: Stanford University Press, 2002.

Otte, T. G., ed. *The Making of British Foreign Policy: From Pitt to Thatcher.* Basingstoke and New York: Palgrave Press, 2002.

Ovendale, Ritchie. *The English-Speaking Alliance: Britain, the United States, the Dominions and the Cold War, 1945–1951.* London: Allen and Unwin, 1985.

Overy, Richard. *The Dictators: Hitler's Germany and Stalin's Russia.* London: Allen Lane, 2004.

Why the Allies Won. London: Jonathan Cape, 1995.

with Andrew, Wheatcroft. *The Road to War,* 2nd ed. London: Penguin Books, 1999.

Paterson, T. G. *Soviet-American Confrontation: Postwar Reconstruction and the Origins of the Cold War.* Baltimore: Johns Hopkins University Press, 1973.

Perlmutter, A. *FDR and Stalin.* Columbia: University of Missouri Press, 1993.

Pleshakov, C. *Stalin's Folly.* Boston: Houghton, Mifflin, 2005.

Pogue, Forrest C. *George C. Marshall: Organizer of Victory, 1943–1945.* New York: Viking, 1973.

Prazmowska, Anita. *Britain, Poland and the Eastern Front, 1939.* Cambridge: Cambridge University Press, 1987.

Britain and Poland, 1939–1943: The Betrayed Ally. Cambridge: Cambridge University Press, 1995.

Raack, R. C. *Stalin's Drive to the West, 1938–1945: The Origins of the Cold War.* Stanford, CA: Stanford University Press, 1995.

Raczynski, Edward. *In Allied London.* London, 1962.

Ramsden, John. *Man of the Century: Winston Churchill and his Legend since 1945.* London: Harper Collins, 2003.

Rees, Laurence. *World War II: Behind Closed Doors: Stalin, the Nazis and the West.* New York: Pantheon Books, 2008.

Reynolds, David. *The Creation of the Anglo-American Alliance, 1937–1941: A Study in Competitive Cooperation.* Chapel Hill: University of North Carolina Press, 1982.

    ed. *The Origins of the Cold War in Europe.* New Haven, CT: Yale University Press, 1994.

    et al. *Allies at War: The Soviet, American and British Experience, 1939–1945.* London: Macmillan, 1994.

    In Command of History: Churchill Fighting and Writing the Second World War. London: Penguin, 2005.

Roberts, Geoffrey. *Stalin's Wars: From World War to Cold War, 1939–1953.* New Haven, CT: Yale University Press, 2006.

Rose, Lisle A. *After Yalta: America and the Origins of the Cold War.* New York: Charles Scribners, 1973.

    Dubious Victory. Kent, OH: Kent State University Press, 1973.

Rothwell, Victor. *Britain and the Cold War, 1941–1947.* London: Jonathan Cape, 1982.

Rubin, Barry. *Paved with Good Intentions: The American Experience in Iran.* New York: Oxford University Press, 1980.

Ruddy, T. Michael. *The Cautious Diplomat: Charles E. Bohlen and the Soviet Union, 1929–1969.* Kent, OH: Kent State University Press, 1986.

Russell, Ruth B. *The United Nations and United States Security Policy.* Washington, DC: Brookings Institution, 1968.

Sainsbury, Keith. *The Turning Point: Roosevelt, Stalin, Churchill and Chiang Kai-shek, 1943: The Moscow, Cairo and Teheran Conferences.* New York: Oxford University Press, 1985.

    Churchill and Roosevelt at War: The War They Fought and the Peace They Hoped to Make. New York: New York University Press, 1994.

Saiu, Liliana. *The Great Powers and Rumania, 1944–1946: A Study in the Early Cold War Era.* New York: East European Monograph distributed by Columbia University Press, 1992.

Schild, Georg. *Bretton Woods and Dumbarton Oaks: American Economic and Political Postwar Planning in the Summer of 1944.* New York: St. Martin's Press, 1995.

Schlesinger, Arthur M., Jr. *The Vital Center: The Politics of Freedom.* Boston: Houghton, Mifflin, 1949.

Service, Robert. *Stalin: A Biography.* London: Macmillan, 2004.

Sharp, Tony. *The Wartime Alliance and the Zonal Division of Germany.* Oxford: Clarendon Press, 1975.

Sherry, Michael. *The Rise of American Air Power: The Creation of Armageddon.* New Haven, CT: Yale University Press, 1987.

Sherwin, Martin. *A World Destroyed: The Atomic Bomb and the Grand Alliance.* New York: Knopf, 1975.

Sherwood, Robert E. *Roosevelt and Hopkins: An Intimate History.* New York: Harper & Bros., 1948.

Silverman, Victor. *Imagining Internationalism in American and British Labor, 1939–1949.* Urbana and Chicago: University of Illinois Press, 2000.

Skard, Sigmund. *The American Myth and the European Mind.* Philadelphia: University of Pennsylvania Press, 1961.

Smith, Gaddis. *American Diplomacy during the Second World War, 1941–1945.* New York: Knopf, 1985.

Smith, M. L., and Peter M. R. Stirk, eds. *Making the New Europe: European Unity in the Second World War.* London: Pinter Publishers, 1990.

Snell, John L., ed. *The Meaning of Yalta: Big Three Diplomacy and the New Balance of Power.* Baton Rouge: Louisiana State University Press, 1956.

Stafford, David. Roosevelt and Churchill: *Men of Secrets.* Woodstock, NY: Overlook Press, 2000.

Steel, Ronald. *Walter Lippmann and the American Century.* Boston: Little, Brown, 1980.

Stephanson, Anders. *Kennan and the Art of Foreign Policy.* Cambridge, MA: Harvard University Press, 1989.

Stettinius, Edward, Jr. *Roosevelt and the Russians: The Yalta Conference.* New York: Doubleday, 1949.

Stoler, Mark A. *Allies and Adversaries: The Joint Chiefs of Staff, the Grand Alliance and U.S. Strategy in World War II.* Chapel Hill: University of North Carolina Press, 2000.

Szwalbe, Stanislaw. *Swiadectwo Czasu.* Warsaw: Wydawnictwo Spoldzielize, 1988.

Taubman, William. Stalin's *American Policy: From Entente to Détente to Cold War.* New York: Norton, 1982.

Taylor, A. J. P. *English History, 1914–1945.* Oxford and New York: Oxford University Press, 1965.

Europe: Grandeur and Decline. Harmondsworth, Middlesex: Penguin Books, 1967.

et al., eds. *Churchill Revised: A Critical Assessment.* New York: Dial Press, 1969.

Terry, Sarah Meiklejohn. *Poland's Place in Europe: General Sikorski and the Origins of the Oder-Neisse Line, 1939–1943.* Princeton, NJ: Princeton University Press, 1983.

Theoharis, Athan G. *The Yalta Myths: An Issue in U.S. Politics, 1945–1955.* Columbia: University of Missouri Press, 1970.

Thomas, Hugh. *Armed Truce: The Beginnings of the Cold War, 1945–1946.* New York: Hamish Hamilton, 1987.

Thomas, R. T. *Britain and Vichy: The Dilemma of Anglo-French Relations, 1940–1942.* New York: St. Martin's Press, 1979.

Thompson, R. W. *Churchill and Morton.* London: Hodder and Stoughton, 1976.

Thorne, Christopher. *Allies of a Kind: The United States, Britain and the War against Japan, 1941–1945.* New York: Oxford University Press, 1978.

Tolstoy, N. *Victims of Yalta*. London: Hodder & Stoughton, 1977.

Tooze, Adam. *The Wages of Destruction: The Making and Breaking of the Nazi Economy*. London: Allen Lane, 2006.

Trachtenberg, Marc. *A Constructed Peace: The Making of the European Settlement, 1945–1963*. Princeton, NJ: Princeton University Press, 1999.

Ulam, Adam. *Expansion and Cooexistence: The History of Soviet Foreign Policy, 1917–1967*. New York: Praeger, 1968.

Umiastowski, R. *Poland, Russia and Great Britain, 1941–1945: A Study of Evidence*. London: Hollis and Carter, 1946.

Urban, G. R. *Stalinism: Its Impact on Russia and the World*. London: St. Martin's Press, 1982.

Volkogonov, D. *Stalin: Triumph and Tragedy*. London: Phoenix Press, 2000.

Walker, J. Samuel. *Henry A. Wallace and American Foreign Policy*. Westport, CT: Greenwood, 1976.

   Prompt and Utter Destruction: Truman and the Use of Atomic Bombs against Japan. Chapel Hill: University of North Carolina Press, 1997.

Wandycz, Piotr. *Soviet-Polish Relations, 1917–921*. Cambridge: Cambridge University Press, 1969.

Ward, Patricia Dawson. *The Threat of Peace: James F. Byrnes and the Council of Foreign Ministers, 1945–1946*. Kent, OH: The Kent State University Press, 1979.

Watt, D. Cameron. *Succeeding John Bull: America in Britain's Place, 1900–1975*. Cambridge: Cambridge University Press, 1984.

Weinberg, Gerhard L. *A World at Arms: A Global History of World War II*. Cambridge and New York: Cambridge University Press, 1994.

Wells, Wyatt. *Antitrust and the Formation of the Postwar World*. New York: Columbia University Press, 2002.

Westad, Odd Arne. *The Global Cold War: Third World Interventions and the Making of Our Times*. Cambridge and New York: Cambridge University Press, 2007.

   Holtsmark, Sven, and Ivor Neumann, eds. *The Soviet Union in Eastern Europe, 1945–1989*. New York: St. Martins Press, 1994.

Wheeler-Bennett, John, and Anthony Nicholls. *The Semblance of Peace: The Political Settlement after the Second World War*. London: Macmillan, 1972.

Wilkins, Mira. *The Maturing of Multinational Enterprise: American Business Abroad from 1914 to 1970*. Cambridge, MA: Harvard University Press, 1974.

Wilmot, Chester. *The Struggle for Europe*. New York: Harper & Bros., 1952.

Winfield, Betty Houchin. *FDR and the News Media*. New York: Columbia University Press, 1994.

Wittner, Lawrence S. *American Intervention in Greece, 1943–1949*. New York: Columbia University Press, 1982.

Woods, Randall Bennett. *A Changing of the Guard: Anglo-American Relations, 1941–1946*. Chapel Hill: University of North Carolina Press, 1990.

   and Howard Jones. *Dawning of the Cold War: The United States Quest for Order*. Athens: University of Georgia Press, 1991.

Woodward, E. L. *British Foreign Policy in the Second World War.* 5 vols. London: Her Majesty's Stationary Office, 1970–71.

Woolner, David. *The Second Quebec Conference Revisited: Waging War, Formulating Peace: Canada, Great Britain and the U.S. in 1944–1945.* New York: St. Martin's Press, 1998.

Wylie, Neville, ed. *European Neutrals and Non-Belligerents during the Second World War.* Cambridge: Cambridge University Press, 2002.

Xydis, Stephen. *Greece and the Great Powers, 1944–1947: Prelude to the Truman Doctrine.* Thessaloniki: Institute for Balkan Studies, 1963.

Yergin, Daniel. *Shattered Peace: The Origins of the Cold War and the National Security State.* Boston: Houghton, Mifflin, 1977.

Zubok, Vladislav, and Constantine Pleshakov. *Inside the Kremlin's Cold War: From Stalin to Khrushchev.* Cambridge, MA: Harvard University Press, 1996.

Articles

Adler, Les, and Thomas G. Paterson. "Red Fascism: The Merger of Nazi Germany and Soviet Russia in the American Image of Totalitarianism, 1930s–1950s." *American Historical Review,* 75 (April, 1970), 1046–64.

Beisner, Robert. "Patterns of Peril: Dean Acheson Joins the Cold Warriors, 1945–1946." *Diplomatic History,* 20 (Summer 1996), 321–55.

Brzezinski, Zbigniew. "How the Cold War Was Played." *Foreign Affairs,* 51 (October 1972), 181–209.

Buhite, Russell. "Soviet-American Relations and the Repatriation of Prisoners of War, 1945." *Historian,* 35 (May 1973), 384–97.

Cantril, Hadley. "Opinion Trends in World War II: Some Guides to Interpretation." *Public Opinion Quarterly,* 12 (Spring 1948), 30–44.

Clemens, Diane Shaver. "Averell Harriman, John Deane, the Joint Chiefs of Staff, and the 'Reversal of Cooperation' with the Soviet Union in 1945." *International History Review,* 14 (May 1992), 277–306.

Davis, Forrest. "Roosevelt's World Blueprint." *Saturday Evening Post,* 115 (April 10, 1943), 20–1, 109–11.

Harbutt, Fraser J. "American Challenge, Soviet Response: The Beginning of the Cold War, February–May, 1946." *Political Science Quarterly,* 96 (Winter 1981–82), 623–39.

Haslam, Jonathan. "Litvinov, Stalin, and the Road Not Taken." In Gabriel Goredetsky, ed., *Soviet Foreign Policy, 1917–1991: A Retrospective.* London: Frank Cass, 1994, 55–62.

Hess, Gary R. "The Iranian Crisis of 1945–1946 and the Cold War." *Political Science Quarterly,* 89 (March 1974), 117–46.

Hughes, E. J. "Winston Churchill and the Formation of the United Nations Organization." *Journal of Contemporary History,* 9, 4 (October 1974), 177–94.

Kennan, George F. "X," "The Sources of Soviet Conduct." *Foreign Affairs,* 25 (July 1947), 566–82.

LaFeber, Walter. "Roosevelt, Churchill and Indochina, 1942–1945." *American Historical Review* 80 (December, 1975), 1277–95.

Larsh, William. "W. Averell Harriman and the Polish Question: December 1943–August 1944." *East European Politics and Societies,* 7 (Fall, 1993), 513–54.

Leffler, Melvyn P. "The Cold War: What Do We Now Know?" *American Historical Review,* 104 (April 1999), 501–24.

Lundestad, Geir. "Empire by Invitation? The United States and Western Europe, 1945–1952." *Journal of Peace Research,* 23 (September 1986), 263–77.

Mark, E. "Revolution by Degrees: Stalin's National Front Strategy for Europe, 1941–1947." Cold War International History Project, Working Paper No. 31, 2001.

"Charles E. Bohlen and the Acceptable Limits of Soviet Hegemony in Eastern Europe: A Memorandum of 18 October, 1945." *Diplomatic History,* 3 (Spring 1979), 201–13.

Miscamble, Wilson D. "Anthony Eden and the Truman-Molotov Conversations, April 1945." *Diplomatic History,* 2, (Spring 1978), 167–80.

Offner, Arnold. "'Another Such Victory': President Truman, American Foreign Policy, and the Cold War,' " *Diplomatic History,* 23 (Spring 1999), 126–55.

Pechatnov, V. O. "'The Allies Are Pressing on You to Break Your Will.' Foreign Policy Correspondence between Stalin and Molotov and Other Politburo Members, September 1945–December 1946." Cold War International History Project, Working Paper No. 26, September 1999.

"The Big Three after World War II: New Documents on Soviet Thinking about Postwar Relations with the United States and Great Britain." Cold War International History Project, Working Paper No. 13, 1995.

Pons, Silvio, "Stalin, Togliatti and the Origins of the Cold War in Europe." *Journal of Cold War Studies,* 3, 2 (Spring 2001).

Resis, Albert. "The Churchill-Stalin Secret 'Percentages' Agreement on the Balkans, Moscow, October, 1944." *American Historical Review,* 83 (April 1978), 368–87.

Reynolds, David, "The Origins of the Cold War: The European Dimension, 1944–1951." *Historical Journal,* 28 (June 1985), 497–515.

Roberts, Geoffrey. "Litvinov's Lost Peace, 1941–1946." *Journal of Cold War Studies,* 4, 2 (Spring, Jr., 2002), 23–54.

Schlesinger, Arthur M., Jr., "Origins of the Cold War." *Foreign Affairs,* 46 (October 1967), 22–52.

Trachtenberg, Marc. "The United States and Eastern Europe: A Reassessment." *Journal of Cold War Studies,* 10,4 (Fall 2008), 94–132.

Ulam, Adam, "Forty Years after Yalta." *New Republic,* 192 (February 11, 1985), 18–21.

Werth, Alexander. "First Contact with Poland." *Russian Review* (March 1946), 13–71.

Yegorova, N. I. "The Iran Crisis of 1945–1946: A View from the Russian Archives." Cold War International History Project, Working Paper No. 15, May 1996.

Index

Adenauer, Konrad, 121
Afghanistan, 85, 268
Albania, 385
Anderson, Sir John, 3
Anders, General W., 380
Anglo-American Petroleum Agreement, 252
Anglo-Persian Oil Company, 108
Anglo-Soviet "Cold War," 380
Anglo-Soviet cultural ties, 171
Anglo-Soviet Public Relations Committee. 99
Anglo-Soviet Trade Union Committee, 99
Anglo-Soviet Treaty (1942)
    anniversary celebrated, 1944, 154
    historical significance of, 74–78
    negotiations for, 40–45, 52–66, 141
    reception of, 69–78
    settlement of, 66–69
Antonescu, Marshal, 187
Argentina, 143, 272
Atlantic Charter, 34, 38, 62, 73, 77–78, 148, 151, 276
atomic bomb, 373
Attlee, Clement, 42, 155, 239
Auden, W. H., 22–23
Australia, 42, 371, 405
Austria, 385

Badoglio, Marshal, 204
Baldwin, Stanley, 16
Ball, Senator Joseph, 258
Bank of England, 242
Barkley, Alben, 322
Baltic states, 35, 41, 60–62, 133, 152
Beard, Charles, 230

Beaverbrook, Lord, 35, 41, 45, 71,93, 239, 335
Beck, Colonel, 170–171, 347
Belgium, 118, 205, 213, 271, 337
Benes, Eduard, 40, 72, 75, 96, 103, 110, 113, 117–119, 132, 140–141, 144, 189, 192, 219
    meeting with Molotov, 1942, 75
    sees vindication in Anglo-Soviet Treaty, 72–73
    self-image as East/West "bridge," 118
    standing with Eden and Foreign Office, 116
    and treaty with Soviets, 118, 137, 140–141
    visit to Churchill in North Africa (1944), 144
Bermuda conference (1942), 236
Bern Incident, 353
Beveridge, Sir William, 122
Beveridge Plan, 221
Bismarck, Otto von, 47, 192
Blaizot Mission, 207
Bliven, Bruce, 17
Board of Education (UK), 99
Bohlen, Charles, 17, 131, 193, 297, 367, 378, 394–395
Bonomi, Ivanoe, 204
Boothby, Robert, 107
Bor-Komorowski, General, 175
Bottai, Guiseppe, 120
Bracken, Brendan, 93, 155, 335
Brazil, 267
Bretton Woods decisions, 223, 235–238
Briand, Aristide, 121
British Broadcasting Corporation, 196
Buhite, Russell, 19

Bulgaria, 153, 166, 177, 186–187, 191,
    195, 197, 286–287
Bull, Hedley, 184
Bullitt, William, 16
Burgess, Michael, 121
Burns, James McGregor, 17, 230
Bush, George W. 20
Butler, R.A., 41
Byrnes, James F.
    appointment as secretary of state,
        374
    at Moscow conference (December
        1945), 375, 380–382
    at New York Security Council meeting
        (1946), 388–392
    at Potsdam, 374
    definition of new "firm" policy
        (February 1946), 395
    diplomacy from appointment to
        Moscow conference (December
        1945), 373–380
    inaugurates firm policy toward Soviet
        Union, 384–386
    pre-Fulton associations with Churchill,
        384–386
    reasons for presence at Yalta, 278
    role at Paris peace conferences (1946),
        397
    role at Yalta, 278
    role in defining Yalta, 320–324
    role in policy transformation, 385–391,
        394–395
    tension with Truman (December 1945),
        375

Cadogan, Alexander, 64–66, 75, 156, 177,
    275–305, 348
Canada, 42, 405
Cantril, Hadley, 270, 276
Carr, E. H., 98, 122
Casablanca conference (1943), 79
Cavendish-Bentinck, Victor, 64
Cazalet, Victor, 42
Chamberlain, Neville, 28, 48–49, 53
Chamberlain, William H., 17
Chiang Kai Shek, 299
China, 212, 299–300, 335, 386
Churchill, Winston L. S.
    and Europe, 80–93
    and Roosevelt, xii–xiii, xv, 9–10, 33,
        45, 128–138, 141–142, 161–166,
        214–217, 229–234, 279–330,
        344–354, 403
    and Stalin, 31–32, 80–93, 128–138,
        143–151, 166, 174–182, 183–210,
        280, 330, 333–344, 349–371,
        384–393, 403

Churchill, Winston L. S. (before Yalta)
    agrees with Stalin on U.N. issues,
        210–211
    arguments in 1944 with Roosevelt over
        economics and strategy, 141–143
    attempts in late 1944 at reconciliation
        with de Gaulle, 207–210
    attempted negotiation with Stalin over
        Poland in early 1944, 143–151
    comparison to Stalin, 80–81
    confrontation conference with de Gaulle before
        D-Day, 155
    consolidation of British "sphere" after
        Tolstoy, 1944, 199–210
    criticism of Soviets at Quebec "Octagon"
        conference, 1944, 162–163
    cultivation of small inner circle in
        Anglo-American relations, 93, 94
    and de Gaulle, 206–210
    discourages protagonists of British-led
        Western Europe, 145, 156–158
    difficulties with Foreign Office (1944),
        195–196
    faith in autonomous postwar Europe
        (1943), 80, 91–93
    flaws in his summitry, 83
    and france, 206–210,
    functional cooperation in Europe with
        Stalin during war, 83–89
    hails Anglo-Soviet treaty (1942), 69–70
    heightened activity in aligning Britain
        to Western Europe (late 1944),
        204–210
    humiliating setbacks at Teheran (1943),
        128–138
    late 1944 policies toward Greece and
        Yugoslavia, 199–200, 203–204
    improved relations with Stalin after
        Tolstoy meeting (1944), 193–196
    initial resistance to Anglo-Soviet treaty
        (1942), 41–42
    meeting at Moscow with Stalin at
        "Tolstoy", (October 1944), 174–182
    misleading postwar characterization of
        October 1944 meeting, 185 n.3
    Paris visit (late 1944), 207
    "percentages" agreement with Stalin
        (October 1944), 176–182
    pressures London Polish government
        (early 1944), 149–150
    prompts to Moscow visit (October
        1944), 167–174
    response to Morgenthau plan, 165
    return to Anglo-Soviet geopolitical
        collaboration (May 1944), 151–154
    tensions with U.S. (late 1944 to
        February 1945), 213–224

visit to Moscow (August 1942) 81–82
visit to United States (December 1941),
32–33.
Churchill, Winston L. S. (Yalta and after)
approach to Yalta, 284–288
assessment of, historically, 401–405
and Bern Incident, 352–353
blamed by Stalin for broken relations
(1946), 392–394
campaign after Yalta to define
conference, 337–341
comparative immunity from Yalta
criticism, 9
concern over Europe's social problems,
356–357
and France at Yalta, 292, 301, 307–309
and Germany at Yalta, 291–295
"Iron Curtain" speech (March 1946),
384–388, 392–393
performance at Yalta reviewed in
Britain, 334–335
pessimism in mid-1945, 366–371
and Poland at Yalta, 295–310
and post-Yalta crisis (1945), 333–372
post-Yalta pressure on Roosevelt, 339,
346–354
report to House of Commons on Yalta,
334
reaction to advent of Truman, 361–368
responses to Declaration on Liberated
Europe, 304, 317
Civil Aviation conference, 236, 245
Clay, Lucius, 397
Clemens, Diane, 18–19, 283, 299
Comintern, 112
Committee on Russia Studies (UK), 99
Communist Party (UK), 99
"confederations" projects in wartime
Europe, 43–44, 59, 62, 71, 96, 118
Polish-Czech and Greek-Yugoslav
associations, 96
Soviet initial acceptance of and later
rejection of, 125–126
conferences
Moscow conference (December 1941),
33–40
Washington conference (December
1941), 32–33
Moscow conference (August 1942), 81–82
Moscow conference (October 1943),
123–127
Teheran conference (November–
December 1943), 127–138
Dumbarton Oaks conference (August–
September 1944), 159–160, 260–269
Quebec conference (September–
October 1944), 161–167

Moscow conference (October 1944),
174–182
Yalta conference (February 1945),
280–330
Potsdam conference (July–August
1945), 373–374
London conference (September 1945), 375
Moscow conference (December 1945),
381–382
Paris conferences (1946), 397
Congress of Friendship and Collaboration
with the Soviet Union, 197
Paris conferences (1946), 367
Congress of Vienna, 1, 25, 30
Conservative Party (UK), 27, 41, 339
Conte, Artur, 7, 229
Cooper, Duff, 156–157, 337
Coudenove-Kalergi, Count, 121
Council of Europe, 233
Cranborne, Lord, 155, 352
Crimean War, 30
Cripps, Sir Stafford, 32, 41, 45, 57
ambassador in Moscow, 32
as supporter of Anglo-Soviet Treaty, 41, 45
on second front, 57
Croce, Bernadetto, 204
Crowe, Sir Eyre, 18–29
Curzon Line, 25, 42, 119, 135–136, 144–145,
150, 283, 286, 295–297, 338, 347
Cyrenaica, 379, 397
Czechoslovakia, 40, 73, 75, 96, 110,
137–138, 140–141, 178, 188–189

Dakar, 250–251
Dallek, Robert, 17, 20, 214, 230
Dalton, Hugh, 357
Davies, Joseph, 367, 371
Deane, John, 16
Declaration of the United Nations, 236, 267
Declaration of National Independence, 236
Declaration on Liberated Europe
Churchill's characterization of, 338, 347
content of, 313
introduction of, at Yalta, 304, 309
response of Stalin and Molotov to,
314–320
significance of, 360, 400–401
significance of, at Yalta, 314
Truman takes literal view of, 360
uses of, by Churchill and Foreign
Office, 348
uses of, in Roosevelt/Byrnes post-Yalta
presentations, 4, 320–322
Denmark, 192
Democratic Party (U.S.), 18, 19
Dimitrov, Georgi, 112–113
Divine, Robert, 258, 261, 263

Dixon, Piers, 156, 331, 334
Dodecanese Islands, 379, 397
Draper, Theodore, 20
Dreiser, Theodore, 70
Dumbarton Oaks conference, 1944,
    159–160, 260–269, 403

"East/West" conception defined, ix–xii
Eastern Europe, 112–113, 132–133
Eden, Anthony
    accepts Soviet "bargain" approach to
        negotiation, 43
    August 1944 paper anticipating
        Moscow Order, 168–169
    campaign for Anglo-Soviet Treaty
        (1942), 52–69
    champions European-oriented policies
        in Britain, 95–97
    character assessed, 38–39
    comments on Yalta and Roosevelt's
        role, 305
    credited for Anglo-Soviet treaty, 71
    and Iran, 202–203
    mission to Moscow and relations with
        Stalin (December 1941), 32–40
    Molotov's view of, 38
    presses European issues with Molotov
        at Moscow (1943), 123–127
    promotes Anglo-Turkish ties after
        Tolstoy (1944), 201–202
    relations and discussions with Maisky
        (1943), 90
    seeks Anglo-Soviet concord over Iran,
        202–203
    and Turkey, 201–202
    visit to U.S. and outcome (March 1943),
        90–91
Ehrenburg, Ilya, 82, 362
Eisenhower, Dwight, 56, 88, 355, 365
Emergency High Commission for
    Liberated Europe, 275–276, 313
Europe
    Anglo-Soviet division of, 176–182
    Cordell Hull's views on, 125
    ideas of, during the war, 120–123
    limited knowledge of U.S., 46–50
    responses in, to Anglo-Soviet treaty,
        72–73
    reactions to Yalta, 334–337
    Roosevelt's indifference toward, at
        Teheran, 130–138
    tendency of leaders to reinsure, 192–193
"Europe/America" conception, defined,
    x–xxiv
European Advisory Commission, 126,
    156, 234, 291, 359
European cultural relations with the
    United States, 46–52

Evatt, H. V., 156
exile governments (other than Polish
    government) in Britain:
    Benes's role, 118–119, 140–141
    de Gaulle's preoccupations, 119
    Spaak's role in Western European unity
        movement, 117–118, 145–147
    relations with British government 115–117
    visits to the U.S., 117

Far East, 110, 127, 195, 299–302, 308,
    374–375, 383
Farewell Address (Washington), 227, 347
Finland, 35–37, 60, 62, 110, 191
Flynn, Ed, 278
Folly, Martin, 36–37
Fontaine, Andre, 7
food conference (1943), 236
Forrestal, James, 361
France
    de Gaulle supported by most French
        people as leader, 206
    in context of British alliance building,
        206–210
    Poland, attitudes toward (1939), 22–23
    seen as indispensable for Western bloc,
        206
    Yalta discussion about, 292
Franco, Francisco, 215
Fraser, Peter, 335
Freidel, Frank, 229
French National Committee, 146, 155
Freston Mission (SOE), 190
Fulbright, William, 259

Gaddis, John Lewis, xii, 17
Galbraith, John Kenneth, 240
Gallipoli, 82
Gasperi, de, Alcide, 121
Gaulle, Charles de
    Anglophobia of, 119
    British supporters (1944), 154–155
    historical consciousness, 405
    humiliations before D-Day, 155
    meeting with Molotov, 1942, 75
    reactions to Anglo-Soviet Treaty, 72
George VI, King, 70
Germany, 192, 374, 400
    discussion of postwar fate at Yalta, 291–295
    discussions on, at Potsdam, 373–374
    favored as prime agenda topic before
        Yalta, 217
    postwar fate of, British views (1944),
        169–170
    reactions in, to Anglo-Soviet Treaty, 72
    wartime attitudes toward European
        unity, 120–121

Great Britain
   abdications in Soviet sphere after
      Tolstoy meeting, 186–190
   attitudes toward Poland and Eastern
      Europe, 1939 and historically, 22–23
   character of British "sphere" in Europe,
      199–210
   cultural activities with wartime Soviet
      Union, 99
   divisions between "integrationists"
      and "accomodationists," 144–147,
      155–158
   efforts to create a commercial nexus
      with Soviet Union, 220–222
   expectations before Yalta of Anglo-
      Soviet-led Europe, 218–224
   European-oriented political and media
      establishment, 93–99
   Foreign Office and London Poles
      (1944), 170–173
   Foreign Office commitment to
      Anglo-Soviet alliance, 95–97
   Foreign Office draws Churchill back to
      Anglo-Soviet cause (1944), 152
   Foreign Office outlook favors Europe
      and Anglo-Soviet line, 95–98
   and France, 206–210
   and Greece, 199–202
   historical and geopolitical/strategic ties
      with Russia/Soviet Union, 30–33
   and Iran, 202–203
   limited knowledge of U.S., 46–50
   limited knowledge of Soviet Union,
      171–172
   mixed public, parliamentary, and press
      reactions to Yalta, 334–335
   positive response to Anglo-Soviet treaty
      (1942), 71–72
   Post-Hostilities Planners and Germany's
      future, 157
   pre-Yalta tensions with United States,
      210–224
   pro-Soviet sentiment in (1942–44),
      100–101
   public attitudes toward allies, 99–101
   public interest in European unity, 121–122
   response to German invasion of Poland,
      23–26
   response to recognition of Lublin
      (1945), 216
   Soviet "Cold War" against, 380–381
   tendency to focus on Europe rather than
      United States, 95–101
   tensions with United States over Five
      Senators outburst (1943), 238
   tensions with U.S. over pre-Yalta
      European actions, 210–224

"Tolstoy" conference at Moscow
      (1944), 186–190
   and Turkey, 201, 202
   traditional foreign policies, 28–29
   value of its historical archival resources,
      xxi–xxii
Greece, 86, 108, 153, 163, 166–167,
      187–188, 191, 199–200, 203–204,
      212–213, 271–272, 286–288, 333,
      349, 365, 369, 379
   British "sphere" includes it (May 1944),
      153
   Churchill's concern about (October
      1944), 166–167
   Churchill raises alarm with Americans
      (Quebec, 1944), 163
   fears of Soviet expansion (1945), 333
   included in British "sphere" in Moscow
      Order (October 1944), 199–200,
      203–204
   Maisky's reassurances about (1943), 108
   prompt to Moscow "Tolstoy"
      conference (1944), 166–167
   Soviet pressures on (from May 1945),
      365–369, 379
   Stettinius's public criticism of British
      actions in (1944), 212–213,
      271–272, 286–288
   valued association, for Britain, 86
Gorky, Maxim, 48
Grew, Joseph, 323
Grey, Sir Edward, 28
Gromyko, Andrei, 262–263, 267, 274,
      287, 389–390
Gunther, John, 51

Hakimi, Ebrahim, 381–382, 388
Halifax, Lord, 41, 53, 60–61, 63, 69, 90, 97,
      152, 164, 214–215, 229, 239, 354–341
Harper, John, 51, 130, 230, 233
Harriman, Averell
   appointment as ambassador in Moscow,
      142
   approves new "firm" policy (1946), 391
   assessment of Roosevelt before Yalta, 271
   frustrations in Moscow (1944), 193
   role at Yalta, in Far East negotiation,
      299, 308
   suggests Hopkins mission to Moscow
      (1945), 367
Harriman, Kathleen, 305
Harvey, Oliver, 150, 268
Hathaway, Robert, 213–214
Henderson, Hubert, 242
Hickerson, John, 275
Hirohito, Emperor, 212
Hiroshima, 373

Hiss, Alger, 15, 305
Hitler, Adolf, 27, 39, 46, 48, 52, 104, 112,
   212, 281–282
Home Intelligence Survey (UK), 100
Hoover, Herbert, 322
Hopkins, Harry
   assists Churchill-Roosevelt exclusivity, 93
   mission to Stalin (1945), 367–369, 402
   and Quebec conference (1944), 161
Horthy, Admiral, 188
Hull, Cordell, 34, 53, 67, 123–127
   151–152, 213, 234, 246, 258, 264
Hungary, 36, 110, 113–114, 178, 188–189

Ickes, Harold, 240
India Office (UK), 202, 234, 379
Indochina, 207
International Labor Organization
   conference, 236
Iran, 88, 202–203, 268, 333, 377–378
   Bevin and Byrnes warn Stalin of looming
      U.N. confrontation, 381–382
   British premonitions of future trouble,
      202–203
   Churchill resists notion of U.S. troops
      in, 88
   protest in Security Council (January
      1946), 381–383
   Soviet pressures against (1945),
      377–379
   Soviets refuse to negotiate with Eden
      over (October 1944), 202–203
   Soviets thought to fear U.N.
      intervention prospect (1944), 268
   U.S. promotes return of, to Security
      Council (March 1946), 389
   U.S./Soviet Security Council confrontation
      over (April 1946), 389–394
Italy, 87–89 108, 110, 118, 192, 212, 251,
   257, 272, 288, 337, 363, 397

Japan, 40, 52, 56–57, 77, 89, 186,
   299–300, 373–375
Johnson, Lyndon, 18
Judt, Tony, 280

Kalinin, Mikhail, 69
Katyn massacres, 79, 86–87, 96, 118, 287,
   301, 311, 339
Kennan, George F., xii, 193, 383–384,
   393–394
Kerr, Clark, 82, 116, 149, 151, 154, 201,
   298, 343, 351, 362
Keynes, John Maynard, 220, 240,
   243–244, 248
   and Bretton Woods agreements, 244
   desire for closer Anglo-American
      politico-economic intimacy, 243

economic delegation leadership (1944),
   243–247
Khrushchev, Nikita, 393
Kimball, Warren, 230, 286
King, Admiral Ernest, 162
Kirkpartick, Jeanne, 16
Kohl, Helmut, 8
Kollantai, Alexandra, 102, 362
Konrad, George, 8
Korea, 212, 308
Krock, Arthur, 64, 74
Kursk-Orel, Battle of, 96, 113

Labour Party (UK), 98–99
Laloy, Jean, 7
Lane, Arthur Bliss, 271–272
Laski, Harold, 99, 314
Law, Richard, 307
League of Nations, 160, 261, 266, 295, 314
Leahy, William, 250, 289, 326, 361, 385
Lebanon, 218, 355
Lend–Lease, 233, 238, 241, 244
Lenin Library gift, 171
Levering, Ralph, 356
Lie, Trygve, 145
Lippmann, Walter, 17, 64, 74, 98, 253, 363
Litvinov, Maxim, 54, 69, 102, 160, 191,
   211, 218
   commission on postwar policy
      assignment, 108–109
   pre-Yalta articles (in 1944), 160, 211
   Second Front and postwar political
      talks with Roosevelt (1942), 54–55
Locarno Pact, 25
Lodge, Henry Cabot, 259
London foreign ministers conference
   (1945), 375
Lothian, Lord, 121
Louis, Wm. Roger, 234, 250
Luce, Henry, 259
Lundestad, Geir, 234
Lvov, 295, 297

MacLeish, Archibald, 277, 279
Mahan, Admiral, 249–250
Maisky, Ivan, 36, 44–45
   commission on postwar Soviet policy
      report, 108–112
   reparations issue presented at Yalta
      (1945), 293, 307
   respect for, conveyed by Molotov, 109
   and stage setting for looming tripartite
      conferences (1943), 106–108
Malia, Martin, 103
Mark, Edouard, 105, 112
Marks, Frederick, 15, 230
Marshall, George, 56, 58, 67, 233
Matthews, H. Freeman, 213

Massigli, M., 336
Mastny, Voytech, 342
media
    American press attitudes toward
        internationalism (1944), 253–254
    Anglo-American press and radio wars
        (late 1944) 253–254
    British press and its European focus,
        98
    mixed British press response to Yalta,
        334–335
    Orwell's critique of British press on
        Warsaw Uprising, 1944, 159
    Polish press, its character and problems
        in wartime London, 172–173
    responses of various elements to
        Anglo-Soviet Treaty (1942), 67–78
Messer, Robert, 320
McCarthy, Joseph, 15
McCormick, Anne O'Hare, 9, 141,
    253–254, 354
Metal Reserves Corporation (U.S.), 252
Mexico, 252
Michael, King (Rumania), 343
Middle East oil issues, 143
Mikolajczyk, Stanislaw
    pressure from Churchill (early 1944),
        148–150
    pressure from Churchill and Stalin
        (Moscow, 1944), 179–181
Mitterand, Francois, 8
Molotov, Vyacheslav
    calls Anglo-Soviet treaty a
        "cornerstone," 154
    characterization of Eden, 38
    negotiation of Anglo-Soviet Treaty, 55–69
    response to British views of Yalta,
        343–346, 351
    role at Yalta, 293, 302–304
    three-month "spheres'" deal (1944), 153–154
    in United States (1942), 66–68
Monnet, Jean, 122
Montefiore, Simon Sebag, 318
Montreux Convention, 85, 136–137, 195
Moran, Lord, 129, 305
Morgenthau, Hans, 51
Morgenthau Henry, 165–166, 240–241
    pressures Britain on postwar finances,
        240–245
    promotes pastoralization of postwar
        Germany (1944), 165–166
Morgenthau Plan, 165–166
Morrison, Herbert, 239
Moscow conference, 1944 ("Tolstoy"),
    167, 174–182, 217, 220
Moscow foreign ministers conference
    (1943), 123–127

Moscow Order
    consolidation of, 183–224
    rationale for and characterization of,
        140, 183–184
    widespread support for, as future
        European framework, 218–229
Mussolini, Benito, 35, 46, 48, 52, 120

Nazi-Soviet Pact (1939), 20, 30, 37, 78
Netherlands, 205
Newsome, W. Brian, 26
New Zealand, 42, 371, 405
Niebuhr, Reinhold, 224
Nisbet, Robert, 15
Northern Tier, 86, 332, 403
Norway, 192, 205, 366
Nowak, Jan, 147

Office of Strategic Services (OSS), 89
Orwell, George, 100, 159, 224
Overlord/D-Day, 128–129, 155, 159

Pacific theater, 211–212
Paderewski, Ignacy, 264
Palmerston, Lord, 60, 171
Pan-American Airways, 253
Pares, Sir Bernard, 171
Paris conference (1946), 397
Paris peace conference (1919), 1, 25, 42, 297
Parker, Ralph, 98
Pasvolsky, Leo, 274–276
Pearson, Drew, 213
Petain, Marshal, 87
Peter, King (Yugoslavia), 147
Petroleum Reserve Corporation (U.S.), 252
Pieck, Wilhelm, 341
Poland
    British and French attitudes toward
        (1939), 22–30
    British constraints on Polish
        government (1944), 170–174
    British responses to (1939), 22–29
    Churchill's plans for Polish troops,
        173–174
    Churchill-Stalin discussions about, at
        Moscow (1944) 174–175, 179–182
    difficulties of London Polish
        government with British
        authorities, 170–174
    fruitless Anglo-Soviet negotiations over
        (early 1944), 143–151
    German invasion of (1939), 22–23
    future broached at Teheran conference
        (1943), 135–138
    Katyn massacre issues, 175
    Mikolajczyk at Tolstoy conference
        (October 1944), 179–182

Poland (*cont.*)
  Polish press in London, 172–173
  Warsaw Uprising (1944), 175
Portugal, 118, 146, 379
Post-Hostilities Planners (UK), 97, 157,
    187 202
Potsdam conference, 2, 332, 373–374
Powell, Anthony, 116
Priestley, J. B., 50
Progressive Citizens of America, 18

Qavam, Sultaneh el, 388–389, 392
Quebec conference, 1944 ("Octogon"),
    161–167

Rakosi, Matyas, 114
Rapallo conference, 78
Reagan, Ronald, 19
Reconstruction Finance Corporation
    (U.S.), 252
Republican Party (U.S.), 15, 107, 245, 258
Resis, Albert, 177
Reston, James, 248, 261
Ribbentrop, Joachim, 282, 335
Revel, Jean-Francois, 7
Reynaud, Paul, 206
Reynolds, David, 9, 47
Roberts, Frank, 156
Roberts, Geoffrey, 318
Roman Catholic Church, 121, 278
Roosevelt, Eleanor, 367
Roosevelt, Franklin D.
  accepts Anglo-Soviet treaty, 61
  and American international
      engagements, 400–401, 403
  announces United Nations plans (June
      1944), 159?
  anxiety over waning support for
      internationalism before Yalta,
      271–279
  approach to Yalta, 282, 286, 311–313
  approves Hull's 1943 Moscow
      performance, 123–127
  assessment of, historically, 399–404
  attitudes toward the British Empire,
      210, 234–251
  attitudes toward Europe, 233–234
  calls Dumbarton Oaks conference,
      159–160
  character of correspondence with Stalin
      (1941–45), 89–90
  Churchill, relations with, xii–xiii, xv,
      9–10, 128–138, 161–166, 214–224,
      229–234, 270–279, 280–330,
      344–354
  conference with Churchill at Quebec
      (September 1944), 161–167

distinctive approach to the war, 227–238
endorses, then rejects, Morgenthau
    Plan, 165–166
expected Anglo-Soviet domination of
    postwar Europe, 218–219
fosters exclusive relationship with
    Churchill, 93
death of, 354
explanations of his apparent postwar
    scenario, 238
and Far East at Yalta, 299–300
and France at Yalta, 292, 301, 307–308
and German issues at Yatla, 291–295
historian's views of, 229–231, 234
move from traditional to radical
    diplomacy at Yalta, 301–320
negotiation with Litvinov (1942), 54–55
negotiation with Molotov (1942)
    67–68
offers second front (spring 1942), 67–68
original focus on Germany for Yalta,
    217
overconfidence at Dumbarton Oaks, 264
perceptions of health of at Yalta, 305
policy approaches, 227–238
and Polish issues at Yalta, 295–310
and post-Yalta crisis, 333, 344–360
private sessions at Teheran with Stalin,
    132–134
problems caused by erupting criticisms
    of Anglo-Soviet behavior, 210, 224
report to Congress on Yalta (1945),
    324–325
reputation influenced by images of
    Yalta, 4–21
response to Anglo-Soviet treaty
    proposals (1942), 54–61
returns to detachment from European
    politics after Teheran, 141–142
role as artist in politics, 231
role as decision maker, 232–233
role as political broker, 232
role as wartime political manager, 231
role at Teheran conference (1943),
    127–138
sharpening dilemma before Yalta, 257
social missteps at Yalta, 291, 309
and staged emergence of coherent
    postwar-oriented "web" (1941–45),
    235–237
Stalin, relations with, 54–57, 89–90,
    128–138, 215–217, 261–279,
    280–330, 400–401
and United Nations, 159, 256–279
uses of the Declaration on Liberated
    Europe at and after Yalta, 304,
    309, 314–322

Royal Air Force, 84
Rubber Reserves Corporation (U.S.), 252
Rumania, 35–37, 60, 62, 153, 166, 177,
    195, 186–188, 287, 343, 349, 385, 387
Russell, Senator Richard, 246
Ruthenia, 119, 178

Sainsbury, Keith, 134
Salazar, Antonio, 118, 146
Sarfatti, Margherita, 48
Sargent, Orme, 97, 152, 157, 177, 221,
    307, 348, 370, 372
Saudi Arabia, 252
Schlesinger, Arthur M., Jr. 17, 213–214,
    269, 273–274, 281, 284, 289, 293,
    295–299, 308, 311, 316, 323
Schmidt, Helmut, 19
Schuman, Robert, 121
Second Front issues, 84, 129, 131, 358
Senarclens, Pierre de, 7
Servan-Schreiber, Jacques, 7
Seton-Watson, R.W., 26
Sforza, Count, 204
Shaw, George Bernard, 70
Sherwin, Martin, 164
Sikorski, Wladyslaw, 61, 115–116
Skard, Sigmund, 46
Skidelsky, Robert, 240–241, 243
Smith, Bedell, 392
Smith M. L., 120
Smuts, Jan, 145–146, 156–157, 161, 288
    attitude toward Anglo-Soviet Treaty
        (1942), 42, 73
    call for British-led Western Europe and
        Commonwealth, 145–156
    urges Churchill to focus on Europe's
        future, 161
Solzhenitsyn, Alexander, 9
Soviet atomic spies, 383
Soviet-Czech treaty, 141–144, 189
Soviet Union
    campaign against British interests
        launched (June 1945), 369–372
    celebration of Anglo-Soviet treaty
        (1942), 69–71
    character of Soviet "closed" sphere in
        Eastern Europe (1944–45), 186–199
    Dimitrov's role in Eastern European
        policy, 112–114
    diplomatic establishment, 102
    exclusive closed sphere in Bulgaria and
        Rumania, 186–187
    explanations of Soviet attitudes at
        Dumbarton Oaks conference,
        264–269
    limits of post–Cold War Soviet
        evidentiary revelations, xix, xx, 102

Litvinov's 1944 articles reflecting
    concern over U.N. proposals, 211
Maisky's commission report (January
    1944), 109–112
Maisky's role in late 1943 stage setting,
    106–108
negotiations and attitudes at
    Dumbarton Oaks conference
    (1944), 260–265
political character, 102–104
post-crisis reconciliation with U.S.
    (June 1945), 369
pressure applied to Hungary and
    Czechoslovakia, 188
pre-Yalta tensions with U.S., 214–224
primacy of Stalin, 102–105
relations with Britain closer after
    Tolstoy meeting (1944), 191–192
renewed strategic vulnerability (early
    1942), 63–64, 66–69
Stalin's policies and apparent objectives
    in Europe, 105–106, 112–114
Stalin's "imperium" in Eastern Europe,
    186–191
warm gestures to British after Tolstoy
    meeting (Moscow, 1944), 196–197
Spaak, Paul-Henri, 116–119, 145–147,
    156, 219
    disappointment over British reluctance
        over Western Europe, 147
    proponent of British-led Western
        Europe, 117–118, 145–147
Spain, 146, 205–206, 339
Spinelli, Altiero, 122
Spykman, Nicholas, 259
Stalin, Joseph
    and Churchill, 31–32, 80–93, 128–138,
        143–151, 166, 174–182, 183–210,
        280–330, 341–372, 384–393, 403
    and Roosevelt, 54–57, 85–90, 128–138,
        215–217, 261–279, 280–330,
        351–354, 400–403
Stalin, Joseph (before Yalta)
    apparent objectives in Eastern Europe,
        102–106, 112–114
    approach to Yalta, 284, 286–288
    improved relations with Churchill after
        Tolstoy meeting, 193–196
    comparatively thin correspondence with
        Roosevelt, 88–89
    completes advantageous Soviet-Czech
        treaty (December 1943), 140–141
    desire for agreement with Britain
        (1941–42), 32
    favors British role in postwar Pacific,
        211–212, 308
    hosts Churchill (August 1942), 81–82

Stalin, Joseph (before Yalta) (*cont.*)
  introductory meetings with Churchill
    and Roosevelt at Yalta, 289
  meets with Churchill at Moscow
    (Tolstoy) (October 1944),
    174–182
  military/strategic concerns at Yalta,
    290–291, 294–295
  negotiations with Churchill over Poland
    (early 1944), 143–151
  objections to U.S. plans for United
    Nations, 214
  presses British for agreement (1942),
    40–45
  rejects Roosevelt's 1944 entreaties
    on veto and membership issues,
    261–262
  shows "bargain" diplomatic strategy,
    43, 197, 311
  reaches out to Roosevelt on "bargain"
    basis after Tolstoy, 197–198
  talks with Eden in Moscow (December
    1941), 34–38
Stalin, Joseph (at and after Yalta)
  basic concerns at Yalta, 286–287
  campaign against Britain (1945–46),
    369–373, 376–382, 392, 396–397
  decision to recognize Lublin regime,
    270
  evaluation of, historically, 400–404
  and Far Eastern and Pacific issues at
    Yalta, 299–300
  and France at Yalta, 292, 301, 307–308
  and German issues at Yalta, 291–295
  and Hopkins mission (1945), 367–368
  introductory meetings with Churchill
    and Roosevelt at Yalta, 289
  and Iranian issues, 377–382, 388–392
  military/strategic concerns at Yalta,
    290–291, 294–295
  and Polish issues at Yalta, 295–310
  preoccupations with Big Three and
    Great Power unity, 290–291, 294,
    325
  and post-Yalta crisis, 333–372
  reaction to Western powers view of
    Yalta, 343–346, 351–362, 366,
    401–403
  response to Declaration on Liberated
    Europe at Yalta, 314–320
  and Security Council confrontations
    (March/April 1946), 388–392
  and United Nations conference at San
    Francisco, 364–365
  and United Nations issues at Yalta,
    298–299
Stalingrad, 52

Stanley, Oliver, 239
Stead, W. T. 46, 254
Steiner, Zara, 29
Stettinius, Edward R., Jr., 271, 284–288,
    293, 311, 314, 327
  and Anglo-American crisis (December
    1944), 213–214
  and conduct of Dumbarton Oaks
    conference, 261–269
  and conduct of San Francisco
    conference, 364–365
  and preparations for Yalta, 273–278
  pre-Yalta focus on U.N. issues, 274–275
  role at Yalta, 293, 295, 302–304, 308
Stimson, Henry, 58, 156, 240, 248–249
Stoler, Mark, 250
Sweden, 73–74, 126, 191, 366
Swing, Raymond Gram, 213, 254, 363
Syria, 208, 355

Tangier, 370
Tansill, Charles, 230
Teheran conference, 2, 248–251, 285
Tennyson, Alfred Lord, 25
Tito, Josip Broz, 147, 178, 203
Theoharis, Athan, 17–18
Thompson, R.W., 10
Thorne, Christopher, 234
Togliatti, Palmiro, 204
Toynbee, Arnold, 26
Trade Union Council (UK), 99
Treaty of Rome, 115
Trieste issue, 363–364
Truman administration, 112
Truman Doctrine, 351
Truman, Harry S.
  accession to presidency, 354
  approval of Byrnes new hard line
    toward Soviets (1946), 391
  chair of Senate National Defense
    Committee, 246–247
  course between Potsdam conference
    and January 1946, 373–380
  frustration in December 1945, 375–376
  and Joseph Davies, 367
  and Hopkins mission, 367–368
  initial militance, 354–355, 360–364
  policy reorientation (February 1946),
    386–388
  pre-Fulton meeting with Churchill, 385
  resists Churchillian strategy (spring
    1945), 364–365
  turn to accommodation with Soviets
    (May 1945), 367–372
Turkey, 42, 61, 73–74, 85–86, 126,
    136–137, 182, 186, 191, 195, 201–202,
    308, 333, 335, 363, 365, 370, 377, 379

Anglo-Soviet reassurances about (1941), 85–86
British fear its gravitation toward Germany, 61
British reassurances after Moscow conference (1944), 201–202
`Churchill's undermining references at Moscow conference (1944), 175, 182, 195
Churchill urges assistance for (1946), 363
discussed at foreign ministers conference (Moscow, 1943), 126
fear of Russian/Soviet designs on the Straits, 42
future discussed at Teheran (1943), 136–138
offered membership in U.N. at Yalta, 308
relief over Anglo-Soviet Treaty (1943), 73
Soviet pressures against (1946), 363

Ulam, Adam, 16, 20
ULTRA, 282
United Nations
concept accepted by Britain and Soviet Union at Moscow conference, 1943
Dumbarton Oaks conference (1944), 159–160, 260–269
Roosevelt announces plans for (June 1944), 159–160
San Francisco conference, 371
United Nations Relief and Rehabilitation Administration, 236
United Nations conference at San Francisco (1945), 267, 319, 337, 351–352, 364, 368
United Nations Security Council, 373, 376, 381, 382–383
London meeting (January 1946), 388–392.
New York meeting (March/April 1946), 388–392
United States
adverse response to Lublin recognition (1944), 215–217
approval of Hull/Roosevelt diplomacy (late 1943), 127, 141
atmosphere in during war, compared to Europe, 225
congressional "nationalism," 245–247
criticisms of British and Soviet actions (late 1944, early 1945), 210–224
disapproval of Soviet-Czech treaty, 1944, 141
economic pressures against Britain, (1944–45), 143, 241–248
evaluations of Teheran conference, 141

deteriorating support for internationalism (late 1944, early 1945), 271–279
and Dumbarton Oaks conference (September–October 1944), 260–269
expansionary state and corporate activity during war, 252–253
"Five Senators" outburst (1943), 238, government/state economic leadership, 252
growing momentum in 1942–44 behind U.N. proposals, 259–260
historical context of U.S. diplomacy, 227–229
its distinctive governmental system, 226
little expectation of direct postwar role in Europe, 218–224
military establishment attitudes (1941–45), 248–251
nationalist, Anglophobic and anti-imperial attitudes, 238–248
New Deal militance (1933–1945), 240–241
positive reception of Anglo-Soviet treaty (1942), 73
preparations for Yalta (1944–45), 255–279
public support for U.N. proposals (1942–44), 258
public opinion, 253–255
Rooseveltian approaches, 227–238
Stettinius's public critique of British diplomacy (1944), 213–215
tendencies toward global economic "envelopment," 254
thin prewar cultural ties with Europe and Britain, 50–52
public disinclination for foreign entanglement, 255
United States Chamber of Commerce, 246

Valery, Paul, 26
Vandenberg, Arthur, 275, 285, 308, 322, 397
Van Kleffens, E. N., 116–118, 145
Vansittart, Robert, 156
Venezuela, 252
Voroshilov, Kliment, 331
Vyshinsky, Andrei, 343

Wallace, Henry, 18, 73, 240
Ward, Geoffrey, 230
Warsaw Uprising, 159, 213, 287, 311
Watt, David, 11
Watt, D. Cameron, xiii, 229
Welles, Sumner, 53

Wells, H. G., 26, 70
West, Rebecca, 26
Western bloc, 118, 144–145, 156–157,
    169, 200
White, Harry Dexter, 240–241
Wilkinson, J. D., 121
Willgress, Dana, 198
Willkie, Wendell, 259, 312
Wilmot, Chester, 9, 229
Wilson, G. M., 76, 152, 186, 204
Wilson, Woodrow, 47, 51, 91, 131, 142,
    194, 213, 218, 228, 247, 259, 265,
    314, 399
Winant, John, 44, 65, 95
Wittmer, Felix, 229
Woods, Randall, 234, 240–243
World War I, 30

Yalta conference
    agreeing on location of, 280
    American images of, 14–18
    Anglo-Soviet issues and tensions at, 306
    American preparations for, 255–279
    bifurcation of meeting, at Roosevelt's
        hands, 310
    Big Three breakdown after, 333–372
    British images of, 9–11
    confusions in historical images of, 1–21
    crisis following, 333–368
    Declaration on Liberated Europe, 304,
        312–330
    discussion of Far Eastern issues at, 299,
        308
    discussion of French issues at, 292
    discussion of German issues at, 291–295
    discussion of military/strategic issues at,
        290–291
    discussion of Polish issues at, 295–310
    discussion of reparations at, 293–294
    discussion of United Nations issues at
        295, 298
    European images of, 6–14
    European powers preparations for,
        210–224
    European sense of victimization at,
        6–11
    evaluations of, 325–330
    getting to and discovering, 280–282
    historiography of, ix–xxiv, 1–21
    overview of, 280–330
    politicization of, 13–14
    preoccupations and strategies of the
        three powers at, 284–288
    presentations by Byrnes and Roosevelt
        at, 320–330
    reception of, in Britain, 334–335
    reception of, in Europe, 336–337
    reception of, in Soviet Union,
        341–344
    reception of, in U.S., 320–330
    recurrent controversies over, 20
    role in postwar U.S. political witch
        hunt, 15–16
    Roosevelt's report to Congress on,
        323–324
    Roosevelt's shaping and symbolic role
        at, 4–6, 9–21
    significance of, 399–403
    steps in the creation of images of,
        11–13, 15–18
Yugoslavia, 108, 147, 153, 197, 203,
    301

Zazlavsky, David, 56, 342
Zhdanovschina, 396
Zhukov, Georgii, 13, 333